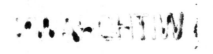

ISBN 975-16-0090-1 (Tk)
975-16-0093-6

BRITISH DOCUMENTS ON OTTOMAN ARMENIANS

VOLUME IV
(1895)

PUBLICATIONS OF THE TURKISH HISTORICAL SOCIETY
SERIAL VII—No. 78[b]

BRITISH DOCUMENTS ON OTTOMAN ARMENIANS

VOLUME IV
(1895)

Ed. By
BİLÂL N. ŞİMŞİR
Member of the Turkish Historical Society

TÜRK TARİH KURUMU BASIMEVİ—ANKARA

1990

T.C.
ATATÜRK KÜLTÜR, DİL VE TARİH YÜKSEK KURUMU
TÜRK TARİH KURUMU YAYINLARI
VII. DİZİ—Sa. 78[b]

İNGİLİZ BELGELERİNDE OSMANLI ERMENİLERİ

CİLT
IV
(1895)

Hazırlayan
BİLÂL N. ŞİMŞİR
Türk Tarih Kurumu Üyesi

TÜRK TARİH KURUMU BASIMEVİ—ANKARA
1990

CONTENTS

INTRODUCTION

The present work, the fourth volume of a series which I have edited since 1982 under the title of *British Documents on Ottoman Armenians*, covers the correspondence relating to the Armenian question in Asiatic Turkey during the second half of 1895. This was a short but difficult period in the relations between Turks and Armenians, as well as between the Ottoman Government and some of the European Great Powers.

The repercussions of the first Sassoun rebellion, organized and provoked by young Hintchak revolutionaries, continued during 1895. The principal aim of the Sassoun insurgents was to secure the intervention of the Great Powers in favour of the Ottoman Armenians. The rebellion gave rise to much anti-Turkish propaganda in European countries. Public opinion in Europe, particularly in Britain, was stirred up; there was a repetition of the outcry that had gone up after the Bulgarian insurrection of 1876. The turcophobes of Europe and America started a campaign to persuade their governments to exert diplomatic pressure on the Ottoman Government in an attempt to compel the Porte to give in to Armenian demands. On the insistence of Britain, a delegation was sent to investigate the situation in the Sassoun region after the rebellion had been suppressed, and in 1895 Britain reopened the subject of Armenian reforms. On 11 May of the same year the British, French, and Russian ambassadors in Istanbul submitted to the Porte a number of reform proposals, along with a memorandum. On 20 July a joint report was drawn up and signed by the consular delegates attached to the Sassoun commission of inquiry.

From the Armenian point of view, all this was another triumph for their network of revolutionary propaganda which they had systematically organized in order to provoke European reaction against Turkey. Emboldened by this success, and encouraged by the reform proposals of the three Powers, the Hintchak revolutionaries decided to begin the final stage of their activities. They were convinced that the proposed reforms could lead to independence. It was reported from Anatolia that in the months of July and August the activities of the Armenian committee had reached such a level that incidents could occur at any time.

Meanwhile in Great Britain Lord Salisbury had been returned to power in June 1895 as Prime Minister and Foreign Secretary. Salisbury now believed that the Ottoman Empire was beyond salvation, that its disintegration was bound to occur in the near future, and that an independent Armenia in eastern Turkey could well be useful to Britain. This was a radical change in the century-old British policy towards Turkey. In order to prevent Russian expansionism towards the south, Britain had previously been the champion of Ottoman territorial integrity, and this policy had suited the interests of the British Empire well. Now that the preservation of the integrity of the Ottoman Empire was no longer in accordance with British interests, Britain was in favour of creating a small Armenian state on Turkish territory to act as a buffer against possible Russian expansion. The ultimate disintegration of the Ottoman Empire finally became part of British foreign policy, and Lord Salisbury insisted that, even if the Armenian question were settled, the Empire of the Sultan was too rotten to exist much longer, so he was planning a final *coup* for it.

Russia was suspicious of British policy. The Russian Government believed that Britain's objective was to gain influence over the Russian Armenians, and thereby foment trouble in the Caucasian provinces of the tsarist empire. The Russian Foreign Minister, Prince Lobanow, said that the Armenian committees were aiming at the creation in Asia Minor of an exceptionally privileged district which would form the nucleus of a future independent Armenian kingdom, and Russia could not agree to this. Lobanow refused to associate his Government with any coercive measure against the Sultan.

On 18 July 1895 Sultan Abdulhamid's own reform plan was announced. The British, French, and Russian ambassadors in Istanbul were informed that:

> His Imperial Majesty, having at heart the welfare of all his subjects, has sent a reiterated order to the Porte to hasten necessary reforms and to ensure good administration, that those reforms which were not contrary to laws and regulations should immediately be put into force, and that Shakir Pasha would supervise and preside over their execution . . .

One month later the Turkish draft of reforms was communicated to the embassies in Istanbul. It was composed of a dozen chapters, and stated *inter alia* that:

> All Ottoman subjects, without distinction, are eligible for the post of Vali (Governor);
> Non-Mussulman assistants will be attached to the Valis where the Vali is a Mussulman;

The Mutessarifs will be Mussulmans or non-Mussulmans;

Non-Mussulman Ottoman subjects will be admitted to administrative posts in proportion to the total members of the Mussulman and non-Mussulman population in each Vilayet;

The police and gendarmerie will be recruited from Ottoman subjects in proportion to the numbers of Mussulman and non-Mussulman inhabitants of the Vilayet, etc.

The Armenians were not in the least satisfied with this plan of reforms, and continued their revolutionary activities. During the summer and autumn of 1895 disturbances were being reported from all over Anatolia. On 30 September the Hintchak committee organized a bloody demonstration in the Ottoman capital with the object of causing disorder and thereby inducing the Powers of Europe to intervene on behalf of the Armenians. During the demonstration the Armenians fired the first shots, killing an army Major and several Privates. Thereupon the police intervened, and in the ensuing battle some sixty Armenians and fifteen gendarmes were killed, and a hundred people were wounded. For a number of days following this exchange incidents continued all over Istanbul.

On 2 October at Trabzon Armenian terrorists shot and wounded the former Governor of Van, Bahri Pasha, and the Trabzon Commander, Hamdi Pasha. This assassination attempt provoked serious clashes between the Turks and the Armenians of the town with the loss of many lives on both sides. In October incidents were reported from a number of towns in Sivas, Mamuretulaziz, Kayseri, Ismid, Erzurum, Trabzon, and Aleppo provinces. In November further incidents occurred in Diyarbakir, Mamuretulaziz, Sivas, Aleppo, and Bitlis provinces. The Armenian revolutionaries were doing their best to procure the intervention of the Powers by provoking all kinds of incidents throughout Anatolia, and in all of these incidents the aggressors were Armenians.

The Ottoman Government was doing its utmost to pacify the country, but the Armenian agitators for their part were determined to disrupt the peace and order of Anatolia.

While the Armenian disturbances continued in Asiatic Turkey, the British Government was preparing to take action against the Sultan by sending in the fleet. In November the British squadrons were getting ready to sail to the Dardanelles, and at the same time the British Government was proposing to the other Great Powers that they should join in a combined naval action. However, this proposal alarmed the Russians who hurriedly decided to mobilize their Black Sea fleet.

Meanwhile the Sultan appointed a new Grand Vizier, and the new

Ottoman Government took a number of measures to cope with the situation. The Sultan on the other hand, believing that the British were behind the Armenian movement, appealed to the British Prime Minister for assistance. He promised that he would carry out reforms, and blamed the Armenians for the delay in their implementation. 'Reforms cannot be carried out as long as they (the Armenians) continue to agitate and create disorder . . . Let then England help me by giving good advice to the Armenians . . .' he said.

The British Government was not at all helpful. On the contrary, they insisted on gunboat diplomacy in order to force the Sultan to introduce the reforms. On 11 November the representatives of the Great Powers met in Istanbul. They decided to send to the Ottoman capital a second '*stationnaire*' or gunboat, and to apply for the Sultan's firman to enable the ships to enter Turkish waters.

To the Sultan the stationing of an additional gunboat in the Ottoman capital was tantamount to foreign naval intervention. He also believed that the presence of these ships in Istanbul at that particular time might encourage the Armenian agitators. The Sultan therefore refused to accept the necessity for another gunboat.

As it was impossible for the Ottoman Sultan to give in to the extravagant demands of a small but very turbulent minority, all the efforts to exert pressure on him through the use of force had ended in a fiasco.

Peking,   BİLÂL N. ŞİMŞİR
26 July 1990.   Member of the Turkish Historical Society

LIST OF THE DOCUMENTS

DOCUMENTS

No. 1

The Archbishop of Canterbury to the Marquess of Salisbury.

LAMBETH PALACE, *July 10, 1895.*

My Lord,   *(Received July 10.)*

I HAVE the honour to write to your Lordship with reference to a letter, dated the 4th June, 1895, which I received from the Earl of Kimberley with respect to the proposed reforms in Armenia.

I had expressed a hope that the so-called Assyrian or Nestorian Christians (who are exposed to precisely the same hardships and dangers at the hands of the Turks and Kurds) might be brought within the scope of the proposed reforms.

Lord Kimberley's letter contained the most welcome assurance that the district of Hekkiari, which is largely inhabited by these Christians, would be so included. Most earnestly do I trust that, in any further settlement of this question, the Patriarch Mar Shimun and his followers, numbering, it is said, some 100,000 souls, will have full consideration given to their sad condition, and be granted the protection that is necessary to their welfare.

I have, &c.

(Signed) EDW. CANTUAR.

F. O. 424/183, pp. 62-63, No. 56

No. 2

The Marquess of Salisbury to Sir P. Currie.

No. 275.

Sir,   FOREIGN OFFICE, *July 10, 1895.*

AT an interview with the Turkish Ambassador to-day I spoke very earnestly to his Excellency on the Armenian question.

I said that it was my earnest desire that the Ottoman Empire should be maintained, and that the rightful prerogatives of the Sultan should be protected from encroachments, but that I saw with regret that His Majesty had taken no steps to meet the just demands of public opinion in Europe and in England in regard to this question.

The essential matter was that provision should be made for securing equitable government to the Armenians. I repudiated all ideas of autonomy as absurd, and I asked no privileges for them, but simple justice between man and man; that Kurds should not oppress Armenians, nor Armenians oppress Kurds. For that purpose I pointed out it was necessary at the present juncture that the eastern provinces of Asia Minor should be placed under a Governor in whom Europe could have confidence. So long as he was a man of firmness, integrity, and loyalty, his religion was a matter of minor importance; but it was essential that he should possess these qualities, and that he should be given a free hand to act as circumstances required without interference from Constantinople. Chakir Pasha did not fulfil these requirements, and no trust was reposed in him. The appointment of Raouf Pasha would be more suitable, but I only mentioned his name as one among many from whom, I doubted not, the Sultan could make his selection.

I then proceeded to tell Rustem Pasha that I maintained the demands which had been presented by the Ambassadors of the three Powers at Constantinople, that I supported entirely the policy which the present Government had inherited from their predecessors in office.

I urged that the Sultan should make as large concessions as possible on the basis of those demands. I impressed upon his Excellency very strongly the perilous position in which it appeared to me that the Ottoman Empire was now placed. I was much struck on coming back to office to find how much ground it had lost in English opinion. It was not that there was any longer any strong excitement on the subject, but a settled conviction was growing that nothing was to be hoped from it in the way of improvement or reform, and that all that could be done was to finish with it. I pointed out that neither Germany, nor Austria, nor Italy were likely to thwart the policy of Great Britain in this matter; that France acted entirely with Russia, and that the sole hold upon existence which the Ottoman Empire retained was the fact that Russia and Great Britain were not wholly agreed. If, by the movement of events, the policy of those Powers and public opinion in the two countries should coincide, the Ottoman Empire must disappear. The danger was therefore extreme, and if the Sultan did not take warning in time, the blow would almost inevitably come upon him, and at a time when he least expected it. I added that I heard of discontent from all parts of the Sultan's dominions, and that the opinion of Europe in general was much less favourable to him than it had been when I previously held office.

I request that your Excellency will report to me at once when you learn that any decision has been taken by the Sultan as to the portions of the scheme of reforms that he can accept.

Should His Majesty remain unwilling to take any steps to satisfy the demands of the Powers, it will be necessary, in view of the situation thus created, for Her Majesty's Government to confer with the Government of Russia as to the course to be taken.

I am, &c.

(Signed) SALISBURY.

F. O. 424/183, p. 63, No. 57

No. 3

Sir P. Currie to the Marquess of Salisbury.

No. 461. THERAPIA, *July 11, 1895.*
My Lord, *(Received July 15.)*
WITH reference to my despatch No. 424 of the 27th June, I inclose a copy of a telegram from Her Majesty's Vice-Consul at Van stating that the Armenians in his district have asked him to represent that the High Commissioner ought to be a European.

A similar opinion is expressed in the document inclosed in Mr. Longworth's No. 88 of the 1st July by the women of Samsoon, and it is evident that the *mot d'ordre* has been given by the Armenian Committees to insist on the uselessness of a Turkish High Commissioner.

I have, &c.

(Signed) PHILIP CURRIE.

F. O. 424/183, p. 87, No. 70

Inclosure in No. 3

Vice-Consul Hallward to Sir P. Currie.

Telegraphic. VAN, *July 11, 1895.*
WITH regard to the appointment of a High Commissioner, the Armenians of Van are very anxious that the European Powers should be acquainted with their conviction that unless he is a European, responsible to the European Powers, and not a Turkish subject, responsible only to the Sultan, the scheme of reforms, which they otherwise cordially accept, will inevitably remain a dead letter.

F. O. 424/183, pp. 87-88, No. 70/1

No. 4

Sir P. Currie to the Marquess of Salisbury.

No. 465.   THERAPIA, *July 14, 1895.*
My Lord,   *(Received July 19.)*

THE Armenian Patriarch has been much distressed by the conduct of some of his Bishops in regard to the recent election of the Catholicos of Cis. They informed the Porte that the election was irregular, and obtained authority to go to Cilicia with the view of holding a new one. The Patriarch maintains that the proceedings were perfectly in order and according to precedent, and has urged the Turkish Government to issue the necessary authority for the meeting of the National Assembly, by which the election of the Catholicos must be ratified before his name is officially submitted to the Sultan.

His Beatitude called upon me yesterday, and spoke with great earnestness of the difficulties of his position. I told him that I could not, of course, interfere in any way in the internal affairs of the Armenian Church, but that I would ask the Grand Vizier, unofficially, to hasten the meeting of the Assembly.

The Patriarch mentioned that over 200 arrests of Armenians of the poorer class had taken place in Constantinople during the last fortnight, the grounds for which were unknown.

He also referred to the fact that, notwithstanding the solemn promises given to me by the Sultan and the late Grand Vizier, that all the Armenian ecclesiastics who were in prison would be released, there were still about fifteen either under surveillance or in actual confinement at Marash, Cesarea, Aleppo, and other places.

I spoke of all these matters privately to the Grand Vizier yesterday, and urged the importance of taking such steps as were possible for calming the irritation which prevailed among the Armenians. I also advised him to show more consideration towards the Patriarch, whom I believed to be a high-minded man, devoted to the interests of the Armenians, but not given to intrigue like so many of his countrymen.

The Grand Vizier said that he had had only one interview with the Patriarch, but that he had been favourably impressed by him. He promised to consider the questions of the meeting of the National Assembly, and the release of the ecclesiastics.

With regard to the arrests in Constantinople, he said they had been made without his knowledge or authority, and that, on hearing of them, he had written to the Minister of Justice to inquire on what grounds such action had been taken.

I have, &c.

(Signed) PHILIP CURRIE.

F. O. 424/183, p. 90, No. 80

No. 5

Sir P. Currie to the Marquess of Salisbury.

No. 298.   CONSTANTINOPLE, *July 17, 1895.*
Telegraphic.   *(Received July 17.)*
WITH reference to my telegram No. 291, I have the honour to state that on receipt of Mr. Hallward's despatch to Mr. Graves No. 51 I communicated the extract respecting the Vali of Van to the Grand Vizier, and again pressed upon him the necessity of the latter's dismissal.

His Highness informed me that no reply had as yet been received from the Sultan, but promised that he would renew his application.

F. O. 424/183, p. 89, No. 75

No. 6

The Marquess of Salisbury to the Archbishop of Canterbury.

My Lord Archbishop,   FOREIGN OFFICE, *July 17, 1895.*
I HAVE the honour to acknowledge the receipt of your letter of the 10th instant, expressing the hope that, in any reforms which may be introduced into the eastern provinces of Asiatic Turkey, full consideration may be given to the condition of the Assyrian Christians in the district of Hekkiari, and that they may be granted the protection necessary to their welfare.

I fear I am unable at present to make any further statement with regard to the position of the Patriarch, Mar Shimun, and his followers, than that contained in Lord Kimberley's communication to your Grace of the 4th ultimo.

A copy of your present letter will, however, be forwarded to Her Majesty's Ambassador at Constantinople.

I am, &c.

(Signed) SALISBURY.

F. O. 424/183, p. 89, No. 76

No. 7

Sir P. Currie to the Marquess of Salisbury.

No. 303.   CONSTANTINOPLE, *July 18, 1895, 11.20 p.m*
Telegraphic.   *(Received July 18.)*

INFORMATION has reached me from a trustworthy source that, despairing of introduction of reforms, the Armenian Revolutionary Committees are determined on provoking another massacre, and are said to be preparing insurrectionary movements in various places.

At Amassia sixteen Armenian Notables who have refused to join the revolutionary party have been condemned to death by the Committee, and one of these Notables, who is a leading Protestant at Marsovan, has been assassinated.

No. 8

Sir P. Currie to the Marquess of Salisbury.

No. 305.   CONSTANTINOPLE, *July 18, 1895, 11 p.m.*
Telegraphic.   *(Received July 18.)*

THE following communication sent to the Porte by the Sultan was read to-day by the Foreign Minister to the Russian, French, and English Dragomans:-

"His Imperial Majesty has at heart the welfare of all his subjects. He has sent reiterated orders to the Porte during the last few days to hasten necessary reforms and to insure good administration.

"Those reforms which are not contrary to Laws and Regulations already in existence His Majesty will immediately put into force, and Shakir Pasha is about to be sent to supervise and preside over their execution.

"Orders to take administrative and police measures to prevent conflicts and to control migrations of Kurds have already been given, and Shakir Pasha, whose presence will be a further guarantee, has also received orders to this effect."

The Foreign Minister stated in answer to inquiries that Shakir Pasha's mission was to carry out the reforms which would be announced in a day or two by the Porte in answer to the last communication from the three Embassies, and that he would start as soon as possible.

His Excellency also requested that an early answer should be given to this communication.

After Mr. Block had left, Turkhan Pasha, in a private conversation with the Russian and French Dragomans, said, "We are most desirous of settling the question;" at the same time expressing the hope that Shakir's nomination would be accepted by England.

Though Shakir's name was not explicitly submitted for approval, it is evidently intended to give the three Embassies an opportunity of concurring.

No objection will, I believe, be raised by the French and Russians.

In my despatch No. 435 of the 1st July, inclosing Colonel Chermside's No. 26, your Lordship will find the latest information as to Shakir Pasha.

F. O. 424/183, pp. 89-90, No. 78

No. 9

Sir P. Currie to the Marquess of Salisbury.

No. 306.   CONSTANTINOPLE, *July 18, 1895, 11.30 p.m.*
Telegraphic.   *(Received July 18.)*

REPORTS stating that animosity between Turks and Christians is increasing daily have been received from Yozgat by the French Embassy.

Our Consuls at Trebizond and Angora confirm the information as to murder of Protestant reported in my telegram No. 303 of the 18th July.

F. O. 424/183, p. 90, No. 79

No. 10

Sir P. Currie to the Marquess of Salisbury.

No. 476. Confidential.   THERAPIA, *July 18, 1895.*
My Lord,   *(Received July 29.)*

I INCLOSE a copy of a despatch addressed to me by Her Majesty's Consul at Trebizond on the 21st May relative to a Petition which had been forwarded to him by Mr. Jewett, the American Consul at Sivas, in regard to the case of two young Armenians accused of being revolutionists, one of whom was shot, and the other was said to have been tortured in prison with the approval of Bekir Pasha, the Mutessasrif of Amassia.

I communicated Mr. Longworth's despatch to Mr. Dwight, of the Bible House, and asked him if he could obtain my confirmation of the account given of the affair in the Petition.

I have now the honour to inclose a letter from him sending me the information that he has received on the subject from the American missionaries in the district, from which it appears that the young men in question had endeavoured to carry out a sentence of death passed by the Revolutionary Committee.

According to the reports received at the Bible House, Bekir Pasha is a man of great vigour, and, though unsparing towards the revolutionists, has shown the utmost firmness on several occasions in retraining the Mussulmans from attacking the Christians.

I have, &c.

(Signed) PHILIP CURRIE.

F. O. 424/183, pp. 119-120, No. 125

Inclosure 1 in No. 10

Consul Longworth to Sir P. Currie.

Sir,   TREBIZOND, *May 21, 1895.*

DR. JEWETT has transmitted to me a long Petition signed by 780 Armenians, dated Amassia, the 3rd instant, the substance of which is as follows.

On the 28th ultimo two young Armenians of good families, the one, Ohan Touloumbajian, age 16, and the other, Ohan Uskudarian, age 18, left town for a village. They wore the dress of mountaineers, and carried each a pistol. After a walk of three hours they met a carriage and wished to engage it. The driver refused to take them, went on, and spoke of them to some villagers as being Armenian brigands or insurgents. They were thereupon pursued, knocked down, and badly hurt. A Turk, Karachaga Hassan by name, a notorious criminal, often in prison, and only let out two months before, happened to pass by, heard what had occurred, and, drawing his revolver, shot Touloumbajian dead. He would have done the same with Uskudarian had not others interfered to save his life.

The lad, as well as the body of his companion, were then taken to Amassia, where Karachaga at once presented himself before the Governor and reported how he had thus cleared the country of two Armenian insurgents. Bekir Pasha, it is alleged, kissed him on the forehead, gave him £T.2, presented him with new weapons, and made him a mounted gendarme, promising him greater favour should he again distinguish himself by such services to the State.

A group was formed and photographed of the two lads, the dead and the living, dressed and armed like brigands, and guarded by twenty gendarmes, a picture which is apparently intended to serve the purpose of rendering Bekir Pasha's report more graphic.

It is furthermore asserted that the Municipal doctor was not allowed to examine the body of the murdered man; that Uskudarian was subjected to torture in prison; that the telegram to the Patriarch on the affair was stopped; and that the Armenian Prelate of Amassia was insulted and threatened for venturing to remonstrate against such proceedings.

I have, &c.

(Signed) H. Z. LONGWORTH.

F. O. 424/183, p. 120, No. 125/1

Inclosure 2 in No. 10

Memorandum on an Amassia Petition transmitted to Sir P. Currie by Consul Longworth, of Trebizond, May 21, 1895.

Confidential.

THIS Petition states that Ohan Touloumbajian and Ohan Uskudarian, of Amassia, attempted to engage a carriage on the highway near Amassia, but were refused by the driver. The driver then spoke of them to some villagers as suspicious characters, when the villagers attacked the two young men, killing one of them and taking the body, together with the survivor, to Amassia, when Bekir Pasha, Governor of Amassia, represented these two young men to be Armenian revolutionists, and rewarded the man who killed Touloumbajian.

A cautious inquiry on the ground reveals the following facts, which may be taken to be substantially capable of proof:-

1. The two young men named did not attempt to engage the carriage, but did attempt to shoot the driver.

2. The villagers came up at the noise of the firing, and killed Touloumbajian, because he would not surrender.

3. The two young men were dressed, not in their ordinary dress, but in the Georgian dress used as uniform by the Armenian revolutionists, with the initials of the Armenian Revolutionary Society embroidered on the sleeves of their coats, and cut upon the stocks of their revolvers.

4. The carriage driver fired upon by the young men had received notice some time before from the Armenian Revolutionary Society that he had been condemned to death by the Council of the Society as a traitor to Amassia.

(Signed) HENRY O. DWIGHT.

F. O. 424/183, pp. 120-121, No. 125/2

No. 11

Sir P. Currie to the Marquess of Salisbury.

No. 307.   CONSTANTINOPLE, *July 19, 1895.*
Telegraphic.   *(Received July 19.)*

DR. JEWETT telegraphed to Consul Longworth from Sivas that a big incendiary fire was reported at Marsovan. A number of Armenians had been arrested, and three assassinated.

F. O. 424/183, p. 91, No. 81

No. 12

Sir E. Malet to the Marquess of Salisbury.

No. 27.   BERLIN, *July 19, 1895, 2.30 p.m.*
Telegraphic.   *(Received July 19.)*

AFFAIRS in Armenia.

Baron von Rotenhan informs me that instructions have been sent to the German Ambassador at Constantinople to urge the Porte strongly to avail themselves of the occasion of your Lordship's accession to office to settle this question in a manner which your Lordship can consider acceptable.

F. O. 424/183, p. 91, No. 82

No. 13

Sir P. Currie to the Marquess of Salisbury.

No. 311.   CONSTANTINOPLE, *July 21, 1895, 11 a.m.*
Telegraphic.   *(Received July 21.)*

MR. SHIPLEY telegraphs to Mr. Graves at Erzeroum that the Government having, as far as he knows, made no attempt to stop them, the tribe of Alai Kuchan are arriving and camping in their pastures of last year. He has not heard of any unusual assembly taking place like that of last year, nor that they are camping in the immediate vicinity of ruined villages.

He adds that on several occasions he has spoken to Shefik Bey, pointing out that if the security of these Armenians is not guaranteed serious responsibility will fall on local authorities. He adds that at Talori and Shatakh there are a few troops.

I propose to ask the Grand Vizier what precautions are being taken to keep the Kurds in order, and to call his attention to the above.

F.O. 424/183, p. 96, No. 85

No. 14

Sir P. Currie to the Marquess of Salisbury.

No. 312.   CONSTANTINOPLE, *July 21, 1895, 11.30 p.m.*
Telegraphic.   *(Received July 21.)*

I WAS informed this evening by M. de Nélidoff that Russian Government have accepted the nomination of Shakir Pasha, and that he proposed to communicate acceptance to Porte to-morrow. On my telling him that I had no instructions from your Lordship on the subject, he said that in that case he was nclined, after consulting with M. Cambon, to inform the Porte that the Russian Government's acceptance was subject to that of the British and French Governments.

I pointed out that if this course was pursued we should be agreeing to the appointment of Shakir Pasha without knowing anything of the powers to be conferred on him, and that, in my opinion, it would be better to reserve our assent until we had been informed of the reforms which the Porte intended to introduce.

The justice of this view was admitted by M. de Nélidoff, and he proposed that we should meet to-morrow at the French Ambassador's to discuss the question. We meet accordingly to-morrow at 2 o'clock in Pera.

F. O. 424/183, p. 96, No. 86

No. 15

Sir P. Currie to the Marquess of Salisbury.

No. 313.   CONSTANTINOPLE, *July 21, 1895, 6.15 p.m.*
Telegraphic.   *(Received July 21.)*

FOLLOWING communication to Porte will be made to-day by Russian Ambassador in reply to that made Turkhan Pasha on the 18th instant to the three Dragomans, as reported in my telegram No. 305 of that day's date:-

"The choice of Shakir Pasha would not be objected to by the Russian Government, but it is necessary that they should know first whether the other two Powers accept his nomination, and also what the reforms are which he will have to supervise, and what powers are conferred to him."

The French Ambassador intends to send a similar reply to-morrow, but I shall await your Lordship's instructions before making any communication.

F. O. 424/183, p. 96, No. 87

No. 16

Sir P. Currie to the Marquess of Salisbury.

No. 320.   CONSTANTINOPLE, *July 24, 1895, noon.*
Telegraphic.   *(Received July 24.)*

MR. HAMPSON telegraphs that the Behranli nomad Kurds having arrived at their pastures, which are two hours distant from Moush, and near those of the inhabitants of the Protestant villages of Hadvoic, soldiers have been sent nominally to prevent a collision, but really to remove Armenians, who have now no place to feed flocks. So far all is quiet in Sasson and Talori, although at least the usual number of nomads are there. He hears that in those directions there are no troops, but in order to maintain order the Government have sent an influential Kurd, who is much mistrusted by the Armenians. It is said that the Sheikh of Zilan is also there.

F. O. 424/183, p. 114, No. 105

No. 17

The Marquess of Salisbury to the Marquess of Dufferin.

No. 384.

My Lord,   FOREIGN OFFICE, *July 24, 1895*

I HAD some conversation to-day with the French Ambassador on the Armenian question. I informed his Excellency that Her Majesty's Government were awaiting the Sultan's declaration as to which of the measures of reform proposed by the Ambassadors at Constantinople he was prepared to concede, but that they could not wait much longer, and that if His Majesty's decision were not shortly made known they would propose that the three Powers should consult together for a further step in advance. My difficulty, however, was that I had not been able to ascertain what course the Russian Government were prepared to adopt.

Baron de Courcel then told me that the Russian Ambassador was ill, or he would have called to-day to inform me that Prince Lobanoff had expressed his firm determination to adhere to the *entente* between Great Britain, France, and Russia, and his full belief that if the three Powers held together the Sultan would yield. In fact, His Majesty had only delayed giving way in consequence of the change of Government here, from which he had hoped to obtain some advantage.

I am, &c.

(Signed) SALISBURY.

F. O. 424/183, p. 114, No. 107

No. 18

The Marquess of Salisbury to the Marquess of Dufferin.

No. 385. Confidential.

My Lord,   FOREIGN OFFICE, *July 24, 1895.*

DURING the conversation recorded in my immediately preceding despatch the French Ambassador took rather excessive pains to assure me that France and Russia desired to keep abreast of us in dealing with the Armenian question. Without professing to be very enthusiastic about the matter, they were thoroughly convinced that after what had passed the three Powers could not allow the Sultan to put the matter aside without effecting a considerable amelioration in the condition of the provinces. His Excellency guarded himself from expressing any desire that the Armenians should be granted a privileged position, or anything else beyond good government.

I am, &c.

(Signed) SALISBURY.

F. O. 424/183, p. 115, No. 108

No. 19

The Marquess of Salisbury to Sir F. Lascelles.

No. 256. Confidential.

My Lord, FOREIGN OFFICE, *July 24, 1895.*

THE Russian Ambassador, who is confined to the house by an accident, sent me a message to-day to the following effect:-

His Excellency had received a letter, dated the 18th instant, from Prince Lobanoff, stating that the Turkish Government were delaying their answer with regard to reforms for the Armenian provinces in the hope of a change of policy on the part of the new Government here. The Prince, however, felt sure that if Great Britain, Russia, and France maintained a united front the Sultan would eventually accede to their demands.

M. de Staal inferred from this that Prince Lobanoff had sent further instructions to the Russian Ambassador at Constantinople.

I am, &c.

(Signed) SALISBURY.

F. O. 424/183, p. 115, No. 109

No. 20

Sir P. Currie to the Marquess of Salisbury.

No. 321. CONSTANTINOPLE, *July 25, 1895, 11 a.m.*

Telegraphic. *(Received July 25, noon.)*

MY telegram No. 319.

Following received from Longworth:-

"All Armenian political prisoners released."

F. O. 424/183, p. 115, No. 110

No. 21

Sir P. Currie to the Marquess of Salisbury.

No. 323.   CONSTANTINOPLE, *July 25, 1895, 10.30 a.m.*
Telegraphic.   *(Received July 25.)*
YESTERDAY I informed the Porte, in accordance with your Lordship's telegram No. 116 of the 23rd July, that, provided that the reforms which Shakir Pasha will have to supervise are adequate and satisfactory, and that the powers given to him are sufficient, we should not object to his appointment, but that, as the selection was not ours, we could not accept any responsibility for it.

F. O. 424/183, p. 115, No. 111

No. 22

Sir P. Currie to the Marquess of Salisbury.

No. 330.   CONSTANTINOPLE, *July 26, 1895, 11 a.m.*
Telegraphic.   *(Received July 26.)*
MR. GRAVES telegraphs that orders were received on the 24th instant that all political prisoners, except those from Talori and Sassoon, should be released.

F. O. 424/183, p. 118, No. 118

No. 23

Sir P. Currie to the Marquess of Salisbury.

No. 331.   CONSTANTINOPLE, *July 26, 1895, 10 p.m.*
Telegraphic.   *(Received July 26.)*
I CONGRATULATED the Sultan to-day, at an audience I had of His Majesty after the Selamlik, on the release of Armenian prisoners on whose behalf I had made representations on various occasions. His Imperial Majesty asked for my assistance in putting this measure before the public in a favourable light.

As regards the reform scheme, His Majesty said that the Council of Ministers would consider it finally on Sunday, and that they would put into execution one by one those reforms which were approved.

I said that, in the opinion of Her Majesty's Government, it was of great importance for the satisfaction of public opinion that the scheme of reforms adopted should be communicated in its entirety to the three Embassies, and that the gravity of the situation made it desirable that this should be done at once. To this His Majesty replied by assuring me that in the course of next week I should receive such a communication, and he added that he was anxious to bring the question to a conclusion, as he was weary of it.

F. O. 424/183, p. 118, No. 119

No. 24

The Marquess of Salisbury to Sir F. Lascelles.

No. 138.

Telegraphic. FOREIGN OFFICE, *July 26, 1895.*

I HAVE received your telegram of yesterday, No. 71, reporting the views entertained by Prince Lobanow on the question of reforms in Asia Minor.

I shall be glad if you will assure his Highness that what Her Majesty's Government are anxious to obtain for the Armenian population is merely justice and the security of life and property, and that the bestowal upon them of any exceptional privilege is neither being pressed nor is it desired by Her Majesty's Government.

F. O. 424/183, p. 118, No. 120

No. 25

Sir P. Currie to the Marquess of Salisbury.

No. 333. CONSTANTINOPLE, *July 27, 1895, 11.20 a.m.*

Telegraphic. *(Received July 27.)*

VICE-CONSUL HAMPSON telegraphed yesterday as follows:-

"Authorities in the Sassoon villages of Guendj Caza, where Armenian relief funds have been distributed, are collecting taxes.

"The funds of the Turkish Relief Commission are chiefly derived from drafts on the taxes of Guendj and Moush."

The attention of the Grand Vizier is being called to this report.

F. O. 424/183, p. 118, No. 121

No. 26

Sir P. Currie to the Marquess of Salisbury.

No. 334.   CONSTANTINOPLE, *July 27, 1895, 11 a.m.*
Telegraphic.   *(Received July 27.)*
    MR. HAMPSON telegraphed yesterday as follows:-
    "Armenian prisoners, thirteen in number, condemned for political offences, were to-day released.
    "All connected with events of last year, including Erko and Mourad, have been kept in prison, and have now been put in chains."
    F. O. 424/183, p. 119, No. 122

No. 27

Sir P. Currie to the Marquess of Salisbury.

No. 337.   CONSTANTINOPLE, *July 27, 1895.*
Telegraphic.   *(Received July 27.)*
    IN reply to my inquiries, Mr. Hampson informed me that none of the persons who gave evidence on the Armenian side before the Commission had been put in prison except Erko, who, before giving evidence, was imprisoned on a trumped-up charge of murder.
    The others are being carefully watched over by Mr. Hampson.
    F. O. 424/183, p. 119, No. 123

No. 28

Sir P. Currie to the Marquess of Salisbury.

No. 338.   CONSTANTINOPLE, *July 28, 1895.*
Telegraphic.   *(Received July 28.)*
    INSTRUCTIONS have been received by the Russian Ambassador from Prince Lobanoff in the sense of your Lordship's telegram No. 124 of 27th July, and M. de Nélidow is ready to resume the concert of the three Embassies in regard to the question of Armenia.
    I have informed the French and Russian Ambassadors that the Sultan promised to me that in the course of this week a communication shall be made to us, and I shall propose that we should jointly insist upon the Sultan keeping this promise.
    I have been informed by the German Ambassador that he has strongly urged His Imperial Majesty to agree to the demands of England in the Armenian

question, and that he has warned him that in the event of his failing to do so the joint pressure put on the Bulgarian Government in regard to Macedonia by the Powers will cease.

F. O. 424/183, p. 119, No. 124

No. 29

Sir F. Lascelles to the Marquess of Salisbury.

No. 193. Confidential.   ST. PETERSBURGH, *July 29, 1895.*
My Lord,   *(Received August 5.)*

ON the receipt on the 20th instant of your Lordship's telegram No. 129 of the previous day, I took an opportunity of speaking to Prince Lobanoff on the subject of the communication which had been sent to the Porte by the Sultan with regard to reforms in Armenia, and the nomination of Shakir Pasha to preside over them.

Prince Lobanoff said he had received a telegram from the Russian Ambassador at Constantinople, which coincided exactly with the telegram addressed to your Lordship by Sir Philip Currie, and his Excellency expressed his opinion that it would be advisable to accept Shakir Pasha's nomination.

I also spoke to Prince Lobanoff of the intention of the Armenian Revolutionary Committees to provoke another massacre, as they despaired of the introduction of reforms, His Excellency had received no information on this subject; and, at his request, I sent him a paraphrase of Sir P. Currie's telegram No. 303, which your Lordship did me the honour to repeat to me in your telegram No. 130 of the 19th instant.

I have, &c.

(Signed) FRANK C. LASCELLES.

F. O. 424/183, p. 154, No. 149

No. 30

Sir P. Currie to the Marquess of Salisbury.

No. 344.   CONSTANTINOPLE, *August 1, 1895, 10 a.m.*
Telegraphic.   *(Received August 1.)*

REFERRING to my telegram of the 28th ultimo, English, Russian, and French Dragomans were summoned by the Minister for Foreign Affairs to the Porte yesterday, when he stated that the Sultan had finally approved the answer as to reforms in Armenia, which would be communicated to the Embassies as soon as it had been translated into French.

F. O. 424/183, p. 136, No. 137
Turkey No. 1 (1896), p. 98, No. 125

No. 31

Sir P. Currie to the Marquess of Salisbury.

No. 488.   CONSTANTINOPLE, *August 1, 1895*
My Lord,   *(Received August 5.)*
     WITH reference to my telegram of the 25th ultimo, I have the honour to
forward to your Lordship copy of a despatch which I have received from Her
Majesty's Consul at Angora respecting the release of Armenian prisoners.
                         I have, &c.
                                        (Signed) PHILIP CURRIE.

F. O. 424/183, p. 138, No. 143

Inclosure in No. 31

Consul Cumberbatch to Sir P. Currie.

Sir,   ANGORA, *July 26, 1895.*
     IN confirmation of my telegram of yesterday's date, I have the honour to
report that on the 24th instant instructions were received by the Governor-General
of Angora to order the release of all Armenian prisoners undergoing their sentences
or awaiting their trial on seditious charges, with the exception of those who may
have been found guilty of murder or any other grave criminal offence such as
making or using bombs, &c.
     In consequence of this general amnesty, I calculate that about thirty of the
Armenians whose trials have taken place since my tenure of this office (October
1893), will be duly released, as well as those condemned by the Special Court, held
at Angora in May 1893, and sent to various fortress-prisons outside this vilayet.
                         I have, &c.
                                        (Signed) H. A. CUMBERBATCH.

F. O. 424/183, p. 138, No. 143/1
Turkey No. 6 (1896) p. 373, No. 483, 483/1

No. 32

Sir P. Currie to the Marquess of Salisbury.

No. 500.   CONSTANTINOPLE, *August 1, 1895.*
My Lord,   *(Received August 5.)*
    I HAVE the honour to forward to your Lordship herewith copy of a despatch which I have received from Her Majesty's Consul at Erzeroum on the subject of the distribution of relief at Sassoon, and inclosing an extract from a private letter from Moush.

I have &c.

(Signed) PHILIP CURRIE.

F. O. 424/183, pp. 138–139, No. 144

Inclosure 1 in No. 32

Consul Graves to Sir P. Currie.

Sir,   ERZEROUM, *July 18, 1895.*
    I HAVE the honour to inform you that Mr. Hallward has reported the departure of Dr. Reynolds from Van for Bitlis and Moush on the 4th instant, and I learn from Mr. Shipley's telegrams that he reached the latter place with the Rev. Mr. Cole on the 9th instant, leaving again for the Sassoon district on the 12th instant.
    I am informed that there is much sickness among the returned refugees, including small-pox, and that the still-unhealed wounds of many of them are in a very bad state from the heat, so that there will be full employment for Dr. Reynolds' medical skill in the hospital, which he and Mr. Cole are organizing at Semal.
    In this connection, I have the honour to transmit copies of an extract from a private letter from Moush, dated the 24th June, which gives a painful account of the privations endured by the Talori people, whose condition is far worse than that of the other Sassoonlis, both because they are more exposed to the attack of the Kurds, and because nothing whatever was done to enable them to plough and sow for this year's summer crops.
    This letter is of special interest, in so far as it gives a definite estimate of the number of destitute persons to be provided for, and of the daily cost of supplying them with a ration of bread.

I have, &c.

(Signed) R. W. GRAVES.

Turkey No. 1 (1895) Part I, p. 131, No. 249, 249/1, 249/2
F.O. 424/183, p. 139, No. 144/1

Inclosure 2 in No. 32

Extract from a Private Letter, dated Moush, June 24, 1895.

TALVORIG is composed of a number of villages, of which thirteen are now absolutely in ruins. No inhabitants remain. No buildings; not so much as a bit of timber. The former inhabitants are wanderers; last winter they took refuge in Psanats district, which comprises more than thirty villages, containing from 20 to 150 houses each, while some of them were scattered about Diarbekir. At the beginning of spring, oppression began at the hands of the nomad Kurds and others, and the villagers then decided that it was best to return to their former homes. There are about 860 of these houseless wanderers, now living in the woods and mountains, in caves and hollow trees, half-naked, and some, indeed, entirely without covering for their nakedness. Bread they have not tasted for months, and curdled milk they only dream of—living as they do upon greens and the leaves of trees. There are two varieties of greens which are preferred, but these are disappearing, as they wither at this season. Living on such food, they have become sickly; their skin has turned yellow, their strength is gone, their bodies are swollen, and fever is rife among them

I will send you a list of the deaths among them.

There is great enmity between the Kurds and these unfortunate people of Talvorig. The former lie in wait for them and shoot them on sight, nor do they allow them to leave the country, so that, shut on every side in their mountains, they will gradually die out. For the sake of humanity let their condition be made known. The authorities do not allow them to wander out and beg, like the remnant of the other Sasson villagers.

In the villages destroyed were eight stone churches with arched roofs. The woodwork of these was collected, piled on the altars, and burned. There were also twelve churches burned which were built wholly or partly of wood, and even the wooden foundations of these were pulled up and burned.

Bedros Tchouroyan, of Upper Talvorig, had two pieces of carpet and a brass vessel, and Hamzé Gamian, of Hosnoud, had two guns. These were sold, and flour purchased for last winter. But the others were and remain destitute, having nothing of value but a few guns.

I do not know what to suggest. There are more than 5,000 of these Sassoon people destitute and hungry. Less than one-fifth are now housed in huts. To give each of them a piece of dry bread daily, £T.40 a-day are wanted. We are trying to help them and give them the means of sowing some of their fields.

The collection of taxes here (at Moush) is being carried out with great severity, and between that and having to support the Sassoon refugees we know not where to turn. Bread is growing dear, and the general misery is on the increase; 600 okes of bread are being distributed daily.

One of the oxen we sent (to enable the refugees to plough) was stolen from Shenik by the Latchkanli Kurds. The nomad Kurds are steadily coming up, and are pitching their tents near the ruined villages: this has been arranged by the authorities. There is danger of serious trouble, for matters only are made worse when the Armenians complain of the Kurds, for the latter say, "You are *our* Armenians; how dare you complain of us?"

F. O. 424/183, pp. 138–140, No. 144/2
Turkey No. 1 (1895) Part I, p. 132, No. 249/2

No. 33

Sir P. Currie to the Marquess of Salisbury.

No. 501.   CONSTANTINOPLE, *August 1, 1895.*
My Lord,   *(Received August 5.)*

I HAVE the honour to forward to your Lordship herewith copy of a despatch which I have received from Her Majesty's Consul at Erzeroum, reporting upon the condition of Bitlis.

I have, &c.

(Signed) PHILIP CURRIE.

F. O. 424/183, p. 140, No. 145
Turkey No. 6 (1896) pp. 373, 374, No. 484, 484/1, 484/2

Inclosure 1 in No. 33

Consul Graves to Sir P. Currie.

Sir,   ERZEROUM, *July 18, 1895.*

I HAVE the honour to transmit herewith to your Excellency copies of an extract from a letter, dated Bitlis, the 10th July, containing some comments upon the dangers to be anticipated at the introduction of the projected scheme of reforms in that district; and also upon the grant of a decoration and promotion to the keeper of the Bitlis prison, the same Abdul-Kader Agha, whose alleged ill-treatment of prisoners is reported in my despatch of the 15th May.

At the same time it is stated that Yakoub Effendi, an official who had endeavoured to protect the inhabitants of the neighbouring village of Mezré, has been dismissed from his post.

I have, &c.

(Signed) R. W. GRAVES.

F. O. 424/183, p. 140, No. 145/1

Inclosure 2 in No. 33

Extract from a Letter, dated Bitlis, July 10, 1895.

I MUST confess that I do not contemplate success unless there is effective European control in all the Departments of the interior; not simply at Constantinople. I fear, too, that, unless there is a strong foreign protection, the transition period will be marked by much bloodshed. If Europe cannot furnish police, she would do well at least to see that the Christians were provided with arms for self-defence. Some are prudently trying to procure such for themselves, but, of course, with a good deal of difficulty and risk. You probably know that there is a growing Society among the Moslems, the members of which vow to shed blood in case the Sultan accepts the scheme of reforms. A week ago, a Moslem in a coffee-house swore that in three days they would cut off the Christians, beginning with the foreigners. It was in a public place, and there were plenty of witnesses, so we decided to speak of the matter, when we called on the Vali Vekil last Saturday. As usual, he promised well, but nothing has yet been done. I feel that it is not a matter to be passed over; and if, after a few more days, I see that no steps have been taken to restrain such a dangerous man, I may telegraph to Constantinople, since they have asked us three successive times by telegraph as to our welfare.

That Mulazim, Abdul Kader Agha, who is at the head of the prison, and is the one who is reponsible for the unspeakable cruelties that have taken place there, has received a decoration, and been promoted to Yusbashi. Yakoub Effendi, the Belediyé Mufettish (Inspector of the Municipality), has received contrary treatment. The Mezra villagers complained to the Government that the Government mules, which were pastured near their village, had been allowed to do a good deal of harm to their crops, &c. This Yakoub was sent to investigate. There he met a Mulazim, and remarked that they had indeed gone beyond all bounds in injuring the villages. Upon this the officer accused Yakoub of defending the Armenians, and reported the matter to the Ferik, who, in turn, reported it to the Vali Vekil, and, as a result, Yakoub was dismissed.

F. O. 424/183, pp. 140–141, No. 145/2

No. 34

Sir P. Currie to the Marquess of Salisbury.

No. 503.   CONSTANTINOPLE, *August 1, 1895.*
My Lord,   *(Received August 5.)*
     I HAVE the honour to forward to your Lordship herewith copy of a despatch which I have received from Her Majesty's Consul at Aleppo, reporting the

imprisonment of two members of the Tarsus Bible Mission, the one for having in his possession "The Revolt of Islam," the other an old Hymn Book containing "Onward Christian Soldiers." I have called the attention of the Grand Vizier to these two cases.

I have, &c.

(Signed) PHILIP CURRIE.

F. O. 424/183, p. 152, No. 147

Inclosure in No. 34

Consul Barnham to Sir P. Currie.

Sir, ALEPPO, *July 18, 1895.*

I HAVE the honour to bring to your Excellency's notice the case of two members of the Tarsus Bible Mission, who are reported by Mr. Christy, President of the Mission, to have been recently sentenced to terms of imprisonment for political offences. One has been sentenced to one year's imprisonment, on the sole ground that among his books was found a copy of Shelley's works containing "The Revolt of Islam."

The other has been condemned at the same time to a year's imprisonment simply for having in his possession an old Hymn Book in which there is a translation of the hymn "Onward, Christian Soldiers."

Owing to misapprehension of the meaning of this piece by the officers of the Government, it had long been omitted from the books used in the Mission Schools, and the offence is limited to the fact that he was found in possession of an old disused book containing the hymn.

I have, &c.

(Signed) HENRY D. BARNHAM.

F. O. 424/183, p. 153, No. 147/1
Turkey No. 6 (1896), pp. 374-375, No. 485, 485/1

No. 35

Sir P. Currie to the Marquess of Salisbury.

No. 504. CONSTANTINOPLE, *August 1, 1895.*
My Lord, *(Received August 5.)*

I HAVE the honour to forward to your Lordship herewith copy of a despatch which I have received from Her Majesty's Consul at Trebizond, reporting the pardon of Armenian political prisoners.

I have, &c.

(Signed) PHILIP CURRIE.

F. O. 424/183, p. 153, No. 148

Inclosure in No. 35

Consul Longworth to Sir P. Currie.

Sir,   TREBIZOND, *July 26, 1895.*
    ON the 24th instant I wired to your Excellency thus: "All Armenian political
prisoners released."
    This Imperial clemency is understood to cover all those who, without having
committed any act against the common law, were either suspected or convicted of
treasonable sedition and conspiracy.
    As regards the Vilayet of Sivas, I am informed by a telegram just received that
forty-five in that town had been released, although pardon could well be extended
to thirty-five of the other political prisoners. I am further informed that the result of
two of the more important trials which took place there on the 25th instant was that
of those arrested for the assault of Hadjee Musta's house eight have been sentenced
to fifteen years' imprisonment, and three to four years; while of those arrested for
the Gavra robbery one was sentenced for life, two to fifteen years, and two to four
years. Those acquitted number four in the first and nine in the second batch of
prisoners.
                         I have, &c.
                                              (Signed) H. Z. LONGWORTH.
    F. O. 424/183, p. 153, No. 148/1
    Turkey No. 6 (1896) p. 375, No. 486, 486/1

No. 36

Sir P. Currie to the Marquess of Salisbury.

No. 345.   CONSTANTINOPLE, *August 2, 1895, 2.30 p.m.*
Telegraphic.   *(Received August 2.)*
    HER Majesty's Consul at Erzeroum telegraphed yesterday as follows:-
    "The Russian Delegate and Mr. Shipley will, in the course of a week or ten
days, have completed their work here, with our assistance. They are at present
engaged with copies of the General Report and Annexes, and in making a collation
of the *procès-verbaux* copied here, of which sixty still remain unsigned.
    "Mr. Shipley should, I conclude, finish the above work before leaving.
    "The fair draft of the General Report signed by the three Delegates, but
without the Annexes, has been dispatched with the French Delegate, who left this
morning.
    F. O. 424/183, p. 136, No. 138
    Turkey No. 1 (1895), Part I, pp. 130-131, No. 248

No. 37

Sir P. Currie to the Marquess of Salisbury.

No. 346.   CONSTANTINOPLE, *August 2, 1895, 7.50 p.m.*
Telegraphic.   *(Received August 2.)*

YESTERDAY the Report of the Commission appointed to consider the proposals for reform made by Russia, France, and England was communicated by the three Dragomans without any observations, and I am forwarding a copy to your Lordship by to-morrow's post.

The communication purports to give the details we asked for on receipt of the Porte's note of the 17th June.

The plan of reforms is dealt with Article by Article, but no reference is made to our Memorandum.

Five years appointment of Valis and any fixed proportion of Christian Kaïmakams and Mutessarifs are refused, but non-Mussulman assistants where necessary are granted.

Election of Mudirs, proposals as to collection of taxes (Chapter 12), are judicial reforms (Chapter 13), Christian officers of gendarmerie, rural police, are refused.

It undertakes to enforce Regulations in the sense of the 2nd paragraph of our proposals as to the Hamidieh (Chapter 10).

It promises to employ sufficient armed force to control the Kurds and to enforce the Regulations as to arms.

It admits recruitment of gendarmes from Moslems and non-Moslems.

It promises a Special Commission on title-deeds.

The appointment of Shakir Pasha and the engagement taken in the 5th paragraph of the Porte's note of the 17th June form the only security for the execution of such reforms as are promised, but the general tone of the communications is that the existing Regulations do not require amendment.

I shall discuss the document with my colleagues to-morrow afternoon.

F. O. 424/183, p. 136, No. 139
Turkey No. 1 (1896), p. 98, No. 126

No. 38

Mr. Elliot to the Marquess of Salisbury.

No. 94.   ATHENS, *August 3, 1895.*
My Lord,   *(Received August 10.)*
    WITH reference to Mr. Egerton's despatch No. 46 of the 4th May, I have the honour to report that the two Armenian proprietors of the "Vatan" newspaper appeared yesterday before the Court of Misdemeanours to answer to the charge of libelling the Sultan, and were discharged on the ground of absence of reciprocity, there not existing in Turkey any penalty for libel against a foreign Sovereign.
    The other charge against them, of publishing a newspaper without authorization, will be heard before the Police Court in a few days.
                                  I have, &c.
                                                      (Signed) F. ELLIOT.
    F. O. 424/183, p. 173, No. 162

No. 39

Sir P. Currie to the Marquess of Salisbury.

No. 565.   THERAPIA, *August 3, 1895.*
My Lord,   *(Received August 7.)*
    I HAVE the honour to inclose a copy of the third answer from the Turkish Government to the Armenian Reform proposals of the three Powers. The previous answers were given on the 2nd and 17th June, and should be read in connection with the one I now forward. The first named stated the intention of the Sultan to extend the administrative reforms to all the vilayets of the Empire. It dealt chiefly with the Memorandum presented by the Embassies, but the ground it took up was substantially the same as that to which the Porte still adheres, with the exception of the appointment of Shakir Pasha to superintend the execution of the reforms.
    The answer of the 17th June conceded this appointment, and added that the Imperial Government declares to the Ambassadors that, whilst safeguarding the sovereign rights of His Imperial Majesty the Sultan and those of his Empire, it is ready to proceed to the immediate execution of the reforms in conformity with the LXIst Article of the Treaty of Berlin, and on the basis of the LXIIIrd Article of the same Treaty.
    It added that, in view of maintaining the principle of equality and of justice, the Imperial Government, when carrying out the organization, would take account of the proportion of the number of its subjects, and that it would concede to the Powers no prerogative beyond that granted to them by the Treaty of Berlin.

The inclosed summary of the Porte's last answer, which has been prepared by Colonel Chermside, gives the substance of the decisions taken on our project of reform Article by Article.

It is probable that so long as Shakir Pasha occupies the post to which he has just been named, the Regulations for the control of the Kurds and the Hamidieh regiments will be more strictly enforced than has hitherto been the case. But the main object which we had in view in proposing the reforms was, as I stated to the Sultan, with the assent of my colleagues on the 5th April last, to secure the good government and contentment of the Armenians by obtaining for them a fair share in the Administration.

I have, &c.

(Signed) Philip Currie.

F. O. 424/183, pp. 155-156, No. 153
Turkey No. 1 (1896), pp. 99-100, No. 130

Inclosure 1 in No. 39

Observations on the Draft of Reforms presented by the Ambassadors of the three Powers for certain Vilayets in Anatolia.

Chapitre I

ARTICLE 1er. Le choix et la nomination de fonctionnaires capables aux postes de Gouverneurs-Généraux et à toutes les autres fonctions publiques, la destitution, le remplacement, et au besoin la mise en jugement de ceux qui seraient reconnus coupables de procédés abusifs sont déjà prévus par les Règlements existants.

Le Gouvernement Impérial entend à porter un soin encore plus grand à ce que les Gouverneurs-Généraux nommés par Iradé Impérial soient choisis également à l'avenir conformément à ces principes réglementaires.

Aux termes du Firman Impérial des réformes octroyé en 1272 tous les sujets de l'Empire à quelque communauté qu'ils appartiennent ont accès selon les règles d'une application générale aux fonctions publiques suivant leurs capacités et aptitudes.

Or, toute personne appelée à occuper les plus importantes fonctions de l'ordre civile comme celles de Vali doit avoir acquis de l'expérience à tous les degrés de la hiérarchie administrative. Si l'on prend surtout en considération la diversité de castes et de mœurs des populations des vilayets dont il s'agit et le fait que d'après les inscriptions des registres du cens, la majorité appartient en tout cas et sous quelque régime que ce soit, à l'élément Musulman, on acquiert la ferme conviction que toute modification du mode actuellement en vigueur pour la nomination des Valis, loin d'améliorer l'administration, entraînerait des complications de nature à compromettre la tranquillité publique. Dans ces conditions, il convient de nommer suivant les exigences locales des adjoints aux Gouverneurs-Généraux, choisis parmi les fonctionnaires non Musulmans appartenant à la partie la plus nombreuse des diverses populations non Musulmanes.

Article 2. Les Valis et autres fonctionnaires ne sont point révoqués tant qu'ils ne sont pas reconnus coupables d'actes de nature à entraîner légalement leur destitution. La preuve en est qu'il y a des Valis et autres fonctionnaires qui conservent leurs postes depuis huit à dix ans. Étant donnée cette règle d'après laquelle personne ne peut être révoquée sans motif légal, on ne voit pas la nécessité d'une restriction ayant pour objet de limiter à un terme de cinq ans la durée des fonctions des Valis.

Article 3. La nomination des adjoints des Gouverneurs-Généraux a été traitée dans la partie finale de l'Article Ier. Leurs attributions se trouvent entièrement et clairement précisées au Chapitre II du Règlement relatif à l'administration générale des Vilayets inséré dans le Dustour.

Chapitre II.

Article 4. De même qu'aux chefs-lieux des vilayets, de même dans la plupart des sandjaks, la majorité appartient aux Musulmans d'après le chiffre proportionnel des habitants. Dans ces conditions, la nomination au poste de Gouverneurs de fonctionnaires Musulmans, capables et compétents paraît tout indiqué. Seulement des non-Musulmans capables et probes peuvent être nommés Mouavins dans tout sandjak où l'État jugerait nécessaire.

Les postes de Caïmacam sont réservés aux diplômés de l'École Civile. Sur le choix du Ministère de l'Intérieur des élèves tant Musulmans que non-Musulmans de cette école sont actuellement nommés par Iradé Impérial aux dits postes. Il convient de maintenir le même système quant au choix de ces fonctionnaires.

Les Musulmans et non-Musulmans qui sans être sortis de l'École occuperaient à l'heure qu'il est des postes de Caïmacam et dont les services et la fidélité seraient éprouvés, pourront être, sur la proposition des Valis appuyée par le Ministère de l'Intérieur, nommés par Iradé Impérial au poste de Caïmacam. On veillera avec le plus grand soin, sur la base de leurs états de services, à ce que ces Caïmacams soient des personnes sans tache et d'une conduite, d'une probité, et d'une fidélité éprouvée aux yeux du Gouvernement. Aux Caïmacams se trouvent attachés des collaborateurs tels que Receveurs des Finances ("Mal-Mudiri"), et Chefs de la Correspondance ("Takrirat Kiatibi"). Créer encore dans tous les cazas des postes spéciaux de Mouavin entraînerait des frais considérables. Du reste, il n'existe pour cela aucune nécessité. En conséquence, plutôt que d'établir partout de pareils postes, il vaudrait mieux les restreindre à certains Caïmacamats ayant une position importante. Dans ce cas, il conviendrait de donner un Mouavin Chrétien au Caïmacam si celui-ci est Musulman et *vice versâ*. Dans les cazas il existe des Conseils d'Administration dont les attributions sont définies au Chapitre IV du Règlement concernant l'administration générale des vilayets et dont les membres Musulmans et non-Musulmans sont élus par les habitants. Ces Conseils sont en état de discuter et de régler les affaires locales de toutes sortes dans tous leurs détails. Il devient dès lors inutile de former dans chaque caza un Conseil spécial chargé de délibérer sur des affaires d'utilité publique et autres.

Le mode d'élection des membres des Conseils d'Administration est indiqué dans les Règlements sur les vilayets et dans celui de l'Administration Communale.

L'organisation communale pourrait se faire conformément aux dispositions des Articles 94 à 106 du Règlement de l'administration générale des vilayets du 9 Janvier, 1286, élaboré sous le Grand Vézirat de feu Aali Pacha, et des Articles 1ᵉʳ à 28 du Règlement sur l'administration communale du 25 Mars, 1292, élaboré sous le Grand Vézirat de feu Mahmoud Nédim Pacha. Cependant le fait que dans les bourgs et villages de l'Empire les populations de différentes classes se trouvent souvent mélangées exclut la possibilité de grouper, comme on en suggère l'idée, les villages d'une même religion dans un même nahié.

L'Administration de chaque nahié par un Moudir et l'institution d'un Conseil chargé d'administrer la commune pourraient se faire également suivant les Règlements susmentionnés.

Seulement ces Règlements contiennent un paragraphe d'après lequel le Conseil Communal pourrait avoir jusqu'à huit membres.

Comme ces membres sont renouvelés par moitié chaque année, il serait plus opportun que le nombre des membres Musulmans et non-Musulmans ne fût que de quatre.

Article 9. Le mode d'élection des Conseils Communaux est soumis aux Règlements précités.

Si tous les habitants d'un nahié sont d'une même classe, il est naturel que les membres du Conseil soient élus parmi les habitants appartenant à cette même classe; si la population d'un cercle communal est mixte, il est également convenable que la minorité soit représentée proportionnellement à son importance, à condition que cette minorité comprenne au moins vingt-cinq maisons.

Article 10. Les Moudirs et les Secrétaires des communes sont déjà rétribués.

Lors de la mise à exécution des mesures ayant pour objet l'organisation des nahiés les appointements seront naturellement fixés dans les limites de l'allocation générale.

Seulement, comme les Règlements en vigueur ne prévoient pas, pour les dépenses locales des communes, l'élaboration d'un budget, cette tâche incombe au chef-lieu des vilayets.

Article 11. Dans l'élection des membres du Conseil Communal les conditions indiquées dans le Règlement concernant l'administration générale des provinces et dans le Règlement des communes doivent être observées.

Il est entendu aussi que les membres à élire ne doivent pas avoir subi de condamnation pour crime ou pour délit politique.

Article 12. L'élection par les habitants des Moudirs des communes à l'instar des membres du Conseil est prévue, il est vrai, par le Règlement de l'administration communale. Mais il n'est pas dit dans ce Règlement que les membres élus choisiront un d'entre eux pour le poste de Moudir et qu'ils en feront part directement au Gouverneur-Général. Au contraire, il est stipulé qu'après que les habitants auront élu aussi le Moudir, son nom sera communiqué par l'entremise du Caïmacam du district dont relève la commune au Mutessarif et par celui-ci au Vali, qui confirmera la nomination par écrit et remplira les formalités nécessaires.

Toutefois la question de savoir si les Moudirs doivent être nommés par l'État ou par voie d'élection est l'objet de controverses même dans certains pays Européens. En égard aux conditions spéciales de l'Empire Ottoman, la nomination de ces Moudirs par l'État serait plus conforme à l'intérêt public. Aussi, le Gouvernement Impérial préfère-t-il le choix et la nomination par l'État des Moudirs des communes à former conformément aux deux Règlements susmentionnés, ainsi que cela se pratique à l'égard des Moudirs déjà existants.

Article 13. Aux termes de l'Article 12 du Règlement de l'administration communale tous ceux qui se trouvent au service du Gouvernement—les professeurs d'école et les prêtres—ne peuvent exercer les fonctions de Moudir.

Article 14. Ce point s'accorde aussi avec l'Article 16 du Règlement de l'administration communale. Le dernier paragraphe est cependant en contradiction avec le même Article, car, dans la partie finale du dit Règlement, il est clairement stipulé que le Moudir et les membres sont rééligibles. En égard au nombre limité de gens capables de remplir dans les communes les fonctions de membres, et au fait que la nomination des Moudirs par le Gouvernement est estimée préférable, le paragraphe réglementaire concernant les membres paraît plus conforme aux exigences de la situation.

Article 15. Les attributions du Moudir et des membres des Conseils Communaux, ainsi que le mode de leur élection et de leur remplacement, sont réglés par les dispositions des Articles 20 à 27 du Règlement sur l'administration des communes.

Article 16. Cet Article est conforme aux Articles spéciaux des Règlements sur l'organisation et l'administration générale des vilayets et du Règlement sur l'administration des communes.

Article 17. Cet Article est conforme aux Règlements sur l'administration des vilayets et des communes.

Chapitre V.

Police

Article 18. Les Règlements en vigueur ne prévoient pas le recrutement parmi les habitants des communes et l'emploi d'agents de police par les Conseils Communaux. Les agents de police d'une commune, s'ils étaient choisis et recrutés parmi les habitants de cette même commune, pourraient y avoir des parents ou alliés, ou être animés d'animosités personnelles à l'égard de certains habitants, ce qui excluerait la possibilité pour eux de remplir consciencieusement les devoirs de leur charge et de se comporter avec impartialité.

La formation au chef-lieu du vilayet de la police et la gendarmerie à recruter parmi les sujets Ottomans honnêtes et dignes de confiance dans la proportion du chiffre général des habitants Musulmans et non-Musulmans de chaque vilayet, l'augmentation selon les besoins locaux des contingents de gendarmerie et de police réservés au district et l'affectation aux chefs-lieux des communes d'un chiffre convenable à détacher de ces contingents paraissent suffisantes pour assurer le but désiré au point de vue de la tranquillité publique.

Article 19. Les agents de police du chef-lieu de la commune agiront naturellement, en matière de police, sous les ordres du Moudir. Si ces agents sont nombreux et s'il y a parmi eux un Commissaire de Police ils devront évidemment se conformer aux Règlements en vigueur. Leurs armes et uniformes seront identiques aux modèles déjà adoptés pour la police. Leurs soldes sont payables par les caisses des districts. Ces agents, rétribués qu'ils sont, devront d'une façon permanente se consacrer à l'accomplissement de leur tâche, sans qu'il leur soit permis de vaquer à leurs affaires personnelles.

Quand les soldats de l'armée régulière en service actif payent dans leurs pays leurs redevances fiscales, il n'y a pas lieu d'exempter les agents de police non-Musulmans du paiement de la taxe d'exonération militaire.

Les agents de police exercent leurs fonctions dans les limites de leurs circonscriptions. L'emploi d'agents montés n'a donc pas de raison d'être et est sans précédent.

Après avoir examiné sur les lieux quel nombre de nouveaux agents de police il serait nécessaire d'employer dans les vilayets il sera procédé à leur recrutement suivant les besoins réels et absolus. Afin d'éviter des dépenses inutiles, il importe de ne point donner à cette mesure plus d'extension que ne le comportent les véritables nécessités. Il est bien entendu que le mode d'emploi, la conduite et les attributions de ces agents doivent rester dans les limites de ce qui se pratique actuellement à l'égard du corps des agents de police et qu'ils ne pourront s'arroger aucun caractère nouveau.

Article 20. Les devoirs de police tels que la surveillance des routes, le maintien de la tranquillité publique, et la sécurité du transport des valises postales incombent à la gendarmerie à pied et à cheval. Il appartient aux autorités centrales des sandjaks et des cazas d'expédier ces gendarmes le cas échéant.

Chapitre VI.

Article 21. Il convient de recruter les gendarmes parmi les habitants Musulmans et non-Musulmans suivant les exigences locales, et de choisir les officiers et les sous-officiers de ce corps dans les cadres de l'armée Impériale. La solde des gendarmes est supérieure à celle des soldats réguliers et celle des officiers équivalente à la solde des officiers de l'armée Impériale. Il est évident que, suivant la règle établie, les soldes et dépenses de la gendarmerie doivent être payées par les caisses des vilayets.

Chapitre VII.

Prisons.

Article 22. Les prévenus sont détenus dans les maisons d'arrêt et les condamnés dans les prisons. C'est aux Valis, Mutessarifs, et Caïmacams de veiller aux conditions hygiéniques des prisons. Les Procureurs-Généraux sont, de leur côté, tenus de faire des inspections à cet égard. Les prisons ont, en outre, un personnel complet de fonctionnaires et de domestiques, tels que Directeur, Secrétaires, Gardiens. On pourrait faire des recommandations pour qu'il soit apporté par ces moyens encore plus de soins à l'administration de l'état des maisons d'arrêt, et des prisons, à la garde desquelles sont préposés des gendarmes et des agents de police. Les tortures et les traitements vexatoires envers les détenus et prisonniers sont interdits de par la loi, qui prescrit les pénalités les plus rigoureuses à l'égard des contrevenants.

Chapitre VIII.

Article 23. L'enquête préliminaire est actuellement effectuée à Constantinople et dans les provinces par les soins des Conseils de Police. Le mode recommandé se trouve d'ailleurs inscrit dans les instructions relatives à l'administration générale des vilayets.

Chapitre IX.

Article 24. La présence dans chaque vilayet d'un Achiret-Memouri chargé de l'administration des Kurdes nomades, de l'arrestation et de la remise des brigands et des criminels n'offre aucun avantage pratique ni ne paraît présenter la perspective d'un projet applicable, attendu qu'il est improbable que les Chefs d'une tribu puissent exercer une influence quelconque sur une autre tribu. En conséquence la poursuite et l'arrestation des brigands et criminels parmi les tribus nomades, leur remise aux Tribunaux doivent être laissées à la gendarmerie et dépendre des ordres donnés et des dispositions adoptées par le Vali. La plupart de ces tribus ne sont pas nomades; leur principal moyen d'existence consistant simplement dans l'élevage des bestiaux, elles se rendent l'été dans leurs pâturages et rentrent en hiver dans leurs foyers situés dans les bourgs et villages. Les localités qu'elles doivent traverser pendant ces migrations seront désignées d'avance, et afin qu'elles ne puissent se livrer à aucun empiètement ou excès sur les biens ou les personnes des habitants sédentaires de ces localités, une force armée suffisante, sous le commandement d'un officier nommé par le Commandant du Corps d'Armée ainsi qu'un détachement de gendarmes et d'officiers désignés par le Vali, seront envoyés sur les lieux. On veillera avec soin à la stricte application à leur égard des dispositions des Règlements sur les feuilles de route et le port d'armes.

Comme garantie que ces tribus ne se porteront à aucun acte contraire aux ordres et recommandations qui leur seront donnés, il est parfois d'usage que les Chefs des tribus envoient au chef-lieu du vilayet ou du sandjak le plus proche un de leurs parents ou alliés jouissant de l'estime et de la confiance de la tribu pour y rester comme otage jusqu'à leur retour dans leurs foyers. Cet usage sera maintenu en vigueur. S'il existe des tribus constamment errantes le Gouvernement aura soin de les encourager à se fixer en leur concédant des terres et des pâturages.

Telles sont les mesures qui peuvent être considérées comme nécessaires.

Les Valis, Mutessarifs, et Caïmacams veilleront avec la plus grande attention à ce que les Chefs des tribus ne soient pas exposés à des insultes ou à des dangers par le fait des intrigues et des calomnies des gens sans aveu.

CHAPITRE X.

Article 25. On a indiqué la façon dont les régiments Hamidiés seraient employés dans le cas où il serait nécessaire de les appeler sous les armes en dehors des périodes déterminées. Les Règlements relatifs à ces régiments étant en train d'être remaniés, les restrictions concernant le port d'armes et d'uniformes en dehors des périodes d'instruction rentrent dans les dispositions des nouveaux Réglements à élaborer. Si des cavaliers Hamidiés en dehors des périodes d'instruction, c'est-à-dire lorsqu'ils ne sont pas sous les armes, venaient à commettre des actes entraînant des poursuites judiciaires, ils sont justiciables d'après l'usage en vigueur des Tribunaux ordinaires.

CHAPITRE XI.

Article 26. Le Gouvernement Impérial prenant en considération la question de la garantie de la propriété immobilière, avait déjà établi comme principe de faire délivrer des titres uniformes par l'Administration des Archives pour les terres et immeubles de toute catégorie en abrogeant l'ancienne règle d'après laquelle, tant à Constantinople que dans les provinces, des titres de diverses formes étaient délivrés pour ces propriétés. C'est ainsi qu'au moyen de la délivrance par l'Administration précitée de titres réguliers soit pour les terrains émiriés et vakoufs, soit pour les immeubles mulks, les droits de propriété des populations ont été garantis. Étant donné que pour l'examen des faits et actes se rapportant à la propriété immobilière il faut avoir une connaissance spéciale des lois sur la matière, cet examen ne saurait être fait par de simples Commissions instituées sur les lieux et composées de membres Musulmans et non-Musulmans. Aussi conviendrait-il de nommer à cet effet des Commissions composées de quatre membres dont deux Musulmans et deux non-Musulmans qui seraient placées, dans les chefs-lieux des vilayets, sous la présidence du Délégué de l'Administration des Archives, et dans les chefs-lieux des sandjaks, sous la présidence du préposé aux propriétés fonciéres.

Ces Commissions auront essentiellement pour mission de reviser les titres authentiques de ceux qui prétendraient avoir des droits de propriété. Cependant, comme il est possible que certaines personnes, par ignorance des dispositions de la loi, ne se soient pas fait délivrer les titres de leurs terrains et immeubles et que par contre d'autres se soient procuré des titres sur des affirmations *ex parte,* il importe de prendre aussi en considération ce point important dans le cours de la revision, d'examiner et de rechercher à telles fins que de droit les circonstances se rattachant à la possession par voie d'achat ou de transfert ou de succession des immeubles et terrains dont les ayants droit ne seront pas procurés dans le temps pour une raison ou une autre des titres de propriété pour ces mêmes immeubles et terrains, de ne priver personne de ses anciens droits parce que des titres ne sont pas produits, de se livrer en ce qui concerne ceux qui se sont procurés d'une façon quelconque des titres sans que leurs droits de propriété aient pu être établis au fond, à des investigations pour savoir comment ils ont pu obtenir ces titres, d'arriver ainsi à mettre les propriétés de chacun à l'abri de toute usurpation, enfin de ne laisser aucune marge à des revendications injustes et à des chicanes et de s'attacher surtout à préserver de toute atteinte les terrains et immeubles Vakoufs.

Voilà en quoi doit consister la tâche principale des dites Commissions.

Leurs résolutions doivent être examinées et approuvées par les Conseils d'Adminitrations des vilayets et des sandjaks. Il conviendrait de déférer aux Tribunaux les affaires qui exigeraient une solution légale. Et pour que cela se fasse conformément au principe de centralisation administrative, quatre personnes choisies parmi les plus honorables, les plus probes, et ayant un passé sans tâche seront envoyées chaque année de la capitale aux vilayets avec mission d'examiner si des procédés contraires au droit et à l'équité ont lieu, et d'en faire connaître le résultat à la Sublime Porte. De cette façon un contrôle sera exercé.

Chapitre XII.

Perception des Dîmes.

Article 27. Que la perception en espèces de tous les produits des dîmes en général soit impossible en égard à la condition des populations, c'est là un point que l'expérience faite à diverses reprises et dans différents endroits a démontré. Le paiement en nature de la dîme à l'époque des récoltes constitue évidemment une facilité pour les habitants. D'ailleurs, aux termes du Règlement qui régit la matière, la mise en adjudication des dîmes par village et leur affermage en cas de demande de la part des habitants, étant admises, le maintien de cette règle paraît s'imposer. Des Percepteurs avaient été nommés dans les temps pour la perception des autres revenus de l'Empire; mais comme ce moyen n'avait pu assurer la rentrée régulière des impôts et un régime normal de nature à offrir des facilités aux populations sous le rapport de l'Administration des Revenus Publics, et que le Gouvernement Impérial avait dû rechercher un mode de perception autre que celui de l'emploi de la force publique, des détachements spéciaux chargés du service de perception avaient été formés. Il a été établi pour principe que ces détachements ne feraient aucune réquisition de fourrages et de vivres dans les endroits où ils se rendraient sous peine de se voir sévèrement punis. Comme le prélèvement et la consignation aux caisses locales des impôts dûs par les populations incombent aux Moukhtars, et aux Receveurs des villages et quartiers élus par les habitants, il est également établi que les hommes faisant partie des détachements de perception n'ont pas à manier d'argent. Dès lors il semble inutile de songer à remplacer ce régime par le mode proposé, d'autant plus que les Percepteurs qu'on voudrait faire choisir et nommer par les Conseils Communaux ne peuvent être autres, ainsi qu'il vient d'être constaté, que les Receveurs et les Moukhtars élus par les habitants.

Article 28. L'essai que le Gouvernement Impérial a fait de l'administration en régie, et non par voie d'affermage des dîmes, loin d'emmener la régularité dans cette branche du service, a donné lieu, au contraire, à des pertes fiscales et à des plaintes de toutes sortes de la part des populations. C'est pour ce motif que le système d'affermage a été rétabli. Seulement, en vue de prévenir toute cause de plainte, une série de clauses et de restrictions ont été insérées au Règlement sur les dîmes. Par exemple, l'affermage en gros des dîmes a été supprimé et remplacé, ainsi qu'il est dit à l'Article précédent, par le système de la mise en adjudication par villages et au nom des habitants pour l'encouragement et la facilité de ces derniers. En outre, de même qu'en cas de difficulté dans l'encaissement des prix d'affermage, le Gouvernement a recours aux Tribunaux, de même les habitants jouissent, d'après la règle en vigueur, de la faculté de s'adresser librement aux Conseils d'Administration et aux Tribunaux en cas de plaintes et de réclamation contre les fermiers.

La corvée se trouve absolument interdite depuis de longues années. Les contre-venants encourent une responsabilité de ce chef. Dès lors il n'y a pas lieu de songer à établir une nouvelle restriction réglementaire à ce sujet. L'établissement de caisses publiques dans les communes a été aussi essayé dans le temps, mais cet essai, loin de donner de bons résultats au point de la régularité des opérations, a été cause que le fisc a subi gratuitement des pertes. Il n'y aurait donc aucun avantage matériel à renouveler cet essai. Il importe de maintenir le régime actuellement en vigueur d'après lequel les dépenses communales fixes inscrites au budget des vilayets sont réglées mensuellement par les caisses des cazas. Les dépenses de vilayets et des sandjaks inscrites au budget sont également réglées par les caisses publiques.

Les frais de construction et de réparation, les allocations de ponts et chaussées, ainsi que les opérations relatives aux prestations en nature et en argent concernent le Ministère des Travaux Publics qui se met à ce sujet en communication avec les vilayets aux fins requises. Quant aux sommes nécessaires pour les dépenses de l'instruction publique, c'est le Ministère de l'Instruction Publique qui les inscrit au Budget et pourvoit à leur réglement en se mettant en communication avec les autorités.

En égard aux Règlements établis, il importe de continuer à procéder aussi à l'avenir suivant cette même règle.

La population n'a jamais eu à fournir gratuitement soit aux fonctionnaires, soit aux troupes Impériales, le logement et les provisions nécessaires à leur entretien. Elle n'a pas été non plus l'objet de mesures de rigueur lors de la perception des impôts. Les arriérés considérables que la population doit chaque année au chef des revenus fiscaux, tels qu'impôts et taxe d'exonération militaire en sont la preuve. Au demeurant, comme il existe des dispositions réglementaires qui défendent la vente pour cause de dettes fiscales ou personnelles de la demeure particulière du contribuable, des terrains nécessaires à sa subsistance, de ses outils et instruments aratoires, de ses bêtes de labour et de ses grains, il n'y a pas lieu d'établir de nouvelles Règles et Lois à cet effet.

CHAPITRE XIII.

Article 29. Il y a dans les communes des Conseils des Anciens ayant pour mission de régler à l'amiable les contestations de peu d'importance, et de réconcilier les parties conformément aux Règlements établis.

Article 30. Dans les cazas il existe des Tribunaux de Première Instance dans les conditions indiquées par la Loi Organique des Tribunaux. Les fonctions de Juges de Paix sont exercées dans les villages par les Conseils des Anciens et dans les communes par les Conseils Communaux. Leur attribution et le degré de leur compétence en matière de réglement d'affaires sont déterminées par la Loi susdite. Il n'y a aucune disposition légale qui prévoie la nomination recommandée des Juges de Paix aux chefs-lieux des cazas et des communes. Il n'y a pas non plus dans les communes et villages des personnes versées dans les questions juridiques. Il ne conviendrait conséquemment pas de nommer des Juges de Paix investis d'attributions si étendues.

Article 31. A l'Article précédent il a été établi qu'il n'y a pas lieu de former des Tribunaux de Paix.

Dès lors il devient inutile de parler de leurs attributions.

Article 32. En matière civile la désignation d'arbitres ne rentre pas dans les attributions des Tribunaux. Aux termes du Code de Commerce les Tribunaux de Commerce nomment des experts dans les procès entre Sociétés. D'ailleurs, comme il a été dit qu'il n'est pas nécessaire de former des Tribunaux de Paix, il n'y a pas lieu d'examiner encore davantage la fixation d'une pareille attribution.

Article 33. D'après les explications qui ont été données sur l'impossibilité et l'inutilité de l'institution de Tribunaux de Paix et sur la nécessité du maintien de l'organisation actuelle de la justice de paix, la conservation des Tribunaux de Première Instance des districts rentre dans l'ordre naturel des choses.

Article 34. Vu l'inutilité des Tribunaux de Paix telle qu'elle ressort des explications qui précèdent, ce que cet Article désigne comme faisant partie de leurs attributions perd toute raison d'être.

Article 35 La nécessité du maintien des Tribunaux de Première Instance dans les cazas a été déjà expliquée. En ce qui concerne les Tribunaux Civils et Criminels des sandjaks les Lois judiciaires ne prévoient pas l'institution de Cours d'Assises ambulantes destinées à connaître des affaires criminelles en lieu et place des Tribunaux Criminels.

On ne peut pas non plus se figurer l'avantage et la possibilité d'une pareille mesure, car les difficultés des communications entraîneraient des pertes de temps dans la tournée d'une Cour de ce genre. Pendant l'hiver les routes seraient interceptées sur certains points; de telle sorte que les procès criminels, notamment les cas de flagrant délit qui exigent une instruction et un jugement à brève échéance, subiraient des retards par suite de la non apparition à temps de la Cour, ce qui, en rendant difficile la réunion de preuves et indices de nature à emmener la conviction, compromettrait les actions criminelles et civiles.

Article 36. Ainsi qu'il ressort des explications données à l'Article précédent, l'organisation de Cours ambulantes est difficile et sans utilité. Il n'y a pas lieu par conséquent de déterminer le mode à suivre dans l'organisation de ces Cours.

Article 37. Puisque le principe même de l'organisation de Cours ambulantes n'a pas été jugé conforme aux exigences de la situation, il n'y a pas lieu de s'occuper de la fixation de leurs attributions.

Article 38. Le principe de la formation de Cours ambulantes n'ayant pas été jugé admissible, l'examen des indications contenues dans cet Article n'a pas de raison d'être.

Article 39. La formation aux chefs-lieux des vilayets d'une Cour Supérieure composée d'un Président et de deux membres constitue une proposition qui ne rentre pas dans les dispositions des Lois judiciaires. Au chef-lieu de chaque vilaye il existe deux Tribunaux d'Appel: l'un Civil, l'autre Criminel, composés chacun d'un Président et de quatre membres, ainsi que des Tribunaux Civils et Criminel de Première Instance composés d'un Président et de deux membres. Le Tribunaux d'Appel examinent les causes civiles et criminelles jugées par le Tribunaux de Première Instance. Quant aux procès criminels qui surgissent dan les chefs-lieux des vilayets, c'est le Tribunal d'Appel qui en connaît le premier.

Les Tribunaux Civils et Criminels de Première Instance composés chacun d'un Président et de deux membres qui se trouvent dans les cazas, connaissent conformément aux Lois Organiques des Tribunaux et aux Codes de Procédure Civile et Criminelle, des procès civils et criminels aux chef-lieux des sandjaks e examinent en appel les Jugements appelables des Tribunaux de Cazas.

L'expérience a démontré la suffisance et l'utilité de l'organisation des Tribunaux provinciaux. Il n'y a donc pas lieu légalement et pratiquement parlan de modifier cette organisation pour former une Cour Supérieure comme celle don il est fait mention plus haut.

Les Jugements rendus par les Tribunaux ordinaires en matière civile e criminelle doivent être absolument libellés en Turc, langue officielle du pays.

Turkey No. 1 (1896), pp. 100-106, No. 130/1

Translation.

CHAPTER I.

ARTICLE 1. The selection and appointment of capable functionaries to the posts of Governors-General and all other public offices, their dismissal, the substitution of others, and, if necessary, the trial of such as may be considered guilty of committing abuses, are already provided for by the existing Regulations.

It is the intention of the Imperial Government to take still greater care that the Governors-General appointed by Imperial Iradé are, in future also, selected in accordance with these established principles.

By the terms of the Imperial Firman of reforms granted in 1272, all the subjects of the Empire, to whatsoever community they belong, are eligible, under the general rules laid down for the performance of public duties, in proportion to their capacity and fitness.

Now, every individual called to fill the most important civil posts, such as that of Vali, must have gained experience in all stages of the administrative hierarchy. Taking into consideration especially the diversity of caste and habits among the populations of the vilayets in question, and the fact that, according to the Returns of the census registers, the Mussulman element forms the majority in every case and under any régime, it is quite evident that any modification of the system now in orce for the appointment of Valis, far from improving the administration, would ntail complications likely to disturb public tranquillity. In these circumstances, it s advisable to appoint, according to local requirements, Assistants to the Governors-General, selected from among the non-Mussulman functionaries belonging to the most numerous of the various non-Mussulman populations.

Art. 2. Valis and other functionaries are not dismissed unless found guilty of acts which legally entail their dismissal. This is proved by the fact that there are Valis and other functionaries who have held their posts eight or ten years. Admitting this rule, that no one can be dismissed without legal cause, there seems no necessity for a restriction the object of which is to limit to a term of five years the duration of appointments of Valis.

Art. 3. The appointment of Assistants to the Governors-General has been dealt with in the last part of Article 1. Their duties are completely and clearly defined in Chapter II of the Regulations relative to the general administration of the vilayets inserted in the "Destur."

CHAPTER II.

Art. 4. As in the chief towns of the vilayets, so in most of the sandjaks, the Mussulmans form the majority of the inhabitants. That being so, the appointment of capable and competent Mussulman functionaries as Governors seems clearly called for. But capable and upright non-Mussulmans may be appointed Moavins in any sandjak where the State considers necessary.

The posts of Kaïmakam are reserved for graduates of the Civil School. Chosen by the Ministry of the Interior, pupils of this school, both Mussulman and non-Mussulman, are now appointed to these posts by Imperial Iradé. It is advisable to adhere to this mode of selecting these functionaries.

Mussulmans and non-Mussulmans, not from the school, who are now filling the post of Kaïmakam, and who are of tried service and loyalty, may, on the recommendation of the Valis, supported by the Ministry of the Interior, be appointed by Imperial Iradé to the post of Kaïmakam. The greatest care will be taken, by examining records of service, that these Kaïmakams shall be of blameless character, and that the Government is satisfied that they are well conducted, honest, and loyal. Attached to the Kaïmakams are coadjutors such as Receivers of Revenue ("Mal-Mudiri") and Chief Clerks ("Takrirat Kiatibi"). The creation in addition in all the cazas of special posts of Moavin would entail considerable expense. Moreover, there is no necessity for it. Instead, therefore, of establishing such posts everywhere, it would be better to limit them to certain Kaïmakamats of importance. In such cases it would be advisable to give a Christian Moavin to the Kaïmakam if the latter is a Mussulman, and vice versâ. In the cazas Administrative Councils exist, whose duties are defined in Chapter IV of the Regulations relative to the general administration of the vilayets, and whose members, Mussulman and non-Mussulman, are elected by the inhabitants. These Councils are in a position to discuss and settle local matters of all kinds in every detail. It is therefore unnecessary to form in each caza a special Council charged to discuss questions of public utility and other matters.

The mode of election of members of the Administrative Councils is set forth in the Regulations concerning the vilayets, and in those concerning the communal administration.

The communal organization might be based on the provisions of Articles 94 to 106 of the Regulations for the general administration of the vilayets of the 9th January, 1286, drawn up under the Grand Vizierate of the late Aali Pasha, and of Articles 1 to 28 of the Regulations on the communal administration of the 25th March, 1292, drawn up under the Grand Vizierate of the late Mahmud Nedim Pasha. But the fact that in the small towns and villages of the Empire populations of different classes are often intermingled excludes the possibility of grouping the villages of the same religion in the same nahié, as suggested.

The administration of each nahié by a Mudir, and the institution of a Council charged with the administration of the commune, might also be effected under the above-mentioned Regulations.

Only these Regulations contain a paragraph according to which the Communal Council may consist of as many as eight members.

As half these members retire each year, it would be more convenient that the number of Mussulman and non-Mussulman members should only be four.

Art. 9. The mode of election of the Communal Councils is governed by the above-quoted Regulations.

If all the inhabitants of a nahié are of the same class, it is natural that the members of the Council should be elected from the inhabitants belonging to that class; if the population of a communal district is mixed, it is equally fitting that the minority should be represented in proportion to its importance, provided the minority comprises at least twenty-five houses.

Art. 10. The Mudirs and Secretaries of the communes already receive remuneration. When the measures for the organization of the nahié are carried out the salaries will naturally be fixed within the limits of the general scheme of payments.

But as the Regulations in force make no provision for the drawing up of a budget for the communal expenses, this task falls to the chief town of the vilayet.

Art 11. In the election of the members of the Communal Council the conditions specified in the Regulations for the general administration of the provinces and in the Regulations for the communes must be observed.

Candidates must not have been sentenced for crimes or political offences.

Art. 12. The Regulations for communal administration provide, it is true, that the Mudirs of the communes, like the members of the Council, shall be elected by the inhabitants. But it is not stated in these Regulations that the members elected shall choose one amongst their numbers for the post of Mudir and inform the Governor-General directly. On the contrary, it is laid down that when the inhabitants have elected the Mudir also, his name shall be communicated through the Kaïmakam of the district to which the commune belongs to the Mutessarif, and by the latter to the Vali, who shall confirm the appointment in writing and complete the necessary formalities.

The question whether Mudirs should be appointed by the state or by election is, however, a disputed point even in some European countries. Looking to the special conditions of the Ottoman Empire, the appointment of these Mudirs by the State would be more in accordance with the public interest. The Imperial Government prefers, therefore, that the State should have the choice and appointment of the Mudirs for the communes to be formed in accordance with the two sets of Regulations above mentioned, as is the practice in the case of the Mudirs already existing.

Art. 13. By the terms of Article 12 of the Regulations for communal administration, persons in the Government service, schoolmasters, and priests cannot hold office as Mudir.

Art. 14. This point also is in conformity with Article 16 of the Regulations for communal administration. The last paragraph, however, does not agree with the Article, for in the concluding part of the said Regulations it is clearly laid down that the Mudir and the members may be re-elected. Considering the limited number of persons in the communes capable of fulfilling the duties of members, and the fact that the appointment of Mudirs by the Government is considered preferable, the paragraph in the Regulations respecting the members seems more in accordance with the requirements of the situation.

Art. 15. The duties of the Mudir and the members of the Communal Councils, as well as the mode of electing and replacing them, are laid down in Articles 20 to 27 of the Regulations for the administration of the communes.

Art. 16. This Article is in conformity with the special Articles of the Regulations for the organization and general administration of the vilayets, and of the Regulations for the administration of the communes.

Art. 17. This Article is in conformity with the Regulations for the administration of the vilayets and communes.

CHAPTER V.

Police.

Art. 18. The Regulations in force do not contain provisions for the recruiting of police agents from among the inhabitants of the communes, or for their employment by the Communal Councils. If the police agents of a commune were chosen and recruited from among the inhabitants of that commune, they might have relatives or friends there, or have feelings of personal animosity against certain inhabitants, which would exclude the possibility of their executing their duties conscientiously, or acting with impartiality.

The formation in the chief town of the vilayet of police and gendarmerie, recruited from honest and trustworthy Ottoman subjects, Mussulman and non-Mussulman, in proportion to the total number of Mussulman and non-Mussulman inhabitants in each vilayet, the increase, according to local requirements, of the contingents of gendarmerie and police allotted to the district, and the assignment to the chief towns of communes of an adequate number of men detached from these contingents, seem sufficient to secure the end desired from the point of view of public tranquillity.

Art. 19. The police agents of the chief town of the commune will naturally act, in police matters, under the orders of the Mudir. If these agents are numerous, and if there is among them a Commissioner of Police, they must clearly be subject to the Regulations in force. Their arms and uniform will be of the pattern already adopted for the police. They will receive their pay from the district treasuries. These agents, being paid, must devote themselves exclusively to the discharge of their duties, and will not be permitted to occupy themselves with their private affairs.

Since soldiers of the regular army on active service pay taxes in their native places, no ground exists for exempting non-Mussulman police agents from payment of the tax of exemption from military service.

The police agents perform their duties within the limits of their districts. The employment of mounted police is therefore uncalled for, and there is no precedent for it.

After it has been ascertained on the spot what number of fresh police agents is required for employment in the vilayets, their recruitment will be proceeded with in accordance with the real and absolute requirements. To avoid unnecessary expense, no greater extension should be given to this measure than absolute necessity warrants. It must be clearly understood that the mode of employment of these agents, their action and duties, must remain within the limits now observed by the corps of police agents, and that they cannot claim any new character.

Art. 20. Police duties, such as the supervision of the roads, the maintenance of public tranquillity, the safe conveyance of the mails, devolve on the gendarmerie, foot and horse. It is the duty of the central authorities of the sandjaks and cazas to send these gendarmes to any place where they are wanted.

Chapter VI.

Art. 21. It is advisable to recruit the gendarmes from among the Mussulman and non-Mussulman inhabitants in accordance with local requirements, and to elect the officers and non-commissioned officers of this corps from the Imperial army. The pay of the gendarmes is higher than that of the regular soldiers, and that of the officers is the same as that of officers of the Imperial army. It is clear that the pay and expenses of the gendarmerie must be paid by the treasuries of the vilayets according to the established rule.

CHAPTER VII.

Prisons.

Art. 22. The accused are detained in the houses of detention, and the convicted in the prisons. It is the duty of the Valis, Mutessarifs, and Kaïmakams to see that the prisons are in a proper sanitary condition. The Procureurs-Généraux are also bound to hold inspections for this purpose. The prisons have a complete staff of officials and servants, such as a Governor, clerks, warders. Instructions might be sent with a view to still greater care being taken, by these means, in the supervision of the condition of the houses of detention and prisons, which are in charge of gendarmes and police agents. Torture and ill-treatment of accused persons and prisoners are forbidden by the law, which imposes the strictest penalties on those who transgress it.

CHAPTER VIII.

Art. 23. Preliminary inquiries are now held at Constantinople and in the provinces by the Councils of Police. The method recommended appears in the instructions relative to the general administration of the vilayets.

CHAPTER IX.

Art. 24. The presence in each vilayet of an Ashiret-Memuri charged with the administration of the nomad Kurds, and the arrest and delivery of brigands and criminals, offers no practical advantage, and does not appear to be a practicable arrangement, as it is improbable that the Chiefs of one tribe can exercise any influence over another tribe. Therefore the pursuit and arrest of brigands and criminals among the nomad tribes, and their delivery to the Tribunals, must be left to the gendarmerie, and depend on the orders given and the steps taken by the Vali. The majority of these tribes are not nomadic; their principal means of subsistence being the breeding of cattle; they go in summer to their pastures, and return in winter to their homes in the small towns and villages. The localities to be traversed by them in these migrations will be indicated beforehand, and to prevent their committing any encroachments or excesses on the property or persons of the residents in these localities, a sufficient armed force, commanded by an officer named by the Commander of the Army Corps, as well as a detachment of gendarmes and officers selected by the Vali, will be sent to the spot. Care will be taken that the provisions of the Regulations as to passes and the carrying of arms are strictly applied to them.

As a guarantee that these tribes will obey the orders given to them, the Chiefs of the tribes sometimes send to the chief town of the nearest vilayet or sandjak one of their kinsmen or friends enjoying the esteem and confidence of the tribe to remain there as hostage until their return home. This custom will continue in force. If there are any tribes which are always wandering, the Government will take care to encourage them to remain stationary by grants of lands and pastures.

The above are the measures which may be regarded as necessary.

The Valis, Mutessarifs, and Kaïmakams will take the greatest care that Chiefs of tribes are not exposed to insults or dangers through the intrigues or calumnies of worthless characters.

CHAPTER X.

Art. 25. The manner of employing the Hamidié regiments, if it is found necessary to call them under arms at other than the regular times, is indicated. As the Regulations concerning these regiments are being revised, the restrictions relative to carrying arms and wearing uniform outside the training times are points which come under the provisions of the new Regulations to be drawn up. If the Hamidié troopers, outside the periods of training, that is, when not under arms, commit acts which render them liable to be prosecuted, they are amenable to the jurisdiction of the ordinary Tribunals.

CHAPTER XI.

Art. 26. The Imperial Government, taking into consideration the question of the security of real property, had already laid down the principle that uniform title-deeds should be issued by the Administration of the archives for land and real property of every description, and that the old system, according to which, both at Constantinople and in the provinces, various kinds of title-deeds were issued for those properties, should be abolished. Thus, by the issue, by the aforesaid Administration, of regular title-deeds, both for "émirié" and "vakouf" lands, and for real property which is "mulk," the rights of property of the populations have been secured. Admitting that, for the examination of matters connected with real property, a special knowledge of the laws on the subject is necessary, such an examination cannot be carried out by mere local Commissions composed of Mussulman and non-Mussulman members. It is therefore advisable to appoint, for this purpose, Commissions composed of four members, two Mussulman and two non-Mussulman, to sit in the chief towns of the vilayets, under the presidency of the Delegate of the Administration of the Archives, and in the chief towns of the sandjaks under the presidency of the Superintendent of Real Property.

It will be the special duty of these Commissions to inquire into the validity of the titles of those whom claim to have proprietary rights. But as it is possible that some people, through ignorance of the law, may not have applied for title-deeds of their lands and real property, and as, on the other hand, others may have obtained title-deeds on *ex parte* declarations, it is necessary to take this important point also into consideration in the process of revision; to inquire into the circumstances connected with the possession, by purchase, transfer, or inheritance, of real property and lands for which, for one reason or another, the owners have not obtained title-deeds; to deprive none of their ancient rights because title-deeds are not forthcoming; to make an investigation in the case of those who by some means obtained title-deeds without their rights of ownership being thoroughly established, in order to discover how they came by those title deeds; to protect, by these means, the property of every one from all usurpation; and, finally, to leave no loop-hole for unfounded claims and fraud; and to take special care to preserve intact the Vakouf lands and other real property.

The above must be the principal task of the aforesaid Commissions.

Their decisions must be examined and approved by the Administrative Councils of Vilayets and Sanjaks. Matters which require to be decided in a Court of law should be referred to the Tribunals; and in order that this may be done in accordance with the principle of administrative centralization, four persons, most honourable and upright men with a blameless past, shall be sent every year from the capital to the vilayets with instructions to ascertain whether anything is being done that is contrary to law or equity, and to report the result to the Sublime Porte. By this means a control will be exercised.

CHAPTER XII.

Collection of Tithes.

Art. 27. The impossibility, in view of the condition of the populations, of collecting in money all the revenues drawn from the tithes generally, has been proved by experience at different times and places. The payment of the tithe in kind at harvest-time is clearly a convenience to the inhabitants. Moreover, as the letting of the tithes by villages, and the farming of them, if a request for such an arrangement is made by the inhabitants, is allowed under the terms of the Regulations governing the subject, the maintenance of this rule appears necessary. Collectors were formerly appointed to collect the other revenues of the Empire; but as this method did not insure the regular receipt of the taxes, or a normal system such as would meet the convenience of the populations in the matter of the administration of the public revenues, and as the Imperial Government were obliged to look for a system of collection that would not necessitate the employment of the public force, special corps were formed, charged with the business in connection with the levy of taxation. The principle has been laid down that no forage or food may be requisitioned by these corps in the localities they visit, under pain of severe punishment. As the Mukhtars and Receivers of the villages and wards, elected by the inhabitants, are responsible for the actual collection, and the delivery to, the local treasuries of the taxes owing by the inhabitants, it is likewise laid down that no money is to pass through the hands of persons belonging to the special staff above mentioned. It therefore seems unnecessary to substitute the arrangement proposed for the system now obtaining, especially as the Collectors, who it is proposed should be chosen and appointed by the Communal Councils, must necessarily be, as has been shown, the Receivers and Mukhtars elected by the inhabitants.

Art. 28. The experiment made by the Imperial Government of collecting the tithes directly, instead of farming them out, far from introducing regularity into this branch of the service, led on the contrary to loss of revenue, and to complaints of all sorts on the part of the populations. For this reason the system of farming out was re-established. Only, in order to avoid any ground for complaint, various clauses and restrictions were inserted in the Regulations concerning the tithes. For instance, the farming out of the tithes on a large scale was abolished, and replaced, as stated under the preceding Article, by the system of farming them out by villages in the name of the inhabitants, for the encouragement and convenience of these latter. Moreover, just as when there is difficulty in obtaining payment of the money due from the tithe-farmers, the Government has recourse to the Tribunals, in the same way, in accordance with the rule in force, the inhabitants have the power of applying freely to the Administrative Councils and the Tribunals in cases of complaints or claims against the farmers.

The corvée has for many years been absolutely prohibited. Offenders in this matter are liable to penalties. There is therefore no occasion to draw up fresh restrictive Regulations on the subject. The establishment of public treasuries in the communes was also tried formerly, but this experiment, far from tending to greater regularity of operations, occasioned gratuitous loss to the Treasury. There would therefore be no material advantage in a renewal of this experiment. It is advisable to maintain the system now in force, by which the fixed expenses of the communes inserted in the budgets of the vilayets are paid every month by the treasuries of the cazas. The expenses of the vilayets and sandjaks inserted in the budget are likewise paid by the public treasuries.

Expenditure on building and repairs, grants for bridges and roads, and the operations connected with contributions in kind and in money, concern the Department of Public Works, which communicates with the vilayets in these matters for all necessary purposes. As regards the sums necessary to meet the expenses of public instruction, they are inserted in the budget by the Department of Public Instruction, which arranges for the payments in communication with the authorities.

Taking into consideration the established Regulations, it is advisable that the present system should remain in force.

The population has never had to provide gratuitously for the officials or Imperial troops lodgings or provisions for their maintenance. Nor has it been harshly treated in connection with the levying of the taxes. The considerable arrears which are owing each year by the population to the Treasury on account of the tax for exemption from military service and other taxes are a proof of this. Moreover, as Regulations are in existence forbidding the sale for debts to the Treasury or personal debts of the private residence of the taxpayer, of the land necessary for his subsistence, of his tools and agricultural implements, of his beasts of labour, or of his seed, there is no occasion for making new Regulations and laws to this effect.

Chapter XIII.

Art. 29. There are in the communes Councils of Elders, whose business it is to settle by friendly agreement disputes of little importance, and to reconcile the parties in accordance with the established Regulations.

Art. 30. There exist in the cazas Courts of First Instance constituted in accordance with the provisions of the Organic Law of the Tribunals. In the villages the duties of Magistrates are discharged by the Councils of Elders, and in the communes by the Communal Councils. Their duties and the extent of their competency in the settlement of cases are defined by the Law above mentioned. No legal provision exists for the appointment, as recommended, of Magistrates in the chief towns of the cazas and communes. Nor are there in the communes and villages persons conversant with legal questions. Consequently, it would not be advisable to appoint Magistrates invested with such extensive powers.

Art. 31. Under the preceding Article, it was shown that no grounds exist for creating Magisterial Courts.

There is, therefore, no need to discuss their functions.

Art. 32. In civil matters, the appointment of Arbitrators does not come within the duties of the Tribunals. Under the Commercial Code, the Commercial

Tribunals appoint experts in suits pending between Companies. Moreover, as it has already been stated that there is no necessity for the creation of Magisterial Courts, there is no need to discuss further the assignment of such a function.

Art. 33. As it has been shown that it is useless and impossible to establish Magisterial Courts, and that it is necessary to maintain the existing organization of the Magistrate's jurisdiction, it follows naturally that the Tribunals of First Instance of the districts must be preserved.

Art. 34. In view of the uselessness of Magisterial Courts, as shown above, the description of their functions in this Article ceases to have any application.

Art. 35. The necessity for maintaining the Tribunals of First Instance of the cazas has already been explained. As regards the Civil and Criminal Tribunals of the sandjaks, the judicial laws do not provide for the institution of movable Courts of Assize, intended to take the place of the Criminal Tribunals in dealing with criminal cases.

It is not apparent what would be the advantage of such an arrangement, or how it could be carried out, for the difficulties of communication would entail loss of time while a Court of this kind was on circuit. In winter the roads would be blocked in some places; so that criminal cases, especially those of persons caught *Flagrante delicto*, which require a speedy trial and sentence, would be delayed by the non-appearance of the Court at the proper time; such delays would make it difficult to collect the evidence in support of the prosecution, and would prevent justice being done in criminal and civil actions.

Art. 36. As shown under the preceding Article, the organization of movable Courts is difficult and useless. There is no occasion, therefore, to settle the manner in which these Courts should be organized.

Art. 37. Since it is not considered advisable to organize movable Courts, there is no need to discuss the duties of such Courts.

Art. 38. As the creation of movable Courts has not been found admissible in principle, this Article need not be considered.

Art. 39. The creation in the chief towns of the vilayets of a High Court, composed of a President and two members, is foreign to the provisions of the judicial Laws. At the chief town of each vilayet there are now two Courts of Appeal, one Civil, the other Criminal, each composed of a President and four members, as well as Civil and Criminal Courts of First Instance, composed of a President and two members. The Courts of Appeal examine civil and criminal cases tried by the Courts of First Instance. As regards criminal cases arising in the chief towns of the vilayets, the Court of Appeal deals with them in the first place.

The Civil and Criminal Courts of First Instance, each composed of a President and two members who are in the cazas, deal, in accordance with the Organic Laws of the Tribunals and the Codes of Civil and Criminal Procedure, with civil and criminal cases in the chief towns of the sandjaks, and examine, on appeal, decisions of the Tribunals of cazas where appeal can be made.

Experience has proved the sufficiency and utility of the organization of the provincial Tribunals. There is therefore no occasion, from a legal or practical point of view, to modify this organization in order to create a High Court such as that mentioned above.

The decisions of the ordinary Tribunals in civil and criminal matters must absolutely be drawn up in Turkish, the official language of the country.

Turkey No. 1 (1896), pp. 107-114, No. 130/1

Inclosure 2 in No. 39

Summary by Colonel Chermside of the Porte's last Answer.

Headings.   *Précis.*

CHAPTER I.

ARTICLE 1. Grants non-Mussulman Muavins.

ARTICLE 1. Acknowledges that post of Vali is open to Christians, but goes so far as to assert that their nomination for various reasons would be undesirable; undertakes to name, where necessary, non-Mussulman assistants to Valis.

Art. 2. Refuses five years' term.

Art 3

Art. 4. Refuses proportion of Christian Mutessarifs demanded.

Admits non-Mussulman Muavins.

Art. 2. Refused five years' term.

Art. 3. Covered by Article 1.

Art. 4. Asserts Mussulman majority exists in most of sandjaks, accordingly Mussulman Mutessarifs appear desirable; does not even state that Christian Mutessarifs will be admitted; admits non-Mussulman Muavins.

Art. 5. Kaïmakams:-
Proportion of Christians asked refused.
Graduates of Civil School, Moslem and Christian, are eligible; present system considered satisfactory. No definite undertaking.

Art. 5. Kaïmakams:-
Graduates of Civil School, Moslem and Christian, can occupy this post on nomination of Minister of the Interior.

No undertaking as to nominating any definite proportion of Christians.

Any actual Kaïmakams, Moslem or Christian, not from the School, can be appointed to the post.

Art. 6. One-third proportion of Mutessarifs and Kaïmakams not accepted.

Art. 6. Maintains existing system generally, but will create post of Muavin in certain cazas.

Headings.   *Précis.*

Will appoint Muavins to assist Kaïmakams where necessary.

Existing Councils maintained instead of proposed reorganization.

Refuses proposed reorganized Council of Caza, and maintains the actual system in force.

Ignores other recommendations, but by inference refuses Council-General.

Art. 7. Maintains organization of nahiés as prescribed in existing Regulations, but not given practical effect to; does not accept proposed reorganization.

Art. 7. Communal organization would be established according to Laws of 1286 and 1292. (These hitherto have only been partially applied.) The modifications proposed are not accepted.

Art. 8. Qualified acceptance of nahié Administration by Mudir and Council.

Art. 8. Nahié Administration by Mudir and Council approved. Suggests only four members; not from four to eight as proposed.

Arts. 9 and 10. Election of nahié Council according to existing Rules. Mudir to be paid. Nahié expenses not to be separate, but charged in vilayet budget.

Arts. 9 and 10. Maintains existing Rules without modifications. Does not make the Mudir an official elected by the people. Allows his pay, but does not admit communal budget.

Art. 11. Election of Communal Council.

Art. 11. Unimportant detail. No remarks to make on Porte's observations. No concessions made.

Art. 12. Election of Mudir by people refused.

Art. 12. Points out the difference of formalities of election of Mudir, as laid down in the existing Regulations and in the project. States that the Government prefers to continue nomination as at present practised.

Art. 13. No observations.

Art. 13. No concession. No remarks to make on Porte's observations.

Art. 14. Prefers existing Regulations to those proposed.

Art. 14. Annual renewal of Council; points out few eligible people in nahié; prefers existing Regulations.

No concessions made.

Art. 18. Rural police refused.

Police and gendarmes to be recruited from Christians and Moslems in proportion to respective numbers of population.

Arts. 15, 16, 17 call for no observations.

Art. 18. Objects to local police proposed in project.

Vilayet gendarmerie to be recruited from all classes in proportion to respective numbers. Contingents to be sent to nahiés; *i.e.,* existing Regulations maintained.

Art. 19. Police in nahié to be organized and administered as at present, where such exists.

Art. 19. Police of nahiés to be under orders of Mudirs, and remain in all respects as at present. They will be paid from district

Headings.   *Précis.*

treasuries. Not to follow other occupations. Exemption of non-Mussulmans from military service tax refused.

Mounted police unnecessary. Agents of police to have exactly the same functions and attributes as under the existing Regulations.

Notes.—The whole of this observation seems based on a misapprehension, *i.e.,* that the rural police proposed in the reform project were intended to be police agents similar to the Turkish police agents employed in cities, and not be merely a local force to replace in a great measure gendarmerie, and maintain public security.

Art. 20. Refusal to assign certain proposed duties to local police.

Art. 20. Reserves to the central authorities the execution of certain duties which it was proposed to take from them and place in the hands of the communal authorities.

Art. 21. Refuses proposal as to reorganization of gendarmerie, except as regards admission of Christians.

Art. 21. Gendarmes to be recruited from Mussulmans and non-Mussulmans. Officers and non-commissioned officers to be taken from the army. No mention made of Christian officers or non-commissioned officers.

Prisons.

Art. 22. Prisons. Separation of accused and convicted.

Warder service, &c.

Art. 22. States that accused and convicted are kept separate. Valis and Mutessarifs are responsible for hygiene. Prisons have complete staffs. More care can be enjoined. Torture, &c., is forbidden. In fact states that the proposals are entirely in accordance with the present Regulations.

Art. 23. Preliminary inquest of accused.

Art. 23. States that a preliminary inquest exists, and that proposal is in accordance with existing Regulations.

Art. 24. Rejects Ashiret-Memouri, but will control emigration with troops and gendarmes, and enforce port d'armes Regulations, &c.

Art. 24. Porte's observation affects to consider that this Article proposes that a tribal Chief should be made responsible for the migrations—a complete misapprehension

Headings.   *Précis.*

—it wishes to leave matter to regular authorities. Points out that many of the pastoral tribes only migrate to summer pastures, and in winter reside in villages. Migrations will be controlled by military detachments and gendarmes, and travelling and port d'armes Regulations will be enforced. The system actually in force will be maintained of tribes occasionally giving hostages to Government during migrations. Refractory tribes who continually contravene these Regulations will be made to settle permanently.

The Valis, &c., will take special care that the Chiefs of tribes are not exposed to insult or outrages.

Art. 25. Hamidieh cavalry Regulations to be amended in sense of proposal.

Clause as to limitation of number of Hamidieh to be employed not accepted.

Art. 25. The manner of employment of Hamidieh troops is prescribed in the Regulations. The Regulations are being recast and the restrictions as to carrying arms and uniforms, when not on duty, by Hamidieh troopers are points which come under the provisions of the new Regulations to be elaborated. When not on duty Hamidieh troopers are amenable to the jurisdiction of the ordinary Courts.

Art. 26. Special Commissions, one President and four members (two Mussulman and two non-Mussulman) to revise title-deeds, and one Commission at vilayet and sandjak head-quarters accepted.

Annual Commission to guarantee rights in future conceded.

Art. 26. States that a very competent Commission is required, and one will be appointed at each vilayet head-quarters, consisting of President, two Moslem and two non-Moslem members.

Resolutions of Commissioners to be submitted to Administrative Councils of vilayet and sandjaks.

An annual Commission to be sent to see if all questions relating to property have been equitably treated.

Art. 27. Rejects proposed system of tax collection; considers present one good and preferable.

Art. 27. Collection of tithe in money has been found impracticable after experience.

The inhabitants can, if they wish, farm their own tithes.

Headings.

Précis.

Collectors were formerly appointed; this system was satisfactory, and the Government, wishing to avoid using the public forces for collection, a special corps has been formed. Its members may not requisition food and forage.

The elected Mukhtars and village Receivers alone have the manipulation of cash, not the corps of Collectors.

Accordingly, it is useless to replace the above system by the proposed one.

Art. 28. Abolition of farming of tithes is not approved; official corvée abolished, but not "prestation;" proposed local assignment of revenues is rejected in favour of the existing system.

The forced sale Regulations of project correspond with the law.

Art. 28. The experiment of the Government in collecting tithes directly instead of farming was unsatisfactory; accordingly, farming has been re-established, with safeguarding clauses; the farming *en gros* is abolished, and the tithes offered for sale village by village; the inhabitants are allowed to buy them. Difficulties are referred to Tribunals and Councils of Administration.

Corvée does not exist. Communal Treasuries have been established, but they were a cause of loss, therefore it would be no good to renew this experiment. It is important to maintain the present system.

The cost of constructions, repairs, road making, &c., as well as "prestation," in kind or money, concern the Minister of Public Works, who corresponds with the Valis on this subject.

Expenses of public instruction are arranged by the Minister of Public Instruction in conjunction with the Valis.

This system should be maintained.

Porte's observation.

Denies population having to give free lodging and provisions, or being badly treated in tax collecting.

Regulations already exist as to not selling up actual residence, necessary land, and tools for debt; therefore, no new Regulations are necessary.

Headings.	*Précis.*
Art. 29. Conseil des Anciens exists.	Art. 29. Points out Conseil des Anciens exists.
Arts. 30, 31, 32, 33, and 34. Rejects Juges de Paix.	Arts. 30, 31, 32, 33, and 34. Courts of First Instance exist in each caza. This arrangement is preferable to Juges de Paix.
Arts. 35, 36, 37, and 38. Rejects Assize Courts and their proposed procedure.	Arts. 35, 36, 37, and 38. Assize Courts not being suitable owing to considerations of communications, climate, &c., the sandjak Courts should remain as now.
Art. 39. Rejects new proposed organization of Superior Tribunal of vilayet.	Arts. 39. Rejects proposed High Court of vilayet as a consequence of the rejection of Assize Courts, and as not being comprised in existing Regulations. Describes in some detail the well-known existing Regulations. Experience has shown sufficiency and utility for existing organization.
Art. 40. Affirms that sentences should be in Turkish. Ignores the Regulation as to translation.	Art. 40. Affirms that Judgments and sentences should be in Turkish, the official language of the country.

Turkey No. 1 (1896), pp. 114-117, No. 130/2

No. 40

Sir P. Currie to the Marquess of Salisbury.

No. 348.   CONSTANTINOPLE, *August 4, 1895, 10.50 a.m.*

Telegraphic.   *(Received August 4.)*

REFERRING to my telegram of the 2nd instant, my French and Russian colleagues consider that the Porte's answer is merely a criticism of our proposals, and not a plan of reforms.

We shall let the Turkish Government know our personal opinions of their answer, adding that we are entirely left in the dark by the communication as regards the reforms which Shakir Pasha is to supervise, but we do not propose to make any joint communication to the Porte until we receive instructions from our Government.

F. O. 424/183, pp. 136-137, No. 140
Turkey No. 1 (1896), p. 99, No.127

No. 41

The Marquess of Salisbury to Sir F. Lascelles.

No. 146.
Telegraphic.   FOREIGN OFFICE, *August 5, 1895.*

FROM my immediately preceding telegram,* your Excellency will have seen that the Ambassadors of the three Powers at Constantinople consider the Sultan's reply to their proposals for Armenian reform so unsatisfactory that they cannot regard it as a serious communication.

Her Majesty's Government think it now very important to learn how far the Russian Government are willing to proceed in putting pressure upon the Porte, as they do not consider that diplomatic means will be of much further avail. They are of opinion that the three Powers cannot withdraw from the enterprise without loss of credit; and they have entertained no doubt that, in consenting to co-operate with them in this matter, their two allies contemplated the possibility of being driven to more energetic measures in the event of the Sultan declining to take any action.

F. O. 424/183, pp. 154-155, No. 151.

* Repeating Sir P. Currie's telegram No. 348 of August 4, 1895.

No. 42

Sir P. Currie to the Marquess of Salisbury.

No. 349.   CONSTANTINOPLE, *August 5, 1895, 10.15 a.m.*
Telegraphic.   *(Received August 5.)*

I RECEIVED the following telegram from Vice-Consul Hampson last night:-

"I have started building operations in the villages of Ghelié-Guzan, Semal, and Shenik, whence I have just returned. Previous to my arrival no work had been commenced, owing to the action of the Turkish Commissioners.

"The hospital work and the distribution of rations was being undertaken by the missionaries, and I trust that now matters will progress favourably. On Tuesday I propose to start for Talori, remaining absent for about a week.

"Would your Excellency kindly inform us whether we may hope for further funds, for although there still remains a sum of nearly 600l. in the hands of the missionaries, much more will be required for the necessary cattle and building operations, and also for the support of the villages during a winter of at least four months, as very little grain could be sown?

"A detailed Report on the present position will shortly be forwarded by the missionaries."

F. O. 424/183, p. 154, No. 150
Turkey No. 1 (1895) Part I, p. 132, No. 250

No. 43

Sir P. Currie to the Marquess of Salisbury.

No. 508.   THERAPIA, *August 5, 1895.*
My Lord,   *(Received August 8.)*
        I HAVE the honour to inclose, for your Lordship's information, the substance
of an unofficial communication made to Mr. Marinitch, the Second Dragoman of
the Embassy, by Nazim Pasha, the Turkish Minister of Police, respecting the
Armenian Revolutionary Societies.
                                    I have, &c.
                                                            (Signed) PHILIP CURRIE.

   F. O. 424/183, p. 171, No. 159

Inclosure in No. 43

Extract from Memorandum by Mr. Marinitch of August 3, 1895.

        THE Minister of Police desires, however, to call the serious attention of his
Excellency the Ambassador to the two Societies which have been formed, one in
London, under the name of "Hentchag", and the other in Switzerland, under the
designation of "Trochag", whose mission it is to hand over to the executioners a
number of innocent and helpless victims, hoping by these bloodthirsty means to
reach a goal entirely apart from that towards which the honest portion of the
Armenian nation are striving. The two Societies in question openly declare
themselves opposed to all lawfully constituted Governments, even against Her
Majesty's Government, although a constitutional and liberal one in the highest
degree.
        The Hentchag Revolutionary Society at London published all kinds of
brochures and seditious pamphlets with the idea of spreading Socialistic
tendencies. Its motto is the destruction of the three institutions which weigh down
humanity: religion, government, and marriage.
        The Society in question was represented at Constantinople by a Committee
whom the Minister succeeded in tracing and suppressing, and Nazim Pasha is
prepared to show his Excellency the Ambassador, if desired, all that was discovered
in the Committee's possession, and now lying under seal, in order that his
statement may be corroborated by facts.
        The Minister begs his Excellency to advise Her Majesty's Government to
cause the police to make a raid upon the Hentchag Society's office in London, and
Her Majesty's Government will then find that the Society is engaged in

disseminating Socialistic ideas of a kind that no regularly constituted Government could possibly tolerate.

The Minister declares that the Socialistic theories now so rapidly gaining ground in Europe do great injury to the various peoples, and that, should they end by permeating the Mussulman population in Turkey, which is for the greater part an ignorant one, the consequences would be disastrous in the extreme.

The Minister of Police perceives with the deepest regret that the Armenian Patriarch, Mgr. Ismirlian, instead of anathematizing the Armenian Anarchical and Socialistic Societies, looks with approval upon the series of crimes perpetrated by them.

Two thousand Armenians have already been done to death by these fanatical Societies, who are still engaged in the pursuit of their anarchical and bloodthirsty ends.

Nazim Pasha begs his Excellency the Ambassador to advise the Patriarch to make every effort to prevent the Hentchag and Trochag Societies continuing their work of destruction.

F. O. 424/183, p. 171, No. 159/1

No. 44

Sir P. Currie to the Marquess of Salisbury.

No. 352.   CONSTANTINOPLE, *August 7, 1895, 10.45 a.m.*
Telegraphic.   *(Received August 7.)*

YESTERDAY the Dragomans were sent for by the Foreign Minister, who communicated to them officially the following:—

"Tout ce qui n'a pas été rejeté dans sa réponse, la Sublime Porte s'engage à exécuter; on exécutera aussi avec leurs modifications les Articles modifiés."

No doubt the objections taken to the vagueness of the terms of the answer of the Porte received on the 2nd August are intended to be met by this communication, but no adequate guarantee for the welfare and security of life and property of the Christian subjects of the Porte, which in the words of Prince Lobanoff are the object of the joint action of the three Powers, is offered by the accepted reforms.

F. O. 424/183, p. 167, No. 155
Turkey No. 1 (1896), p. 118, No. 131

No. 45

The Marquess of Salisbury to Sir P. Currie.

No. 292.

Sir,   FOREIGN OFFICE, *August 7, 1895.*

RUSTEM PASHA called to-day to inform me of the nature of the concessions which the Sultan was prepared to make in reference to the Armenian question. They did not, apparently, go further than an assurance on the part of the Government of Turkey that reforms would be introduced, and that justice would be done. There was no guarantee which would satisfy the public opinion of Europe that these engagements on the part of the Turkish Government would be performed.

I pointed out to his Excellency this defect, but he insisted that any guarantee other than the promise of the Sultan of Turkey would be in prejudice of the rights and inconsistent with the dignity of his Sovereign.

I warned his Excellency in as earnest language as I could employ of the danger to which the Ottoman Empire was being exposed by trifling with questions of this kind. The attempt to avoid the honest performance of the duties of Government by artifices of negotiation which could only put off the evil day was a policy of the results of which Turkey had already had a sinister experience, and which might lead her into grievous calamity.

Rustem Pasha dwelt much on the fact that these troubles were begun by the turbulence or the organized revolt of the Armenians, and that as many crimes were to be laid to their door as to that of the Turkish soldiers.

I replied that, from our point of view, his defence was wholly inapplicable. What we complained of was that the proper duties of Government were not done, that the state of society in many of the provinces was mere anarchy, and that it mattered little in dealing with the justice of these charges whether the outrages were committed by Mussulmans upon Armenians or by Armenians upon Mussulmans. I said the responsibility for this state of things must be considered as ultimately resting upon the Sultan, and that I feared he was surrounded by councillors who concealed the truth from his eyes.

I am, &c.

(Signed) SALISBURY

F. O. 424/183, pp. 167-168, No. 156
Turkey, No. 1 (1896), p. 118, No. 132

No. 46

The Marquess of Salisbury to Sir F. Lascelles.

No. 265.

Sir, FOREIGN OFFICE, *August 7, 1895.*

THE Russian Chargé d'Affaires called upon me to-day to speak about the Armenian question.

I told him how the matter stood, and, in reply, he renewed the assurance which I had already received, that Prince Lobanoff was resolved to act in concert with Her Majesty's Government on this question, it being only understood that nothing in the shape of the creation of an autonomous state in Armenia should be attempted.

I replied that I entirely agreed as to the impossibility of establishing such a state, and the great inexpediency, therefore, of making any efforts in that direction.

The inclination of my mind was, at present, to consider whether there was not some arrangement which we could demand of the Sultan as a legitimate consequence of the provisions of the LXIst Article of the Treaty of Berlin. By that Article we had a right to exercise surveillance, but surveillance did not consist in an Ambassador residing at Constantinople and looking on, but involved some more active and effectual form of vigilance. The problem before us was to devise some machinery for surveillance which would be effective, and which yet should not inflict an unnecessary wound upon the susceptibilities of the Sultan with regard to his prerogatives.

I am, &c.

(Signed) SALISBURY.

F. O. 424/183, p. 168, No. 157
Turkey No. 1, (1896), p. 118-119, No. 133

No. 47

Sir P. Currie to the Marquess of Salisbury.

No. 512. THERAPIA, *August 7, 1895.*

My Lord, *(Received August 12.)*

I HAVE the honour to transmit to your Lordship herewith copy of a despatch addressed to Mr. Longworth, reporting upon the state of affairs at Marsovan, which has been forwarded to me from Trebizond.

I have, &c.

(Signed) PHILIP CURRIE.

F. O. 424/183, p. 176, No. 168
Turkey No. 6 (1896), No. 487, 487/1

Inclosure in No. 47

Letter addressed to Consul Longworth.

Sir,   SIVAS, *July 23, 1895.*

I HAVE to acknowledge your letter and telegram asking me to report on the Marsovan affair. When your telegram came I had just telegraphed to you: "Big incendiary fire reported at Marsovan. Three Armenians assassinated. Numerous Armenians arrested." I made a mistake as to the number assassinated, as you will see, and, perhaps, also in regard to the origin of the fire. I was slow in getting reliable information. Now I can give you something reliable.

Up to the 1st July affairs were quiet. That morning about sunrise Kouyoumdjee Garabet was assassinated by two men near the Protestant Church, whither he was going to attend service.

He was the chief man of the Protestant community, and Chairman of a Council of Thirty who were responsible for the peace of the city. He was very unpopular with the Armenians, and liked by Turkish officials. He is said to have kept a journal of all he heard said by the Armenians of a political nature, and reported it to the Government. He received seventeen wounds, including a bad cut on the head, and his abdomen was partially ripped open. He made some resistance. One of the murderers was traced by blood for some distance to a fountain where he washed. The assassination of Garabet was followed by the arrest of about 200 Armenians, including some women and children. Persons who lived near the scene of the murder, and also persons who had previously been in prison as political suspects, were put in prison. All but a few, perhaps six to ten, were examined and released in a few days. All the Armenians seem to have banded together to shield the murderers, and prevent their being caught. I think Bekir Pasha probably did wisely. His effort was to get hold of the Revolutionary Committee as well as the murderers.

About the 5th July a new preparatory Turkish school building was finished and dedicated. Some shavings and lumber still remained in and about the building. On the 12th July, the Kaïmakam and some other officials met in the school and stayed there, until about 2 o'clock à la Turque in the evening. An hour or two later the building was discovered to be on fire. The fire spread rapidly, and extended to other buildings. The Kaïmakam's house was burned, and in all thirty houses, twenty shops, three khans, and the school were destroyed. The son of the watchman of the school, a Turk, was burned up in the school.

At about 11 o'clock à la Turque in the morning of the 13th July, Kiremidjee Hadjee Serkis Agha, a Gregorian, returning to his home from the fire, was murdered by two men. He was called a "traitor." He was cut up similarly to Garabet. The murderers were not caught. The man who first reported the murder to the Government was put in prison and tortured. Four men who witnessed the murder, but claimed they could not identify the murderers, were put in prison, and a large number of Armenians were arrested. A cordon was put around the city, and for a day or two no one was allowed to leave. Bekir Pasha sent for the assistance of the Kaïmakams of Hadji Keuy and Cavza.

It is said that during the day following the fire the Mahommedans met in the mosques and talked about massacring the Christians. The condition was considered very critical. At Amassia and Tokat, also, an outbreak between Turks and Armenians is apprehended.

The Armenians at Tokat profess to believe that the Turks are incited to attack the Christians by the officers of the vilayet in order to show that the Turks will not accept foreign interference in behalf of the Armenians. I am told that nine loads of powder were recently brought here by soldiers from Erzinghian, and that powder is being freely sold to Turks and Kurds at Zara and Karahissar.

There is renewed talk of mobilizing the army. The condition of things is thoroughly bad, and soon will be worse if something is not done to improve it.

F. O. 424/183, p. 160, No. 157
Turkey No. 1 (1896), pp. 118-119, No. 133

No. 48

Sir P. Currie to the Marquess of Salisbury.

No. 513. CONSTANTINOPLE, *August 7, 1895,*
My Lord, *(Received August 12.)*

I HAVE the honour to forward to your Lordship herewith copy of a despatch which I have received from Her Majesty's Consul at Angora, reporting the latest information received by him with regard to the events at Marsovan.

I have, &c.

(Signed) PHILIP CURRIE.

F. O. 424/183, p. 177, No. 169

Inclosure in No. 48

Consul Cumberbatch to Sir P. Currie.

Sir, ANGORA, *August 2, 1895.*

WITH reference to my despatch of the 19th July, I have the honour to report that the latest information received by me as to events at Marsovan is: (1) that thirty to forty of the Armenians arrested immediately after the murder of Garabet

Aristakesian have been conveyed to Amassia; (2) that another prominent Armenian of Marsovan, viz., Hadji Sarkiss Kiramidjian, has also been murdered, in July by the agents of the Secret Committee, presumably because he was considered a "traitor;" and (3) that another, also a man of some standing in that town, has found it necessary to quit the place owing to the reception of a threatening letter from the Secret Committee.

All these incidents confirm the conviction that the revolutionary element has not disappeared from the Marsovan region, whatever may be the case in other parts.

I have, &c.

(Signed) H. A. CUMBERBATCH.

F. O. 424/183, p. 178, No. 169/1
Turkey No. 6 (1896), p. 377, No. 688, 688/1.

No. 49

Sir P. Currie to the Marquess of Salisbury.

No. 517.   THERAPIA, *August 8, 1895.*
My Lord,   *(Received August 12.)*
WITH reference to my despatch of the 23rd May, transmitting a list of Armenians in prison for political offences, I have now the honour to forward to your Lordship a further Table, drawn up by Mr. Ponsonby, showing the numbers of prisoners released in accordance with the amnesty granted on the 23rd July, and of those still detained in prison.

I am calling the attention of the Grand Vizier to the action of the provincial authorities in keeping political prisoners in confinement in disregard of the Sultan's orders.

I have, &c.

(Signed) PHILIP CURRIE.

F. O. 424/183, p. 185, No. 172
Turkey No. 6 (1896), pp. 377-378, No. 489, 489/1

Inclosure in No. 49

TABLE showing Number of Armenian Political Prisoners released in accordance with the Amnesty granted on July 23, 1895, and of those who are still detained in Prison.

Name of Place.	Prisoners Released.	Prisoners still Detained.	Remarks
Erzeroum	20	16	Including 10 Narman prisoners, and the naturalized American.
Van	Protestants of Saird. 30	51	36 at Van, 15 at Shattakh, for no reason.
Bitlis	13	—	Those connected with events of last year, including Mourad and Erko. None who gave evidence before Commission detained except Erko.
Trebizond	All	—	
Sivas	45	35	Mentioned to whom pardon might well be extended.
Acre	50	7	At Acre.
Tripoli	2	—	
Smyrna	All	—	
Angora	About 30	—	Probable delay in release of Yuzgat prisoners, as Vali is unwilling to assume any responsibility.
Aleppo	6	22	Still remain.
Adana	All	—	
Alexandretta	All	—	Except those described by authorities as criminal and non-political.

F. O. 424/183, p. 185, No. 172/1

No. 50

The Marquess of Salisbury to Sir F. Lascelles.

No. 266.

Sir,   FOREIGN OFFICE, *August 9, 1895.*

THE Russian Chargé d'Affaires informed me to-day that his Government had not yet received the text of the Sultan's reply with regard to reforms in the Armenian provinces, and that until it was in their hands they could express no opinion.

Prince Lobanoff was disposed to entertain the idea of devising "some machinery for surveillance," as suggested in my conversation with M. Kroupensky of the 7th instant, but considered that any such proposal must be clearly and precisely defined before being submitted to the Sultan.

I am, &c.

(Signed) SALISBURY.

F. O. 424/183, p. 173, No. 161

No. 51

Evangelical Alliance to the Marquess of Salisbury.

7, ADAM STREET, STRAND, LONDON, *August 9, 1895.*

My Lord,   *(Received August 10.)*

REFERRING to correspondence between Her Majesty's Foreign Office and the Council of the Evangelical Alliance with reference to the question of religious liberty in Turkey, and especially referring to Lord Kimberley's letter of the 27th May, our Council desire me to lay before your Lordship the following statement.

In my letter of the 19th April I stated that it was the wish of our Committee in Constantinople that a copy of the document which they had prepared at the request of Sir Philip Currie (entitled "Violations of the Hatti Humayoun") should be sent "in confidence" to our Committees in Berlin and in Washington, in order that they might urge their respective Governments to support the representations made by the British Ambassador at Constantinople to the Sultan's Government with reference to the infringements of religious liberty. Lord Kimberley replied that he must first consult Sir Philip Currie before he could give permission for us to use the document in the way indicated.

In his Lordship's letter of the 27th May this consent was given. We had a careful summary of the document made and forwarded to Berlin; but, just as we were about to send another copy to our American Committee, we learned that the entire document prepared for Sir Philip Currie (and including the letter addressed to his Excellency by our Secretary in Constantinople) had been printed and circulated in the United States. We instantly made inquiries as to how this publication had been effected. Our Constantinople Committee replied that one of the American missionaries, a member of the Committee, had sent a copy of the paper, in strict confidence, to his Board of Missions at Boston; but the Secretary of our Committee adds, "I expressly called attention to the fact that there must be no publication, because the document belongs to the British Embassy."

Thus your Lordship will see that our Council are entirely innocent of any complicity in the breach of confidence which has been committed by the publication of the paper. We feel it necessary to make this plain statement of facts to your Lordship, and we have also given publicity to a similar statement in one of the London dailies which had referred to the publication of the document in America.

Her Majesty's Foreign Office will, I am sure, admit that our Council have always acted with the utmost caution in dealing with official correspondence relating to infringements of religious liberty in Turkey; and it has been source of extreme regret to our Council that the American Board of Missions in Boston, having obtained, privately and confidentially, a copy of the paper which had been prepared specially by request of Sir Philip Currie, should have forgotten all the amenities of official life by publishing the document. The deep regret which our Council feel is shared also by our Constantinople Committee.

While writing, may I take the opportunity, in the name of our Council, of expressing their warm gratitude for the prompt and energetic measures which his Excellency the British Ambassador has taken from time to time, and especially in regard to the Ordou Christians during the past year?

Believe me, &c.

(Signed) A. J. ARNOLD,
General Secretary.

F. O. 424/183, p. 174, No. 163

No. 52

Sir F. Lascelles to the Marquess of Salisbury.

No. 196. Confidential.   ST. PETERSBURGH, *August 9, 1895.*
My Lord,   *(Received August 19.)*

IT was only this afternoon that I had an opportunity, since the receipt on the 6th instant of your Lordship's telegram of the previous day, of seeing Prince Lobanoff.

His Excellency, after listening to a paraphrase of your Lordship's telegram, was good enough to read to me a telegram which he had received yesterday from the Russian Chargé d'Affaires in London, giving an account of a conversation which your Lordship had had with him on the subject of the steps which should now be taken at Constantinople as regards Armenian reforms.

Prince Lobanoff said that he had at once telegraphed to M. Kroupensky to the effect that he could not express an opinion on the Sultan's answer until he had seen the text of it. His Excellency reminded me that he had never concealed from me his opinion of the scheme of reforms drawn up by the Ambassadors at Constantinople, which he considered unworkable. In his opinion, the Ambassadors had gone too far. At the same time, after all that had taken place, he was strongly of opinion that the Sultan should be induced to grant some reforms, and he thought that the suggestion which your Lordship had made in your conversation with M. Kroupensky for some sort of "mécanisme de surveillance" might provide a way out of the difficulty. As it was, the Ambassadors had a right of surveillance, and if it was a question of delegating this right to a Committee composed of the Dragomans of the Embassies and certain Turkish officials for the purpose of watching over the introduction of reforms, he would be happy to join in urging such a proposal on the Sultan, who, he believed, would agree to it. If, however, it was intended to create a permanent institution which should undertake the administration of certain provinces in Asia Minor, he should not be able to agree to it. Russia had formerly been in the position of a "Protecting Power" in the Danubian Principalities and in Servia, but she had been unable to secure any real improvement in the administration, and the result had been that she had made herself unpopular with the population, who had looked to her for the redress of their grievances. He would therefore strongly object to any proposal which would in any way render the Russian Government responsible for the administration in any part of the Sultan's dominions, as he considered that such responsibility was greater than any Government should incur.

On my asking Prince Lobanoff how far the Russian Government would be prepared to go in putting pressure on the Sultan in the event of His Majesty refusing to take any steps at all, his Excellency replied that he authorized me to state to your Lordship that the idea of the employment of force was personally repugnant to the Emperor; and, in answer to my further inquiries, his Excellency said that the employment of force by any one of the three Powers would be equally distasteful to the Russian Government. He was, however, of opinion that a firm and united attitude on the part of the three Ambassadors at Constantinople would induce the Sultan to yield, and he had lost no opportunity, both in his conversation with the Turkish Ambassador here and in a private and friendly letter which he had lately had occasion to write to the Grand Vizier, to strongly urge the absolute necessity for the Sultan to take immediate steps for the settlement of this question.

I have, &c.

(Signed) FRANK C. LASCELLES.

F. O. 424/183, p. 189, No. 184
Turkey No. 1 (1896), p. 121, No. 139

No. 53

Sir F. Lascelles to the Marquess of Salisbury.

No. 197. Confidential.   ST. PETERSBURGH, *August 9, 1895.*
My Lord,   *(Received August 19.)*

IN the conversation with Prince Lobanoff, which I had the honour to record in my preceding despatch of this day's date, his Excellency told me that by the last messenger from Constantinople he had received a number of reports from the Turkish police on the subject of recent events in the Armenian provinces. In consequence of the mass of details and the large number of Armenian names, the perusal of these documents was a somewhat wearisome work, but they clearly proved the existence of a widespread revolutionary movement which was strongly supported by the Armenian Committees abroad, and more especially in England.

It was true that it was not possible to place implicit reliance, on Turkish reports, but they had received confirmation from an inquiry which had recently been held in Roumania, which proved that among the Armenians there was a large and active party who cared little for reforms or an improved Administration, but sought to bring about a complete state of anarchy. No form of government, however ideally perfect, could ever satisfy this party, who aimed at the destruction of all authority, and the general distribution of property.

It would therefore be necessary in the attempts we were making to obtain an improvement of the administration, and security for the lives and property of the Christian subjects of the Sultan, to avoid giving any encouragement to this party of disorder. At one moment his Excellency had been apprehensive lest Her Majesty's Government might have been induced to go further in the way of demanding some sort of autonomy for the Armenian provinces than the Russian Government could have approved, but the assurance which I had given him that all that Her Majesty's Government wished was to secure a better government and security for life and property, had convinced him that his apprehensions were unfounded, and it was a matter of great satisfaction to him that your Lordship had assumed so moderate and statesmanlike an attitude on this subject.

His Excellency was also gratified to find that the language which he had held to Husny Pasha on the necessity of the Sultan agreeing to reforms had corresponded entirely with that held by your Lordship to Rustem Pasha.

I have, &c.

(Signed) FRANK C. LASCELLES.

F. O. 424/183, p. 190, No. 185
Turkey No.1 (1896), pp. 121-122, No.140

No. 54

Sir P. Currie to the Marquess of Salisbury.

No. 359.　　　　　　　　　　CONSTANTINOPLE, *August 12, 1895, 7.30 p.m.*
Telegraphic.　　　　　　　　　　　　　　　　*(Received August 12.)*

IT was decided at a meeting I had with my Russian and French colleagues that to-morrow a paper should be presented to the Porte by our Dragomans summarizing in exact terms the reforms which have been accepted in the answers of the Turkish Government.

The Dragomans are to ask the Porte categorically whether these reforms are the measures which are to be put into execution by Shakir Pasha; and on Thursday they are to call for a reply. We propose, on receipt of the assent of the Porte to this paper, to forward it to our Governments, at the same time suggesting additions recommended by the three Ambassadors.

These additions will consist of a permanent Commission of Control, with access of Dragomans; a proportion of Christians in the gendarmerie and the Administration, and rural guards to be chosen locally in each commune.

It appeared from the language held by M. de Nélidoff that Russia would wish to limit the scope of the permanent Commission of Control; but on the other hand M. Cambon read to us a telegram which he had received from Paris stating that the opinion which your Lordship expressed in favour of the Commission to the Russian Chargé d'Affaires had met with the cordial concurrence of Prince Lobanoff.

F. O. 424/183, p. 186, No. 174

No. 55

Sir F. Lascelles to the Marquess of Salisbury.

No. 74.　　　　　　　　　　ST. PETERSBURGH, *August 13, 1895.*
Telegraphic.　　　　　　　　　　　　　　　　*(Received August 13.)*

IN reply to the observations contained in your Lordship's telegram No. 146, Prince Lobanoff has telegraphed to the Russian Representative in London that, before seeing the Sultan's answer, he is unable to express an opinion upon it. Some system of surveillance, as suggested by your Lordship, might, in his Excellency's opinion, obviate the difficulty, but he wishes to be informed of the nature of this surveillance. The formation of a permanent Committee to supervise the administration would render us directly responsible for it, and his Excellency is averse to it, but he is willing to join in urging upon the Turkish Government the desirability of a temporary Committee to superintend the introduction of reforms.

Prince Lobanoff informed me, in reply to my question as to how far the Imperial Government were prepared to go in pressing these reforms upon the

Sultan, that both the Emperor and he himself were strongly against force being used by any or all of the Powers.

F. O. 424/183, p. 186, No. 176

No. 56

The Marquess of Salisbury to Mr. Howard.

No. 401A.

Sir, FOREIGN OFFICE, *August 13, 1895.*

THE French Ambassador called here to-day and asked me about the state of affairs in the Armenian provinces.

I told his Excellency that I was more and more coming to the conclusion that the strongest position for the three Powers to occupy was that assigned to them by the LXIst Article of the Treaty of Berlin, and that we should claim the right of surveillance and all other rights which that provision of the Treaty necessarily carried with it. No genuine surveillance could be exercised by an authority seated at Constantinople; it must be some authority locally resident at Van, Bitlis, or Erzeroum, or at some other suitable spot in the disturbed country. If a Commission consisting of four Turkish members and three Commissioners nominated by the three Powers were appointed to reside in the Armenian provinces with full authority to investigate and report, some security would be obtained for the adoption of reforms and a means of remedy provided should misgovernment again prevail. A Commission of this kind would not, I thought, go beyond the rights conferred by the Treaty of Berlin, and the majority of members being Turkish, there would be no infringement of the Sultan's prerogatives, while if three European Commissioners of sufficient weight and standing were selected they would be able, as they might deem necessary, to direct the proceedings of the Commission. It was essential, however, that each of the Commissioners should have the right of individual investigation and report, and that all facilities necessary for this purpose should be afforded to them.

M. De Courcel was of opinion that on this basis it would be possible to construct an arrangement for adjusting the present difficulties without injury to the rights of the Sultan, and his Excellency thought that Russia might be persuaded to accept some plan such as that indicated. The position of his Government, he observed, was that of an intermediary; whatever course the British and Russian Governments agreed upon, they might feel assured that France would also be ready to adopt.

I am, &c.

(Signed) SALISBURY.

F. O. 424/183, p. 187, No. 177

No. 57

Sir P. Currie to the Marquess of Salisbury.

No. 362.   CONSTANTINOPLE, *August 14, 1895, 11.30 a.m.*
Telegraphic.   *(Received August 14.)*
I HAVE learnt that during the last few days the Palace has assumed a
fanatical tone with respect to the Armenian question. The tenour of a telegram sent
to Rustem Pasha yesterday was that any reforms beyond those which the Porte
have already accepted would constitute an attack on the Mahommedan religion,
and would be an incitement to the Armenians to commit acts of a similar criminal
nature to those perpetrated in Macedonia by the Bulgarians.
F. O. 424/183, p. 182, No. 178

No. 58

Sir P. Currie to the Marquess of Salisbury.

No. 526.   CONSTANTINOPLE, *August 14, 1895.*
My Lord,   *(Received August 19.)*
I HAVE the honour to forward to your Lordship herewith copy of a despatch
which I have received from Her Majesty's Consul at Trebizond respecting ill-
feelings between Turks and Christians at Tokat and Gemerek.
                                   I have, &c.
                                                        (Signed) PHILIP CURRIE.

F. O. 424/183, p. 194, No. 190

Inclosure in No. 58

Consul Longworth to Sir P. Currie.

Sir,   TREBIZOND, *August 5, 1895.*
The following is an extract from a letter, dated Sivas, the 30th ultimo:-
"I have the names of nine prominent and official Turks at Tokat who,
according to exact information obtained from a foreigner, are threatening to
massacre the Christians. An Armenian is pushing them on. Such talk may not lead
to a massacre, but at least it must increase the apprehension and the animosity
between the races, which is already at the point of an outbreak.
"At Gemerek the Armenian churches have been closed for a week past,

because the people say their rights and everything sacred are trampled under foot and cursed by the Turkish officials, and the Church gives them no security or redress.

I have, &c.

(Signed) H. Z. LONGWORTH.

F. O. 424/183, p. 194, No. 190/1
Turkey No. 6 (1896), p. 378, No. 490, 490/1

No. 59

Sir P. Currie to the Marquess of Salisbury.

No. 528.   THERAPIA, *August 15, 1895.*
My Lord,   *(Received August 19.)*
    I HAVE the honour to transmit to your Lordship herewith copy of the joint Report drawn up by the Consular Delegates attached to the Commission appointed to inquire into the events at Sasun, together with Annexes.

I have, &c.

(Signed) PHILIP CURRIE.

F. O. 424/183, p. 203, No. 192
Turkey No. 1 (1895) Part I, p. 132, No. 252, 252/1

Inclosure in No. 59

Report of the Consular Delegates attached to the Commission appointed to inquire into the Events at Sasun.

A la suite des événements dont la région de Sassoun, dépendant des Sandjaks de Mouch et de Guendj, Vilayet de Bitlis, avait été le théâtre pendant l'été de l'année 1894, le Gouvernement Impérial Ottoman décida l'envoi sur les lieux d'une Commission chargée d'y procéder aux enquêtes nécessaires, et obtint des Puissances représentées à Erzeroum l'autorisation pour leurs Consuls de se faire représenter par des Délégués auprès de la dite Commission.

Elle était composée de son Excellence Chefik Bey, Président, Djelal Bey, Madjid Bey, du Général Tewfik Pacha, et Omer Bey, membres, ce dernier ayant cessé ses fonctions le 29 Janvier, par suite de sa nomination au poste de Vali *ad interim* de Bitlis.

Les Délégués du Consul de France, du Consul de la Grande-Bretagne, et du Consul-Général de Russie, à Erzeroum étaient MM. Vilbert, Shipley, et Prjévalsky.

Ils ont l'honneur d'exposer ci-dessous les résultats de l'enquête; mais ils croient indispensable de tracer auparavant une rapide esquisse du pays où les événements se sont déroulés, de déterminer ensuite les rapports unissant les populations indigènes Arménienne et Kurde, pour passer en dernier lieu à l'examen des événements eux-mêmes et à l'appréciation des questions qui en découlent: existence d'une révolte, réalité de massacres, et fixation de responsabilités.

Aperçu du Pays.

Dans la partie sud et sur la lisière de la plaine arrosée par le Kara Sou, un des affluents du Mourad Sou (Euphrate Oriental), et au pied d'une chaîne de montagnes bordant cette plaine du côté sud-ouest se trouve bâtie la ville de Mouch, chef-lieu du sandjak du même nom, dépendant du Vilayet de Bitlis.

Les diverses parties de cette chaîne portant le nom général de montagnes de Mouch, parties situées auprès de la ville même, sont appelées Kourtik-Dagh, Hatcherach Sevsar (Pierres Noires) et leurs versants sud et sud-ouest, opposés à la plaine, se réunissent par l'intermédiare d'une série de hauteurs, de moindre élévation, au grand massif de l'Antok-Dagh et de Tsovasar, formant ainsi une série de vallées et de ravins qu'arrosent les sources du Batman Sou: c'est là que sont situés les villages Arméniens de Kavar, Shatak et Talori.

Dans une de ces vallées qui contourne ensuite l'Antok-Dagh du côté nord-ouest, et à sa partie supérieure se trouvent Chenik, Semal et Alian, distants l'un de l'autre d'une demi-heure, et de trois à trois heures et demie de Mouch; également, dans la partie supérieure d'une seconde vallée, passant au sud-ouest de l'Antok-Dagh, et entre cette dernière montagne et celle de Tsovasar, on rencontre les six villages de Shatak: Kop, Guermav, Iritsank, Tapik, Kiagashin, Chouchamerg, puis Agpi, Hetink sur les flancs du Tsovasar-Dagh; enfin en face d'Agpi, et dans un rayin transversal, Guéliéguzan, compris dans les villages de Kavar, et séparé de Chenik et Semal par des hauteurs nommées Keupru-Cherif-Han et Tchaï, qui rattachent l'Antok-Dagh aux montagnes de Mouch; c'est par ces hauteurs que passent les sentiers reliant Chenik et Semal à Guéliéguzan.

Plus loin que ce dernier village et qu'Agpi, dans la direction du sud-ouest, les ravins que forment les contreforts très escarpés et boisés de l'Antok-Dagh renferment les villages d'Ergart, Tsorir, Spangank, les quartiers qui composent Talori, nommés: Dawalik, Pourh, Hosnoud, Hartk, Hakmank, Kholovit, Halorink, Talori même dit Ekoudoun, dit Verin Kiegh, puis Ichhantzor dit Aktchesser, Sevit, Ingouznak, et les quartiers qui dépendent de ces divers villages. Le plus éloigné est celui de Talori, dont les quartiers situés à une ou deux heures l'un de l'autre sont à cinq ou six heures de Guéliéguzan, et auquel il est relié par deux chemins: l'un direct par la montagne, et passant par le ravin de Guéliésan et Afkart, l'autre par le ravin d'Agpi, Hetink, et Spagank.

Les villages de Kavar Chenik, Semal, et Guéliéguzan, dont Alian n'est qu'un quartier, dépendent du Caza de Mouch, les villages de Shatak, Agpi, Hetink, Spagank, Tsorir, Ergart, de celui de Sassoun et tous les autres du caza de Koulp.

On trouvera un supplément (ch. No. 1), et tel qu'il résulte des renseignements fournis par l'enquête, le détail, approximatif du nombre de maisons et d'habitants que cette région renferme.

Relations de la Population Arménienne et Kurde.

L'ensemble du pays, dont il vient d'être donné un rapide aperçu, présente des terrains fertiles, de riches pâturages propices à l'élèvement d'un nombreux bétail, et du côté de Talori même se rencontrent des minerals de fer, exploités par les villageois qui fabriquaient et fournissaient aux régions environnantes les ustensiles de travail nécessaires.

La population Arménienne qui habite cette partie du Vilayet de Bitlis est entourée par une grande quantité de villages Kurdes du côté de Sassoun, Khian et Koulp; en été venant de la direction de Diarbekir, et Silivan aux montagnes ci-dessus énumérées: Tsovasar, Antok et Kourtik Dagh, pour y paître leurs troupeaux, arrivent les tribus semi-sédentaires Kurdes dont les deux principales sont les Bekrauli, et les Badikanli composées de nombreuses subdivisions (Kabilé) qui portent des noms différents.

Grâce au groupement des villages Arméniens, à la configuration même du sol et, d'autre part, aux rivalités existant entre les Kurdes eux-mêmes, les habitants de Kavar et de Talori avaient pu, jusqu'ici, se maintenir sur le pied de bonnes relations avec leurs voisins et visiteurs Kurdes; ils vivaient, selon l'expression d'un témoin, comme des frères "de terre et d'eau" et les difficultés qui s'élevaient entre eux, occasionnées par des vols de bétail tour à tour emporté et repris, finissaient toujours par être tranchées au gré des parties intéressées.

Il est juste d'ajouter que si les relations de Kurdes à Arméniens présentaient un caractère satisfaisant c'est que de long date ceux-ci, pour trouver aide et protection, en cas de besoin auprès des Aghas Kurdes, leur payaient, proportionnellement à leurs ressources, une redevance annuelle connue sous le nom de "hafir" et consistant à leur remettre une certaine partie de tout ce qu'ils récoltent, des têtes de bétail, de l'argent en nature, en y ajoutant des effets d'habillement, des instruments aratoires, &c. Quand un paysan Arménien marie sa fille, son Agha perçoit sous le nom de "hala" la moitié de la somme versée, selon les habitudes du pays, par le fiancé aux parents de la future.

Chaque village ou chaque maison dépend d'un ou plusieurs Aghas, qui regardent des diverses perceptions comme un droit de propriété, au point qu'ils se le transmettent par voie d'héritage ou par vente à l'amiable.

Si l'Arménien refuse de payer pour un motif quelconque, l'Agha l'y contraint par la force en lui volant son bétail ou en lui causant quelque dommage; les Aghas des villages de Kavar et de Talori étaient principalement les Aghas Kurdes de Sassoun (Kharzan).

Telle est du moins la façon dont les Arméniens avec une unanimité presque absolue ont présenté le "hafir;" mais il convient d'ajouter que des témoignages eux-mêmes il résulte que les exigences de ce tribut, si elles s'appliquaient aux gens de Talori et de Khian étaient beaucoup plus faibles à Guéliéguzan, Semal, et Chenik, dont un habitant dit que le "hafir" n'y était pas payé.

Les Kurdes et leurs Aghas entendus par la Commission d'Enquête déclarent ne même pas connaître le mot de "hafir" et sa signification, affirment qu'un pareil tribut a cessé d'exister depuis une cinquantaine d'années et expliquent la perception opérée par certains Aghas sur les Arméniens comme une redevance dûe par l'exploiteur du sol au propriétaire du fond.

Néanmoins, le fait que le "hafir" existait jusque dans ces dernières années est prouvé par la déclaration du nommé Taleb Effendi, un des agents de l'autorité à Mouch, qui, chargé de fréquentes missions dans ces pays, doit être au courant, et qui parle dans sa déposition d'un Kurde s'étant rendu, il y a deux ans, à Talori, dit-il textuellement, "pour y percevoir le 'hafir.' "

Les explications données à cet égard par une communication officielle, émanant du Conseil Administratif de Mouch et qui n'a été lue qu'en partie, d'ailleurs, dans la séance de la Commission en date du 7 Juin, 1895, ne sauraient être considérées comme probantes et présentant un caractère d'indépendance absolue.

Dans les trois ou quatre dernières années, les relations entre les villages Arméniens en question et les Kurdes commencèrent à prendre un caractère d'hostilité qu'il est permis d'attribuer à deux causes: d'une part, chez les Kurdes la propagande religieuse de leurs Cheiks, reconciliant entr'elles les tribus jusqu'alors en mésintelligence et leur interdisant toute querelle motivée par la protection qu'elles exerçaient, à l'encontre les unes des autres, sur les Arméniens; d'autre part, l'agitation causée parmi ceux-ci par des hommes tels que Damadian, leur représentant leur sujétion aux Kurdes comme une sorte d'esclavage contre lequel ils ne trouvaient aucune protection auprès du Gouvernement, et les poussant à secouer le joug: l'année 1893 donne une preuve de cet état d'hostilités ouvertes dans l'attaque combinée des tribus Kurdes sur Talori.

Exposé des Evénements de Sassoun en 1894.

C'est sur ces entrefaites qu'au printemps de 1894 un Arménien, nommé Hamparsoum Boyadjian, originaire du Vilayet d'Adana, et ayant fait ses études de médecine à Constantinople et à Genève, arriva dans la région de Talori, prenant, pour n'être pas reconnu, le nom de Mourad. Accompagné d'une bande armée parmi laquelle se trouvait un ancien compagnon de Damadian, avec lequel il s'est l'ailleurs rencontré, il parcourait les villages de la région et ceux de Kavar pour y exercer la médecine à ce qu'il prétend, et engager les Arméniens à se délivrer des mauvaises coutumes de "hafir, hala" qui les assujettissaient aux Kurdes. Mais ni lui ni aucun de ses cinq compagnons à qu'il avait donné des fusils de guerre et des munitions, n'ont pu expliquer de façon plausible leur séjour dans les montagnes, et la déposition de l'un d'eux fait comprendre que s'il était sorti de la voie droite, c'est à la suite de l'oppression dont soit sa famille, soit lui-même avait eu à se plaindre de la part des Kurdes.

Presque tous les témoins Arméniens nient connaître même le nom de Mourad. Les Kurdes ou les témoins ayant des attaches officielles ne parlent de lui que par oui-dire. Dans ces circonstances l'enquête ne présente pas les données nécessaires pour se rendre un compte parfaitement exact de ses faits et gestes. Tout ce qu'il est permis de conclure c'est qu'il visitait les régions de Kavar et de Talori où il avait sa résidence principale, ainsi que les villages environnants, se promenant avec ses compagnons, mais rarement dans les montagnes, et donnant, comme il le reconnaît lui-même, des conseils touchant directement les rapports d'Arméniens à Kurdes. D'après le nommé Tono, de Talori, en effet, il engageait les premiers à rendre dent pour dent aux seconds, et à ne pas payer leurs impôts au Gouvernement pour attirer son attention.

En outre, le contenu du cahier trouvé sur Mourad lui-même, composé de pièces de vers patriotiques en Arménien, d'une biographie de Damadian, exposant les agissements de ce dernier, encore que ces écrits ne soient pas de Mourad, les notes au crayon entr'autres, qu'il reconnaît être de sa main et qui sont le début d'une lettre relatant le commencement des événements de 1894, prouvent indubitablement qu'aussi bien que Damadian, Mourad est venu dans ces pays avec un but politique caché et en essayant de provoquer des rencontres entre les Arméniens et les Kurdes. D'ailleurs ces excitations ne paraissent guère avoir eu pour résultat, acquis par l'enquête, que l'incident d'Aktchesser, au mois de Juin 1894, et d'où de Caïmacam de Koulp, qui 'y était allé pour percevoir les impôts et arrêter quelques individus, fut obligé de se sauver, et de plus, quelques méfaits qui auraient été commis par les Arméniens sur les Kurdes.

Un grand nombre d'accusations de différent genre: vols, meurtres barbares, viol, &c., ont été soulevées contre les premiers. Le détail, ainsi que le degré de confiance qu'elles méritent, s'en trouvera consigné dans le supplément (ch. No. 2); les Soussignés doivent reconnaître comme ayant été réellement commis, pendant l'été de 1894, le vol des deux bœufs du nommé Ahmé Ahmo de Nedrân, le meurtre de deux Kurdes: l'un de Inekân, et l'autre de Karikân; l'attaque sur les tentes du nommé Hassan Chaouki, et le 28 Juillet (v. s.) 1894, sur celles des Kurdes Velikanli, habitant Moush, cette dernière provoquée par des querelles antérieures au sujet de bétail volé et repris.

Ces attentats paraissent avoir eu pour auteur la bande des compagnons de Mourad, qui devaient être en réalité plus nombreux que les cinq hommes arrêtés avec lui et parmi lesquels se trouvaient selon toute vraisemblance quelques Arméniens de Kavar et de Talori.

Ces faits dans leur ensemble, le dernier surtout, où trois Musulmans furent tués ou blessés, ne pouvaient manquer, grossis et exagérés, d'exciter chez les Kurdes une agitation que rend visible la déposition de Hichman Agha, disant qu'un Kurde Velikanli courut chez les Bekranli pour leur exposer la situation critique qui leur était faite par les Arméniens, et la déclaration de Cherho, Agha des Bekranli, expliquant que si les Badikanli prirent part aux combats qui suivirent, ce n'était pas pour aider aux Bekranli, leurs ennemis de la veille, mais pour venger tous les méfaits dont eux-mêmes avaient eu à souffrir de la part des Arméniens.

Quoiqu'il en soit, les Kurdes se rassemblèrent à Kavar et à Talori et, surtout dans ce dernier endroit, leur nombre paraît avoir été considérable; à quelle influence déterminante doit-on l'attribuer? Les données de l'enquête ne permettent de rien affirmer, des déclarations isolées, d'après lesquelles ce rassemblement aurait été causé par les excitations des agents de l'autorité, dont le Cheik Mehemet de Zeilan aurait été l'intermédiaire, ne pouvant être regardées comme suffisantes dans un cas aussi important, et la présence à Guéliéguzan de celui-ci, le premier des Cheiks Kurdes, quoique affirmée par quelques témoignages, ne paraissant pas prouvée.

A la suite de l'agitation qui s'était produite parmi les Kurdes, les Karikanli veulent attaquer les Arméniens, mais ils en sont empêchés par l'intervention des troupes régulières, détachées au nombre de deux compagnies d'infanterie à Merguémouzan, situé à trente minutes de Chenik. Il est à noter que cette alerte devait forcément obliger les Arméniens à prendre leurs précautions contre la possibilité d'attaques ultérieures.

Peu de temps après les Bekranli, au nombre de soixante à quatre-vingts environ, se rendent avec leurs Aghas, Omer et Cherho, au dit campement de Merguémouzan, et à leur retour tombent sur Chenik et Semal, dont les habitants se retirent sur les hauteurs de Keupru-Cherif-Han et de Tchaï, ainsi que les gens d'Alian qui se réunissent à eux et les combats commencent entre Kurdes et Arméniens. C'était de 1er Août, (v. s.) 1894.

Au moment où ces combats eurent lieu, quelle fut la conduite des compagnies de troupes régulières chargées de maintenir l'ordre dans cette partie du pays et campées à Merguémouzan, à une demi-heure de distance de Chenik? Elle a reçu deux explications: d'une voix presque unanime, les villageois accusent les soldats d'avoir, réunis aux Kurdes, participé à l'attaque dont Chenik et Semal auraient été l'objet. Mais le Commandant de ces troupes, le Capitaine Hadji Moustapha Effendi, nie connaître l'existence des combats, affirmés par les dépositions des Kurdes et Arméniens qui y prirent part, et dit seulement qu'un matin il apprit que pendant la nuit une partie des Bekranli avait été assaillie par les Arméniens, le neveu d'Omer Agha tué et, ajoute-t-il, "son cadavre mutilé apporté au camp."

Les Bekranli et Badikanli, eux aussi, nient que les troupes se soient mêlées aux combats et disent que, cernés par les Arméniens, ils se trouvèrent dans l'impossibilité de donner aucun avis aux soldats de Merguémouzan.

Cependant les Soussignés ne sauraient accepter cette explication, attendu que les Badikanli, dont les pâturages se trouvent du même côté de Chenik que le campement, purent recevoir la nouvelle du combat et au nombre d'une centaine, à les en croire, venir se joindre aux Bekranli.

En outre, le chef du détachement qui ajoutait foi, comme le prouvent sa déposition et celle de Fevzi Effendi, aux bruits répandus auparavant, suivant lesquels les Arméniens étaient dans l'intention d'exterminer les soldats qu'il commandait à Merguémouzan et qui sur ces entrefaites avaient été portées à un bataillon, ce qu'il a toujours caché, devait être forcément amené à prendre des mesures de précaution et de surveillance qui auraient dû lui permettre d'être informé de ce qui se passait aux alentours et en particulier de la lutte assez importante, par suite du nombre des combattants, engagée à proximité de son propre campement.

Pour ces différents motifs, les Soussignés, prenant en considération que l'accusation, portée contre les troupes de Merguémouzan d'avoir participé à l'attaque des Kurdes émane des Arméniens seuls, ne peuvent la considérer comme absolument prouvée, mais en admettant qu'en réalité elles se soient abstenues, le fait avoué et reconnu par lui d'être resté dans l'inaction, lors d'événements graves et proches, qu'il ne pouvait pas ne pas connaître, condamne la conduite du chef des troupes, aussi gravement que si elles eussent pris une part directe à l'action.

Les événements ci-dessus racontés, l'incident d'Aktchesser, quelques attaques sur les Kurdes et en dernier lieu sur les Velikanli, joints au bruit que les Arméniens voulaient même se porter sur les troupes de Merguémouzan, qu'une de leurs bandes était dans l'intention de tuer le Caïmacam de Sassoun à Shatak, enfin la lutte avec les Kurdes Bekranli et le départ subséquent des Arméniens sur l'Antok-Dagh, tout cela, réuni à la présence parmi eux de Mourad et de ses compagnons, laquelle n'était pas un secret pour les autorités, fut considéré par elles comme une révolte ouverte contre le Gouvernement qui décida l'envoi de troupes, dans le but de disperser les rebelles et de s'emparer de leur chef Mourad et de ses acolytes.

Quelques bataillons furent concentrés à Mouch et un détachement, sous le commandement du Colonel Tewfik Bey, qui reçut les instructions directes du Muchir du IVe Corps d'Armée, Zeki Pacha, et qui se trouva ensuite sous les ordres d'Edhem Pacha, Commandant Militaire de Mouch, fut organisé. Il se composait de deux bataillons et quart d'infanterie, une peloton de dragons, avec deux canons de montagne, plus une trentaine de zaptiés.

Parti de Mouch le 13 Août (v. s.), 1894, ce détachement alla se réunir près de Chenik aux deux compagnies campées à Merguémouzan, qui, quelques jours auparavant avaient été renforcées et atteignaient un bataillon.

Ce que firent et ce que devinrent les Arméniens depuis leur fuite sur l'Antok-Dagh jusqu'au jour où le détachement quitta Mouch n'a pas été parfaitement éclairci.

La lettre trouvée dans les papiers de Mourad et qui lui était adressée de l'Antok-Dagh par le prêtre Ohannès, de Semal, Kirko, fils de Mossé, de Chenik, et Ohan, fils de Nigo, permet de conclure que pendant une période de douze jours, à dater du commencement des événements, soit le 1er ou le 2 Août, les Arméniens ne cessèrent de lutter avec les Kurdes dont ils restèrent vainqueurs, mais que le onzième jour, épuisés par les combats précédents, ils durent, vers le soir, céder aux attaquants Husséindsik, quartier de Guéliéguzan, puis Guéliéguzan même, que le village fut ensuite brûlé. Leur situation était alors désespérée.

En même temps, de la déposition de Tewfik Bey et de quelques autres, il résulte que le 14 Août (v. s.) le détachement, quittant Chenik de bon matin et arrivé le même jour à Guéliéguzan, eut en route une rencontre qui se borna à un échange de coups de fusil, et qu'en atteignant Husséindsik, les Arméniens qui occupaient le village en furent délogés après un court combat. Est-ce le même combat que celui dont fait mention la lettre précitée? Ce document, qui mérite foi complète, étant donné les circonstances où il a été écrit, parle d'un combat qui durait jusqu'au soir, que ce même soir Guéliéguzan était brûlé et que les Arméniens étaient près d'être anéantis.

En résumé, les événements, tels qu'ils se dégagent avec difficulté des données très approximatives de l'enquête, se présentent de la façon suivante:

Dans ces dernières années, les relations entre les Arméniens de Kavar et de Talori et les Kurdes, s'étaient sensiblement altérées; un agitateur politique, Hamparsoum Boyadjian, dit Mourad, en profite pour former une bande qui se livre à quelques méfaits sur les Kurdes; ceux-ci excités se rassemblent, tombent sur les Arméniens et les combats commencent.

Le Gouvernement, considérant la conduite des Arméniens comme une révolte ouverte, envoie des troupes, qui les dispersent, et s'emparent de Mourad.

La question de la résistance que les Arméniens auraient opposée aux troupes à Guéliéguzan et à Guéliésan n'a pas été suffisamment éclaircie. Dans le premier de ces deux endroits, comme on l'a expliqué plus haut, il est plus probable que les Arméniens avaient évacué le village avant l'arrivée du détachement; dans le second, il n'est pas possible de dire, s'il y a eu résistance en masse, ou quelques cas de résistance isolée.

Le fait que les Kurdes se trouvaient avec les troupes, et que celles-ci n'ont rien fait pour les éloigner peut être considéré comme prouvé.

Il reste à examiner si les Arméniens étaient en réalité en révolte contre le Gouvernement, si la répression a été proportionnée à la gravité du mouvement, et, dans le cas où elle aurait dépassé les bornes de l'humanité, à qui incombent les responsabilités.

Les preuves citées à l'appui de l'existence d'une révolte sont les suivantes:-

La propagande de gens, tels que Damadian et Mourad;

La formation de bandes armées depuis le commencement du mois de Mai 1894;

L'état d'hostilité ouverte contre les agents du Gouvernement se traduisant par l'incident d'Aktchesser, l'attentat sur le Caïmacam de Sassoun à Kiagashin, l'expulsion des zapités par les habitants d'Agpi et de Hetink, le refus datant de quinze ou vingt ans, opposé par les gens de Talori, d'admettre des employés sur leur territoire, et de payer leurs impôts.

La préparation de la poudre, et sa distribution, ainsi que celle du plomb;

Le rassemblement des Arméniens sur l'Antok-Dagh, d'où ils descendaient pour molester et attaquer les Kurdes;

L'incendie mis par eux-mêmes à leurs propres villages;

La résolution d'exterminer les soldats campés à Merguémouzan, et, enfin, leurs attaques sur les troupes Impériales à Guéliéguzan et à Guéliésan.

On ne peut nier l'existence d'une propagande ni la présence de Mourad avec ses compagnons, parmi les gens de Kavar et de Talori, et la participation des premiers aux combats soutenus par les Arméniens.

Conditions de l'Enquête.

La Commission, composée comme il est dit ci-dessus, a tenu 107 séances du 24 Janvier au 21 Juillet, 1895, et entendu 190 témoins, qu'il est possible de répartir de la façon suivante:-

Vingt-trois agent de l'autorité civile ou ayant des attaches avec elle, deux officiers de l'armée régulière, six membres du clergé Arménien, soixante-et-un Kurdes, deux Arméniens de Mouch, soixante-dix-huit Arméniens de Kavar, dix-huit Arméniens de Khian.

Mais de ce grand nombre de témoignages la majeure partie ne présente qu'une très faible valeur:

Les agents de l'autorité civile ou militaire, les membres du clergé Arméniens, les deux Arméniens de Mouch, donnent de longs détails sur la propagande révolutionnaire qui aurait été faite dans le pays par l'agitateur Mourad et ses prédécesseurs et sur les méfaits commis par les Arméniens, mais évitent de parler de l'affaire de Sassoun, et quelques-uns d'entre eux font même des déclarations mensongères à ce sujet.

D'un autre côté, les Arméniens de Kavar et de Talori nient pour la plupart connaître Mourad, même de nom, passent sous silence soit par peur ou pour tout autre motif, les agissements du premier et de ses compagnons, et tout ce qu'ils craignent pouvoir ensuite leur être reproché—luttes avec les Kurdes et les troupes régulières.

Les Arméniens de Khian, ainsi qu'un certain nombre de témoins venus de ce côté, répètent d'une façon générale un récit identique dans des termes identiques; l'un même, Recho, fils de Boghos de Keguervan, se donnant comme Kiahia, sans l'être, Pollo, fils d'Avédis, comme Kiahia de Nedran, qui ne renferme que deux maisons Arméniennes; Boghos, fils de Khazar, de Guéliémansour, comme membre du Conseil des Anciens, et personne ne l'y connaît, toutes circonstances faisant douter de l'identité des personnes qui comparaissent.

La plupart de ces témoins ayant été choisis par l'intermédiaire des autorités de Koulp et de Guendj, que la Commission d'Enquête avait invitées à lui envoyer des personnes ayant connaissances des événements, ce mode de comparaître ne pouvait en aucune façon être garant de la sincérité de leurs déclarations.

Des 78 Arménians de Kavar, 35 sont de Chenik, 15 sont de Semal, 11 sont de Guéliéguzan, 1 est de Spagank, 2 sont de Agpi, et 3 sont de Talori, plus 11 prisonniers faits dans ce dernier endroit, et dont les témoignages ne sauraient en conséquence être regardés comme indépendants l'un de l'autre.

La comparaison de ces chiffres démontre que les événements de Talori, dont la Commission, en dépit des suggestions des Soussignés, a toujours refusé de rechercher l'origine possible et les motifs dans les faits de 1893, ont été, pour ainsi parler, laissés de côté par elle, que son attention s'est portée particulièrement sur le village de Chenik alors que les allégations relatives aux faits qui se seraient passés à Guéliéguzan même, entre Guéliéguzan et Talori et à Talori auraient dû attirer et retenir ses principaux efforts.

De ces soixante-dix-huit Arméniens à l'exception de ceux d'entr'eux venus de leur plein gré et de ceux appelés pour vrifier leur existence, le choix a appartenu aux autorités locales; et pendant leur séjour ils se trouvaient sous la surveillance et à la disposition de la police. C'est un zaptié qui rencontre au bazar Girbo et Khatcho, fils de Manouk de Chenik et que les mène devant la Commission. A plusieurs reprises les Soussignés ont attiré l'attention de la Commission, auprès de laquelle l'accès a toujours été difficile, sur l'intérêt qui se présentait, pour la recherche de la vérité, à se mettre en contact direct avec la population et à ne laisser de la sorte aucun intermédiaire, aucune influence s'interposer entre elle-même et les témoins que la Commission avait à entendre. Mais les Soussignés doivent constater que leurs efforts dans ce sens sont toujours restés infructueux et ils étaient cependant justifés: le Moukhtar d'Alvarindj reçoit de la Commission l'ordre d'amener directement devant elle un réfugié de Spagank, qui se trouvait dans son village: il en est empêché par la police, ainsi que cela ressort des procès-verbaux, cette ingérence va jusqu'à s'exercer dans le local même de la Commission où des témoins sont, soit menacés, soit intimidés par les agents de l'autorité employés à son service.

Dès le début de l'enquête la Commission avait établi deux catégories: l'une de suspects accusés, l'autre de témoins ou informateurs entre les personnes qu'elle entendait, distinction contre laquelle les Soussignés n'ont pas manqué de protester et qui s'est fait sentir jusque dans le mode même d'interrogatoire des personnes ayant comparu.

Dans ces conditions, il est compréhensible que l'enquête, malgré sa durée et le nombre des témoins entendus, n'ait fourni relativement qu'une faible quantité de résultats certains, et sa continuation, d'ailleurs, étant donné la façon dont elle n'a cessé d'être menée n'aurait pas permis d'espérer une découverte plus large de la vérité.

(Signé) M. Vilbert.
H. S. Shipley.
M. Prjevalsky.

Mouch, *le 20 Juillet, 1895.*
F. O. 424/183, pp. 203-216, No. 190/1
Turkey No. 1 (1895) Part I, pp. 134-146, No. 252/1

Chapitre II.—Actes de vol, de fait de Meurtre, de Brigandage, et d'Illégalité, que les Arméniens ont été accusés d'avoir commis pendant l'été de 1894.

D'après un grand nombre de témoins entendus par la Commission, les Arméniens de Kavar et de Talori, obéissant aux conseils et aux instigations de Mourad, auraient, dès le début du printemps de 1894, formé des bandes armées qui se seraient livrée à une série de crimes de tout genre contre les Kurdes et auraient même commis certains délits d'insoumission à l'égard du Gouvernement, ainsi que d'autres actes ayant été considérés par celui-ci comme des préparatifs à la révolte.

L'examen des actes ci-dessus mentionnés constitue le contenu de ce chapitre.

(A.)—*Actes de Vol, Brigandage, et Meurtre contre les Kurdes.*

(a.) Vol des effets des Kurdes Badikanli, Meho, et Temo, emportés de la maison de Girbo de Chenik.

Il résulte des dépositions des nommés Youssouf-ben-Ali, Mehemet-ben-Haïdar, et Peto-ben-Tako de Kouhislam (Procès-verbaux Nos. 54 et 55) que le 5 Mai, 1894, ils rencontrèrent près de Guéliéguénim une bande d'Arméniens armés ayant à leur tête Kirko, Moukhtar de Chenik.

Ils virent, en même temps, des bêtes de somme, chargés d'effets et le même jour ils apprirent à Guéliémansour que les dits effets qui appartenaient aux Kurdes Badikanli, Meho et Temp, avaient été enlevés de la maison de Girbo de Chenik.

Il convient de faire observer que de tous les Badikanli et les habitants de Guéliémansour entendus devant la Commission pas un seul n'a mentionné ce vol et que le susdit Peto, fils de Tako, un des témoins ci-dessus mentionnés, a donné à ce sujet des dépositions contradictoires. Girbo, fils de Manouk (Procès-verbal No. 65) qui, ainsi qu'on peut en conclure de la déposition du Caïmacam de Koulp (Procès-verbal No. 66) est le Girbo dans la maison duquel le vol a été commis, n'y a fait aucune allusion quoiqu'il ait montré beaucoup d'empressement à attribuer d'autres méfaits aux Arméniens.

Dans ces conditions le fait même du vol d'effets de Temo et Meho ne peut pas être regardé comme prouvé.

Quant à la rencontre près de Guéliéguénim d'une bande composée de quarante Arméniens en armes ayant Kirbo à leur tête, l'enquête ne donne pas d'indices directes qui appuyent ou qui informent les déclarations à ce sujet de trois habitants de Kouhislam: elles pourraient trouver une confirmation indirecte dans l'attaque à laquelle cette même bande se serait portée à cette même place cinq jours plus tard, soit le 10 Mai, sur une caravane se rendant à Mouch; mais comme il sera démonstré ci-dessous cette attaque elle-même paraît douteuse.

L'apparition d'une bande armée ayant le Moukhtar de Chenik à la tête, après l'annonce que disent en avoir faite à Guéliémansour par Youssouf, Mehemed, et Peto devait infailliblement attirer l'attention des habitants de ce village, cependant treize d'entre eux entendus devant la Commission n'en ayant fait aucune mention, l'existence même de cette bande ne doit pas être considérée comme démontrée.

(b.) Attaque sur une caravane de porteurs se rendant à Mouch.

D'après les déclarations de cinq Kurdes, interrogés par la Commission (Procès-verbal No. 58), une attaque aurait lieu le 10 Mai à Guéliéguénim sur une caravane de porteurs se rendant à Mouch, quarante charges de blé enlevées, quatre Musulmans blessés, dont l'un serait mort quelques jours après. Plainte à ce sujet fut portée à Mouch le 11 Mai (Procès-verbal No. 59).

Quoique des dispositions aient été prises sur le papier pour la poursuite des gens accusés, l'absence de suites effectives données à cette affaire, malgré la gravité des déclarations des plaignants, tendrait à démontrer que les renseignements pris par les autorités locales ne vinrent pas à l'appui des accusations formulées dans la plainte et que l'attaque en question n'eut pas lieu dans les conditions exposées, pas plus qu'elle n'eut les conséquences alléguées par les requérants.

Une plainte datée aussi le 11 Mai, 1894, et lu dans la séance du 5 Février, 1895, confirme cette supposition. Elle parle également d'une attaque par les Arméniens de Chenik au nombre de quinze, parmi lesquels Kirko, sur les habitants des mêmes villages de Djaks et Tiakhs, auxquels appartiennent les cinq témoins ci-dessus mentionnés; quinze charges de blé auraient été enlevées. Deux des signataires de cette seconde requête portent le même nom que ceux de deux des cinq témoins en question, l'un des individus présents ayant éprouvé à donner son vrai nom un embarras qu fut partagé par ces compagnons.

La Commission n'a pas fait d'enquête au sujet de cette attaque, se bornant à entendre les plaignants, et sans nier la réalité du fait lui-même que démontre la plainte portée en son temps, il y a lieu de considérer comme restées obscures les conditions dans lesquelles cette attaque aurait eu lieu.

(c.) L'enlèvement des moutons de Dervich Agha, de Khochekan, et la blessure faite alors à son fils Ibrahim qui en serait mort ensuite.

L'enquête à ce sujet ne possède que la déclaration de Dervich Agha lui-même (Procès-verbal No. 27). Cette attaque si elle s'est produite, ne pouvait pas rester ignorée d'autant plus qu'elle aurait pu être regardée comme un acte de vengeance des Arméniens contre Dervich Agha, qui avait pris une part directe à l'arrestation de Damadian, cependant Omer-ben-Pourto est le seul (Procès-verbal No. 30) qui en aurait entendu parler. Taleb Effendi (Procès-verbal No. 12) qui donnait sa déposition en se rapportant à des notes écrites ne cite pas cette affaire parmi la longue série de crimes qu'il impute aux Arméniens.

L'absence de plainte en son temps de la part de Dervich Agha, qui, il le déclare lui-même, connaissait les agresseurs et possédait des témoins de l'incident, ne permet pas d'accorder foi à son récit, car malgré l'explication qu'il donne de son silence il pouvait toujours espérer que les autorités, vu ses services, donneraient toutes les suites voulues à sa plainte.

L'enquête à ce sujet n'a pas été poursuivie par la Commission.

(d.) Le viol et le meurtre barbare environ le 10 Juin, 1894, de Hedo, femme de Moussa Abdoullah, de Molla Meleki.

Ce crime forme le sujet des dépositions du mari de la victime (Procès-verbal No. 65), et d'Ahmet-ben-Récho (Procès-verbal No. 67). Le Caïmacam de Koulp (Procès-verbal No. 66) confirme le fait de la remise d'une requête y ayant trait, et Ali de Guéliéguzan (Procès-verbal No. 68), parent de la victime, a entendu parler de ce meurtre quelques jours avant les événements sur l'Antok-Dagh. Taleb Effendi (Procès-verbal No. 12) dans sa déposition cite également le meurtre barabre de Hedo, femme de Moussa, mais il ajoute que le mari lui-même fut tué, et il place ce double assassinat parmi les événements de l'année 1893, le regardant comme une cause des combats qui se produisirent cette même année entre Kurdes et Arméniens.

Ni Réched (Procès-verbal No. 24), ni Mehmet-ben-Mirzo (Procès-verbal No. 33), ni Meho (Procès-verbal No. 69), les parents de la femme tuée, en énumérant les actes de violence dont les Arméniens se seraient rendus coupables à l'égard des Kurdes, ne font aucune mention de cet incident qui, s'il avait eu vraiment lieu, ne pouvait échapper à leur attention. De plus, il est difficile d'admettre que le vol de deux bœufs chez le nommé Ahmo-ben-Ahmé de Nederan ait pu provoquer une plus grande impression sur les Kurdes qu'un meurtre qui aurait été commis dans de circonstances aussi barbares. Cependant le vol de ces bœufs a trouvé une mention dans presque chaque déposition faite par un Kurde ou Arménien de Khian ou Koulp devant la Commission, tandis que pour le meurtre en question les seules dépositions sont celles ci-dessus mentionnées.

L'absence d'enquête à ce sujet et en son temps, reconnue par le Caïmacam de Koulp lui-même, est avec le récit invraisemblable en soi que fait le mari de la victime, une raison sérieuse qui donne à douter que cette accusation contre les Arméniens soit fondée.

En conséquence, les Soussignés ne sauraient regarder cet incident comme un des faits acquis devant la Commission.

(e.) La déclaration unique et très indéterminée de Nadir Agha (Procès-verbal No. 13) au sujet de l'enlèvement par les Armeniens d'une femme Kurde qui après avoir subi de mauvais traitements aurait été relâchée au bout de deux jours, ne présente pas les données voulues pour arriver à une conclusion quelconque.

(f.) Meurtre barbare près de Guéliéguénim d'un Kurde dont le cadavre aurait été apporté au camp de Merguémouzan entre le 14 et 17 Juillet (Procès-verbal No. 5).

Cette allégation n'a pas été confirmée ni par les dépositions du Capitaine Moustapha Effendi (Procès-verbal No. 9), ni par celle de Medjid on-Bachi (Procès-verbal No. 5), dont la conversation avec un soldat et niée ensuite par Medjid lui-même aurait fourni l'occasion du rapport qui a trait à cet incident.

(g.) Le meurtre par des Arméniens du fils d'Amo, Kurde de Khochekan, et dont le cadavre écorché, d'après le Capitaine Moustapha Effendi, aurait été amené au camp, n'a pas été mentionné dans une seule déposition devant la Commission qui cependant a entendu un très grand nombre de Kurdes Badikanli et autres. Seul Serkiz, fils de Hamza (Procès-verbal No. 42), du village de Hartk, près Talori, dit d'une façon indéterminée que les Armeniens non seulement tuaient les Kurdes mais encore écorchaient les victimes.

Dans ces circonstances, l'accusation dont il s'agit ne peut pas être considérée comme prouvée.

(h.) Le meurtre au commencement du mois de Juin du Kurde Temich-ben-Mehemet et mutilation du cadavre.

Le nommé Ressoul-ben-Merdjo (Procès-verbal No. 20) est venu de lui-même devant la Commission porter plainte à ce sujet, mais se bornant à de simples dénonciations n'a fourni aucune preuve à l'appui des accusations qu'il a jetées sur les Arméniens.

Aucun des trois Kurdes de Guéliéguzan (Procès-verbaux Nos. 24, 68, et 69) ne fait allusion à ce meurtre quoique d'après Ressoul lui-même ce serait les Kurdes de Guéliéguzan qui les premiers lui en auraient fait part.

Les dépositions des trois Kurdes de Djadjas, voisin du village où demeurait la victime, accusent le fait seul du meurtre mais ne désignent pas les auteurs (Procès-verbal No. 69).

De plus, à en croire Ressoul, il résiderait de façon permanente à Djadjas et par conséquent aurait vu lui-même le cadavre mutilé. Mais il résulte des dépositions de Dervich Agha (Procès-verbal No. 27) que le dit Ressoul habite Mouch depuis longtemps et qu'il a participé avec son frère Mamo à la prise de Damadian.

Dans ces circonstances, en admettant le fait même d'un meurtre dont l'existence d'ailleurs n'a pas été suffisamment démontrée, aucune preuve n'est avancée que ce meurtre ait été commis par les Arméniens.

(i.) Le meurtre de Selim (Procès-verbal No. 20) qui d'après les dépositions de son fils Abdullah aurait eu lieu ai mois de Juillet 1894, a été commis en réalité en 1893 pendant les événements de Talori, ce qui résulte de la déposition du dit Abdullah lui-même rapprochée de celle de Taleb Effendi (Procès-verbal No. 12).

La Commission n'a pas poursuivi l'enquête sur cet incident.

(j.) L'attaque sur le Kurde Mehmet de Tapik.

(k.) L'enlèvement de bestiaux chez Ako-ben-Abro.

(l.) L'attaque sur Moussa-ben-Sado.

(m.) Le meurtre d'un Kurde dont environ 150 moutons furent enlevés (Procès-verbaux Nos. 5, 69, 72, 24).

Chacune de ces quatre accusations ne repose que sur des dépositions uniques et indéterminées qui ne permettent de formuler une conclusion.

(n.) L'enlèvement par une bande d'Arméniens armés de deux bœufs appartenant à Ahmo-ben-Ahmé, du village de Nederen, forme le sujet de dépositions nombreuses, indépendantes les unes des autres, parmi lesquelles les principales sont celles d'Osman-ben-Tolo, Arakel, fils de Tavo, Ali-ben-Abdo (Procès-verbal No. 59), Gulavi-ben-Abdo (Procès-verbal No. 60), Tato et Serko (Procès-verbaux Nos. 62 et 63).

Il en ressort de façon incontestable que ce vol a eu lieu et qu'il était le fait d'une bande armée d'Arméniens qui se retirèrent ensuite vers l'Antok-Dagh. Mais il est à noter que les dites dépositions relatives à la poursuite par les Kurdes des Arméniens ravisseurs démentient que les Arméniens de Chenik, Semal, et Guéliéguzan n'étaient ni au moment de l'enlèvement même, ni immédiatement après réunis sur l'Antok-Dagh.

(o.) Le meurtre barbare de Husséin-ben-Kalo, du village d'Inekan.

D'après le récit du Capitaine Moutsapha Effendi (Procès-verbal No. 9) ce fut le cadavre mutilé d'un homme de Khian habitant dans le voisinage de Merguémouzan qui fut apporté au camp; la victime qui était allée sur l'Antok-Dagh chercher deux bœufs qu'elle avait perdus y fut assassinée.

Arakel, fils de Tavo (Procès-verbal No. 59), Tato (Procès-verbal No. 62), disent avoir entendu parler par les Kurdes partis à la recherche des bœufs d'Ahmo Ahmé du meurtre d'un Kurde d'Inekan, Osman-ben-Talo, Ali-ben-Abdo, Gulavi-ben-Abdo, Maksoud-ben-Hassan, Salih-ben-Omer, Mamo-ben-Temo (Procès-verbal Nos. 59, 60, et 65), confirment le fait du meurtre et du transport du cadavre mutilé à Merguémouzan.

En examinant toutes ces dépositions on voit que tous ces témoins parlent du même fait. Sako (Procès-verbal No. 17) a entendu dire par les zaptiés, au temps des événements mêmes, qu'un cadavre mutilé avait été amené au camp. Dans ces circonstances, le fait doit être considéré comme prouvé; attendu qu'il résulte des dépositions précitées que c'était au moment de la poursuite par les Kurdes de la bande d'Arméniens qui avaient enlevé les bœufs d'Ahmo Ahmé, il est possible que cet homme ait été tué par elle.

Quant au récit de Gulavi-ben-Abdo (Procès-verbal No. 60) qui, se disant témoin oculaire, a donné les plus minutieux détails des actes de cruauté révoltante qu'il aurait vu commettre par les Arméniens, il ne convient pas d'y ajouter foi, car ce même Gulavi-ben-Abdo, ayant d'après sa propre déclaration accompagné le cadavre jusqu'au camp de Merguémouzan, il est impossible qu'il n'ait pas donné ces détails avec les noms des assassins soit à ses compagnons, soit au Capitaine Moustapha Effendi. Etant donné les contradictions très sérieuses existant entre le déposition de ce dernier et celles des autres témoins relativement aux conditions dans lesquelles la mort du dit Kurde aurait eu lieu, les circonstances environnant cet incident restent très vagues et n'ont pas été suffisamment éclaircies par l'enquête.

(p.) Le meurtre du Kurde Karikanli Sili-ben-Kasso.

On doit considérer le fait du meurtre de cet homme, confirmé même par Attam (Procès-verbal No. 77) comme prouvé.

En ce qui regarde les auteurs de l'attenat et les détails on ne saurait prendre au sérieux les dépositions de Hazzo, de Spagank (Procès-verbal No. 70), et Gulavi-ben-Abdo (Procès-verbal No. 60), et en l'absence de témoignages directs considérer cette dernière question comme élucidée par l'enquête.

Toutefois la disparition de Silo-ben-Kasso sur des terrains situés près de villages Arméniens, les déclarations des villageois qui nient en avoir aucune connaissance, alors que les dires du susdit Attam prouvent que ce fait ne pouvait être ignoré d'eux, la présence enfin parmi les Arméniens de la bande de Mourad, donnent lieu de fortement soupçonner les Arméniens du meurtre dont il s'agit.

(q.) Attaque sur les tentes de Hassan Chaouki (Procès-verbal No. 90) accompagnée d'un vol de bétail, deux hommes ayant été blessés, cette attaque mentionnée aussi fréquemment dans les dépositions entendues que celle ayant eu pour résultat l'enlèvement des deux bœufs d'Ahmo Ahmé et les meurtres de deux Kurdes d'Inekan et de Karikan est confirmé par la déposition de Hassan Chaouki lui-même et par celle de Tato, de Guéliémansour (Procès-verbal No. 62), qui de plus affirme que cet incident même aurait été la cause des rencontres ultérieures entre les Kurdes et les Arméniens. Étant donné les dépositions unanimes au sujet de cette attaque, elle doit être admise comme s'étant réellement produite, et les auteurs comme étant des Arméniens.

(r.) Attaque sur les tentes d'Émin-ben-Kasso.

D'après Emin-ben-Kasso lui-même (Procès-verbal No. 28), Mirzo-ben-Ali et Salih-ben-Ali (Procès-verbal No. 29), cette attaque aurait eu lieu environ le 15 Août aux pâturages nommés Chen près de Chenik et Semal et aurait été suivie par l'enlèvement d'environ 300 moutons, par la mort de quatre Kurdes, et la blessure de trois autres.

Des dépositions de Suleïman-ben-Mollah Ahmet et Ahmo-ben-Mehemet (Procès-verbal No. 72) il résulterait au contraire que cette attaque aurait eu lieu au mois de Juillet.

Si l'on prend en considération la situation dans laquelle se trouvaient les Arméniens le 15 Août sur l'Antok-Dagh et de plus l'endroit où l'attaque alléguée aurait eu lieu, c'est-à-dire près de Chenik, du côté opposé à l'Antok-Dagh, on doit la regarder comme impossible et étant donné que les Kurdes nient avoir soutenu aucun combat avec les Arméniens sauf les deux seuls jours à Tchaï, il est très probable que la perte d'hommes attribuée par Émin-ben-Kasso à l'incident en question n'ait été qu'un résultat des combats qui eurent lieu pendant le première moitié d'Août.

Si au contraire l'attaque avait lieu au mois de Juillet, comme prétendent les témoins Suleïman et Ahmo précité il est alors inexplicable qu'un accident entraînant des conséquences aussi graves n'ait été l'objet d'aucune mention dans les autres témoignages Kurdes et qu'Omer-ben-Pourto (Procès-verbal No. 30) si bien renseigné n'en ait pas même entendu parler.

(s.) L'attaque sur les tentes d'Amo Meho de Latchekan aux pâturages du Kourtik-Dagh à deux heures de distance des villages de Chenik et Semal.

Les plus minutieux détails au sujet de cette attaque on été donnés par Amo Meho lui-même (Procès-verbal No. 28), mais quoique très graves n'ont trouvé de confirmation que dans quatre témoignages Badikanli (Procès-verbaux Nos. 71 et 72).

L'affaire en question à ce qu'affirmait le plaignant, se serait passée à Kourtik-Dagh, mais dans ce cas elle n'aurait pu rester ignorée du Capitaine Moustafa Effendi; cependant nu celui-ci ni les autres Kurdes qui énumèrent les méfaits Arméniens n'en font mention, et le Capitaine aussi bien que ces derniers sont absolument muets au sujet des cadavres mutilés des trois Kurdes qui, à en croire Ahmo, auraient été apportés à Merguémouzan.

Cet incident ne doit pas être pris plus en considération que le précedent.

(t.) L'enlèvement du bétail de Farho-Oghlou, Kurde d'Inekan.

Il résulterait des dépositions y relatives (Procès-verbaux Nos. 30, 49, 59, 66, 67, et 91) que ce vol aurait été commis par une bande d'Arméniens des villages de Kavar et de Talori. A cette accusation les Arméniens répondent simplement par des dénégations et les récits Kurdes se contredisent eux-mêmes sur quelques points.

Etant donné les exagérations et les inventions remarquées dans le récit de semblables attaques, il ne paraît pas possible, sans nier que celle-ci ait eu lieu, de se prononcer à son endroit, surtout si l'on prend en considération que les deux principaux témoins de l'incident, Sophi Mehemet et Suleïman de Guedorni (Procès-verbal No. 70) donnent ensuite un récit tout à fait invraisemblable au sujet de la question suivante, savoir:-

(u.) La perception des Arméniens pendant deux années sur des Musulmans

d'argent et de produits agricoles à titre de redevances pour l'Église Arménienne.

Étant donné la situation respective des Kurdes et des Arméniens dans le pays, les premiers étant les maîtres on doit considérer cette accusation qui porte non sur un cas isolé de brigandage, mais s'étend à une période de deux années, comme une pure invention, ayant toute l'apparence d'avoir été imaginée pour servir de contrepoids aux déclarations des Arméniens relatives au hafir que les Kurdes perçoivent d'eux.

(v.) La conversion au Christianisme opèrée de force par Mourad sur trois Kurdes de Guéliéguzan et sur la famille de Hazzo de Spagank.

Cette accusation malgré les récits circonstanciés mais pleins de contradictions et d'invraisemblances, dont elle est l'objet de la part d'Ali, Mého de Guéliéguzan, et Hazzo de Spagank (Procès-verbaux Nos. 68, 69, et 70), confirmée d'après ouï-dire par Taleb Effendi, ne présente rien qu'une calomnie.

Ces faits sont inadmissibles, si l'on songe aux conditions du pays, le district où ces conversions auraient été oporées étant à proximité immédiate de Mouch, et entouré par des villages Kurdes où les soi-disant victimes auraient pu aisément se réfugier.

(w.) Le meurtre de Hadji Agha, Kurde Bekranli, dont le cadavre mutilé aurait été apporté au camp de Merguémouzan.

D'après le Capitaine Moustapha Effendi (Procès-verbaux Nos. 9 et 80), Hadji Agha aurait été tué pendant l'attaque des Arméniens sur les Bekranli, venant à leurs pâturages d'été, mais toutes les autres dépositions à ce sujet, y compris celles des Bekranli eux-mêmes, ne confirment ni le fait de mutilation du cadavre ni celui du combat dans les conditions relatées par le Capitaine Moustapha Effendi. Seul Cherho, Agha des Bekranli (Procès-verbal No. 87), déclare que les cadavres de trois Kurdes tués pendant le premier jour de la lutte avaient été mutilés par les Arméniens, mais il nie que les Bekranli aient eu des relations avec les troupes à Merguémouzan, tandis que de son côté le Capitaine qui les commandait nie avoir eu connaissance d'un combat ayant duré deux jours entre les Arméniens et Kurdes. Vu ces contradictions évidentes et les exagérations démonstrées plus haut au sujet de mutilation de cadavres par les Arméniens, on ne peut considérer cette accusation comme digne de foi.

(x.) Obstructions, pour les Musulmans, du fait des Armeniens, de routes directes de Khian à Mouch pendant deux ans.

Les dépositions à ce sujet de Salih Agha, Ressoul, Dervich Agha, Salih-ben-Zoro, Medjid Effendi, et Temo (Procès-verbaux Nos. 14, 20, 27, 28, 49, et 51) sont de simples allégations insuffisamment appuyées sur des faits probants.

(y.) L'attaque sur les Kurdes Velikanli le 28 Juillet (v. s.),1894 (Procès-verbaux Nos. 4, 7, 9, 12, 13, 14, 17, 20, 30, 36, 41, 51, 59, 73, 74, 75, et 98).

Les nombreuses dépositions à ce sujet tant Arméniennes que Kurdes établissent le fait d'une telle attaque de la part des gens de Chenik, et accompagnée de la mort de trois Kurdes et ne diffèrent que sur les motifs. Les Arméniens les trouvent dans un vol de bétail commis d'abord par les Kurdes tandis que les autres dépositions attribuent l'attaque aux excitations de Mourad et à l'état de révolte où se trouvaient alors les Arméniens. Mais le fait qu'ils restituèrent par égard pour le Gouvernement le bétail enlevé à cette occasion, en se bornant à se plaindre des Velikanli aux agents des autorités venus à Chenik, ainsi que leur attitude à l'égard de ces mêmes agents, montrent bien que cette attaque n'avait pas le caractère révolutionnaire qu'on lui à prêté et n'était que le résultat d'une dispute entre les deux parties intéressées.

Quant à l'accusation de viol de femmes à cette occasion portée contre les Arméniens, elle émane du seul Simonen Oghlou (Procès-verbal No. 98), qui en aurait fait part à Fevzi Effendi, mais n'a pas été confirmée par celui-ci, envoyé spécialement pour examiner l'incident et ne saurait être acceptée sur l'affirmation unique du dit Simonen Oghlou.

(z.) Les paroles injurieuses proférées par les bandes Arméniennes contre la religion Musulmane.

Ce fait a été signalé dans beaucoup de dépositions, les témoins ajoutant qu'en même temps des Arméniens criaient le nom de Mourad, comme celui du leur chef, et Mourad lui-même n'a pas nié que la chose fût possible, vu les habitudes du pays.

Quoique les témoignages relatifs à cette accusation émanent d'un seul côté, on peut admettre que des injures aient été proférées par les Arméniens au cours de leurs rixes avec les Kurdes.

(B)—*Actes d'Insoumission des Arméniens à l'égard du Gouvernement et autres agissements considérés par celui-ci comme préparatoires à la Révolte.*

(a.) Attaque sur le Caïmacam de Koulp, au village d'Aktchesser, environ le 20 Juin (v.s.), 1894.

Le récit fait à ce sujet par le Caïmacam lui-même et confirmé par la déposition des gens de sa suite (Procès-verbaux Nos. 66, 67) ne paraît que peu vraisemblable, attendu qu'une réunion de plusieurs centaines d'Arméniens armés de Kavar et de Talori joints à ceux d'Aktchesser même, attaquant un Agent du Gouvernement du rang de Caïmacam n'aurait pas pu ne pas être considéré comme un acte de révolte ouverte; cependant, malgré la gravité du cas, on ne voit pas qu'une mesure quelconque ait été prise à la suite de ce grave incident, ce qui permet de penser qu'il était de proportions beaucoup plus modestes que celles qui lui ont été attribuées par le Caïmacam.

D'autre part, comme il ressort du commencement d'une lettre prise sur Mourad, qu'il y eut une opposition réelle de la part des villageois à l'arrestation de leurs Chefs, le fait en question ne peut être regardé autrement que comme un acte d'insoumission envers les Agents du Gouvernement.

Aucun des habitants d'Aktchesser n'ayant été appelé devant la Commission, l'enquête ne présente qu'un des côtés de la question.

(b.) Attaque affirmée par le Caïmacam de Sassoun comme ayant été méditée contre sa personne à Kiagashin (Procès-verbal No. 52).

L'enquête ne présente aucune déposition indépendante de celle du Caïmacam lui-même et aucun habitant du village de Kiagashin n'ayant été produit devant la Commission malgré la demande des Délégués, ceux-ci ne peuvent regarder ce fait comme établi, d'autant plus que le Caïmacam ne basait ses propres affirmations que sur les simples informations d'un de ses Agents.

(c.)Expulsion de Chenik de Fevzi Effendi, Commandant de Gendarmerie, envoyé à l'occasion de la rixe entre les habitants de ce village et les Kurdes Velikanli, et allégué par Anton Effendi, Vicaire de l'Évêque Catholique de Mouch (Procès-verbal No. 43).

Cette accusation n'a pas été confirmée par Fevzi Effendi même. Les déclarations du prêtre Parsegh disant que des Agents du Gouvernement tels qu'Ali Effendi, Taleb Effendi et autres envoyés pour donner des conseils aux villageois de Kavar et de Talori auraient été chassés par ces derniers, n'ont pas trouvé davantage de confirmation dans les dépositions faites devant la Commission, Taleb Effendi lui-même ayant nié s'être rendu dans ces districts pendant l'été 1894.

(d.) Refus par les habitants de Talori d'admettre chez eux pendant quinze ans les agents de l'autorité.

La déposition à ce sujet de Medjid Effendi et du Caïmacam de Koulp (Procès-verbaux Nos. 49 et 66) ce dernier allant jusqu'à affirmer qu'à cause de cette conduite il n'a pu envoyer des agents pour constater l'état des villages détruits de Talori, est en absolue contradiction avec la déposition de Mahmoud Onbachi (Procès-verbal No. 75) qui affirma que pendant son service comme gendarme il passait par Talori sans être aucunement inquiété par les Armeniens.

Mais en admettant que le fait avancé fut vrai, il faudrait en voir le cause dans la situation génerale du pays et ne pas rejeter la faute sur les Armeniens vu leur situation au milieu des Kurdes et leur faiblesse numérique.

(e.) Attaque méditée par les Arméniens sur les troupes de Merguémouzan.

La plupart des dépositions à cet égard ne reposant que sur des oui-dire et le Capitaine Moustafa Effendi se basant uniquement sur les informations reçues d'un certain Kurde de Sassoun par l'intermédiaire d'un zaptié, le fait de préméditation d'une attaque sur les soldats ne présente que le caractère d'une simple rumeur.

Les déclarations relatives à ce sujet des témoins Rechid, Ali, et Hazzo (Procès-verbaux Nos. 23, 69, et 70), vu leur caractère invraisemblable et contradictoire, ne peuvent pas être considérées comme fournissant un appui quelconque à l'accusation, d'autant plus que leur présence parmi les Armeniens sur l'Antok-Dagh est des plus douteuses.

(f.) Refus des habitants d'Agpi et Hetink de payer leurs impôts en 1894.

Cette accusation a été portée par le seul Caïmacam de Sassoun (Procès-verbal No. 52), et l'enquête n'a pas été faite à ce sujet. Simo, d'Agpi (Procès-verbal No. 81), a nié le fait.

(g.) Introduction de poudre et de plomb à Talori (Procès-verbaux Nos. 49, 53, 69, et 75).

L'enquête en fournit deux cas: l'un constaté par les agents secrets de Medjid Effendi, l'autre vu par les gens de Khian, qui auraient rencontré une bande avec les porteurs des munitions en question. En dépit des affirmations des témoins précités, les conditions dans lesquelles ils ont comparu devant la Commission et les détails de leur récit ne permettent pas de le considérer comme vraisemblable.

(h.) Enfouissement des effets, ustensiles de ménage, &c., au printemps de 1894, de la part des gens de Kavar, et présenté dans de nombreux témoignages comme préparatoire à la révolte.

Les Arméniens ont expliqué cette habitude, d'ailleurs ancienne, par la crainte du vol des Kurdes venant dans leurs environs à leurs pâturages d'été.

Translation.

IN consequence of the events of which the district of Sasun, included in the Sandjaks of Mush and Ghendj, in the Vilayet of Bitlis, had been the scene during the summer of the year 1894, the Imperial Ottoman Government decided to send to the spot a Commission charged to hold the necessary inquiry there, and obtained from the Powers represented at Erzeroum authority for their Consuls to be represented by Delegates attached to the Commission.

The Commission was composed of his Excellency Shefik Bey, President; Djelal Bey, Madjid Bey, General Tewfik Pasha, and Omer Bey, members, the last named ceasing to act on the 29th of January, on being nominated to the post of Vali of Bitlis *ad interim.*

The Delegates of the French Consul, the British Consul, and the Russian Consul-General at Erzeroum were respectively MM. Vilbert, Shipley, and Prjcvalsky. They have the honour to set forth below the results of the inquiry, but they think it indispensable to being by taking a rapid survey of the country in which the events took place, and then to investigate the relations between the native Armenian and Kurdish populations, finally passing to the examination of the events themselves, and the consideration of the questions rising from them, namely, whether there was really a revolt, whether massacres did actually occur, and who should be held responsible.

Survey of the Country.

In the southern part, and on the edge of the plain watered by the Kara Su, one of the affluents of the Murad Su (Eastern Euphrates), and at the foot of a chain of mountains bordering this plain on the south-west, is situated the town of Mush, the chief town of the sandjak of the same name, in the Vilayet of Bitlis.

The various portions of this chain (which is known as the Mountains of Mush) lying near the town itself, are called Kurtik-Dagh, Hatsherash Sevsar ("Black Rocks"); their southern and south-western slopes facing the plain are joined by a series of heights of lesser altitude to the great range of the Antok-Dagh and Tsovasar, thus forming a series of valleys and ravines watered by the springs of the Batman-Su; it is there that the Armenian villages of Kavar, Shatak, and Talori are situated.

In one of these valleys, eventually running round the north-west side of the Antok-Dagh, and in its upper extremity, are Shenik, Semal, and Alian, at half-an-hour's distance from one another, and three to three-and-a-half hours from Mush. Similarly situated at the upper end of a second valley, which runs to the south-west of the Antok-Dagh, and between this mountain and Mount Tsovasar, are the six villages of Shatak: Kop, Ghermav, Iritsank, Tapik, Kiagashin, and Shushamerg, then Agpi and Hetink on the side of the Tsovasar-Dagh; and then, facing Agpi, and in a transversal ravine, is Ghelieguzan, one of the villages of Kavar, separated from Shenik and Semal by heights named Keupru-Sherif-Han and Chaï, which connect the Antok-Dagh with the Mountains of Mush; the paths leading from Shenik and Semal to Ghelieguzan pass over these heights.

Beyond Ghelieguzan and Agpi, to the south-west, the ravines forming the very steep and wooded spurs of the Antok-Dagh contain the villages of Ergart, Tsorir, Spagank, the wards composing Talori, named Dawalik, Purh, Hosnud, Hartk, Hakmank, Kholovit, Halorink, Talori itself, known as Ekudun, or Verin Kiegh, then Ishhantazor, known as Akchesser, Sevit, Inguznak, and the wards belonging to these various villages. The most distant is that of Talori, the wards of which, situated at one or two hours' distance from each other, are five or six hours from Ghelieguzan, with which two paths connect it: one by the mountain direct, passing by the ravine of Gheliesan and Afkart, the other by the ravine of Agpi, Hetink, and Spagank.

The villages of Kavar, Shenik, Semal, and Ghelieguzan, of which Alian is only a ward, belong to the Caza of Mush, the villages of Shatak, Agpi, Hetink, Spagank, Tsorir, and Ergart to that of Sasun, and all the rest to the Caza of Kulp.

The approximate numbers of houses and inhabitants in this district, as shown by the evidence furnished by the inquiry, will be found in the Annexes (Chap. I).

Relations of the Armenians with the Kurds.

The country, of which a short sketch has just been given, contains fertile tracts and rich pastures well adapted for rearing large numbers of cattle, and on the Talori side there are even iron mines, worked by the villagers, who used to manufacture the necessary agricultural implements and supply them to the surrounding districts.

The Armenian population inhabiting this portion of the Vilayet of Bitlis is surrounded by a large number of Kurdish villages on the side of Sasun, Khian, and Kulp. In the summer the half-settled Kurdish tribes, of which the two chief are the Bekranli and the Badikanli, with many subdivisions (Kabilé) bearing different names, come from the direction of Diarbekir and Silivan to the mountains of Tsovasar, Antok, and Kurtik-Dagh, mentioned above, to pasture their herds.

Thanks to the grouping of the Armenian villages, and the configuration of the ground, and also to the rivalry existing among the Kurds themselves, the inhabitants of Kavar and Talori had, up to this time, been able to maintain good relations with their neighbours and visitors the Kurds; they lived, to use the expression of a witness, like brothers "of earth and water," and the difficulties which arose among them, due to thefts of cattle alternately carried off and retaken, always ended by being settled to the satisfaction of the parties interested.

It should be added that if the relations of the Kurds with the Armenians were of a satisfactory character, it was because the latter, in order to secure assistance and protection from the Kurdish Aghas in case of need, had for a long period paid them an annual due, in proportion to their resources, known by the name of "hafir," and consisting of a certain portion of all their crops, cattle, silver, ore, with the addition of articles of clothing, agricultural implements, &c. When the daughter of an Armenian peasant marries, his Agha levies, under the name of "hala," half the sum paid by the bridegroom, by the custom of the country, to the bride's parents.

Every village and house is dependent on one or more Aghas, who look upon the different levies made as a proprietary right, going so far as to hand it on as an inheritance, or to sell it by private contract.

If an Armenian refuses for any reason to pay, the Agha compels him to do so by force, stealing his cattle, or doing him some injury. The Aghas of the villages of Kavar and Talori were chiefly the Kurdish Aghas of Sasun (Kharzan).

This, at any rate, is the description which the Armenians almost unanimously gave of the hafir, but it is only right to add that the evidence given goes to show that, though the requirements of this tribute may have pressed upon the people of Talori and Khian, they were much less severe at Ghelieguzan, Semal, and Shenik, an inhabitant of which latter place stated that the "hafir" was not paid there.

The Kurds and their Aghas heard before the Commission declare that they do not even know the word "hafir" or its meaning, state that no such tribute has existed for fifty years, and explain the levies made by certain Aghas on the Armenians as a debt due from the tiller of the soil to its proprietor.

Nevertheless, the fact that the "hafir" existed to within the last few years is proved by the declaration of Taleb Effendi, one of the agents of the authorities at Mush, who, having been sent on frequent missions into these districts, ought to be well informed, and who, in his deposition, speaks of a Kurd having gone two years ago to Talori for the purpose, he says in so many words, "of levying hafir."

The explanations given on the subject in an official communication emanating from the Administrative Council of Mush, read, but only in part, at the sitting of the Commission on the 7th June, 1895, cannot be considered as proof, or as being of an absolutely independent character.

For three or four years past the relations between the Armenian villages in question and the Kurds had begun to assume a hostile character, which may be attributed to two causes: on the side of the Kurds, the religious propaganda of their Sheiks which reconciled the tribes hitherto on bad terms, and prohibited all quarrels arising from the protection which any one tribe might extend over the Armenians to the disadvantage of another; and on the side of the Armenians the agitation fomented by such men as Damadian, who represented to them their subjection to the Kurds as a sort of slavery against which the Government afforded them no protection, and stirred them up to cast off the yoke. The year 1893 affords a proof of this state of open hostility in the combined attack of the Kurdish tribes on Talori.

Account of the Events at Sasun in 1894.

Such was the state of things when, in the spring of 1894, an Armenian named Hamparsum Boyadjian, a native of the Vilayet of Adana, who had studied medicine at Constantinople and Geneva, arrived in the district of Talori, taking the name of Murad to avoid recognition. Accompanied by an armed band, amongst whom was an ancient comrade of Damadian—also an acquaintance of his—he traversed the villages of the district, as well as those of Kavar, for the purpose of practising medicine, as he states, and persuading the Armenians to free themselves from the evil custom of "hafir, hala," which kept them in subjection to the Kurds. But neither he nor any of his five companions, whom he had provided with military guns and ammunition, have been able to give a satisfactory explanation of their sojourn in the mountains; and one of them practically admits in his evidence that if he had left the paths of honesty it was owing to the oppression which either himself or his family had had to endure at the hands of the Kurds.

Almost all the Armenian witnesses deny any knowledge even of the name of Murad. The Kurds, or witnesses with official connections, only speak of him from hearsay. Under these circumstances, it is impossible to get a very clear idea of his proceedings from the slender evidence given at the inquiry. The only conclusion that can be drawn is that he visited the regions of Kavar and Talori, which he made his principal residence, as well as the surrounding villages, moving about with his companions, but not often in the mountains, and giving counsels directly affecting, as he himself admits, the relations of the Armenians with the Kurds. According to the man Tono, of Talori, he, in fact, encouraged the former to give as good as they got to their adversaries, and to attract the attention of the Government to themselves by refusing to pay their taxes.

Moreover, the contents of the note-book found upon Murad, consisting of patriotic verse in Armenian, and a biography of Damadian, giving an account of his acts, though they may not have been written by Murad, prove beyond doubt—by the pencil notes, amongst other things, admitted by him to be in his handwriting, and forming the introduction of a letter on the beginning of the events of 1894—that Murad, no less than Damadian, came into the country with a concealed political end in view, and with the intention of provoking encounters between Armenians and Kurds. No result, however, as far as the inquiry could elicit, appears to have ensued from these incitements except the incident of Akchesser, in the month of June 1894, when the Kaïmakam of Kulp, who had gone to that place to collect the taxes and arrest certain individuals, was obliged to fly, and several outrages said to have been committed by Armenians on Kurds.

The former have been accused of a large number of crimes of different kinds: thefts, barbarous murders, rape, &c. Details on these points, as well as observations on the degree of credence they deserve, will be found in the Annexes (Chap. II).

The Undersigned must recognize as having really taken place in the summer of 1894 the theft of two oxen of the man Ahme Ahno, of Nedran, and the murder of two Kurds, one belonging to Inekân, the other to Karikân, the attack on the tents of the man Hassan Shauki, and on the 28th July (o. s.), 1894, on those of the Velikanli Kurds inhabiting Mush, the latter attack being provoked by former quarrels about cattle that had been stolen and recaptured.

These crimes seem to have been committed by the band accompanying Murad, which must in reality have numbered more than the five men arrested with him, and among whom in all probability some Armenians from Kavar and Talori were to be found.

These facts taken together, and particularly the last-mentioned attack, in which three Mussulmans were killed or wounded, could not fail, when made much of and exaggerated, to arouse among the Kurds an amount of agitation which is seen from the deposition of Hichman Agha, who states that a Velikanli Kurd went to the Bekranli to inform them of the critical situation in which they were placed by the Armenians, and from the declaration of Sherho, Agha of the Bekranli, explaining that the Badikanli took part in the ensuing conflicts, not to assist the Bekranli, who had just before been their enemies, but to avenge all the misdeeds which they had themselves had to submit to at the hands of the Armenians.

Whatever the facts may be, the Kurds assembled at Kavar and Talori, and their number appears to have been considerable, especially at the latter place. The question is: To what cause is this movement to be ascribed? The results of the inquiry admit of no positive statement on the subject; for some isolated declarations to the effect that this meeting was caused by the instigations of Government agents, through the intermediary of Sheik Mehement of Zeilan, cannot in a case of such importance be regarded as being of sufficient value, nor does the presence of the latter, who is the chief of the Kurdish Sheiks, at Ghelieguzan, although affirmed by several witnesses, appear to be proved.

In consequence of the agitation which had arisen among the Kurds, the Karikanli wished to attack the Armenians, but were prevented by the intervention of the regular troops, two infantry companies of which were sent to Merghemuzan, thirty minutes distant from Shenik. It should be noted that the effect of this alarm was to make it absolutely necessary for the Armenians to take precautions against the possibility of subsequent attack.

Shortly afterwards the Bekranli, to the number of about sixty or eighty, betook themselves with their Aghas, Omer and Sherho, to the above-mentioned encampment at Merghemuzan, and on their return fell upon Shenik and Semal, the inhabitants of which retired to the heights of Keupru-Sherif-Han and Chaï, with the people of Alian who joined them, and the conflicts between Kurds and Armenians began. This was the 1st August (o. s.), 1894.

At the time these encounters took place, what was the attitude of the companies of regular troops charged to keep order in that part of the country, and encamped at Merghemuzan, distant half-an-hour from Shenik? Two explanations have been given; the villagers almost unanimously accuse the soldiers of having joined the Kurds and taken part in the attack directed against Shenik and Semal. But the Commandant of these troops, Captain Hadji Mustapha Effendi, denies all knowledge of the encounters mentioned in the depositions of the Kurds and Armenians who took part in them, and merely says that one morning he learnt that during the night a body of Bekranli had been attacked by the Armenians, the nephew of Omer Agha killed, and, he adds, "his mutilated corpse brought into the camp."

The Bekranli and Badikanli also deny that the troops took part in the encounters, and say that, being surrounded by the Armenians, they found it impossible to communicate with the soldiers at Merghemuzan.

But the Undersigned cannot accept this explanation, seeing that the Badikanli, whose pastures lie on the same side of Shenik as the encampment, managed to hear of the fight, and that 100 of them, according to their own account, were able to come and join the Bekranli.

Moreover, the head of the detachment, who gave credence, as proved by his deposition and that of Fevzi Effendi, to the reports previously circulated, which attributed to the Armenians the intention of exterminating the soldiers under his command at Merghemuzan, and whose strength had in the meanwhile been increased to a battalion, a fact he always kept secret, must of necessity have taken measures of precaution and supervision, which would have kept him informed of events in the vicinity, and especially of the fight which was taking place in proximity to his own camp, and which was sufficiently important from the number of combatants.

For these different reasons, taking into consideration the fact that the accusation brought against the troops at Merghemuzan of having taken part in the attack of the Kurds emanates from the Armenians alone, the Undersigned cannot regard it as absolutely proved; but admitting that the troops really held aloof, the fact, avowed and admitted by the Commander of the troops, of having remained passive during serious events which took place close to him, and of which he could not have been in ignorance, is as weighty a condemnation of his conduct as if the troops had directly anticipated in the engagement.

The events narrated above, the Akchesser incident, some attacks on the Kurds, and, lastly, on the Velikanli, joined to the report that the Armenians intended even to attack the troops at Merghemuzan, that one of their bands designed to kill the Kaïmakam of Susan at Shatak, finally, the fight with the Bekranli Kurds and the subsequent departure of the Armenians for the Antok-Dagh,—all this, joined to the presence among them of Murad and his companions, which was no secret to the authorities, was considered by them as an open revolt against the Government, who resolved to send troops with the object of dispersing the rebels and seizing their leader Murad and his associates.

Some battalions were concentrated at Mush, and a detachment was organized, under the command of Colonel Tewfik Bey, who received instructions direct from the Mushir of the 4th Army Corps, Zekki Pasha, and was afterwards under the orders of Edhem Pasha, Military Commandant of Mush. This force consisted of two and a quarter battalions of infantry, a detachment of dragoons, with two mountain guns, and about thirty zaptiehs.

Starting from Mush on the 13th August (o. s.), 1894, this force proceeded to join, near Shenik, the two companies in camp at Merghemuzan, who, a few days previously, had been reinforced to the strength of a battalion.

It has not been clearly ascertained what the Armenians did, or what became of them, from the time of their flight to the Antok Dagh to the departure of the detachment from Mush.

The letter found among Murad's papers, and addressed to him from the Antok-Dagh by the priest Ohannes of Semal, by Kirko of Shenik, the son of Mosse, and by Ohan, the son of Nigo, makes it appear from that during a period of twelve days from the commencement of the events, that is, from the 1st or 2nd August, the Armenians never ceased fighting the Kurds, whom they overcame; but that on the eleventh day, exhausted by the previous conflicts, they were forced towards evening to give up to their assailants Husseindsik, a ward of Ghelieguzan, then Ghelieguzan itself, and that the village was then burned down. Their position then became desperate.

At the same time it appears from the deposition of Tewfik Bey, and of others, that on the 14th August (o. s.) the detachment of troops, starting early in the morning from Shenik, and arriving the same day at Ghelieguzan, had on their march an encounter which was merely an exchange of shots, and that on their reaching Husseindsik the Armenians who occupied the village were dislodged from it after a short fight. Is this the same fight as the one mentioned in the above letter? This document, which is worthy of full credence on account of the circumstances in which it was written, mentions a fight which lasted till the evening, and says that or the same evening Ghelieguzan was burnt, and that the Armenians were nearly annihilated.

To sum up, the course of events, such as they appear extracted with difficulty from the very uncertain data collected at the inquiry, seems to have been as follows:-

During the last few years the relations between the Armenians at Kavar and Talori and the Kurds had undergone a considerable change; a political agitator, Hamparsum Boyadjian, called Murad, takes advantage of this to form a band which commits certain misdeeds against the Kurds; the latter are excited and assemble, attack the Armenians, and the fight commences.

The Government regard the conduct of the Armenians as an open revolt, and send troops, who disperse them and capture Murad.

The question of the resistance said to have been offered by the Armenians to the troops at Ghelieguzan and Gheliesan has not been sufficiently elucidated. At the former of these two places, as explained above, it is more probable that the Armenians had evacuated the village before the arrival of the detachment; at the latter, it is impossible to say whether there was united resistance, or whether there were some instances of isolated resistance.

The fact that the Kurds were with the troops, and that no steps were taken by the latter to make them withdraw, may be considered as proved.

There remain to be examined the questions whether the Armenians were really in revolt against the Government; whether the measures of repression were in proportion to the gravity of the movement; and, if those measures went beyond what humanity permitted, on whom the responsibility falls.

The facts brought forward in proof of the existence of a revolt are as follows:-

The propaganda of men such as Damadian and Murad;

The formation of armed bands since the beginning of May 1894;

The state of open hostility against the Government officials, shown by the Akchesser incident, the attempt on the Kaïmakam of Sasun at Kiagashin, the expulsion of zaptiehs by the inhabitants of Agpi and Hetink, the refusal, for the last fifteen or twenty years, of the people of Talori to allow officials to enter their territory or to pay taxes;

The manufacture of powder, and its distribution, as also that of lead;

The assembling of the Armenians on the Antok-Dagh, whence they came down to molest and attack the Kurds;

The burning by them of their own villages;

The resolve to exterminate the soldiers encamped at Merghemuzan, and, lastly, the attacks of the Armenians on the Imperial troops at Ghelieguzan and Gheliesan.

The existence of a propaganda, the presence of Murad and his companions among the people of Kavar and Talori, and the participation of the former in the fights in which the Armenians were engaged, cannot be denied.

Circumstances of the Inquiry.

The Commission, composed as above stated, held 107 sittings from the 24th January to the 21st July, 1895, and heard 190 witnesses, who may be divided as follows:-

Twenty-three persons employed by the civil authorities or connected with them; 2 officers of the regular army; 6 members of the Armenian clergy, 61 Kurds; 2 Armenians from Mush; 78 Armenians from Kavar; 18 Armenians from Khian.

But little value attaches to the greater part of this mass of evidence.

The Government employés, civil or military, the members of the Armenian clergy, and the two Armenians from Mush give copious details respecting the revolutionary propaganda said to have been carried on in the country by the agitator Murad and his predecessors, and respecting the misdeeds of the Armenians, but avoid speaking of the Sasun affair, and some of them even make false statements on this subject.

On the other hand, the Armenians from Kavar and Talori for the most part deny that they know Murad, even by name, and observe silence, through fear or some other reason, on the subject of his doings and those of his companions, and on all matters for which they are afraid they may be afterwards blamed, such as the fights with the Kurds and the regular troops.

The Armenians from Khian, as well as a certain number of other witnesses from that part, repeat generally an identic story in identic terms; one of them even, Resho, son of Boghos of Keghervan, styling himself a Kiahia, although he is not one; another, Pollo, son of Avedis, styling himself Kiahia of Nedran, where there are but two Armenian houses; Boghos, son of Khazar of Gheliemansur, calling himself member of the Council of Elders, though no one there knows him; all these are circumstances which create doubts as to the identity of the people who appeared.

Most of these witnesses having been selected through the intermediary of the authorities of Kulp and Ghendj, who were asked by the Commission of Inquiry to send them persons with knowledge of the events, the circumstances under which they appeared as witnesses could not be a guarantee of the good faith of their declarations.

Of the 78 Armenians from Kavar, 35 are from Shenik, 15 are from Semal, 11 are from Ghelieguzan, 1 is from Spagank, 2 are from Agpi, and 3 are from Talori, besides 11 men who were taken prisoners in the latter place, and whose depositions could not therefore be regarded as independent of each other.

A comparison of these figures shows that the events of Talori, the possible origin and causes of which the Commission, in spite of the suggestions made by the Undersigned, always refused to seek in the occurrences of 1893, were, so to speak, set aside, and that the attention of the Commission was especially directed to the village of Shenik, while the statements relative to events said to have taken place at Ghelieguzan itself, between that place and Talori, and at Talori, should have principally attracted their attention and occupied them.

The selection of these seventy-eight Armenians was left to the local authorities, with the exception of two of them, who came of their own accord, and of those who were summoned for the purpose of verifying their existence; and during their stay they were under the supervision and at the disposal of the police. It was a zaptieh who met Girbo and Khacho, sons of Manuk of Shenik, in the bazaar and brought them before the Commission. On several occasions the Undersigned drew the attention of the Commission, access to which was always difficult, to the importance, in order to discover the truth, of putting themselves in direct touch with the people, and of thus not allowing any intermediary or any influence to come between themselves and the witnesses whose evidence the Commission had to take. But the Undersigned must place it on record that their efforts in this sense were always fruitless, though they were justified in making them. The Mukhtar of Alvarindj was ordered by the Commission to bring directly before them a refugee of Spagank, who was then in his village, but he was prevented by the police, as shown by the *procès-verbaux*. This interference even extended to the meeting-place of the Commission, where winesses were threatened and intimidated by the Government agents attached to its service.

From the commencement of the inquiry the Commission divided the witnesses into two classes: one composed of accused suspects, the other of witnesses or informers, a distinction against which the Undersigned did not fail to protest, and which was noticeable even in the mode adopted for the examination of witnesses.

In these circumstances, it is comprehensible that the inquiry, notwithstanding its duration and the number of witnesses heard, should have produced relatively but few certain results; moreover, considering the manner in which it was conducted throughout, no hopes could be entertained that is continuance would have led to an ampler discovery of the truth.

(Signed) M. VILBERT.
H. S. SHIPLEY.
M. PRJEVALSKY.

MUSH, *July 20, 1895.*

CHAPTER II.—ACTS OF MURDER, BRIGANDAGE, AND LAWLESSNESS ATTRIBUTED TO THE ARMENIANS DURING THE SUMMER OF 1894.

According to a large number of witnesses heard by the Commission, the Armenians of Kavar and Talori, yielding to the advice and instigation of Murad, are said to have formed since the beginning of spring 1894 armed bands, which committed a series of crimes of all sorts against the Kurds, and even some acts of insubordination against the Government, as well as other acts which were regarded by the latter as preparatory to a revolt.

This chapter deals with the acts above mentioned.

(A.)—*Acts of Theft, Brigandage, and Murder directed against the Kurds.*

(a.) Theft of property belonging to the Badikanli Kurds, Meho and Temo, and carried away from the house of Girbo of Shenik.

It appears from the depositions of Yussouf-ben-Ali, Mehemet-ben-Haïdar, and Peto-ben-Tako of Kuhislam (*Procès-verbaux* Nos. 54 and 55), that on the 5th May, 1894, they met near Ghelieghenim a band of armed Armenians led by Kirko, Mukhtar of Shenik.

They saw at the same time beasts of burden laden with property, and they learnt on the same day at Gheliemansur that the said property had belonged to the Badikanli Kurds, Meho and Temo, and had been carried off from the house of Girbo of Shenik.

It is well to call attention to the fact that of all the Badikanli and inhabitants of Gheliemansur who were heard before the Commission, not one mentioned this robbery, and that the above-named Peto, son of Tako, one of the witnesses mentioned above, gave contradictory evidence on this subject. Girbo, son of Manuk (*Procès-verbal* No. 65), who, as may be concluded from the deposition of the Kaïmakam of Kulp (*Procès-verbal* No.66), is the Girbo in whose house the robbery was committed, made no allusion to it, although he showed himself very ready to attribute other misdeeds to the Armenians.

Under these circumstances, the fact even of the robbery of property belonging to Temo and Meho cannot be considered as proved.

As to the meeting near Ghelieghenim with a band composed of forty armed Armenians led by Kirko, the inquiry affords no direct indication either confirming or rebutting the declarations of three inhabitants of Kuhislam on the subject; they may be said to receive indirect confirmation from the attack said to have been made by this same band at the same place five days later, on the 10th May, on a caravan going to Mush: but, as will be shown later, the attack itself seems doubtful.

The appearance of an armed band, with the Mukhtar of Shenik at its head, after the information said to have been given about it at Gheliemansur by Yussuf,

Mehemed, and Peto, must infallibly have attracted the attention of the inhabitants of that village, yet, as thirteen of them who were heard before the Commission made no mention of it, the existence even of this band must not be considered as established.

(b.) Attack on a caravan of carriers going to Mush.

According to the statements of five Kurds who were examined by the Commission (Procès-verbal No. 58), an attack was made on the 10th May at Ghelieghenim on a caravan of carriers going to Mush, forty loads of corn were carried off, and four Mussulmans were wounded, of whom one died some days later. A complaint on the subject was made at Mush on the 11th May (Procès-verbal No. 59).

Although orders were given on paper for the pursuit of the accused, the absence of any real action in this case, in spite of the serious statements of the complainants, would seem to show that the information obtained by the local authorities was not such as to confirm the accusations laid in the complaint, that the attack in question did not take place under the conditions stated, and that its consequences were not such as were alleged by the complainants.

A complaint, also dated the 11th May, 1894, which was read at the sitting of the 5th February, 1895, confirms this supposition. It mentions likewise an attack made by the Armenians of Shenik, fifteen in number, and amongst them Kirko, on the inhabitants of the same villages of Djaks and Tiakhs, to which the five witnesses above mentioned belonged. Fifteen loads of corn were said to have been carried off. Two of the signatories of this second Petition bear the same names as those of two of the five witnesses in question, and one of the individuals present felt a hesitation in giving his real name which was shared by his companions.

The Commission made no investigation into this attack, but confined themselves to hearing the complainants, and, without denying the reality of the incident itself, which is shown by the complaint made at the time, the circumstances of this attack must be considered as not having been cleared up.

(c.) The lifting of the sheep belonging to Dervish Agha, of Khoshekan, and the wound then inflicted on his son Ibrahim, which resulted later in his death.

On this subject the only statement elicited by the inquiry was that of Dervish Agha himself (Procès-verbal No. 27). If this attack took place, it could not remain unknown, more especially as it might have been regarded as an act of vengeance on the part of the Armenians against Dervish Agha, who had been directly concerned in the arrest of Damadian; yet Omer-ben-Purto alone (Procès-verbal No. 30) had heard it mentioned. Taleb Effendi (Procès-verbal No. 12), who referred to written notes while make his depositions, does not mention this matter in the long list of crimes with which he charges the Armenians.

The failure of Dervish Agha to lay a complaint at the time, though knowing, as he declares, the aggressors, and having witnesses of the incident, induces disbelief in his story, for, in spite of the explanation which he gives of his silence, he had always reason to hope that the authorities, considering his services, would take all necessary action on his complaint.

The inquiry into this affair was not pursued by the Commission.

(d.) The violation and barbarous murder, about the 10th June, 1894, of Hedo, wife of Mussa Abdullah, of Molla Meleki.

This crime forms the subject of the depositions of the husband of the victim (Procès-verbal No. 65), and of Ahmet-ben-Recho (Procès-verbal No. 67). The Kaïmakam of Kulp (Procès-verbal No. 66) confirms the fact of the delivery of a Petition on the subject, and Ali of Ghelieguzan (Procès-verbal No. 68), a relative of the victim, had heard this murder spoken of some days before the events on the Antok-Dagh. Taleb Effendi (Procès-verbal No. 12), in his deposition, likewise mentions the barbarous murder of Hedo, wife of Mussa, but he adds that the husband was himself killed, and he places this double assassination among the events of the year 1893, regarding it as a cause of the combats which took place that same year between Kurds and Armenians.

Neither Reshed (Procès-verbal No. 24) nor Mehmet-ben-Mirzo (Procès-verbal No. 33), nor Meho (Procès-verbal No. 69), relatives of the woman who was killed, in enumerating the acts of violence said to have been committed by the Armenians against the Kurds, make any mention of this incident, which, had it really occurred, could not have escaped their notice. Besides, it is difficult to admit that the theft of two beasts from the man Ahmo-ben-Ahme of Nederan could have made a greater impression on the Kurds than a murder said to have been committed under such barbarous circumstances. Yet the theft of these beasts was mentioned in almost every deposition made before the Commission by a Kurd or an Armenian of Khian of Kulp, whilst the only depositions dealing with the murder in question are those above mentioned.

The absence of inquiry into this matter at the time, admitted by the Kaïmakam of Kulp himself, together with the account, improbable on the face of it, given by the husband of the victim, afford serious reason for doubting whether this accusation against the Armenians is well founded.

Consequently, the Undersigned cannot regard this incident as one of the facts established before the Commission.

(e.) The solitary and very vague statement of Nadir Agha (Procès-verbal No. 13) respecting the abduction by the Armenians of a Kurdish woman, who after being subjected to bad treatment was said to have been released at the end of two days, does not furnish the information requisite for arriving at any conclusion.

(f.) The barbarous murder near Ghelieghenim of a Kurd whose corpse was said to have been taken to the camp at Merghemuzan between the 14th and 17th July (Procès-verbal No. 5).

This allegation was not confirmed in the depositions of either Captain Mustafa Effendi (Procès-verbal No. 9) or of Medjid on-Bachi (Procès-verbal No. 5), whose conversation with a soldier, which was subsequently denied by Medjid himself, was said to have occasioned the report on the subject of this incident.

(g.) The murder by the Armenians of the son of Amo, a Kurd of Khoshekan whose flayed corpse was, according to Captain Mustafa Effendi, brought into camp, was not mentioned in a single deposition before the Commission, though they heard a very great number of Badikanli and other Kurds. Serkiz, son o Hamza (*Procès-verbal* No. 42), of the village of Hartk, near Talori, alone stated hesitatingly that the Armenians not only killed the Kurds, but also flayed the victims.

In these circumstances the accusation in question cannot be considered as proved.

(h.) The murder early in June of the Kurd Temish-ben-Mehemet, and the mutilation of the corpse.

One Ressul-ben-Merdjo (*Procès-verbal* No. 20) appeared of his own accord before the Commission to make a complaint on this subject, but confined himself to simple denunciations, and brought no proof in support of his accusations against the Armenians.

None of the three Kurds of Ghelieguzan (*Procès-verbaux* Nos. 24, 68, and 69 make any allusion to this murder, although, according to Ressul, the Kurds o Ghelieguzan were the first to inform him of it.

The depositions of the three Kurds of Djadjas, a village near that in which the victim lived, mention the fact of the murder only, but do not name its authors (*Procès-verbal* No. 69).

Further, Ressul states that he lives permanently at Djadjas, and consequently himself saw the mutilated corpse. But the depositions of Dervish Agha (*Procès-verba* No. 27) show that the said Ressul has lived for a long time at Mush, and that he took part with his brother Mamo in the capture of Damadian.

In these circumstances, even admitting the fact of a murder, of which however, there is not sufficient evidence, no proof is forthcoming that this murder was committed by the Armenians.

(i.) The murder of Selim (*Procès-verbal* No. 20), which, according to the depositions of his son Abdullah, took place in July 1894, was really committed in 1893 during the events of Talori, as is shown by comparing the deposition of the said Abdullah with that of Taleb Effendi (*Procès-verbal* No. 12).

The Commission did not inquire further into this incident.

(j.) The attack on the Kurd Mehmet of Tapik.

(k.) The lifting of cattle belonging to Ako-ben-Abro.

(l.) The attack on Mussa-ben-Sado.

(m.) The murder of a Kurd, 150 of whose sheep were lifted (*Procès-verbaux* Nos. 5, 69, 72, and 24).

Each of these four accusations rests only on solitary and vague depositions, which do not allow of any conclusion being arrived at.

(n.) The lifting by a band of armed Armenians of two oxen belonging to Ahmo-

)en-Ahme, of the village of Nederen, forms the subject of numerous depositions ndependent one of another, the chief among them being those of Osman-ben-Tolo, Arakel, son of Tavo, Ali-ben-Abdo (*Procès-verbal* No. 59), Gulavi-ben-Abdo (*Procès-verbal* No. 60), Tato and Serko (*Procès-verbaux* Nos. 62 and 63).

It is quite clear from these depositions that this robbery took place, and that it was committed by an armed band of Armenians, who afterwards retired in the direction of the Antok-Dagh. But it is noteworthy that the said depositions respecting the pursuit of the Armenian plunderers by the Kurds deny that the Armenians of Shenik, Semal, and Ghelieguzan were, either at the time of this cattle-lifting, or immediately afterwards, assembled on the Antok-Dagh.

(*o.*) The barbarous murder of Hussein-ben-Kalo, of the village of Inekan.

According to the statement of Captain Mustafa Effendi (*Procès-verbal* No. 9), it was the mutilated corpse of a man of Khian, residing in the vicinity of Merghemuzan, that was brought into camp; the victim had gone to the Antok-Dagh in search of two oxen which he had lost, and was there assassinated.

Arakel, son of Tavo (*Procès-verbal* No. 59), and Tao (*Procès-verbal* No. 62) say that they heard the murder of a Kurd of Inekan spoken of by the Kurds who went in pursuit of the beasts of Ahmo Ahmé; Osman-ben-Talo, Ali-ben-Abdo, Gulavi-ben-Abdo, Maksud-ben-Hassan, Salih-ben-Omer, and Mamo-ben-Temo (*Procès-verbaux* Nos. 59, 60, and 65) confirm the fact of the murder and of the mutilated corpse being brought to Merghemuzan.

An examination of all these depositions shows that all these witnesses are referring to the same incident. Sako (*Procès-verbal* No. 17) heard it said by the zaptiehs, at the time of the events, that a mutilated corpse had been brought into camp. In these circumstances the fact must be held as proved: seeing that the depositions above mentioned show that it occurred at the time the Kurds were pursuing the band of Armenians who had carried off the beasts of Ahmo Ahme, it is possible that the man was killed by that band.

As to the story of Gulavi-ben-Abdo (*Procès-verbal* No. 60), who, calling himself an eye-witness, gave most minute details of acts of revolting cruelty which he saw committed by the Armenians, no reliance should be placed on it, for as this same Gulavi-ben-Abdo, according to his own statement, accompanied the corpse to the camp at Merghemuzan, it is impossible that he should not have given these details, with the names of the assassins, either to his companions or to Captain Mustafa Effendi. Considering the very serious manner in which the deposition of the latter contradicts those of the other witnesses as to the circumstances attending the death of the said Kurd, the details of this incident remain very vague, and have not been sufficiently cleared up by the inquiry.

(*p.*) The murder of the Karikanli Kurd Silo-ben-Kasso.

The fact of the murder of this man, confirmed as it is by Attam (*Procès-verbal* No. 77) must be considered as proved.

As to the authors of the deed and its details, the depositions of Hazzo of

Spagank (*Procès-verbal* No. 70), and of Gulavi-ben-Abdo (*Procès-verbal* No. 60) cannot be taken seriously, and in the absence of direct evidence this last point cannot be considered as cleared up by the inquiry.

Nevertheless, the disappearance of Silo-ben-Kasso on ground close to Armenian villages, the declarations of the villagers denying all knowledge of it though the statement of the aforesaid Attam proves that the fact must have been known to them, and, lastly, the presence amongst the Armenians of Murad's band afford strong grounds for suspecting the Armenians of the murder in question.

(*q.*) The attack on the tents of Hassan Shauki (*Procès-verbal* No. 90) accompanied by a theft of cattle and the wounding of two men. This attack, which is mentioned in the depositions as frequently as that which resulted in the carrying off of the two oxen of Ahmo Ahme and the murders of two Kurds of Inekan and of Karikan, is confirmed by the depositions of Hassan Shauki himself, and of Tato of Gheliemansur (*Procès-verbal* No. 62), the latter asserting further that this same incident was the cause of the subsequent encounters between the Kurds and the Armenians. Considering the unanimous depositions on the subject of this attack, it must be accepted as having really taken place, and its authors as having been Armenians.

(*r.*) The attack on the tents of Emin-ben-Kasso.

According to Emin-ben-Kasso himself (*Procès-verbal* No. 28), Mirzo-ben-Ali and Salih-ben-Ali (*Procès-verbal* No. 29), this attack took place about the 15th August at the pastures called Shen, near Shenik and Semal, and was followed by the lifting of some 300 sheep, the death of four Kurds, and the wounding of three others.

The depositions of Suleiman-ben-Mollah, Ahmet, and Ahmo-ben-Mehemet (*Procès-verbal* No. 72) show, on the contrary, that this attack occurred in July.

Taking into consideration the situation in which the Armenians found themselves on the 15th August on the Antok-Dagh, and, further, the spot where the alleged attack took place, that is to say, close to Shenik, on the side furthest from the Antok-Dagh, it must be regarded as impossible, and, considering that the Kurds deny the fact of any fight with the Armenians, excepting only the two days at Tchai, it is very probable that the loss of life attributed by Emin-ben-Kasso to the incident in question was but a result of the fights which occurred during the first half of August.

If, on the other hand, the attack took place in July, as stated by the above-named witnesses Suleiman and Ahmo, it is inexplicable that an accident involving such serious consequences should not have been mentioned in the other Kurdish evidence, and that Omer-ben-Purto (*Procès-verbal* No. 30), who was so well informed, should not even have heard it spoken of.

(*s.*) The attack on the tents of Amo Meho of Latshekan at the pastures of the Kurtik-Dagh, two hours' distance from the villages of Shenik and Semal.

Most minute details on the subject of this attack were given by Amo Meho himself (*Procès-verbal* No. 28), but though very serious they were only corroborated by the evidence of four Badikanlis (*Procès-verbaux* Nos. 71 and 72).

According to the complainant the occurrence in question took place at Kurtik-Dagh, but in that case it could not have remained unknown to Captain Mustafa Effendi; yet neither he nor the other Kurds who enumerate the Armenian misdeeds make any mention of it, and the Captain as well as these latter are absolutely dumb on the subject of the mutilated corpses of the three Kurds, which, if Ahmo may be believed, were brought to Merghemuzan.

This incident does not merit consideration any more than the preceding one.

(t.) The lifting of the cattle of Farho-Oghlu, a Kurd of Inekan.

From the depositions respecting this (*Procès-verbaux* Nos. 30, 49, 59, 66, 67, and 91) it would appear that this robbery was committed by a band of Armenians from the villages of Kavar and Talori. To this accusation the Armenians simply oppose denials, and the Kurdish accounts contradict themselves on some points.

Considering the exaggerations and inventions noticeable in the accounts of similar attacks, without denying that this one took place, it does not appear possible to decide on its locality, especially if the fact be taken into consideration that the two principal witnesses of the incident, Sofi Mehemet and Suleiman of Ghedorni (*Procès-verbal* No. 70), go on to furnish an altogether improbable account of the following incident, viz:-

(u.) The collection by the Armenians from Mussulmans, for the space of two years, of money and agricultural produce under the name of dues for the Armenian Church.

Considering the respective status of Kurds and Armenians in the country, the former being the masters, this accusation, not bearing on an isolated case of brigandage, but extending over a period of two years, must be regarded as a pure invention, with every appearance of having been created as a counterpoise to the statements of the Armenians relative to the "hafir" which the Kurds collect from them.

(v.) The compulsory conversion to Christianity by Murad of three Kurds of Ghelieguzan and of the family of Hazzo of Spagank.

Notwithstanding the accounts, circumstantial, yet full of contradictions and improbabilities, given on the subject of this charge by Ali, Meho of Ghelieguzan, and Hazzo of Spagank (*Procès-verbaux* Nos. 68, 69, and 70), and confirmed on hearsay by Taleb Effendi, it is simply a calumny.

These facts are incredible if the state of the country be considered, the district in which these conversions are said to have taken place being in close proximity to Mush, and surrounded by Kurdish villages where the supposed victims might easily have taken refuge.

(w.) The murder of Hadji Agha, a Bekranli Kurd, whose mutilated corpse is said to have been brought into the camp at Merghemuzan.

According to Captain Mustafa Effendi (*Procès-verbaux* Nos. 9 and 80), Hadji

Agha was killed during the attack by the Armenians on the Bekranli on their way to their summer pastures, but the other depositions on this subject, including those of the Bekranli themselves, do not confirm either the fact of the mutilation of the corpse or that of the fight in the circumstances related by Captain Mustafa Effendi. Shercho, Agha of the Bekranli (*Procès-verbal* No. 87), alone states that the corpses of three Kurds, killed in the first day's fighting, were mutilated by the Armenians, but he denies that the Bekranli had any relations with the troops at Merghemuzan, whilst, on his side, the Captain who commanded them denies any knowledge of a fight of two days' duration between the Armenians and Kurds. In view of these evident contradictions, and the exaggerations shown above respecting the mutilation of corpses by the Armenians, this charge cannot be regarded as worthy of belief.

(*x.*) The closing to the Mussulmans, by the Armenians, of direct routes from Khian to Mush during two years.

On this subject the depositions of Salih Agha, Ressul, Dervish Agha, Salih-ben-Zoro, Medjid Effendi, and Temo (*Procès-verbaux* Nos. 14, 20, 27, 28, 49, and 51) are simple allegations insufficiently supported by facts.

(*y.*) The attack on the Velikanli Kurds on the 28th July (o. s.), 1894 (*Procès-verbaux* Nos. 4, 7, 9, 12, 13, 14, 17, 20, 30, 36, 41, 51, 59, 73, 74, 75, and 98).

The numerous depositions on this subject, Armenian as well as Kurdish, establish the fact of such an attack by the people of Shenik, accompanied by the death of three Kurds, and only differ as to its motives. The Armenians attribute it to a robbery of cattle committed, in the first instance, by the Kurds, whilst the other depositions attribute the attack to the instigations of Murad, and the state of revolt in which the Armenians then were. But the fact that, out of respect to the Government, they restored the cattle carried off on this occasion, while confining themselves to lodging a complaint against the Velikanli with the Government agents who had come to Shenik, and their attitude towards these same agents, show pretty clearly that this attack did not bear the revolutionary character attributed to it, and was only the result of a dispute between the two parties concerned.

As to the accusation brought against the Armenians of the violation of women on this occasion, it emanates solely from Simonen Oghlu (*Procès-verbal* No. 98), who communicated it to Fevzi Effendi, but it was not confirmed by the latter, who was specially sent to investigate the incident, and cannot be accepted on the solitary assertion of the said Simonen Oghlu.

(*z.*) The injurious expressions used by the Armenian bands against the Mussulman religion.

This fact has been mentioned in many depositions, the witnesses adding that, at the same time, the Armenians shouted the name of Murad as that of their Chief, and Murad himself did not deny that the thing was possible, considering the customs of the country.

Although the evidence respecting this accusation comes from one side only, it may be allowed that insults were uttered by the Armenians in the course of their conflicts with the Kurds.

(B.)—*Acts of Insubordination on the part of the Armenians towards the Government, and other Proceedings regarded by the latter as preparatory to Revolt.*

(a.) Attack on the Kaïmakam of Kulp, at the village of Akchesser, about the 20th June (o. s.), 1894.

The account of this matter given by the Kaïmakam himself, and confirmed by the deposition of his subordinates (*Procès-verbaux* Nos. 66 and 67), seems hardly probable, seeing that an attack made by a body of some hundreds of armed Armenians of Kavar and Talori, united to those of Akchesser itself, on a Government agent of the rank of Kaïmakam, could not but be considered as an act of open revolt; yet, notwithstanding the gravity of the case, no steps appear to have been taken in consequence of this serious incident, and this warrants the conclusion that is proportions were much more modest than those attributed to it by the Kaïmakam.

On the other hand, as it appears from the beginning of a letter found on Murad that there was a real resistance on the part of the villagers to the apprehension of their leaders, the incident in question cannot be regarded otherwise than as an act of insubordination against the Government officials.

As none of the inhabitants of Akchesser were summoned before the Commission, the inquiry only shows one side of the question.

(b.) Attack stated by the Kaïmakam of Sasun to have been planned against him personally at Kiagashin (*Procès-verbal* No. 52).

The inquiry includes no deposition independent of that of the Kaïmakam himself, and as, in spite of the demand of the Delegates, no inhabitant of the village of Kiagashin was produced before the Commission, they cannot regard this fact as established, more especially as the Kaïmakam based his own assertions entirely on information received from one of his subordinates.

(c.) Expulsion from Shenik of Fevzi Effendi, Commandant of Gendarmerie, sent there on the occasion of the quarrel between the inhabitants of the village and the Velikanli Kurds, and spoken of by Anton Effendi, Vicar of the Catholic Bishop of Mush (*Procès-verbal* No. 43).

This charge did not receive confirmation from Fevzi Effendi himself. Nor were the statements of the priest Parsegh that Government agents, such as Ali Effendi, Taleb Effendi, and others, who were sent to give advice to the villagers of Kavar and Talori, were expelled by the latter, confirmed in the depositions taken before the Commission, and Taleb Effendi himself denied having gone to these districts during the summer of 1894.

(d.) Refusal of the inhabitants of Talori during a period of fifteen years to allow Government officials to visit them.

On this subject the depositions of Medjid Effendi and the Kaïmakam of Kulp (*Procès-verbaux* Nos. 49 and 66), the latter going so far as to declare, that owing to this conduct he was unable to send agents to ascertain the state of the ruined villages of Talori, absolutely contradict that of Mahmoud on-bashi (*Procès-verbal* No. 75), who declared that during his service as gendarme he passed through Talori without being in any way molested by the Armenians.

But even admitting that the fact alleged was true, the cause must be sought for in the general state of the country, and the Armenians must not be blamed, having regard to their position in the midst of the Kurds, and their numerical weakness.

(e.) Attack on the troops at Merghemuzan, planned by the Armenians.

As most of the depositions on this subject are based only on hearsay, and as Captain Mustafa Effendi relies solely on information received from a certain Kurd of Sasun through a zaptieh, the reported planning of an attack on the soldiers must be considered as a mere rumour.

The statements of the witnesses Reshid, Ali, and Hazzo, on this subject (*Procès-verbaux* Nos. 23, 69, and 70), considering their improbable and contradictory nature, cannot be regarded as giving any support to the accusation, more especially as their presence among the Armenians on the Antok-Dagh is extremely doubtful.

(f.) Refusal of the inhabitants of Agpi and Hetink to pay their taxes in 1894.

This accusation was made by the Kaïmakam of Sasun alone (*Procès-verbal* No. 52), and no inquiry was made into the matter. Simo of Agpi (*Procès-verbal* No. 81) denied the fact.

(g.) Introduction into Talori of powder and lead (*Procès-verbaux* Nos. 49, 53, 69, and 75).

Two cases appear in the inquiry: one alleged by the secret agents of Medjid Effendi; the other seen by the people of Khian, who are said to have met a band with persons carrying the ammunition in question. Notwithstanding the assertions of the above-mentioned witnesses, the circumstances attending their appearance before the Commission, and the details of their story, do not admit of its being regarded as probable.

(i.) Hiding of property, household utensils, &c., in the spring of 1894, by the people of Kavar, represented in numerous depositions as preparatory to revolt.

The Armenians explained this practice, which is an old one, as the outcome of fear of robbery by Kurds who came into their neighbourhood to their summer pasturages.

No. 60

Sir P. Currie to the Marquess of Salisbury.

No. 365. Confidential.   CONSTANTINOPLE, *August 16, 1895, 3.45 p.m.*
Telegraphic.   *(Received August 16.)*
    RUSTEM PASHA has reported at length to Porte his conversation with your Lordship on the 14th instant, and your statement that the least the Powers could accept would be a Commission consisting of three Europeans and four Turks.
    I mentioned to M. Cambon your conversation with French Ambassador on the 15th instant. He did not think that Russia would support such a Commission as you proposed.
    A telegram has been received by the Russian Ambassador from Prince Lobanoff, who states that in principle he has adhered to your Lordship's idea, that we should limit our action to superintending the measures which the Turks will take and the responsibility for which should be left to them. The Prince awaits the development of your Lordship's idea.
    F. O. 424/183, pp. 187-188, No. 179

No. 61

Sir F. Lascelles to the Marquess of Salisbury.

No. 76.   ST. PETERSBURGH, *August 16, 1895.*
Telegraphic.   *(Received August 16.)*
    I HAVE the honour to acknowledge the receipt of your Lordship's telegram No. 150, and have communicated its substance to Prince Lobanoff, leaving, at his request, a paraphrase of its contents with him. His Excellency informs me that when he had received the reply of the Sultan he telegraphed to the Russian Embassy in London stating that it was merely an analysis of the Scheme of Reforms elaborated by the Ambassadors at Constantinople. He had never looked on that Scheme in the light of an ultimatum to the Sultan, whom we could not therefore force to adopt it. In his opinion direct responsibility for the administration of Asia Minor should be avoided by us. His Excellency also inquired, with regard to the Commission suggested by your Lordship, whether it was to be temporary or permanent, the impression I gathered being that although Prince Lobanoff thought that the present difficulty might be solved by means of some sort of Committee of Surveillance, he would be averse to an institution of a permanent nature. He expressed it as his opinion that the Sultan would now give way, and that the introduction of reforms would really be proceeded with.
    F. O. 424/183, p. 188, No. 180

No. 62

The Marquess of Salisbury to Sir F. Lascelles.

No. 269A.

Sir,   FOREIGN OFFICE, *August 16, 1895.*

THE Russian Chargé d'Affairs communicated to me this afternoon a message from Prince Lobanoff, stating that the reply of the Turkish Government relative to the proposed reforms in the Armenian Provinces, which had just reached him, was merely an analysis, Article by Article, of the Scheme prepared by the three Ambassadors, and did not indicate the measures which Shakir Pasha was authorized to produce. Nevertheless, the Russian Government having never regarded the project of the Ambassadors in the light of an ultimatum, did not consider it desirable that the Powers should endeavour to impose it upon the Porte, with whom they preferred to leave the whole responsibility of the measures to be adopted. From this point of view, the idea which I had suggested that the Powers should limit their action to the organization of "une surveillance", appeared to the Russian Government in entire accordance with the requirements of the LXIst Article of the Treaty of Berlin.

I told M. Kroupensky that the three Ambassadors at Constantinople were also urging the nomination of a due proportion of Christian functionaries, and that the Valis should be appointed for a term of five years, and I said that I thought they should be supported on these points. I said, however, that if the negotiations were broken off it would probably be on the question of adequate surveillance, and on this point I repeated my suggestion that the Commission of Surveillance should be a body sitting at some town in the Armenian provinces, and that it should consist of four Turkish and three European members.

I added that if the Turkish Government refused to comply with this demand they must understand that Her Majesty's Government would not be satisfied to accept the refusal.

I am, &c.

(Signed) SALISBURY.

F. O. 424/183, p. 188, No. 181
Turkey No. 1 (1896) p. 120, No. 138

No. 63

Sir P. Currie to the Marquess of Salisbury.

No. 529.   CONSTANTINOPLE, *August 16, 1895.*
My Lord,   *(Received August 25.)*
    I HAVE the honour to forward to your Lordship herewith copy of a despatch which I have received from Her Majesty's Consul at Erzeroum respecting difficulties attending the farming of tithes in the Vilayet of Bitlis.
                            I have, &c.
                                        (Signed) PHILIP CURRIE.

F. O. 424/183, p. 235, No. 204

Inclosure 1 in No. 63

Consul Graves to Sir P. Currie.

Sir,   ERZEROUM, *August 1, 1895.*
    I HAVE the honour to transmit herewith to your Excellency copy of an extract from a letter, dated Bitlis, the 24th July, on the subject of the present difficulties attending the farming of the tithes in that province, which may be expected to extend to other provinces included in the scope of the projected reforms as harvest approaches. Tithe farmers hesitate to speculate in the purchase of tithes which they may no longer be permitted to render more profitable in the old illicit ways, and the villagers fear to buy in their own tithes, in default of proper protection from the predatory Kurds.
    Thus the prolonged suspense on the subject of the reforms seems likely to involve the Government in serious financial embarassment, for, apart from the tithe question, I am informed that in some districts the population seem disposed to withhold, or at least delay, the payment of "verghi" and other taxes, in the hope of profiting by the reformed fiscal arrangements.
                            I have, &c.
                                        (Signed) R. W. GRAVES.

F. O. 424/183, p. 235, No. 204/1

Inclosure 2 in No. 63

Extract from a Letter, dated Bitlis, July 24, 1895.

THE matter of farming out the villages is coming up. The hungry villagers are threshing out their wheat and trying to eke out a living. The Government forbids them to measure the wheat, and tries to force them to buy up their own villages. The "Multazims" do not come forward as readily as other years to buy the villages, for fear, perhaps, that they will not be able to use force in getting more than their right. If the villagers should take them on themselves, then the Kurds, who stand in some awe of the "Multazims," would feel free to help themselves. Thus the villagers are ground between the two stones—the Kurds, if they buy their own villages, and the extortions of the "Multazims" if they do not buy themselves. Meanwhile they cannot eat of their crops under fear of heavy penalties.

F. O. 424/183, p. 235, No. 204/2
Turkey No. 6 (1896), p. 379, No. 491, 491/1, 491/2

No. 64

Sir P. Currie to the Marquess of Salisbury.

No. 368.   CONSTANTINOPLE, *August 18, 1895, 3.40 p.m.*
Telegraphic.   *(Received August 18.)*

MR. HAMPSON informed me to-day by telegraph that, despite his remonstrances with the Mutessarif, unexampled severity was being shown in tax-collecting in the plain of Moush. Great cruelty is being shown to the Christians, on the special ground that they complained to the Commission. The Mudirs of Avrana and Avsakdur and Hadji Feim, Reshid and Iskender, captains of police, are the worst offenders.

F. O. 424/183, p. 189, No. 183
Turkey No. 1 (1895) Part I, p. 132, 133, No. 251

No. 65

Sir P. Currie to the Marquess of Salisbury.

No. 369.   CONSTANTINOPLE, *August 19, 1895, 10.45 p.m.*
Telegraphic.   *(Received August 19.)*

WITH reference to my telegram of the 12th instant, our summary has come back from the Porte, but the reforms which they had accepted in their note have been still further curtailed.

The document will be sent home on Thursday.

F. O. 424/183, p. 231, No. 193
Turkey No. 1 (1896), p. 122, No. 141

No. 66

The Marquess of Salisbury to Sir P. Currie.

No. 135.
Telegraphic.   FOREIGN OFFICE, *August 19, 1895.*

I HAVE received your telegram of yesterday, reporting that the taxes are being collected with unparalleled severity from the Christians in the Plain of Moush.

I presume that, in concert with the French and Russian Ambassadors, you will demand that the officials found guilty of this inhuman conduct should be dismissed or suspended.

Your Excellency may inform the Turkish Government that it will not be possible to withhold this information from Parliament, and that the worst impression will be created in the public mind in this country and in Europe, unless it can be announced that the Porte has adopted proper measures with a a view to prevent such abuses.

F. O. 424/183, pp. 231-232, No. 194
Turkey No. 1 (1895) Part I, p. 190, No. 253

No. 67

The Marquess of Salisbury to Sir P. Currie.

No. 136.
Telegraphic.   FOREIGN OFFICE, *August 19, 1895.*

I HAVE received, through the Russian Chargé d'Affaires, the reply of the Russian Government to the statements concerning Armenian reforms which I made in my conversation with M. Kroupensky on the 16th instant.

As regards the term of office of the Valis, and the organization of the Gendarmerie, Prince Lobanoff is of opinion that the Sultan is likely to show himself particularly recalcitrant on these points, and that it would not be possible for the Powers, without exceeding the rights conferred by the Treaty of Berlin, to peremptorily insist upon the acceptance of the demands made in regard to them.

His Excellency sees no objection to the proposal that the "Mixed Commission of Surveillance" should sit at Bitlis, Van, or Erzeroum, and that each member should be entitled to make investigations of his own for communication to the Commission.

F. O. 424/183, p. 232, No. 195
Turkey No. 1 (1896), p. 122, No. 142

No. 68

Sir P. Currie to the Marquess of Salisbury.

No. 535.   CONSTANTINOPLE, *August 20, 1895.*
My Lord,   *(Received August 25.)*
    I HAVE the honour to forward to your Lordship herewith copy of a despatch
which I have received from Her Majesty's Consul at Erzeroum, transmitting an
extract from a private letter from one of the American missionaries in Bitlis giving
an account of the state of affairs in that town.

                               I have, &c.
                                         (Signed) PHILIP CURRIE.

    F. O. 424/183, p. 238, No. 207

Inclosure 1 in No. 68

Consul Graves to Sir P. Currie.

Sir,
                                           ERZEROUM, *August 9, 1895.*
    I HAVE the honour to transmit herewith to your excellency an extract from a
private letter, dated Biltlis, 31st July, from one of the American missionaries in that
town, giving an account of the present condition of affairs there, and especially of
the annoyance and danger to which the missionaries are still exposed owing to the
neglect or weakness of the authorities.
    The report as to the expected arrival of the Russian Vice-Consul for Van at
Bitlis was evidently due to a mistake.
    The gentleman meant is a Russian traveller named Vassilien, who arrived
yesterday at Erzeroum, having visited Bitlis on his way from Van. He is, I am told,
engaged on a mission of purely scientific research.
                               I have, &c.
                                         (Signed) R. W. GRAVES.

    F. O. 424/183, p. 238, No. 207/1

Inclosure 2 in No. 68

Extract from a Private Letter dated Bitlis, July 31, 1895.

    ON Thursday, the 21st instant, twenty political prisoners were released here.
On Sunday three others, who were in for long terms, were also released. I have
word from Sairt that the two remaining brothers and the women (charged with the

murder of Shakir Tchaoush) were released on Thursday. Since theirs was not a political offence their release is probably due to efforts made there.

The six boys that have now been in prison nearly two months for having mistaken a Kurdish girl for an Armenian, and tried to get the authorities to rescue her, are not released nor even brought to trial. The treatment of these Armenians stands out all the more strongly from some experience of my own.

Four weeks ago, one Khalid Effendi in a coffee-house threatened that in three days they would cut off the Christian population, beginning with us foreigners. As there were good witnesses forthcoming, we thought it wise to mention the fact to the Vali Vekil when calling on him several days later. He took the name and address down, but nothing was done.

A few days later Mr. Cole called on business and again referred to this man, who was continuing his vile threats about town. The Vekil said he was not worth paying any attention to, but he would have him called and give him a good reprimand. Even this was not done.

Last Thursday I was out riding, with a man riding not far behind me, when a stone about as large as a man's fist came flying from the edge of a field above me and came near hitting me. I at once turned round and saw that the thrower was one of three young men, Turks, on a roof some distance away. Besides my man, there were other persons present who saw it and could act as witnesses. I at once went to the Government head-quarters. The Alai Bey was not there, but a subordinate officer sent two zaptiehs along with me to secure the culprits. After a good deal of parleying it seems they came away without doing anything.

On Monday I called on the Alai Bey and told him what had happened, and that I found that nothing had been done. He seemed to have heard nothing about it. He at once called in the subordinate officer and reprimanded him for not having told him. The latter said he had forgotten to do so; that the tax-collector of that ward had gone security for the young man. He at once ordered them to be brought there. I also referred to the case of Khalid Effendi, and he ordered him to be brought. I then came away, but subsequently the Bey sent for me. It was to say that he had put Khalid Effendi into prison; that he knew he was a vile man, &c. As to the matter of the young men who had thrown the stone, they admitted that they had thrown one large stone, but it was not at me. They, as watermen, were having a quarrel among themselves; it was at one of their number that they were throwing, and the stone happened to come near me. I did not see how he could keep a serious face while making this explanation. I told him I did not believe it, that I was sure no other person was near me for them to throw at. At the same time I was not so anxious to have these persons punished as I was to have a guarantee that I would not be molested while riding about the city. He begged that I would let the matter drop, as this was a doubtful case, and he could assure me that nothing of the kind would happen again. Feeling somewhat satisfied that Khalid Effendi had been imprisoned, I decided to let the matter drop, and bade the Bey farewell.

The next day I found that Khalid Effendi had not even been kept overnight—probably he was kept in a room for an hour or two, while there was any danger of my being there. If he had been an Armenian, you could have depended on imprisonment and harassing worse than has been inflicted on the six Armenian boys. I wish Europe could comprehend that it is simply impossible for a Moslem to grant justice as between a Christian and a Moslem, and to expect them to be an active partner in carrying out reforms is the sheerest nonsense. It is a dangerous experiment this, trying to get such a majority to live on equal terms with Christians without providing adequate protection from outside. We shall see. On Monday the Armenian Notables who were let out on bail some months ago were called to the Vekil and Military Pasha, and informed that an Imperial pardon had been granted them, whereupon one of their number said that they would not admit that they had any fault for which to receive forgiveness. They would accept no pardon. At this the officials were rather crestfallen, and finally said, "Give at least an oath of fealty to the Government." "This," they said, "we will do as we always have done." Another of their number said, "We have endured all those months of imprisonment and have suffered great losses, but we see many of those who were the cause of this still continuing in office as before;" as though any attention would ever be paid to their complaints while the Courts are under Turkish rule.

I was at Tadvan last Sunday. Seven zaptiehs were there collecting taxes in the old way, feeding their horses to the full with clover, killing a kid, and demanding the best of food for all for nothing, beating the poor men that could not pay or would not serve them as they wished.

The Russian Consul is expected here from Van to-day. The Government has asked one of the leading Armenians to take him as a guest, but he has refused, saying that for seeing the English Consul last autumn we have suffered untold miseries, we cannot take the risk of entertaining this one. It is probable that the Armenians will not call on him when he comes, but merely send word that they do not dare to carry out their great wish of seeing him. The matter of inviting the Armenians to entertain him I am not sure of, but their giving such a reason for not calling on him is probable.

F. O. 424/183, pp. 238–239, No. 207/2

No. 69

Sir P. Currie to the Marquess of Salisbury.

No. 534.   CONSTANTINOPLE, *August 20, 1895.*
My Lord,   *(Received August 27.)*
       WITH reference to my telegram No. 330 of the 26th July I have the honour to forward to your Lordship herewith copies of despatches which I have received from

ier Majesty's Consul at Erzeroum, respecting the amnesty of political prisoners in Erzeroum, Van, and Bitlis.

I have, &c.

(Signed) PHILIP CURRIE.

F. O. 424/183, p. 255, No. 219

Inclosure 1 in No. 69

Consul Graves to Sir P. Currie.

Sir,   ERZEROUM, *July 25, 1895.*

I HAVE the honour to report that orders were received here by telegraph on the 24th instant for the release of all political prisoners, with the exception of any who might be connected with the events of last year in the districts of Sassoun and Talori. On the receipt of these orders twenty political prisoners were set at liberty, while sixteen others, who are charged with offences which may fairly be classed as political, are still detained in prison. Among these are the remaining ten Narman prisoners, most of whom have now been nearly four years in gaol without any trial save the mock court-martial of March 1893, and also the naturalized American citizen Harout Simonian, mentioned in my despatch of the 8th instant—together with the other persons captured with him in the affair near Kara Kilisseh, reported in my despatch of the 13th ultimo.

I have, &c.

(Signed) R. W. GRAVES.

F. O. 424/183, p. 255, No. 219/1

Inclosure 2 in No. 69

Consul Graves to Sir P. Currie.

Sir,   ERZEROUM, *August 8, 1895.*

WITH reference to my despatch of the 25th ultimo I have the honour to report the following further particulars respecting the amnesty to Armenian so-called political prisoners:-

At Erzeroum, in addition to the twenty prisoners released in the first instance, the Russian Armenian, named Arshag, mentioned in my despatch of the 11th ultimo, who is a deserter from the Russian Army, was to have been handed over to the Russian Consul-General, but succeeded in escaping from his guards at the Government house, and has not been recaptured.

Ten Narman prisoners and the five remaining members of the band captured about two months ago near the Russian frontier, including the naturalized American citizen, Harout Simonian, still remain in prison.

From Baiburt I learn that the four political prisoners detained there have been released.

I have no certain information from Erzingian, but am told that Hadji Calous Halkan, Oghlou, and the other Armoudan prisoners, are still detained as common-law offenders.

The Karakilisseh prisoners who wished to embrace the Orthodox faith mentioned in my despatch to your Excellency of the 10th May, were removed to Bayazid, where they are said to be still detained.

From Van I have not received full details, though Mr. Hallward informs me in a private letter that, amongst others, the prisoner Karrekin refered to in my despatches Nos. 11 and 17, Confidential, of this year, and one Maksabedian accused of sharing in a plot against the life of Bahri Pasha, were released on the 30th ultimo, while a number of prisoners who should have profited by the amnesty are still in gaol.

At Bitlis twenty prisoners were released on the 25th, and three more on the 28th ultimo, while the six young Armenians arrested for endeavouring to obtain the release of a supposed Christian girl from the hands of the Kurds, as reported in the inclosure to my despatch of the 24th June, are still detained without trial.

From Moush Mr. Hampson informs me, in a despatch of the 26th ultimo, copies of which I have the honour to transmit herewith to your Excellency, that thirteen prisoners, whose names he furnishes, have been set at liberty, while fourteen others, including "Mourad," and eleven Talori men, Erko, one of the strongest Armenian witnesses before the Commission of Inquiry, and one other, are still in prison, and are being treated with greater severity than heretofore.

With regard to Erko's case, it is to be hoped that his speedy release may be procured from the Porte, as I learn from Mr. Shipley that there can be little doubt that the charge of murder brought against him was trumped up in order to punish him for having fearlessly presented himself before Abdullah Pasha, on the first arrival of the Turkish Commissioners at Moush, at a time when the other survivors of the Sassoun affair were successfully terrorized into silence by the local authorities. So that, if the interested Powers are able to afford any protection to Sassoun witnesses from the consequences of their evidence, this man, if anyone, should be made to profit by it. Mr. Hampson notes the significant fact that of twenty-two Talori prisoners—the only prisoners made during the Sassoun events of 1894—eleven have died during an imprisonment of less than a year, and that three out of eight alleged accomplices of Damadian had also died in prison.

Lastly, from Kharpout, I am informed in a private letter from Mr. Boyajian, that all the prisoners there (the number given in his despatch to your Excellency of the 5th April, was twenty-four) have been released, excepting six, three of whom are to be re-tried on a charge of murder, and the three others should, he thinks, have been released under the terms of the amnesty. Mr. Boyajian does not give any particulars as to prisoners in other parts of the Kharpout Vilayet, or in the Vilayet of Diarbekir.

I have, &c.

(Signed) R. W. GRAVES.

F. O. 424/183, pp. 255–256, No. 219/2

Inclosure 3 in No. 69

Vice-Consul Hampson to Consul Graves.

Sir,   MOUSH, *July 26, 1895.*

AS I had the honour to inform you by telegram to-day, thirteen Armenians in prison here on political charges have been set at liberty.

Their names are as follows:-

Deacon Moyses, of Ziaret; Deacon Harutune, of Erzeroum; Zachar, of Moush; Zachar, of Talori; Bedros, of Ardgonk; Hagop, of Enguznak; Ghandil, of Guvars; in prison since August 1894, on charge of concealing Damadian in Sovrp Garabet Monastery.

Boghos, of Bitlis; Mardiros, of Ketakom; Azo, of Geliésan; Mirkho, of Koulp; Boghos; in prison since March 1891, for being friends of Damadian.

The first condemned for 101 years, others 5 years. Micaïl, Mardiros, and Nooro, arrested at same time, died in prison.

Krikor, of Moush, in prison since December 1894.

I understand that the above were released in consequence of telegraphic orders from Constantinople that all Armenian prisoners not accused of murder or other grave crimes should be set free.

There now remain in prison here fourteen Armenians: "Mourad" (Dr. Hamparsoumian); eleven of Damadian's companions who were arrested in Talori last year (the other eleven have died in prison); Erko, who was one of the strongest witnesses on the Armenian side before the Commission of Inquiry, but was arrested, before giving evidence, on a trumped up charge of murder; and an Armenian who was arrested sometime ago on a pretence that he had robbed Kurds.

I learn that "Mourad" and his companions are now being treated with considerably greater severity than heretofore.

I have, &c.

(Signed) CHARLES S. HAMPSON.

P.S.—I hear that certain Armenian political prisoners have also been released at Bitlis, but, so far, have been unable to obtain details.

C. S. H.

F. O. 424/183, pp. 256–257, No. 219/3

No. 70

Sir P. Currie to the Marquess of Salisbury.

No. 371.   CONSTANTINOPLE, *August 20, 1895, 12.30 p.m.*
Telegraphic.   *(Received August 20.)*
    YESTERDAY I met my Russian and French colleagues, to discuss the
communication which we had received from the Porte, and which was referred to in
my telegram to your Lordship of the 12th instant. They agreed with me that not
only does the summary of accepted reforms as revised by the Porte show no
progress, but some concessions which were made in previous notes are actually
withdrawn.
    We have no intention under the present circumstances of discussing the
reforms any further, but shall reply, if pressed, that we await the instructions of our
Governments, in whose hands the matter now rests.
    F. O. 424/183, p. 232, No. 197
    Turkey No. 1 (1896), pp. 122–123, No. 143

No. 71

Sir P. Currie to the Marquess of Salisbury.

No. 532.   CONSTANTINOPLE, *August 20, 1895.*
My Lord,   *(Received August 25.)*
    I HAVE the honour to forward to your Lordship herewith copy of a despatch
which I have received from Her Majesty's Consul at Erzeroum, inclosing a
despatch from Her Majesty's Vice-Consul at Van, reporting the dismissal of Bahri
Pasha, Vali of Van, and pointing out the necessity of removing his creatures.
                                        I have, &c.
                                                        (Signed) PHILIP CURRIE.

    F. O. 424/, p. 235, No. 205
    Turkey No. 6 (1896) p. 329, No. 492

Inclosure 1 in No. 71

Consul Graves to Sir P. Currie.

Sir,   ERZEROUM, *August 6, 1895.*
    I HAVE the honour to transmit herewith to your Excellency copy of a
despatch which I have received from Her Majesty's Vice-Consul at Van, reporting

the dismissal of Bahri Pasha, the Vali of Van, with observations upon that Governor's administration of the province since his arrival in March 1892. Mr. Hallward also points out the urgent necessity for getting rid of Bahri Pasha's creatures, especially Nouri Effendi, the Chief of Police, and the judicial functionaries whose corruption, inefficiency, and fanaticism have disgraced the administration of justice in Van of recent years.

I have, &c.

(Signed) R. W. GRAVES.

F. O. 424/183, p. 236, No. 205/1
Turkey No. 6 (1896) p. 380, No. 492/1

No. 72

Sir P. Currie to the Marquess of Salisbury.

No. 533.   CONSTANTINOPLE, *August 20, 1895.*
My Lord,   *(Received August 25.)*

WITH reference to my despatches of the 20th March and of the 14th April, I have the honour to forward to your Lordship herewith copy of a despatch which I have received from Her Majesty's Consul at Erzeroum respecting the bad condition of Christians in Kharput and Palu.

I have, &c.

(Signed) PHILIP CURRIE.

F. O. 424/183, p. 237, No. 206

Inclosure 1 in No. 72

Consul Graves to Sir P. Currie.

Sir,   ERZEROUM, *August 6, 1895.*

I HAVE the honour to transmit herewith to your Excellency extracts from letters which I have received from Mr. Boyajian, Acting British Vice-Consul for Diarbekir, but not resident at Kharput, dated the 15th and 22nd July respectively, which give a bad account of the present condition of the Christian population in the country districts of Kharput and in the neighbouring Caza of Palu, which belongs to the Vilayet of Diarbekir.

The acts of oppression committed by the local Beys and by the Kaïmakam of Palu upon the inhabitants of Habab, mentioned in the second extract from Mr.

Boyajian's letters, formed the subject of my despatch to your Excellency of the 3rd
March, and my despatch of the 26th March, 1895.

I have, &c.

(Signed) R. W. GRAVES.

F. O. 424/183, p. 237, No. 206/1

Inclosure 2 in No. 72

Acting Vice-Consul Boyajian to Consul Graves.

Extract.   KHARPUT, *July 15, 1895.*

THE Vali is taking good care to preserve order in the town, but the state of
things in the cazas and villages is as bad as ever. The condition of the Christians is
really intolerable. An Armenian was recently murdered in Peri, the chief place of
Charsandjak Caza. A Moslem was suspected of the crime. Another Armenian at
Perchange was so severely beaten by a Moslem that he died from the effects. The
dead bodies of both the victims were brought here, and the Governor-General was
petitioned. His Excellency ordered a *post-mortem* examination in both cases, which
was held after a fashion, and a verdict given of "Death from natural causes." Thus
the affair was closed, and pronounced by the authorities, as is the fashion now, to be
another trick of the Armenians.

It is stated on good authority that the zaptiehs are committing all kinds of
exactions and outrages upon the Armenians in the villages, and horrible things are
reported to me from the Palu Caza as perpetrated by the zaptiehs and the
Kaïmakam of the caza.

F. O. 424/183, pp. 237–238, No. 206/2
Turkey No. 6 (1896) p. 381, No. 493, 493/1, 493/2

Inclosure 3 in No. 72

Acting Vice-Consul Boyajian to Consul Graves.

Extract.   KHARPUT, *July 22, 1895.*

I AM informed that the Armenians of Habab, a village in the Palu Gaza, lately
sent a telegram to His Majesty the Sultan, complaining of two Beys of Palu, who are
in the habit of sending Kurds to their village to perpetrate outrages of every sort,
and pray either to be delivered from their hands, or to be granted permission to
remove to another place. A copy of this Petition is sent also to the Grand Vizier.

F. O. 424/183, p. 238, No. 206/3
Turkey No. 6 (1896) p. 382, No. 493/3

No. 73

The Marquess of Salisbury to Sir P. Currie.

No. 304.

Sir,   FOREIGN OFFICE, *August 21, 1895.*

THE Turkish Ambassador called on me to-day, and urged very strongly the impossibility of the Sultan giving way to the demand for a Mixed Commission of Surveillance in connection with the introduction of Armenian reforms. Indeed, his Excellency threatened me, not obscurely, with a probable change of policy on the part of Turkey, which would lead her to place herself entirely in the hands of Russia.

His Excellency discussed the question in this sense for more than an hour, but he did not use any argument with which your Excellency is unacquainted. The point upon which he principally relied was the injury which any such concession would do to the prestige of the Sultan in the eyes of his Moslem subjects.

I could only answer in return that the demand for this Commission was the very smallest guarantee which the Governments concerned must exact in fulfilment of the rights conferred upon them under the 61st Article of the Treaty of Berlin. If the Commission involved an encroachment on the prerogative of the Sultan, that encroachment took place seventeen years ago, when he ratified the Treaty.

I expressed my great regret at the obstinacy shown by His Majesty upon this point. I said a guarantee was absolutely necessary to us, and it was the least with which we could be content. I deplored his attitude, as I thought it might bring great dangers upon Turkey, but I did not hold out any hope that we should withdraw or abate the demand we had made in this respect.

I am, &c.

(Signed) SALISBURY.

F. O. 424/183, p. 233, No. 198

No. 74

Sir P. Currie to the Marquess of Salisbury.

No. 538.   CONSTANTINOPLE, *August 21, 1895.*

My Lord,   *(Received August 25.)*

I HAVE the honour to forward to your Lordship herewith a copy of a despatch which I have received from Her Majesty's Consul at Erzeroum, transmitting despatches from Her Majesty's Vice-Consul at Moush reporting the incursions of Kurds on Armenian pastures, and their subsequent removal.

I have, &c.

(Signed) PHILIP CURRIE.

F. O. 424/183, p. 240, No. 208

Inclosure 1 in No. 74

Consul Graves to Sir P. Currie.

Sir,   ERZEROUM, *July 31, 1895.*

I HAVE the honour to transmit herewith to your Excellency copies of despatches which I have received from Her Majesty's Vice-Consul at Moush, reporting on the arrival of nomad Kurds in the Sassoon and Talori districts and the forcible removal of the Armenians of Hadavorig from their pastures by the Moush authorities, on the pretext of avoiding disturbances between them and the Bekranli tribe of Kurds.

I have, &c.

(Signed) R. W. GRAVES.

F. O. 424/183, p. 240, No. 138/1
Turkey No. 1 (1895) Part I, p. 190, No. 255, 255/1

Inclosure 2 in No. 74

Vice-Consul Hampson to Consul Graves.

Sir,   MOUSH, *July 24, 1895.*

WITH reference to Mr. Shipley's telegram to you of the 20th instant, and my telegram to Her Majesty's Embassy, repeated to you, of yesterday, respecting the presence of nomad Kurds in the Sassoon and Talori districts in spite of a promise given by the Porte to the Russian Ambassador to prevent their entry this year, as communicated to the Russian Consul-General at Erzeroum, I have the honour to report that, as far as I can ascertain at present, the facts are as follows:-

No attempt having been made on the part of the Government to prevent them, nomad Kurds of the Bekranli, Badikanli, Reshkotanli, and Latchkanli tribes, to at least the usual number, and, it is said, in larger numbers than usual, have pitched their tents on their habitual pasture-grounds in Sassoon and Talori. I hear also that women and children are conspicuously absent among them this year, but whether this is true or not I am unable to say.

There are no troops in the two districts named; and the only step taken by the authorities to maintain order is to send an influential Kurd of this town, Hajji Deib by name, nominally to keep the Kurds quiet. This man enjoys anything but a good reputation here. It is said that the Sheikh of Zeilan is also with the Bekranli Kurds in the mountains. However, so far, there appears to have been no trouble.

As an instance of the means adopted to prevent collisions between the Kurds and the Armenian villagers, I may quote the following:-

For some years past certain of the Bekranli Kurd have adopted as their pasturage ground close to the pasturages belonging, by right to "Tapu," to the inhabitants of Hadavorik, a Protestant Armenian village some two hours distant from Moush. The Kurds having arrived last week, about a company of soldiers were sent to forcibly remove the Armenians from their pasturages, where they already were. These people have now nowhere to feed their flocks, which are considerable.

If, in order to prevent collisions, the Armenians are to be forced to vacate their pasturages and leave them to the Kurds, the method will, no doubt, be effective, as the former will be forced to quit these districts.

I have, &c.

(Signed) CHARLES S. HAMPSON.

F. O. 424/183, p. 240, No. 208/2

Inclosure 3 in No. 74

Vice-Consul Hampson to Consul Graves.

Sir,   MOUSH, *July 30, 1895.*

WITH reference to my despatch of the 24th instant, I have the honour to state that the Kurds were quietly told to vacate the pastures of the inhabitants of Hadavorik, the latter having threatened to telegraph to the Grand Vizier on the subject.

I reported the above by telegraph to Her Majesty's Embassy, repeated to yourself, to-day.

I have, &c.

(Signed) CHARLES S. HAMPSON.

F. O. 424/183, p. 241, No. 208/3
Turkey No. 1 (1895) Part I, p. 195, No. 255/2, 255/3

No. 75

Sir P. Currie to the Marquess of Salisbury.

No. 540.   THERAPIA, *August 21, 1895*
My Lord,   *(Received August 25.)*

WITH reference to my telegram of the 19th instant, I have the honour to transmit herewith to your Lordship copy of the paper summarizing the reforms accepted in the Porte's previous answers, which was presented to the Minister for Foreign Affairs by the Dragomans of the three Embassies on the 13th instant, and also a copy of the reply which I have received, entitled "Résumé du Contre-Projet du Gouvernement Impérial."

The differences between this reply and the summary of concessions may be classed under three heads:-

1. The withdrawal of reforms already conceded in the previous answers, as in the case of the absolute rejection of the eligibility of Christians for the posts of Valis and Mutessarifs granted in paragraph 4 of the Porte's answer of the 2nd June, which expressly states that non-Mussulmans will be admitted to administrative posts in each vilayet in proportion to the members of the Mussulman and non-Mussulman population.

2. The abrogation of numerous enactments and Regulations which have existed for many years, although they may have been allowed to remain a dead letter, as in the above-quoted case of the rejection of the eligibility of Christians to the higher administrative posts, and also in the case of the appointment of Mudirs, who, according to the Regulations, were to be chosen from the population, but are now to be named by the Imperial Government without any such restriction.

3. The abrogation of Regulations actually existing and hitherto enforced, as in the case of the reassertion without comment of any kind of the publication exclusively in Turkish of judicial sentences, whereas the law specially states that they shall be accompanied by a translation in the local language, and also in the case of certain points in connection with the organization of nahiés.

The present communication, like the answer of the 1st August, is altogether more reactionary than the earlier replies, and in some cases no longer makes concessions even in form.

So far from insuring to the Christians a larger share in the administration, the so-called reforms now promised by the Porte formally reserve to the Moslems a still more exclusive control of the Executive than that prescribed by the present Regulations.

I have, &c.

(Signed) PHILIP CURRIE.

F. O. 424/183, p. 241, No. 209
Turkey No. 1 (1896), p. 123-124, No. 146

Inclosure 1 in No. 75

Summary of Concessions embodied in the Turkish Draft of Reforms.

CHAPITRE I.—VALIS.

ARTICLE 1. Les Valis seront nommés par le Gouvernement. Tous les sujets Ottomans, sans distinction, ont accès au poste de Vali.

Art. 2. La durée des pouvoirs des Valis n'est pas limitée.

Art. 3. Des adjoints non-Musulmans seront nommés auprès des Valis, conformément aux Lois et Règlements.

Ils ont pour attribution, aux termes du Chapitre II du Règlement sur l'administration des vilayets (Aristarchi, vol. 3, p. 13), de coopérer aux affaires générales du vilayet, et d'en préparer l'expédition.

CHAPITRE II.—MUTESSARIFS.

Art. 4. Les Mutessarifs seront Musulmans ou non-Musulmans.

Ils pourront être assistés de Moavins, qui seront Chrétiens si les Mutessarifs sont Musulmans.

CHAPITRE III.—CAÏMACAMS.

Art 5. Les Caïmacams seront choisis par le Ministère de l'Intérieur parmi les diplômés de l'École Civile, sans distinction de religion.

Les Caïmacams actuellement en fonctions et reconnus capables pourront, quoique non diplômés de cette école, continuer leur carrière dans l'Administration.

Art. 6. Des sujets Ottomans non-Musulmans seront admis aux postes administratifs proportionnellement au chiffre total des populations Musulmanes et non-Musulmanes de chaque vilayet.

Dans les cazas "ayant une position importante," des Moavins ayant une religion différente de celle du Caïmacam seront nommés.

Sont maintenus les Conscils Administratifs du sandjak et du caza, composés de membres de droit et de membres élus.

CHAPITRE IV.—NAHIÉS.

Art. 7. L'organisation des nahiés sera mise en vigueur selon les prescriptions des Articles 94 à 106 du Règlement sur l'administration générale des vilayets du 9 Janvier, 1286, et des Articles 1 à 28 du Règlement sur l'administration communale de 25 Mars, 1292.

Art. 8. Chaque nahié sera administré par un Moudir et un Conseil composé de quatre membres élus parmi les habitants. L'un d'eux sera adjoint. Il y aura, en outre, un Secrétaire.

Art. 9. L'élection des membres du Conseil de nahié se fera proportionnellement aux classes de la population.

Art. 10. Les Moudirs et les Secrétaires des nahiés seront rétribués.

Art. 11. Les candidats au Conseil du nahié devront remplir les conditions prescrites par la loi.

Art. 12. Les Moudirs seront nommés par le Gouvernement, et choisis parmi les habitants du nahié, selon les stipulations de l'Article 10 du Règlement sur l'administration des communes (Aristarchi, vol. 5, p. 61).

Art. 13. Les fonctionnaires, les professeurs, et les prêtes ne peuvent être Moudirs.

Art. 14. Les membres du Conseil sont renouvelés par moitié chaque année et rééligibles. Le Moudir restera en fonction deux ans, et ses pouvoirs pourront être renouvelés.

Art. 15. Les attributions de Moudir et des Conseils sont réglées par les Articles 20 à 27 du Règlement sur l'administration des communes.

Art. 16. Chaque village aura un Moukhtar; s'il y a plusieurs quartiers plusieurs classes d'habitants, il y aura un Moukhtar par quartier et par classe.

Art. 17. Aucun village ne pourra relever de deux nahiés à la fois.

Chapitre V.—Police.

Art. 18. La police et la gendarmerie seront recrutées parmi les sujets Ottomans dans la proportion du chiffre général des habitants Musulmans et non-Musulmans du vilayet. Des contingents suffisants seront affectés à chaque subdivision administrative, y compris le nahié.

Art. 19. Les agents de police affectés au service du nahié agiront sous les ordres du Moudir. Leur solde sera payée par les caisses des districts.

Les agents non-Musulmans continueront à payer la taxe d'exonération du service militaire.

Art. 20. C'est la gendarmerie qui est chargée de maintien de l'ordre et de l'escorte de pa poste.

Chapitre VI.—Gendarmerie.

Art. 21. Les gendarmes seront recrutés parmi les habitants Musulmans et non-Musulmans de l'Empire proportionnellement au chiffre total des populations des différentes religions dans chaque vilayet.

Malgré la promesse contenue dans le paragraphe 4 final de la réponse de la

Porte du 2 Juin, 1895, la Porte écarte les Chrétiens des grades d'officiers et de sous-officiers dans la gendarmerie.

CHAPITRE VII.—PRISONS.

Art. 22. Il sera apporté plus de soins à l'application des Règlements concernant la tenue des prisons et le traitement des détenus et des prisonniers.

CHAPITRE VIII.—COMITÉ D'ENQUÊTE PRÉLIMINAIRE.

Art. 23. Le Comité d'Enquête préliminaire fonctionnera suivant les prescriptions de l'Article 11 des Instructions sur l'administration des vilayets. (Aristarchi, vol. 5, p. 53.)

CHAPITRE IX.—CONTRÔLE DES KURDES.

Art. 24. Les localités de migration des Kurdes seront fixées d'avance, et un officier avec une force armée suffisante et de gendarmes accompagnera la tribu dans sa migration. Un Commissaire de Police lui sera adjoint.

Les Kurdes donneront des otages pendant leurs migrations.

Les Règlements sur les feuilles de route et le port d'armes seront appliqués aux Kurdes.

S'il y a des tribus "constamment errantes," le Gouvernement les engagera à se fixer en leur concédant des terres.

Le droit d'élection et d'éligibilité n'appartient pas aux individus faisant partie des populations non sédentaires.

CHAPITRE X.—CAVALERIE HAMIDIÉ.

Art. 25. Le port d'armes et d'uniformes par les cavaliers Hamidiés, en dehors des périodes d'instruction, seront défendus par des Règlements militaires à élaborer.

Dans les mêmes circonstances ils sont justiciables des Tribunaux ordinaires.

CHAPITRE XI.—TITRES DE PROPRIÉTE.

Art. 26. On instituera au chef-lieu de vilayet et des sandjaks des Commissions pour la revision des titres de propriété. Ces Commissions seront composés de quatre membres (deux Musulmans et deux non-Musulmans) et présidées par le Directeur des Archives ou le préposé aux immeubles.

Leurs décisions seront soumises aux Conseils Administratifs.

En outre, quatre délégués seront envoyés chaque année de Constantinople au vilayets pour examiner les irrégularités qui auraient pu surgir dans les affaires d propriété.

Chapitre XII.—Perception des Dîmes et Impôts.

Art. 27. Des "détachements spéciaux" sont chargés de la perception de impôts, pour éviter l'emploi de la force publique. Ces détachements ne peuven faire aucune réquisition de fourrages et de vivres. Le prélèvement et la consignatio des impôts aux caisses de l'État incombent aux Moukhtars et aux Receveurs de villages et quartiers élus par les habitants.

Les membres des "détachements spéciaux" n'ont pas à manier d'argent.

Art. 28. La perception de la dîme se fera par voie d'affermage. L'affermage e gros reste aboli et a été remplacé par le mise en adjudication par villages et au non des habitants avec recours aux Tribunaux en cas de difficultés.

La prestation en nature et en argent est maintenue.

Le budget de l'Instruction Publique dans chaque vilayet est fixé par l Ministère de l'Instruction Publique.

La vente pour cause de dettes fiscales ou personnelles de la demeure d contribuable, des terrains nécessaires à sa subsistance, de ses instruments d travail, de ses bêtes de labour, et de ses grains demeure interdite.

Chapitre XIII.—Justice.

Art. 29. Il y aura dans chacune des localités du nahié un Conseil des Ancien présidé par le Moukhtar et dont la mission sera de concilier à l'amiable le contestations entre les habitants.

Arts 30, 31, 32, 33, 34, 35, 36, 37, 38, et 39. L'organisation; judiciair demeurera telle qu'elle est à présent.

Art. 40. Les jugements seront exclusivement libellés en langue Turque. L'Article 26 des Instructions sur les vilayets (Aristarchi, vol. v, p. 56) déclare que les jugements seront libellés en Turc et seront accompagnés, suivant les besoins d'une traduction en langue locale.

Turkey No. 1 (1896), pp. 124–126, No. 146/1

Translation.

Chapter I.—Valis.

ARTICLE 1. The Valis will be appointed by the Government. All Ottoman subjects, without distinction, are eligible for the post of Vali.

Art. 2. The duration of the powers of the Valis is not limited.

Art. 3. Non-Mussulman Assistants will be attached to the Valis, in accordance with the Laws and Regulations.

In accordance with the terms of Chapter II of the Regulations concerning the administration of the vilayets (Aristarchi, vol. iii, p. 13), their function is to assist in the general business of the vilayet and to attend to its despatch.

CHAPTER II.—MUTESSARIFS.

Art. 4. The Mutessarifs will be Mussulmans or non-Mussulmans.

They may be assisted by Moavins, who will be Christians if the Mutessarifs are Mussulmans.

CHAPTER III.—KAÏMAKAMS.

Art. 5. The Kaïmakams will be chosen by the Ministry of the Interior from among persons holding diplomas of the Civil School, without distinction of religion.

Kaïmakams now holding office and considered efficient may, even if they do not hold diplomas of that School, continue their career in the Government service.

Art. 6. Non-Mussulman Ottoman subjects will be admitted to administrative posts in proportion to the total numbers of the Mussulman and non-Mussulman population in each vilayet.

In cazas "having an important position," Moavins of a different religion from that of the Kaïmakam will be appointed.

The Administrative Councils of the sandjak and the caza, composed of ex officio and elected members, are retained.

CHAPTER IV.—NAHIÉS.

Art. 7. The organization of the nahiés will be carried out according to the provisions of Articles 94 to 106 of the Regulations for the general administration of the vilayets of the 9th January, 1286, and Articles 1 to 28 of the Regulations for the communal administration of the 25th March, 1292.

Art. 8. Each nahié will be administered by a Mudir and a Council composed of four members elected from among the inhabitants. One of them will be the Assistant. There will also be a Secretary.

Art. 9. The members of the Council of the nahié will be elected from the different classes of the population in proportion to their numbers.

Art. 10. The Mudirs and the Secretaries of the nahiés will receive salaries.

Art. 11. Candidates for membership of the Council of the nahié must fulfil the conditions prescribed by law.

Art. 12. The Mudirs will be appointed by the Government and chosen from the inhabitants of the nahié, according to the provisions of Article 10 of the Regulations for the administration of the communes (Aristarchi, vol. v, p. 61).

Art. 13. Officials, professors, and priests cannot be Mudirs.

Art. 14. Half of the members of the Council retire annually and are eligible for re-election. The Mudir will hold office for two years, and his powers may be renewed.

Art. 15. The functions of the Mudir and of the Councils are regulated by Articles 20 to 27 of the Regulations for the administration of the communes.

Art. 16. Each village will have a Mukhtar; if there are several wards and several classes of inhabitants, there will be a Mukhtar for each ward and for each class.

Art. 17. No village can belong to two nahiés.

Chapter V.—Police.

Art. 18. The police and the gendarmerie will be recruited from Ottoman subjects, in proportion to the numbers of Mussulman and non-Mussulman inhabitants of the vilayet. Sufficient contingents will be assigned to each administrative subdivision, including the nahié.

Art. 19. The police agents assigned to the nahié will act under the orders of the Mudir. They will be paid out of the district treasuries.

The non-Mussulman police agents will continue to pay the tax for exemption from military service.

Art. 20. The duties of keeping order and of escorting the post are assigned to the gendarmerie.

Chapter VI.—Gendarmerie.

Art. 21. The gendarmes will be recruited from the Mussulman and non-Mussulman inhabitants of the Empire in the proportion of the numbers of the populations of the different religions in each vilayet.

In spite of the promise made in the fourth and last paragraph of the reply of the Porte dated 2nd June, 1895, the Porte excludes Christians from the ranks of officers and non-commissioned officers in the gendarmerie.

Chapter VII.—Prisons.

Art. 22. More care will be taken to carry out the Regulations concerning the management of prisons and the treatment of persons under the provisional detention and prisoners.

CHAPTER VIII.—COMMITTEE OF PRELIMINARY INQUIRY.

Art. 23. The Committee of Preliminary Inquiry will act in accordance with the provisions of Article 11 of the Instructions for the administration of the vilayets. (Aristarchi, vol. v, p. 53).

CHAPTER IX.—CONTROL OF THE KURDS.

Art. 24. The places of migration of the Kurds will be fixed beforehand, and an officer with a sufficient armed force and gendarmes will accompany the tribe during its migration. A Police Commissary will be attached to him.

The Kurds will give hostages during their migrations.

The Regulations concerning passes and the carrying of arms will be applied to the Kurds.

If there are any tribes which are always wandering, the Government will call on them to settle, and will grant them lands.

Persons belonging to the non-sedentary population are not entitled to take part in elections or to be elected.

CHAPTER X.—HAMIDIÉ CAVALRY.

Art. 25. The carrying of arms and the wearing of uniforms by persons belonging to the Hamidié cavalry, at times other than the periods of training, will be forbidden by military Regulations to be drawn up.

In the same circumstances they are amenable to the jurisdiction of the ordinary Tribunals.

CHAPTER XI.—*Titles to Property.*

Art. 26. Commissions for the revision of titles to property will be established in the chief towns of the vilayets and sandjaks. These Commissions will be composed of four members (two Mussulmans and two non-Mussulmans), and will be presided over by the Director of Archives or the Superintendent of Real Property.

Their decisions will be submitted to the Administrative Councils.

Further, four delegates will be sent every year from Constantinople to the vilayets to investigate any irregularities which may have occured in matters connected with property.

CHAPTER XII.—LEVYING OF TITHES AND TAXES.

Art. 27. "Special detachments" are charged with the levying of the taxes, to avoid the employment of the public force. These detachments cannot requisition forage or provisions. It is the duty of the Mukhtars and the Receivers of the villages and wards, elected by the inhabitants, to collect the taxes and deliver them to the State treasuries.

No money must pass through the hands of the members of the "special detachments."

Art. 28. The tithe will be levied by farming. Farming on a large scale remains abolished, and is replaced by farming out the tithe by villages and in the name of the inhabitants, with the right of appeal to the Tribunals in case of difficulties.

The payment of contributions in kind and in money will continue.

The budget of Public Instruction in each vilayet is fixed by the Ministry of Public Instruction.

As hitherto, it is forbidden to sell, on account of debts to the Treasury or personal debts a taxpayer's house, the land necessary for his maintenance, his implements, his beasts of labour, or his seeds.

CHAPTER XIII.—JUSTICE.

Art. 29. There will be in each place in the nahié a Council of Elders presided over by the Mukhtar. Its duty will be to settle disputes among the inhabitants by friendly arrangement.

Arts. 30, 31, 32, 33, 34, 35, 36, 37, 38, and 39. The judicial organization will remain as it is at present.

Art. 40. Judgments will be drawn up in Turkish only. Article 26 of the Instructions for the vilayets (Aristarchi, vol. v, p. 56), states that judgments will be drawn up in Turkish, and will, if necessary, be accompanied by a translation in the local language.

Turkey No. 1 (1896), pp. 127–129, No. 146/1

Inclosure 2 in No. 75

Résumé du Contre-Projet du Gouvernement Impérial.

CHAPITRE I.—VALIS.

ARTICLE 1. Les Valis seront Musulmans et nommés par Iradé Impérial.

Art. 2. La durée des pouvoirs des Valis n'est pas limitée.

Art. 3. Des adjoints non-Musulmans seront nommés auprès des Valis, ainsi que cela est prévu au Chapitre II du Règlement de l'Administration Générale des Vilayets.

Ils ont pour attributions aux termes du dit Chapitre II de coopérer aux affaires générales du vilayet et d'en préparer l'expédition.

Chapitre II.—Mutessarifs.

Art. 4. Les Mutessarifs seront Musulmans et là où le Gouvernement Impérial e jugera nécessaire il nommera auprès d'eux des Mouavins Chrétiens.

Chapitre III.—Caïmacams.

Art. 5. Les Caïmacams seront choisis par le Ministére de l'Intérieur parmi les diplômés de l'École Civile sans distinction de religion et nommés par Iradé mpérial.

Les Caïmacams Musulmans et non-Musulmans actuellement en fonction et reconnus capables pourront, quoique non diplômés de cette école, continuer leur carrière dans l'Administration.

Art. 6. En vue de maintenir d'une façon équitable le principe de justice et d'égalité, le Gouvernement Impérial, lorsqu'il aura à'procéder à l'organisation, agira en tenant compte de la proportion du nombre de ses sujets.

Dans les cazas "ayant une position importante" des Mouavins, ayant une religion différente de celle de Caïmacam, seront nommés. Sont maintenus les Conseils Administratifs du sandjak et du caza composés de membres de droit et de membres élus.

Chapitre IV.—Nahiés.

Art. 7. L'organisation des nahiés sera mise en vigueur selon les prescriptions des Articles 94 à 106 du Règlement sur l'administration générale des vilayets du 9 Janvier, 1286, et des Articles 1 à 28 du Règlement sur l'administration communale du 25 Mars, 1292.

Art. 8. Chaque nahié sera administré par un Moudir et un Conseil composé de quatre membres élus par les habitants.

Art. 9. L'élection des membres du Conseil de nahié se fera proportionnellement aux classes de la population. Si la population de cercle communal est mixte, la minorité devra être représentée proportionnellement à son importance relative à condition qu'elle comprenne aux moins vingt-cinq maisons.

Art. 10. Les Moudirs et les Secrétaires des nahiés sont retribuées.

Art. 11. Les candidats au Conseil de nahié devront remplir les conditions prescrites par les Règlements de l'administration générale des vilayets et de l'administration communale.

Art. 12. Les Moudirs seront choisis et nommés par le Gouvernement Impérial.

Art. 13. Les fonctionnaires, les professeurs, et les prêtres ne peuvent être Moudirs.

Art. 14. Les membres du Conseil seront renouvelés par moitié chaque année et rééligibles.

Art. 15. Les attributions du Moudir et des Conseils sont réglées par les Articles 20 à 27 du Règlement sur l'administration des communes, sauf que les Moudirs seront, comme il est dit plus haut, nommés par le gouvernement Impérial.

Art. 16. Chaque village aura un Moukhtar; s'il y a plusieurs quartiers et plusieurs classes d'habitants, il y aura un Moukhtar par quartier et par classe.

Art. 17. Aucun village ne pourra relever de deux nahiés à la fois.

Chapitre V.—Police.

Art. 18. La police et la gendarmerie seront recrutées parmi les sujets Ottomans dans la proportion du chiffe général des habitants Musulmans et non-Musulmans du vilayet. Des contingents suffisants seront affectés à chaque subdivision administrative, y compris le nahié.

Art. 19. Les agents de police affectés au service du nahié agiront sous les ordres du Moudir et seront commandés par les Commissaires. Leurs armes et leurs uniformes seront identiques aux modéles déjà adoptés pour la police.

Art. 20. C'est la gendarmerie qui est chargée de maintien de l'ordre et de l'escorte de la poste.

Chapitre VI.—Gendarmerie.

Art. 21. Les gendarmes seront recrutés parmi les habitants Musulmans et non-Musulmans suivant les exigences locales, et les officiers et sous-officiers de ce corps choisis dans les cadres de l'armée Impériale.

La gendarmerie est entretenue et soldée aux frais du vilayet. La solde des gendarmes est supérieure à celle des soldats de l'armée Impériale et celle des officiers équivalente à la solde des officiers de l'armée Impériale.

Chapitre VII.—Prisons.

Art. 22. Il sera apporté plus de soins à l'application des Règlements concernant la tenue des prisons et le traitement des détenus et des prisonniers.

Chapitre VIII.—Comité d'Enquête Préliminaire.

Art. 23. Le Comité d'Enquête Préliminaire fonctionnera suivant les prescriptions de l'Article 11 des Instructions sur l'administration des vilayets.

CHAPITRE IX.—CONTRÔLE DES KURDES.

Art. 24. Les localités de migration des Kurdes seront fixées d'avance et un officier avec une force armée suffisante et des gendarmes accompagnera la tribu dans sa migration. Les Kurdes donneront des otages pendant leurs migrations.

Les Règlements sur les feuilles de route et le port d'armes seront appliqués aux Kurdes.

S'il y a des tribus "constamment errantes," le Gouvernement les engagera à se fixer en leur concédant des terres.

CHAPITRE X.—CAVALERIE HAMIDIÉ.

Art. 25. Le port d'armes et d'uniforme par les cavaliers Hamidié, en dehors des périodes d'instruction, seront défendus par les Règlements militaires à élaborer.

Dans les mêmes circonstances ils sont justiciables des Tribunaux ordinaires.

CHAPITRE XI.—*Titres de Propriété.*

Art. 26. On instituera au chef-lieu de vilayet et des sandjaks des Commissions pour la revision des titres de propriété. Ces Commissions seront composées de quatre membres (deux Musulmans et deux non-Musulmans), et présidées par le Directeur des Archives ou le préposé aux immeubles.

Leurs décisions seront soumises aux Conseils d'Administration.

En outre, quatre délégués seront envoyés chaque année de Constantinople aux vilayets pour examiner les irrégularités qui auraient pu surgir dans les affaires de propriétés.

CHAPITRE XII.—PERCEPTION DES DÎMES ET IMPÔTS.

Art. 27. Des "détachements spéciaux" sont chargés de la perception des impôts pour l'éviter l'emploi de la force publique. Ces détachments ne peuvent faire aucune réquisition de fourrages et de vivres. Le prélèvement et la consignation des impôts aux caisses de l'État incombent aux Moukhtars et aux Receveurs des villages et quartiers élus par les habitants.

Les membres des "détachements spéciaux" n'ont pas à manier d'argent.

Art. 28. La perception de la dîme se fera par voie d'affermage. L'affermage en gros reste aboli, et a été remplacé par le mise en adjudication par villages, et au nom des habitants avec recours aux Tribunaux en cas de difficultés.

La prestation en nature et en argent est maintenue.

Le budget de l'Instruction Publique dans chaque vilayet est fixé par le Ministére de l'Instruction Publique.

La vente pour cause de dettes fiscales ou personnelles de la demeure de contribuable des terrains nécessaires à sa subsistance, de ses instruments de travail, de ses bêtes de labour, et de ses grains demeure interdite.

CHAPITRE XIII.—JUSTICE.

Art. 29. Il y a dans chacune des localités un Conseil des Anciens, présidé par le Moukhtar, et dont la mission est de concilier à l'amiable les contestations entre les habitants, contestations prévues par les lois judiciaires.

Arts. 30, 31, 32, 33, 34, 35, 36, 37, 38, et 39. L'organisation judiciaire demeurera telle qu'elle est à présent.

Art. 40. Les Jugements seront exclusivement libellés en langue Turque.

Turkey No. 1 (1896), pp. 129–131, No. 146/2

Translation.

Summary of the Counter-Scheme of the Imperial Government.

CHAPTER I.—VALIS.

ARTICLE 1. The Valis will be Mussulmans, and will be appointed by Imperial Iradé.

Art. 2. The duration of the powers of the Valis is not limited.

Art. 3. Non-Mussulman Assistants will be attached to the Valis, as provided in Chapter II of the Regulations for the general administration of the vilayets.

According to Chapter II above mentioned, their duties are to assist in the general business of the vilayet and to attend to its despatch.

CHAPTER II.—MUTESSARIFS.

Art. 4. The Mutessarifs will be Mussulmans, and the Imperial Government will attach Christian Moavins to them where considered necessary.

CHAPTER III.—KAÏMAKAMS.

Art. 5. The Kaïmakams will be chosen by the Ministry of the Interior from among persons holding diplomas of the Civil School, without distinction of religion, and will be appointed by Imperial Iradé.

Mussulman and non-Mussulman Kaïmakams now holding office and considered efficient may, even if they do not hold diplomas of that School, continue their career in the Government service.

Art. 6. With a view to uphold in a equitable manner the principle of justice and equality, the Imperial Government, when it proceeds to the organization, will take into account the proportion of the numbers of the different classes of its subjects.

In cazas "having an important position" Moavins of a different religion from that of the Kaïmakam will be appointed. The Administrative Councils of the sandjak and the caza, composed of *ex officio* and elected members, are retained.

Chapter IV.—Nahiés.

Art. 7. The organization of the nahiés will be carried out according to the provisions of Articles 94 to 106 of the Regulations for the general administration of the vilayets of the 9th January, 1286, and Articles 1 to 28 of the Regulations for the communal administration of the 25th March, 1892.

Art. 8. Each nahié will be administered by a Mudir and a Council composed of four members elected by the inhabitants.

Art. 9. The members of the Council of the nahié will be elected from the different classes of the population in proportion to their numbers. If the population of the communal district is mixed, the minority shall be represented in proportion to its importance, provided that it comprises at least of twenty-five houses.

Art. 10. The Mudirs and the Secretaries of the nahiés will receive salaries.

Art. 11. Candidates for membership of the Council of the nahié must fulfil the conditions prescribed by the Regulations for the general administration of the vilayets and the Regulations for the communal administration.

Art. 12. The Mudirs will be chosen and appointed by the Imperial Government.

Art. 13. Officials, professors, and priests cannot be Mudirs.

Art. 14. Half of the members of the Council retire annually, and are eligible for re-election.

Art. 15. The functions of the Mudir and of the Councils are regulated by Articles 20 to 27 of the Regulations for the administration of the communes, except that the Mudirs will be appointed by the Imperial Government, as stated above.

Art. 16. Each village will have a Mukhtar; if there are several wards and several classes of inhabitants, there will be a Mukhtar for each ward and for each class.

Art. 17. No village can belong to two nahiés.

Chapter V.—Police.

Art. 18. The police and the gendarmerie will be recruited from Ottoman subjects in proportion to the total numbers of Mussulman and non-Mussulman inhabitants of the vilayet. Sufficient contingents will be assigned to each administrative subdivision, including the nahié.

Art. 19. The police agents assigned to the nahié will act under the orders of the Mudir, and will be commanded by the Commissaries. Their arms and uniforms will be of the pattern already adopted for the police.

Art. 20. The duties of keeping order and of escorting the post are assigned to the gendarmerie.

Chapter VI.—Gendarmerie.

Art. 21. The gendarmes will be recruited from the Mussulman and non-Mussulman inhabitants according to local requirements, and the officers and non-commissioned officers of this corp will be chosen from the Imperial army.

The gendarmerie is kept and paid at the expense of the vilayet. The pay of the gendarmes is higher than that of the soldiers of the Imperial army, and the pay of the officers is the same as that of the officers of the Imperial army.

Chapter VII.—Prisons.

Art. 22. More care will be taken to carry out the Regulations concerning the management of prisons and the treatment of persons under provisional detention and prisoners.

Chapter VIII.—Committee of Preliminary Inquiry.

Art. 23. The Committee of Preliminary Inquiry will act in accordance with the provisions of Article 11 of the Instructions for the administration of the vilayets.

Chapter IX.—Control of the Kurds.

Art. 24. The places of migration of the Kurds will be fixed beforehand, and an officer with a sufficient armed force and gendarmes will accompany the tribe during its migration. The Kurds will give hostages during their migrations.

The Regulations concerning passes and the carrying of arms will be applied to the Kurds.

If there are any tribes which are always wandering, the Government will call on them to settle and will grant them lands.

Chapter X.—Hamidié Cavalry.

Art. 25. The carring of arms and the wearing of uniforms by persons belonging to the Hamidié cavalry, at times other than the periods of training, will be forbidden by military Regulations to be drawn up.

In the same circumstances they are amenable to the jurisdiction of the ordinary Tribunals.

Chapter XI.—Titles to Property.

Art. 26. Commissions for the revision of titles to property will be established in the chief towns of the vilayets and sandjaks. These Commissions will be composed of four members (two Mussulmans and two non-Mussulmans) and will be presided over by the Director of Archives or the Superintendent of Real Property.

Their decisions will be submitted by the Administrative Councils.

Further, four delegates will be sent every year from Constantinople to the vilayets to investigate any irregularities which may have occured in matters connected with property.

Chapter XII.—Levying of Tithes and Taxes.

Art. 27. "Special corps" are charged with the levying of the taxes, to avoid the employment of the public force. These corps cannot requisition forage or provisions. It is the duty of the Mukhtars and the Receivers of the villages and wards, elected by the inhabitants, to collect the taxes and deliver them to the State treasuries.

No money must pass through the hands of the members of the "special corps."

Art. 28. The tithe will be levied by farming. Farming on a large scale remains abolished, and is replaced by farming out the tithe by villages, and in the name of the inhabitants, with the right of appeal to the Tribunals in case of difficulties.

The payment of contributions in kind and in money will continue.

The budget of Public Instruction in each vilayet is fixed by the Ministry of Public Instruction.

As hitherto, it is forbidden to sell, on account of debts to the Treasury or personal debts, a man's house, the land necessary for his maintenance, his implements, his beasts of labour, or his seeds.

Chapter XIII.—Justice.

Art. 29. There is in each place a Council of Elders, presided over by the Mukhtar. Its duty is to settle disputes among the inhabitants by friendly arrangement in cases where the disputes are foreseen by law.

Arts. 30, 31, 32, 33, 34, 35, 36, 37, 38, and 39. The judicial organization will remain as it is at present.

Art. 40. Judgments will be drawn up in Turkish only.

F. O. 424/183, pp. 241-246, No. 209/1

Turkey No. 1 (1896), pp. 132–134, No. 146/2

No. 76

Mr. Howard to the Marquess of Salisbury.

No. 273. Confidential.   PARIS, *August 22, 1895.*
My Lord,   *(Received August 24.)*
M. HANOTAUX said to me to-day that he could tell me privately, and not for publication in a Blue Book, that he highly approved of your Lordship's proposal for a Commission of Supervision as a settlement of the Armenian difficulty; and he especially approved of the suggestion that the members of the Commission should reside in the districts where disorders, &c., were likely to arise.

He had personally always thought that the former scheme submitted to the Porte was too extensive, contained too many details, and, in fact, was too long for any Government, let alone Turkey, to accept, so to speak, at once. His idea had been for the three Powers concerned to agree as to the minimum they would and could demand under the Treaty of Berlin, and then to obtain the acceptance of that minimum. Your Lordship's proposal was in accordance with this idea, and it would have his loyal support.

I have, &c.,

(Signed) HENRY HOWARD.

F. O. 424/183, p. 234, No. 201

No. 77

Sir P. Currie to the Marquess of Salisbury.

No. 542.   THERAPIA, *August 22, 1895.*
My Lord,   *(Received August 26.)*
I HAVE the honour to transmit to your Lordship herewith copy of a Petition which I have received from the Moslem inhabitants of Constantinople, complaining of the existing state of Government, and demanding the enforcement of Article 73 of the Constitution.

I have, &c.

(Signed) PHILIP CURRIE.

F. O. 424/183, p. 251, No. 212.

Inclosure in No. 77

Petition from the Moslem Inhabitants of Constantinople.

Traduction.

Très honoré Ambassadeur,

L'AMITIÉ entre les Gouvernements n'est jamais sentimentale, mais elle est toujours basée sur des intérêts communs. C'est pourquoi il est de rigueur que les relations de l'Angleterre avec la Turquie soient toujours dans des meilleurs termes. Dans tout l'Empire Ottoman s'il y a quelqu'un qui n'entend, ou bien qui ne veut entendre cette sentence politique, ce n'est que Sa Majesté Impériale le Sultan.

Toute sorte de progrès étant impossible sous un système de politique comme le nôtre, il est évident que comme toutes nos affaires, la politique aussi reste à la merci des vagues illusions, et sous la dépendance des caprices inconstants de celui qui gouverne. C'est ainsi que la politique suivie entre les deux États amis n'a été et n'est autre chose qu'une idée personnelle et éventuelle du Sultan.

Les marques d'amitié que la population Anglaise nous témoigne suffit pour nous montrer combien elle reconnaît l'importance de ces faits, et nous empêche de faire cas des visions de Rosebery aussi bien que celles du Sultan.

Nous avons vu dernièrement l'Angleterre s'immiscer dans nos affaires de l'intérieur et cela en proclamant la réforme.

Nous avons applaudi le but, mais nous avons fort regretté du choix de la méthode, la soi-disant réforme n'étant demandée que pour un certain amas de personnes.

Il est impossible de ne pas comprendre que l'application d'une pareille méthode est sur tous les rapports forcément dangereaux pour un Gouvernement hétérogène comme le nôtre.

Forcer pour cela le Gouvernement ça ne serait pas du tout logique. Perdre l'influence de tous les Islams pour une si fameuse réforme, c'est commettre là une des plus graves fautes politiques, dont la réparation plus tard coûterait bien cher. En tout cas le Gouvernement Anglais a l'air de vouloir introduire chez nous des réformes. En bien! si l'Angleterre trouve réellement que notre réforme lui convienne (ce qu'il n'y a lieu de s'en douter), et si les Anglais pour un caprice particulier du Sultan, ou bien encore pour quelques cris injustes et insignifiants d'une poignée d'Arméniens, les Anglais, disons-nous, trouvent qu'il ne serait pas avantageux de déplaire à tous les Islams en général, et à toute la population Musulmane de Turquie en particulier; et si, enfin, le Gouvernement Britannique veut réellement être gentil envers les Islams et assurer le bonheur de tous nos concitoyens non-Musulmans nous, pour le salut commun, nous proclamons l'exécution de la loi constitutionnelle que le Sultan communique officiellement à toutes les Puissances Européennes lors de son avènement au trône.

Dans un Gouvernement hétérogène comme le nôtre il n'y a d'autre salut que la mise en exécution de cette loi.

Pour le bonheur de toutes les nations, pour que chacun puisse librement jouir de ses droits il n'y d'autre moyen que l'ouverture de la Chambre!

Aucune autre réforme n'est possible!

Pour notre bien et avec notre salut, pour que nous puissions être de l'Angleterre des amis utiles, nous demandons de l'honorable Ambassadeur, et des hommes d'État de l'Angleterre, qu'ils forcent notre Gouvernement au nom de toute le population Musulmane de l'Empire, pour la mise en exécution de l'Article 73 de la Constitution!

Nous sommes persuadés que l'honorable Ambassadeur, par l'énergie qui le caractérise, fera tout son possible pour s'attirer les remerciements de tout le peuple Islam* en particulier, et de toutes les nations en général.

De la part de toute la population Musulmane de Constantinople.

F. O. 424/183, pp. 251-252, No. 212/1

*Ottomans de Turquie.

No. 78

Mr. Barrington to the Marquess of Salisbury.

No. 254.   VIENNA, *August 22, 1895.*
My Lord,   *(Received August 26.)*

COUNT GOLUCHOWSKI told me yesterday that, the Turkish Ambassador having opened the subject of Armenia with him, a conversation about it had ensued in which he had freely expressed his opinion of the inexpediency of the Porte's turning a deaf ear to the representations of the three Powers who had taken the matter up at Constantinople. Count Goluchowski told the Ambassador that his advice was given as that of a disinterested friend and well-wisher, who had no desire to see the Turkish Empire fall to pieces, an end to which it would assuredly come if it persisted in an evasive policy as regarded reforms, the necessity for which had become palpable. He was willing enough, he said, to believe in the good intentions of the Sultan, and in the earnestness of the Grand Vizier, whom he knew to be a sensible and capable man, but he could not close his eyes to the fact that the provincial administration was detestable, and could not help doubting whether the real truth concerning it ever reached the Sultan, and whether the Grand Vizier was able to counteract the hidden influences brought to bear on His Majesty.

On this point the Turkish Ambassador was rather disposed to admit the possibility of such being the case, as the intrigues which unfortunately went on in the Palace might perhaps lead to the interception of intelligence which those who sought Imperial favour might deem to be of a displeasing nature to the Sultan himself. His Excellency then alluded to the attitude of England, and Count Goluchowski said that in his opinion your Lordship could follow no other line, in view of the state of feeling which had been aroused in the country, and of the course of action that had been adopted hitherto. Your Lordship's language, he told the Ambassador, struck him as the natural display of a certain irritation at the hilatoriness shown by the Porte, and its indisposition to accept friendly counsels, which were given really in its own interest. Moreover, though your Lordship had spoken plainly in public, the utterance was in thorough consonance with language previously used to the Sultan's Representative in London, and if that had been faithfully reported, your Lordship's subsequent speech could afford no ground of surprise.

Altogether the Turkish Ambassador did not get much encouragement to hope for a more favourable opinion of Turkish policy being expressed at the Foreign Office here, and the recommendation strongly impressed upon his Excellency for conveyance to his Government was that the Porte should make the concessions demanded of it, if it did not wish to run the risk of worse things befalling it.

I may mention that I happened to meet the Turkish Ambassador before I saw Count Goluchowski, and that I inferred from his Excellency's observations that the change of Government in England had led to expectations that the question of Armenian reforms would not be urged on the Porte with the same insistance as before. To me, too, he expressed some disappointment at the stringent tenour of your Lordship's speech in the House of Lords. I said that such an anticipation as he seemed to have formed, and which might have been shared by his Government, notwithstanding the language held to his colleague in London, rather pointed to the necessity of disabusing the Porte of the idea that a change of persons involved a change of principle; and I added that what Her Majesty's Government sought was the introduction of a system to secure not special privileges, but reasonable justice, for the Sultan's Armenian subjects, which would afford guarantees against the perpetration on them of the terrible acts of cruelty to which they had been exposed with no means of redress.

His Excellency appeared to look on the question as a merely insurrectionary one, fomented and exaggerated by Committees abroad, and he seems, or professed, to be quite ignorant of the measures that had been resorted to for quelling the disturbance.

I have, &c.

(Signed) WILLIAM A. C. BARRINGTON.

F. O. 424/183, pp. 252-253, No. 213

No. 79

Sir P. Currie to the Marquess of Salisbury.

No. 373.   CONSTANTINOPLE, *August 23, 1895, 2.30 p.m.*
Telegraphic.   *(Received August 23.)*

ACCORDING to instructions contained in your Lordship's telegram No. 135 of the 19th August, Mr. Marinitch made a representation to Turkhan Pasha yesterday respecting the conduct of the Moush officials.

His Excellency denied the truth of the reports, but took down the substance of the communication for inquiry.

The French and Russian Dragomans supported Mr. Marinitch in general terms, and called special attention to the fact that the three Ambassadors had declared their intention of extending protection to the witnesses examined before the Moush Commission.

> *F. O. 424/183, p. 233, No. 200*
> *Turkey No. 1 (1895) Part I, p. 190, No. 254*

No. 80

Sir E. Malet to the Marquess of Salisbury.

No. 191. Confidential.   BERLIN, *August 24, 1895.*
My Lord,   *(Received August 26.)*

IN the course of conversation yesterday Baron von Marschall said he had seen Tewfik Pasha, the Turkish Ambassador, three days ago, and had urged him strongly to advise the Porte to make concessions with regard to Armenia, and to yield with a good grace to the advice tendered by her Majesty's Government.

His Excellency said that, in his opinion, the scheme of reforms proposed by the three Powers, was very moderate in its scope, and that it was in the interest of Turkey to accept the same without further delay.

His Excellency feared that Tewfik Pasha, who was "un homme du Palais," might think twice before he reported his remarks to the Sultan; he had, however, done his best to explain to him the views of the German Government on the subject.

I have, &c.

(For Sir E. Malet)
(Signed) MARTIN GOSSELIN.

F. O. 424/183, p. 253, No. 214

No. 81

Sir P. Currie to the Marquess of Salisbury.

No. 375.   CONSTANTINOPLE, *August 24, 1895, 9.15 p.m.*
Telegraphic.   *(Received August 24.)*
DANISH BEY, Director of the Consular Department at the Porte, has been appointed as assistant to Shakir Pasha on the Commission. The other members are Aides-de-camp of the Sultan and officials of the Imperial Chancery, and no Christian is attached to it.

Shakir Pasha leaves for Erzeroum to-morrow.

F. O. 424/183, p. 234, No. 203
Turkey No. 1 (1896), p. 123, No. 145

No. 82

Sir P. Currie to the Marquess of Salisbury.

No. 543.   CONSTANTINOPLE, *August 24, 1895.*
My Lord,   *(Received September 2.)*
WITH reference to my despatch to the Earl of Kimberley of the 19th June, I have the honour to forward to your Lordship herewith copy of a despatch which I have received from Her Majesty's Consul at Aleppo respecting the revolutionary movement at Suedia. I have approved Mr. Barnham's action in urging on the Vali of Aleppo the necessity of adopting measures for the protection of Christians at Antioch.

I have, &c.

(Signed) PHILIP CURRIE.

F. O. 424/183, p. 391, No. 244
Turkey No. 6 (1896) p. 386, No. 500, 500/1

Inclosure in No. 82

Consul Barnham to Sir P. Currie.

Confidential.
Sir,   ALEXANDRETTA, *August 7, 1895*
I HAVE the honour to inform your Excellency, with reference to my telegram of this date, that the British Vice-Consul at Antioch, in a report dated the 30th ultimo, states that two Armenian muleteers from the village of Beilan had that day

been arrested for having in their custody two loads, consisting of boxes of Martini-Henry cartridges. They were found in an unfrequented part of the country near Antioch, proceeding in the direction of the villages of Suedia.

In a second report, dated the 1st instant, Mr. Donek informs me that two more arrests had taken place on the previous day, when two loads were seized at the village of Harbiyé, 3 miles south of Antioch, together with a package of letters. In the four boxes of which the loads consisted were Martini-Henry cartridges, breeches of guns, locks, and screws.

There was considerable excitement at Antioch in consequence of these arrests. A large crowd of Moslems proceeded at once to the Armenian quarter with the intention of forcing an entrance into the Armenian church, where it was suspected that arms had been concealed. Search was made in the church by Government officials, but nothing of the kind having been discovered, the crowd dispersed.

On the following day (1st August) the Heads of the Armenian Church sent identical telegrams to the Grand Vizier, Vali of Aleppo, and the Patriarch, reporting the occurrence, and complaining of the threatening attitude of the Moslem population.

The same day the Roman Catholic priest of Huda Beg, one of the Suedia villages, was roughly handled by a Moslem crowd, who wished to search him for arms as he was entering the city gate, and he was compelled to take refuge at the French Vice-Consulate.

Mr. Donek writes that he personally feels anxious for the safety of British subjects at Antioch, as the Moslems are openly saying that these troubles have been promoted by the English.

Considering the fact that the Christian population in Antioch is a mere handful as compared with the Mussulman, that the Armenian revolutionary party apparently is planning an insurrection in that country, in which case the patience of the Moslem population will be sorely tried, I have thought it right to acquaint the Vali with Mr. Donek's views of the situation, and begged him to take all necessary steps with a view to quiet the Moslem inhabitants.

With a knowledge of the avowed intentions of the Armenian revolutionary party as stated in the pamphlet quoted in the margin,* and of the facts reported in my despatch of the 1st June last, I think it probable that an insurrection will shortly break out at Suedia.

Possibly it is the intention of the revolutionary leaders to give the signal for its outbreak, only under certain contingencies; but as arms have been introduced into the country in large quantities, and men have been drilling, with the expectation of having to fight, it is probable that on the first act of violence on the part of the authorities there will be bloodshed. I should say that the extent of the movement will depend upon the action of the Ansariyé felleheen, who form the majority among the population of the district. They are the Mussulman sect, intensely hostile to the Turks, and especially ill-disposed to some of the leading Turkish Notables of Antioch. They particularly resent the conscription for the army.

We had heard nothing of the revolutionary movement during the last six weeks. Acting on the reports received from the Kaïmakam of Antioch, the Vali had exaggerated the gravity of the situation in his telegrams to the Palace, or rather, seeing that, in spite of the dispatch of troops to Suedia, and of gun-boats to the coast, nothing material was discovered, he was held to have exaggerated it, and was censured accordingly. The troops were withdrawn about six weeks ago, the gun-boats three weeks ago.

Nothing material had been discovered by the troops, though it is a fact that, while they were searching the suspected villages, the ringleaders were there in disguise mingling among the villagers, and no one attempted to betray them.

As regards the extent to which arms have been introduced into the country, I have information that a large quantity were actually passed through the Custom-house at Alexandretta, hidden in consignments of cloth.

I have just received information that a boat-load of arms is about to land on the Suedia coast, and that one of the Turkish gun-boats has, at the same time, resumed guard.

Eight persons have been forwarded to Aleppo under arrest. One of these is an Armenian holding an American passport, in whose luggage a sum of 800 liras was discovered. When examined before the Kaïmakam of Antioch he declared that it was money for the relief of distressed Armenians.

I have, &c.

(Signed) HENRY D. BARNHAM.

F. O. 424/183, pp. 391-392, No. 244/1
Turkey No. 6 (1896) p. 387, No. 500/1

*"The Voice of the Armenian Revolutionists," by Avetis Nazarbek.

No. 83

Sir P. Currie to the Marquess of Salisbury.

No. 380. Secret.   CONSTANTINOPLE, *August 26, 1895, 2.15 p.m.*
Telegraphic.   *(Received August 26.)*

I AM informed, from a private source, that one section of the Palace officials still counsel resistance to English advice, on the ground that Russia will not act with us, and that your proposals are only meant to frighten His Majesty; but another section maintain that such resistance is dangerous.

The Sultan himself is getting very uneasy about your Lordship's language to

Rustem Pasha, and his Iradés to the Porte have become more subdued in tone the last two days.

The Grand Vizier, so far as he dares, favours reform.

The Sultan is receiving warnings from his secret police of the serious discontent existing among the Mussulman population.

F. O. 424/183, p. 254, No. 216

No. 84

The Marquess of Salisbury to Sir P. Currie.

No. 138.
Telegraphic. FOREIGN OFFICE, *August 26, 1895.*

I HAVE received your despatch No. 528 of the 15th instant, inclosing a copy of the Joint Report drawn up by the Consular Delegates on the Sassoon Commission of Inquiry.

It will of course be necessary that this Report should be laid before Parliament.

On the 24th instant I forwarded copies to you in print, and I should be glad to know how soon the final text and copies of the Annexes may be expected.

Unless you see any objection, I propose to ask at once whether the French and Russian Governments will assent to the eventual publication of the Report. It is probable that the consent of the two Powers may be more easily obtained if applied for at once.

F. O. 424/183, p. 254, No. 217

No. 85

The Marquess of Salisbury to Sir P. Currie.

No. 139.
Telegraphic. FOREIGN OFFICE, *August 26, 1895.*

I WAS informed to-day by the Russian Chargé d'Affaires that his Government consider it undesirable to insist on the reorganization of the gendarmerie and the fixed term of office for the Valis in the Armenian provinces. The Russian Government still adhere to the opinion that the introduction of Christians into the gendarmerie of the provinces, whether they be mingled with the Mahommedans or formed into separate companies, would be a cause of disturbance and sanguinary strife.

F. O. 424/183, pp. 255, No. 218
Turkey No. 1 (1896), p. 134, No. 148

No. 86

Sir P. Currie to the Marquess of Salisbury.

No. 381.   CONSTANTINOPLE, *August 27, 1895, 10.45 a.m.*
Telegraphic.   *(Received August 27.)*
WITH reference to your Lordship's telegram No. 138, I see no objection to asking the consent of the French and Russians to the publication of the Report. Mr. Shipley has arrived, and I hope to send home a revised copy with the Annexes by the end of the week.

F. O. 424/183, p. 257, No. 220

No. 87

Sir P. Currie to the Marquess of Salisbury.

No. 546.   CONSTANTINOPLE, *August 27, 1895.*
My Lord,   *(Received September 2.)*
I HAVE the honour to forward to your Lordship herewith copy of a despatch with I have received from Her Majesty's Consul at Trebizond respecting the proceedings of the Vali of Sivas.

I have, &c.

(Signed) PHILIP CURRIE.

F. O. 424/183, p. 395, No. 246

Inclosure in No. 87

Consul Longworth to Sir P. Currie.

Sir,   TREBIZOND, *August 19, 1895.*
KHALIL BEY'S unaccountable proceedings at Sivas are thus referred to by Dr. Jewett in his letter of the 14th instant:-
"A man who pretends to know says that the Vali is assisting to organize a Turkish revolutionary demonstration, either for the purpose of showing that reforms cannot be introduced for the Armenians without destroying the peace of the whole Empire, or some other reason. I mention it simply that we may see what the truth is when events declare themselves, if they ever do."

I have, &c.

(Signed) H. Z. LONGWORTH.

F. O. 424/183, p. 395, No. 246/1

No. 88

Sir P. Currie to the Marquess of Salisbury.

No. 383.　　　　　　　　　　　　　　CONSTANTINOPLE, *August 27, 1895, 12.15 p.m.*
Telegraphic.　　　　　　　　　　　　　　　　　　　*(Received August 27.)*

WITH reference to your Lordship's telegram of the 26th instant, no reforms are now being pressed on the Porte by my colleagues and myself.

The demand for five years' tenure of Valis was met by a statement that they were appointed with a view to remaining more than five years if they conducted themselves well.

Small numbers of Christians have been from time to time employed in the gendarmerie as at Van as late as 1888, and possibly later.

This point has been throughout accepted in principle by the Porte, but the latter have declined to define the proportion.

The Porte have accepted the reorganization of the gendarmerie, but on their own lines.

F. O. 424/183, p. 257, No. 221
Turkey No. 1 (1896), pp. 134-135, No. 149

No. 89

Sir P. Currie to the Marquess of Salisbury.

No. 544.　　　　　　　　　　　　　　　　CONSTANTINOPLE, *August 27, 1895.*
My Lord,　　　　　　　　　　　　　　　　　　　*(Received September 2.)*

I HAVE the honour to transmit herewith to your Lordship a despatch from Her Majesty's Consul at Erzeroum, forwarding the letter in which Mr. Shipley, the British Delegate to the Bitlis Commission, submits the Joint Report drawn up by his colleagues and himself on the proceedings of the Commission.

I have much pleasure in calling your Lordship's attention to the satisfactory manner in which Mr. Shipley performed the arduous duties intrusted to him.

The work of the Delegates was performed under conditions which entailed no small amount of personal inconvenience, and I submit that the way in which it was carried out, and the perfect harmony which prevailed between them during the whole time of their association, reflect the greatest credit upon them.

I beg to recommend Mr. Shipley's services to your Lordship's approval.

I have, &c.

(Signed) PHILIP CURRIE.

F. O. 424/183, p. 393, No. 245
Turkey No. 1 (1895) Part I, P. 193, No. 260

Inclosure 1 in No. 89

Consul Graves to Sir P. Currie.

Sir,   ERZEROUM, *August 12, 1895.*

I HAVE the honour to transmit herewith to your excellency copies of a despatch which has been addressed to me by Mr. Shipley, British Delegate with the Commission of Inquiry into the events of Sasun in 1894, on his submitting the General Report of the Delegates upon those events.

The Report itself, with its Annexes, has been instrusted to M. Prjevalsky, the Russian Delegate, by whom it is being carried to Constantinople.

After a careful study of this document, and of the daily Joint Reports of the Delegates upon which it is based, I can only express my entire agreement with their conclusion, as far as they go, and bear my testimony to the unselfish zeal and energy with which they have all laboured so long—under conditions of almost unparalleled difficulty and hardship—in order to arrive at this result.

At the same time, I venture to point out certain respects in which, as was only to be expected from the conditions under which the inquiry was made, the Report of the Delegates has fallen short of an entire elucidation of the Sasun affair, from its earliest beginning up to the date of writing, when, by administrative pressure of every kind, and under the disguise of superintending their relief, the Turkish authorities are still endeavouring to consummate the ruin of the Christians of Sasun and Talori.

1. Owing to the persistent refusal of the Turkish Commissioners to take evidence on the subject, no inquiry was made into the attack of the Kurds on Talori in 1893, which, in my belief, had for its direct result the agitation of "Mourad" and his fellows, their isolated acts of hostility towards the Kurds, and of insubordination towards Government officials, and the subsequent terrible reprisals of the latter in 1894. The Delegates were therefore only able to express a guarded opinion upon this concatenation of events.

2. No attempt whatever was made by the Commission to throw light upon the movements of troops or the superior orders under which the Commanding officers acted; consequently, the precise share of the regular troops in the masssacre of Christians, without distinction of age or sex, rests upon the evidence of Armenians only. This fact has prevented our Delegates from doing more than formally express their conviction that such massacre took place, without attempting to fix the personal responsibilities for its execution.

3. Although it is clear from what has been recorded in the daily Joint Reports, as well as from outside information, that strong pressure was brought to bear by intimidation or promises of reward, to influence the evidence of Armenian witnesses, in their final Report the Delegates have refrained from insisting upon the fact that, not only is there a strong presumption that the evidence on the

government side had been prepared beforehand by the local authorities, but proofs were actually adduced that evidence was previously submitted to the Commissioners before being given formally in the presence of the European Delegates.

4. On the question of torture and acts of revolting atrocity, in the absence of independent corroborating evidence, and in consequence of the reluctance of the Commissioners to go into them, it was impossible for the Delegates to do more than declare that they remain in obscurity.

The lack of direct authority vested in the Delegates rendered them powerless to remedy these voluntary shortcomings of the Turkish commissioners. In the consequent absence of legally conclusive proofs, their quasi-judicial position, and the necessity imposed upon each of them of not claiming to record as proved more than was certain to be admitted as such by his colleagues, has compelled them to render an open verdict upon these important points, or refrain from touching upon them at all.

Individually, however, there is no impropriety in their expressing their matured opinions on these subjects, and Mr. Shipley proposes to embody his own in a Memorandum to be submitted to your Excellency after his return to Constantinople.

In conclusion, I desire to express my acknowledgments of Mr. Shipley's services during his long and arduous mission. I am in a position to say that such success as the Delegates have been able to achieve is largely due to the prudence, tack, and unfailing straightforwardness shown by Mr. Shipley in his relations with his colleagues, of whose conduct towards himself he speaks in the warmest terms; and I have also the thank him for valuable assistance most cordially rendered to myself during his residence at Erzeroum before and after the inquiry at Moush.

I have, &c.

(Signed) R. W. GRAVES.

F. O. 424/183, pp. 393-394, No. 245/1
Turkey No. 1 (1895) Part I, p. 194, No. 260/1

Inclosure 2 in No. 89

Mr. Shipley to Consul Graves.

Sir,   ERZEROUM, *August 10, 1895.*
I HAVE the honour to submit to you herewith, in accordance with instructions, the Joint Report on the events in Sasun of last year,* drawn up by Messrs. Prjevalsky, Vilbert, and myself, Delegates of the Russian, French and British Consulates at Erzeroum respectively to the Bitlis Commission appointed by the Turkish Government to inquire into the events in question.

Owing to the great pressure of work entailed by the necessity of completing the revision of the Protocols of the above-mentioned Commission, I am unavoidably compelled to postpone the consideration of certain points in the above Report to which I think particular attention should be drawn, leaving them to be embodied in a Memorandum which I propose to submit subsequently to Her Majesty's Ambassador at Constantinople.

I would only at present remark that the conclusions arrived at in our Report above referred to were arrived at in entire agreement with my colleagues, to whose unselfish and strenuous co-operation with myself I feel it my duty to bear the fullest witness.

It only remains for me to acknowledge my great obligations for the asistance which I have on all occasions met with from yourself. The information, in particular, placed by you at my disposal has proved to be of the utmost value to me, owing to your intimate knowledge of the districts coming under the scope of the inquiry.

I have, &c.

(Signed) H. S. Shipley.

F. O. 424/183, p. 394, No. 245/2
Turkey No. 1 (1895) Part I, p. 195, No. 260/1, 260/2

No. 90

Sir P. Currie to the Marquess of Salisbury.

No. 548.   Therapia, *August 27, 1895.*
My Lord,   *(Received September 2.)*

I HAVE the honour to inclose herewith translation of an extract from the Turkish newspaper "Saadet," reporting a reconciliation effected between hostile nomad tribes in the Vilayet of Van.

I have, &c.

(Signed) Philip Currie.

F. O. 424/183, p. 396, No. 248

Inclosure in No. 90

Extract from the "Saadet" of August 25, 1895.

Translation.

IN consequence of a misunderstanding which lately arose between the tribes of the Beit-esh-Shebab Caza, in the Vilayet of Van, and the nomad tribe of the

Kindan, who for that reason avoided the pastures situated within the caza in question and wandered from place to place, an Imperial Iradé was issued ordering that Captain Emin Agha, of the Vilayet Merkez, together with the Vice-Kaïmakam, Mustapha Agha, should proceed to the pasture-lands referred to and effect a reconciliation between the dissentient parties.

Thanks to the efforts of these officials, the misunderstanding has now been removed, and friendly relations have been re-established.

The Kindan tribe have returned to their pasture-land at Kani-Mas, and have pitched their tents. In pledge of the intertribal reconciliation a banquet was given, at which members of the various tribes were present, and Emin and Mustapha Aghas have reported to the Vali that this banquet was a great success, and the name of the Sultan was received with acclamation.

The Vali, in reply, as signified his approval to the officials in question.

F. O. 424/183, p. 396, No. 248/1
Turkey No. 6 (1896) p. 388, No. 502, 502/1

No. 91

Sir P. Currie to the Marquess of Salisbury.

No. 383. Confidential.   CONSTANTINOPLE, *August 28, 1895, 10.50 a.m.*
Telegraphic.   *(Received August 28.)*

SAÏD PASHA, ex-minister for Foreign Affairs, was sent yesterday by the Sultan to the three Embassies to say that His Majesty was now disposed to grant the Commission of Control, on the understanding that it should be under the presidency of the Foreign Minister, and that the Dragomans should only communicate with it through him.

I was out when Saïd Pasha called, but he saw my two colleagues, who declined to discuss the matter, saying that it was in the hands of the Governments.

Turkish Ambassador at Paris reports that he had urged M. Hanotaux to exert his influence with England in favour of Turkey, but latter had declined to do so, stating, at the same time, that French government would examine and give its opinion on the steps which the Turkish Government proposed to take if they were communicated immediately.

F. O. 424/183, p. 258, No. 223

No. 92

Sir P. Currie to the Marquess of Salisbury.

No. 550.   THERAPIA, *August 28, 1895.*
My Lord,   *(Received September 2.)*
    I HAVE the honour to report that the former Kaïmakam of Bolanik, Ismaïl
Hakki Effendi, has been appointed Kaïmakam of the Caza of Sasun.
                              I have, &c.
                                              (Signed) PHILIP CURRIE.

F. O. 424/183, p. 397, No. 249

No. 93

Sir P. Currie to the Marquess of Salisbury.

No. 387.   CONSTANTINOPLE, *August 28, 1895, 1.50 p.m.*
Telegraphic.   *(Received August 28.)*
    WITH reference to my telegram of to-day No. 386, the ex-Foreign Minister,
Saïd Pasha, has again been to see me. He had been intrusted with the following
message from the Sultan, whom he had just seen:-
    "If the government agree that the Commission of Control should always be
under the presidency of the Minister for Foreign Affairs, and that the Dragomans
should only communicate with the commission through the Ministry for Foreign
Affairs, the Porte would accept the proposals of the three Powers on the following
points: Institution of rural guards; proposals respecting gendarmerie; proportion of
Christians to be employed in the Administration; nomination of Mudirs by the
government from the local authorities; improvement of prisons."
    I said that I would inform your lordship of Saïd Pasha's communication, but
that I had no authority either to discuss these proposals or to make any new ones.
    F. O. 424/183, p. 258, No. 224

No. 94

Mr. Howard to the Marquess of Salisbury.

No. 281.   PARIS, *August 28, 1895.*
My Lord,   *(Received August 29.)*
    I COMMUNICATED to M. Hanotaux this evening the substance of your
Lordship's telegram No. 108 of this day's date respecting the publication of the
Report of the Delegates on the Moush inquiry.

M. Hanotaux, who said that he had just read this Report, stated that, as Minister of Foreign Affairs, he could not of course object to the publication of the same, as such a step was a question of English internal policy. Personally, however, while acknowledging your Lordship's superior wisdom and experience, he was of opinion that it would be well to postpone the publication of the Report if possible for at least a week.

It had struck him on reading the Report that the conclusions of the Delegates were necessarily vague on many points, and that, consequently, if the publication took place, which would lead to universal discussion in the press, both parties could, and no doubt would, make capital out of the Report, which would, in his opinion, weaken the action of the three Powers concerned, and might make the Porte still more disinclined to accept any of the reforms demanded.

His Excellency had this morning received a telegram from M. Cambon, stating that after an interview with Saïd Pasha, the former Minister of Foreign Affairs, he thought that he saw signs of the Porte really weakening and giving way, and M. Hanotaux was of opinion that it would be very advantageous if the publication of the Report could be delayed for a few days in order to see whether this would really prove to be the case.

His Excellency then suggested that Sir Philip Currie might be instructed to inform the Porte that Her Majesty's Government had decided to publish the Report, as possibly such an instruction might hasten the acceptance of the reforms demanded by the Powers.

I informed his Excellency that I would report his remarks immediately to your Lordship.

I have, &c.

(Signed) HENRY HOWARD.

F. O. 424/183, pp. 260-261, No. 229

No. 95

Sir F. Lascelles to the Marquess of Salisbury.

No. 80.   ST. PETERSBURGH, *August 28, 1895.*
Telegraphic.   *(Received August 28.)*

THIS afternoon the Russian Minister for Foreign Affairs informed me of the language which he had given the Russian Chargé d'Affaires instructions to use to your Lordship. He trusts that an agreement is not far off. With regard to the two points at issue, M. de Nélidoff has reported that the question of the duration of the appointment of the Valis was one which could be dropped by the Representatives of the Powers, and the principle that the Gendarmerie should be recruited among the non-Mussulman and Mussulman inhabitants was accepted in the Project presented by the Porte. No further difficulty is, therefore, anticipated with regard to these matters.

Prince Lobanoff added that, although he would have preferred the Surveillance Committee should sit at Constantinople, in a conciliatory spirit and to avoid making difficulties, he had accepted your Lordship's proposal, but the Russian Ambassador at Constantinople had pointed out to him that a claim to be represented on the Committee might be put in by the other Powers who signed the Treaty of Berlin, the Committee being based on that Treaty, and, supposing this were to happen, your Lordship's proposed committee of four Turks and three Europeans would no longer be possible. Prince Lobanoff does not like the idea of a Committee composed of a larger number of persons.

F. O. 424/183, pp. 258–259, No. 220
Turkey No. 1 (1896), p. 135, No. 150

No. 96

The Marquess of Salisbury to Sir P. Currie.

No. 144.
Telegraphic.   FOREIGN OFFICE, *August 28, 1895.*
ACCORDING to a telegram published to-day from Reuter's Agent at Constantinople, a Turkish Colonel and his escort were attacked by brigands in the neighbourhood of Kemakh, south-west of Erzinghian. The sergeant of the escort is reported killed. The authorities attributing this attack to the Armenians, have dispatched to the district a large number of troops, who are reported to be attacking villages and monasteries, and perpetrating other deeds of violence. The telegram adds that the inhabitants have appealed to the foreign Ambassadors at Constantinople.

I should be glad to learn whether information to this effect has reached your Exellency.

F. O. 424/183, p. 259, No. 227
Turkey No. 6 (1896) p. 385, No. 497

No. 97

Sir F. Lascelles to the Marquess of Salisbury.

No. 209. Confidential.   ST. PETERSBURGH, *August 28, 1895.*
My Lord,   *(Received September 2.)*
I HAD a long conversation this afternoon with Prince Lobanoff on the subject of Armenian reforms. His Excellency began by stating, in reply to my inquiries,

that Shakir Pasha had at last left Constantinople, which he presumed meant that the Sultan had become alarmed, and had seen the necessity of doing something to settle the question. His Excellency thought that this might be partly due to a conversation he had recently had with the Turkish Ambassador here, who had asked him whether it was true that Russia had adopted the English demands. Husny Pasha had become much perturbed on hearing that this was the case, and had expressed his surprise and regret that the Russian Government had adopted such a course. Prince Lobanoff had replied that there was nothing surprising in the matter, as the action now taken was entirely justified by the Treaty of Berlin, and the Turkish Government had only themselves to blame for not having introduced reforms earlier. They had, he believed, been led to hope that the recent change of Government in England might have brought about a modification of the views of Her Majesty's Government, and that your Lordship would be less inclined to press the demands of the Ambassadors on the Porte. In this, however, the Turkish Government had been mistaken, and, in his Excellency's opinion, the demands which had been put forward were the minimum which your Lordship, in view of the state of public opinion in England, could accept.

Prince Lobanoff said that it was rather hard that Husny Pasha should reproach him after the line he had taken in attempting to moderate the action of Her Majesty's Government, who at one time seemed on the point of taking isolated action in the matter, which he feared might have led to great complications, and, indeed, have reopened the whole Eastern question.

I thanked Prince Lobanoff for the information he had given me, and fully admitted the moderating character of the action he had taken.

His Excellency then went on to say that he hoped we were now very near a satisfactory understanding. He repeated to me almost textually the language which he had instructed the Russian Chargé d'Affaires in London to hold to your Lordship with regard to the two points still under discussion, viz., the maintenance in office of the Valis for five years and the reorganization of the gendarmerie.

With regard to the first, his Excellency had received a report from M. de Nélidoff, saying that the Ambassadors, in discussing the subject, had agreed that this point was one of those which would be easiest to drop; and, with regard to the second, he perceived that the Turkish counter-project admitted the recruitment of gendarmes among both Mussulmans and non-Mussulmans. He did not think, therefore, that either of those two points would give rise to much further difficulty, and is gathered from M. Kroupensky's telegrams that your Lordship shared his views as to the danger of enrolling Mussulmans and Christians either together or in separate bands.

Prince Lobanoff reminded me that he had been of opinion that it would have been more desirable that the Committee of Surveillance should remain at Constantinople, and that he had agreed to your Lordship's proposal that it should sit at Van, Bitlis, or Erzeroum rather from a wish to avoid raising difficulties and to how a conciliatory spirit than from a conviction of its desirability. He still thought that the presence of the Committee in some town in Asia Minor might encourage the Armenian Committees abroad to continue their agitation, and he feared that the Committee of Surveillance would be flooded with demands, many of which would probably be unfounded and very difficult to investigate. However this might be, there was another aspect of the affair which had been suggested to him by M. de Nélidoff, and which would be fatal to your Lordship's proposal that the Committee should be composed of three Europeans and four Turks.

The arrangement was based on the Treaty of Berlin, and each of the Signatory Powers of that Treaty would have the right of being represented on the Committee. It would be difficult enough to get three Europeans and four Turks to work together, but a Committee of twice those numbers would certainly do more harm than good, and might constitute a real danger.

I told Prince Lobanoff that I would not fail to report his views to your Lordship, and he begged me to do so. I had, therefore, the honour on my return from the Ministry for Foreign Affairs, to forward to your Lordship my telegram of his day's date.

In conclusion, Prince Lobanoff again expressed the hope that an arrangement might shortly be arrived at. He was sincerely anxious that the matter should be settled so as to prevent complications in the Armenian provinces of Turkey, which, in consequence of her geographical position and direct interest in the question, was a matter of paramount importance to Russia.

I have, &c.

(Signed) FRANK C. LASCELLES.

F. O. 424/183, pp. 401-402, No. 256
Turkey No. 1 (1896), p. 137, No. 156

No. 98

Sir P. Currie to the Marquess of Salisbury.

No. 388. CONSTANTINOPLE, *August 29, 1895, 2 a.m.*
Telegraphic. *(Received August 29.)*

WITH reference to my telegram of yesterday No. 387, by order of the Sultan, Saïd Pasha returned at midnight to withdraw the proposal made by him in the morning. He was charged to say instead, that if the Powers accepted the Commission as modified, the Porte would discuss the five other points.

Saïd Pasha said that the change had been brought about by intrigues, and he expressed the utmost shame at having to give such a message.

Should I receive any more messages in regard to Armenian reforms, I shall refuse to transmit them officially.

F. O. 424/183, p. 261, No. 230

No. 99

Sir P. Currie to the Marquess of Salisbury.

No. 551.   THERAPIA, *August 29, 1895*
My Lord,   *(Received September 2.*

I HAVE the honour to transmit herewith copy in paraphrase of a telegram which I have received from Her Majesty's Consul at Erzeroum, stating that Mr Hampson ascertained, on visiting the Talori villages, that the thirteen wards which compose that group, twelve, consisting of 425 houses, had been totally destroyed while the thirteenth, which contained thirty houses, had only been plundered.

I would call your Lordship's attention to the fact that the Delegates on the Moush Commission of Inquiry have understated the number of houses destroyed in the Talori district.

I have, &c.

(Signed) PHILIP CURRIE

F. O. 424/183, p. 397, No. 250

Inclosure in No. 99

Consul Graves to Sir P. Currie.

Telegraphic.   ERZEROUM, *August 26, 1895*

MR. HAMPSON has ascertained that the Kurds still practise the levy of "hafir".

With reference to the statistics given in the Annex of Delegates' Joint Report, the report on the Talori villages drawn up by Mr. Hampson shows that, of the thirteen wards which compose that group, and were visited by him, twelve, consisting of 425 houses, had been totally destroyed, while the thirteenth, which contained thirty houses, had been only plundered.

F. O. 424/183, p. 397, No. 250/1

No. 100

Sir P. Currie to the Marquess of Salisbury.

No. 552.   THERAPIA, *August 29, 1895.*
My Lord,   *(Received September 2.)*

I HAVE the honour to transmit herewith copies of two despatches which I have received from Her Majesty's Consul at Aleppo, reporting outrages on Armenians at Killis and Beilan.

I am calling the attention of the Sublime Porte to the threatening attitude of the Moslem population, as reported in the above-mentioned despatches.

I have, &c.

(Signed) PHILIP CURRIE.

F. O. 424/183, p. 397, No. 251

Inclosure 1 in No. 100

Consul Barnham to Sir P. Currie.

Sir,   ALEPPO, *August 11, 1895.*

I HAVE the honour to inform your Excellency that I have received a joint letter from the Armenian, Greek, and Protestant ecclesiastics of Killis, reporting a brutal outrage committed upon an Armenian near that town. The writers preface their report by saying that Christians of all sects suffer from the insolence of the Mussulman inhabitants, that their women are insulted at the public baths, and that, in some cases, knives have been drawn by Turks in the public streets.

On the 2nd instant, Aghdaz Oghlou Ibrahim, while watering his olive garden, was attacked by the caretaker of a neighbouring vineyard, named Chakir Osman, and others, who beat him so severely that his life is in danger; they smeared his face with filth, placed him on a donkey, facing the tail, which they made fast round his waist with the aid of a cord. His arms were secured behind his back, and his legs under the donkey's belly, and in this position he was driven along the high road into the town of Killis, while his tormentors ran alongside shouting, "This is the respect due to Giaours."

He was thus paraded through the streets and market of Killis as far as the Government House, being the object of every kind of insult from the crowd.

The writers state that Chakir Osman has been imprisoned, but that his companions are at large.

I will take the first suitable opportunity of speaking to the Vali unofficially about the aggressive behaviour of the Moslem population at Killis.

I have, &c.

(Signed) HENRY D. BARNHAM.

F. O. 424/183, p. 398, No. 251/1

Inclosure 2 in No. 100

Consul Barnham to Sir P. Currie.

Confidential.

Sir,   ALEXANDRETTA, *August 15, 1895.*

I HAVE the honour to report that, being here for a few days on the business of the Consulate, I yesterday received a visit from the chief Armenian priest of this town, who handed me a Petition, the substance of which he begged me to bring to your Excellency's notice.

On the 3rd instant the exiled priests Stepan and Kevork returned to Beilan, and he having been charged by the Patriarchate with the affairs of the Armenian Church in Beilan during their absence, proceeded to meet and welcome them, accompanied by their relatives and friends, and by the school children. As they entered Beilan a crowd of Turkish boys collected and stoned them, and several of the children and some women were badly hurt. The boys kept shouting out the words, "Iradé vardur Giaiourlari Kirajaiz" ("It is the Sultan's order, we will smash the Giaours"), accompanied by curses upon the Armenians and their religion.

When the Government was informed of the occurrence, police were sent, and some of the stone-throwers arrested, but they were released two hours later.

The Vali was informed by telegraph, and he sent strict orders to the Kaïmakam to punish the offenders, but the latter replied by sending a mazbata, signed by the members of the Council of Administration, stating that the facts had been exaggerated, and that the public peace had not been disturbed. An Armenian member of the Council, who can neither read not write, but who had been forced to affix his seal to the mazbata, without having knowledge of its contents, sent in his resignation the following day.

The Petition next refers to certain outrageous acts committed by Nouri Effendi, the Mufti of Beilan, who burnt down the hedge surrounding his neighbour's vineyard (an Armenian), and made use of the following language in the market-place at Beilan, addressed to an Armenian named Avidis, "As for you Giaours, please God, I will crush the leaders among you before long."

I have tested the truth of these statements, and believe them to be correct. It is evident that if young Turkish lads make use of the language quoted they must have learnt it from their parents, and, if so, there can be no doubt that the Turks at Beilan are brooding over this Armenian question, and mean mischief. I have within the last week reported to your Excellency similar incidents at Antioch, Killis, and Beilan, and there can be no question that the situation throughout the vilayet is very serious.

The American Vice-Consul writes that troubles have occurred at Zeitoun, but he has not been able to ascertain of what nature.

In my report of the 9th instant I have expressed my belief that an Armenian nsurrection would probably occur at Suedia, but I think I have understated the matter, and that there will also be outbreaks in other parts of the vilayet. I understand this from the language of the priest who presented the Petition above referred to. It appears to be the intention of the revolutionary leaders to give the signal for insurrection, should the reforms sanctioned by the Sultan fall short of their demands. But, in the meantime, with such a state of feeling as is shown by the Turks, outbreaks will probably occur before the reforms are promulgated.

Moreover, the Macedonian question may precipitate an outbreak. The Armenians are watching the course of events in Macedonia with great anxiety, fearing lest that question should assume such proportions as to absorb the attention of the Powers, and cause them to neglect their interests, or give them a second place.

I have, &c.

(Signed) HENRY D. BARNHAM.

F. O. 424/183, pp. 398-399, No. 251/2

No. 101

Sir P. Currie to the Marquess of Salisbury.

No. 553. CONSTANTINOPLE, *August 29, 1895.*

My Lord, *(Received September 2.)*

I HAVE the honour to forward to your Lordship herewith copy of a despatch which I have received from her Majesty's Consul at Trebizond, reporting outrages on Armenians at Ketcheyourd.

I have, &c.

(Signed) PHILIP CURRIE.

F. O. 424/183, p. 399, No. 252

Inclosure in No. 101

Consul Longworth to Sir P. Currie.

Sir, TREBIZOND, *August 19, 1895.*

THE following is an instance of misgovernment, as reported by Dr. Jewett:-

"At Ketcheyourd, or near there, district of Zara, two Kurds had been killed. The Kaïmakam of Zara sent, 30th July, a policeman and four brigands to the village. They searched and plundered the village, arrested and terribly maltreated twenty Armenians.

"'To escape further outrage, the rest of the inhabitants (Armenians) came with their wives and their children to Sivas. They were driven off, however, by the police, and sent back to their village."

I have, &c.

(Signed) H. Z. LONGWORTH

F. O. 424/183, p. 399, No. 252/1

No. 102

Sir P. Currie to the Marquess of Salisbury.

No. 389.   CONSTANTINOPLE, *August 29, 1895, 10.40 a.m*
Telegraphic.   *(Received August 29.)*

THE facts of the incident near Erzinghian are correctly stated in Reuter's telegram.

I have received the following telegram from Her Majesty's Consul at Erzeroum on the subject:-

"The Armenian Archbishop at Erzeroum has received by special messenger letters signed by the Episcopal Vicar, the Protestant preacher, and the members of the Armenian Council of Erzinghian. These letters state that about the 12th August some unknown brigands attacked and robbed a Turkish Lieutenant-Colonel near Kemakh, and killed a sergeant of the escort. The Turkish authorities declare that the crime was committed by Armenians, and the Marshal Zeki Pasha has dispatched a large body of soldiers in pursuit. These soldiers are reported to be plundering villages and monasteries, and committing all kinds of outrages. Several arrests have been made among the Armenians of Erzinghian. The signatories recall the horrors of the Sasun massacres, and pray for protection against the local authorities and the soldiers. I consider that the Erzinghian Armenians, who are completely cowed, would not have dared to make such an appeal except under extreme pressure, and the matter must therefore be serious."

I made representations to the Porte on the 26th, as also did my French and Russian colleagues, and am now awaiting their answer.

F. O. 424/183, p. 261, No. 231

No. 103

Sir P. Currie to the Marquess of Salisbury.

No. 390.   CONSTANTINOPLE, *August 29, 1895, 7.55 p.m.*
Telegraphic.   *(Received August 29.)*

THE Sublime Porte have received a telegram from their Ambassador at St.
Petersburgh stating that Prince Lobanoff informed him on the 27th instant that
Russia accepted England's proposal to appoint a Commission of Surveillance,
consisting of three Europeans and four Turks, under the Treaty of Berlin. Prince
Lobanoff had said this was the smallest concession which he could make to your
Lordship's demands, and that unless he did so England and Turkey would be left
alone face to face.

M. de Nélidow also tells me that the proposal of the Commission has been
accepted by Prince Lobanoff.

F. O. 424/183, p. 262, No. 232

No. 104

Sir P. Currie to the Marquess of Salisbury.

No. 393.   CONSTANTINOPLE, *August 29, 1895, 3.45 p.m.*
Telegraphic.   *(Received August 29.)*

WITH reference to my telegram of yesterday, I am informed by the Grand
Vizier that telegraphic orders have been sent to Erzinghian to the effect that the
Armenians arrested on account of the Kemakh incident are to be released.

F. O. 424/183, p. 263, No. 235
Turkey No. 6 (1896), p. 385, No. 499

No. 105

Sir P. Currie to the Marquess of Salisbury.

No. 556. Confidential.   THERAPIA, *August 29, 1895.*
My Lord,   *(Received September 2.)*

WITH reference to my telegram of the 24th August, the Minister for Foreign
Affairs informed the Dragomans of the three Embassies, on Saturday last, that
Marshal Shakir Pasha was to start on the following day, and his Excellency added
that he hoped that the good-will shown by the Turkish Government in taking this
step would give satisfaction to the Powers. The three Dragomans received this
communication without remark.

The Turkish newspapers have since announced the departure of Shakir Pasha. His Staff consists of Danish Bey, Head of the Consular Department at the Porte, who goes as his assistant; Ihsan Bey, Councillor of the Turkish Embassy at Tehran, and it is stated, two Aides-de-camp of the Sultan, together with several Secretaries and employés from the Palace Chancellerie.

Shakir Pasha is expected to proceed to Erzeroum, thence to Van, Bitlis, Mamouret-el-Aziz, and Diarbekir, and will spend the winter at Kharput, visiting Sivas in the spring.

I have, &c.

(Signed) PHILIP CURRIE.

F. O. 424/183, p. 400, No. 255
Turkey No. 1 (1896), p. 136, No. 155

No. 106

Sir P. Currie to the Marquess of Salisbury.

No. 554.   CONSTANTINOPLE, *August 29, 1895.*
My Lord,   *(Received September 2.)*

WITH reference to my despatch of the 7th August, I have the honour to forward to your Lordship herewith copy of a despatch which I have received from Her Majesty's Consul at Trebizond, reporting further on misgovernment at Marsovan.

I have, &c.

(Signed) PHILIP CURRIE.

F. O. 424/183, p. 399, No. 253

Inclosure in No. 106

Consul Longworth to Sir P. Currie.

Sir,   TREBIZOND, *August 19, 1895.*

ON the 30th ultimo I sent your Excellency copy of a letter on the state of affairs at Marsovan. I have now, in continuation, to give the following extract of a letter dated Sivas, the 14th instant:-

"It appears that the fire at Marsovan is not really believed by the officials to have been set by the Armenians. It may have been wholly accidental, and the 'Belidieh Reïs' has been thought responsible for it.

"The conduct of affairs at Marsovan has been very bad. Indiscriminate arrests, torture, and most inefficient measures have been used. Bekir Pasha came and stormed, threatened openly to make a second Sasun of Marsovan, and left again without accomplishing anything.

"The soldiers are generally obnoxious, telling the people that their days are numbered. About 100 remain in prison at Marsovan, eight are in chains, and about half are sick with the itch or some other disease."

I have, &c.

(Signed) H. Z. Longworth.

Turkey No. 6 (1896) p. 390, No. 506, 506/1
F. O. 424/183, p. 400, No. 253/1

No. 107

Sir P. Currie to the Marquess of Salisbury.

No. 555.   Therapia, *August 29, 1895.*
My Lord,   *(Received September 2.)*

I HAVE the honour to report that the Ministry of Justice state that a monk and three priests who were undergoing imprisonment at Van have now been summoned to Constantinople, and set at liberty after taking an oath of fidelity to the Sultan.

I have, &c.

(Signed) Philip Currie.

F. O. 424/183, p. 400, No. 254
Turkey No. 6 (1896) p. 391, No. 507

No. 108

Sir P. Currie to the Marquess of Salisbury.

No. 557.   Therapia, *August 29, 1895.*
My Lord,   *(Received September 9.)*

ON the strength of information received from Marsovan I recently made representations to the Grand Vizier respecting the cruelty inflicted on Armenians imprisoned there, on account of recent murders and supposed incendiarism, with the object of extorting confessions from them.

I also mentioned to his Highness the case of the only competent medical man in Marsovan, who has been ordered to leave that town for Amassia, though not charged with any offence.

Saïd Pasha promised to cause inquiries to be made in the matter.

I have, &c.

(Signed) PHILIP CURRIE.

F. O. 424/183, p. 412, No. 278
Turkey No. 6 (1896) p. 393, No. 513

No. 109

Sir P. Currie to the Marquess of Salisbury.

No. 391.   CONSTANTINOPLE, *August 30, 1895, 11.30 a.m.*
Telegraphic.   *(Received August 30.)*

IN the course of a confidential conversation which I have had with the Austrian Ambassador on the subject of the Armenian question, Baron de Calice gave me to understand that the action of the three Powers has throughout been unofficially supported by Austria, who will continue to act in this spirit; and that, while reserving the equal rights of all the Signatory Powers, nothing will be done to endanger the success of your Lordship's proposal of a Mixed Commission. The Austrian Government, which is anxious to assist Her Majesty's Government, would not, in the event of the future of the present proposal, be unfavourable to an International Commission of all the Treaty Powers under Article LXI of the Treaty of Berlin, should the three Powers see fit to suggest it.

F. O. 424/183, p. 262, No. 233

No. 110

Sir P. Currie to the Marquess of Salisbury.

No. 394.   CONSTANTINOPLE, *August 30, 1895, 3.45 p.m.*
Telegraphic.   *(Received August 30.)*

WITH reference to my telegram to your Lordship of the 23rd instant:-

I have made a further representation to the Grand Vizier respecting the cruelty of Captain Reshid Effendi towards the Christians upon receipt of a fresh telegram from Vice-Consul Hampson on the subject.

In consequence of my renewed representations, his Highness has caused a telegram to be sent dismissing that officer from his post.

F. O. 424/183, p. 263, No. 237
Turkey No. 1 (1895) Part I, p. 193, No. 257

No. 111

Sir F. Lascelles to the Marquess of Salisbury.

No. 83.   St. Petersburgh, *August 31, 1895.*
Telegraphic.   *(Received August 31.)*

WHEN Prince Lobanoff accepted your Lordship's proposal for the formation of a Committee of Surveillance, his Excellency imagined that this Committee was quite distinct from the Committee of Control proposed by the Ambassadors in their scheme of reform, and that the former superseded the latter. It appears that there is some uncertainty as to whether this is the case, and Prince Lobanoff has asked me if his view is accurate. I said that in order to make sure I would refer the question to your Lordship, but that I was under the impression that his Excellency was correct.

F. O. 424/183, p. 263, No. 238
Turkey No. 1 (1896), p. 135, No. 152

No. 112

Sir. P. Currie to the Marquess of Salisbury.

No. 396.   Constantinople, *September 1, 1895, 10.40 a.m.*
Telegraphic.   *(Received September 1.)*

THE following is the tenour of a verbal communication which Turkhan Pasha came yesterday evening to make to the three Embassies:-

The Turkish Commission of Control as proposed by the three Ambassadors would be accepted by the Sultan on the understanding that the Dragomans would restrict their communications with the Commission to the reforms adopted by the Porte.

The nomination or election of Mudirs from the local Notables, the institution of rural guards, and the appointment of Christians, in proportion to their numbers, to the Administration and Gendarmerie would also be accepted.

I said that a Commission with European members had now been demanded by the Powers.

The Minister for Foreign Affairs replied that a commission with European members was quite out of the question, and he urged that his proposals should be telegraphed to your Lordship.

I declined to do so unless the Foreign Minister put them in writing. This, without further instructions, he did not venture to do.

F. O. 424/183, p. 264, No. 239
Turkey No. 1 (1896) p. 136, No. 153

No. 113

The Marquess of Salisbury to Sir F. Lascelles.

No. 164.
Telegraphic.   FOREIGN OFFICE, *September 1, 1895.*
    I HAVE received your Excellency's telegram of the 31st ultimo.
    Prince Lobanoff is quite right in supposing that the Committee of Surveillance suggested by me is quite distinct from, and is intended to supersede, the Committee of Control suggested in the Scheme of Reforms presented by the Ambassadors.
    F. O. 424/183, p. 264, p. 241
    Turkey No 1 (1896), p. 136, No. 154

No. 114

Sir F. Lascelles to the Marquess of Salisbury.

No. 84.   ST. PETERSBURGH, *September 2, 1895.*
Telegraphic.   (*Received September 2.*)
    I HAVE been informed by Prince Lobanoff that he has received a telegram from M. de Nélidoff stating that the Porte, in order to evade your Lordship's proposal of a Committee of Surveillance, have consented to the Committee of Control, as suggested by the three Ambassadors, and to the five disputed points in the scheme of reforms. M. de Nélidoff considers that this new communication practically accepts with slight modifications the demands of the Ambassadors, and Prince Lobanoff hopes that, as it is most necessary that the question should be concluded as soon as possible, a settlement may shortly be arrived at.
    F. O. 424/183, p. 402, No. 257
    Turkey No 1 (1896), p. 138, No. 157

No. 115

Sir P. Currie to the Marquess of Salisbury.

No. 399.   CONSTANTINOPLE, *September 3, 1895, 11.55 a.m.*
Telegraphic.   (*Received September 3.*)
    I HAVE told Mr. Graves, in reply to his request for instructions as to the attitude he should adopt towards Shakir Pasha, that he should call upon the Pasha

when he arrives at Erzeroum, but that, if questioned, he should say that no instructions respecting his mission have been received by him.

Instructions of a similar nature are being sent by my colleagues.

F. O. 424/183, p. 402, No. 258

No. 116

Sir P. Currie to the Marquess of Salisbury.

No. 401.   CONSTANTINOPLE, *September 3, 1895, 8 p.m.*
Telegraphic.   *(Received September 3.)*

ON the strength of information received from Mr. Hallward that fifty-one Armenians were still in prison at Van, I made representations to the Grand Vizier, and his Highness has sent telegraphic orders to the Vali that all those detained for political offences should be at once released.

F. O. 424/183, p. 402, No. 259

No. 117

Sir P. Currie to the Marquess of Salisbury.

No. 562.   CONSTANTINOPLE, *September 3, 1895.*
My Lord,   *(Received September 9.)*

I HAVE the honour to forward to your Lordship herewith copy of a despatch which I have received from Her Majesty's Consul at Trebizond respecting the state of affairs in the inland districts of the Vilayet of Trebizond.

I have, &c.

(Signed) PHILIP CURRIE.

F. O. 424/183, p. 413, No. 280

Inclosure in No. 117

Consul Longworth to Sir P. Currie

Sir,   TREBIZOND, *August 27, 1895.*

THE following extracts from Dr. Jewett's letter of the 21st instant confirm more or less what has been told me at Trebizond respecting the extent of (1) the fire at Amassia, (2) the disturbance at Tamzara, and (3) the doings of an armed Armenian band near Erzinghian:—

"On last Saturday night an extensive fire occurred at Amassia, starting about midnight and lasting six hours. The following buildings were destroyed: 58 houses, 165 shops, 2 khans, 1 mosque, 1 medresseh, 1 tomb, 1 tekieh, 1 Turkish school, and 1 old unoccupied Government house; 31 of the houses were Mahommedan, 17 Armenian, and 10 Greek; 90 shops were Mahommedan, 62 Armenian, and 18 Greek. The origin of the fire is not known, but it is suspected that it was set by Armenians.

"Five or six days ago, at Tamzara, two hours from Karahissar, some Turks started a quarrel with some Armenian women in regard to the manufacture of wine. The Turks objected to the odour of the wine. Words and sticks were freely used, but no one was severely injured. Ten Turks were arrested.

"The Armenians seized the occasion to close their shops, and said they had no confidence in the Government to protect them.

"At Gurun an officer of police quarrelled with a shop-keeper, used violent language against the Armenians, and the Armenians say he drew his revolver and said it would be of no consequence if he killed a few Christians. The Armenians said they feared they would be attacked by the Turks, and they closed their shops. The officer is under arrest.

"At Derende also a quarrel occurred.

Between Karpoot and Erzinghian a Kaïmakam Director of a model farm was attacked by a band of sixty well-armed Armenians. The Armenians killed and wounded some of the Kaïmakam's escort and stole 300 liras. Probably you already know about it.

"It is said that a very grave affair occurred at Karpoot, but I do not know about it.

"At Manjuluk a quarrel of little consequence occurred between Turks and Armenians.

"It appears that the Armenians are trying to start trouble, but so far they have not succeeded very well."

I have, &c.

(Signed) H. Z. Longworth.

F. O. 424/183, p. 413, No. 280/1

No. 118

Sir P. Currie to the Marquess of Salisbury.

No. 567.   CONSTANTINOPLE, *September 3, 1895.*
My Lord,   *(Received September 9.)*
    I HAVE the honour to forward to your Lordship herewith a copy of a despatch which I have received from Her Majesty's Consul at Erzeroum, respecting alleged arrests and ill-treatment of Armenians at Keghi.
    Your Lordship will observe that this information is gleaned from Armenian sources only.
                                                    I have, &c.
                                            (Signed) PHILIP CURRIE.

F. O. 424/183, p. 417, No. 284

Inclosure in No. 118

Consul Graves to Sir P. Currie.

Sir,   ERZEROUM, *August 23, 1895.*
    I HAVE the honour to report that the Armenian Archbishop of Erzeroum has received a letter and telegrams from his Vicar in Keghi, a caza lying to the south-west of Erzeroum, complaining of the ill-treatment of the Armenians there by the local authorities. It appears that an unsigned letter fell into the hands of the authorities, which contained congratulations upon the supposed acceptance by the Porte of the scheme of reforms and upon the success of the recent appeal of the Catholicos Khirmian to the Emperor of Russia.
    On the strength of this, thirteen Armenians of Keghi were arrested within the last few days, and an inquiry was held by the Cadi, the Juge d'Instruction, Feïzullah Bey and Eyoub Bey, the second Clerk of the Court. It is said that the prisoners have been severely beaten and otherwise ill-used by their orders, for the purpose of forcing them to make statements incriminating the Vicar, who has been active in drawing official attention to local abuses, as reported in my despatch of the 1st April, 1895.
    The Vicar, whose name is Aristakes Vartebet, was then summoned before the Kaïmakam and Medjles and taxed with seditious conduct, which he strenuously denied, and complained of the cruel treatment of the prisoners, for which he states the Cadi assumed all the responsibility in full council, saying that the men were beaten by his express orders. He adds that at the present moment every kind of abuse and exaction is being committed in the collection of Government taxes.
    I am not in possession of any independent information at present confirming

the Vicar's statements, but all the news which reached me from Armenian sources is to the effect that the present condition of the Christians in the Keghi Caza is most deplorable.

I have, &c.

(Signed) R. W. GRAVES.

F. O. 424/183, pp. 417-418, No. 284/1

No. 119

Sir P. Currie to the Marquess of Salisbury.

No. 568.   THERAPIA, *September 3, 1895.*
My Lord,   *(Received September 9.)*
    I HAVE the honour to transmit herewith copy of a despatch from Her Majesty's Consul at Erzeroum, inclosing an extract from a letter from Mr. Boyajian respecting Armenian agitation in Kharput. I would wish to call your Lordship's attention to Mr. Graves' statements as to the plans of the Hindchag Society, of which I have received confirmation from various quarters.

I have, &c.

(Signed) PHILIP CURRIE.

F. O. 424/183, p. 418, No. 285

Inclosure 1 in No. 119

Consul Graves to Sir P. Currie.

Sir,   ERZEROUM, *August 20, 1895.*
    I HAVE the honour to transmit herewith to your Excellency an extract from a private letter which I have received from the Acting British Vice-Consul at Kharput, dated the 5th August, reporting the appearance in that place of several Armenian agitators of the Hindchag Society, who are inciting the Armenians of the town and neighbouring villages to sedition and violence.

    In Erzeroum and Van, with the exception of several armed bands which crossed the Russian frontier during the month of June, the party of action among the Armenians have kept very quiet of late, having been persuaded that a contrary course would only prejudice the Armenian cause, and impede diplomatic action for the introduction of reforms. It is, however, more than probable that, if disappointed in their expectations, they will renew their agitation with increased violence, and endeavour to provoke reprisals on a scale certain to involve European intervention.

I have, &c.

(Signed) R. W. GRAVES.

F. O. 424/183, p. 418, No. 285/1

Inclosure 2 in No. 119

Extract from a private Letter, Kharput, August 5, 1895.

IT appears that there are now in this place several Armenians belonging to the Hindchagian Society, who are trying to organize revolutionary Committees here and in the villages, and, as I understand, they have in a measure succeeded. They are inciting the people to violent action; since the liberation of the political prisoners this party has become bolder, and they are making foolish demonstrations. They say they will attack the prison and liberate the six men still imprisoned by force. Twice they went down to Mezré in procession in considerable numbers, and treated their Bishop very badly when he advised them to disperse and not engage in so rash an undertaking. They are scattering papers here and there, threatening the life of those whom they suspect of opposing them. Should they continue this reckless course, I am afraid of a serious result. The Moslems, I hear, have already sent a telegram to the Palace complaining of the attitude of the Armenians. That their action will do much harm is very evident; but it appears that they are not inclined in any way to listen to advice, unless force is used by the Government.

I have also learned that recently the Dersim Kurds attacked two Armenian villages at Chemish Gezek, and carried off all that the poor villagers possessed.

F. O. 424/183, p. 418, No. 285/2

No. 120

Sir P. Currie to the Marquess of Salisbury.

No. 402.
Telegraphic.

CONSTANTINOPLE, *September 3, 1895, 8 p.m.*

(Received September 3.)

KEMAKH incident.

With reference to my telegrams of the 29th ultimo respectively, the Turkish Government is sending a Circular note giving their version of the incident.

According to it some Armenian brigands having attacked a Turkish Colonel, a band consisting of only 120 men were sent in pursuit of them. The brigands were captured, but no villages or convents were pillaged, nor were any other outrages committed by the troops.

F. O. 424/183, p. 402, No. 260
Turkey No. 6 (1896), p. 391, No. 509

No. 121

Sir P. Currie to the Marquess of Salisbury.

No. 564.   CONSTANTINOPLE, *September 3, 1895.*
My Lord,   *(Received September 9.)*

I HAVE the honour to forward to your Lordship herewith copy of a despatch which I have received from Her Majesty's Vice-Consul at Moush respecting abuses in tax collection in Moush.

I have, &c.

(Signed) PHILIP CURRIE.

F. O. 424/183, p. 414, No. 281.

Inclosure in No. 121

Vice-Consul Hampson to Consul Graves.

Sir,

I REGRET to have to state that the reports of the brutal manner in which the taxes are being collected in the villages throughout this district grow worse and worse. The zaptiehs, who demand the whole taxes for the year up to March next, ill-treat the inhabitants—men, women and children, sell all their property at absurd prices, and destroy what is unsaleable.

At Awran, a village in the Moush Plain, they forcibly entered the houses at night, dragged the naked women from their beds and threw them into a stream. They tied ropes round the men's necks and led them to the water and forced them to drink. In short, the tax-collecting is everywhere conducted in a shameful manner. The worst offender appears to be a certain Reshid Effendi, Lieutenant of Police.

At Agpik, a Sasun village, which was robbed but not burnt last year, the same thing has been going on.

I have called the Mutessarif's attention to these facts, but fear that under the present system little improvement can be hoped for.

I have, &c.

(Signed) C. S. HAMPSON.

F. O. 424/183, p. 414, No. 281/1
Turkey. No. 1 (1895), Part I, p. 196, No. 264, 264/1

No. 122

Sir P. Currie to the Marquess of Salisbury.

No. 569.   THERAPIA, *September 3, 1895.*
My Lord,   *(Received September 9.)*
    I HAVE the honour to transmit to your Lordship herewith copy of a despatch which I have received from Her Majesty's Consul at Erzeroum, inclosing a despatch from Her Majesty's Vice-Consul at Moush on the subject of the relief operations in Sassoon. I would draw your Lordship's favourable attention to the great services which Dr. Reynolds is rendering without regard for his own personal interests.
    I have expressed to Mr. Hampson my approval of the steps he has taken to forward the work of relief in Sassoon.
                                                           I have, &c.
                                                           (Signed) PHILIP CURRIE.

F. O. 424/183, p. 419, No. 286
Turkey No. 1 (1895) Part I, p. 197, No. 265, 265/1, 265/2

Inclosure 1 in No. 122

Consul Graves to Sir P. Currie.

Sir,   ERZEROUM, *August 19, 1895.*
    I HAVE the honour to transmit herewith to your Excellency copy of a despatch which I have received from Her Majesty's Vice-Consul at Moush on the subject of the relief operations in Sassoon. Before Mr. Hampson's arrival the work of relief seems to have been brought almost to a standstill by the obstructive policy of the local authorities, but his energy has already overcome some of the difficulties, especially in the matter of providing shelter for the survivors of last year's massacre in the Kavar villages at least.
    I would venture to suggest that the dismissal of the Mutessarifs of Moush and Guendj, and their replacement by officials not identified in any way as they have been with the policy of extermination of the Sassoonlis, are steps which should have been taken months ago if the Sublime Porte had been really anxious to dissociate itself from such a policy.
                                                           I have, &c.
                                                           (Signed) R. W. GRAVES.

F. O. 424/183, p. 419, No. 286/1

Inclosure 2 in No. 122

Vice-Consul Hampson to Consul Graves.

Sir,   MOUSH, *August 5, 1895.*

I HAVE the honour to report that, in obedience to his Excellency Sir P. Currie's telegraphic instructions of the 29th ultimo, I left Moush on the 1st August for Sassoon, to superintend in person the distribution of relief. Previous to my departure the Mutessarif informed me that orders had been received from the Grand Vizier that the Turkish Relief Commission were to consult and work with me in the distribution.

I proceeded directly to Semal. On entering the pretty and fertile Sasson valley the pitiable state of things became at once evident; not a house is standing throughout the valley, which includes Semal, Shenik, and Guelieguesan. Even the houses scattered on the hill-sides at considerable distances from the actual villages had been hunted out and burned. A few fields are in cultivation with the grain sown late when the first relief arrived; but though the crops look well, they are, of course, very few, and even those are in many cases so backward that it is doubtful if they will ripen. At the very best these crops will not suffice to support the villages for more than two months. An ox or a cow is a very rare sight, and not a sheep or a hen is to be seen, though the mountains are crowded with flocks belonging to the nomad Kurds, many of them stolen from the villages last year.

On arriving at Semal I found the missionaires settled there distributing rations to the starving villagers who came to them from all sides; while Dr. Reynolds has established a small hospital in huts of branches put up among the ruins, and is treating a considerable number of patients both for old wounds and for small-pox (which is rife) and other diseases. There was not a sign of any commencement of building, and on inquiring the reason I was told that the Turkish Commissioners had forbidden the villagers to touch their houses. I immediately set the people of Semal to work repairing some of the walls, and, when the Turkish Commissioners came to see me that evening, talked very seriously to them at the way in which they had neglected their duties, and insisted that they should at once take steps to bring the timber for roofing purposes, which the Mutessarif had assured me I should find ready, but of which there was no sign.

Next day (2nd August) I went over to Shenik, where I found exactly the same condition of things. Having set people to work on their walls I rode about one hour further to a hill above Guelieguesan, as I had heard that nomad Kurds were occupying that village, having turned out the Christian inhabitants. I found this statement to be true, and saw myself the Kurds and their flocks swarming in the village and hurring away when they saw us looking at them from above. On the way within half-hour from Shenik I had seen the tents of the nomads on the mountains, the may belonging to the village cut and carried off by the Kurds, and the flocks of the latter feeding on the pastures of the Armenians.

On returning to Semal that evening I spoke very strongly to the Commissioners on the subject, pointing out what a disgraceful thing it was that the nomad Kurds should be allowed to behave thus close to the Commission and the zaptiehs in attendance on them. Next day, in my absence, Hajji Tahil (referred to in previous despatches as having been sent to keep the Kurds in order) and the Major in command of the company stationed between here and Sassoon came down from the mountains to see me. The Commissioners repeated to them my observations, and they at once started off to inquire into the matter, but I have not yet heard with that result.

On Saturday, the 3rd August, I went to Gueleiguesan. It is hard to realize that this beautiful village, in a rich valley, high among the mountains, shaded by large walnut trees, was the scene last year of an awful massacre, but the burned houses, the death-pits, the human bones still to be found, and the grave of the priest Ohannes are there as witnesses. Here also I at once set the people to work building.

Yesterday I returned to Moush, and start again to-morrow viâ Semal, Aliantsik, and Guelieguesan for Talori, the visit of which will occupy about a week.

From what I have seen so far, it is evident that next to nothing has been done in the way of permanent relief, or to enable the villagers to remain in their villages this winter. The missionaries have done what they were allowed to do in the way of keeping the people alive and aiding the sick; but this is not enough. The first thing to be done is undoubtedly to secure necessary shelter for the villagers before bad weather commences, i.e., within the next two months. A certain number of professional masons are absolutely necessary to set things going in each village, and these the Mutessarif has now promised to allow to go up.

After shelter has been secured, it will be necessary to consider how the people are to be supported for at least four months of the winter, and also how to supply them with such cattle, sheep, &c., as are absolutely necessary for their existence. On these points I have requested the missionaries to draw up detailed reports for each village in Sassoon which I hope to be able to forward next week, and the following week to send a similar report for the Talori district, where I hear things are very bad, and the Kurds returning to their old practices.

In any case, it is quite evident that large sums of money will be needed if any effective relief is to be granted, and I would appeal strongly for prompt help. So far the funds collected from Armenian sources are unavailable owing to the hostility of the authorities.

It is right that I should mention what serious sacrifices Dr. Reynolds is making in order to assist the relief work. His practice in Van is large and profitable, and this he is totally abandoning.

I telegraphed the substance of the proceding to Her Majesty's Embassy last night.

(Signed) C. S. HAMPSON.

F. O. 424/183, pp. 419-420, No. 286/2
Turkey No. 1 (1895) Part I, p. 198, No. 265/2

No. 123

Sir P. Currie to the Marquess of Salisbury.

No. 403.   CONSTANTINOPLE, *September 4, 1895, 11.20 a.m.*
Telegraphic.   *(Received September 4.)*

I HAD already reported to your Lordship in my telegram No. 396 of the 1st instant the communication referred to by Prince Lobanoff in his conversation as repeated to me in your Lordship's telegram No. 150 of yesterday.

I cannot agree in regarding it as a complete acceptance of the demands of the three Ambassadors. It does not provide for a Christian Assistant to the High Commissioner, and leaves the latter without any definite instructions, and entirely under Palace control. It restricts the scope of the permanent Commission, and omit all mention of the following points:-

Control over appointments of Valis; reform of prisons; provisions for protection of Armenians outside the six vilayets; retention of part of the revenues for local purposes; reform of the Tribunals.

The Grand Vizier, however, informs me that the Sultan has now ordered him to take the matter in hand, and I consider that, if your Lordship would authorize me to press for a complete acceptance of the original reform of proposals, I should probably, in return for an abandonment of the proposed Mixed Commission, be able to obtain some further concessions from His Imperial Majesty. My colleagues are not favourable to the Mixed Commission. They think that only force would induce the Sultan to accept it, and that if sent to the provinces the European Commissioners would have no power over their Turkish colleagues, who would refer every demand to Constantinople, where it would have to be fought out by the Embassies.

Whatever reforms are adopted, we ought, I think, to insist on their being embodied in a formal Decree, and, if they are not to be a dead letter, we should at once appoint military Vice-Consuls.

It would be difficult for the Russians to oppose any measures, short of an attack on the Dardanelles, which we might take to force the Sultan to improve the condition of the Armenians. At the same time, there can be no doubt that the Russians do not like our interference in the Armenian question, and the influence we have acquired over the Christian population in Asia Minor, which looks exclusively to England for help.

F. O. 424/183, pp. 403-404, No. 263

No. 124

Sir P. Currie to the Marquess of Salisbury.

No. 572. Confidential.   THERAPIA, *September 4, 1895.*
My Lord,   *(Received September 9.)*
    THE Armenian Patriarch sent me a message a few days ago pointing out the dangers and sufferings to which the Armenian population in the Asiatic provinces would be exposed during the coming winter if the measures of reform proposed by the Powers were not shortly carried out.

    I suggested that his Beatitude should address a confidential letter embodying his views to the three Ambassadors.

    I have now the honour to inclose a copy of a communication on the subject which I have received from his Beatitude.

I have, &c.

(Signed) PHILIP CURRIE.

P.S.—A similar letter has been addressed to the Russian and French Ambassadors.

P. C.

F. O. 424/183, p. 421, No. 287

Inclosure in No. 124

The Armenian Patriarch to Sir P. Currie.

Confidentielle.
M. l'Ambassadeur,   CONSTANTINOPLE, *le 22 Août (3 Septembre), 1895.*
    LES informations qui affluent des provinces de la Turquie habitées par les Arméniens établissent l'aggravation croissante de l'état des choses. En dépit des assurances des communiqués officiels, meurtres, déprédations, enlèvements de femmes et d'enfants, tortures dan les prisons, conversions par force, profanations des choses saintes, exactions inouïes des gendarmes collecteurs et des fermiers continuent à frapper la population Arménienne. Par endroits, des attaques ont lieu contre les Chrétiens de la part de la populace, et des menaces de massacre général grondent.

    La compassion des nations et des États Chrétiens qui ont provoquée les souffrances de la population Arménienne, tourne, semble-t-il, en une cause de vengeances et de persécutions aussi longtemps que tarde la mise en exécution des mesures destinées à améliorer le déplorable État dénoncé. La population dépouillée des moyens de se défendre et abandonnée à son sort, en face d'une populace surexcitée, armée et certaine de la protection des fonctionnaires, implore de secours tout d'une voix.

En présence de ces appels désespérés j'ose, M. l'Ambassadeur, encore une fois, solliciter votre haute et bienveillante attention sur une situation aiguë, grosse de dangers, et vous demander la grâce d'exposer à la généreuse et vaillante Puissance que vous représentez la gravité de cette situation. C'est dire combien est urgente la nécessité, avant que le mal ne soit devenu irrémédiable et que l'hiver, en interrompant complétement les communications des provinces Arméniennes avec le dehors, ne vienne y assurer un libre champ à tous les méfaits, d'aviser aux moyens propres à établir sur des bases définitives l'ordre, la tranquillite dans les pays, et à mettre, une fois pour toutes, un terme aux persécutions.

En vous confiant au soin du Tout-Puissant, j'ai, &c.

Le Patriarche des Arméniens de Turquie,
(Signé) Madtéos.

F. O. 424/183, p. 421, No. 287/1

No. 125

Sir P. Currie to the Marquess of Salisbury.

No. 404.   Constantinople, *September 4, 1895, 11.30 a.m.*
Telegraphic.   *(Received September 4.)*

IT is reported that Alai Bey, who left Bitlis a fortnight ago for Sasun in command of a body of eighty soldiers in order to restrain the Kurds, had a fight with them near Psank and killed twelve or thirteen of them.

F. O. 424/183, p. 404, No. 264

No. 126

Sir P. Currie to the Marquess of Salisbury.

No. 405.   Constantinople, *September 4, 1895, 11.30 a.m.*
Telegraphic.   *(Received September 4.)*

WITH reference to my telegram of the 30th ultimo, No. 394:-

The Acting Vali has informed Her Majesty's Vice-Consul at Moush that the Turkish Government has ordered the dismissal of the five officials named.

F. O. 424/183, p. 404, No. 265

No. 127

The Marquess of Salisbury to Sir F. Lascelles.

No. 280. Confidential.

Sir,   FOREIGN OFFICE, *September 4, 1895.*

I HAVE received your Excellency's despatch No. 209, Confidential, of the 28th ultimo, recording your conversation on that day with Prince Lobanoff on the subject of Armenian reforms.

I notice that in alluding to the reorganization of the Gendarmerie, the Prince said that he gathered from the telegrams received from the Russian Chargé d'Affaires in London that I shared his views as to the danger of enrolling Mussulmans and Christians, either together or in separate bands.

There must have been some misapprehension on M. Kroupensky's part in regard to this point. I have not expressed to him any opinion on the question of mixture of Mussulman and Christian gendarmes, and I should be obliged if your Excellency would take an opportunity of explaining this to Prince Lobanoff.

I am, &c.

(Signed) SALISBURY.

F. O. 424/183, p. 404, No. 266

No. 128

Memorandum communicated by Rustem Pasha, September 4, 1895.

DIX-SEPT brigands Arméniens déguisés ayant attaqué près de Kemakh le Lieutenant-Colonel Réchid Bey, ont tué un seirgent, blessé un autre individu de sa suite, et volé £T.300 et quelques effets. Deux détachements de soixante hommes furent envoyés à leur poursuite; et l'un d'eux ayant atteint les bandits du côté de Tchanlivank une fusillade s'ensuivit pendant laquelle quatre de ces derniers furent tués, un blessé, et trois arrêtés vivants. Les troupes ont eu de leur côté deux officiers et trois soldats blessés légèrement. De l'aveu même des brigands capturés, sur lesquels on a retrouvé l'argent et les effets, leur bande avait été formée dans le but de susciter des troubles.

Les coupables ont été déférés aux Tribunaux et la justice suivra son cours.

Il est absolument inexact que quatre bataillons aient été dépêchés à la poursuite des malandrins. Les deux détachements se composaient seulement de soixante hommes. La version que les troupes Impériales avaient attaqué des villages et couvents et commis des actes de violences est dénué de tout fondement.

CONSTANTINOPLE, *le 3 Septembre, 1895.*

Translation.

SEVENTEEN Armenian brigands in disguise attacked Lieutenant-Colonel Réchid Bey near Kemakh, killed a sergeant, wounded another member of his suite, and stole £T.300, and some effects. Two detachments of sixty men were dispatched in pursuit, one of which overtook the bandits in the direction of Tchanlivank, and a skirmish took place, in which four of the latter were killed, one wounded, and three captured. On the side of the troops, two officers and three soldiers were slightly wounded. The captured brigands, on whom was found the money and the property stolen, themselves admitted that their band was formed with the object of creating disturbances.

The offenders were handed over to the Tribunals, and justice will take its course.

It is absolutely untrue that four batallions were sent in pursuit of the miscreants. The two detachments only consisted of sixty men. There is no foundation for the statement that the Imperial troops attacked villages and convents, and committed acts of violence.

CONSTANTINOPLE, *September 3, 1895.*

F. O. 424/183, p. 403, No. 261

Turkey No. 6 (1896) p. 392, No. 510

No. 129

Prince Lobanoff to M. Kroupensky.

(Communicated to Foreign Office, September 4.)

LA Porte consent, pour éviter la Commission de Surveillance proposée par Lord Salisbury, à admettre les communications directes des Drogmans avec la Commission de Contrôle recommandée dans le projet des Ambassadeurs et céde sur la presque totalité de nos demandes avec des modifications relativement peu importantes. Nous croyons qu'on pourrait être satisfait de ce résultat pour terminer l'affaire Arménienne, mais aimerions prélablement connaître l'opinion du Cabinet Britannique.

Le 4 Septembre, 1895.

Translation.

IN order to avoid the Commission of Supervision proposed by Lord Salisbury, the Porte agrees to allow direct communications between the Dragomans and the Commission of Control recommended in the Ambassadors' scheme, and gives way to nearly all our demands, with certain comparatively unimportant modifications.

We think that we may be satisfied with this in order to close the Armenian question, but should be glad to know first what is the opinion of the British Cabinet.

September 4, 1895.
F. O. 424/183, p. 403, No. 262
Turkey No. 1 (1896), p. 138, No. 159

No. 130

Sir P. Currie to the Marquess of Salisbury.

No. 573.   THERAPIA, *September 5, 1895.*
My Lord,   *(Received September 9.)*
    I HAVE the honour to transmit to your Lordship herewith a copy of a Memorandum drawn up by M. Marinitch, giving the Turkish version of the state of affairs in the Sasun and Talori villages, as communicated to him by the Minister for Foreign Affairs, on the authority of the Vali of Bitlis.

I have, &c.

(Signed) PHILIP CURRIE.

F. O. 424/183, p. 422, No. 288

Inclosure in No. 130

Memorandum by M. Marinitch.

THE Sublime Porte has communicated to me the following information reported by the Acting Vali of Bitlis:-

"The fate of the populations of Sasun and Talori has been somewhat ameliorated by the distribution of relief to them. It is not correct that these people had to feed themselves only with vegetables, as, up to this moment, there has been distributed to them through the Commission sitting at Moush, the amount of 372,000 piastres.

"The Commission at Guendj has begun to distribute relief also.

"It is equally incorrect that the Kurds have stolen the cattle distributed to these inhabitants, on the contrary, it is the Mousin Oghlons, Armenians of the village of Shenik, who have carried away from the tribe of the village of Vezneder three sheep, one ox, and one cow, and have stolen the horse and the ox belonging to a Kurd of the Cadezon tribe.

"This fact has been admitted by the Armenians, Agop and Kerpo and his companions of Guéliégugan and of Ghelialian. The stolen cattle have been restored to their owners by the above-mentioned Commission. To re-establish good order and public tranquillity, a regiment of Imperial troops and an Ulema called Hadji Talib Effendi, were sent to the spot before the return of the Kurds from their pasturages. A close watch is being kept everywhere.

"Among the seven wards of Talori, three have agreed to accept the help which is being distributed, and four have stated that they could not accept it."

(Signed) H. Marinitch.

September 3, 1895.
F. O. 424/183, p. 422, No. 228/1

No. 131

Sir P. Currie to the Marquess of Salisbury.

No. 574.   Therapia, *September 5, 1895.*
My Lord,   *(Received September 9.)*

WITH reference to my despatch No. 552 of the 29th ultimo, reporting outrages committed on Armenians at Killis and Beilan, I have the honour to inform your Lordship that I instructed Mr. Marinitch to call the serious attention of the Minister for Foreign Affairs to the threatening attitude of the Moslem population of Antioch, Killis, and Beilan, as represented in the two reports from Her Majesty's Consul at Aleppo inclosed in my above-mentioned despatch.

Tourkhan Pasha professed his unwillingness to believe that such language as that reported by Mr. Barnham could have been made use of by the Mahommedan population, but promised to lay the matter before the Grand Vizier for his Highness' consideration.

I have, &c.

(Signed) Philip Currie.

F. O. 424/183, p. 422, No. 289

No. 132

Sir P. Currie to the Marquess of Salisbury.

No. 409.   Constantinople, *September 6, 1895, 7.45 p.m.*
Telegraphic.   *(Received September 6.)*

THE French Vice-Consul at Sivas has communicated to the French Ambassador the following report of excesses committed by Armenians in that district:-

"The Judge of Karahissar, who, in consequence of complaints made against him by the Armenians, had been removed by the Vali from his post, was proceeding to Sivas escorted by three zaptiehs, when a band of Armenians fell on him, wounded the escort, carried the Judge off to the mountains, where he was tortured and his body cut to pieces. The authorities thereupon sent a Captain and nine soldiers against the Armenians, but the Captain was dangerously wounded and six soldiers killed. They have now sent a force of twenty-eight Circassians to deal with them.

"There is a well-armed band of Armenians, about thirty or forty strong, in the environs of Sivas, and a guard conveying money belonging to the Régie has been robbed by Armenians.

"There is much excitement among the Mussulman population."

This and the Kemakh incident confirm the statement heard on many sides that the Armenian Revolutionary Committee intend to force on a crisis if the reforms are delayed.

F. O. 424/183, p. 405, No. 268

No. 133

The Marquess of Salisbury to Sir P. Currie.

No. 151.
Telegraphic.   FOREIGN OFFICE, *September 6, 1895.*

I HAVE received your Excellency's despatch No. 403 of the 4th instant, relative to Armenian reforms.

If the reforms demanded by the Ambassadors are offered to you in full by the Porte in writing, or if the only omissions made are, in your opinion, unimportant, I should feel bound, in view of what passed in the spring, to accept the offer; but I have no confidence in any Commission consisting entirely of Turkish subjects; and I am afraid that the work would have to be recommenced in a few years.

I concur in your view that the concessions made by the Turkish Government should be embodied in a formal Decree, and that we should insist on the appointment of military Vice-Consuls.

F. O. 424/183, p. 405, No. 269

No. 134

The Marquess of Salisbury to Sir P. Currie.

No. 311.
Sir,   FOREIGN OFFICE, *September 6, 1895.*

I HAVE received your Excellency's despatch No. 544 of the 27th ultimo, forwarding despatches from Her Majesty's Consul at Erzeroum and the British Delegate to the Sasun Commission, and the joint Report drawn up by Mr. Shipley and his colleagues on the proceedings of the Commission.

I have much pleasure in requesting you to express to Mr. Shipley my satisfaction at the manner in which he has performed his duties, and my entire approval of his proceedings.

I am, &c.

(Signed) SALISBURY.

F. O. 424/183, p. 405, No. 270

No. 135

The Sublime Porte to Rustem Pasha.

CONSTANTINOPLE, *le 6 Septembre, 1895.*

(Communicated by Rustem Pasha, September 9.)

DANS le cas où il se trouverait parmi les officiers de gendarmerie, les agents de police, et les gardes champêtres Chrétiens des individus qui, se laissant circonvenir par les manœuvres et les intrigues des Comités Arméniens, manqueraient à leurs devoirs de fidélité, et, abusant de leur qualité, se porteraient, contrairement aux sentiments d'humanité, à des insultes et à des vexations à l'égard des Musulmans, ou qui prêteraient une aide matérielle ou morale aux agitateurs, le Gouvernement Impérial, sans préjudice de son droit d'avoir recours à l'action publique, se réserve, en cas de récidive et s'il le juge nécessaire, d'en aviser les trois Puissances et de se concerter à cet égard officieusement avec leurs Ambassadeurs.

Translation.

CONSTANTINOPLE, *September 6, 1895.*

IF there are, among the Christian officers of gendarmerie, police agents, or rural policemen, any persons who, being led away by the manœuvres and intrigues of the Armenian Committees, fail in their duty, and, abusing their powers in a spirit of inhumanity, insult or persecute Mussulmans, or who give material or moral assistance to agitators, the Imperial Government, without prejudice to its right to take public action, reserves the right, in case the offence is repeated, and if it considers it necessary, to inform the three Powers, and to concert with their Ambassadors unofficially on the subject.

F. O. 424/183, p. 425, No. 294
Turkey No. 1 (1896), p. 141, No. 165

No. 136

The Sublime Porte to Rustem Pasha.

CONSTANTINOPLE, *le 6 Septembre, 1895.*

(Communicated by Rustem Pasha, September 9.)

VOTRE Excellence sait qu'à la suite du Mémorandum et du projet de réformes qui nous avaient été présentés par les trois Ambassadeurs, nous leur avions remis, de notre côté, un contre-projet élaboré par la Commission Ministérielle et sanctionné par Iradé Impérial. Copie de ce contre-projet a été envoyé à votre Excellence en son temps.

Il nous est revenu depuis que, trouvant les points acceptés par nous insuffisants, on allait nous faire certaines demandes concernant six autres points qui, exclus et discutés en Conseil des Ministres, on été avec la sanction Impériale acceptés dans la forme suivante:—

1. Les avis et communications que les Drogmans auront à faire à la Commission devront se borner aux réformes dont l'application a été décidée par le Gouvernement Impérial pour les six vilayets et ne point s'en écarter;

2. A l'exception des Valis et des Mutessarifs, qui devront être Musulmans, des fonctionnaires Chrétiens seront nommés proportionnellement au chiffre des populations;

3. Il y aura dans chaque nahié des gardes champêtres. Le nombre en sera fixé par les Gouverneurs-Généraux sans pouvoir excéder le chiffre de cinq pour chaque nahié. Il va sans dire que dans les nahiés habités par des populations différentes, ils seront mixtes. Ces gardes champêtres seront choisis par le Conseil de Nahié. Leur uniforme et leur armement seront arrêtés par le Département de la Guerre;

4. Les Règlements existant sur les prisons seront strictement observés et appliqués;

5. Il y aura des officiers Chrétiens dans la police et la Gendarmerie; et

6. Les Moudirs des nahiés seront, conformément aux Règlements, élus parmi les members des Conseils des Nahiés.

Je prie votre Excellence de voir immédiatement son Excellence le Ministre des Affaires Étrangères et de lui faire part de ce qui précède.

Votre Excellence aura soin de déclarer en même temps que le Gouvernement Impérial ayant pris acte des assurances données tant ici par les trois Ambassadeurs au nom de leurs Gouvernements que par ceux-ci à nos Ambassadeurs accrédités auprès d'eux "comme quoi il ne pouvait même leur passer par l'idée de faire des propositions pouvant porter attenite aux droits souverains de notre auguste Maître et à l'indépendance de l'Empire," il est évident que les six vilayets en question ne pourront acquérir dans l'avenir aucun caractère privilégié; et si, par impossible, une idée pareille venait un jour à surgir, le Gouvernement profitera des assurances précitées.

F. O. 424/183, pp. 424-426, No. 295

Turkey No. 1 (1896), p. 140, No. 164

Translation.

CONSTANTINOPLE, *September 6, 1895.*

YOUR Excellency is aware that after the receipt of the Memorandum and scheme of reforms presented to us by the three Ambassadors, we communicated to them a counter-scheme drawn up by the Ministerial Commission and sanctioned by Imperial Iradé. A copy of this counter-scheme was transmitted to your Excellency in due course.

We have since been informed that, the points accepted by us being considered insufficient, certain demands were about to be made to us in regard to six other points, which, excluded and discussed at the Council of Ministers, have, with the Imperial sanction, been accepted in the following form:-

1. The notifications and communications which the Dragomans may make to the Commission must be limited to the reforms which the Imperial Government has decided to introduce in the six vilayets, and must not deal with any other subject.

2. Apart from the Valis and Mutessarifs, who must be Mussulmans, Christian officials will be appointed in proportion to the numbers of the different populations.

3. There will be rural policemen in every nahié. Their number will be fixed by the Governors-General, but must not exceed five for each nahié. In nahiés inhabited by different populations, they will of course be taken from both. These rural policemen will be chosen by the Council of the nahié. Their uniform and arms will be settled by the Department of War.

4. The existing Regulations concerning prisons will be strictly observed and applied.

5. There will be Christian officers in the police and gendarmerie.

6. The Mudirs of the nahiés will be elected from the members of the Councils of nahiés, in accordance with the Regulations.

I request your Excellency to see his Excellency the Minister of Foreign Affairs immediately, and communicate to him what is stated above.

Your Excellency will take care to state at the same time that, the Imperial Government having taken note of the assurances given here by the three Ambassadors in the names of their Governments, and by the latter to our Ambassadors accredited to them, "that they had never had any idea of making proposals which might be prejudicial to the sovereign rights of our august Master and the independence of the Empire," it is evident that the six vilayets in question cannot at any future time acquire a privileged character; and if, which is impossible, such an idea should ever arise, the Government will take advantage of the assurances just quoted.

Turkey No. 1 (1896), p. 141, No. 164

No. 137

Sir P. Currie to the Marquess of Salisbury.

No. 411.   CONSTANTINOPLE, *September 7, 1895, 9.30 p.m.*
Telegraphic.   *(Received September 7.)*

WITH reference to my telegram No. 410 of to-day's date and your Lordship's telegram No. 151 of yesterday, I have the honour to inform your Lordship that I am preparing a list of the important points of the reforms demanded by the Ambassadors which are omitted from the Porte's offers, and shall submit the same to your Lordship by telegraph.

F. O. 424/183, p. 406, No. 271

No. 138

The Marquess of Salisbury to Sir F. Lascelles.

No. 281A.
Sir,   FOREIGN OFFICE, *September 7, 1895.*

THE Russian Chargé d'Affaires called here on the 4th instant and communicated the substance of a telegram from Prince Lobanoff on the last proposal made by the Porte respecting Armenian reforms.

I inclose a copy of this communication, in which you will perceive that the Prince expresses his opinion that the proposal concedes most of our demands, with only unimportant modifications. He thinks therefore that it might be accepted as a satisfactory settlement of the question, but he invites the opinion of Her Majesty's Government on the subject.

The French Ambassador called on the following day, and stated that M. Hanotaux was equally of opinion that, if possible, advantage should be taken of this offer to settle the question.

In reply to these communications, the French Ambassador and the Russian Chargé d'Affaires have been informed that, in my opinion, if the Porte offers in writing to accept the reforms proposed by the Ambassadors, with only unimportant omissions, the three Governments should accept the offer, though I have little confidence in any Commission composed exclusively of Turkish subjects.

I have laid stress on the importance of the offer being made in writing, and containing a substantial acceptance of the demands made by the Ambassadors, if it is to be taken in lieu of the Mixed Commission.

It is clear on examination that the verbal offer made on the 31st ultimo by the Turkish Minister for Foreign Affairs falls far short of this. It omits the proposed

control over the appointment of the Valis, the provisions for protection o
Armenians outside the six vilayets, the reform of the Tribunals and prisons, the
application of part of the revenues to local purposes, and the Christian Assistant to
the High Commissioner.

Sir P. Currie hears, however, that the Sultan has authorized the Grand Vizier
to take the matter in hand, and thinks that by pressure further concessions my be
obtained.

I am, &c.

(Signed) SALISBURY

F. O. 424/183, p. 406, No. 272

No. 139

Sir P. Currie to the Marquess of Salisbury.

No. 412.   CONSTANTINOPLE, *September 8, 1895, 3.20 p.m.*
Telegraphic.   *(Received September 8.)*

I HAVE the honour to submit the following list of points contained in the
proposals of the Ambassadors of the 11th May which are omitted by the Porte.

I would propose, with your Lordship's approval, to put them forward as
requiring satisfactory solution before the question of withdrawing your Lordship's
proposal of the appointment of a Mixed Commission can be taken into
consideration.

As regards the plan of reforms, I would insist upon the following:-

1. That the disqualification of Christians for the post of Vali should be
omitted.

2. That, as regards the Mutessarifs, Chapter II should be maintained.

3. That a fixed minimum of Christian employés, based on the population
should be established for each vilayet.

4. That official members should be excluded from the Administrative
Councils.

5. That the Regulations for rural guards should be those laid down in Chapter
V, and that their numbers should be decided according to local requirements.

6. That the first charge on the local revenues should be the cost of the local
administration.

7. That judicial sentences should be accompanied by Armenian translations.

As regards the Memorandum I would insist:-

1. That there should be some guarantee that the Valis will be properly chosen.

2. That the proposal as to the return of the emigrants and their reinstatement
in their lands should be adopted.

3. That pending criminal cases should be settled by Special Commissions.

4. That Article 6, respecting the inspection of prisons, should be put in force.

5. That the powers of the High Commissioner should be satisfactorily defined, and that a Christian Assistant should be attached to him.

6. That the functions assigned to the Commission of Control should be adequate, and that the Ambassadors should have the right of representing abuses to the Commission through their Dragomans.

7. That the proposals as to the Armenians in the other vilayets of Asiatic Turkey should be adopted.

I would further stipulate that the reforms should be embodied in an Imperial Decree.

As regards the appointment of military Vice-Consuls, I do not apprehend any difficulty in obtaining their recognition by the Porte.

F.O. 424/183, pp. 406-407, No. 273
Turkey No. 1 (1896), pp. 139-140, No. 163

No. 140

Sir P. Currie to the Marquess of Salisbury.

No. 586.   CONSTANTINOPLE, *September 9, 1895.*
My Lord,   *(Received September 16.)*

I HAVE the honour to forward to your Lordship herewith copy of a despatch which I have received from Her Majesty's Consul at Angora, transmitting a Memorandum respecting an affray between Christians and Mussulmans at Cæsarea.

I have, &c.

(Signed) PHILIP CURRIE.

F. O. 424/183, p. 432, No. 315

Inclosure 1 in No. 140

Consul Cumberbatch to Sir P. Currie.

Sir,   ANGORA, *September 2, 1895.*

I HAVE the honour to send your Excellency the inclosed Memorandum on an incident that has taken place near Cæsarea, which, besides showing the state of feeling that exists between Christian and Mussulman, may lead to further trouble in that quarter.

I have, &c.

(Signed) H. A. CUMBERBATCH.

F. O. 424/183, p. 432, No. 315/1

Inclosure 2 in No. 140

Memorandum by Consul Cumberbatch.

THE 26th August was being celebrated by the Armenians at Cæsarea as a Church Feast Day and as the anniversay of the Patron Saint of the Dévérenk Monastery, situated near that town.

Crowds of Armenians assembled at the monastery, and the roads leading to it were lined with Turkish onlookers.

The return of one or two Armenian prisoners, recently liberated under the general amnesty, was the occasion of a certain amount of demonstration on the part of their co-religionists, whose spirits were further raised by the circulation of a report that on the anniversary of the Sultan's accession the Firman would be issued granting certain reforms.

In the midst of the excitement, which was no doubt helped by too free libations, a drunken Armenian, returning from the monastery, made use of insulting language to some Turks on the roadside, whereupon five of the latter sprang on him and gave him a sound beating. Other Armenians interfered, and a general *mêlée* ensued, but was not accompanied by any serious injuries.

The Turks were ultimately driven off, but they were heard to threaten revenge.

About two or three hours later four Armenians, who had been in no way connected with the affray, were returning to Césarea through a quarter of the village of Talass called Kichikeny, and had stopped to water their horses at a fountain. Their names are Garabet, Nevshéhirlian, Garabet Gouyoumdjian, Khatcher Dillaryan, and Zacchéos Malazyan.

They may or may not have been drinking, but one or two of them were perhaps noisy.

Suddenly a crowd of Turks rushed out from behind the fountain and attacked them, first with stones, until they had got them out of their saddles, and then with knives and clubs.

They were all four badly cut by stones on the head, and had deep wounds and many bruises. One was badly slashed on the wrist and head with a dagger, and one had a bad stab in the arm, but none of the wounds are dangerous.

I have not had time to learn what steps the authorities have taken in the matter.

(Signed) H. A. CUMBERBATCH.

ANGORA, *September 3, 1895.*
F. O. 424/183, pp. 432-433, No. 315/2

No. 141

Sir P. Currie to the Marquess of Salisbury.

No. 588. Confidential.   THERAPIA, *September 10, 1895.*
My Lord,   *(Received September 16.)*

MGR. AZARIAN, the Armenian Catholic Patriarch, called upon me a few days ago and expressed the gratitude he felt for the appointment of a British Vice-Consul in the Vilayet of Bitlis.

The presence of Mr. Hampson had, he said, been a great protection to the Christians against the persecution to which they were subjected.

His Beatitude went on to say that his flock had taken no part in the political agitation which had existed among the Gregorian Armenians, and that he himself had endeavoured to act as a mediator between the latter and the Turkish government.

Matters, however, had now gone so far, and the treatment of the Armenian Catholics had become so intolerable, that they had been forced to throw in their lot with their Gregorian brethren.

He regretted that the Gregorian Patriarch refused to hold any communiation with him, and begged that I would use my influence to bring about a reconciliation between them. He was most anxious that any question which existed between the two Churches should be settled amicably without reference to the Turkish Tribunals.

I am informed that this remarkable change in the attitude of Mgr. Azarian, who does not bear a high reputation for honesty, and is looked upon by the Armenians as a traitor, has been brought about by means of a threat, addressed to him by the Revolutionary Committee, that if he persisted in his opposition to their cause he would be put to death.

I have, &c.

(Signed) PHILIP CURRIE.

F.O. 424/183, p. 433, No. 316

No. 142

Sir P. Currie to the Marquess of Salisbury.

No. 589. Confidential.   THERAPIA, *September 10, 1895.*
My Lord,   *(Received September 16.]*

MGR. ISMIRLIAN, the Armenian Patriarch, called upon me on the 7th instant and expressed his great satisfaction at the report which had reached him that your Lordship had addressed a demand to the Turkish Government for the appointment of a Commission with European members, and that the Russian Government were supporting it.

I said that it was true that your Lordship considered that such a Commission would be the best security for the execution of reforms, but that the Turks had now made further concessions in the direction of the reforms proposed by the Ambassadors, which did not include the appointment of European Commissioners; that further negotiations would take place, and that it was uncertain what their result might be.

Her Majesty's Government were most anxious to do their best for the security of the life and property of the Christians, but they were acting in the matter in agreement with Russia and France, and it was necessary that the solution arrived at should be acceptable to those Powers.

I asked the Patriarch whether he had any information as to the designs attributed to the Armenian Revolutionary Committees. He said that he had no definite knowledge on the subject, but that the sufferings of the Armenians were more severe than ever; that the anger of the Turkish authorities at the support given to the Armenians by England and other Powers showed itself in ever-increasing acts of cruelty and oppression; that the Christian population were being driven to despair, and that, from desperate men, violent acts must be expected. It was only the promulgation of reforms under pressure from European Powers which could restore any tranquillity to the Armenian provinces.

I have, &c.

(Signed) PHILIP CURRIE.

F. O. 424/183, p. 434, No. 317

No. 143

Sir P. Currie to the Marquess of Salisbury.

No. 590.   THERAPIA, *September 10, 1895.*
My Lord,   *(Received September 16.)*
THE Foreign Minister communicated to the Dragomans of the three Embassies yesterday the substance of a telegram which had been forwarded to the Turkish Ambassadors in London, St. Petersburgh, and Paris, stating that the Ottoman Government were prepared to accept six points of the proposals of the Ambassadors in addition to those mentioned in the Turkish counter-project.

A copy of the telegram and of the declaration annexed to it are inclosed herewith.

After making this communication, Turkhan Pasha expressed to Mr. Marinitch his earnest hope that Her Majesty's Government would be satisfied with these six points. The Turkish Government, he said, had full confidence in the sense of justice which animates the British government, who would no doubt remember that they had great commercial interests involved in the Ottoman Empire, which rendered it imperative that the Armenian question should once and for all be definitively settled, and peace and good order restored in those provinces. He added, confidentially, that if, contrary to expectation, the Armenian Revolutionary Committees, which are now intriguing both in Turkey and in foreign countries, were to take advantage of the employment of Christian officers in the gendarmerie, police, and administration to commit excesses upon the Mussulman portion of the population, the sublime Porte could not tolerate such proceedings, and if they were persisted in, would confer with the three Embassies in order that the latter should use their best influence to put a stop to them.

Referring to the recent violent acts of Armenian bands in the neighbourhood of Erzinghian and Sivas, Turkhan Pasha requested Mr. Marinitch to call the attention of Her Majesty's Embassy to the series of crimes which are being committed by the Armenian Revolutionary Committees with the object of provoking reprisals, and so bringing about a state of things which would call for further foreign intervention, in the hope that still greater concessions might thereby be obtained from the Sultan. His Excellency said that instructions had been sent to the provincial authorities directing them to use their best efforts to prevent reprisals on the part of the Mussulman population, but, he added, that such crimes must inevitably provoke retaliation, and would still further embitter the present situation. The death, for instance, of four Mussulmans might bring about that of twenty Armenians. It was essential that these misdeeds should be put a stop to, and the fact that attacks were now made upon the public officials was most serious.

Turkhan Pasha concluded his remarks by saying that the Armenian population was formerly a very peaceful one, but had now become discontented and unsettled owing to the sympathy of England and other Powers. For the reasons he had stated the Sublime Porte was desirous of bringing the question to an end, and had therefore accepted these reforms. But they could go no further, and it was essential that Europe should accept them also, and that the Armenians should be warned that they have nothing more to expect in the way of concessions.

I have, &c.

(Signed) Philip Currie.

F. O. 424/183, pp. 434-435, No. 318

No. 144

Sir P. Currie to the Marquess of Salisbury.

No. 591.   CONSTANTINOPLE, *September 10, 1895.*
My Lord,   *(Received September 16.)*
    I HAVE the honour to forward to your Lordship herewith copy of a despatch which I have received from Her Majesty's Consul at Erzeroum, inclosing extracts from private letters from Mr. Boyajian respecting the Armenian agitation in Kharput.

I have, &c.

(Signed) PHILIP CURRIE.

    F. O. 424/183, p. 435, No. 319

Inclosure 1 in No. 144

Consul Graves to Sir P. Currie.

Sir,   ERZEROUM, *August 30, 1895.*
    WITH reference to my despatch of the 20th instant, I have the honour to transmit herewith to your Excellency extracts from private letters which I have received from the Acting British Vice-Consul at Kharput, giving further evidence of the existence in that place of a political agitation among the Armenians, which threatens to produce dangerous results if not speedily checked.

I have, &c.

(Signed) R. W. GRAVES.

    F. O. 424/183, p. 435, No. 319/1

Inclosure 2 in No. 144

Acting Vice-Consul Boyajian to Consul Graves.

Private.
Extract.   KHARPUT; *August 12, 1895.*
    THREE days ago an Armenian came to the Rev. Mr. Barnam and said that he was delegated by 400 Armenians to demand from him the delivery of the printing press to them, and added that in case of refusal they would attack the office and take the press by force.
    Mr. Barman gave notice to the authorities, upon which the man was arrested. He refused to give the names of those who sent him to Mr. Barnam, and was consequently detained.
    Some years ago the Armenians of Husseinig, a village at the foot of the

Kharput Hill, hung a bell in their church and rang it. To this a certain Pasha, the chief man in the place, objected, and complained to the then Vali, and the Vali obtained an order from Constantinople to stop the bell, and it was stopped. About a fortnight ago the Armenians in large numbers crowded to the church and rang the bell. Again the Moslems became enraged and appealed to the Vali, and the Vali gave orders that the bell should not be rung before an order was procured from Constantinople. The Armenians do not regard this order, and they go on ringing the bell, saying that as they have bells in the town, in Mezré, and in many other villages, they should not be prevented, especially as in Husseinig four-fifths of the population are Armenians.

No. 145

Sir P. Currie to the Marquess of Salisbury.

No. 413.   CONSTANTINOPLE, *September 10, 1895, 10.40 a.m.*
Telegraphic   *(Received September 10.)*
    HER Majesty's Vice-Consul at Moush has again telegraphed to me that the authorities are treating Mourad and the other Talori prisoners with great cruelty. According to the report of the governor himself, out of the twenty-two Talori prisoners, eleven had died since last September. I am making strong representations to the Porte as to the treatment to which these prisoners are submitted.
    F. O. 424/183, p. 426, No. 296

No. 146

Sir P. Currie to the Marquess of Salisbury.

No. 414.   CONSTANTINOPLE, *September 10, 1895, 7.25 p.m.*
Telegraphic.   *(Received September 10.)*
    THE Grand Vizier, in consequence of my representations, is sending stringent orders by telegraph to the Vali of Bitlis to prevent any ill-treatment of Mourad and other prisoners, and to ameliorate the sanitary state of prisons.
    He has ordered the Vali to report why the prisoners have been kept so long without trial, and to make a personal inspection of the condition of the prisons.
    F. O. 424/183, p. 426, No. 297

No. 147

Sir F. Lascelles to the Marquess of Salisbury.

No. 219. Confidential.   St. Petersburgh, *September 10, 1895.*
My Lord,   *(Received September 16.)*

BY my telegram No. 83 of the 31st ultimo I had the honour to report to your Lordship the substance of a conversation which I had had with Prince Lobanoff on the previous evening on the subject of Armenian reforms. His Excellency told me that he had heard from Constantinople that that Committee of Control suggested in the Ambassadors' scheme of reforms was still being discussed, although he had understood that that Committee had been superseded by the Committee of Surveillance proposed by your Lordship, and it was in the belief that such was the case that he had accepted your Lordship's proposal. He was now anxious to know whether the view he had taken was correct.

I replied that I had formed exactly the same opinion as his Excellency, but in order that there might be no doubt on the subject, I would at once submit the question to your Lordship.

On the receipt of the 2nd instant of your Lordship's telegram No. 164, I called upon Prince Lobanoff to inform him that his impression was quite correct.

His Excellency then communicated to me a telegram which he had received from M. De Nélidoff, and which explained the matter. The Sultan had been so much alarmed at your Lordship's proposal that he had declared himself willing to accept not only the Committee of Control suggested by the Ambassadors, but also the five points which were under discussion. M. Nélidoff also reported that this new communication from the Sultan amounted to a practical acceptance of the Ambassadors' demands with insignificant modifications. His Excellency dwelt at some length on the desirability of bringing the question to a speedy conclusion, and expressed the hope that an opportunity now offered for doing so.

On the afternoon of the 7th instant I had a further interview with Prince Lobanoff, who showed me a telegram which he had received from the Russian Chargé d'Affaires in London, which, however, did not enable him to gather exactly what your Lordship's views were. His Excellency insisted upon the great desirability of putting an end to a question which had already dragged on too long, and which was inciting agitation not merely in the Armenian provinces, but throughout the whole of the Turkish Empire. He had reason to know that the French Government entirely shared this view, and he sincerely hoped that your Lordship would not allow an opportunity, which seemed a favourable one for settling the matter definitively, to be lost. He was aware that Sir Philip Currie did not appear to be satisfied, and was perhaps disappointed that the scheme of which he had been the principal author had not been accepted in its entirety, but he thought that it would be a pity if a question of *amour-propre* should prevent a settlement that was desirable from every point of view.

I replied, perhaps with some vivacity, that there could be absolutely no question of *amour-propre*, and that if Sir Philip Currie raised objections to the present proposal of the Sultan, it was only that he foresaw that it would not be a satisfactory or final settlement of the question.

Last night I had the honour of receiving your Lordship's telegram No. 172, repeating a telegram from Sir Philip Currie with regard to the six points which had been accepted in addition to those contained in the Turkish counter-project, and on meeting Prince Lobanoff at dinner to-night I asked him whether he had anything more to tell me with regard to this question.

His Excellency replied that he was most anxious to know what view your Lordship took of this communication from the Porte, and that he was awaiting with the greatest interest a telegram from M. Kroupensky on the subject.

I have, &c.

(Signed) FRANK C. LASCALLES.

F. O. 424/183, p. 443, No. 323

No. 148

Sir P. Currie to the Marquess of Salisbury.

No. 593.   THERAPIA, *September 11, 1895.*
My Lord,   *(Received September 16.)*

IN my despatch No. 557 of the 29th ultimo, I had the honour to inform your Lordship that I had made representations to the Grand Vizier respecting the cruelties alleged to have been inflicted on the Armenian prisoners at Marsovan, and that I had drawn to his Highness' special attention to the case of Dr. Melkom Altoumian.

His Highness promised to make enquiries into the matter, and I now have the honour to transmit to your Lordship translation of the telegram sent by the Vali of Sivas to the Grand Vizier in reply to his inquiries.

I have, &c.

(Signed) PHILIP CURRIE.

F. O. 424/183, p. 441, No. 321

Inclosure in No. 148

The Vali of Sivas to the Grand Vizier.

Telegraphic. *Undated.*

INSTRUCTIONS have constantly been sent to the proper authorities that the Armenian prisoners should not suffer, and that violence should not be done to them. The complaints that the prisoners at Marsovan have been tortured in order to extort confessions are merely accusations which, for some time past, the Armenians are in the habit of making against the Government officials and the Mussulman population. Inquiries, however, having been made respecting this matter, the Mutessarif of Amassia has telegraphed that the accusations that these prisoners had been beaten or tortured is utterly void of foundation. The circumstances of the case are, that the Patriarchate having telegraphed to the trustees of the Armenian Church at Marsovan that the prisoners had been granted a free pardon, the members of the Armenian Lay Council went to the Government Offices and asked for the release of the prisoners. The local authorities stated in answer that no such order had as yet been received, upon which the prisoners began to create a disturbance. The authorities gave the latter to understand that they would, of course, be set at liberty the moment the necessary instructions were received, but that it was out of place to insist on being released before the orders to that effect had been received. The authorities at the same time advised them not to create a disturbance, whereupon order was restored. Later on, upon the receipt of the Imperial Iradé, those of the prisoners included in the amnesty were set at liberty. The complaint, therefore, that these prisoners had been beaten or tortured is due either to the above circumstance, or is one of the calumnies merely which Armenians generally are now making use of against the authorities, as has already been stated to the Porte in previous reports.

With regard to Melkom Altoumian, I beg to say that I have already had the honour on three occasions to report to the Porte fully on that individual by telegraph. This man was formerly the municipal doctor at Marsovan, and was at the same time medical assistant at the American school. He further built a house near the school in question as an appurtenance. His house was subsequently set fire to and destroyed with the object of fixing crime either on the Government officials or upon the Mussulman population. Altoumian was imprisoned for having given medical attendance to members of the Revolutionary Committees. He is the brother of Dr. Erminian, who was granted free pardon last year. He is also the brother-in-law of Dr. Karakine, who was to be appointed Dragoman of the French Vice-Consulate at Sivas, and upon whose antecedents I had the honour to report by telegraph in May last. Altoumian is, further, a relative of Dr. Dikron, upon whom a sentence of death was passed at Yozgat, and the members of his family are considered to be seditious. He himself is a suspicious character, and has been more than once imprisoned by order of the Court, and subsequently released.

It was ascertained, from a report received from the Mutessarif of Amassia, that so long as this man remained at Marsovan, the local authorities would be compelled to consider him as under suspicion, should any disturbances take place in that town. He was accordingly dismissed from his post as municipal doctor at Marsovan; and an intimation was conveyed to him to take up his residence in Amassia, his birthplace, where he would be at liberty to practise his profession. M. Altoumian consented to go, but as he was obliged to proceed to Marsovan from time to time on business, he expressed the desire to be allowed to reside again in that city. His wish to live at this latter place is concealing some seditious design; and as he does not possess any real property in Marsovan, he will not be allowed to reside there, the local authorities having, moreover, stated, that it would be more convenient that he should reside at Amassia and practise there as a doctor.

F. O. 424/183, pp. 441-442, No. 321/1

No. 149

Sir P. Currie to the Marquess of Salisbury.

No. 416.   CONSTANTINOPLE, *September 11, 1895, 10.35 a.m.*
Telegraphic.   *(Received September 11.)*

IN continuation of my telegram No. 405 of the 4th September, Her Majesty's Vice-Consul at Moush now telegraphs that the Mutessarif appears to openly disregard the orders of the Vali, as, in spite of the latter's assurances, only two Mudirs have been dismissed by the Mutessarif, and Reshid and the other two police officers are still employed in collecting taxes.

I shall make a further representation to the Grand Vizier on the matter.

F. O. 424/183, p. 426, No. 299

No. 150

Sir P. Currie to the Marquess of Salisbury.

No. 417.   CONSTANTINOPLE, *September 11, 1895, 10.35 a.m.*
Telegraphic.   *(Received September 11.)*

MR. GRAVES telegraphs reporting the arrival of Shakir Pasha at Erzeroum, and saying that he called on him the next day. Shakir Pasha will in a few days proceed to Bayazid, returning thence to Erzeroum, and leaving again for Sivas and Erzinghian.

His Excellency, in his conversation with Mr. Graves, complained that the difficulties of his task were increased by the present bad feeling between Mussulmans and Christians, which he feared had been fostered by some Government officials.

He spoke a good deal about road construction, and also said that he intended to appoint 210 Christian gendarmes in the Vilayet of Erzeroum, besides other Christian officials, but added that money was scarce.

Mr. Graves confined himself to agreeing with him on the necessity of establishing means of communication and restoring security in the first instance, and refrained from entering into any discussion as to his mission.

F. O. 424/183, p. 427, No. 300

No. 151

Sir P. Currie to the Marquess of Salisbury.

No. 418. Confidential.   CONSTANTINOPLE, *September 11, 1895, 11.10 a.m.*
Telegraphic.   *(Received September 11.)*

I HAVE this morning received a message from the Armenian Patriarch stating that he considers that the reluctance of the Sultan to accept the proposals of the 11th May shows distinctly that the guarantees then asked for would not be sufficient to secure the execution of the reforms, and begging me in consequence to communicate to your Lordship his ardent hope and prayer that your proposal of an International Commission will not be dropped.

F. O. 424/183, p. 427, No. 301

No. 152

Sir F. Lascelles to the Marquess of Salisbury.

No. 223. Confidential.   ST. PETERSBURGH, *September 11, 1895.*
My Lord,   *(Received September 16.)*

IN obedience to the instructions contained in your Lordship's despatch No. 280, Confidential, of the 4th instant, I have explained to Prince Lobanoff that your Lordship, in your conversation with the Russian Chargé d'Affaires in London on the subject of Armenian reforms, had expressed no opinion on the question of the mixture of Mussulman and Christian gendarmes, and it was therefore not accurate to state that your Lordship shared his Excellency's views as to the dangers of enrolling Mussulmans and Christians either together or in separate bands.

Prince Lobanoff replied that he had received a letter from M. Kroupensky, stating that Sir Thomas Sanderson had spoken to him on the subject, and that it was quite true that your Lordship had expressed no opinion, and had limited yourself to saying, on hearing Prince Lobanoff's views on the subject, "il se pourrait qu'il ait raison." His Excellency added that M. Kroupensky had reported the conversation accurately, and that it was he himself who, on learning that your Lordship admitted that he might be right, had given a wider interpretation to your Lordship's words.

I have, &c.

(Signed) FRANK C. LASCELLES.

F. O. 424/183, p. 444, No. 324

No. 153

Sir P. Currie to the Marquess of Salisbury.

No. 419. Confidential   CONSTANTINOPLE, *September 11, 1895, 11.25 a.m.*
Telegraphic.   *(Received September 11.)*

LAST Saturday the Armenian Patriarch paid me a visit, and yesterday he had an interview with M. de Nélidow. His Beatitude informs me that his Excellency's language was to the effect that he could not at present see any prospect of real reforms, and that some later opportunity of establishing them must be looked for; that the most that could be done at present for the Armenians was to appease the irritation and hatred prevailing between them and the Mussulmans.

M. de Nélidow had mentioned that he had with his own hand drawn up the XVIth Article of the Treaty of San Stefano, and that it was none of his doing that the LXIst Article of the Treaty of Berlin was substituted for it, the intention of its authors being to use it as an arm against Russia.

Hitherto M. de Nélidow has always told the Patriarch that he and his Government would do all within the bounds of possibility for the Armenians, so that his present language would seem to denote a change of attitude on his part.

F. O. 424/183, p. 427, No. 302

No. 154

Sir F. Lascelles to the Marquess of Salisbury.

No. 92.   ST. PETERSBURGH, *September 11, 1895.*
Telegraphic.   *(Received September 11.)*

PRINCE LOBANOFF hopes that the Turkish acceptance of the six points mentioned in your Lordship's telegram No. 172 may be considered as satisfactory, and is very anxious to know your Lordship's views on the subject.

F. O. 424/183, p. 427, No. 303

No. 155

The Marquess of Salisbury to Sir P. Currie.

No. 320.

Sir,   FOREIGN OFFICE, *September 11, 1895.*

THE Turkish Ambassador called at the Foreign Office on the 9th instant, and communicated, on behalf of the Turkish Government, two papers, of which I transmit copies to your Excellency, announcing the acceptance by the Porte, with certain modifications, of six of the points included in the scheme of Armenian reforms originally proposed by the Ambassadors of the three Powers at Constantinople. These points are additional to those contained in the Turkish counter-project.

Rustem Pasha called again to-day, and was informed that I was sincerely desirous of bringing the Armenian question to a conclusion, but that, in my opinion, it could only be ended by the Sultan affording some sort of guarantee for the lives and property of the inhabitants of the provinces affected. There were two methods by which this object might be attained. One method was that set forth in the scheme submitted by the Ambassadors at Constantinople, which consisted in providing that, among the functionaries of all sorts, a certain proportion should be Christians, and that, in places where the high officials were Mussulmans, they should have a Christian as their assistant, and *vice versâ*. The other method consisted in allowing the continuance of the present Mussulman administrative organization under the inspection of a Commission resident in the province, and composed partly of European Commissioners, who should be able to report abuses to the Ambassadors at Constantinople.

I am, &c.

(Signed) SALISBURY.

F. O. 424/183, p. 428, No. 304
Turkey No. 1 (1896), p. 142, No. 168

No. 156

The Marquess of Salisbury to Sir F. Lascelles.

No. 176.

Telegraphic.   FOREIGN OFFICE, *September 11, 1895.*

THE telegram from the Russian Chargé d'Affaires to which Prince Lobanoff referred, as reported in your Excellency's telegram of the 8th instant, only contained the substance of Sir P. Currie's telegram of the 4th instant respecting Armenian reforms, and of my answer of the 6th.

In my opinion, the offer of the Turkish Government must be a substantial acceptance in writing of all the more important proposals madeby the three Ambassadors at Constantinople before it can be regarded by us as a substitute for the Mixed Commission.

F. O. 424/183, p. 428, No. 305
Turkey No. 1 (1896), p. 143, No. 169

No. 157

The Marquess of Salisbury to Sir F. Lascelles.

No. 178.
Telegraphic.   FOREIGN OFFICE, *September 11, 1895.*

I CONCUR in Prince Lobanoff's view that a settlement of this Armenian question is highly desirable. It can, however, only be brought to a conclusion by some sort of security being afforded by the Sultan to the inhabitants of these provinces for life and property.

There are two ways by which this object may be attained.

One method is that advised by the Ambassadors of the three Powers at Constantinople, which consists in requiring that among the functionaries of all kinds there should be a proportion of Christians, and that where the high officials are Mussulmans they should have a Christian for their Assessor, and *vice versâ*

The other method consists in allowing a continuance of the present Mussulman administrative organization under the supervision of a Commission resident in the province, and composed partially of European Commissioners, who should be able to report abuses to the Ambassadors at Constantinople. This was the suggestion of Her Majesty's Government. It received the approval of the Governments of France and Russia, and was recommended verbally to the Turkish Government.

Her Majesty's Government are willing to negotiate on either the one of the other of these forms of guarantee, but at present no definite offer of either in writing has reached them.

F. O. 424/183, pp. 428-429, No. 306
Turkey No. 1 (1896), p. 143, No. 170

No. 158

Sir P. Currie to the Marquess of Salisbury.

No. 592.   CONSTANTINOPLE, *September 11, 1895.*
My Lord,   *(Received September 16.)*
    I HAVE the honour to forward to your Lordship herewith copy of a despatch
which I have received from Her Majesty's Consul at Erzeroum, inclosing Mr.
Hampson's Report on his tour through Sasun and Talori.
    I have communicated copies of this despatch, with its inclosures, to the French
and Russian Ambassadors.
                              I have, &c.
                                               (Signed) PHILIP CURRIE
    F. O. 424/183, p. 436, No. 320

Inclosure 1 in No. 158

Consul Graves to Sir P. Currie.

Sir,   ERZEROUM, *August 26, 1895.*
    I HAVE the honour to transmit herewith to your Excellency copy of a
despatch which I have received from Her Majesty's Vice-Consul at Moush,
reporting upon the tour which he has just completed through Sasun and Talori.
    From the accompanying sketch-map your Excellency will see that Mr.
Hampson has visited all the most important points signalized by massacre and
atrocity in 1894. Besides passing several days between Semal, Shenik, and
Guelieguzan, which received the visit of the Commission of Inquiry last May, Mr.
Hampson has traversed the ravine of Gueliesan, and seen the traces of massacre in
the shape of human remains which still strew the track. He proceeded thence to
Ishkentsor or Aktchesser, where the alleged attack by the Armenians on the
Kaïmakam of Koulp took place, and afterwards visited all the thirteen wards
comprising Talori in succession. His information as to the number of houses
destroyed in this group of villages may be taken as conclusive; and as it differs
widely from the figures given in the Annex to their Joint Report by the Consular
Delegates, who did not reach Talori, I though it advisable to telegraph its
substance to your Excellency to-day, adding that Mr. Hampson ascertained that
the Kurds are still in the habit of levying "hafir" on the district, notwithstanding
the attempt to demonstrate before the Commission of Inquiry that the practice was
unknown, or at least obsolete.
    Passing to the east of the Talori River, Mr. Hampson skirted the district of
Kurdish Sasun, which he found as usual in a state of lawless turmoil, and

proceeded through the Hetink and Aghpik groups of villages to Shatakh, and so back to Moush viâ Semal.

In concluding his long and interesting Report, Mr. Hampson indicates as measure essential to the future prosperity of Sasun and Talori, after their present necessities have been relieved, the prevention of Kurdish incursions and outrages, and the abolition of the "hafir;" to effect which it would be necessary to reduce Kurdish Sasun, which he describes as the source of all the past troubles, and to remove some of the most turbulent Chiefs. But I would point out that it is idle to expect any honest endeavour to carry out this or any remedial policy from the present Mutessarifs of Moush and Guendj, between whose sandjaks the district under report is divided; not that matters are likely to be mended under any successors who may be appointed to replace them, until a radical change is effected in the current from head-quarters, which now influences and directs every action of provincial Governors in this part of the Ottoman Empire.

I have, &c.

(Signed) R. W. Graves.

F. O. 424/183, pp. 436-437, No. 320/1
Turkey No. 1 (1895), Part I, p. 199, No. 266, 266/1, 266/2

Inclosure 2 in No. 158

Vice-Consul Hampson to Consul Graves.

Sir,   Moush, *August 18, 1895.*

I RETURNED yesterday from a tour in the Sasun and Talori districts, as I had the honour to announce to yourself and Her Majesty's Embassy. As you will see from the inclosed sketch-map, which, without any pretensions to geographical correctness, gives, I hope, a truer idea of the relative positions of the places named than any map I have seen, I visited all the principal parts of the district. The mountainous nature of the country, consisting of alternate high ridges and deep valleys, many of them thickly wooded with walnuts, oaks, willows, mulberries, figs, and vines, and abounding in streams, and the entire absence of any but the roughest footpaths, make travelling a matter of great difficulty.

Some idea of the variations of elevation traversed may be gathered from the following approximate figures of height above sea-level:-

	Feet
Semal	6,000
Mountains south of Guelieguzan (at point crossed)	8,000
Valley of Talori stream	3,500
Mount Sovasor (at point crossed)	8,200

It may well in the first place to give some explanation of the terms "Sasun" and "Talori," as to which much confusion seems to exist.

The term "Sasun" though properly only applicable to the caza of that name, belonging to the Sandjak of Moush, and extending from the Komlik Mountains on the north to the borders of Sairt on the south, and from the Talori Su on the west to Maratong on the east, the residence of the Kaïmakam being at Hasso, is commonly used for the whole region south of Moush as far as Sairt, Khyan, and Koulp on the south, and extending to the neighbourhood of the town of Guendj on the west, and to Modeki and Mount Maratong on the east. Of this country the greater part is known as Armenian Sasun, but a small corner in the north-east, of which the principal place is a group of villages, or wards, the largest being Boshkan and Kevashdik (the residences respectively of the notorious Aghas Halil and Hishman, who are generally at war among themselves), in all about 150 houses, which are sometimes collectively spoken of as the village of Sasun, is known as Kurdish Sasun. It is inhabited by Kurds who refuse to recognize any Government, pay no taxes, and live in a state of complete lawlessness and rebellion, no one, Government official or other, being able to enter their district. Here, as pointed out later, is the nest of most of the troubles in these parts.

The name Talori only covers the various "mahalés," or wards, which form the village of Talori, viz.:—

Merquer (25 houses); Eko-dun and Talori (60 houses); Hakmank (15 houses); Halorink (50 houses); Mezré (35 houses); Zorir (15 houses); Devalink (40 houses); Tevalid (40 houses); Hosnoud (15 houses); Pourkh (50 houses); Hartho (35 houses); Ergank (30 houses); and Hartk (45 houses); and belongs to the Sandjak of Guendj, with Ishkentson and the neighbouring places.

Semal, Shenik, Guelieguenim, Aliantsik, Guelieguzan are administered directly from Moush.

I think that the term "Gavar," or "Kavar" has also been wrongly understood as applying to some special district. This is not so. "Kavar" is an Armenian word meaning a small district or group of villages, not in any way necessarily recognized officially as a separate division. There is no district specially known as Kavar. Shenik, Semal, and the neighbouring villages are talked of as a "kavar;" equally Shatakh and Psanats (Psank) are "kavars" of Sasun Caza; Talori is a "kavar" of Guendj.

I have endeavoured in the following report of my journey to state, after the name of each village, the number of houses of which it formerly consisted. It has been impossible in most cases to obtain any definite information as to the numbers massacred last year. It is hoped that many of the former inhabitants are still scattered in neighbouring districts. That large numbers perished seems certain, the whole of the region being absolutely surrounded by Kurds and soldiers, under the direction of the Mutessarif of Guendj, and of Major Sali Effendi, now in command of the detachment on the mountains near Moush. Nobody and nothing belonging to the Armenians was purposely spared. From twenty to fifty from each village appeared to be the idea of the number who lost their lives.

On the 6th August I again left Moush for Semal, where I stayed that night. Shortly after my arrival, Hajji Mejmeddin Effendi, a rich and intelligent Kurd of Bitlis, who has great influence among his compatriots, also arrived. He was accompanied by Taleb Effendi, of certain notoriety during the Commission of Inquiry. As his Excellency the Ambassador informed me in his telegram of that day's date, they had been sent from Bitlis to inquire into the condition of Sasun and Talori. I had some conversation with them on the subject, and met them again in the camp of the Guendj Mutessarif, near Ishkentsor. The building operations were going on steadily at Semal, but no timber had yet arrived.

On the 7th I left Semal with Mr. Cole, viâ Shenik and Aliantsik, a ward of Guelieguzan, for the latter place. We found the building advancing everywhere, but there was much typhoid fever in Shenik.

On the 8th we went on over the shoulder of Mount Antok by a very rough road to Ishkentsor, passing the top of the valley of Gueliésan, where large numbers of Armenians were butchered by the soldiers and Kurds last year. I found various human remains still lying about close to the track.

In Ishkentsor (40 houses) nearly every building had been destroyed, as also in Enguznak (20 houses), Ardgorik, and Sevid. The inhabitants complained bitterly of the attempts to collect taxes from them in their present miserable condition; but I found that these had ceased for the last ten days, and when I saw the Mutessarif of Guendj next day he told me that he had received orders not to collect taxes at present in those parts. The villagers complained also of the "hafir," a tribute which they have to pay to the neighbouring Kurdish Aghas. In this district the worst tyrants appear to be Suleiman (or Selo) Agha and his family. The former lives at Sindah, in the Khyan district, and is a notorious ruffian.

Leaving Ishkentsor on the 9th, we proceeded to Merquer (25 houses), the highest of the wards of Talori, stopping on the way to lunch with the Mutessarif of Guendj, an old man, quite unfit for his work, and whose record is anything but good. He is also, as above stated, under very bad influences. With him were Hajji Mejmeddin and Taleb Effendis, and they had some 70,000 piastres for distribution among the wards of Talori. The inhabitants had, however, so far refused to accept the money of those whom they considered as the butchers of their relatives and friends. At Hajji Mejmeddin's request I spoke to the people of Talori on the subject, and the money was subsequently distributed, after which the two envoys from Bitlis immediately returned home, this being apparently the end of their mission.

At Merquer, which was one of the centres of the military force employed last year in the work of destruction, the position of the mountain guns which were fired down the ravine, more for bravado than for any practical results to be obtained, being evident, the desolation was complete, and here, as in every ward of Talori which I subsequently visited, not a house is standing. I should state that the villages of this district have all the appearance of having been very well off, many of the houses having two and even three stories. As is the case in the Kurdish villages now, the welcome extended to us everywhere, bands of twenty to fifty nomad Armenians meeting us on our approach to every village, and escorting and helping us along the road, proved how much they appreciated the sympathy and help given to them by England.

From Merquer we proceeded through the ruined wards of Eko-dun and Talori (together 60 houses), Hakmank (15) and Devalink (40), to the edge of the Talori stream, in a deep gorge below Tevalid (40).

Here we remained over Sunday, the 11th, being continually surrounded by crowds from the neighbourhood, whom, as above stated, we eventually persuaded to accept the relief funds distributed by the Mutessarif. The priest of Devalink is a certain Stepan, who appeared as a false witness before the Commission of Inquiry on behalf of the Kurds, and is a paid Government spy. An instance of his having appropriated certain sums belonging to the villagers having been brought to my notice, and Stepan himself having shamelessly admitted it, I was able to frighten him into returning the same, and into promising to amend his ways.

On the 12th we went on through Pourkh (50 houses), round the rock of Ferferkar, celebrated among Armenians as the place of refuge of Damadian and "Mourad," passing above the Devil's Bridge to Hartk (45 houses), a beautiful village, but also entirely ruined, having been both burnt and fired with cannon.

Having heard that the Kurds in the district west and south-west of Mount Maratong were committing all sorts of outrages, I now determined to turn back and visit that region, especially as I knew that the Kaïmakan of Sasun was there, and as I had good reason to believe that the nest and source of most of the Kurdish lawlessness was to be found in that neighbourhood. On the 13th, therefore, leaving Spagank (50 houses) on the north, and crossing the Talori Su close to the cave where Mourad was betrayed and captured, I proceeded viâ Erghank (or Erghart, 30 houses), the Kurdish village of Arghik, Kistan (nearly abandoned ten years ago, now 4 houses), and Tertank (8 houses), to the mountains above the monastery of Komats, and the villages of Cheftinik and Hauzorik, where I pitched my camp.

The villages passed this day had not been burned last year, but are suffering much at the hands of Kurds; and the fact that we were approaching the strongholds of the latter became evident, one Agha riding up to us and insolently demanding cartridges, another, who lives in the rich Kurdish village of Jernalink, but who was staying, an unwelcome and expensive guest, in the Christian village of Tertank, ordering the villagers not to allow us to alight there.

We stayed over the 14th above Cheftinik, and I had several long and interesting conversations with the Kaïmakam, Ismaïl Bey, an able, energetic, and honest man, who has an excellent record wherever he has been. Mr. Cole had known him as Kaïmakam of Boulanik.

He informed me that it was quite true that the nest of all the Kurdish troubles was in this district. As mentioned in the beginning of this despatch, the Kurds of Kurdish Sasun consider themselves independent, and those of this region are nearly as bad.

The respect neither Government officials nor any one else, but do as they please, living on the Armenians, turning them out of their villages, ill-treating them in every way, and stealing and destroying their property. The nearest roads are unsafe.

Ismaïl Bey complained that, with all the good-will possible, he was quite unable to keep order. He has only fourteen zaptiehs in a caza which is large, the country most difficult, and including places like Kurdish Sasun. He has no troops at his command. All he could do was to report the lawlessness and his own powerlessness to the Mutessarif. Either the caza should be divided into smaller districts, with strong officials and an efficient force of zaptiehs, or he should be granted at least fifty good zaptiehs and a strong detachment of military stationed there all the year round.

The instances of Kurdish outrages brought to my notice are far too numerous to quote. In a word, they laugh at the pretence of control which exists. Only four days before my arrival the Kurds had murdered a man at Psank (Halilan), and turned all the Christians out of the village, of which they had taken possession. The Kaïmakam had only four zaptiehs in the neighbourhood, and could do nothing. Three days later a Kurd had fired at and wounded a woman in the village in which the Kaïmakam was staying because she tried to prevent him from entering and robbing her house. In February last, Halil, son of Bishar, the Kurd Agha of Boshkan and Pevek (the same Halil Agha before mentioned), seized an Armenian, Astour, son of Der Hachadour of Komk, and kept him in irons in his house for forty-five days, beating and torturing him with hot irons, &c., every day, until he paid 1,000 piastres, 25 sheep, 2 oxen, 2 cows, &c. The result of a complaint to the Kaïmakam was that Halil consented to restore 500 piastres and 25 lambs in the place of the 25 sheep. I saw Astour and his scars. These are only examples of the endless cases which I heard of. To show the insolence of the Kurds, I may add that, some villagers having gone to fetch hay for my horses, some Kurds who met them, hearing that the hay was for me, refused to let them bring it. When I reported this to the Kaïmakam he said, "What can I do? They often refuse to allow things to be brought to me." Till this region is reduced to some semblance of order it seems hopeless to think of any peace or security in Sasun and Talori.

On the 15th August we took the mountain road over Mount Sovasor, which leads from Hasso to Moush, from which we had a good view over the rebel Kurdish district, passing close above the principal villages. Turning down to the west we reached Hetink (40 houses) which had been entirely ruined last year. Some seven or eight houses have been since rebuilt, and more crops have been sown than in most of the devastated villages, but considerable relief will still be needed there, especially as the seed for the fields sown was obtained from the Kurds, who have a lien on a proportion of the crops, which, if permitted, they are sure to exact in a very liberal manner. The missionaries propose to endeavour to buy off this lien at a reasonable price. From this place most of the villagers managed to escape with their lives, only eighteen having been killed.

On the 16th August we went to Kelarash and Teghik, which, with Hidan and Aghpik, form the four wards of the village known by the last name, and which formerly contained 69 houses; of these, only 28 are now standing, 16 having escaped burning last year, and 12 having been since rebuilt. Thence we returned, through Tapik and Kegashend, which had only suffered from loss of cattle and property last year, to Semal.

The Kurds resident in Tapik, after I had passed, ill-treated the Christians who had dared to come and speak to me. Immediately on my return here I demanded from the Mutessarif the punishment of the offenders, which he has promised. If this promise is not fulfilled I shall report again to you, as I consider it important that an example should be made.

In Semal and in Shenik the building is progressing well, several houses only waiting for timber to be roofed in. This, however, has not yet arrived, though the Mutessarif has been there in person during the past week, and, outwardly at least, pushed on the building. A certain number of masons from Moush are now at work, but have so far received no wages, though the Turkish Relief Commission undertook to pay them. The Mutessarif continues to show hostility to the missionaries, amounting to personal rudeness, and endeavours to misrepresent their actions to the people.

I am glad to be able to state that the nomad Kurds have been forced to move on, at least from the mountains close to Moush.

In concluding this Report of my journey, I have the honour to state that, in my opinion, when once the inhabitants of the district visited have been relieved from the dire want to which they were reduced by the events of last year, and re-established—not in the position in which they were before (that cannot be expected all at once)—but in such a position as will enable them to live and work to regain what they have lost, the requirements and best means for which object Mr. Cole is reporting on, there will be one chief measure to secure their comfort and prosperity: this is the prevention of Kurdish incursions and outrages, and the abolition of the system of "hafir," or tribute, extorted by certain Kurdish Aghas. To effect this it is, I consider, absolutely necessary to reduce Kurdish Sasun and the neighbouring Kurdish villages to something like order and obedience.

This I believe would be no difficult task if energetic measures were adopted. A small military force would suffice. Certain of the more powerful Chiefs would have to be removed permanently from these regions, notably Halil, Hishman, and Suleiman Aghas, all referred to above, and a strong hand would have to be kept over the remainder.

If this were done I see no reason why Sasun and Talori should not become flourishing and rich districts.

I have, &c.

(Signed) CHARLES S. HAMPSON.

F. O. 424/183, pp. 437-440, No. 320/2
Turkey No. 1 (1895), Part I, pp. 200-203, No. 266/2, 266/3

No. 159

Sir P. Currie to the Marquess of Salisbury.

No. 595.   THERAPIA, *September 12, 1895.*
My Lord,   *(Received September 16.)*

I HAVE the honour to transmit to your Lordship herewith copy of a note which I have received from the Armenian Patriarch, repeating in writing the message communicated to your Lordship in my telegram No. 418 of yesterday's date, with regard to the proposed superintendence of the execution of reforms in the Armenian provinces by an International Commission.

I have, &c.

(Signed) PHILIP CURRIE.

F. O. 424/183, p. 442, No. 322

Inclosure in No. 159

The Armenian Patriarch to Sir P. Currie.

M. l'Ambassadeur,   CONSTANTINOPLE, *le 30 Août (12 Septembre), 1895.*

AU cours de l'entrevue que votre Excellence a bien voulu m'accorder Samedi dernier j'ai eu particulièrement l'honneur d'exprimer le désir que l'idée, si sagement conçue, savoir, que le Haut Commissaire chargé de veiller à l'exécution des réformes dans les provinces habitées par les Arméniens doit être un Européen, et que des membres Européens, doivent se trouver au sein de la Commission de Contrôle, ne soit point abandonnée.

Considérant que la garantie de l'application du projet, la tranquillité des populations, de l'état actuel des choses dépendront, d'une manière essentielle et absolue, de la dite combinaison, j'ose, M. l'Ambassador, recourir aujourd'hui encore à votre Excellence, et implorer la grâce que vous vouliez bien solliciter, par la voie télégraphique, la bienveillante attention de sa Seigneurie le Premier Ministre Britannique, le Marquis de Salisbury, sur le désir ci-haut exprimé, et me seconder de nouveau, dans cette décisive circonstance, de vos généreux efforts et de votre grande autorité.

Les sympathies et la protection prodiguées par votre Excellence envers notre nation, qui sait les apprécier à leur plus noble valeur, m'autorisent à penser que ma présente demande trouverait bon accueil auprès de votre Excellence.

En vous confiant à la garde du Très-Haut, je vous prie d'agréer, &c.

Le Patriarche des Arméniens de Turquie,

(Signé) MADTÉOS.

F. O. 424/183, p. 442, No. 322/1

No. 160

Sir F. Lascelles to the Marquess of Salisbury.

No. 95.   ST. PETERSBURGH, *September 13, 1895.*
Telegraphic.   *(Received September 13.)*

PRINCE LOBANOFF, to whom I have communicated the substance of your Lordship's telegrams of the 11th instant, told me that he had strongly urged the Turkish Ambassador, on his communicating the instructions just sent by the Porte, that the offer of his Government should be put in writing.

The question, in his Excellency's opinion, is now so far advanced as to allow of his leaving for Contrexeville to-night. He expects to remain about six weeks abroad.

F. O. 424/183, p. 429, No. 308
Turkey No. 1 (1896), p. 143, No. 171

No. 161

The Duke of Westminster to the Marquess of Salisbury.

GROSVENOR HOUSE, LONDON, *September 14, 1895.*
My Lord,   *(Received September 17.)*

I HAVE the pleasure to transmit herewith a third remittance of 1,000*l.* from the Armenian Relief Fund, which the Committee will be much obliged by your Lordship causing to be transmitted to Sir Philip Currie, to be applied, under his Excellency's direction, for the distressed Armenians in the Sasun region.

The Committee venture to hope that the assurances given by Mr. Curzon in the House of Commons on the 3rd instant relative to the attitude of the Turkish authorities towards the relief distributors in the Sasun will be verified, as the Patriarch of Constantinople (Mgr. Ismirlian) greatly fears that the number of deaths, already considerable, will increase during the coming winter if the Turkish authorities persist in placing obstacles in the way of relief distribution, and continue to encourage the Kurds to harass and plunder the Armenian villagers who have been doing their utmost to support their destitute countrymen during the past twelve months.

Attention having repeatedly been called in the public press, and also in letters addressed to this Committee, to the reprehensible conduct of the Porte in dealing with the complaints of the starving Armenians, I have, in the name and on behalf of the Committee, to beg the very earnest and careful consideration of your Lordship to the pressing question of compensation to the survivors for the loss of houses, homesteads, oxen, flocks, and crops, which the Porte appears to be unwilling to grant.

It is not the desire of the Committee to make any unreasonable request, but they cannot help thinking that your Lordship will agree with the expressions, almost unanimous in the British press, that the time for diplomatic representations has expired, and that coercive measures are demanded in the interests of the honour of this nation as well as in the interest of humanity.

I have, &c.

(Signed) WESTMINSTER,
Vice-President and Chairman of Executive Committee, Armenian Relief Fund.
F. O. 424/183, pp. 444-445, No. 326

No. 162

The Sublime Porte to Rustem Pasha.

CONSTANTINOPLE, *le 14 Septembre, 1895.*
Télégraphique.   *(Communicated by Rustem Pasha, September 14.)*

NOUS désirons comme Lord Salisbury que la question qui nous occupe soit réglée dans le plus bref délai. Des deux méthodes qu'elle indique, la seconde, à savoir l'institution sur les lieux d'une Commission d'Inspection composée en partie de Commissaires Européens, ne saurait en aucune façon être acceptée par nous parce qu'elle porterait atteinte aux droits souverains de Sa Majesté Impériale le Sultan, notre auguste Maître, que les trois Puissances nous ont assuré à maintes reprises vouloir respecter et parce qu'elle constituerait une ingérence évidente dans nos affaires intérieures.

Reste la première, qui consisterait à nommer dans une certaine proportion des fonctionnaires Chrétiens dans les vilayets en question. Or, ainsi qu'il est spécifié dans le second des six points que nous avons acceptés en dernier lieu, le Gouvernement Impérial consent à nommer dans les dites provinces des fonctionnaires Chrétiens proportionnellement au chiffre de la population.

Votre Excellence sait que l'Empire se divise en grandes contrées désignées sous le nom de vilayets administrées par des Gouverneurs-Généraux. Auprès des

Gouverneurs-Généraux des six vilayets en question se trouveront des Adjoints Chrétiens (voir l'Article 1ᵉʳ de notre Contre-Projet).

Les vilayets se divisent eux-mêmes en plusierus départements ("sandjaks"). Les Gouverneurs les plus importants de ces départements auront à côté d'eux des Adjoints Chrétiens.

Quant aux subdivisions des dits départements dénommés cazas (districts), les Sous-Gouverneurs qui se trouvent à leur tête seront nommés sans distinction de religion. Cependant dans les cazas d'une certaine importance si le Sous-Gouverneur est Musulman, son Adjoint sera Chrétien et vice versa (voir l'Article 4 de notre Contre-Projet).

Les districts ("cazas") se conposent de plusieurs communes ("nahiés") qui seront administrées par des Moudirs (Maires) sans distinction de religion et élus parmi les membres des Conseils Communaux (voir le dernier des six points).

Pour ce qui est des autres branches administratives provinciales, des fonctionnaires Chrétiens y seront nommés proportionnellement au chiffre de la population (voir le second des six points).

De plus, il y aura des officiers Chrétiens dans la police et la gendarmerie (voir le cinquième des points).

Je crois superflu de m'étendre sur les autres réformes résultant de notre Contre-Projet dont le résumé a dû être communiqué à Lord Salisbury par Sir Philip Currie, ainsi que sur les trois autres des six points acceptés en dernier lieu, qui se trouvent spécifiés dans un de mes précédents télégrammes, dont le plus important a trait aux communications à faire par les Drogmans à la Commission (voir le premier point).

Le désir de Lord Salisbury, qui est d'associer les Chrétiens aux Musulmans dans l'administration des six vilayets en question, se trouvant ainsi réalisé, nous aimons à espérer que sa Seigneurie voudra bien considérer la question comme résolue.

Translation.

Telegraphic.   CONSTANTINOPLE, *September 14, 1895.*

WE, like Lord Salisbury, are anxious that the question which occupies us should be settled as soon as possible. Of the two methods for its solution, the second, that is, the establishment on the spot of Commission of Inspection partly composed of European Commissioners, cannot possibly be accepted by us, because it would be derogatory to the sovereign rights of His Imperial Majesty the Sultan, our august Master, which the three Powers have assured us repeatedly they wish to respect, and because it would clearly constitute an interference in our internal affairs.

There remains the first method, which consists in the appointment of a certain proportion of Christian officials in the vilayets in question. As stated in the second of the six points which we have recently accepted, the Imperial Government agrees to appoint in the said provinces Christian officials in proportion to the number of the population.

Your Excellency knows that the Empire is divided into large provinces called vilayets, administered by Governors-General. Associated with the Governors-General of the six vilayets in question there will be Christian Assistants (see Article 1 of our counter-scheme).

The vilayets are divided into several departments ("sandjaks"). With the most important Governors of these departments will be associated Christian Assistants.

As to the subdivisions of the departments, called cazas (districts), the Sub-Governors in charge of them will be appointed without distinction of religion. But, in the more important cazas, if the Sub-Governor is a Mussulman his Assistant will be a Christian, and *vice versâ* (see Article 4 of our counter-scheme).

The districts ("cazas") are composed of a number of communes ("nahiés") which will be administered by Mudirs (Mayors) without distinction of religion, elected from the members of the Communal Councils (see the last of the six points).

As regards the other provincial administrative posts, Christian officials will be appointed to them in proportion to the number of the population (see the second of the six points).

There will, moreover, be Christian officers in the police and the gendarmerie (see the fifth point).

It is not necessary for me to recapitulate the other reforms named in our counter-scheme, the substance of which has no doubt been communicated to Lord Salisbury by Sir P. Currie, or the remaining three of the six points recently accepted, which are specified in one of my former telegrams, and the most important of which relates to the communications to be made by the Dragomans to the Commission (see the first point).

Lord Salisbury's wish to associate the Christians with the Mussulmans in the administration of the six vilayets in question being thus realized, we trust that his Lordship will consider the question settled.

F. O. 424/183, pp. 429-430, No. 309
Turkey No. 1 (1896), pp. 143-145, No. 172

No. 163

Sir P. Currie to the Marquess of Salisbury.

No. 599.   CONSTANTINOPLE, *September 17, 1895.*
My Lord,   *(Received September 23.)*
      I HAVE the honour to forward to your Lordship herewith, copy of a despatch
which I have received from Her Majesty's Consul at Erzeroum, reporting the
existence of an anti-Christian Secret Society among the Moslems at Moush.
                                    I have, &c.
                                                  (Signed) PHILIP CURRIE.

      F. O. 424/183, p. 451, No. 339

Inclosure 1 in No. 163

Consul Graves to Sir P. Currie.

Sir,   ERZEROUM, *September 3, 1895.*
      I HAVE the honour to transmit herewith to your Excellency copy of a
despatch which I have received from Her Majesty's Vice-Consul at Moush,
reporting that he has been informed of the existence of a Secret Society among the
worst class of Moslems at Moush, pledged to oppose by violence the introduction of
reforms benefiting the Christian population, and that their threats have been
particularly directed against himself.
      I may recall to your Excellency that the Bitlis missionaries have repeatedly
alluded to the existence of a similar Association in that city, while in Erzeroum
threats of this nature have been frequently uttered within the last few months by
bad characters among the Moslem townsmen, encouraged thereto by some of the
lower class officials and religious Sheikhs. No present apprehension need be felt,
provided the civil and military authorities do their duty in repressing any outward
manifestation of such ideas, but any failure to do so on their part would be attended
by imminent danger of grave disorders, for which local Governors and
Commanders should at once be held personally responsible.
                                    I have, &c.
                                                  (Signed) R. W. GRAVES.

      F. O. 424/183, p. 451, No. 399/1

Inclosure 2 in No. 163

Vice-Consul Hampson to Consul Graves.

Sir,   Moush, *August 26, 1895.*

I CONSIDER it my duty to inform you that I have been frequently warned of late, from what I believe to be trustworthy sources, of the existence of a Society amongst the worst characters of the Moslems of this town for violent action against the Christians, especially in case the projected reforms are accepted by the Government. I am told that their threats are particularly directed against myself.

While personally attaching little importance or belief to these stories, I have thought it right to inform the Mutessarif of what I had heard, leaving it to him, if he thought necessary, to provide an extra guard for my camp at night.

I may add that the Military Commander here, when calling upon me yesterday, expressed the wish that, when I went to Sasun or such regions, I would allow him to send a sufficient number of soldiers with me in case of accidents. The object of this wish is probably at least twofold.

I have, &c.

(Signed) CHARLES S. HAMPSON.

P.S.—The Mutessarif has informed me that he will send a zaptieh to my camp every night.

C. S. H.

F. O. 424/183, p. 451, No. 339/2

No. 164

Sir P. Currie to the Marquess of Salisbury.

No. 598.   CONSTANTINOPLE, *September 17, 1895.*
My Lord,   *(Received September 23.)*

WITH reference to my despatch No. 556, Confidential, of the 29th ultimo, I have the honour to forward to your Lordship herewith, copy of a despatch which I have received from Her Majesty's Consul at Trebizond, giving further information respecting the mission of Shakir Pasha.

I have, &c.

(Signed) PHILIP CURRIE.

F. O. 424/183, p. 450, No. 338

Inclosure in No. 164

Consul Longworth to Sir P. Currie.

Sir,   TREBIZOND, *September 10, 1895.*
ALLOW me to make a few remarks in continuation of my despatch of the 2nd
instant.

Shakir Pasha's mission, it would appear, includes this as well as the inland
vilayets. It seems, however, that his authority is very limited as regards economic
questions and pecuniary difficulties. If this be so, his task as a whole is likely to
prove extremely arduous, if not futile. Signs of a discouraging nature have already
begun to manifest themselves. Anxious though he be to introduce improvements,
he finds that without expenditure, improvements cannot be introduced. The
following is a case in point tending to show that his procedure has only brought as
yet a lively exchange of telegrams. The Marshal had with reason found the
Trebizond-Erzeroum road above Ardassa and below Baïburt in a disgraceful
condition. He wired to the Vali to have it immediately repaired at all cost. Cadri
Bey replied that he would be delighted to do so if funds were supplied. Shakir Pasha
then telegraphed to Constantinople, and the Minister of Public Works urgently
applied to the Vali for an estimate. Cadri Bey answered to this that he had already
sent it months ago, and so the matter rests at present. What makes this particularly
aggravating to Cadri Bey is the fact for the repair of this very section he had
amassed with difficulty £T.8,000, which, as usual, was appropriated by the central
Government with provocative unconcern as to local requirements.

Shakir Pasha is thinking, I understand, of proposing some considerable
changes in the administrative divisions of the country. He will suggest, it is said, the
inclusion of Trebizond in the Erzeroum Vilayet, and Sasun in that of Sivas. Apart
from military advantages, few others are likely to accrue from such an
arrangement. What would seem to me more recommendable for consideration is
the formation of the strip of coast from the Russian frontier to the Bosphorus, into a
distinct maritime province with a midway capital, such as the ports of Sinope or
Vona possessing a large, deep, and well-sheltered harbour.

Thus, with a nucleus of reforms in the interior, with trade routes tapping the
rich plains, with industries employing the indigent, and with general security for
life, property, and honour, an era of prosperity unknown for centuries might be
introduced into this unhappy country.

I have, &c.

(Signed) H. Z. LONGWORTH.

F. O. 424/183, p. 450, No. 338/1

No. 165

Sir P. Currie to the Marquess of Salisbury.

No. 423.   CONSTANTINOPLE, *September 17, 1895, 10.30 a.m.*
Telegraphic.   *(Received September 17.)*

WITH reference to my telegram No. 416 of the 11th instant, I have now the honour to report that Vice-Consul Hampson has informed me by telegraph of the dismissal of the three police officers.

F. O. 424/183, p. 445, No. 327

No. 166

Sir P. Currie to the Marquess of Salisbury.

No. 424.   CONSTANTINOPLE, *September 18, 1895, 7.30 p.m.*
Telegraphic.   *(Received September 18.)*

THE Russian Ambassador called this afternoon and informed me of the proposal of the French Government that the three Ambassadors should jointly consider the best means of utilizing the Porte's last proposals respecting Armenian reforms.

M. de Nélidoff, who has not received any instructions on the subject, asked if I was authorized to join in such a proceeding. I said that I had not heard of the proposal.

For the last few days I have been confined to the house, and therefore have not seen French Ambassador.

F. O. 424/183, p. 445, No. 328

No. 167

The Marquess of Salisbury to Sir P. Currie.

No. 323.
Sir,   FOREIGN OFFICE, *September 18, 1895.*

I HAVE received your Excellency's despatch No. 569 of the 3rd instant relative to the steps which are being taken for the relief of the distressed Armenians of the Sasun district.

I concur in your approval of the action of Her Majesty's Vice-Consul at Moush, as reported in his despatch of the 5th ultimo to Her Majesty's Consul at Erzeroum, and I have heard with much satisfaction of the philanthropic efforts

which Mr. Hampson states are being made by Dr. Reynolds in furtherance of th
work of relieving the Sasunlis.

F. O. 424/183, p. 445, No. 329

No. 168

Sir P. Currie to the Marquess of Salisbury.

No. 604.   CONSTANTINOPLE, *September 19, 1895*
My Lord,   *(Received September, 23.*

    I HAVE the honour to forward to your Lordship herewith copy of a despatcl
which I have received from Her Majesty's Consul at Aleppo reporting that a
collision occurred last week between Turks and Armenians at Ouzerlon anc
Tchoukmerziven.

I have, &c.

(Signed) PHILIP CURRIE

F. O. 424/183, p. 457, No. 342

Inclosure in No. 168

Consul Barnham to Sir P. Currie.

Sir,   ALEPPO, *September 6, 1895*
    I HAVE the honour to inform your Excellency that a collision occurred las
week between Turks and Armenians at Ouzerlon and Tchoukmerziven, in the
Caza of Pyas, Vilayet of Adana. This news has reached me through the Vice-
Consulate of Alexandretta, and is embodied in a letter written from Ouzerlon to the
British Vice-Consul by a certain Dr. H. K. Peltekian, as follows (3rd September):-

    "There are several mixed Armenian and Turkish villages near here. The
Turks and Armenians are constantly fighting. This afternoon there was a great
fight, in which several were shot on both sides. I have been dressing the wounds of
men and women all the afternoon. I am a citizen of the United States, and came
here with my wife to visit some friends. I consider that our lives are in danger. I
have been to the telegraph office, but they refuse to accept my telegram, and have
written to the American Vice-Consul at Alexandretta for help and advice."

    With reference to the above, I would observe that the Armenians of these two
villages have the reputation of being turbulent, and are probably to blame for what
has taken place.

    I have written to the Vali of Adana asking him in a friendly way to take
precautions to insure the peace.

I have, &c.

(Signed) HENRY D. BARNHAM.

F. O. 424/183, p. 457, No. 342/1

No. 169

Sir P. Currie to the Marquess of Salisbury.

No. 606.   THERAPIA, *September 19, 1895.*
My Lord,   *(Received September 23.)*

WITH reference to my despatch No. 582 of the 9th instant respecting the imprisonment of six Armenian boys at Bitlis, I have now the honour to report that the Vali of Bitlis telegraphed to the Grand Vizier on the 12th instant stating that no boys but three men were imprisoned at Bitlis for having attempted to rape a Moslem woman.

He added that they were arrested on the 27th May last on an order from the Court, and their trial is about to be concluded. Their guilt is proved by the fact that they themselves have admitted that they thought that they were raping an Armenian woman.

The Vali added that, owing to the feeling prevailing in the vilayet, such an act was regarded as a most serious offence against public morals, and that the arrest of the culprits had had the effect of calming public feeling, which was greatly incensed against them.

        I have, &c.

        (Signed) PHILIP CURRIE.

F. O. 424/183, p. 457, No. 343

No. 170

Sir P. Currie to the Marquess of Salisbury.

No. 612.   THERAPIA, *September 19, 1895.*
My Lord,   *(Received September 23.)*

WITH reference to my despatches Nos. 567 and 583 of the 3rd and 9th instant respecting the arrest of thirteen Armenians in Keghi, I have now the honour to report that the Vali of Erzeroum has telegraphed the following explanation to the Sublime Porte.

Two letters were seized by the authorities, one signed by a certain Kircor Antrahian, the other unsigned, both containing matter of a compromising nature. The culprits were arrested, but the priest Aristahes and other leading inhabitants of Keghi tried to conceal some of the authors of the letters, and eventually enabled them to effect their escape. The trial of the culprits is now proceeding. The priest Aristahes had made three appeals to the Court to endeavour to persuade them to modify their opinion as to the guilt of the accused. Thirteen Armenians had given evidence against him. The Vali further states that there is no foundation for the complaints of the ill-treatment of the prisoners by order of the Kadi and other officials.

I have, &c.

(Signed) PHILIP CURRIE.

F. O. 424/183, p. 458, No. 344

No. 171

The Marquess of Salisbury to Sir P. Currie.

No. 327.

Sir,   FOREIGN OFFICE, *September 19, 1895.*

MOREL BEY called at the Foreign Office yesterday to inquire, on the part of the Turkish Ambassador, whether I had any reply to make to the communication from the Porte respecting Armenian reforms, a copy of which was left with me by his Excellency on the 14th instant.

Rustem Pasha has been informed that I think the further negotiations on the subject had better be carried on at Constantinople, where up to the present they have been conducted.

I am, &c.

(Signed) SALISBURY.

F. O. 424/183, p. 447, No. 334
Turkey No. 1 (1896), p. 147, No. 176

No. 172

Sir P. Currie to the Marquess of Salisbury.

No. 429.   CONSTANTINOPLE, *September 24, 1895, 11.20 a.m.*

Telegraphic.   *(Received September 24.)*

MR. HAMPSON telegraphs to me that the Turkish authorities are preventing the missionaries from bringing any large timber for building at Semal and Shenik, and that they have not a sufficient store themselves.

I have requested the Grand Vizier to telegraph to the local authorities to do all in their power to help on the building.

F. O. 424/183, p. 458, No. 345

No. 173

The Marquess of Salisbury to the Marquess of Dufferin.

No. 458.

My Lord,   FOREIGN OFFICE, *September 24, 1895.*

THE French Ambassador called at the Foreign Office on the 20th instant to ask what was the state of the negotiations with regard to the introduction of reforms in the provinces of Asiatic Turkey inhabited by Armenians.

His Excellency was received in my absence by Mr. Bertie, who informed him of my recent communications with Sir F. Lascelles and Rustem Pasha, and that I had caused the Russian Government to be told that I considered that the offer of the Porte must be a substantial acceptance in writing of all the more important proposals of the three Ambassadors before it could be regarded as a substitute for my proposal for the appointment of a Mixed Commission.

Mr. Bertie also said that I had informed Rustem Pasha, with reference to a telegram from the Porte which was communicated by his Excellency on the 14th instant, and of which I inclose a copy, that I thought the negotiations had better be carried on at Constantinople as before.

Mr. Bertie read to Baron de Courcel Sir P. Currie's telegram of the 18th instant, stating that he had been informed by the Russian Ambassador at Constantinople that the French Government had suggested that the three Ambassadors should jointly consider the best means of utilizing the proposals of the Porte respecting Armenian reforms.

M. de Courcel observed that this was not quite a suggestion of his Government, but that they were inclined to advocate the mode of proceeding indicated, subject to my concurrence. His Excellency added that Prince Lobanoff had informed M. Hanotaux that he had sent instructions of that nature to the Russian Ambassador at Constantinople.

M. de Courcel said that the French Government were anxious to continue the accord of the three Powers at Constantinople, and he inquired whether I would be content with the acceptance—a formal acceptance—by the Porte of the proposals of the three Ambassadors, or rather the six points, as it was very important to close the question as soon as possible.

Mr. Bertie read to Baron de Courcel my telegram to Sir F. Lascelles of the 11th instant, in which I stated that I considered that the offer of the Porte must be a substantial acceptance in writing of all the more important proposals of the three Ambassadors before we could regard it as a substitute for the Mixed Commission.

M. de Courcel did not think there would be any difficulty in obtaining from the Porte an acceptance in writing, but he raised a question of form, not under instructions, but personally, viz., whether the Powers could insist upon a written and signed acceptance of a project which, though communicated to the Porte, had not been signed by the Ambassadors or sent in a signed note.

I have informed M. de Courcel that I consider that we must not only have the assurances of the Porte in writing, but that they must contain satisfactory concessions with respect to the appointment of a Christian "Adjoint" of the Commissioner, and of Christian "Adjoints" of the Valis, if Moslems, and with respect to admitting Christians to a share of all offices below that of Vali, down to the rural police.

I am, &c.

(Signed) SALISBURY.

F. O. 424/183, pp. 458-459, No. 346
Turkey No. 1 (1896), p. 147-148, No. 177

No. 174

The Marquess of Salisbury to Sir F. Lascelles.

No. 293.
Sir,   FOREIGN OFFICE, *September 24, 1895.*

THE Russian Chargé d'Affaires called at the Foreign Office on the 21st instant, and was received in my absence by Mr. Bertie.

M. Kroupensky said that Prince Lobanoff had instructed him by telegraph, after an interview which his Excellency had had with the French Minister for Foreign Affairs, to inquire what was my definite opinion on the telegram from the Porte, relative to Armenian reforms, dated the 14th September, which had been communicated to me by the Turkish Ambassador. I inclose a copy of the telegram from the Porte.

M. Kroupensky stated that Prince Lobanoff was of opinion that the document constituted an acceptance of the most important points of the scheme of reforms communicated to the Porte by the three Ambassadors, and that it might be accepted by the Powers.

Mr. Bertie informed M. Kroupensky that the reply given to Rustem Pasha had been that I thought that the futher negotiation had better be carried on at Constantinople as before.

M. Kroupensky said that Prince Lobanoff would be glad to know my personal opinion on Rustem Pasha's communication, and whether I would accept it if the three Ambassadors at Constantinople recommended it.

Mr. Bertie replied that, in my opinion, any acceptance by the Porte of the demands of the Ambassadors must be in writing.

I have informed M. Kroupensky that, if Her Majesty's Ambassador at Constantinople reported to me that the Sultan had *in writing* accepted the material

)ortions of the scheme of the three Ambassadors, I should be content; that the)roposals which have proceeded from the Porte up to this time have been studiedly ndefinite in all respects, and obviously insufficient in some; for instance, the appointment of Christian Valis or Mutessarifs is not admitted.

I am, &c.

(Signed) SALISBURY.

F. O. 424/183, p. 459, No. 347
Turkey No. 1 (1896), p. 148, No. 178

No. 175

Sir P. Currie to the Marquess of Salisbury.

No. 621.   CONSTANTINOPLE, *September 25, 1895.*
My Lord,   *(Received September 30.)*
    I HAVE the honour to forward to your Lordship herewith copy of a despatch which I have received from Her Majesty's Consul at Erzeroum, forwarding a despatch from the late Mr. Boyajian at Kharpout respecting representations made o the Governor-General on the subject of the misconduct of the Police Commissioner of Arabkir.

I have, &c.

(Signed) PHILIP CURRIE.

F. O. 424/183, p. 469, No. 363

Inclosure 1 in No. 175

Consul Graves to Sir P. Currie.

Sir,   ERZEROUM, *September 13, 1895.*
    I HAVE the honour to transmit herewith to your Excellency copy of a despatch which I have received from the late Acting British Vice-Consul at Kharpout, reporting the representations which he made to the Governor-General, Raouf Pasha, on the subject of the misconduct of the Police Commissioner of Arabkir, and his Excellency's answer.
    The conclusion drawn by Mr. Boyajian is that, although Raouf Pasha is accounted one of the best Turkish Governors, yet he has shown a manifest desire to screen the offending police officer, of whose guilt Mr. Boyajian felt no doubt; that unworthy and corrupt officials thrive under his administration, and that the Christians of the villages at least continue to suffer ill-treatment and violence of

every description at the hands of Kurds and gendarmes, while their complaint remain unheeded.

I have, &c.

(Signed) R. W. Graves

F. O. 424/183, p. 469, No. 363/1

Inclosure 2 in No. 175

Acting Vice-Consul Boyajian to Consul Graves.

Sir,   Kharpout, *August 30, 1895*

I HAVE the honour to inform you that I have had lately a private interview with Raouf Pasha, the Governor-General of this place. In the course of conversation on the general state of things, I took the opportunity of calling his Excellency's attention to the subjects mentioned in one of my private letters to you, namely, the most revolting deeds committed by the Commissioner of Police in Arabkir, who murdered an Armenian in his own house, and before the eyes of the victim's old mother, and insulted two Armenian women by exhibiting and himself putting on their underclothes in their presence, and in the presence of several others, and making at the same time indecent remarks.

In reply, his Excellency remarked that the Commissioner was acting perfectly within the bounds of his duty in killing the man, as that Armenian was one of the desperate revolutionists and a fugitive; that having learned one day that this Armenian was concealed in his own house, the Commissioner, in company with several gendarmes, proceeded there and invited the culprit to surrender; instead of obeying the summons, he (the Armenian) fired upon the gendarmes, upon which they fired, and the man was killed. His Excellency added that in his estimation the said Commissioner was a brave man, who did his duty very faithfully during the time that Arabkir was in a disturbed state, and that he deserved acknowledgement of his services, and he had applied for his promotion. As to the second point, Raouf Pasha informed me that an inquiry regarding it was addressed to him from Constantinople, upon which he asked the Kaïmakam of Arabkir to inform him, who in his turn stated that the accusation was altogether unfounded, and he (the Vali) replied so to the question of the Porte. But his Excellency further stated, "Supposing that the accusation was true, what sort of punishment could be inflicted on the offender beyond an admonition, and perhaps an imprisonment for four or five days?"

On this point I took the liberty to remind his Excellency that the act in question was not committed by an ordinary official, but by the Commissioner of Police, who is charged with the duty of protecting the life, property, and honour of the public. When he commits such an indecent act, which is plainly against public morality, his punishment ought naturally to be severer than that described by him. To this his Excellency assented.

I need hardly state that the information the Vali received concerning the points above stated differ widely from that obtained from different sources. Using the mildest expression, he has been misinformed by the Kaïmakam of the caza. The Commissioner of the Police, together with the gendarmes, entered the house, and the Armenian, feeling that they were going to take his life, seized his gun in self-defence, but did not fire. They rushed upon him, threw him to the ground, and pierced him with their bayonets. His poor old mother, seeing the precarious state of her son, fell on him with the view to protecting him, and she also received a wound.

I have only to remark that, however courteous and pleasant the interview was, yet the effort of the Governor-General to shelter the horrible acts of the Commissioner in question greatly astonished me. Raouf Pasha has always been considered as one of the best Valis, his integrity and sense of justice being above suspicion; yet with all this nothing, or very little, has been done in this vilayet; unworthy and corrupt officials have been living and thriving under his administration, and though Armenians have not been persecuted lately for political reasons, and there appears to be comparative tranquillity in the town, yet in the villages the Christians are continuing to suffer ill-treatment and violence of every description at the hands of Kurds and gendarmes, and I regret to state that their complaints remain unheeded.

I have, &c.

(Signed) T. Boyajian.

F. O. 424/183, p. 470, No. 363/2

No. 176

Sir P. Currie to the Marquess of Salisbury.

No. 625. THERAPIA, *September 25, 1895.*
My Lord, *(Received September 30.)*

WITH reference to my despatch No. 623 of the 25th September, I have the honour to inform your Lordship that the Grand Vizier has communicated to Mr. Marinitch a telegram which he received from the Vali of Bitlis on the 12th instant in reply to his inquiries with regard to the abuses in the collection of taxes in the plain of Moush.

The Vali declares that the complaints against the zaptiehs are unfounded, and that there is no truth in the statement that the property of the villagers is being sold or destroyed. He adds that the taxes are being collected in a perfectly proper manner, and that the villagers are subjected to no sort of oppression or vexatious treatment.

I have represented to the Grand Vizier that Mr. Hampson visited the villages in person, and ascertained for himself that the complaints were well founded, and I have called his attention to the practice followed by the Vali of Bitlis of denying all charges without regard to the truth.

His Highness has promised that he will not fail to communicate further with the Vali.

I have, &c.

(Signed) PHILIP CURRIE.

F. O. 424/183, p. 474, No. 367

No. 177

Sir P. Currie to the Marquess of Salisbury.

No. 626.   THERAPIA, *September 25, 1895.*
My Lord,   *(Received September 30.)*
IN view of the fearful mortality which, according to a Report of the Vali of Bitlis, was prevalent in the Moush prison, I sent my Dragoman to the Grand Vizier to represent to his Highness the necessity of remedying the insanitary state of that prison, which confirmed all the worst stories current in Europe in connection with the imprisonment of innocent Christians, which is one of the worst features of the misgovernment of the Asiatic provinces of Turkey. Mr. Marinitch was to urge more particularly that the Talori prisoners, if the criminal folly of retaining them in prison at all was persisted in, should be at once removed to healthy quarters, and treated, not as condemned criminals, but as untried prisoners. Should this not be promptly done, the details would have to be published in Europe.

His Highness, on receiving the verbal communication, at once telegraphed to the Vali of Bitlis, instructing his Excellency to inspect the prisons himself, to ameliorate the condition of the Talori and other prisoners, and to report why the Armenians have been imprisoned, and why they have not yet been tried.

I have the honour to inclose copy of a telegram received from the Vali in reply to the Grand Vizier's inquiries.

I have since made further representations to the Grand Vizier on the insanitary condition of the same prison, and his Highness has again telegraphed to the Vali of Bitlis calling his serious attention to the subject.

I have, &c.

(Signed) PHILIP CURRIE.

F. O. 424/183, p. 474, No. 368

Inclosure in No. 177

Extract from Mr. Marinitch's Memorandum of September 16, 1895.

Telegram from Vali of Bitlis to Grand Vizier.

IT is true that the prisons in the Bitlis vilayet are not internally arranged and managed in accordance with the new system; but they are, nevertheless, kept according to the rules of justice and humanity. He himself (the Vali) on his first arrival in the vilayet had personally inspected the prisons, and had caused new clothes to be given to the Talori prisoners, who were in the greatest state of destitution. He had further caused matting to be placed on the ground, and the municipal doctor is constantly disinfecting the premises and seeing that all sanitary conditions are fulfilled. When the Government offices are constructed the conditions of the prisons at Bitlis, Moush, and other towns in the vilayet will also be ameliorated and enlarged. The authorities are taking every measure in order that the prisoners at Bitlis, Moush, and elsewhere should not be subject to ill-treatment, and for that purpose the prisons are constantly being inspected. No torture whatever has been inflicted either upon Mourad, leader of the revolutionary movement, or upon the other prisoners.

The deaths which occurred last year in the prisons were due to typhus and cholera, diseases which were then prevalent. Nobody up to the present moment has been arrested or imprisoned without any legal reason being adduced. All arrests and imprisonments, therefore, are being made by law.

In consequence of the Talori insurrection two Armenians among those arrested, viz., Mourad Hampartsoun and Ohannes, have been condemned to death. The Armenians Aram, Kevork, Kiragos, Caspar, Boghos, and Tony Obo-Boghos were condemned to fifteen years' confinement in a fortress. The Armenians Hatcho and another Hatcho were condemned to imprisonment.

The judicial proceedings connected with the trial of these prisoners were forwarded to the Court of Cassation, and although the Proctor-General applied to the Minister of Justice on the 17th July and 24th August last, asking whether these prisoners were to profit or not by the general amnesty, the Minister in question has not, as yet, sent a reply on this subject. This is the reason, adds the Vali, why these individuals are still in prison.

The Proctor-General further stated that the prisons are supervised by guardians and gendarmes, and that no effort is spared in order that they should be kept in good condition.

F. O. 424/183, p. 475, No. 368/1

No. 178

Sir P. Currie to the Marquess of Salisbury.

No. 627.   THERAPIA, *September 25, 1895*
My Lord,   *(Received September 30.*
    WITH reference to my despatch No. 604 of the 19th instant, inclosing a
despatch from Her Majesty's Consul at Aleppo respecting an alleged conflic
between Turks and Armenians at Ouzerton and Tchoukmerzivan, I have the
honour to inform your Lordship that I caused inquiries to be made from the
Minister for Foreign Affairs as to whether any news had reached the Sublime Porte
confirming this report.
    His Excellency Turkhan Pasha stated, in reply, that he had heard nothing o
it, adding that if such a conflict had occurred the Minister of the Interior would
have been sure to have informed him of it.
                                      I have, &c.
                                                    (Signed) PHILIP CURRIE

    F. O. 424/183, p. 475, No. 369

No. 179

Sir P. Currie to the Marquess of Salisbury.

No. 430.   CONSTANTINOPLE, *September 25, 1895, 11.5 a.m*
Telegraphic.   *(Received September 25.)*
    HER Majesty's Consul at Erzeroum telegraphs that Shakir Pasha left that
town yesterday for Bayazid. He is expected to return in about three weeks to
Erzeroum.
    F. O. 424/183, p. 460, No. 348
    Turkey No. 1 (1896), p. 149, No. 179

No. 180

Sir P. Currie to the Marquess of Salisbury.

No. 630.   CONSTANTINOPLE, *September 25, 1895.*
My Lord,   *(Received September 30.)*
    I HAVE the honour to forward to your Lordship herewith copy of a despatch

which I have received from Her Majesty's Consul at Erzeroum, reporting the arrival of Shakir Pasha in that town.

I have, &c.

(Signed) PHILIP CURRIE.

F. O. 424/183, p. 468, No. 362
Turkey No. 1 (1896), p. 149, No. 181

Inclosure in No. 180

Consul Graves to Sir P. Currie.

Sir,   ERZEROUM, *September 10, 1895.*

I HAVE the honour to report that Shakir Pasha arrived yesterday morning at Erzeroum, where an official reception was given to his Excellency, at which the Christian communities, excepting the small body of native Greeks, were conspicuous by their absence.

This afternoon I called upon his Excellency, who received me very cordially, and told me that he intended to leave for Bayazid in a few days, returning to Erzeroum, and then proceeding to Erzinghian and Sivas.

In the course of a long conversation, Shakir Pasha spoke a great deal on the subject of road construction, and told me that he intended to appoint 210 Christian gendarmes to reinforce the Erzeroum gendarmerie, which is below its proper strength, besides appointing other Christian officials; but he added that the measures he hoped to introduce were costly, and money scarce, and that difficulties of his mission were greatly increased by the bad feeling which now exists between Mussulmans and Christians, fostered in many cases, he feared, by the action of the Government officials.

I abstained from entering into any discussion with his Excellency on the subject of his mission, merely expressing agreement with him as to the necessity of restoring security, and establishing means of communication in the first place.

I had the honour to report the substance of the above to your Excellency by telegraph to-day.

I have, &c.

(Signed) R. W. GRAVES.

F. O. 424/183, p. 469, No. 362/1
Turkey No. 1 (1896), p. 149, No. 181/1

No. 181

Sir P. Currie to the Marquess of Salisbury.

No. 432.   CONSTANTINOPLE, *September 26, 1895, 11 a.m*
Telegraphic.   *(Received September 26.,*

MR. GRAVES telegraphs to me confidentially that several more Armenian revolutionary agents have lately arrived from Russia, and that their activity is increasing in Erzeroum.

They are now said to receive their orders from London. They utter threats of violence against the Armenian Notables who still act as members of the Administration Council, and demand money from them for purposes of agitation.

F. O. 424/183, p. 463, No. 352

No. 182

Sir P. Currie to the Marquess of Salisbury.

No. 433.   CONSTANTINOPLE, *September 26, 1895, 12.40 p.m.*
Telegraphic.   *(Received September 26.)*

I TAKE your Lordship's statement to the Russian Chargé d'Affaires, as recorded in your telegram No. 160 of the 24th instant, "that you would be content if I reported that the Sultan had, in writing, accepted the material portions of Ambassadors' scheme," as leaving me free to use my discretion as to the points to be insisted on. I propose, accordingly, to endeavour to obtain my colleagues' support to as many of the points mentioned in my telegram No. 412 of the 8th instant as I can.

With reference to your Lordship's telegram No. 162 of yesterday, I have the honour to report that my colleagues have not as yet informed me that they have received any instructions as to making a further communication to the Porte respecting Armenian reforms.

F. O. 424/183, p. 463, No. 353

No. 183

Sir P. Currie to the Marquess of Salisbury.

No. 629.   CONSTANTINOPLE, *September 26, 1895.*
My Lord,   *(Received September 30.)*

I HAVE the honour to forward to your Lordship herewith copy of a despatch which I have received from Her Majesty's Consul at Trebizond, reporting the death of the Karahissar Public Prosecutor.

I have, &c.

(Signed) PHILIP CURRIE.

F. O. 424/183, p. 476, No. 370

Inclosure in No. 183

Consul Longworth to Sir P. Currie.

Sir,   TREBIZOND, *September 16, 1895.*

THE following is an extract from Dr. Jewett's letter, dated Sivas, the 11th instant, describing how the Karahissar Public Prosecutor was put to death by an armed band:-

"There is not very much news to report. I have sent by the last two posts to Mr. Terrell copies of twelve telegrams received by the Archbishop and the Vali reporting recent troubles and hardships in the surrounding towns and villages, and also an account of the murder of the Procureur of Karahissar. Some further details in regard to the latter affair may interest you. The Procureur ('Mudiumumi-Mouavini') had been removed by the Vali in consequence of many complaints against him by the Armenians. He and the Chief Secretary of Choroum, with their families and two zaptiehs, were on their way to Sivas. Passing through a narrow defile on the road near Zara (4th September), they were fired upon by a party of men from behind the rocks and trees. One zaptieh was killed, the other was wounded in the hand and struck on the head by a spent bullet. He left. The Secretary was seriously wounded. The men came out from their shelter and proceeded to rob the whole party. They took about 250*l.* from the Mouavin, and 18*l.* from the Secretary ('Kiatib'). Later they returned the 18*l.* to the Kiatib, said they had nothing against him, and were very sorry that he had been wounded. They then took the Mouavin off from the road, organized a court-martial, tried him, and sentenced him to death under the 54th Article of the Penal Code. He was shot through the head. The murderers are undoubtedly Armenians. The Government has sent out a lot of zaptiehs to arrest them, but they have not been caught, and are not likely to be found in the region where the Government is searching for them.

"Some of the Armenians say quite boldly that the days of tranquillity and inactivity for this region are over. There is said to be a well-armed band of forty Armenians somewhere around the city ready for business. The Revolutionary Committee is making 'forced loans' from the wealthy Armenians, and it is said that the Armenian Archbishop has been obliged to pay 50l. to save his head, and he has given his resignation to the Patriarch."

I have, &c.

(Signed) H. Z. LONGWORTH.

F. O. 424/183, p. 476, No. 370/1

No. 184

The Marquess of Salisbury to the Marquess of Dufferin.

No. 460.

My Lord,   FOREIGN OFFICE, *September 27, 1895.*

THE French Ambassador and the Russian Chargé d'Affaires called here together on the 23rd instant, and were received by Sir Percy Anderson. They explained that they were not making a joint representation, but as they had come to talk on the same subject, they thought it more convenient not to speak separately.

Baron de Courcel said that I was no doubt aware that M. Hanotaux and Prince Lobanoff were agreed as to the course to be adopted at Constantinople, my concurrence in which they were most anxious to obtain. His Excellency showed Sir P. Anderson an instruction which he had received from M. Hanotaux. It states that Sir P. Currie had thrown out, in conversation with M. Cambon, the idea that the three Ambassadors might address a communication to the Porte, taking note of the concession of the six points (recorded in Sir P. Currie's telegram No. 410 of the 7th instant), adding any others which they might consider essential, and saying that unless they received a written acceptance in fifteen days, the project of the local Mixed Commission would be revived. M. Hanotaux approved of this idea as a basis, and had authorized M. Cambon to join in a note, adding to the six points already conceded, a seventh stipulating for the appointment of Christian "Adjoints" to the Mussulman Valis and Mutessarifs, and *vice versâ*.

M. Kroupensky said that Prince Lobanoff had sent similar instructions to the Russian Ambassador at Constantinople.

Sir P. Anderson asked if the instructions were clear about a written answer. Baron de Courcel said that in fact the Turkish Ambassador at Paris had sent a note.

Sir P. Anderson then observed that he understood that one of my reasons for preferring that the negotiations should continue at Constantinople was because the Turkish Representatives abroad have never sufficient powers, and that consequently a written communication from the Porte would be essential. His

Excellency said that this was a strong point, and that he thought there would be no difficulty about it.

On Sir P. Anderson inquiring whether the seventh point as to the "Adjoints" was to be identical with the original demand made by the Ambassadors, M. Kroupensky said he thought that the Porte had already accepted it. Sir P. Anderson replied that no satisfactory assurance on the point had been received. Baron de Courcel concurred, and said that they would be ready to support the original demand.

In reply to a remark made by Sir P. Anderson that he could not say whether Her Majesty's Government would not press for further concessions, Baron de Courcel wished it to be clearly understood that the two Governments had agreed to add the seventh point, but were not prepared to go further. He added that M. Hanotaux proposed to leave a large discretion to the Ambassadors as to the form of their communication to the Porte.

Sir P. Anderson asked what view was taken of the fifteen days' notice said to have been suggested by Sir Philip Currie, with the alternative in case of non-compliance.

His Excellency hesitated, but eventually said that it would be preferred that nothing should be said about it, and that there should be no menace. It would indeed, he remarked, be unnecessary, as M. Hanotaux felt sure that the Porte would accept the seven points.

Both Baron de Courcel and M. Kroupensky expressed their anxiety to know whether Sir P. Currie would receive similar instructions.

They have been informed that his Excellency knows the views of Her Majesty's Government exactly, and will explain them fully to his French and Russian colleagues.

On the following day Baron de Courcel called again, and said that he wished to make a correction in his communication. He explained that the seventh point would not refer to the "Adjoints" to the Valis and Mutessarifs; he understood that that demand was already accepted in principle by the Porte; the addition point on which the Ambassadors would be told to insist would be the appointment of a Christian "Adjoint" to the High Commissioner.

I am, &c.

(Signed) SALISBURY.

F. O. 424/183, pp. 463-464, No. 355

No. 185

The Marquess of Salisbury to Sir F. Lascelles.

No. 297.

Sir, FOREIGN OFFICE, *September 27, 1895.*

THE Russian Chargé d'Affaires called at the Foreign Office on the 25th instant, and, referring to the answer he had received to his communication of the 21st instant respecting Armenian reforms, as recorded in my despatch, to your Excellency, No. 293 of the 24th, informed Mr. Bertie that he had compared notes with the French Ambassador, and found that the communication I had made to his Excellency did not quite correspond with that he himself had received as regards the points on which I still held it necessary to obtain satisfactory assurances from the Porte.

I inclose a copy of my despatch to Lord Dufferin recording the communication made to Baron de Courcel.

M. Kroupensky said that whereas in the reply to him the prohibition of Christian Valis or Mutessarifs had been instanced as showing the insufficiency of the Turkish assurances, Baron de Courcel had only been told that I considered that there must be satisfactory concessions with respect to putting a Christian "Adjoint" by the side of the High Commissioner, and by the side of the Valis when they are Mussulmans.

M. Kroupensky was anxious to have this apparent discrepancy explained.

Mr. Bertie pointed out that the Porte had stated as the second of the six points conceded by them that "Except the Valis and Mutessarifs who *must* be Mussulmans, Christian functionaires will be named in proportion to the number of the population;" that I had quoted this as showing the insufficiency of the Turkish answer, but that this reference did not necessarily imply that I insisted on the Vali being a Christian. The Turkish statement barred Christians from employment both as Vali and Mutessarif, and was therefore manifestly insufficient, even were it admitted that the former should always be a Mussulman.

Mr. Bertie added that all these details were to be dealt with at Constantinople, and could be discussed by the Russian and French Ambassadors there with Sir P. Currie, who knew exactly, and would explain to them, the views of Her Majesty's Government.

M. Kroupensky expressed the wish that the point he had raised should be submitted to me, and I have informed him that what is desired by Her Majesty's Government is that:-

1. All Valis *may* be Christian.

2. There *must* be an adequate proportion of Christian Mutessarifs.

3. Whenever the Vali or the Mutessarif is Mussulman, there *must* be a Christian "Adjoint."

I am, &c.

(Signed) SALISBURY.

F. O. 424/183, pp. 464-465, No. 356

No. 186

Sir P. Currie to the Marquess of Salisbury.

No. 436.   CONSTANTINOPLE, *September 28, 1895.*
Telegraphic
FOLLOWING received from Hampson yesterday:-
"Erko of Shenik was released on bail yesterday."
F. O. 424/183, p. 465, No. 357

No. 187

Sir P. Currie to the Marquess of Salisbury.

No. 437.   CONSTANTINOPLE, *September 28, 1895, 7.30 p.m.*
Telegraphic.   *(Received September 28.)*
THE Sultan has at last taken a step in the right direction: he has dismissed the Vali of Erzeroum, and appointed in his place Raouf Pasha, Vali of Kharpout.
F. O. 424/183, p. 465, No. 358

No. 188

Sir P. Currie to the Marquess of Salisbury.

No. 438.   CONSTANTINOPLE, *September 30, 1895, 3 p.m.*
Telegraphic.   *(Received September 30.)*
THE Armenian Revolutionary Committee has addressed a letter to me and my French and Russian colleagues stating that the Armenians in Constantinople are about to make a pacific demonstration with the object of making public their wishes for reforms in the Armenian provinces.
The Committee hopes that, in view of the pacific character of the

demonstration, there will be no intervention of the police or armed forces, which might have regrettable consequences, for which the writers disavow all responsibility.

F. O. 424/183, p. 476, No. 371

No. 189

Sir P. Currie to the Marquess of Salisbury.

No. 439.   CONSTANTINOPLE, *September 30, 1895, 5.10 p.m.*
Telegraphic.   *(Received September 30.)*

STAMBOUL has been the scene of serious disturbances to-day; shots were fired, and some Armenians were killed by the police.

F. O. 424/183, p. 477, No. 372

No. 190

The Marquess of Salisbury to Sir P. Currie.

No. 165.
Telegraphic.   FOREIGN OFFICE, *September 30, 1895.*

WILL it be possible for your Excellency to come to England about the 14th October without inconvenience?

Her Majesty's Government are of opinion that it will be necessary to consult you personally as to the position of the Armenian question.

F. O. 424/183, p. 477, No. 373

No. 191

The Marquess of Salisbury to Sir P. Currie.

No. 166.
Telegraphic.   FOREIGN OFFICE, *September 30, 1895.*

I HAVE received your Excellency's telegram No. 433 of the 26th instant relative to Armenian reforms.

It is very desirable that you should, as you propose, endeavour to obtain the support of the French and Russian Ambassadors to as many of the points mentioned in your telegram No. 412 of the 8th ultimo as may be possible.

I do not think that the Russian Government are disposed to press the Porte for any further concessions, but it is possible that they may do so under the advice of the Russian Ambassador at Constantinople.

F. O. 424/183, p. 477, No. 374

No. 192

The Marquess of Salisbury to the Marquess of Dufferin.

No. 466.

My Lord, FOREIGN OFFICE, *September 30, 1895.*

THE French Ambassador called at the Foreign Office on the 24th instant.

Baron de Courcel stated that he considered my views as to what should be required from the Turkish Government in the matter of Armenian reforms, as set forth in my despatch to your Excellency of the 24th instant, as coinciding with those of his Government.

His Excellency thought that the note which M. Hanotaux and Prince Lobanoff proposed should be addressed by the three Ambassadors to the Porte would elicit a written answer.

He said that the French Government were anxious that the Ambassadors should proceed at once, so that the question might be closed. His Government has received information that the Armenian Committees intend to foment disturbances in Turkey.

I am, &c.

(Signed) SALISBURY.

F. O. 424/183, p. 477, No. 375
Turkey No. 1 (1896), p. 150, No. 182 (Extract)

No. 193

Sir P. Currie to the Marquess of Salisbury.

No. 441. CONSTANTINOPLE, *October 1, 1895, 11.45 p.m.*

Telegraphic. *(Received October 1.)*

IN reply to your Lordship's telegram No. 165 of the 30th ultimo, I would suggest that, even should Russia stand aloof, I ought, before starting for London, to inform the Ottoman Government that, subject to such modifications as the three Powers may agree to, Her Majesty's Government will insist on the publication and execution of the Reforms of the 11th May. If your Lordship approves, I will speak to the Grand Vizier in this sense, and let it be known that I have done so, as otherwise my departure may appear to confirm statement circulated by the Palace that Her Majesty's Government has dropped the Reforms. A belief that such is the case would drive the Armenians to desperation.

I should also wish to be instructed whether I should, when making the above communication to the Grand Vizier, at the same time mention that your Lordship has summoned me home or whether I should allow sufficient time to elapse for me to receive a reply to my first communication before giving them this additional information. If I adopted the latter course, they would attribute my departure to the absence of a satisfactory answer from the Sublime Porte, and I have little doubt that the Sultan would make considerable concessions in order to prevent my leaving.

F. O. 424/184, p.1, No. 2

No. 194

Sir P. Currie to the Marquess of Salisbury.

No. 442.   CONSTANTINOPLE, *October 1, 1895, 8.30 p.m.*
Telegraphic.   *(Received October 1.)*

I HAVE received the following account of the riots which took place yesterday in Stamboul from a trustworthy eye-witness:-

About 2,000 Armenians, mostly young men of the middle class, assembled near the Porte with the object of presenting a Petition to the Grand Vizier. The gendarmerie stopped them, and the officer in command summoned them to disperse, and, on their refusing to do so, gave the order to seize their leader. The Armenians carried revolvers and knives, all of one pattern. Shots were exchanged, and the officer of the gendarmerie was killed. About fifteen gendarmes and sixty Armenians fell. The police then dispersed the Armenians, pursuing them and arresting large numbers.

The Softas and other Turks, who had been supplied with clubs, set on the Armenians in the streets and beat many of them to death under the very eyes of the police. About 500 Armenians were arrested. Other demonstrations took place at the same time in different parts of Stamboul. 1,000 armed Armenians with women and children have taken refuge in the church of Patriarchate, where they are besieged by the police.

The police treated the prisoners with the greatest brutality; the Cavass of the British Consulate saw four men brought into the courtyard of the Ministry of Police and bayoneted in cold blood. The Grand Vizier sent twice for the Patriarch yesterday, who, however, did not obey His Highness' summons. Nothwithstanding official statements that order has been restored, there has been several murders of Musulmans and Armenians to day in Stamboul and Galata.

The attitude of the Moslem population causes great uneasiness and apprehension is felt as to the safety of the Christians.

F. O. 424/184, p. 2, No. 3

No. 195

Sir P. Currie to the Marquess of Salisbury.

No. 634.   CONSTANTINOPLE, *October 1, 1895.*

My Lord,   *(Received October 7.)*

I HAVE the honour to forward to your Lordship herewith copy of a despatch which I have received from Her Majesty's Consul at Erzeroum, reporting Mr. Hampson's return from Bitlis, and the state of affairs there and on the road.

I have caused the facts to be communicated to the Grand Vizier.

I have, &c.

(Signed) PHILIP CURRIE.

F. O. 424/184, p. 8, No. 27

No. 196

Sir P. Currie to the Marquess of Salisbury.

No. 443.   CONSTANTINOPLE, *October 2, 1895, 2.30 p.m.*

Telegraphic.   *(Received October 2.)*

A JOINT communication has been made by the Ambassadors to the Porte on the subject of the riots in Stamboul. We mention the facts which have been brought to our knowledge, and which I reported to your Lordship in my immediately preceding telegram.

We urge that the disorders should be repressed by the forces of the Government alone, and with the least possible bloodshed; and protest against private persons being encouraged or allowed to attack Armenians, and against the cold-blooded murder of prisoners by the police.

F. O. 424/184, p. 2, No. 4

No. 197

Sir P. Currie to the Marquess of Salisbury.

No. 444.   CONSTANTINOPLE, *October 2, 1895, 2.45 p.m.*
Telegraphic.   *(Received October 2.)*

MY telegram of yesterday, No. 442.

It appears that the police charged the Armenians and struck them with the butts of their muskets and flat of their swords, and seized upon their leaders; but there seems no doubt that it was the Armenians who fired the first shot.

F. O. 424/184, p. 2, No. 5

No. 198

Sir P. Currie to the Marquess of Salisbury.

No. 445.   CONSTANTINOPLE, *October 2, 1895, 7.55 p.m.*
Telegraphic.   *(Received October 2.)*

THE Khans inhabited by Armenians in many quarters of Constantinople were, with the connivance of the police, attacked last night by Turks, headed by Softas, and the occupants murdered. There is every reason to believe that the excesses will continue. The churches are full of fugitive Armenians, and are surrounded by the police. Terror reigns in the capital and its suburbs, and wholesale arrests are being made.

The Foreign Minister received the representation made this afternoon on behalf of the Ambassadors with indifference. He declared that none of the facts alleged by us had occurred, and that every measure had been taken to guarantee order and public security.

The Government accuses the Patriarch of fomenting the troubles, whereas his Secretary assures me that he solemnly adjured his people to abstain from violence.

I am secretly informed, on high authority, that the Sultan himself has given private orders to the Ministers of War and Police to treat the Armenians with the utmost rigour, while, on the other hand, it has been officially announced that great leniency would be shown them.

The Porte have sent a Circular to their Representatives abroad grossly misrepresenting the real state of affairs.

F. O. 424/184, p. 3, No. 6

No. 199

Sir P. Currie to the Marquess of Salisbury.

No. 446.　　　　　　　　　　　　CONSTANTINOPLE, *October 2, 1895, 8 p.m.*
Telegraphic.　　　　　　　　　　　　　　　　*(Received October 2.)*

ON Mr. Marinitch informing me this evening of the manner in which the Foreign Minister received the representation made on behalf of the Ambassadors this afternoon, as reported in my immediately preceding telegram, I sent the following telegram to the Grand Vizier:-

"J'appelle l'attention de votre Altesse et celle du Gouvernement Impérial sur la communication faite aujourd'hui par les premiers Drogmans de cinq Grandes Puissances à son Excellence le Ministre des Affaires Étrangères. Selon les nouvelles qui me parviennent de tous côtés des massacres d'Arméniens ont eu lieu dans les khans qu'ils habitent sur plusieurs points de la capitale et la terreur règne dans Constantinople et ses faubourgs.

"Loin de s'améliorer l'état des choses s'aggrave et je me vois dans la nécessité d'y appeler l'attention sérieuse de mon Gouvernement."

F. O. 424/184, p. 3, No. 7

No. 200

The Marquess of Salisbury to the Marquess of Dufferin.

No. 117.
Telegraphic.　　　　　　　　　　　　FOREIGN OFFICE, *October 2, 1895.*

IT is necessary, in order to enable the negotiations at Constantinople for the introduction of reforms in the provinces inhabited by Armenians to proceed, that further instructions should be sent to the Ambassadors.

I request your Excellency to propose to the Government to which you are accredited to instruct their Ambassador at Constantinople to concert with the other two Ambassadors in regard to the points in the scheme communicated to the Porte on the 11th May last, which in their opinion are necessary for the protection of the lives and property of the Armenians and to report the result of their consultation.

F. O. 424/184, p. 3, No. 8

No. 201

Sir P. Currie to the Marquess of Salisbury.

No. 450.   CONSTANTINOPLE, *October 3, 1895, 12.20 p.m.*
Telegraphic.   *(Received October 3.)*
   MR. LONGWORTH telegraphs that the ex-Vali of Van, Bahri Pasha, and the Commandant of Trebizond were walking together in the town, when some unknown person fired a revolver at them, and both received wounds in the leg.
   F. O. 424/184, p. 4, No. 10

No. 202

Sir P. Currie to the Marquess of Salisbury.

No. 452.   CONSTANTINOPLE, *October 3, 1895, 6.50 p.m.*
Telegraphic.   *(Received October 3.)*
   MY telegram of yesterday No. 446.
   It is said that the Armenians intend making another demonstration. However, things seemed quieter last night, though there are still very few Armenians to be seen about, and their shops remain closed, and the churches are still full of fugitives.
   The arrests continue.
   F. O. 424/184, p. 4, No. 11

No. 203

The Marquess of Salisbury to Sir P. Currie.

No. 169.
Telegraphic.   FOREIGN OFFICE, *October 3, 1895.*
   I HAVE received your Excellency's telegram No. 441 of the 1st instant relative to the proposed reforms in the provinces inhabited by Armenians.
   It might, I think, be better to reserve till later the announcement that you are going to England.

I approve of the statement which you propose to make to the Grand Vizier, but I should wish you to substitute for the words "small modifications" the words "modifications to detail."

F. O. 424/184, p. 4, No. 12

No. 204

Sir P. Currie to the Marquess of Salisbury.

No. 648.   CONSTANTINOPLE, *October 3, 1895.*
My Lord,   *(Received October 7.)*

WITH reference to my despatch No. 298 of the 9th May, I have the honour to forward to your Lordship herewith copy of a despatch which I have received from Her Majesty's Consul at Aleppo respecting the position of Christians at Djibin, in the Sandjak of Urfa.

I have, &c

(Signed) PHILIP CURRIE.

F. O. 424/184, p. 20, No. 35

Inclosure in No. 204

Consul Barnham to Sir P. Currie.

Sir,   ALEPPO, *September 16, 1895.*

WITH reference to my despatches of the 3rd and 29th April last, I have the honour to again bring to your Excellency's notice the position of the Christians at Djibin, in the Sandjak of Urfa.

I have already reported that a young Armenian girl had been carried off from the village, that her brother had avenged her by killing her seducer, and that thirty of the villagers were imprisoned at Khalfat for complicity in his death.

Of these, four have since been condemned to long terms of imprisonment, the remainder having returned to Djibin about a month ago. The Kurd who was killed belongs to a village near at hand, Omerli, in the Caza of Khalfat, and the men of Omerli have declared a war of revenge against the people of Djibin.

When those who had been acquitted had returned but a few days to Djibin, the Kurds came down from Omerli, and laid before the Armenians three alternatives:-

1. That all of them should turn Moslem.

2. That four virgins should be surrendered to the men of Omerli.

3. That payment should be made to the family of the murdered Kurd of 25,000 piastres.

Failing compliance with one of these alternatives they would be massacred.

Some of the villagers then went to the Kaïmakam of Khalfat and asked for protection, but they were sent away with the answer that what they had suffered was slight punishment for having caused the death of a Moslem.

They then wrote a Petition to the Vali of Aleppo, and sent copies of the Petition to every Consulate, with a request that the Consuls would intercede with the authorities on their behalf.

I forwarded the Petition to the Vali on the 28th ultimo, stating that, as the facts complained of were exceedingly grave, I hoped his Excellency would think it an act of friendship that I should bring them to his notice. I have had no reply, and have no positive knowledge that the Vali took action in the matter. Whether he did so or not, the result is unsatisfactory, for I yesterday received information that, in consequence of fresh troubles, the villagers have been obliged to send all their young women to the care of friends in Biredjik and Urfa, and entire families are leaving the place.

I have, &c.

(Signed) HENRY D. BARNHAM.

F. O. 424/184, p. 20, No. 35/1

No. 205

Sir P. Currie to the Marquess of Salisbury.

No. 650.   THERAPIA, *October 3, 1895.*
My Lord,   *(Received October 3, 1895.)*

AS I telegraphed to your Lordship on the 30th ultimo, a communication bearing the seal of the "Hindchag", the Armenian Revolutionary Committee, was addressed to the Embassies on the 28th ultimo, stating that a strictly peaceful demonstration was about to be made by the Armenians in order to express their desire for reforms. A copy of this communication is inclosed, together with a Memorial received from the same source, which appears to be a copy of an Address drawn up for presentation to the Porte.

The demonstration took place on the 30th ultimo, but unhappily it had not the peaceful character attributed to it.

The demonstrators were armed with pistols and knives of a uniform pattern which had no doubt been issued to them by the organizers of the movement.

There is good reason to suppose that the object of the "Hindchag" was to cause disorder and bloodshed with the view of inducing the Powers of Europe to intervene on behalf of the Armenians.

It is stated that 3,000 persons took the Sacrament in the various Armenian churches on the preceding Sunday in order to be prepared for death.

I am told that the Patriarch besought the congregation at the Cathedral church of Koum Kapou in the most earnest manner to abstain from deeds of violence, and to trust to the efforts which were being made on their behalf by some of the Powers, but his discourse was ill-received. A young Armenian springing up shouted, "We have waited long enough," and a rush was made towards the Patriarch, who took hasty refuge in his private apartments.

On the morning of the 30th ultimo, crowds of Armenians assembled in various quarters of the town, the largest assemblage being in the Armenian quarter of Koum Kapou. They proceeded towards the Porte in numbers, estimated by eye-witnesses at about 2,000, though this is probably an exaggeration.

The authorities appear to have taken some steps to organize a counter-demonstration, and it was observed that an unusual number of Softahs and other Turks armed with sticks were collected in the streets.

The police appear to have made some effort to induce the crowd to retire peaceably.

According to the statement made by the Minister of Police to one of the Dragomans of the Embassy, he deputed Server Bey, a Major in whom he had special confidence, to urge the crowd to disperse.

On their refusing to do so, and stating their intention of proceeding to the Porte, he ordered his men to drive back the crowd with the flat of their swords and the butt-end of their muskets. At the same time, two mounted gendarmes seized upon the leader of the procession, who carried the Memorial which it was intended to present to the Porte. Shots were then exchanged. It is said that the first which was fired proceeded from the Armenians and killed the Major of Gendarmes.

After a time, the Armenians fled in all directions, leaving many of their number on the ground—about thirty of the police, including four officers, were killed or wounded in the course of the day. The flying mob was pursued by the police and the Softahs, and other Turks then joined in the fray.

Prince Albert of Schleswig Holstein Sonderburg Glücksburg and the nephew of the German Ambassador, who happened to be passing, saw close to their carriage an Armenian whose arms were held by several men while others beat him on the head with sticks, when he fell to the ground in an insensible condition, a zaptieh advanced and finished him by firing two shots into his body.

Similar acts are reported by other witnesses and it was specially noted that the police stood by and even held the victims while they were beaten to death by private individuals.

The wounded prisoners appear to have been treated with great brutality and the porter of the British Consulate, who had gone to the Ministry of Police on business, saw four men brought in by the police and bayonetted as soon as they entered the gates of the courtyard.

The most serious feature of this unfortunate outbreak appears to be the violence exercised by the Softahs and other Turks with the consent, if not by the directions, of the authorities. This violence still continued yesterday. Armenians were attacked in all directions and many appear to have been killed. In one instance which occured in Galata they resisted their assailants and shots were fired on both sides. Several khans, occupied by Armenians in various parts of the town, have also been invaded and the inmates massacred.

If these proceedings are not promptly put a stop to, it is to be feared that the lives of other Christians, and even of foreigners, may be in danger. Many Armenians have taken refuge in the churches; the rest generally remain in their houses. In the church of the Patriarchate at Koum Kapou from 500 to 1,000 armed men are collected.

Urgent messages have been sent to the Patriarch to send them away, but he has protested his inability to do so, and the issues are guarded by gendarmes.

An informal meeting took place yesterday morning at the house of the Austrian Ambassador, at which my Russian and German colleagues and I were present. It was decided to make the communication, of which a copy is inclosed, to the Foreign Minister, and this was accordingly done yesterday afternoon.

On learning from my Dragoman that Turkhan Pasha had received our representations with apparent indifference, and according to his usual habit had denied the truth of the facts brought to his knowledge, I thought it desirable to communicate at once with the Grand Vizier, who had been summoned to the Palace before the Dragomans arrived at the Porte. I accordingly sent him the telegram, of which a copy is inclosed.

I have, &c.

(Signed) PHILIP CURRIE.

F. O. 424/184, pp. 20-22, No. 36

No. 206

Sir P. Currie to the Marquess of Salisbury.

No. 453.   CONSTANTINOPLE, *October 4, 1895, 10.50 a.m.*
Telegraphic.   *(Received October 4.)*

MR LONGWORTH telegraphs that one of the two Armenians who fired on Bahri Pasha, as reported in my telegram No. 450 of yesterday, has been arrested. No further arrests have been made, and public order has not been disturbed.

F. O. 424/184, p. 4, No. 13

No. 207

Sir P. Currie to the Marquess of Salisbury.

No. 454.   CONSTANTINOPLE, *October 4, 1895.*
Telegraphic.   *(Received October 4, 7.5 p.m.)*

I CALLED to-day at the private house of Kiamil Pasha, who had expressed a wish to see me at once.

I spoke of the excesses committed during the last few days by the police and by private Mussulmans in Constantinople against unoffending Armenians, of the massacres in khans and houses, of the continued arrests, and of the condition of the prisons, which I proposed to visit, as I did under your Lordship's orders in 1876.

I strongly urged that some steps should be immediately taken to reassure the Armenians and to enable them to return, without fear of further outrages, to their homes and their occupations.

His Highness seemed imperfectly acquainted with the facts, but declared his determination to have a fair inquiry made into them, and he offered to allow any one whom I might depute to assist in the inquiry.

With regard to the Armenian question, his Highness expressed a strong opinion as to the necessity of an early settlement. He appeared to be under the impression that there was an agreement on all points between the Powers and the Porte.

I told him that some further points remained to be discussed, and I specially insisted on the importance of the reforms being promulgated in an Imperial Decree.

I made the communication authorized by your Lordship's telegram No. 169 of the 3rd October.

F. O. 424/184, p. 5, No. 14

No. 208

Sir P. Currie to the Marquess of Salisbury.

No. 456.   CONSTANTINOPLE, *October 4, 1895, 9.40 p.m.*
Telegraphic.   *(Received October 4.)*

MY Russian and French colleagues have been instructed by their respective Governments to address a note to the Porte in which they take act of the reforms which the Sublime Porte has already accepted, and ask, in addition, for a Christian Assistant to the High Commissioner and to the Vali, this latter point being already conceded.

At a meeting I had with them this evening, I said that your Lordship had proposed that we should be authorized to concert as to further points, and that I did not, therefore, feel justified in joining in the note which they proposed to address to the Porte.

F. O. 424/184, p.5, No.16

No. 209

M. Kroupensky to the Marquess of Salisbury.

(Received October 5.)

LE Chargé d'Affaires de Russie est chargé par son Gouvernement de communiquer à Lord Salisbury que l'Ambassadeur de Russie à Constantinople a reçu des instructions qui l'autorisent de se joindre à ses collègues d'Angleterre et de France pour adresser à la Porte une note collective qui ferait état des concessions déjà accordées par le Sultan et de celles sur lesquelles l'accord paraît s'être fait entre les trois Gouvernements, c'est-à-dire, l'adjonction de Chrétiens aux Valis et au Haut Commissaire et la participation des Chrétiens aux emplois publics.

Le Gouvernement Impérial pense que les désordres qui viennent de se produire à Constantinople rendent plus urgent que jamais d'accélérer la conclusion des négociations ayant trait à la question Arménienne.

LONDRES, *le 5 Octobre, 1895.*

Translation.

THE Russian Chargé d'Affaires is directed by his Government to inform Lord Salisbury that the Russian Ambassador at Constantinople has received instructions which authorize him, in concert with his English and French colleagues, to address a collective note to the Porte, stating the concessions already granted by the Sultan, and those in regard to which an agreement appears to have been arrived at by the three Governments, that is to say, the appointment of Christian assistants to the Valis and the High Commissioner, and the participation of Christians in the public service.

The Imperial Government consider that the disorders which have just occurred at Constantinople render it more imperative than ever to expedite the settlement of the negotiations relative to the Armenian question.

F. O. 424/184, p. 7, No. 23
Turkey No. 1 (1896), p. 151, No. 186

No. 210

Sir P. Currie to the Marquess of Salisbury.

No. 460. CONSTANTINOPLE, *October 6, 1895, 7.20 p.m.*
Telegraphic. *(Received October 6.)*

THE joint note of the Ambassadors was presented at the Porte to-day.

Nothing has been done by the Government to restore the public confidence, arrests are still made, and the general feeling of uneasiness continues, and it is rumoured that serious events may be looked for.

Artin Pasha went to-day, by order of the Sultan, to the Patriarchate, and with the assistance of the Patriarch endeavoured to persuade the refugees to leave the churches. This they refused to do, the Revolutionary Committee, it is said, having advised to remain. The Committee have also ordered Armenians to keep their places of business closed, with the result that many payments are suspended.

F. O. 424/184, p. 8, No. 26

No. 211

Sir P. Currie to the Marquess of Salisbury.

No. 652. Confidential. THERAPIA, *October 6, 1895.*
My Lord, *(Received October 11.)*

I HAVE the honour to transmit herewith copy of a Report by Mr. Shipley, Dragoman of this Embassy, containing an account of an interview which he had, by my instructions, with the Armenian Patriarch on the 4th October.

I have, &c.

(Signed) PHILIP CURRIE.

F. O. 424/184, p. 34, No. 68

Inclosure in No. 211

Report by Mr. Shipley.

Confidential.

IN accordance with the instructions of his Excellency the Ambassador, I called yesterday, accompanied by a cavass of the Embassy, on the Armenian Patriarch, Mgr. Ismirlian, at the latter's residence at Koum Kapou.

After the usual inquiries as to the health of his Beatitude, I informed the latter that I had been instructed by his Excellency to assure his Beatitude that his

Excellency took the deepest interest in the present state of the Armenians; that his Excellency would do what lay in his power to put a stop to the arrest and murder of innocent people; that he would make the strongest representations on the subject to the Grand Vizier, whom he was visiting that day; and that his Excellency sympathized very fully with the trouble and difficulty in which his Beatitude was placed.

Finally, that his Excellency was aware of and had reported to Her Majesty's Government the efforts made by his Beatitude to restrain violence, and that his Excellency, bearing in mind the suffering which retaliation might inflict on innocent persons, as well as the fact that violence would alienate the sympathies of Europe, hoped that his Beatitude would not fail to continue these efforts.

I also made his Beatitude acquainted with the substance of the communication to the Sublime Porte by the Embassies under date of the 2nd October, reading out to his Beatitude the concluding paragraph.

His Beatitude, in reply, begged me to convey to his Excellency his deepest thanks for the sympathy shown by his Excellency not only to himself but to the Armenian cause, and further expressed the most earnest hope that his Excellency would find a radical remedy for the existing state of things. His Beatitude then went on to say that as the recent events were due to the utterly desperate and wretched condition into which the Armenians had fallen, there could be no hope that the present state of things would cease in any vilayet if the reforms were not under the direct control and guarantee (his Beatitude laying great emphasis on the latter word) of either the six European Powers collectively or any one of them.

As regards the necessity of restraining further violence, on which I told his Beatitude that your Excellency laid particular stress, the Patriarch said he would do what he could, but stated, at the same time, that it was out of his power to guarantee anything. The Armenian communities were coming to him and saying, "You see our desperate condition; we know that during nine months you have done your best, but what is going to be done?"

The Armenians were beside themselves, arrested as they were, thrown into prison, and shut up through fear in their churches.

His Beatitude, in reply to a question of mine as to whether any more demonstrations were likely to take place, while admitting that things were now a little quieter, stated that he would offer no guarantee that they would remain so in view of the desperation of the Armenians to which his Beatitude repeatedly referred.

I may mention that his Beatitude, though disposed to take an extremely despondent view of the situation, was evidently more cheerful at the end of the interview, and was, I think, most grateful to his Excellency for the expression of sympathy I had been instructed to convey.

His Beatitude furnished to me at the above interview the following particulars respecting recent events.

Up to the present eighty-one bodies had been given up to the Patriarchate by the Turkish authorities, of which two had had their throats cut. More bodies were being sent in that day, the exact number of which his Beatitude could not give until evening. The medical reports concerning these and other cases would in due course be furnished to the various Embassies.

In the Kassim Pasha affair the Turkish authorities had not delivered up any bodies, but he estimated the number of victims at from thirty to forty.

At Kara Geumrih, near the mosque of Mehmed Fatih, twenty-five Armenians had been killed, as well as a young girl and two women, one of the latter being pregnant.

As regards the latter case, the facts, according to his Beatitude, given on the authority of the chief Armenian medical attendant, Dr. Tirakian by name, were that the abdomen was cut open. The woman was taken to the hospital in question, where the doctor succeeded in extracting the infant, the woman then expiring.

Of 150 men known to be at Tchoukour Tchesmé Han, no traces had been found since 4.30 p.m. on Tuesday. Of these twelve had been killed by the official report, and their bodies handed over; none of these bodies, however, belonged to the men of Palu, of whom it was known that a certain number were among the 150 referred to, or they would have been known by their dress.

As regarded the Armenians in the churches, there were, his Beatitude stated, no cordons, military or otherwise, placed round them to prevent the Armenians from coming out. The latter, however, who took refuge there, principally at night, were afraid to come out owing to their fear of being either arrested or assassinated.

I may mention, in conclusion, that I visited the church at Koum Kapou, and found a great number of Armenians inside. They seemed, however, to be well looked after, and not wanting for food.

I omitted to state, with regard to the Tchoukour Tchesmé Han affair, that his Beatitude informed me that an eye-witness, whose name he refrained from giving, stated that he had seen eight chariots with dead bodies.

I myself saw at the Patriarchate a man, Caloust by name, who bore evident traces of ill-usage.

F. O. 424/184, p.p. 35-36, No. 68/1

No. 212

Sir P. Currie to the Marquess of Salisbury.

No. 653.   THERAPIA, *October 6, 1895.*
My Lord,   *(Received October 11.)*
    I HAVE the honour to transmit herewith copy of a letter which has been
addressed by the Armenian Patriarch to the Representatives of the Great Powers
appealing for their assistance in the re-establishment of order.

                                              I have, &c.
                                              (Signed) PHILIP CURRIE.

    F. O. 424/184, p. 36, No. 69

Inclosure in No. 212

The Armenian Patriarch to Sir. P. Currie.

Confidentielle.   PATRIARCAT ARMÉNIEN,
M. l'Ambassadeur,   CONSTANTINOPLE, *le 4 Octobre, 1895.*
    DEPUIS Lundi dernier, 17 (29) Septembre, la population Arménienne de la
capitale est en prioe à la panique et se trouve précisément dans l'état auquel sont
condamnés, depuis longtemps, ses compatriotes des provinces. Ce jour, un groupe
de nos nationaux s'est réuni pour aller soumettre une pétition à la Sublime Porte et
implorer le terme de leurs souffrances, de même que dans la matinée; l'office
terminé, un autre groupe, comprenant des femmes originaires des provinces, s'était
présenté à nous et était parti sur nos promesses encourageantes.
    Cependant, du côté de la Sublime Porte, selon nos informations, la démarche
des pétitionnaires est empêchée par la force des armes, et là ont lieu des scénes
sanglantes; de nombreux Arméniens sont cruellement tués, d'autres sont blessés,
arrêtés et vont emplir les prisons.
    Devant ces faits, devant les assassinats survenus çà et là et les mouvements
menaçants d'individus à l'apparence de Softas, un certain nombre d'Arméniens
viennent se réfugier dans la cathédrale.
    Les jours et les nuits suivants, surtout à la faveur des ténèbres et de la solitude,
des massacres ont lieu. On égorge nuitamment des ouvriers Arméniens dans un
han de Tchoukour-Tchesmé (Stamboul), un groupe de provinciaux Arméniens
dans un han à Kassim-Pacha; dans maints quartiers et villages, à Galata, à
Guédik-Pacha, à Hasskeui, à Makrikeui, à Cunkapan, à Caragheumruk, à
Tophané, à Atpazar des innocents sont assassinés, entre autres notre Yassakdji
Avediss, à 8 heures du soir, à son retour de Yeni-Kapou au Patriarcat, et tout près
du corps de garde.

La populace saisit le texte de chercher des armes comme un mot d'ordre, pour envahir les demeures et en égorger les habitants sans défense, sous les yeux indifférents de la police.

Des personnes en grand nombre ont également disparu.

Il n'a pas encore été possible de préciser le nombre des personnes tuées, blessées, arrêtées et disparues; il paraît considérable, bien que jusqu'à ce matin seize cadavres seulement ont été livrés pour être enterrés.

On demande sécurité de tous côtés; les écoles, les maisons de commerce, et les boutiques restent closes et la faim menace les familles pauvres. La terreur va se généralisant, et de même que la population de Stamboul s'était réfugiée dans la Cathédrale, du côté de Péra et de Galata, une population, parmi laquelle des femmes et des enfants, poussée par la peur, s'en va se refugier dans les églises de ces localités, comme dans des asiles inviolables.

Le Gouvernement nous demande avec instance de disperser cette population, mais ni les exhortations, ni les promesses ne lui inspirent assez de confiance pour la déterminer de sortir, tant qu'elle continue à apprendre que de nouveaux crimes se commettent jour et nuit et que des prisonniers succombent aux mauvais traitements. Dans ces conditions comment nous serait-il possible de lui fermer les portes de nos églises, et de la priver de l'unique asile peut-être qui lui reste.

En présence de cette situation désespérée, au nom de l'humanité, au nom de la Chrétienté et de la civilisation Européenne, nous recourons à votre Excellence et vous implorons à l'effet de prendre en sérieuse considération le présent état des choses et de déterminer par l'intervention de votre haute autorité, l'adoption des mesures nécessaires pour rétablir d'une façon réelle l'ordre et la sécurité, calmer toute cette population, évacuer les églises, et, grâce à une enquête impartiale, révéler les crimes commis, découvrir les personnes disparues, relâcher les prisonniers, infliger des punitions exemplaires à tous les auteurs, complices et agents des massacres des Chrétiens.

En confiant votre Excellence à la garde du Très-Haut et invitant sur elle les bénédictions Divines, j'ai, &c.

Le Patriarche des Arméniens de Turquie,
(Signé) MADTÉOS.

F. O. 424/184, pp. 36-37, No. 69/1

No. 213

Sir P. Currie to the Marquess of Salisbury.

No. 655.   THERAPIA, *October 6, 1895.*
My Lord,   *(Received October 11.)*

WITH reference to my telegrams Nos. 443 and 445 of the 2nd October, I have the honour to transmit to your Lordship copy of a Memorandum by Mr. Marinitch giving an account of the interview at which the Dragomans of the Great Powers made joint representations to the Minister for Foreign Affairs respecting the recent disturbances in Constantinople.

I have, &c.

(Signed) PHILIP CURRIE.

F. O. 424/184, p. 38, No. 71

Inclosure in No. 213

Memorandum by Mr. Marinitch.

IN accordance with your Excellency's instructions I waited last Wednesday with my Austrian, French, Italian, and German colleagues upon the Minister for Foreign Affairs, and took part in the join representation made in consequence of the excesses committed by zaptiehs, and more especially by private Mussulmans during and after the affray of last Monday in Stamboul when the Armenians made their so-called peaceful demonstration.

Turkhan Pasha stated, in reply, that he did not know whether excesses, such as those complained of, had actually been committed. But his Excellency declared that the Turkish Government had taken, and were still taking, every possible measure to entirely restore order and tranquillity in the capital, and that he could guarantee that public security was perfectly assured.

In answer, I stated that I regretted to see that his Excellency did not understand the great importance of the joint representation made by the five Embassies, nor the gravity of the situation, which calls for immediate and more efficacious measures.

My Italian colleague mentioned to Turkhan Pasha the wholesale massacre of Armenians at Kassim-Pasha, which his Excellency professed not to have heard of.

The French Dragoman simply referred to the conversation he had had in the morning with the foreign Minister, and M. Testa, the German Dragoman, stated that the eye-witnesses being persons of whose credibility no doubt could be entertained, the facts complained of were in the opinion of the Embassies fully established.

Turkhan Pasha thereupon repeated his former statements, which, as you Excellency will perceive, were not such as a Minister for Foreign Affairs should have made in answer to so strong a representation at so critical a moment.

THERAPIA, *October 5, 1895.*

F. O. 424/184, p. 39, No. 71/1

No. 214

Sir P. Currie to the Marquess of Salisbury.

No. 461.   CONSTANTINOPLE, *October 7, 1895, 11.55 p.m.*
Telegraphic.   *(Received October 7.)*

THE Sultan sent Zekki Pasha, Grand Master of Artillery, to me this evening, to say that the proximity of the English fleet encouraged the Armenian Revolutionary Committee in their action, and to beg me to give orders for its removal to some more distant port, *e.g.,* Salonica. Order, he said, could not be restored as long as the fleet remained at Lemnos. The Armenian Committee hoped by provoking the Turkish population to bloodshed to force Her Majesty's Government to bring the fleet to Constantinople, and demand autonomy for the Armenians.

I replied that it was not in my power to issue orders respecting movements of the fleet. The present disturbance of public order was due to the excesses committed by the Turkish population with the connivance of the police, even though the trouble originated with the action of the Armenians, and it was for the Turkish Government to restore order and confidence. If the answer returned to Porte to the note of the Ambassadors, asking what measures had been taken to calm the agitation prevailing among Mussulmans and Armenians, proved satisfactory, I would inform Her Majesty's Government of its purport, at the same time reporting His Imperial Majesty's desire that the fleet might be moved from Lemnos.

On Zekki Pasha asking whether I would support this request, I replied that the decision lay entirely with Her Majesty's Government, but that it could hardly be expected in the present critical state of affairs in the capital that they would consent to move the fleet.

During our conversation, Zekki Pasha repeatedly insisted on the fact that the first shot had been fired by the Armenians, and I replied that the wholesale massacres and arrests of innocent Armenians which had taken place could not be justified by the criminal act of a few revolutionists.

He admitted that regrettable excesses had occurred, but asserted that their continuance was now rendered impossible owing to the military patrols which had been established.

F. O. 424/184, p. 26, No. 38

No. 215

Sir P. Currie to the Marquess of Salisbury.

No. 656.   Therapia, *October 7, 1895.*
My Lord,   *(Received October 11.)*
    WITH reference to my telegram No. 460 of the 6th instant, I have the honour
to transmit herewith copy of the collective note of the six Embassies presented to
the Porte on the 6th October respecting the present state of insecurity in
Constantinople.
                                        I have, &c.
                                        (Signed) Philip Currie.

F. O. 424/184, p. 39, No. 72

Inclosure in No. 215

Collective Note.

    EN présence des événements dont la ville de Constantinople a été le théâtre
depuis cinq jours, les Représentants des Grandes Puissances ont dû se préoccuper
des conséquences qui pourraient résulter de la durée de cet état de trouble.
    Il existe au sein de la population Arménienne de la capitale une excitation et
une inquiétude qui ne paraissent pas se calmer. Quelle que soit la cause à laquelle
on puisse les attribuer il semble qu'au lieu de diminuer elles ne fassent
qu'augmenter chaque jour. Aussi d'après le bruit public est-il à craindre qu'on
n'assiste à de nouveaux incidents.
    En outre l'inquiétude causée par les mesures prises contre les Arméniens qui
n'étaient pas mêlés au mouvement, les arrestations en masse, les sévices dont
plusieurs ont été l'objet, ont déterminé nombre d'entre eux à se réfugier dans les
églises dont ils ne veulent pas sortir s'ils n'obtiennent des garanties sérieuses pour
leur liberté et leur vie. Il est évident que la prolongation d'un pareil état de choses
ne peut qu'augmenter l'agitation des esprits et constitue une cause permanente de
conflits.
    Un fait grave surtout est à noter: c'est qu'à la suite de la dispersion de la
manifestation de Lundi dernier un grand nombre d'individus n'appartenant ni à la
police ni à l'armée, des Softas, des Kurdes établis à Constantinople, de simples
particuliers dans mandat, se sont armés, ont poursuivi les Arméniens et se sont
livrés même contre des Chrétiens appartenant aux autres communautés à des
agressions de tout genre. On signale de leur part de nombreuses attaques aux
propriétés et des faits de pillage et de meurtre. L'autorité loin de mettre un terme à
leurs excès a tout l'air de les avoir encouragés. Quelques Ambassades ont pu

enregistrer des sévices subis par plusieurs de leurs nationaux; toutes ont eu connaissance des arrestations arbitraires et des actes de brutalité commis par des agents de police et des zapités.

Quel que repréhensible que puissent être les actes accomplis par les manifestants, de pareils excès ne sauraient être excusés.

En outre la police elle-même a gravement méconnu les devoirs d'équité et de modération qui s'imposent aux représentants de la force publique. Tous les témoignages concordent à démotrer qu'elle à pratiqué les arrestations sans mesure, sans contrôle, et sans aucune vérification de l'identité des personnes. Un grand nombre de passants inoffensifs ont été appréhendés et jetés en prison sous le simple prétexte qu'ils étaient ou paraissaient Arméniens. La police s'est livrée sur les détenus à des excès de tout genre. Partout ils ont été victimes des plus mauvais traitements, de coups et de blessures, et plus d'une fois les agents ont tué des prisonniers sans défense.

La Sublime Porte conviendra que tous ces faits sont de nature à causer la plus grande émotion parmi les colonies Européennes établies à Constantinople.

Ils autorisent à penser que si cette situation se prolongeait la sécurité publique serait gravement et irrémédiablement compromise et que l'agitation en s'étendant pourrait gagner les provinces de l'Empire.

Les Représentants des Puissances se voient dans l'obligation de demander à la Sublime Porte quelles mesures elle a prise pour calmer l'inquiétude et l'agitation qui se sont emparées des populations Musulmane et Arménienne, pour prévoir ainsi le retour des lamentables incidents de ces jours derniers et mettre les Chrétiens et les colonies étrangères à l'abri d'éventualités périlleuses.

Ils ont aussi le désir de prêter leur concours au Gouvernement Ottoman afin de rétablir de part et d'autre la tranquillité dans les esprits. Ils pensent que des enquêtes immédiates sur les événements dont Constantinople vient d'être le théâtre, sur l'état des prisons, sur la conduite des agents de police et des gendarmes, et que la mise en liberté des nombreux prisonniers contre lesquels ne s'élèves aucune charge sérieuse seraient les meilleurs moyens de calmer l'agitation actuelle.

Ils sont prêts à assister et à seconder le Gouvernement Impérial dans ses enquêtes et à lui transmettre toutes les informations qu'ils ont pu recueillir. Ils ne doutent pas que la Sublime Porte ne prenne enfin les mesures nécessaires pour mettre un terme à un état de choses dont la conscience Européenne ne manquerait pas de s'indigner s'il devenait évident que l'inaction de l'autorité encourage de regrettables passions.

Les Représentants des Puissances estiment qu'il est urgent d'arriver aux moyens d'assurer à la population Chrétienne de la capitale une sécurité que les faits cités plus haut et tant d'autres ont si gravement compromise depuis quelques jours. Ils ont la ferme confiance que le Gouvernement Impérial soucieux de démontrer que son esprit de justice et son autorité peuvent exercer une action efficace dans des circonstances aussi graves les mettra promptement en mesure de rassurer leurs

Gouvernements respectifs au sujet d'événements qui préoccupent à juste titre l'opinion publique et qui ne manqueront pas de soulever en Europe la plus vive émotion.

Le 6 Octobre, 1895.
F. O. 424/184, pp. 39-40, No. 72/1

No. 216

Sir P. Currie to the Marquess of Salisbury.

No. 464.   CONSTANTINOPLE, *October 8, 1895, 2.40 p.m.*
Telegraphic.   *(Received October 8.)*

I THINK that all the essential points in the proposals of the 11th May are dealt with in the recommendations of the three Ambassadors reported in my immediately preceding telegram. It seems hopeless in the present state of the finances to demand that local administration should be made a first charge on the revenue of the vilayets, and we have therefore dropped that point.

F. O. 424/184, p. 26, No. 39

No. 217

Sir P. Currie to the Marquess of Salisbury.

No. 465.   CONSTANTINOPLE, *October 8, 1895, 6.40 p.m.*
Telegraphic.   *(Received October 8.)*

ABOUT 2,000 Armenians have taken refuge in the Patriarchate and the Armenian churches in Constantinople. The police have surrounded the buildings, and allow no food to be taken in.

In consequence of an appeal made on behalf of the refugees, the three Ambassadors have offered to intervene and endeavour to settle the difficulty, and have requested the Porte to give orders in the meantime for the suspension of the blockade.

F. O. 424/184, pp. 26-27, No. 40

No. 218

Sir P. Currie to the Marquess of Salisbury.

No. 468.
Telegraphic.

CONSTANTINOPLE, *October 8, 1895, 11.55 p.m.*
(Received October 8.)

WITH reference to my telegram of yesterday's date No. 461, I have the honour to inform your Lordship that I received a further visit from Zekki Pasha this evening. He was the bearer of a request from the Sultan that I would use my influence to put an end to the disturbances caused, according to His Imperial Majesty, by the violence of the Armenians. I informed Zekki Pasha of the telegram which the six Embassies had this afternoon addressed to the Porte, proposing to use their good offices in regard to those who had taken refuge in the churches, and I said that if we received solemn assurances that no one would molest the refugees, we would advise them to give up their arms and return to their homes.

Zekki Pasha then went on to say that the Sultan had determined to offer his devoted friendship to England and to follow her advice, and repeated His Majesty's request that the fleet might be moved from Lemnos, adding that, under these circumstances, he could not doubt that Her Majesty's Government would immediately comply with His Majesty's request.

I replied that this was not the first time that the Sultan had given similar assurances which had not been fulfilled. If, however, His Majesty really wished to follow England's advice, he would find Her Majesty's Government quite ready to counsel him for the benefit of the Ottoman Empire. He must, however, prove the sincerity of his intentions not merely by words, but by deeds.

I did not think that for the present any change in the position of the fleet would be made, but when the reforms demanded by the Powers had been promulgated and satisfactory steps taken for restoring order, I felt sure that Her Majesty's Government would make no difficulty in meeting His Majesty's wishes on this point.

Zekki Pasha said that the Sultan would receive me if I would attend the Selamlik on Friday.

The proximity of the fleet is evidently disturbing His Majesty very much, and there are grounds for hoping that, if I and my colleagues are at once authorized to press for the acceptance of the reforms as laid down in my telegram No. 463 of the 8th instant, we might, without much delay, succeed in carrying them through.

F. O. 424/184, p. 27, No. 43

No. 219

The Marquess of Salisbury to the Marquess of Dufferin.

No. 483.
My Lord,   FOREIGN OFFICE, *October 8, 1895.*

THE French Ambassador informed Mr. Bertie, on the 6th instant, that your Lordship had made a communication to M. Hanotaux relative to Armenian reforms in accordance with the instructions contained in my telegram No. 117 of the 2nd instant.

M. Hanotaux had informed Baron de Courcel that, in compliance with my suggestion, he had instructed M. Cambon, by telegraph, to concert with the British and Russian Ambassadors at Constantinople in regard to the final proposals to be presented to the Porte, it being understood that the points included in the scheme presented by the Ambassadors on the 11th May last should be the subject of their examination, and that they should refer the results of their deliberations to their respective Governments.

M. Hanotaux was anxious to know whether my suggestion had been communicated in writing to the Russian Government, as it had been by you to the French Government. He was very desirous of avoiding any uncertainty which might delay the conclusion of the negotiations with the Porte, and Prince Lobanoff, M. Hanotaux said, appeared to share his views on this point.

Mr. Bertie informed Baron de Courcel that the instructions to Sir F. Lascelles were telegraphed to St. Petersburgh, and that his Excellency had replied by telegraph on the 4th instant that M. Chichkine had informed him that, in consequence of a telegram from Prince Lobanoff, instructions in the sense requested by me had been sent to M. de Nélidoff.

I am, &c.

(Signed) SALISBURY.

F. O. 424/184, p. 28, No. 44

No. 220

Sir P. Currie to the Marquess of Salisbury.

No. 469.   CONSTANTINOPLE, *October 9, 1895, 10.15 a.m.*
Telegraphic.   *(Received October 9.)*

IN reply to the joint note presented by the Embassies on the 6th instant, as reported in my telegram No. 460 of that day's date, the Sublime Porte has addressed a note to us stating the measures that have been adopted to prevent any fresh disturbances and to assure the security of the Christians and foreign colonies.

These measures are as follows:

Patrols of soldiers and police circulate night and day in the streets for the maintenance of order.

Warnings have been issued and the public has been recommended, through the medium of the newspapers, to keep the peace. The Sheikh-ul-Islam has exhorted the Softas in the same sense.

F. O. 424/184, p. 28, No. 45

No. 221

Sir P. Currie to the Marquess of Salisbury.

No. 470. CONSTANTINOPLE, *October 9, 1895, 10.15 a.m.*
Telegraphic. *(Received October 9.)*

IN reply to the telegram from the Embassies proposing our good offices in the matter of the refugees in the churches, as reported in my telegram No. 463 of yesterday, the Porte has telegraphed thanking us for our offer, but denying that the police have prevented food being brought into the churches.

They are willing to confer with the Ambassadors as to the best means of dealing with the difficulty.

F. O. 424/184, p. 28, No. 46

No. 222

Sir P. Currie to the Marquess of Salisbury.

No. 473. CONSTANTINOPLE, *October 9, 1895, 7.10 p.m.*
Telegraphic. *(Received October 9.)*

MY telegram No. 470 of yesterday.

The foreign Minister met the Ambassadors at the French Embassy this afternoon to give us the answer of the Sublime Porte to the offer of our good services in the matter of the refugees in the churches.

Saïd Pasha, speaking in the name of the Ottoman Government, gave us his word that the refugees would be allowed to leave the churches on condition of their giving up any arms they might possess, and that they would be neither arrested nor molested, but might return freely to their homes.

The Dragomans of the Embassies will to-morrow visit the different Armenian churches and inform the refugees of the assurances given by the Imperial Government and encourage them to go home. Every precaution will be taken to prevent disturbances, and the Dragomans will act in communication with the Minister of Police.

F. O. 424/184, p. 29, No. 49

No. 223

Sir P. Currie to the Marquess of Salisbury.

No. 474.   CONSTANTINOPLE, *October 9, 1895, 7.20 p.m.*
Telegraphic.   *(Received October 9.)*

M. CAMBON informs me that the French Government have sent him a telegram approving the recommendations of the three Ambassadors as to the points to be insisted on in the proposals of the 11th May (*vide* my telegram No. 463 of the 8th October).

He has also heard that recommendations meet with Prince Lobanoff's approval.

F. O. 424/184, p. 29, No. 50

No. 224

Sir P. Currie to the Marquess of Salisbury.

No. 659. Confidential.   CONSTANTINOPLE, *October 9, 1895.*
My Lord,   *(Received October 14.)*

I HAVE the honour to forward to your Lordship herewith copy of a letter which I have received from the Armenian Patriarch praying that the execution of Armenian Reforms should be under European control.

A similar letter was addressed to the other Embassies.

I have, &c.

(Signed) PHILIP CURRIE.

F. O. 426/184, p. 48, No. 87

Inclosure in No. 224

The Armenian Patriarch to Sir P. Currie.

Confidentielle.   PATRIARCAT ARMÉNIEN, CONSTANTINOPLE, *le 6 Octobre,1895.*
M. l'Ambassadeur,

A L'OCCASION du projet des reformes proposées par les trois Grandes Puissances, en vue des provinces habitées par les Arméniens, nous avons eu, à plusieurs reprises, l'honneur d'appeler la bienveillante attention de leurs Excellences les Ambassadeurs de ces Puissances sur la nécessité de placer l'exécution du projet sous la surveillance et le contróle directe des Puissances Européennes.

Des faits évidents continuent à démontrer d'une maniére pitoyable qu'il ne sera pas possible de tirer du dit projet le profit attendu, tant que cette condition essentielle n'y sera pas annexée et que l'exécution en sera abandonnée au mode ordinaire. L'extrême gravité de la situation nous fait un devoir de revenir sur ce point, bien que nous soyons profondément impressionné par le spectacle douloureux étalé sous nos yeux.

Considérant, en effet, que la condition du contrôle constitue simplement une question de vie et de mort pour une population Chrétienne, persécutée et noyée dans le sang; considérant qu'à cette condition seule pourra se réaliser le désir manifesté, dans un si noble esprit, par les Grandes Puissances de l'Europe généreuse et civilisée de mettre fin aux souffrances de cette population et d'établir l'ordre et la sécurité dans le pays, nous osons, M. l'Ambassadeur, recourir à votre Excellence et implorer de vous la grâce d'appeler sur ce point, avec votre haute intelligence, la sollicitude de votre Gouvernement, afin que les Grandes Puissances Européennes veuillent bien soumettre l'exécution du projet de réformes à leur contrôle collectif ou même au contrôle de celles entre elles qu'elles jugeraient convenable de charger de ce soin.

En confiant votre Excellence, &c.

Le Patriarche des Arméniens de Turquie,
(Signé) MADTÉOS.

F. O. 424/184, p. 19, No.87/1

No. 225

Sir P. Currie to the Marquess of Salisbury.

No. 660.   CONSTANTINOPLE, *October 9, 1895.*
Mr Lord,   *(Received October 14.)*

I HAVE the honour to forward to your Lordship herewith copy of a despatch which I have received from Her Majesty's Vice-Consul at Moush, reporting the dismissal of police officers complained of with reference to abuses in tax collection.

I have, &c.

(Signed) PHILIP CURRIE.

F. O. 424/184, p. 49, No. 88

Inclosure in No. 225

Vice-Consul Hampson to Sir P. Currie.

Sir,   Moush, *September 16, 1895.*
    WITH reference to my despatch of the 9th instant, I am glad to report that the
three Captains of Police, Reshid, Hajji Fïm, and Iskender have now been
dismissed.
    I hear that even now the Mutessarif has assured them that this is only a
temporary measure.
    I may add that many of the zaptiehs (privates) have not received any pay for
the last eight months.
                                            I have, &c.
                                            (Signed) Charles S. Hampson.

    F. O. 424/184, p. 49, No. 88/1

No. 226

Sir P. Currie to the Marquess of Salisbury.

No. 661. Confidential.   Therapia, *October 9, 1895.*
Mr Lord,   *(Received October 14.)*
    WITH reference to my despatch No. 653, Confidential, of the 6th instant, I
have the honour to transmit a Report drawn up by Mr Shipley of a further visit
which, by my instruction, he paid to the Patriarchate on the 6th instant.
                                            I have, &c.
                                            (Signed) Philip Currie.

    F. O. 424/184, p. 50, No. 89

Inclosure in No. 226

Memorandum by Mr. Shipley.

Very Confidential.
    I PROCEEDED to-day to the Armenian Patriachate, as instructed by his
Excellency the Ambassador, and found his Beatitude in the company of Artin
Pasha.
    The latter, to whom I handed your letter, after a short reference to recent
events, dwelling, however, on the fact of the massacres and the desperate condition
of the Armenians, begged me to convey to his Excellency the following facts.

He, Artin Pasha, had had two audiences of the Sultan, at the first of which, viz., last night, His Majesty had ordered him to visit the Patriarch, and, acting in accord with the latter, assure, on the part of His Majesty, the Armenians shut up in the churches, that nothing would happen to them if they came out and dispersed. Artin Pasha further stated that while at the first audience he learned that a Report had been drawn up by Kiamil, Turkhan, Rifaat, and Riza-Pashas, and presented to His Majesty, recommending a blockade of the churches and to allow no one either to go in or come out—the pretext made use of being that the official communication recently published in the papers had had no attention paid to it by the Armenians.

On receiving His Majesty's order, Artin Pasha proceeded the same night to the Patriarchate, and in the presence of his Beatitude spoke to three or four of the Armenians shut up in the church at Koum Kapou, and informed them that the Sultan had given him, Artin Pasha, full power to act, to promise them an amnesty, in fact, to give them all the necessary assurances if they would come out quietly.

To this the Armenians replied: "We believe you and the Patriarch, but you yourself may have been deceived. We have no confidence in him who sent you; we are in Turkey;" and although he, Artin Pasha, for the space of three hours, endeavoured to persuade them he did not succeed, although he states they were shaken. He and the Patriarch had further told the Armenians that they could go out gradually by sixes or so at a time, and that if anything happened to any one of them the churches would still be open to them as a refuge. The Armenians, however, were not persuaded, and demanded the immediate execution of the reforms for which they had been waiting nine months.

Artin Pasha then returned to the Sultan, and informed the latter that although he and the Patriarch had done all in their power, they had only succeeded in shaking, not convincing, the Armenians. At this second audience, Artin Pasha informed me, he had most earnestly begged the Sultan not to give the order for the blockade of the churches, pointing out to His Majesty the dangers to which it would give rise, such as the fanaticism of the Mussulmans residing near the Patriarchate (a danger upon which the Patriarch also strongly insisted to me)—the people who would starve and thereby become desperate, and the Sultan upon these representations countermanded the order at once.

Artin Pasha then went on to say most confidentially that the Sultan's *amour propre* was now concerned; His Majesty wished to show his Ministers that he had been able to solve the difficulty by peaceful means. He, Artin Pasha, however desired me to point out to his Excellency that the Sultan might at any moment be obliged to give way, owing to the persistence of the Ministers, and to the fact, which would be strongly insisted on by the latter, that no notice had been taken of the official communication above referred to.

Artin Pasha added that the Sultan now thought that the blockage had been counselled in order to expressly create a state of panic and disturbance which in turn would be made use of to dethrone him. Artin Pasha further stated that it was Kiamil Pasha who had strongly insisted on the necessity of the blockade, going so far as to declare that he would resign if the measures in question were not adopted. On this account, it was Kiamil Pasha who would be the next Minister to be dismissed.

Under these circumstances, therefore, Artin Pasha desired me to inform your Excellency that the matter was one of the greatest urgency; that together with the Patriarch he begged me to say to his Excellency that the deputation of the Armenians above alluded to have said they would believe England, and that, in consequence, if his Excellency would only cause it to be conveyed to these Armenians that no harm could come to them, and that the reforms would be immediately published, they would at once come out and go peaceably to their occupations.

Both Artin Pasha and his Beatitude spoke of the deep gratitude felt by every Armenian towards England, and of the influence over them possessed by the latter country.

At the close of the interview, I asked his Beatitude whether he himself thought that any harm would come to Armenians if they came out. His Beatitude replied that, speaking as Armenian Patriarch, he was obliged to say that Abdul Hamid had made so many promises to the Armenians, none of which had been fulfilled, that he himself hesitated to believe.

Artin Pasha, on the other hand, thought that this time the Sultan was sincere, since his own person was at stake, and advised, therefore, his Excellency to send some kind of message to the Armenians, as to whose desperation there was no doubt whatever.

(Signed) H. S. SHIPLEY.
(Received October 6, 1895.)

F. O. *424/184, pp. 50-51, No. 89/1*

No. 227

Sir P. Currie to the Marquess of Salisbury.

No. 663.   CONSTANTINOPLE, *October 9, 1895.*
My Lord,   *(Received October 14.)*
WITH reference to my telegram No. 432 of the 26th September, I have the honour to forward to your Lordship herewith copy of a despatch which I have received from Her Majesty's Consul at Erzeroum, reporting increase of Armenian agitation in that town.

I have, &c.

(Signed) PHILIP CURRIE.

F. O. *424/184, p. 51, No. 90*

Inclosure in No. 227

Consul Graves to Sir P. Currie.

Confidential.

Sir,   ERZEROUM, *September 25, 1895.*

I HAVE the honour to report that the Armenian revolutionary agents belonging to the Hintchag and Tashnaktsagan organizations are daily growing more active at Erzeroum, and that several fresh agitators are reported to have arrived here recently from Russia.

I am informed that they have threatened one or two of the Armenian Notables who are members of the Administrative Council of the vilayet with violence if they continue to sit on the Council, and have demanded money of them to be used for the purposes of their agitation, such as buying arms, &c.

Though these agents are mostly Russian Armenians, and their organizations are to be found in Tiflis, Kars, and other towns of the Caucasus Government, it is said that they are now acting under orders emanating from a Committee established in London.

I had the honour to report the substance of the above to your Excellency by telegraph to-day.

I have, &c.

(Signed) R. W. GRAVES.

F. O. 424/184, p. 51, No. 90/1

No. 228

Sir P. Currie to the Marquess of Salisbury.

No. 664.   THERAPIA, *October 9, 1895.*

My Lord,   *(Received October 14.)*

I HAVE the honour to transmit herewith copy of a despatch which I have received from Her Majesty's Consul at Erzeroum respecting the distribution of relief funds in Sasun. Dr. Reynold's Report, forming the inclosure to Mr. Graves' despatch, has been sent to the President of the Local Armenian Relief Fund, by whom it will be communicated to the Duke of Westminster.

I have, &c.

(Signed) PHILIP CURRIE.

F. O. 424/184, p. 52, No. 91

Inclosure in No. 228

Consul Graves to Sir P. Currie.

Sir,   ERZEROUM, *September 26, 1895.*

WITH reference to my despatch of the 18th instant, I have the honour to transmit herewith Dr. Reynold's Report on relief operations in Sasun for the week ended the 16th September, which reached Moush too late for Mr. Hampson to write any covering despatch to it.

The work of rebuilding seems to progress satisfactorily, the chief difficulty being the lack of timber for roofing, which the local authorities had engaged to supply, and expense exceeding 500*l.* is likely to fall on the relief funds under this head; while the need of clothing and bedding is being urgently felt on account of the colder weather, which has set in. Dr. Reynolds confirms Mr. Hampson's estimate of 15,000*l.* as absolutely necessary to keep the Sasun people alive over the winter, and enable them to provide for the future; and he appeals urgently for funds to be sent in time to get the winter supplies into the suffering district before the roads are closed.

If the sum required is forthcoming from various sources, I would suggest that the missionaries should be informed by telegraph without delay that they can expend the funds now in hand without fear upon matters of immediate necessity, and begin to place their orders for winter provisions to be held in readiness for immediate transport.

I have, &c.

(Signed) R. W. GRAVES.

F. O. 424/184, p. 52, No. 91/1

No. 229

Sir P. Currie to the Marquess of Salisbury.

No. 665.   CONSTANTINOPLE, *October 9, 1895.*
My Lord,   *(Received October 14.)*

I HAVE the honour to forward to your Lordship herewith copy of a despatch which I have received from Her Majesty's Consul at Erzeroum, giving an account of the progress of Shakir Pasha's Mission, and inclosing summary of the latter's scheme for the reorganization of police, gendarmerie, and prisons.

I have, &c.

(Signed) PHILIP CURRIE.

F. O. 424/184, p. 52, No. 91/1

Inclosure 1 in No. 229

Consul Graves to Sir P. Currie.

Sir,   ERZEROUM, *September 27, 1895.*

AS I had the honour to report to your Excellency by telegraph on the 24th instant, Shakir Pasha with his suite left Erzeroum that day for Bayazid. His Excellency was also accompanied by Mr. Sachtleben, an American gentleman who has passed four or five months at Erzeroum endeavouring to throw light upon the circumstances under which the late Mr. F. Leng met his death last year in Alashgird, and by the Rev. W. Chambers, of Erzeroum, who volunteered to assist Mr. Sachtleben in his search. Shakir Pasha has promised to afford Mr Sachtleben all possible assistance, and it will be interesting to see whether he will now clear this matter up, as he certainly has the power of doing, or whether he will allow the local authorities to persist in obstructing the course of justice by denying any knowledge of Mr. Leng's fate, and concealing all traces of this supposed murder.

Since the arrival of Shakir Pasha's Mission on the 9th September, his Excellency has certainly been active in inquiry into every branch of administration. He has visited the prison, and expressed himself very strongly on the miserable conditions of its inmates, as well as on the neglect of the judicial authorities, whereby prisoners are allowed to remain for years awaiting trial. He also put seals on all the Government safes with a view to audit, but as they were nearly all empty no useful purpose was served by this measure. A programme is also being prepared under his direction for the construction of new road, and for the repair and maintenance of the one road which already exists, that from Trebizond to Erzeroum. His Excellency has also made a recommendation as to the working of the coal-mines in this neighbourhood, which I hardly think practical, namely, that it should be undertaken by the Municipality of Erzeroum.

The subjects, however, which had received his closest attention are the organization of the gendarmerie, police and prison organizations, and the creation of a corps of "tahsildars" for tax-collecting purposes. The Erzeroum official paper has just published his scheme dealing with these questions, a summary of which I have the honour to inclose herewith.

The most noticeable fact in connection with Shakir Pasha's Mission is the absolute refusal of the Armenians to have anything to say to it. They took no part in the official reception given to his Excellency on his arrival at Erzeroum, nor has the Armenian Archbishop, as Head of the community, called upon him, and he is said to be much incensed against his Beatitude, and to have reported very unfavourably of him to Constantinople.

My Russian colleague has endeavoured to persuade the Archbishop to meet Shakir Pasha, and to accept any advantages or concessions the latter might make to the Armenians, but without success. Five Armenian Notables summoned in succession to serve as members of the Commission for the Reorganization of the Gendarmerie, Prisons, &c., have declined that honour. A young Armenian Catholic, similarly invited, was about to accept, but was dissuaded therefrom by the advice, not unmixed with menace, of his Gregorian neighbours, and Shakir has had to content himself with a Greek grocer as the only Christian member of his Commission. Not a single Armenian recruit has presented himself for enrolment in the gendarmerie or police, although it is said that an offer was made to an Armenian tradesman of the town of 10*l.* bounty for every Armenian recruit he would bring before the Commission up to ten in number.

It must be added that in the present temper of the Armenians, who are being worked upon by revolutionary agents from the Caucasus, any of them who accepted Shakir Pasha's overtures would do so at some personal risk. Under these circumstances, and in default of funds to carry out even the meagre programme which has been put forward, it is not surprising if Shakir Pasha shows signs of discouragement, while local opinion is almost unanimous to the effect that the drafting of this programme is all that he will accomplish, and that the Commission will eventually be withdrawn, like so many preceding Turkish Reform Commissions, leaving a bill for its expenses, amounting to over 1,000*l.* a-month, to be settled by the local Treasury, when it is able, as the only record of its passage.

I have, &c.

(Signed) R. W. GRAVES.

F. O. 424/184, p. 53, No. 92/1

Inclosure 2 in No. 229

Summary of Scheme published by Erzeroum Official Paper.

A COMMISSION is formed of military officers and Mussulman and Christian members, under the direction of his Excellency Shakir Pasha, comprising one military officer as President, and two members, one Moslem and one Christian, from among the respectable Notables, whose duty it will be to recruit the necessary number of gendarmes to make up the present deficiency in the gendarmerie from the non-Moslem population; to reorganize the gendarmerie regiment so formed, and to tell it off to its proper stations.

Gendarmerie.—Four "tabours" (battalions) will be formed, one for each of the Sanjaks of Erzinjan, Bayazid, and Erzeroum, and the fourth at head-quarters at Erzeroum.

Each "tabour" will comprise three cavalry "beuluks" (companies).

Composition of Beuluks.

	Cavalry.	Infantry.
Beuluk Aghassi (Captain)	1	1
1st Lieutenants	1	1
2nd Lieutenants	1	1
Chaoushes (sergeants)	5	4
Beuluk Emini (sergeant)	1	1
Onbashis (corporals)	10	8
Privates	50	64
	69	80
	9 companies	7 companies
	621 ‗‗‗‗‗ 560	
	= 1,181	
1 Colonel, Alaï Bey	1	
1 Alaï Kiatibi (Regimental clerk)	1	
Majors (Tabour Aghassi)	4	
Tabour Kiatibi (Company clerks)	4	
Total	1,191	

(N.B.—It will be seen that this Table only provides for nine cavalry beuluks, whereas, in the preceding paragraph, it is stated that there will be four tabours, each comprising three cavalry beuluks, $4 \times 3 = 12$.—R.W.G.)

The number of men now wanting is to be made up of Christians, who will be distributed among the different companies.

The head-quarters "beuluk" of foot gendarmerie to be employed for prison and guard-house duties, Government-house, and town patrols.

The cavalry "beuluks" will serve alternately, one for country duty, one detached for the sanjaks, where most needed, and one at head-quarters. The sanjak "tabours" to be detailed for road duties and cordons in the cazas.

New gendarmes not to be recruited from the people of the district where the "tabour" serves. Gendarmes no longer to be employed for tax-collecting, as special "tahsildars" will now be appointed.

Christians desirous of serving to present themselves before the Commission, and after satisfying the latter of their good character, &c., they will be enlisted, sworn in, and told off to their respective "beuluks." No difference will be made between them and their Mussulman comrades. Similar recruiting commissions will be formed in the sanjaks to that at Erzeroum.

Police and Tahsildars.—Recruits who can read and write can join the police, and those acquainted with arithmetic can be enrolled as "tahsildars" (collectors).

Gendarmes already in service who possess these qualifications can be appointed as police or "tahsildars."

Cazas not divided into "nahiés" will have one "chaoush" and three "tahsildars." In those cazas which are divided into "nahiés" besides one "tahsildar" for each "nahié," the caza will have three or four "tahsildars;" and in the capital of the sanjak there will be one "bash chaoush," two "chaoushes," and four "tahsildars," while in the capital of the vilayet there will be a "chief tahsildar," two "chaoushes," and six "tahsildars," enrolled from Mussulmans and Christians alike, able to read and keep accounts. They will be placed under the orders of the "Mal Mudiris." They are not to call in the assistance of the gendarmerie; their duties in tax-collecting do not comprise the actual handling of the money, which will be collected by the members of the Councils of Elders, and brought by the Headmen to the caza capital. Regulations will be drawn up later for the "Mal Mudirs'" departments.

Police.—Each "nahié" will have one police agent. Each caza at least three police agents, under a third class commissary. Each sanjak at least five police agents, one second class and two third class commissaries. At the capital of the vilayet there will be ten police agents under one chief commissary, two second class and two third class commissaries.

Municipal Guards.—The duties of municipal guards are to attend to the maintenance of order and cleanliness in the streets, in which they will be assisted wherever necessary by the police.

Prison Warders.—The capital of each caza will have one prison warder, the capital of each sanjak will have eight, and the capital of the vilayet twelve. There will be a chief warder in the vilayet and sanjak capitals. Their duties are to guard the gaols, and perform the necessary prison services, and to keep the prisons clean; they will be placed directly under the Director of Prisons, without whose orders, in writing, no one can be imprisoned or released from prison.

Persons arrested by police or gendarmes cannot be detained more than twenty-four hours without a warrant from the judicial authorities, the Director of Prisons being held responsible if this rule is infringed. Persons arrested summarily can only be detained for twenty-three hours, after which a written Report must be sent in on the subject to the Procureur-Général and the chief local authority.

25 REBI-UL-EVVEL, 1313 *(September 1 (13), 1895).*

F. O. 424/184, pp. 54-55, No. 92/2

No. 230

Sir P. Currie to the Marquess of Salisbury.

No. 666.   CONSTANTINOPLE, *October 9, 1895.*
My Lord,   *(Received October 14.)*
    WITH reference to my despatch No. 586 of the 9th September, I have the
honour to forward to your Lordship herewith copy of a despatch which I have
received from the Acting British Consul at Angora, reporting that no steps have
been taken by the authorities at Cæsarea to investigate the affray which recently
took place between Mussulmans and Christians in that neighbourhood.
                              I have, &c.
                                           (Signed) PHILIP CURRIE.

F. O. 424/184, p. 55, No. 93

Inclosure in No. 230

Acting Consul Fontana to Sir P. Currie.

Sir,   ANGORA, *October 2, 1895.*
    WITH reference to Mr. Consul Cumberbatch's despatch to your Excellency
of the 2nd ultimo, setting forth the details of an attack made by armed Mussulmans
at Talas, near Cæsarea, upon four young Armenians whose names he specifies, I
have the honour to report that, according to information received by me from the
district in question, no investigation whatever has been made by the Cæsarea
authorities with a view to the arrest of the guilty parties. The originators of the
attack are said to be the son-in-law of the Talas Chief of Police, the son of a local
Turkish Notable, and a vineyard "bekji."
    I have made representations upon the subject to the Vali, who has promised to
have the necessary investigations made, and to inform me of the result, which I
shall not fail to at once report to your Excellency.
                              I have, &c
                                           (Signed) RAPHAEL A. FONTANA.

F. O. 424/184, p. 55, No. 93/1

No. 231

Consul Cumberbatch to Sir P. Currie.

Sir,   ERZEROUM, *October 9, 1895.*
WITH reference to Mr. Consul Graves' despatch of the 27th ultimo, I have
the honour to transmit the substance of an article which has appeared in the local
official Gazette in connection with Shakir Pasha's mission.

I may also add that a plan has been drawn up by his Excellency's orders, and
transmitted to Constantinople for approval, for the administrative reorganization
of the villages in the Erzeroum plain. There will be three nahiehs, one of which is to
be composed chiefly of Armenian villages, and will have an Armenian Mudir with a
Turkish Mouavin, whilst in the other two the position will be reversed.

These measures, which may probably be followed by similar ones, whether
executed or not, are evidently intended to be considered in the light of reforms.
                                                   I have, &c.
                                          (Signed) H. A. CUMBERBATCH.

F. O. 424/184, p. 173, No. 284/1

Inclosure in No. 231

Extracts from Erzeroum Official Gazette.

THE Commission, presided over by Danish Bey, appointed by Shakir Pasha
to inquire into certain branches of the local Administration, found the accounts of
the various financial Departments in order, but saw fit to recommend measures for
the more regular payment of salaries.

In the Judicial Department, it was found that there were no Mustandiks
(Examining Officers) attached to the Caza Tribunals, but that their work was
being done by members of those Courts. This needed remedy, and in future the
elected members (Intikhab) of the Courts should not be allowed to take their seats
unless they knew how to read and write. It was also notified that no one was to be
imprisoned without the necessary legal order.

This report having been submitted to the Vali, his Excellency issued Circular
instructions accordingly.

The technical school, which has been closed for several years, is to be reopened
for the benefit of poor boys who wish to learn a trade.

Civilians not being allowed into the military hospital any longer owing to
superior orders, the President of the Municipality has been instructed by Shakir
Pasha to build a special hospital for civilians.

Officials having been sent to examine and report on the roads leading from Erzeroum to the principal towns in the province, orders have been issued for repairs to be effected on those leading to Gumush-haneb, Erzinghan, and Bayazid, and guard-houses to be erected at intervals.

A special road to the forest of Ispir, for the transport of fuel, is recommended by Shakir Pasha, as well as the working of the coal mine near Erzeroum by the Municipality.

F. O. 424/184, p. 173, No. 284/2

No. 232

Sir P. Currie to the Marquess of Salisbury.

No. 669.

My Lord,

THERAPIA, *October 10, 1895.*

(Received October 14.)

I HAVE the honour to inform your Lordship that the Russian and French Governments having authorized their respective Ambassadors to concert with me the points in the "Projet de Réformes" of the 11th May which we consider necessary for the protection of the life and property of the Armenians, we held a meeting on the 7th instant, and I have the honour to transmit to your Lordship herewith a copy of the provisions which we agreed to recommend to our Governments as necessary.

I have, &c.

(Signed) PHILIP CURRIE.

F. O. 424/184, p. 56, No. 95
Turkey No. 1 (1896), p. 157, No. 196

Inclosure in No. 232

Provisions recommended to the Governments of Great Britain, France, and Russia, as necessary for the Protection of the Life and Property of the Armenians.

THE reforms will be formulated in a General Act which will be drawn up in agreement with the Powers, and inserted in the Imperial Decreee promulgating them.

2. A Christian Assistant to Shakir Pasha, whose name should be unofficially submitted to the Powers.

3. The participation of Christians in the administration to be specified, and the posts of Vali and Mutessarif to be open to Christians.

4. The Dragomans to have the right of addressing to the Commission of Control any complain, communication, or information which the Embassies may

think desirable, but to be debarred from asking for any reforms beyond those granted in the Decree.

The Commission of Control to fix the number of Christian functionaries in proportion to the population for each vilayet.

5. Christian Assistants to be attached to Mahommendan Valis and Mutessarifs.

6. The right of the Ambassadors to remonstrate against the appointment of incapable, dishonest, or fanatical Valis to be reserved in the note to the Porte.

7. The number of rural guards to be fixed by the Vali on the recommendation of the Mudir and in conformity with local requirements.

8. A note to be addressed by the Ambassadors to the Porte taking act of the promises made respecting prisons, arbitrary arrests, amnesty, reinstatement of emigrants, regulations for the Hamidié cavalry, and insisting upon their complete and immediate execution.

9. A stipulation that the principles of the reform scheme will be applied to all the sandjaks and cazas of Asia Minor where the Christians form a notable part of the population.

F. O. 424/184, p. 57, No. 95/1
Turkey No. 1 (1896), p. 158, No. 196/1

No. 233

Sir P. Currie to the Marquess of Salisbury.

No. 476.   CONSTANTINOPLE, *October 10, 1895, 11 a.m.*
Telegraphic.   *(Received October 10.)*

MR. CUMBERBATCH telegraphs from Erzeroum that the Vali, having received news of the recent disturbances at Constantinople, and of the attempt on the life of Bahri Pasha at Trebizond, and fearing the unusual state of ill-feeling among both Christians and Mahommedans, has taken precautionary measures to prevent any outbreak.

During the last few days two supposed informers have been assassinated at Erzeroum and one at Erzingan, the murders being attributed to revolutionary agents.

F. O. 424/184, p. 31, No. 55

No. 234

Sir P. Currie to the Marquess of Salisbury.

No. 477. CONSTANTINOPLE, *October 10, 1895, 12.10 p.m.*
Telegraphic. *(Received October 10.)*

HER Majesty's Vice-Consul at the Dardanelles has reported by telegraph, under date of the 9th October, 5 P.M., that great activity prevails in all the forts there; that several hundreds of soldiers have arrived from Constantinople; that extra torpedoes have been laid down on both sides of the Straits; and that he hears that the cannons are loaded, and pointed in their different positions down the Straits.

F. O. 424/184, p. 31, No. 56

No. 235

Sir P. Currie to the Marquess of Salisbury.

No. 478. CONSTANTINOPLE, *October 10, 1895, 12.10 p.m.*
Telegraphic. *(Received October 10.)*

MR. HAMPSON telegraphed yesterday from Mush that there is considerable fear of disorder there, but that the town is being well patrolled. He adds that the Mutessarif of Bajazid has exchanged with the Mutessarif of Mush.

F. O. 424/184, p. 31, No. 57

No. 236

Sir P. Currie to the Marquess of Salisbury.

No. 479. CONSTANTINOPLE, *October 10, 1895, 12.10 p.m.*
Telegraphic. *(Received October 10.)*

HER Majesty's Consul at Trebizond telegraphed at 6 P.M. last night that the day had passed in false alarms, but that no disturbances had taken place.

F. O. 424/184, p. 31, No. 58

No. 237

The Marquess of Salisbury to Sir E. Monson.

No. 54.
Telegraphic.   FOREIGN OFFICE, *October 10, 1895.*

I HAVE received your telegram No. 71 of yesterday, conveying a message from Count Goluchowski to the effect that, in view of the present crisis at Constantinople, Austria wishes to act in accord with England, and that it is therefore essential that he should know exactly the present situation between the three Powers and the Porte with regard to Armenian reforms, and the precise views of Her Majesty's Government.

The information furnished to your Excellency to-day, in my telegrams Nos. 50 to 53 inclusive, together with other correspondence already sent to you, will enable you to explain to Count Goluchowski the present state of the negotiations on the subject of the reforms.

Pray thank his Excellency in my name for his offer of assistance, and tell him that I shall be very glad if instructions can be sent to the Austrian Ambassador at Constantinople to consult with Her Majesty's Ambassador as to the way in which the support of the Austrian Government can be most effectively given.

F. O. 424/184, p. 33, No. 63

No. 238

The Marquess of Salisbury to Sir P. Currie.

No. 179.
Telegraphic.   FOREIGN OFFICE, *October 10, 1895.*

IN my immediately preceding telegram I repeated to you a telegram from Her Majesty's Ambassador at Vienna, reporting a communication from the Austrian Minister for Foreign Affairs on the gravity of the present situation in Turkey, and his Excellency's opinion that not a moment should be lost in bringing collective pressure to bear on the Porte to insure the protection of all Christians.

I should be glad to learn your Excellency's views on this communication from Count Goluchowski.

F. O. 424/184, p. 33, No. 64

No. 239

The Marquess of Salisbury to Sir P. Currie.

No. 180.
Telegrapic.   FOREIGN OFFICE, *October 10, 1895*.

I HAVE received your telegrams Nos. 463, 464 and, 474 of the 8th and 9th instant respectively, with reference to the further points in the scheme of Armenian reforms which the Ambassadors of Great Britain, France, and Russia have submitted to their respective Governments, and to which they consider it is essential to obtain the consent of the Porte.

As soon as the necessary instructions have reached the Russian Ambassador enabling him to join in the necessary representations to the Porte, your Excellency is, of course, authorized to proceed immediately on the lines recommended by you in concert with your French and Russian colleagues.

You will see from Sir E. Monson's telegram, repeated to you in my telegram No. 178 of to-day, that the Austrian Government take a very serious view of the present situation, and have expressed a wish to give their support to our proposals for reforms in Armenia. I have suggested to Count Goluchowski that the Austrian Ambassador at Constantinople should confer with you as to the mode in which Austria can most effectively support us in our present negotiations.

F. O. 424/184, p. 33, No. 65

No. 240

The Marquess of Salisbury to Sir F. Lascelles.

No. 308.
Sir,   FOREIGN OFFICE, *October 10, 1895*.

THE Russian Chargé d'Affaires called at the Foreign Office on the 5th instant and handed to Sir Percy Anderson a *note verbale*, of which I transmit a copy herewith, stating that the Russian Ambassador at Constantinople had been authorized to join his British and French colleagues in addressing a collective note to the Porte on the subject of Armenian reforms.

Sir Percy Anderson informed M. Kroupensky that Sir P. Currie had reported that the Russian and French Ambassadors had received their instructions, and that at his suggestion they had telegraphed to their Governments to inquire whether they would be given latitude to concert as to further points beyond those contemplated in the instructions sent to them, one of which would be the publications of the reforms by Imperial Degree.

I am, &c.

(Signed) SALISBURY.

F. O. 424/184, p. 34, No. 66

No. 241

The Marquess of Salisbury to Sir F. Lascelles.

No. 308A.

Sir,   FOREIGN OFFICE, *October 10, 1895.*

THE Russian Ambassador called at the Foreign Office to-day and communicated to Sir T. Sanderson a telegram from his Government relative to the proposal made by the British, French and Russian Ambassadors to address a fresh note to the Porte demanding certain further concessions in regard to the reforms to be introduced in the Armenian provinces.

The Russian Government suggest that it might be more prudent, in view of the disturbed state of things at Constantinople, that the three Ambassadors should only call upon the Porte to adhere in principle to their proposals, leaving the details to be discussed when the excitement had calmed down.

I have informed M. de Staal that I consider it very desirable to leave it, as far as possible, to the discretion of the Ambassadors to decide as to the course of procedure, since, being on the spot, they are the best judges of what the situation renders desirable. The greater the latitude given to them the better will be the chance of bringing the matter to a successful termination.

I am, &c.

(Signed) SALISBURY.

F. O. 424/184, p. 34, No. 67

No. 242

Sir E. Monson to the Marquess of Salisbury.

No. 286.   VIENNA, *October 10, 1895.*

My Lord,   *(Received October 12.)*

I FOUND Count Goluchowski yesterday very much disturbed by telegrams received from Constantinople and Trebizond as to an outbreak of murderous fanaticism at the latter port, which, his Excellency said, taken in conjunction with the horrors which have been committed in the Turkish capital, inspired him with grave apprehensions that the lives of Christians throughout Turkey might shortly be in imminent peril.

Count Goluchowski said that he had just sent telegrams to the Imperial Ambassadors at all the great capitals, instructing them to inquire and report at once the views of the Government to which they are accredited, and stating that he is of opinion himself that all the Ambassadors at the Porte should collectively bring the strongest pressure to bear upon the Turkish Government, and insist upon ffective measures being taken to protect all Christians in the Ottoman dominions. The Sultan and his Government should be explicitly informed that they will be held esponsible for whatever happens.

Count Gulochowski charged me to state to your Lordship that he thinks the gravity of the situation cannot be exaggerated, and that instant action is necessary not only in the above sense but in compelling the Sultan to come to an agreement with England, France, and Russia on the question of Armenian reforms.

He said that Austria had hitherto held aloof, but that a catastrophe seemed approaching in which her interests would be concerned; and he wishes to act in accord with your Lordship he will be glad to be placed in possession of your exact views and intentions.

His Excellency's language was throughout very forcible.

I have, &c.

(Signed) EDMUND MONSON.

F. O. 424/184, pp. 47-48, No. 83

No. 243

Sir P. Currie to the Marquess of Salisbury.

No. 673.   THERAPIA, *October 10, 1895.*

My Lord,   *(Received October 14.)*

WITH reference to my despatch No. 656 of the 7th October, I have the honour to transmit herewith copy of a Circular *note verbale,* addressed by the Sublime Porte to the six Embassies in reply to the collective note presented by the latter respecting the present state of insecurity in Constantinople.

I have, &c.

(Signed) PHILIP CURRIE.

F. O. 424/184, p. 59, No. 98

Inclosure in No. 243

Note Verbale.

Circulaire.

DANS la note verbale qu'ils ont adressé au Ministère Impérial des Affaires Etrangères à la date du 6 de ce mois à propos des incidents qui se sont dernièrement produits à Constantinople, MM. les Représentants des Grandes Puissances lui font part de la préoccupation que leur inspirent les conséquences qui pourraient résulter de ces états de trouble.

La cause de la persistance de cette agitation qui préoccupe MM. les Représentants étrangers est, comme on le sait, l'obstination d'un certain nombre d'Arméniens à rester enfermés dans trois églises. On est donc fondé à espérer que si des conseils de la part de MM. les Représentants des Grandes Puissances exhortant les Arméniens á rentrer dans le calme venaient se joindre aux mesures prises par le Gouvernement Impérial, l'ordre et la tranquillité ne tarderaient pas à être complètement rétablis.

Le fait que depuis le premier jour de ces incidents les Musulmans ne se sont point portés à des sévices contre les Arméniens est une preuve que tant qu'ils ne seront pas attaqués par ceux-ci, ils ne prendront l'initiative d'aucune agression.

Mais si par suite de la grande étendue de la capitale des Arméniens attaquent inopinément les Musulmans et autres habitants sur des points qui leur paraîtraient propices, il est tout naturel que ceux-ci, en attendant l'arrivée de la force publique, cherchent à se défendre eux-mêmes.

MM. les Représentants des Grandes Puissances peuvent être sûrs que si un certain nombre d'Arméniens se sont réfugiés dans les églises dont ils ne veulent pas sortir sans avoir obtenu des garanties sérieuses pour leur liberté et leur vie, ce n'est point, comme ils le prétendent, parce que des Arméniens qui n'étaient pas mêlés au mouvement ont été arrêtés et plusieurs d'entre eux maltraités, mais bien parce que leur but réel est d'augmenter la surexcitation provoquée par les incidents qu'ils ont suscités et de préparer ainsi la voie à un autre mouvement encore plus grave; les coups de pistolet qu'ils ne cessent de tirer jour et nuit dans les églises et ailleurs et les rumeurs alarmantes qu'ils répandent en sont la preuve.

Le Lundi, jour où le mouvement a commencé, des Arméniens armés surgirent en masse et se mirent à manifester, tirant et blessant un Commandant de Gendarmerie et les Musulmans qu'ils rencontraient. Repoussés par la police, ils se dispersèrent mais pour aller se rassembler de nouveau sur d'autres points où ils attaquèrent encore la population. Les mutins étant en plus grand nombre que les agents de police et gendarmes présents, les Musulmans durent riposter et se défendre eux-mêmes.

Dans un pareil moment d'effervescence, il se peut que des représailles aient eu lieu comme cela arrive, du reste, dans les pays les plus civilisés de l'Europe, mais quant aux agressions qui se sont produits contre des Chrétiens appartenant aux autres communautés, il est prouvé qu'elles sont le fait des Arméniens mêmes. Toutefois, comme aucune plainte n'a été formulée à propos d'actes de pillage commis pas plus par des Musulmans que par des Arméniens, la nouvelle concernant la perpétration de pareils faits ne peut pas être fondée.

En vue de mettre un terme à cet état de choses, le Gouvernement Impérial n'a négligé aucune mesure; il a fait publier dans les quartiers de la ville des recommandations et conseils efficaces invitant la population Musulmane à s'abstenir de tout acte d'agression sous peine des punitions les plus sévères, des avis dans le même sens adressés au public en général, out été insérés à diverses reprises dans les journaux et des patrouilles de soldats, d'agents de police, et de gendarmes ne cessent de circuler dans les rues. Dès lors l'allégation d'aprés laquelle l'autorité semblerait avoir encouragé les Musulmans à commettre des excès est inadmissible, ce qui est prouvé par le Communiqué officiel paru dans les journaux le second jour des incidents.

Il a été constaté par une enquête que deux étrangers seulement ont été par suite de certaine ressemblance arrêtés pendant les recherches faites par la police pour la découverte des prévenus, mais leur identité ayant été établie ils ont été aussitôt relâchés. La Préfecture de Police repousse formellement l'assertion comme quoi des détenus auraient été maltraités, blessés, ou tués par ses agents.

Quant à la croyance que si cette situation se prolongeait l'agitation en s'étendant pourrait gagner les provinces de l'Empire, elle est fondée. En effet, à en juger du contenu de certains écrits subversifs trouvés sur les agitateurs Arméniens, des instigations révolutionnaires avaient dû être faites préalablement dans les provinces puisque aussitôt après les incidents surgis dans la capitale, des faits séditieux ont commencé à se produire aussi dans quelques vilayets, faits qui sont réprimés au fur et à mesure qu'ils surgissent.

Pour ce qui est des mesures prises par la Sublime Porte pour prévenir le retour d'incidents regrettables, et mettre les Chrétiens et les colonies étrangères à l'abri d'éventualités périlleuses, des recommandations efficaces ont été faites,, ainsi qu'il a été dit plus haut, au public par la voie des journaux et aux étudiants en théologie par son Altesse le Cheik-ul-Islam; des conseils et avertissements ont été adressés dans les quartiers aux habitants; et des patrouilles de soldats, d'agents de police, et de gendarmes montés et non montés circulent jour et nuit dans les rues pour le maintien de l'ordre.

Certes, cet état de choses ne peut prendre fin que si les Arméniens renoncent à leurs menées révolutionnaires. Il est évident qu'en empêchant la fourniture de vivres à ceux lui sont réfugiés dans les églises, on les obligerait à les évacuer, mais les autorités impériales espérant arriver à les en déloger par la persuasion n'ont pas voulu jusqu'ici pousser plus loin les dispositions adoptées et elles ne cessent de faire à cet effet des recommandations tant au Patriarcat qu'aux Notables de la communauté.

Le Gouvernement Impérial remercie MM. les Représentants étrangers de leur désir de lui prêter leur concours pour rétablir la tranquillité dans les esprits. Une Commission a été déjà chargée d'examiner les motifs de l'arrestation des détenus et tous ceux dont la mise en liberté est jugée nécessaire cont immédiatement relaxés.

SUBLIME PORTE, *le 8 Octobre, 1895.*

F. O. 424/184, pp. 59-60, No. 98/1

No. 244

Sir P. Currie to the Marquess of Salisbury.

No. 675.   THERAPIA, *October 10, 1895*
My Lord,   *(Received October 14.)*

THE fall of the Grand Vizier, Saïd Pasha, was very sudden, though not unexpected.

On several occasions when he had tendered his resignation to the Sultan it had been refused, but on the 2nd instant he was summarily dismissed. The immediate circumstance of his fall, as related to me by himself, were as follows:-

In consequence of the disturbances in Constantinople he had been ordered to sleep at the Palace.

On the day of his fall he had presented a Report to the Sultan on the Armenian difficulty, and had been in constant communication with His Majesty in regard to it.

These communications were prolonged during the night until at 3 o'clock A.M., without previous warning, the First Chamberlain of the Sultan came to demand the surrender of his official seal.

Kiamil Pasha had already been summoned, and was at once appointed Grand Vizier.

Saïd Pasha immediately sent for a hired carriage, and retired to his own house unattended and unhonoured.

His Majesty appears from the first to have been displeased at the advice tendered to him by Saïd Pasha, who took a very gloomy view of the situation, and, so far as he was allowed to do so, expressed his opinion strongly to his Imperial master.

In the interviews which I have had with Saïd Pasha he has impressed me very favourably. During the years which he has passed in seclusion he appears to have studied and reflected much, and the views he expresses are enlightened and statesmanlike.

He possesses in a high degree the confidence of Mussulmans as well as Christians, and is generally regarded as the first statesman in the Empire.

His successor, Kiamil Pasha, has a high reputation for ability, but the same confidence is not felt in his probity as in that of Saïd Pasha.

He is of a more supply nature than his predecessor, and it is possible that this may give him an advantage in dealing with the Sultan.

I have, &c.

(Signed) PHILIP CURRIE.

F. O. 424/184, p. 61, No. 100

No. 245

Mr. Egerton to the Marquess of Salisbury.

No. 123.   ATHENS, *October 10, 1895.*
My Lord,   *(Received October 15.)*

THE Government press in Athens, in comments on the late events at Constantinople, represent the excitement of the Armenians as having been artificially fostered, and dwells upon the friendliness with which the authorities in that capital are treaing the Greek Christians.

The duty of the Greek Government, says the "Palingenesia" (not M. Delyanni's own paper, but edited by a supporter of his), is to shut its ears against wild reports, and watch events. The attempts of the Armenians, nothwithstanding the encouragement received from London, will fail. It is folly to hope to form an Armenian barrier against Russian advance in Asia; even if it were formed, it would be even weaker than the Bulgarian barrier, which England with such feverish haste erected, and which has been proved to be composed of straw. Consequently, the demand for reforms, if such reforms are to be applied by the Turkish Government, is illusory; if England were really in earnest, and succeeded in forming an independent Armenia, the fate of the Armenians would not improve; they might change masters, but, like the Cypriotes, they would labour in servitude and make no progress.

To this an independent paper, the "Estia," answers that it is clear the present Ministry is endeavouring to make advances to the Franco-Russian alliance: the presence of Prince Nicolas at Miremont, the voyage of M. Nicolas Delyanni to Copenhagen, the report from Paris of the conclusion of a Greek Loan under the guarantee of Russia, and the violent attack in the Government paper on English policy in the East all point to this; and the article concludes by saying that the personal feelings of the Prime Minister for France should not be allowed to influence the policy of the country, which policy should be the result of cool judgment. The article concludes that it is to be regretted that the events above mentioned should have occurred if no policy had been deliberately chosen, and it behoves the Government to pay more attention to the language of the press over which it has influence.

I merely allude to these articles as they might be mentioned in the European press, though I think they have no other interest.

The Greek mind cannot comprehend the humanitarian view of the Armenian question, and thinks it a political game, each party working for its own hand. The only time M. Skouzès has spoken to me on the subject I told him, though I had no later information, I was satisfied that the Great Powers were acting in unison at Constantinople, and that what they insisted upon would be done.

As for M. Delyanni's predelictions, he is a remnant of the foolish days when

Greek politicians attached themselves to foreign Missions, and there were English
French, and Russian parties; but from the complaints of the French Charge
d'Affaires to me of the impossibility of getting any results to his representations to
the Minister, I fancy that beyond a few vixenish utterances against England, which
he may imagine must be agreeable to its supposed rival for the affection of Greece
M. Delyanni's French sympathies do not lead him very far.

I have, &c.

(Signed) Edwin H. Egerton

F. O. 424/184, pp. 62-63, No. 103

No. 246

Sir P. Currie to the Marquess of Salisbury.

No. 486.   Constantinople, *October 11, 1895, 11.25 a.m*
Telegraphic.   *(Received October 11.)*

IN reply to your Lordship's telegram No. 178 of the 10th October repeating a
telegram received from Her Majesty's Ambassador at Vienna, I think that the
three Embassies who have been acting in complete accord, will no doubt find their
hands greatly strengthened by their success in clearing the churches of refugees.

The Sultan and his Government seem now to realize the danger of the
situation, and will probably be ready to follow our advice.

In the event of any further troubles in the provinces we shall not fail to press
the Government to adopt such measures as we may deem advisable. Both the
Sultan and the Patriarch have sent this morning to express their gratitude for our
action in clearing the Armenian churches, and their belief that it will have a good
effect in restoring confidence.

F. O. 424/184, p. 46, No. 77

No. 247

Sir P. Currie to the Marquess of Salisbury.

No. 488.   Constantinople, *October 11, 1895, 8 p.m.*
Telegraphic.   *(Received October 11.)*

IN continuation of my telegram No. 482 of yesterday, I have the honour to
inform your Lordship that the Dragomans having again visited the churches, have
now been successful in inducing all the refugees to leave.

Their total number amounted to 2,414; of whom about 12 per cent carried
arms.

F. O. 424/184, p. 46, No. 78

No. 248

Sir P. Currie to the Marquess of Salisbury.

No. 489. CONSTANTINOPLE, *October 11, 1895, 9.10 p.m.*
Telegraphic. *(Received October 11.)*
THE Dragomans were to-day informed by the Minsiter of Police that a Commission had been named to inquire into the cases of all prisoners arrested in connection with the recent disturbances, and to release immediately all who are not accused of any serious crime. The Minister undertook to examine any cases of murder that might be brought before him and expressed his readiness to punish any officials guilty of torturing the prisoners, if proofs were furnished by the Embassies.

F. O. 424/184, p. 46, No. 79

No. 249

Sir E. Monson to the Marquess of Salisbury.

No. 72. VIENNA, *October 11, 1895.*
Telegraphic. *(Received October 11.)*
I HAVE the honour to report, with reference to telegram No. 54 from your Lordship, that the Austro-Hungarian Ambassador in Constantinople will be addressed by Count Goluchowski in the sense suggested by you. His Excellency is very grateful for the information which your Lordship's telegrams placed me in a position to give him.

His Excellency says that it is difficult for him to come forward prominently on the subject of Armenian reforms owing to the persistence of Germany in an attitude of indifference, as he is unwilling that the Sultan should believe that, on this question, divergent views are held by the members of the Triple Alliance, but he will instruct Baron Calice to do all he possibly can to impress on the Sultan that the proposals of the three Ambassadors must be accepted by him.

F. O. 424/184, p. 47, No. 81

No. 250

The Marquess of Salisbury to Sir E. Monson.

No. 57.
Telegraphic.   FOREIGN OFFICE, *October 11, 1895, 4.30 p.m.*
    I CONSULTED Her Majesty's Ambassador at Constantinople on the communication made to you by the Austrian Minister for Foreign Affairs respecting the present situation in Turkey, and reported in your telegram No. 70 of the 9th instant.
    In my immediately preceding telegram I repeat to you Sir P. Currie's reply, and I shall be glad if you will communicate its substance to Count Goluchowski. It appears from this telegram that matters are progressing satisfactorily for the present at Constantinople.
    F. O. 424/184, p. 47, No. 82

No. 251

Sir P. Currie to the Marquess of Salisbury.

No. 676.   CONSTANTINOPLE, *October 11, 1895.*
My Lord,   *(Received October 21.)*
    I HAVE the honour to forward to your Lordship herewith copy of a despatch which I have received from Her Majesty's Consul at Trebizond reporting the suppression of disorder following the attempted murder of Bahri Pasha and Hamdi Pasha.
                                    I have, &c.
                                    (Signed) PHILIP CURRIE.
    F. O. 424/184, p. 70, No. 128

Inclosure in No. 251

Consul Longworth to Sir P. Currie.

Sir,   TREBIZOND, *October 5, 1895.*
    MY telegrams of the 2nd and 3rd instant will have informed your Excellency of Wednesday's regrettable occurrence.
    It was obviously an attempt to take away the life of Lieutenant-General Bahri Pasha, who, as ex-Vali of Van, is returning to Constantinople. When walking about 4 P.M. along the main street of the town, accompanied by the Trebizond

Commandant, Hamdi Pasha, the Persian Consul-General, Rezi Khan, and the Telegraph Inspector, Hadjee Omer Effendi, a man sprang out of a narrow passage and emptied his revolver at him. He received a flesh wound on the thigh, while Hamdi Pasha had his ankle pierced by a bullet, but neither of them are much hurt. The would-be assassin, joined by a companion, made his escape, firing behind on his pursuers, and hitting thus, though slightly, an Armenian and a Turkish boy.

The dastardly assault was as daring as it was reckless of all consequences. Had it occurred at the landing-place, where the troops were under arms in honour of Bahri Pasha's departure, it would have been most assuredly followed by very serious disorders. There is, as usual in such cases, a mass of circumstantial but conflicting statements regarding this incident. I cannot therefore come to any conclusion as to who did it and why it was done. The Turks suspect the Armenians, and the Armenians suspect the Turks.

One of the two supposed men has been caught, but his friends declare that they can satifactorily prove an *alibi*. He is an Armenian coffee-shop keeper, Armenag Gasparian by name, who for taking a prominent part in the disturbance of the 25th May was dismissed from the service of the Bishopric.

The affair, as was to be expected, caused a considerable amount of sensation and excitement, while rumours of massacres at Constantinople tended to aggravate matters. In connection with these reports, I would like here to express my thanks for your Excellency's telegram of the 3rd instant. It enabled me at least to calm the feelings of the better classes by stating that nothing like from 2,000 to 3,000 lives had been sacrificed. The appointment of Kiamil Pasha as Grand Vizier, I may add, had also a salutary effect in my relations with the officials, known as he is to have English tendencies.

Such were the feelings when last night some men, on plunder intent, mustered large bands of armed Moslems from the neighbouring villages and commenced to attack Christian houses, breaking doors and windows, firing volleys in the streets and terrifying the peaceable inhabitants. At the same time a Turk was badly wounded by, it is alleged, two Armenians, from which the report spread that the Mahommedans were being massacred. The townsmen were then up in arms. There must have been at least 3,000 rowdies with knives, pistols, guns, and revolvers rushing frantically through the streets. It was extremely doubtful whether the 500 soldiers, aided by a small number of police and gendarmerie, could possibly made head against such a rabble. The Christians crowded into the Consultates and public buildings, and we were all on the alert awaiting an attack. Three of the ringleaders, however, were happily arrested, and many were unmercifully beaten, not only by the soldiers, but by the Vali himself, and thus within two hours the crowds were made to disperse. It was with relief, therefore, that I found myself able to telegraph to your Excellency this morning that order had been restored promptly, to which I may now add that no lives were lost in the disturbance.

A Consular meeting was held in the forenoon. We met at the Austrian Consulate-General, and consulted together on the situation. It was decided that we should all drive in a body through the town to the Government House and make in person our representations to the Vali. Five carriages were engaged for the purpose. In the first were seated the Austrian and Persian Consul-Generals, in the second the Italian Consul and myself, in the third the French and Russian Consuls, in the fourth the Greek and Belgian Consuls, and in the fifth the Spanish Vice-Consul and my Dragoman. Though in plain clothes, some would like to think that our procession was as a spectacle imposing enough to calm the fears of the Christians and strike fear into the hearts of the Turks! Be this as it may, we saw Cadri Bey and expressed to him our appreciation of his own efforts, those of the evil and military authorities, and those of the Mahommedan Notabilities, all of whom by their exertions had courageously and successfully prevented a massacre of the Christians.

His Excellency related at some length the events of the night, and spoke hopefully of the future, referring to me as being fully aware of the measures taken to insure public security. He, moreover, promised to have the troops reinforced, the gendarmerie increased, the disreputable characters arrested, and the Consulates, Missions, and churches, where people take refuge, efficiently protected.

I will not lengthen out this despatch any further. It is now near midnight and the town is quiet. Nothing can be heard but the frequent tramp of the patrols, the regular beat of the watchmen, and the distant clatter of the vedettes.

I have, &c.

(Signed) H. Z. Longworth.

F. O. 424/184, pp. 70-71, No. 128/1

No. 252

Sir P. Currie to the Marquess of Salisbury.

No. 490.   Constantinople, *October 12, 1895, 12.30 p.m.*
Telegraphic.   *(Received October 12.)*

HER Majesty's Consul at Trebizond telegraphed to-day that it is estimated by local authorities that in Tuesday's disturbance there were killed 182 Armenians and 11 Turks, and wounded 19 Armenians, 26 Turks, and 1 Greek.

F. O. 424/184, p. 48, No. 84

No. 253

Sir P. Currie to the Marquess of Salisbury.

No. 491.　　　　　　　　　CONSTANTINOPLE, *October 12, 1895, 8.10 p.m.*
Telegraphic.　　　　　　　　　　　　　　*(Received October 12.)*

WITH reference to my telegram No. 488 of the 11th October, I have the honour to report that a few refugees have returned to the church in Pera, as they were refused admission to their former lodgings by the Turkish landlords. The Dragomans informed the Minister of Police, who at once sent orders that these refugees should be admitted to their houses.

Their engagement in regard to the refugees appear to be loyally carried out by the Turkish authorities, and they have ceased making arbitrary arrests.

F. O. 424/184, p. 48, No. 85

No. 254

Telegram from the Porte to the Turkish Embassy in London.

CONSTANTINOPLE, *le 12 Octobre, 1895.*
(Communicated by Morel Bey, October 14.)

LE 20 Septembre dernier deux Arméniens de Trébizonde ont tiré sur Bahri Pacha, ex-Vali de Van, et le Commandant Militaire, et les ont blessés. Les assaillants ont été arrêtés. Deux jours après un Arménien ayant blessé dans une rixe un soldat, des désordres se sont produits, mais ils ont été reprimés grâce aux mesures adoptées par les autorités Impériales. Cependant quatre jours après, les Arméniens ayant inopinément attaqué les Musulmans, des troubles ont éclaté de nouveau à Méidani-Charki, point très fréquenté de la ville, et les Musulmans et les Arméniens en sont venus aux mains. A la suite des coups de feu tirés par des Arméniens sur les agents de police et les officiers de la gendarmerie qui avaient été chargés de leur donner des conseils d'apaisement, qui ne furent nullement écoutés, la bagarre a pris de telles proportions qu'il y a eu de part et d'autre des morts et des blessés, dont le nombre pour les Musulmans est de onze morts et vingt-cinq blessés, et un soldat blessé; et pour les Arméniens est de 182 morts, dont cinq femmes et dix-neuf blessés, dont quatre femmes. Depuis, l'ordre et la tranquillité ont été rétablis.

F. O. 424/184, pp. 61-62, No. 101

No. 255

Consul-General Grant to the Marquess of Salisbury.

No. 12.   WARSAW, *October 12, 1895.*
My Lord,   *(Received October 15.)*

I HAVE the honour to report to your Lordship that the "Warshawski Dniewnik," which seldom misses an opportunity of venting its animosity against England, has a leading article, in its issue of the 27th ultimo (9th instant), on the Armenian question and the recent events at Constantinople, which concludes as follows:-

"There is no doubt that the appointment of Kiamil Pasha is an important concession to England, but its practical results are doubtful. Although Russia, France, and England are acting in concert in the Armenian question, their interests are far from being the same. What England wants in Armenia is sufficiently well known, and it is not only contrary but hostile to Russian interests. If France and Russia have joined England in the Armenian question, it has only been in order to mitigate her excessive demands and control her action. We may hope that the Sultan will understand the danger to the Porte itself of the English pretensions, and that the appointment of Kiamil Pasha will not lead to serious practical results. To give the Armenians an extensive political autonomy, or to create an independent Armenian kingdom, as has been demanded on the 30th September by the agitators arrived from London, would be a cowardly retreat before a handful of rebels, the instruments of English policy.

"Armenia, no doubt, needs some interior reforms, but these reforms should not interfere with the principle of the sovereign right of the Sultan, and should not afford to England the possibility of making Armenia her property and an ontpost against Russia. Yet such are the plans and the aspirations of England."

This is how the Government newspaper of Warsaw enlightens the subjects of the Emperor as to the action of Great Britain in the Armenian question.

I have, &c.

(Signed) HENRY GRANT.

F. O. 424/184, p. 63, No. 104

No. 256

Sir P. Currie to the Marquess of Salisbury.

No. 493.   CONSTANTINOPLE, *October 14, 1895, 10.20 p.m.*
Telegraphic.   *(Received October 14.)*

YESTERDAY the Minister for Foreign Affairs came to Therapia and had a
long meeting with the three Ambassadors on the subject of Armenian reforms.

We communicated to him the several points of our additional demands, and
we agreed that he should return to-day accompanied by Munir Bey, Secretary-
General of the Ministry of Foreign Affairs for Turkish correspondence, who would,
in concert with our three Delegates, draw up a draft of the Act in which the reforms
are to be embodied for publication.

This has now been done, and the three Ambassadors, together with Saïd
Pasha, have revised the draft.

Nothing further is needed except the final sanction of His Imperial Majesty.

Saïd Pasha, after having seen the Sultan, will meet us again to-morrow.

F. O. 424/184, p. 62, No. 102

No. 257

Sir P. Currie to the Marquess of Salisbury.

No. 679.   THERAPIA, *October 14, 1895.*
My Lord,   *(Received October 21.)*

ON the morning of the 11th instant, the Dragomans of the British, French,
and Russian Embassies called upon the Minister of Police in order to settle various
details connected with the measures to be adopted by the police for the evacuation
of the churches by Armenian refugees, and to ascertain from his Excellency
whether there was any truth in the report that five Armenians had been killed by
Softas on the At Meidan on the 9th instant.

Nazim Pasha assured them, in reply, that these reports were entirely
unfounded, and stated that most stringent orders had been issued in accordance
with the instructions of the Sublime Porte, that no further arrests of Armenians
should be made, and that any Armenians arrested by mistake should be at once
released. This measure, adopted in consequence of the engagement entered into by
the Sublime Porte, with the Representatives of the Great Powers, would, in his
opinion, completely paralyze the action of the police, and he must in consequence
decline to be answerable for the maintenance of public order.

It was impossible, he continued, to regard the movement of the 30th
September as a pacific demonstration, as maintained by the Armenians; it was

simply a means of provoking a general rising at Constantinople, attended by massacre and bloodshed, which might necessitate the intervention of the Great Powers. Similar insurrectionary movements might be expected in the provinces of the Empire, especially in the towns of Aleppo and Adana.

His Excellency then proceeded to call attention to an article in a revolutionary paper which had appeared in New York about a fortnight before the incident of the 30th September, showing clearly the object which the Armenians had in view. The Constantinople Committee were, he said, specially active in fomenting the revolutionary spirit, and it was they who extorted money from the Armenians and obliged them to keep their shops shut. Their names were well known to the police, and might, if neccesary, be communicated to the Embassies; at the same time his Excellency considered it his duty to call the attention of the Ambassadors to the necessity of devising some means to enable him to take vigorous action against them, either by bringing them to justice, or by banishing them from the Empire.

According to information which he had received, an insurrectionary movement of a far more serious nature than that of the 30th September, might shortly be expected at Constantinople if he was not allowed to take the necessary precautions for preventing it, and the situation was rendered doubly critical by the fact that these revolutionary ideas were certain, sooner or later, to penetrate to the Mussulman population, which was only too ready to receive them.

His Excellency, in conclusion, stated his opinion that no measure of reforms would satisfy the Armenians, and that even if administrative autonomy were granted to them, they would still clamour for more.

I have, &c.

(Signed) PHILIP CURRIE.

F. O. 424/184, pp. 71-72, No. 129

No. 258

Sir P. Currie to the Marquess of Salisbury.

No. 495.   CONSTANTINOPLE, *October 15, 1895, 3 p.m.*
Telegraphic.   *(Received October 15.)*

WITH reference to my telegram No. 480 of the 10th October:

There is a rumour that 10,000 men are to be sent to reinforce the garrison of the Dardanelles, but as yet no steps have been taken.

Additional submarine mines have not yet been dispatched; but additional earth-works have been commenced near Namajieh, Kafes Point, and on the hill behind Anatoli Medjidieh.

F. O. 424/184, p. 64, No. 106

No. 259

Sir P. Currie to the Marquess of Salisbury.

No. 496.   CONSTANTINOPLE, *October 15, 1895, 7.25 p.m.*
Telegraphic.   *(Received October 15.)*

GREAT activity is being shown by the Armenian Revolutionary Committee, and it is stated by the police that a further demonstration is being planned by them.

The Armenian shopkeepers had reopened their shops to-day, but they have been ordered to close again.

Forty-seven prisoners have up to the present moment been released by the Commission referred to in my telegram No. 489 of the 11th October, and Mr. Lister has received permission to visit the prisons on Wednesday.

F. O. 424/184, p. 64, No. 107

No. 260

Sir P. Currie to the Marquess of Salisbury.

No. 681.   THERAPIA, *October 15, 1895.*
My Lord,   *(Received October 21.)*

I HAD the honour of being received in audience by the Sultan on the 11th instant.

His Imperial Majesty expressed his gratitude for the assistance I had given, in concert with the other Ambassadors, towards the restoration of order in the capital. He went on to say that the sympathy which had been shown in England for the Armenians has had the effect of encouraging them in acts of violence, and complained bitterly of the attacks made upon him in the English press.

I replied that I could not assume any responsibility for articles which appeared in the newspapers, but that His Majesty might rest assured that Her Majesty's Government has never encouraged acts of violence, and that their interference in the Armenian question had been solely directed to obtaining an amelioration of the condition of the Armenians in the Asiatic provinces. It was, I said, the ardent desire of Her Majesty's Government that the question of reforms should be brought to a speedy conclusion, with the view of putting an end to the existing state of tension and uneasiness.

The French and Russian Ambassadors had, as well as myself, been authorized to make certain proposals for the final settlement of the question to the Imperial Government, and we had invited the Minister for Foreign Affairs to confer with us. I trusted that His Imperial Majesty would authorize Saïd Pasha to deal with the question.

IIis Majesty replied that he had no objection to such a course, but that he wished me first to see Marshal Zeki Pasha, who had already called upon me twice in the course of last week, and who enjoyed the full confidence of His Majesty.

I replied that I should, of course, be very happy to receive any one whom His Majesty might send to me, but that, in the matter of reforms, I was acting in accord with my colleagues, and that I could not, therefore, discuss them separately.

His Majesty said that the communications with which Zeki Pasha would be charged were of a private and confidential nature.

I again repeated that Her Majesty's Government attached the greatest importance to the settlement of the reform question; that, in view of the strong pressure of public opinion, they could not consent to any further postponement of it; and that I felt sure that until it was brought to a conclusion they would be unwilling to discuss any other question.

I urged especially the importance of the publication of the reforms as a means not only of satisfying public opinion in Europe, but also of calming the agitation among the Armenians themselves.

I assured His Majesty that in insisting, as they felt bound to do, on a prompt compliance with the recommendations of the three Governments, Her Majesty's Government had no hostile feeling towards His Majesty or his Mussulman subjects; on the contrary, they believed that a reform in the administration of the Asiatic provinces was essential to the very existence of the Empire, and they desired that these reforms should be carried out in such a manner as not to wound the susceptibilities of the Moslem population.

His Majesty avoided giving any definite reply to my observations, but repeated his wish that I should see Zeki Pasha, who would call upon me on the following day.

I have, &c.

(Signed) PHILIP CURRIE.

F. O. 424/184, pp. 73-74, No. 131

No. 261

Sir P. Currie to the Marquess of Salisbury.

No. 497.   CONSTANTINOPLE, *October 15, 1895, 4.30 p.m.*
Telegraphic.   *(Received October 15.)*

WITH reference to my telegram of yesterday, at a further conference which took place to-day with Saïd Pasha and Munir Bey, the wording of the Act embodying the reforms was finally settled so far as concerns the Ambassadors and the Porte.

To-morrow it will be submitted to the Council of Ministers, and then the Iradé of the Sultan is all that will be required.

F. O. 424/184, p. 65, No. 108
Turkey No. 1 (1896), p. 158, No. 198

No. 262

The Marquess of Salisbury to Sir E. Monson.

No. 98.
Sir,   FOREIGN OFFICE, *October 16, 1895.*
COUNT DEYM called at the Foreign Office this afternoon, having returned to England earlier than he had expected.

He had apparently been sent back by Count Goluchowski, who was much disquieted by the condition of things at Constantinople. The object, however, of his return was to some extent anticipated, because the confidential information of the close of the Armenian negotiations had at that time reached the Foreign Office.

He appeared to be apprehensive of danger from two directions.

He feared that if our negotiations did not come to a successful issue, and the Sultan was obdurate, England might take measures of a coercive character which would raise the whole Eastern question.

But he appeared also to be apprehensive that there is impending a fundamental change of opinion on the part of the allies of Austria in regard to the elements of that question. He spoke of the members of the Triple Alliance, but I thought that his language in many points was applicable only to England. He seemed to think that Austria's allies were no longer desirous of maintaining the Turkish Empire, and he appeared to have been affected by some speculations published in England pointing to the retirement of this country altogether from the Mediterranean as a field of political action.

He then spoke of the impossibility of Austria ever being a party to such a change of opinion, and urged the importance of maintaining the Turkish Empire for the longest possible period, as Austria could never tolerate the presence of Russia on the Bosphorus.

I concurred with him in this general statement of policy, which, I said, had for a long time been the policy professed and supported by England, and to which England still adhered, and I told him that there was no fear of any movement of public opinion in this country which would result in the withdrawal of the English naval forces from the Mediterranean.

I am, &c.

(Signed) SALISBURY.

F. O. 424/184, p. 67*, No. 116†

No. 263

The Marquess of Salisbury to Sir P. Currie.

No. 352.
Sir,   FOREIGN OFFICE, *October 16, 1895*
    I HAVE received your Excellency's despatch No. 642 of the 2nd instant
relative to the continued detention at Van of Erko of Shenik and other Armenian
political prisoners, and their alleged ill-treatment in prison.
    I approve the representations which you made to the Grand Vizier on the
subject.
                                    I am, &c.
                                                              (Signed) SALISBURY.
        *F. O. 424/184, p. 67, No. 116**

No. 264

Sir P. Currie to the Marquess of Salisbury.

No. 505.   CONSTANTINOPLE, *October 17, 1895, 10.30 a.m.*
Telegraphic.   *(Received October 17.)*
    IN Constantinople there is much ferment among the Mussulmans, but their
animosity appears for the moment to be directed less against the Christians than
the Sultan. A strong feeling is said to exist in favour of a revival of the Constitution
of 1877.
    The strong patrols of military render any serious outbreak here unlikely. The
Revolutionary Committee issues orders to the Armenians which it enforces by
threats, and by its action keeps alive the state of alarm which has existed ever since
the commencement of the present disturbances. The reports which have reached
the various Embassies from all parts of the Asiatic provinces show a very disturbed
and critical state of affairs, which might at any moment lead to massacres of the
Christians. The authorities in the provinces appear to be doing their best to
maintain order, but the forces at their disposal are generally inadequate. The
Ambassadors met yesterday to compare notes on the situation, when it was decided
that the Dragomans of the Austrian, Russian, and British Embassies should
proceed to-day to the Patriachate, and urge the Patriarch on behalf of the six
Embassies to do all that is in his power to put a stop to the dangerous action of the
agitators.
    The Ambassadors hope that this message will strengthen his Beatitude's
hands in dealing with the agitation, as it is known that his own views are entirely
against it.

At the same time, the French, German, and Italian Dragomans are to make arrangements for the disposal of the arms left by the refugees in the churches; these arms to be conveyed to the Ministry of War, and deposited there under the seal of the Embassies for the present.

F. O. 424/184, p. 67, No. 116

No. 265

Sir P. Currie to the Marquess of Salisbury.

No. 682.   THERAPIA, *October 16, 1895.*
My Lord,   *(Received October 21.)*

I HAVE received from the Italian Embassy the inclosed translation of a Turkish Proclamation recently posted up by Mussulmans in Constantinople.

I hear that a Turkish lawyer named Ajem Izzet, who is one of the leaders of the „Jeune Turquie" party, has been arrested as the author of this document. It is asserted that he refused to answer any questions, and said that the authorities might put him to death, but that others "would spring up like mushrooms to follow his example," and that the day for suppressing all expression of Mussulman opinion had gone by.

I have, &c.

(Signed) PHILIP CURRIE.

F. O. 424/184, p. 74, No. 132

Inclosure in No. 265

Turkish Proclamation posted up by Mussulmans in Constantinople.

Translation.
Citoyens,

LE mouvement égoïste des Arméniens, et la part qu'ils ont prise dans les massacres de plusieurs malheureux nous ont profondément affligés. Il est évident que la situation actuelle est la conséquence des maux de l'Administration présente.

Le Sultan Hamid, pour cacher ses fautes, veut montrer coupables et fautifs les Musulmans devant le monde civilisé. Le temps est venu d'obtenir nos droits légitimes que la législation Mahométane et la Constitution qui nous a été octroyée nous donnent pour la sauvegarde de notre honneur et de notre vie. En avant! En nous donnant la main donnons une plus grande extension à notre union et à notre accord. Effaçons la tâche infligée par l'Administration tyrannique sur l'Islam Ottoman.

F. O. 424/184, p. 74, No. 132/1

No. 266

Sir P. Currie to the Marquess of Salisbury.

No. 684.   THERAPIA, *October 16, 1895.*
My Lord,   *(Received October 21.)*

ON the 8th instant I received a telegram from Her Majesty's Consulate in Constantinople stating that the Armenian ecclesiastical authorities of Pera begged for my intervention in consequence of the police having blockaded their church, in which about 2,000 persons had taken refuge, and that no food was allowed to enter.

I at once consulted my Austrian colleague (as Doyen of the Corps Diplomatique) and M. Nélidoff. They had received no information themselves, but they agreed that the matter was serious, and that united action on the part of all the Embassies was desirable.

This opinion being fully shared by our other colleagues, a telegram signed by the five Ambassadors and the Italian Chargé d'Affaires was dispatched without delay to the Minister of Foreign Affairs tendering our good offices for the solution of the difficulty. His Excellency replied next day denying that the entry of food into the churches had been forbidden, but accepting our offer of intervention.

Saïd Pasha met the Ambassadors at the French Embassy the same afternoon, and gave us his word, in the name of the Turkish Government, that if the refugees would lay down their arms they would be allowed to return freely to their homes, and not be arrested or molested. It was agreed that the Dragomans of the six Embassies should visit the Armenian churches in Pera and other quarters where refugees were collected, and should communicate to them the above assurances, and urge them to leave.

I have the honour to inclose a Memorandum by Mr. Marinitch, reporting how the Dragomans accomplished their mission.

The successful and unanimous action of the Embassies in a matter which was causing serious uneasiness both to the authorities and to the Christian population has produced a salutary effect, and cannot fail to increase the influence which the united action of the Representatives of the Great Powers is capable of exerting.

I have already reported to your Lordship that the Sultan expressed his gratitude for the assistance rendered to his Government both personally and through the Foreign Minister, and I have now the honour to inclose a copy of a letter of thanks which my colleagues and I have received from the Armenian Patriarch.

The Dragomans appear to have discharged their task with much tact and skill. Mr. Marinitch especially deserves great credit for his share in quieting the fears of the refugees. He was chosen to address the people in the church of Pera as the mouthpiece of his colleagues, and I am assured by impartial persons that it was greatly owing to his clear and forcible language that confidence was restored, and that the Armenians were induced to depart quietly to their homes.

I have, &c.

(Signed) PHILIP CURRIE.

F. O. 424/184, p. 80, No. 134

Inclosure 1 in No. 266

Memorandum by Mr. Marinitch.

Confidential.

IN accordance with your Excellency's instructions, herewith returned, I undertook on Thursday last, with my colleagues of the Embassies of the Great Powers, the difficult task of persuading the Armenians to leave the churches, where they had taken refuge, to return to their houses.

We met first at the British Embassy in Pera in order to ascertain whether the police authorities had received their instructions to afford the necessary assistance to us in carrying out the task intrusted to us, and whether the members of the Ephoria were to be found at the church of Pera, which was to be visited first.

When this was done we proceeded to the said church and communicated to the Ephors the object of our mission. These gentlemen at once placed themselves in communication with some of the refugees, and it was agreed that we should go to the church, where the Bishop would speak to the people who had gathered there.

In view of the fact that the speech made by this Prelate had no great effect upon the people, I was requested to address them, and I did so. Thereupon some thirty women and children began to leave the church. One of the refugees, however, who had left and run after them, succeeded in inducing them to return. Great confusion then arose, most of the refugees refusing to leave the church, stating that they were afraid to return to their dwellings. I was again requested to address the people, who had now assembled in the churchyard, but my words were not heard owing to the cries of the people, who, as far as I have been able to learn, were listening to the bad advice given by certain of the refugees, who, fearing apparently to be looked upon as ringleaders, and seized by the police, were endeavouring to prevent the others from leaving the church.

We thereupon retired into a room with the Ephors and the Bishop, in order to consider what was to be done in face of the refusal of the refugees to quit the church. The Ephors advised us not to insist for the present, so as to give the ignorant people time to talk over the real object of our visit. M. Maximoff, the Russian Dragoman, requested the Ephors to give the people clearly to understand the serious consequences as regards themselves which would ensue if they lost such an opportunity of leaving the church under the assurances given by the Porte to the Great Powers that none of them would be arrested or molested.

We then left the church at Pera and proceeded to the Cathedral of Koum Kapou, where the Patriarch on learning our arrival requested us to wait upon his Beatitude, which we did accordingly.

M. Maximoff explained to Mgr. Ismirlian the object of our mission and the unsuccessful result of the steps taken by us at the Pera church. His Beatitude expressed his deepest regret and offered to use his best efforts in order to enable us to carry out successfully our instructions.

Thereupon we entered the Cathedral of Koum Kapou and set to work without loss of time. We addressed the people and found that they made no opposition to returning to their homes. Several of the refugees were conversant with the Russian idiom which led us to believe that they were Armenians of Russian origin and most of them, we found, were wearing caps instead of the Turkish fez. They then began to return to their homes leaving their arms in the custody of the clergy. Those who, fearing to be looked upon as rioters by the police, were reluctant to leave the church, we supplied with a kind of "sauf-conduit". Within two hours we succeeded in clearing the church of its inmates, and according to the list drawn up 450 men and women actually returned to their homes.

We then returned to the Pera church and found that our advice had not proved altogether useless, as 400 men and women had left the church in question for their homes. But as it was too late for the others to gain their dwellings in safety, we caused them to remain where they were for that night, promising to come back the following day to resume our work. Having done this we left for Therapia.

The next day, Friday, we reached the church at Pera at 9 o'clock in the morning, and having at once resumed proceedings succeeded within five hours in inducing all the refugees to leave the church, not, however, without fresh difficulties created by certain individuals who may be looked upon as the instigators of the recent events. Those who still hesitated to leave we supplied with a sort of "sauf-conduit." All arms were left in the church. The total number of the men and women who thus returned to their homes amounted to 1,150, among them being persons belonging to various classes of the community.

Thence we proceeded to the Galata church. Here the evacuation began without any serious difficulty after the Armenian priest had made the people clearly understand the object of our mission. The Armenians who had gathered in this church were of the lower class, and it was evident that most of them had gone there merely to escape ill-treatment.

Here we gave very few "sauf-conduits". Their arms remained in the church. We further discovered two flags made with black paper, which were hanging in the form of a cross on the wall of the staircase, and over the chair of the President of the Council, bearing the following inscription: "Vivent les dévoués Hintchakistes!" These flags were removed at our request.

Within two-and-a-half hours we succeeded in inducing the refugees, to the number of 550, men and women, to return to their homes.

Meanwhile, M. Bay, of the French Embassy, who, acting under our instructions, had procceded to the church at Hasskeui to see how matters stood there, returned and reported that he had induced the remaining refugees, to the number of 164, to return to their homes, no arms apparently having been found upon them, and very few "sauf-conduits" having been given to them.

We then left for the church at Scutari, where the refugees, amounting to some fifty-five persons, were easily persuaded to return to their houses. Only a few women and children, living in an exclusively Mussulman quarter, refused to go out. But it was agreed between us and the representative of the Patriarchate that they should be provided on the day following with other dwellings and removed there.

We did not visit the Pancaldi church as the Patriarch Azarian had, on Friday morning, informed the Dragoman of the French Embassy that the refugees there, amounting to forty-five, had returned to their homes.

I beg to subjoin certain of the conditions demanded by some of the refugees in the Pera church before consenting to leave, which, however we refused to take into consideration.

According to our information only 12 per cent of the refugees were found with arms in their possession. The cavasses of the Embassies did not, of course, allow anybody to leave the churches without first carefully searching them for their arms which, we ascertained, were not of one pattern, as asserted by the Turkish authorities.

Lists of the refugees were drawn up, and will be forwarded to the respective Embassies.

The emblems of mourning which were hanging on the doors of the several churches were at once removed by our orders.

I may add that, from what I observed, the greater part of the refugees, both men and women, were resolved to resist and die if efforts had been made by the Turkish authorities to compel them to leave the churches by force.

Before concluding, I think it my duty to mention that the police officials who were placed at our entire disposal afforded to us unhesitatingly their whole support.

(Signed) H. MARINITCH.

October 12, 1895.
F. O. 424/184, pp. 81-82, No. 134/1

Inclosure 2 in No. 266

The Armenian Patriarch to Sir P. Currie.

M. l'Ambassadeur,   *Undated.*

GRACE aux bons offices et aux bienveillantes assurances de leurs Excellences MM. les Ambassadeurs des six Grandes Puissances Européennes, les malheureux réfugiés dans certaines églises, à la suite des horribles événements de ces jours derniers, viennent de quitter leurs asiles et de se disperser avec le calme et la tranquillité désirables. C'est un devoir sacré et bien doux à notre cœur de vous exprimer notre très profonde gratitude aussi bien pour votre généreuse intervention, qui a eu pour effet d'écarter un grave péril imminent, que pour sentiments de sympathie personnelle prodigués par vous à notre égard dans les douloureuses conjonctures que nous traversons. Nous exprimons également nos vifs remercîments à MM. les Drogmans attachés à votre Ambassade qui ont su accomplir avec un tact si appréciable, la délicate mission de rassurer une population affolée par la peur et le désespoir.

Permettez-nous d'ajouter, Excellence, que nous avons trop de foi dans votre sagacité pour oser vous implorer que vous veuillez bien continuer vos nobles soins, afin que des mesurers efficaces soient adoptées sans autre délai à l'effet de mettre fin à la situation menaçante actuelle, de prévenir le retour de tueries d'innocents, de faire cesser les excès commis dans les prisons, d'empêcher, enfin, que les tristes faits qui viennent de se dérouler sous nos yeux ne puissent avoir leur contre-coup dans les provinces, qui serait terrible.

F. O. 424/184, pp. 82-83, No. 134/2

No. 267

Sir P. Currie to the Marquess of Salisbury.

No. 685.   THERAPIA, *October 16, 1895.*
My Lord,   *(Received October 21.)*

WITH reference to my despatch No. 681 of yesterday, I have the honour to state that Marshal Zeki Pasha called upon me by order of the Sultan on the 12th instant.

He said that His Majesty was desirous of restoring the friendly and intimate relations which formerly existed between Turkey and England, and that, with this view, he wished to make a special appeal to me as British Representative for my assistance in the present juncture of affairs. In my conversation with His Majesty on the previous day, I had mentioned that Her Majesty's Government would insist on certain reforms in addition to those which had already been conceded by His

Majesty. The Sultan could not understand the object which England had in view, more especially as he understood that the Russian Government had expressed themselves as satisfied with the reforms already granted. His Excellency was instructed to represent the danger of offending his Mussulman subjects, to which the Sultan would be exposed by making concessions to the Armenians.

I replied that Her Majesty's Government were acting in accord with the Governments of France and Russia, who had sent instructions to their Representatives here identical with those I had received. The additional concessions that we should ask for were few in number, and involved no question of principle. I added that Her Majesty's Government did not demand anything that would be repugnant to the feelings of the Mussulman population, for I could not suppose that the admission of the Christians to public employment in proportion to their numbers, which was already sanctioned in theory by existing laws, could have any such effect. For my own part, I could promise that nothing should be inserted in the Act embodying the reforms which could justly offend Moslem susceptiblities.

Zeki Pasha asked me to give him a list of our demands, but I declined to do this on the ground that, as I was acting in concert with the Ambassadors of France and Russia, I should not be justified in anticipating the communication that we should jointly make to the Foreign Minister as soon as he was authorized to call upon us.

Zeki Pasha having again pressed me to give some assurances that would reassure the Sultan, I repeated that the only safe course for His Majesty to pursue was to promulgate the reforms with the least possible delay. Public opinion in England was pressing for strong measures, and was calling upon Her Majesty's Government to make use of the fleet to enforce the demands of England. It was my earnest wish that the Sultan should be saved from the dangers that threatened him and his Empire, but I feared that this would be impossible if His Majesty did not give his consent to a prompt settlement of the question.

I have, &c.

(Signed) PHILIP CURRIE.

F. O. 424/184, p. 83, No. 135

No. 268

Sir P. Currie to the Marquess of Salisbury.

No. 506.　　　　　　　　　　　　　　　CONSTANTINOPLE, *October 17, 1895, 1 p.m.*
Telegraphic.　　　　　　　　　　　　　　　　　　*(Received October 17.)*

MR. LONGWORTH telegraphed to-day that the military at Trebizond regard the Consulate with suspicion, and that he is helpless. He asks if nothing can be done for people who served Consulate, who he is certain are innocent. I have telegraphed to ask if he means that Consulate servants have been arrested.

He says that no Turks but many Armenians are being arrested and tried by court-martial, and that it is thought some will be shot.

F. O. 424/184, p. 67, No. 117

No. 269

Sir P. Currie to the Marquess of Salisbury.

No. 507.   CONSTANTINOPLE, *October 17, 1895, 7.10 p.m.*
Telegraphic.   *(Received October 17.)*

AN official intimation has just reached me that an Iradé sanctioning the reforms as settled between the Minister for Foreign Affairs and the Ambassadors has been issued by the Sultan.

F. O. 424/184, p. 68, No. 118

No. 270

Sir P. Currie to the Marquess of Salisbury.

No. 508.   CONSTANTINOPLE, *October 17, 1895, 7.30 p.m.*
Telegraphic.   *(Received October 17.)*

THE following was received to-day from the British Consul at Aleppo:-

"Revolutionary agents have ordered Armenians of Suedia who are away from their homes to come back at once to the district, in order to be ready for an outbreak."

F. O. 424/184, p. 68, No. 119

No. 271

Sir P. Currie to the Marquess of Salisbury.

No. 509.   CONSTANTINOPLE, *October 17, 1895, 11 a.m.*
Telegraphic.   *(Received October 17.)*

THERE have been no further disturbances at Trebizond. The Russian gun-boat "Terets" arrived there on the 14th instant.

F. O. 424/184, p. 68, No. 12

No. 272

Sir P. Currie to the Marquess of Salisbury.

No. 687. THERAPIA, *October 17, 1895.*
My Lord, *(Received October 21.)*
    I HAVE the honour to transmit herewith copies of despatches which I have received from Her Majesty's Consul at Aleppo respecting the political situation at Aintab and Djibbin.
    I am bringing the various abuses reported as existing in the administration of that district to the notice of the Grand Vizier.
                  I have, &c.

                  (Signed) PHILIP CURRIE.

F. O. 424/184, p. 84, No. 136

Inclosure 1 in No. 272

Consul Barnham to Sir P. Currie.

Sir, ALEPPO, *October 4, 1895.*
    I HAVE the honour to forward herewith, for the favour of your Excellency's perusal, copy of a letter which I have received from the Rev. M. G. Papazian, Protestant Minister at Aintab, and Professor H. Krikorian, of Aintab College, reviewing the various abuses which exist in the administration of that part of the Aleppo Vilayet.
    Dr. Fuller, the Present of Aintab College, in transmitting this letter, remarks: "I believe it to be a correct and very moderate statement of facts."
    The incidents related are repeated all over the Empire, but in drawing your Excellency's attention specially to the concluding paragraph, I would say that I have had much corroborative evidence lately that the situation in Aintab is extremely critical, and in Marash.
    Aghassé, the leader of the Hunchagists, has been in Aintab since the month of August, and a very large number of Armenians have in consequence joined the revolutionary party.
    The professors of Aintab College have had the greatest difficulty in preventing the college boys from taking part in the movement, and have aided the American missionaries in their constant endeavour to discourage it.
                  I have, &c.

            (Signed) HENRY D. BARNHAM.

F. O. 424/184, p. 84, No. 136/1

Inclosure 2 in No. 272

The Rev. M. Papazian and Professor Krikorian to Consul Barnham.

Sir,   AINTAB, *October 1, 1895.*

THE special efforts which we understand are now being made to secure reforms in the administration of the Government in this land seem to make it proper for us, through you, to solicit the attention of the British Government to the following facts, of the entire accuracy of which we are prepared to furnish the most indubitable proofs, and which are only a small part of a large number of similar facts which might be easily collated.

1. The Aleppo Vilayet is believed to contain approximately 100,000 Christians and 500,000 Moslems.

These Christians are found chiefly in the regions about Marsh, Zeitoun, Urfa, Aintab and Antioch, and their general condition is that of great and increasing poverty and oppression. This is specially true with regard to the mountain villages about Marsh and Zeitoun, and also with regard to Jibbin, a village some fourteen hours north-east of Aintab. It will not be denied that the general policy of the Government in all this region has been, and is still, to enforce the largest possible and most unrelenting exaction of taxes, with very little regard for, or protection of, individual rights, and almost no attempt to alleviate or improve the general situation.

While such a policy is to the last degree irksome and oppressive to the whole population, there are also many cases in which special discrimination is made against Christians, and under which their hardships are particularly great.

Specifications.

1. In Aintab an annual tax for roads has been assessed and collected for more than twenty years. During the past nine years the people of Aintab have paid the Government under this head more than 1,500 Turkish liras, and to-day the city has no made roads connecting it with any other place, and work to this end has been even attempted on no more than 6 miles near to Aintab, where the roads were already comparatively good.

2. For the past ten years 2,000 liras a-year has been collected by the Government from Aintab for the schools of any sort; and such as are maintained are practically of no benefit to Christians.

3. In the collection of the tithes the greatest abuses are commonly practised. Instead of one-tenth not unfrequently a fourth and even a-half of the income is taken, and in some cases more than three-fourths have been seized.

4. Christians arrested on suspicion of political plottings have been threatened and irregularly mulcted sometimes to the amount of 400 or 500 liras in a single case.

5. In Inndajak, a Christian village seven hours from Marash, the regulations imposed with regard to cutting and selling lumber have been such as practically to ruin this chief industry of the village and reduce the people to the last extremity of poverty.

6. In Jibbin, for the murder of one Moslem killed in a quarrel in which the two parties were about equally to blame, and in which Moslems had at least equal responsibility with Christians, twenty-seven Christians were imprisoned, of whom twenty were in prison eleven months, two died in prison, and four were finally convicted and condemned to fifteen years' imprisonment each, and not a Moslem has been in any way punished.

7. It is increasingly difficult, and now nearly impossible for Christians to secure permission for the establishment of schools, or for the erection of school or church buildings, and in some cases schools and churches have been arbitrarily closed.

8. Insult, abuse, violence, and threatening of Moslems against Christians has greatly increased of late, and all attempts to secure the adequate punishment of Moslem offenders in such cases are utterly futile.

(a.) Within the past three months there have been in Aintab three wanton attacks by Moslems on wedding parties in Christian houses, in which many Christians were shamefully abused and severely beaten, and for which no satisfaction has been secured.

(b.) In the same city, and within the same time, there have been three cases of sodomy violently perpetrated by Moslems upon Christian boys, two of whom were about 11, and one 16 years of age, and for this no punishment has been inflicted, although the most energetic representations have been made in the case to the Government.

9. It is a well understood fact that the idea and hope is generally cherished among the lower classes of Moslems that under certain circumstances, not unlikely to occur, a general rising of Moslems, and an indiscriminate massacre of Christians will be undertaken, and these and not a few Moslems in high office and authority have given free expression to sentiments calculated to encourage and   flame this idea. In view of these and other similar facts which we need not now name, we desire most earnestly to solicit and implore the intervention of the British Government in such a way as may best and most speedily secure the protection of the Christian people of this vilayet.

We have, &c.

(Signed) Rev. M. G. Papazian.
Professor H. Krikorian, *of Aintab College for Central Turkey.*

F. O. 424/184, p. p. 84-85, No. 136/2

No. 273

Sir P. Currie to the Marquess of Salisbury.

No. 694.   THERAPIA, *October 17, 1895.*
My Lord,   *(Received October 21.)*

WITH reference to my telegram No. 497 of the 15th instant, I have the honour to transmit to your Lordship a copy of the Act embodying the reforms for the six vilayets inhabited by Armenians, as drawn up by the Delegates of the three Embassies, in conjunction with Munir Ber, the Secretary-General of the Foreign Department, and revised by the three Ambassadors and Saïd Pasha.

It is intended that this document should be promulgated in the form of an Annex to an Imperial Decree (probably a letter addressed to the Grand Vizier) which will notify the appointment of a High Commissioner, the amnesty, the arrangements for the return of the emigrants, and the application of the principles laid down in the Act to the other districts of Asiatic Turkey which contain a considerable proportion of Christians.

The terms in which the above provisions will be stated in the Decree have also been agreed upon, and will be found at the end of the Act.

I have, &c.

(Signed) PHILIP CURRIE.

F. O. 424/184, p. 95, No. 140

Inclosure in No. 273

Act embodying the Reforms for the six Vilayets inhabited by Armenians, as drawn up by the Delegates of the three Embassies in conjunction with Munir Bey, the Secretary-General of the Foreign Department, and revised by the three Ambassadors and Saïd Pasha.*

CHAPITRE I.—VILAYETS ET MUTESSARIFATS.

ARTICLE 1. Auprès de chaque vilayet (Gouvernement-Général) sera nommé un Mouavin non-Musulman conformément aux dispositions du Chapitre II du Règlement sur l'Administration Générale des Vilayets du 29 Chewal, 1286.†

Il sera chargé conformément à ce Règlement de coopérer aux affaires générales du vilayet et d'en préparer l'expédition.

Art. 2. Seront également nommés des Mouavins non-Musulmans auprès des

---

* This is the Scheme of Reforms communicated by the Porte to Sir P. Currie on the 26th October, and sent home in his No. 704 of October 22, 1895.   † See Appendix.

Mutessarifs et des Caïmacams Musulmans dans les sandjaks et les cazas où cette mesure sera justifiée par l'importance de la population Chrétienne.

Chapitre II.—Caïmacams.

Art. 3. Les Caïmacams seront choisis sans distinction de religion par le Ministère de l'Intérieur parmi les diplômés de l'École Civile et nommés par Tradé Impérial.

Art. 4. Seront maintenus dans l'Administration ceux qui, étant actuellement en fonctions, seront reconnus capables bien que non-diplômés.

Dans le cas où il n'y aurait pas en ce moment un nombre de non-Musulmans diplômés de l'École Mulkié suffisant pour permettre de faire les nominations reconnues nécessaires, ces postes seront occupés par des personnes au service du Gouvernement qui, quoique non-diplômées, seront reconnues aptes à remplir les fonctions de Caïmacam.

Chapitre III.—Proportion des Chrétiens dans les Fonctions Publiques.

Art. 5. Les fonctions administratives seront confiées aux sujets Musulmans et non-Musulmans proportionnellement aux chiffres des populations Musulmanes et non-Musulmanes de chaque vilayet.

Le nombre des fonctionnaires non-Musulmans de l'Administration de la Police et de la Gendarmerie sera fixé par la Commission Permanente de Contrôle.

Chapitre IV.—Conseils des Sandjaks et Cazas.

Art. 6. Les Conseils Administratifs des sandjaks et des cazas composés de membres élus et de membres de droit sont maintenus et fonctionneront conformément à l'Article 61 du Règlement sur l'Administration Générale des Vilayets de 1286,* et aux Articles 77 et 78 de la Loi des Vilayets de 1867, d'après lesquels ils ont été constitués.*

Leurs attributions sont fixées par les Articles 90, 91, et 92 du Règlement sur l'Administration Générale des Vilayets,† et par les Articles 38, 39 et 40 des Instructions relatives à l'Administration Générale des Vilayets du 25 Mouharrem, 1293.†

Chapitre V.—Nahiés.

Art. 7. Les nahiés seront organisés conformément aux prescriptions des Articles 94 à 106 du Règlement sur l'Administration Génerale des Vilayets de

* See Appendix.

1286,‡ et des Articles 1 à 19 du Règlement sur l'Administration des Communes du 25 Mars, 1292.‡

Art. 8. Chaque nahié sera administré par un Moudir et un Conseil composé de quatre membres élus parmi les habitants.

Le Conseil choisira parmi ses membres un Moudir et un Adjoint. Le Moudir devra appartenir à la classe qui forme la majorité des habitants et l'Adjoint à l'autre classe. Le Conseil aura, en outre, un Secrétaire.

Art. 9. Si les habitants d'un nahié sont d'une même classe les membres du Conseil seront élus exclusivement parmi les habitants appartenant à cette même classe; si la population du Cercle Communal est mixte la minorité devra être représentée proportionnellement à son importance relative à condition qu'elle comprenne au moins vingt-cinq maisons.

Art. 10. Les Moudirs et les Secrétaires des nahiés sont rétribués.

Art. 11. Les candidats aux Conseils des Nahiés devront remplir des conditions prévues par l'Article 10 du Reglement sur l'Administration des Communes.§

Art. 12. Les Imams, les prêtres, les professeurs d'écoles, et tous ceux qui se trouvent au service du Gouvernement ne pourront être élus Moudirs.

Art. 13. Le Conseil sera renouvelé par moitié chaque année. Ses membres ainsi que le Moudir seront rééligibles.

Art. 14. Les attributations du Moudir et des Conseils des Nahiés sont réglées par les Articles 20 à 27 du Règlement sur l'Administration des Communes.‖

Villages des Nahiés.

Art. 15. Chaque village du nahié aura un Moukhtar. S'il y a plusieurs quartiers et plusieurs classes d'habitants il y aura un Moukhtar par quartier et par classe.

Art. 16. Aucun village ne pourra relever de deux nahiés à la fois.

CHAPITRE VI.—JUSTICE.

Art. 17. Il y aura dans chque localité un Conseil des Anciens présidé par le Moukhtar et dont la mission sera de concilier à l'amiable les contestations entre les habitants, contestations prévues par les lois judiciaires.

Art. 18. Les fonctions de Juges de Paix sont exercées dans les villages par les Conseils des Anciens et dans les communes par les Conseils Communaux. Leurs attributions et le degré de leur compétence sont déterminés par la loi.

† Ibid.   ‡ Ibid.   § Ibid.   ‖ Ibid.

Art. 19. Des Inspecteurs Judiciaires dont le nombre ne sera pas moindre de six et qui seront par moitié Musulmans et non-Musulmans, seront chargés dans chaque vilayet d'accélérer le jugement de tous les procès en cours et de surveiller l'état des prisons conformément au Règlement de . . . . .

Les inspections devront être faites en même temps par deux Inspecteurs, dont l'un Musulman et l'autre non-Musulman.

CHAPITRE VII.—POLICE

Art. 20. Les agents de la police seront recrutés parmi les sujets Musulmans et non-Musulmans de l'Empire proportionnellement aux chiffres des populations Musulmane et non-Musulmane du vilayet.

Art. 21. Des contingents suffisants seront affectés à chaque subdivision administrative, y compris le nahié.

Les agents de police du nahié sont placés sous les ordres du Moudir et commandés par des Commissaires.

Leurs armes et leurs uniformes seront indentiques aux modèles déjà adoptés.

CHAPITRE VIII.—GENDARMERIE.

Art. 22. Les officiers, sous-officiers, et soldats de la gendarmerie seront recrutés parmi les habitants Musulmans et non-Musulmans de l'Empire, proportionnellement aux chiffres des populations Musulmane et non-Musulmane de chaque vilayet.

La gendarmerie sera soldée et entretenue aux frais de la caisse du vilayet.

La solde des gendarmes est supérieure à celle des soldats de l'armée Impériale, et celle des officiers équivalente à la solde des officiers de l'armée Impériale.

Art. 23. Las gendarmerie est chargée du maintien de l'ordre et de l'escorte de la poste.

CHAPITRE IX.—GARDES-CHAMPÊTRES.

Art. 24. Le Conseil du Nahié choisira des gardes-champêtres dans les différentes classes de la population.

Leur nombre sera fixé par la Commission Permanente de Contrôle, conformément aux besoins de chaque nahié, sur le rapport du Moudir et la proposition du Vali.

Leur uniforme et leur armement seront arrêtés par le Départment de la Guerre.

Chapitre X.—Prisons et Comité d'Enquête Préliminaire.

Art. 25. Les Règlements existants sur la tenue des prisons et des maisons d'arrêt seront strictement exécutés.

Art. 26. Le Comité d'Enquête Préliminaire prévu par les Articles 11 et 12 des Instructions relatives à l'Administration Génerale des Vilayets* est appelé à fonctionner de la façon la plus régulière.

Chapitre XI.—Contrôle des Kurdes.

Art. 27. Les localités de migration des Kurdes seront fixées d'avance de façon à éviter tout dommage aux habitants de la part des Achirets. Un officier ayant sous ses ordres une force armée suffisante et des gendarmes accompagnera chaque tribu dans sa migration. Un Commissaire de Police lui sera adjoint.

Les Kurdes remettront à l'autorité des ôtages pendant leurs migrations.

Les Règlements sur les feuilles de route et le port d'armes seront appliqués aux Kurdes.

Les tribus nomades et errantes seront engagées à se fixer sur des terres qui leur seront concédées par le Gouvernement.

Chapitre XII.—Cavalerie Hamidié.

Art. 28. Le port d'armes et d'uniformes par les cavaliers Hamidiés en dehors des périodes d'instruction est prohibé.

En dehors de ces périodes, les cavaliers Hamidiés sont justiciables des Tribunaux ordinaires.

Un Règlement Militaire qui déterminera tous les détails de leur service sera elaboré sans retard.

Chapitre XIII.—Titres de Propriété.

Art. 29. Il sera institué au chef-lieu du vilayet et des sandjaks des Commissions pour la revision des titres de propriété.

Ces Commissions seront composées de quatre membres (deux Musulmans et deux non-Musulmans), et présidées par le Directeur des Archives ou le préposé aux Immeubles.

Leurs décisions seront soumises aux Conseils d'Administration.

En outre, quatre Délégués seront envoyés chaque année de Constantinople

* See Appendix.

dans les vilayets pour examiner les irrégularités qui auraient pu surgir dans les affaires de propriétés.

Chapitre XIV.—Perception des Impôts.

Art. 30. Pour éviter l'emploi de la force publique, des agents spéciaux, qui ne pourront faire aucune réquisition de fourrages ni de vivres, et qui n'auront aucun maniement de fonds, remettront aux Moukhtars et aux Receveurs des villages et quartiers élus par les habitants, les feuilles sur lesquelles sont inscrits les impôts dus par chaque habitant.

Les Moukhtars et Receveurs susnommés seront seuls chargés de la perception des impôts et de leur consignation aux caisses de l'État.

Chapitre XV.—Dîmes

Art. 31. La perception de la dîme se fera par voie d'affermage. L'affermage en gros demeure aboli et est remplacé par la mise en adjudication par villages et au nom des habitants.

En cas de difficulté, ceux-ci pourront recourir aux Tribunaux. Dans le cas où personne ne se présenterait pour l'affermage des dîmes de certains villages, ou bien si le prix offert était inférieur à la valeur réelle des dîmes à adjuger, ces dîmes seront administrées en régie, conformément au l'èglement sur la matière.

La corvée étant abolie la prestation en nature et en argent est maintenue pour les travaux d'utilité publique.

Le budget de l'Instruction Publique dans chaque vilayet est fixé par le Ministère de l'Instruction Publique.

La ventre pour cause de dettes fiscales ou personnelles de la demeure du contribuable, des terrains nécessaires à sa subsistance, de ses instruments de travail, de ses bêtes de labour, et de ses grains demeure interdite.

Chapitre XVI.—Commission Permanente de Contrôle.

Art. 32. Il sera institué à la Sublime Porte une Commission Permanente de Contrôle composée par moitié de membres Musulmans et non-Musulmans, et chargée de surveiller l'exacte application des réformes.

Les Ambassades feront parvenir à cette Commission, par l'intermédiaire de leurs Drogmans, les avis, communications, et renseignements qu'elles jugeront nécessaires, dans les limites de l'application des réformes et des mesures prescrites par le présent Acte.

Lorsque le Sublime Porte et les Ambassades seront d'accord pour considérer la Commission comme ayant accompli son mandat, elle sera dissoute.

Paragraphes figurant dans le Décret.

Paragraphe 1.—Haut Commissaire de Surveillance pour l'Application des Réformes.

(Traduction.)

Un fonctionnaire digne de considération à tous égards sera nommé et envoyé sur les lieux à titre de Haut Commissaire (Mufettich) par le Gouvernement Impérial avec mission spéciale de surveiller l'exécution des réformes et de présider à leur application.

En cas d'absence ou d'empêchement ce Haut Commissaire sera remplacé provisoirement par un autre haut fonctionnaire Musulman désigné par Sa Majesté Impériale.

Le Haut Commissaire Impérial sera accompagné dans sa mission par un Adjoint (Moavin) non-Musulman.

Paragraphe 2.—Amnistie.

Sa Majesté Impériale le Sultan, ayant accordé, le 23 Juillet, 1895, une amnistie aux Arméniens accusés ou condamnés pour des faits politiques, cette mesure sera appliquée à tous ceux qui auraient été incarcérés avant cette date, et qui seraient encore détenus, et qui ne seraient pas convaincus de participation directe à des crimes de droit commun.

Paragraphe 3.—Rentrée des Emigrés.

Les Arméniens qui auraient été expulsés ou éloignés de leur pays ou qui auraient émigré en pays étranger, pourront rentrer librement en Turquie, après que leur nationalité Ottomane et leur bonne conduite auront été démonstrées.

Paragraphe 4.—Situation des Non-Musulmans dans les autres Vilayets de l'Anatolie.

Des mesures conformes aux principes ci-dessus seront appliquées dans les cazas tels que Zéitoun et Hadjin.

APPENDIX

Articles in the Turkish Règlement, &c., referred to in the Project of Reforms of October 15, 1895.

Chapitre I.—Article 1.

Règlement l'Administration Générale des Vilayets du 29 Chewal, 1287.

Article 17. Les Muavins ont pour devoirs d'aider les Valis dans leur pouvoir exécutif général du vilayet.

Ces devoirs consistent à coopérer avec le Vali dans toutes les affaires ressortissant des-attributions de ce dernier, désignées dans le Chapitre I, à étudier les papiers qui seront adressés par les divers bureaux du vilayet ainsi que les autres lettres et documents dont le Vali lui permettra de prendre connaissance, à les renvoyer aux bureaux respectifs, à soumettre au Vali, par l'entremise du Directeur des Archives, un résumé des pièces décrétées, à écrire sur le dos des documents relatifs aux affaires intérieures du vilayets l'avis et la décision du Gouvernement Géneral, et à soumettre à la décision du Vali les questions qui exigent l'opinion personnelle de ce dernier.

Les fonctions du Muavin peuvent être aussi déléguées à un autre fonctionnaire du chef-lieu du vilayet.

Chapitre IV. Article 6.

Règlement sur l'Administration Génerale des Vilayets du 29 Chewal, 1287.

Art. 61. Pour la délibération sur les affaires relatives à l'administration génerale et particulière des vilayets, lesquelles seront spécifiées dans les Chapitres suivants, ont été institués un Conseil Général convoqué une fois par an au siège du vilayet, et les Conseils d'Administration permanents siégeant dans les chef-lieux des vilayets, des arrondissements, et des cantons. Outre ces Conseils, les villages et nahiés ont des Conseils particuliers pour leurs affaires respectives, et chaque ville et bourg ont de même à part leurs Conseils spéciaux pour le réglement des affaires particulières propres à chaque communauté ainsi que de leurs affaires municipales.

Loi des Vilayets de 1867.

Art. 77. Le Chef de la Magistrature, le Contrôleur-Géneral, le Directeur de la Corresponance, le fonctionnaire attaché à la Cour Civile et Criminelle, le Mufti, le Cadi, et les Chefs religieux des communautés non-Musulmanes, siégeant de droit au Conseil d'Administration du chef-lieu du vilayet, se réunissent en Comité Electoral sous le présidence du Vali. Ce Comité choisit sur la liste des sujets Ottomans résidant tant aux chef-lieux du vilayet et des sandjaks que dans les chefs-lieux des cazas, payant 500 piastres, au moins, de contributions directes, jouissant de crédit et de considération dans le vilayet et sachant lire et écrire, des personnes en nombre égal au triple de celui des membres à nommer au Conseil d'Administration Centrale et à la Cour Civile et Criminelle.

La liste des éligibles est réduite dans les chefs-lieux des sandjaks, conformément aux prescriptions relatives à l'élection des Conseillers et des Mumeiz des sandjaks et des cazas.

Les procès-verbaux contenant le résultat de ces opérations électorales et transmis par les chefs-lieux des sandjaks, sont adressés au Vali qui soumet à la Sublime Porte les noms des personnes qu'il aura choisies, d'après les règles établies aux Articles précédents. Les élections sont confirmées par lettres Vizirielles.

Art. 78. Les quatre Conseillers des cazas de chaque sandjak se réunissent au chef-lieu du sandjak, un mois avant la convocation du Conseil-Général qui sera tenu chaque année au centre du vilayet, pour procéder à l'élection, sur la liste des habitants tant des chef-lieux du sandjak que de ces cazas, de trois personnes réunissant les conditions d'éligibilité des Conseillers et appelées à faire partie du Conseil-Général. Elles se rendent au siège du Gouvernement Central sur l'invitation du Mutessarif.

Les Conseillers des cazas, qui se sont rendus au chef-lieu du sandjak pour y élire les membres du Conseil-Général, leur remettent et font parvenir, par leur intermédiaire, au Vali, toutes les demandes des cazas relatives aux travaux d'utilité publique, à l'agriculture, au commerce, et autres matières pouvant faire l'objet des délibérations du Conseil.

Règlement sur l'Administration Génerale des Vilayets du 29 Chewal, 1287.

Art. 90. Les affaires dont il est parlé dans le Chapitre II et qui se rapportent à l'administration de l'arrondissement sont du ressort de ce Conseil, à savoir, le contrôle, d'après les Règlements spéciaux, des revenus et dépenses de l'arrondissement; la revision des comptes des caisses d'épargne; la surveillance et la conservation des biens mobiliers et immobiliers du Gouvernement; l'examen, dans la limite de sa juridiction, des différends surgis entre les employés Gouvernementaux; la création des routes vicinales dans les cantons; l'adjudication des revenus publics et la conclusion des contrats et achats, qui sont, d'après les lois ou les ordres spéciaux du Gouvernement, du ressort du Mutessarifat. Les affaires qui, conformément à la loi, ne sont pas de la compétence du Mutessarifat sont référées au Conseil Administratif du vilayet.

Le Conseil délibère aussi sur les questions relatives à l'agriculture, au commerce, à l'instruction et aux travaux d'utilité publique, ainsi que sur les questions concernant les institutions utiles et la santé publique. Les questions de la répartition dans les cantons et de la rentrée des impôts, dont, à la suite d'une décision du Gouvernement, il serait chargé par le Conseil d'Administration du vilayet, ainsi que les documents que les Gouvernements des cantons lui adresseront relativement aux questions susmentionnées, font également l'objet des délibérations du Conseil.

Les décisions de ce Conseil sont consignées en Mazbatas qui sont transmis au Mutessarif.

Art. 91. La forme des délibérations, la rédaction des procès-verbaux, et le mode de procédure de ces Conseils sont déterminés dans les Articles du Chapitre II sous le titre "Dispositions Génerales."

Art. 92. Les attributions de ce Conseil sont: le contrôle des recettes et dépenses du canton; la revision des comptes des caisses d'épargne; l'adminstration et la conservation de tous les biens mobiliers et immobiliers de l'État; la répartition dans les quartiers et villages des impôts, d'après les décisions du Conseil Administratif de l'arrondissement; la prise de toute mesure relative à la santé publique; l'examen, dans les limites de sa juridiction, des procès surgis entre les fonctionnaires publics; la construction de routes vicinales dans les villages et les nahiés; l'adjudication des revenus publics et la conclusion des contrats et achats, dont le Caïmakam est directement autorisé par la loi ou en vertu d'un ordre spécial. Pour les affaires qui ne sont pas du ressort du Caïmakamat, il s'en réfère au Conseil d'Administration de l'arrondissement.

Le Conseil soumet au Caïmakam de l'arrondissement les Mazbatas contenant ses décisions.

Instructions relatives à l'Administration Générale des Vilayets du 25 Mouharrem, 1293.

Art. 38. Les Conseils d'Administration présidés par les Valis dans les vilayets, par les Mutessarifs dans les sandjaks, et par les Caïmacams dans les cazas, connaissent des affaires administratives concernant l'État et le pays. Leur devoir consiste à donner librement leur avis sur les affaires qui sont soumises à leurs délibérations conformément à la loi et à l'usage.

Art. 39. Les membres des Conseils d'Administration ne sont pas responsables d'une exécution contraire à leurs décisions. Ils doivent toutefois s'abstenir de tout abus dans l'exercice de leurs fonctions. La responsabilité résultant des actes exécutés, contrairement aux décisions des Conseils Administratifs ou de décisions annulées ou ajournées sans motifs, retombera sur les fonctionnaires chargés du Pouvoir Exécutif.

Art. 40. Dans le cas où les membres des Conseils d'Administration reconnaîtraient des irrégularités ou des injustices dans le service administratif, ils pourront communiquer, par un Rapport à la Sublime Porte, le résultat des constatations qu'ils auront effectuées, en se tenant dans les limites de la stricte justice. Tout individu qui serait l'objet de vexations exercées contre sa personne ou d'injustices commises contre ses intérêts, de la part d'un fonctionnaire public ou d'un simple particulier, a le droit de s'en plaindre directement à la Sublime Porte. Toutefois, s'il constaté que ces plaintes sont le résultat d'une animosité personnelle, le calomniateur sera passible des peines édictées par la loi.

CHAPITRE V.—ARTICLE 7.

Règlement sur l'Administration Générale des Vilayets du 29 Chewal, 1287.

Art. 94. Ces Conseils sont composés des membres des Démogeronties du nahié et des villages placés dans la circonscription du gouvernement du nahié. Chaque Démogerontie n'enverra dans le Conseil que quatre de ses membres au plus. Le Conseil est convoqué, à des époques fixées, dans le chef-lieu du nahié.

Art. 95. La durée de chaque session de ces Conseils ne peut pas dépasser une semaine. Ils sont convoqués quatre fois par an à des époques choisies et fixées par le Gouverneur-Général.

La Mudir du nahié est le Président de ce Conseil.

Art. 96. Le Caïmacam, sur l'ordre du Gouverneur de l'Arrondissement, informe le Mudir du nahié du temps de la convocation du Conseil.

Art. 97. Le Mudir invite les membres qui doivent siéger dans ce Conseil et qui seront pris dans les Démogeronties des villages placés dans la circonscription du nahié et ouvre les débats. Le nombre des membres que chaque Démogerontie de village enverra au Conseil ne peut être plus de quatre.

Art. 98. Les décisions des Conseils du nahié sont prises à la pluralité des voix. En cas d'égalité des votes, la voix du Président forme la majorité,

Art. 99. Si les membres convoqués ne sont pas présents à l'époque fixée pour l'ouverture des séances, le Mudir peut en ajourner à une semaine l'ouverture. Ce délai passé, si les membres arrivés, par rapport au nombre des villages qui forment le nahié, constituent la majorité, c'est-à-dire si le nahié se compose par exemple de cinq villages et que trois des villages seulement ont envoyé leurs délégués, les débats peuvent être commencées.

Art. 100. Ces Conseils s'occupent des institutions d'utilité publique dont l'exécution est désirée et peut être obtenue avec le concours manuel et pécuniaire de la population des villages du nahié. Ils s'occupent également de la construction des routes entre les villages, ainsi que des questions relatives aux pâturages, aux forêts et bois appartenant en commun aux villages du nahié, et des questions que les Démogeronties des villages soumettront au Conseil relativement à l'agriculture, à l'industrie, et au commerce. La multiplication et la conservation des outils d'agriculture et des bêtes de labour ainsi que la salubrité publique et le reglement les affaires municipales communes entre les villages, sont aussi des devoirs de ces Conseils. Ils s'occupent en outre du contrôle des décisions des Démogéronties quant à la répartition des impôts, et ils examinent les demandes ayant trait à la modification de cette répartition.

Le résultat des débats du Conseil du nahié est transmis par-le Mudir au Caïmacam du canton.

Art. 101. Les décisions prises au sein de ce Conseil ne sont pas exécutoires. Elles sont mises à exécution suivant que le Caïmacam en autorisera le Mudir.

Art. 102. La partie technique des travaux à exécuter, tels que routes vicinales, édifices publics et d'intérêt général, dont la création a été arrêtée par le Conseil du nahié et approuvé par le Gouvernement cantonal, regarde ce Gouvernement-ci. Sous ce rapport le Conseil du nahié n'intervient dans ces affaires que pour examiner les questions dont il serait saisi par le Gouvernment cantonal, et pour transmettre par l'intermédiaire du Mudir le résultat de ses délibérations à ce sujet.

Art. 103. Il est interdit aux Conseils des nahiés de statuer sur des procès, d'infliger des amendes et de se saisir de toute question en dehors des limites et de se saisir de toute question en dehors des limites de leurs attributions, prescrites dans les Articles précédents.

Art. 104. La partie des revenus municipaux du canton revenant aux nahiés, sera allouée à l'exécution des travaux d'utilité publique décidés par les Conseils des nahiés.

Le produit des offrandes et des dons des particuliers sera ajouté à la somme précitée et ce capital sera gardé dans le chef-lieu du nahié sous la surveillance des membres du Conseil Communal.

Art. 105. Les membres du Conseil à la clôture des débats de chaque session rentrent dans leurs villages respectifs.

Outre les réunions régulières le Mudir peut, sur l'invitation du Caïmacam et en cas d'une affaire urgente, convoquer en session extraordinaire les membres du Conseil, qui sont tenus à se rendre à l'invitation.

Art. 106. Les membres du Conseil ne peuvent se réunir à l'insu du Mudir ni s'entendre et provoquer des réunions communes avec les membres du Conseil d'un nahié voisin. Dans le cas contraire ils seront tenus responsables par-devant la loi.

Réglement sur l'Administration des Communes du 28 Mouharrem, 1292.

Art. 1. Les villages, les fermes, et les maisons isolées dépendant de chaque district, formeront plusieurs cercles eu égard à leur situation portant le nom des cercles communaux.

Art. 2. Les cercles communaux se divisent en deux catégories; la première contient les cercles qui se composent d'un seul village et l'autre ceux qui comprennent de plusieurs villages. Les cercles de la première catégorie seront composés de villages contenant plus de 200 maisons; ceux de la deuxième comprennent les villages et les quartiers contenant jusqu'à 200 maisons. Le villages contenant plus de cinquante maisons pourront former des cercles de la première catégorie, après avoir accompli les conditions énoncées dans le neuvième Article; toutefois les villages qui contienuent moins de cinquante maisons, ne pouvant former un cercle à part, seront annexés aux autres.

Art. 3. Il est entendu que les villages formant le cercle communal ne pourron être éloignés de l'endroit qui sera choisi comme chef-lieu que de trois heures au plus.

Art. 4. Aucun village ne pourra être annexé en parti à un autre cercle communal, quel que soit le nombre de ses habitants. En cas même qu'un village dépendant d'un caza se trouve situé près d'un autre caza, il ne pourra faire partie du cercle communal de ce dernier.

Art. 5. Si le cercle communal comprend un seul village, il prend le nom de ce village; mais quand il est composé de plusieurs villages, et d'autres habitation isolées, il prend le nom du plus grand, qui est aussi le chef-lieu du cercle; toutefois les villages compris dans le cercle ne pourront changer leurs noms.

Art. 6. Les propriétés immeubles, terrains, pâturages, et autres terres qui se trouvent dans le village compris dans le cercle communal des deux catégories susmentionnées ne subiront aucune modification, et resteront sous l'administration de ce cercle communal.

Art. 7. Chaque cercle communal aura un Mudir et un Conseil, composé de quatre membres au minimum et huit au maximum, élus par les habitants; l'un de ces membres exercera les fonctions de l'Adjoint du Mudir. Le Conseil aura en outre un Secrétaire.

Art. 8. Les villages compris dans les cercles communaux auront, comme par le passé, chacun un Mukhtar. Si un village contient plusieurs quartiers, et ses habitants sont divisés en différentes classes, il y aura un Mukhtar pour chaque quartier et pour chaque classe des habitants.

Art. 9. Les Mudirs et leurs adjoints, ainsi que les membres des Conseils des cercles communaux, exerceront, sans aucune rétribution, leurs fonctions; cependent, les habitants du cercle donneront annuellement une somme convenable aux Mudirs en compensation de leurs dépenses. Une somme convenable sera allouée annuellement au Secrétaire du Conseil, ainsi le montant des émoluments à donner chaque année, et le mode de leur répartition et perception seront contrôlés par les autorités supérieures du chef-lieu.

Art. 10. Les Mudirs et les membres du cercle communal devront être sujets Ottomans, avoir des intérêts dans la localité, être âgé à plus de 30 ans, et choisi parmi ceux qui paient une contribution annuelle à l'État de 100 piastres au minimum, et qui n'ont pas subi une condamnation.

Art. 14. Le Mudir du cercle doit savoir lire et écrire, mais comme ces Mudirs seront élus par les habitants, et jouiront conséquemment de leur confiance, ces derniers en seront garants et responsables. Après l'élection des Mudirs leur nomination sera approuvée par le Gouverneur-Général de vilayet, auquel le fait sera référé par le Caïmacam et le Mutessarif.

Art. 12. Les Imams, les prêtres, les professeurs d'écoles, et tous ceux qui se trouvent au service du Gouvernement, ne pourront être élus Mudirs.

Art. 13. Si les habitants du cercle d'une commune sont d'une même classe, le Mudir, les membres, et l'Adjoint seront élus exclusivement parmi les habitants appartenant à cette même classe. Si le village contient des habitants mixtes, les membres du Conseil seront moitié Musulmans, moitié non-Musulmans. Le Mudir sera élu parmi la classe qui forme la majorité des habitants, et l'adjoint parmi l'autre classe.

Art. 14. Le Mudir et les membres du Conseil seront élus parmi les habitants qui ont les qualités énoncées dans les Articles 10 et 11; ainsi, si le cercle est composé d'un seul village, ses habitants se réunissent à un jour fixe et font l'élection du Mudir et des membres du Conseil; et si le cercle est composé de plusieurs villages, ceux des habitants de chaque village qui jouissent de la considération et de la confiance du public réunis au chef-lieu du cercle choisissent le Mudir et les membres du Conseil.

Art. 15. Le Mudir et les membres du Conseil dans leur première réunion choisiront par majorité de voix un Adjoint, qui en l'absence du Mudir exercera les fonctions de ce dernier; d'ailleurs il sera considéré comme les autres membres.

Art. 16. Les Mudirs seront changés toutes les deux années, et les membres seront changés chaque année en moitié. Le Mudir et les membres pourront être réélus. Si les membres du Conseil sont moitié Musulmans et moitié non-Musulmans, ils seront aussi changés en moitié, et leurs successeurs seront pris parmi ceux qui appartiennent à leur classe.

Art. 17. Si le poste du Mudir et de membre reste vacant, pour accomplir le reste de leur service ils seront nommés à leur place ceux qui ont eu le plus de voix au moment de l'élection.

Art. 18. Les Mukhtars seront élus parmi les habitants indiqués et hommes de confiance et seront remplacés chaques année.

Art. 19. Si des plaintes étaient élevées contre un membre ou tout le Corps Administratif et ces plaintes étaient constatées par le Tribunal ou seraient examinés, ces employés seront remplacés.

CHAPITRE V.—ARTICLE 11.

Règlement sur l'Administration des Communes

Art. 10. Les Mudirs et les membres du cercle communal devront être sujets Ottomans, avoir des intérêts dans la localité, être âgé à plus de 30 ans, et choisis parmi ceux qui paient une contribution annuelle à l'État de 100 piastres au minimum, et qu n'ont pas subi une condamnation.

CHAPITRE V.—ARTICLE 14.

Règlement sur l'Administration des Communes.

Art. 20. Les Conseils des cercles se réuniront au moins deux fois par semaine.

Art. 21. Le Mudir est chargé de l'exécution sur l'avis du Conseil des ordres et instructions qui lui seront délivrés par le chef-leiu du district dont rélève le cercle communal; il portera en outre à la connaissance des habitants les ordres supérieurs; il fera un Rapport et le transmettra au Caïmacam du district dont rélève le cercle, dans lequel il mentionnera les demandes des habitants et le résultat des enquêtes préparatoires qu'il exécutera en cas qu'un crime aura été commis dans le village; il procédera aussi, avec le concours des habitants à l'arrestation des coupables de crime lorsqu'il n'y a pas des gendarmes dans ces endroits, et les enverra au chef-lieu du district.

Art. 22. Les Conseils Communaux auront à aviser aux moyens assurant le maintien des bons rapports parmi les habitants; pourront résoudre à l'amiable les procès civils de peu d'importance et procéder à la réconciliation en cas qu'une rixe aurait éclatée parmi les habitants. Cependant ils n'auront pas le droit de procéder à l'examen des procès du ressort des Tribunaux et d'arranger à l'amiable les procès concernant les crimes et les délits. Si l'on constatait l'apparition de brigands et de voleurs et qu'on aurait conséquemment besoin de force publique, les Mudirs des Conseils auront recours à la station militaire la plus poche, ou au chef de la gendarmerie qui sera installée conformément à l'Article 28.

Art. 23. Les Conseils Communaux ont aussi pour attribution de percevoir des contribuables et d'envoyer au Gouvernement les revenus du fisc; ils sont donc chargés d'encaisser ces revenus et de déposer le somme à la caisse du chef-lieu du district; s'ils rencontrent de difficultés dans la perception, ils auront recours au préposés des revenus du caza; en cas de non réussite de ces derniers, ils demanderont le concours de chef-lieu du caza.

Art. 24. Il y aura dans le chef-lieu de cercle communal un registre, dans lequel seront inscrits, d'après un Tableau envoyé du caza, les taxes, l'impôt de l'exonération militaire, les dîmes et aures contributions du chaque village.

Art. 25. Les Conseils Communaux feront tout leur possible pour encaisser à temps et intégralement les revenus du fisc des villages compris dans le cercle; à la fin de chaque année ils auront à rendre compte de tous les revenus ainsi que des sommes déposées à la caisse du caza.

Art. 26. Le Secrétaire du cercle communal est chargé aussi des affaires de la comptabilité; il est en outre autorisé de délivrer en cas de besoin des certificats revêtus du sceau des membres du Conseil pour des affaires autres que celles concernant la collection des revenus. Les Secrétaires seront admis au service après avoir donné un garant.

Art. 27. Les Conseils Communaux auront un sceau spécial.

Chapitre X.—Article 26.

Instructions relatives à l'Administration Générale des Vilayets.

Art. 11. Les Valis prendront, avant tout, les dispositions nécessaires pour constituer les Conseils dans la forme recommandée. Ils désigneront les Directeurs et les gardiens des prisons. Ils établiront ensuite, dans le chef-lieu des vilayets et des sandjaks, un Comité d'enquête préliminaire composé d'un Président et de deux membres Musulmans et non-Musulmans.

Art. 12. Ces Comités auront pour mandat de s'enquérir des causes qui ont motivé l'arrestation, par les zaptiés, des prévenus et d'ordonner qu'ils soient emprisonnés et interrogés, dans les cas où l'acte qui leur est attribué serait de nature à entrainer des pénalités édictées par la loi; de faire mettre immédiatement en liberté, sous caution, ceux dont la conduite ne motiverait pas l'application de la loi; de veiller à ce que personne ne soit retenu sans nécessité en prison.

F. O. 424/184, pp. 95-103, No. 140/1

No. 274

The Marquess of Salisbury to Sir P. Currie.

No. 184.
Telegraphic.   Foreign Office, *October 18, 1895, 5.45 p.m.*

I HAVE received your telegram No. 507 of the 17th instant, reporting the issue of the Sultan's Iradé which sanctions the scheme of Armenian reforms as settled between the Turkish Minister for Foreign Affairs and the Ambassadors of Great Britain, France, and Russia at Constantinople.

I have to convey to you my hearty congratulations on the success obtained by your Excellency.

I should be glad to learn without delay the terms of the Imperial Iradé, or of the arrangement sanctioned by it.

F. O. 424/184, p. 68, No. 121

No. 275

Sir P. Currie to the Marquess of Salisbury.

No. 510.   CONSTANTINOPLE, *October 19, 1895, 10.45 a.m.*
Telegraphic.   *(Received October 19.)*
HER Majesty's Consul at Trebizond telegraphs that only his Turkish scribe
has been arrested, as he had kept his two other Armenian employés in the
Consulate. I have instructed Mr. Marinitch to make representations to the Grand
Vizier on this arrest of a servant of Her Majesty's Consulate, and to request his
Highness to give orders that such things should not occur again.
F. O. 424/184, p. 68, No, 122

No. 276

Sir P. Currie to the Marquess of Salisbury.

No. 511.   CONSTANTINOPLE, *October 19, 1895, 11.20 a.m.*
Telegraphic.   *(Received October 19.)*
THE messenger who left on Thursday is taking the text of the scheme of
reforms requested in your Lordship's telegram No. 184.
F. O. 424/184, p. 69, No. 123

No. 277

Sir. P. Currie to the Marquess of Salisbury.

No. 512.   CONSTANTINOPLE, *October 19, 1895, 11.30 a.m.*
Telegraphic.   *(Received October 19.)*
I HAVE just received a visit from the Secretary of the Armenian Patriarch,
who came to express his Beatitude's gratification at the acceptance of the reforms,
and his sincere thanks for all that has been done by Her Majesty's Embassy on
behalf of the Armenians. The Patriarch promises to do his utmost to induce his
people to co-operate heartily with a view to securing the successful working of the
scheme, and to abstain in the future from revolutionary agitation. As long as the
reforms were still under discussion, he felt it his duty to press for additional
guarantees, but he trusts that what has been obtained will be sufficient to secure the
life and property of the Armenians.
F. O. 424/184, p. 69, No. 124

No. 278

Sir P. Currie to the Marquess of Salisbury.

No. 513.   CONSTANTINOPLE, *October 19, 1895, 11.40 a.m.*
Telegraphic.   *(Received October 19.)*

YOUR Lordship's telegram No. 165 of the 30th ultimo.

Subject to your Lordship's approval, I propose to leave for England on the 24th instant for a stay of about two weeks, now that the Sultan has accepted the reforms.

F. O. 424/184, p. 69, No. 125

No. 279

Sir P. Currie to the Marquess of Salisbury.

No. 514.   CONSTANTINOPLE, *October 20, 1895, 3.5 p.m.*
Telegraphic.   *(Received October 20.)*

THE day before yesterday, after the Selamlik, the Sultan gave an audience to M. de Nélidoff. His Majesty seemed to be in very bad spirits. He expressed his firm determination to put into execution what he had promised, but he was afraid that the other classes of his subjects might cause him grave difficulties by their demands. He used rather bitter language about pressure which the Powers had brought to bear on him in order to make him execute laws which were already a part of Turkish legislation, and also complained of the Armenian Patriarch. He said he had proofs that his Beatitude was the prime mover of the reform agitation, and he had shown himself unworthy of his position.

The Russian Ambassador combated this view of the Patriarch's conduct.

F. O. 424/184, p. 69, No. 126

No. 280

Sir P. Currie to the Marquess of Salisbury.

No. 515.   CONSTANTINOPLE, *October 20, 1895, 7.50 p.m.*
Telegraphic.   *(Received October 20.)*

WITH reference to my telegram No. 507, I have the honour to inform your Lordship that the Sublime Porte has addressed me an official note inclosing a letter from the Grand Vizier to the Shakir Pasha. This document communicates the reforms agreed upon between the three Embassies and the Minister for Foreign

Affairs, instructs him to superintend their execution, and states that they have also been communicated to the six vilayets.

A comparison of the French and Turkish texts is now being made.

To-morrow I shall meet the Russian and French Ambassadors in order to settle the terms of our reply. We intend to address a note to the Porte in which we shall reserve our right to object to the appointment of unfit persons as Valis, and we shall take note of any other points which may seem to require it.

F. O. 424/184, p. 70, No. 127

No. 281

Sir P. Currie to the Marquess of Salisbury.

No. 516.   Constantinople, *October 21, 1895, 10 a.m.*
Telegraphic.   *(Received October 21.)*

YESTERDAY my Austrian colleague gave me to understand that the Triple Alliance Powers would probably demand from the Porte an official communication of the Armenian reforms, and also claim the right of communicating with the Commission of Control through their Dragomans on the same footing as the other three Embassies.

He did not think that Austria, for her part, would make much use of the right, but she had a just claim to most-favoured-nation treatment.

I said that I did not think her right could be contested.

Baron Calice has throughout given a friendly support to the reform negotiations.

F. O. 424/184, p. 103, No. 141

No. 282

Sir P. Currie to the Marquess of Salisbury.

No. 517.   Constantinople, *October 21, 1895, 5.30 p.m.*
Telegraphic.   *(Received October 21.)*

I HAD an interview to-day with the Minister for Foreign Affairs and the Grand Vizier. The officials they think of for the Commission of Control are good. The present governor of Smyrna, Hassan Fehmi, will very likely be President; he went some time ago on a mission to London. I was satisfied with their language as to the execution of the reforms.

F. O. 424/184, p. 104, No. 142

No. 283

Sir P. Currie to the Marquess of Salisbury.

No. 518. Confidential.   CONSTANTINOPLE, *October 21, 1895, 7.25 p.m.*
Telegraphic.   *(Received October 21.)*

THE Grand Vizier admitted the gravity of the alleged discontent existing among Mussulmans, on my asking him about it to-day. He had represented the matter, but with little effect, as it seemed, to his Imperial Majesty. Great numbers of arrests are said to have been effected.

But I hear that the Moslem population have received the reforms, of which only parts have been published, favourably. They ask why all parts of the country should not enjoy them equally.

F. O. 424/184, p. 104, No. 143

No. 284

Sir P. Currie to the Marquess of Salisbury.

No. 519.   CONSTANTINOPLE, *October 21, 1895, 7.40 p.m.*
Telegraphic.   *(Received October 21.)*

I HAVE received a telegram from Mr. Russell, at the Dardanelles, on the subject of my telegram to your Lordship No. 495.

He says it is uncertain whether floating mines have been laid. They have nearly completed a masked battery of considerable strength on the hill not far from the Mejidieh fort, and have already got twelve cannon and mortar in position.

On the Asiatic side, at the Hamidie and Sultanie forts, and at the Namazie fort on this side, fresh torpedoes have been laid. Like the old ones, they are in iron cases.

The troops sent from Constantinople were artillery.

F. O. 424/184, p. 104, No. 144

No. 285

The Marquess of Salisbury to Sir P. Currie.

No. 187.
Telegraphic.   FOREIGN OFFICE, *October 21, 1895, 11 p.m.*

I HAVE received your telegram No. 516 of the 21st instant stating that according to a communication made to you by your Austrian colleague the Governments of Austria, Germany, and Italy will probably claim the right of communicating with the Commission of Control in connection with the Armenian Reforms Act on the same footing as Great Britain, France, and Russia.

I approve your Excellency's reply on the subject to Baron Calice. If the claim is put forward by the three Powers, Her Majesty's Government will be ready to give it their support.

F. O. 424/184, p. 104, No. 145

No. 286

Sir P. Currie to the Marquess of Salisbury.

No. 699.   CONSTANTINOPLE, *October 21, 1895.*

My Lord,   *(Received October 29.)*

I HAVE the honour to forward to your Lordship herewith copy of a despatch which I have received from the Acting Consul at Angora, reporting the murder of the Assistant Procureur-Général of Choroum by Armenian highwaymen.

I have, &c.

(Signed) PHILIP CURRIE.

F. O. 424/184, p. 121, No. 192

Inclosure in No. 286

Acting Consul Fontana to Sir P. Currie.

Sir,   ANGORA, *October 12, 1895.*

I HAVE the honour to report, for the information of your Excellency, that a short time ago the Assistant Procureur-Général of Choroum, in the Sandjak of Yuzgat, whilst proceeding to Sivas with his family, and accompanied by the director of a branch office of the Régie, was waylaid and murdered by a band of Armenians armed with rifles. The Régie official was wounded in the knee, but received no other injury, and was allowed to continue his journey.

The Sivas authorities, upon hearing of the outrage, lost no time in dispatching a force of nine zaptiehs, under the command of a Mulazim, in pursuit of the highwaymen, with orders to bring them in dead or alive. The band was overtaken, and a sharp fight ensued, in which the Mulazim and seven of his men were killed, the other two being severely wounded.

Nothing definite is known here as to the motive for the attack upon the Assistant Proctor; he is believed, however, to have been instrumental in the condemnation, at various times, of a large number of Armenians.

I have, &c.

(Signed) RAPHAEL A. FONTANA.

F. O. 424/184, p. 121, No. 192/1

No. 287

Sir P. Currie to the Marquess of Salisbury.

No. 520.   CONSTANTINOPLE, *October 22, 1895, 7.20 p.m.*
Telegraphic.   *(Received October 22.)*
WE have information that at Trebizond and Akhissar the Turks were encouraged by the military and police to massacre the Armenians, on the ground that the latter intended to attack the Mussulmans, and it is believed by many that the orders to do so were sent from the Palace.

To-day the Grand Vizier informed Mr. Marinitch that the Armenians at Andrin and Zeitoun, in the Vilayet of Aleppos, had attacked the Turks; that some of them were mounted and carried army rifles. He promised to communicate further details to-morrow.

The Armenians of Zeitoun and the neighbouring villages, like the Sasunlis, are mountaineers, and more formidable than most of their race, and I fear that the statements telegraphed to the Grand Vizier may be preliminary to a massacre.

Could the Admiral be authorized to send some ships to Alexandretta or one of the neighbouring ports in the event of matters getting worse?

I intend to warn the Grand Vizier to-morrow of the serious consequences of allowing further slaughter, but I think it would be advisable that the Powers should act in concert to prevent such a calamity.

F. O. 424/184, p. 105, No. 146

No. 288

Colonial Office to Foreign Office.

DOWNING STREET, *October 22, 1895.*
Sir,   *(Received October 23.)*
I AM directed by the Secretary of State for the Colonies to transmit to you, for the information of the Marquess of Salisbury, with reference to the letter from your Department of the 20th ultimo, a copy of a despatch from the Acting High Commissioner of Cyprus on the subject of the alleged export of arms and ammunition from Cyprus for Armenia.

I am, &c.

(Signed) R. H. MEADE.

F. O. 424/184, p. 105, No. 148

Inclosure 1 in No. 288

Administrator Young to Mr. Chamberlain.

Confidential.   GOVERNMENT COTTAGE, MOUNT TROODOS, CYPRUS.
Sir,   *(Received October 2, 1895.)*

I HAVE the honour to acknowledge the receipt of your Confidential despatch of the 31st July last transmitting a despatch received by the Marquess of Salisbury from Her Majesty's Ambassador at Constantinople, regarding the alleged importation into Armenia of arms and ammunition from Cyprus, and requesting me to furnish you with any observations I have to offer with respect to the statements made in the Report of the United States' Consular Agent at Aleppo.

2. I have the honour to inform you that I have made careful inquiry into these statements, and, as regards the statement that about 300 Armenian workmen had arrived in Cyprus in search of work, and had since returned to their homes, the Report of the United States' Consular Agent does not say when they came to Cyprus, but I cannot find that any number of Armenian workmen have, within the past year, visited the island, and I cannot but believe that the information given to the United States' Consular Agent was incorrect.

3. It appears that about a year ago Armenians commenced to arrive in small parties by the Messageries steamer from Marseilles; some twenty-seven arrived in this way; they were well dressed, spoke English, and stated that they came from America.

4. During the winter a party of eighteen arrived from Beyrout by an Austrian Lloyd steamer, and others have from time to time been conveyed here by the same line; also, a number have arrived by the Bells steamers direct from Alexandria.

5. The exact number cannot be ascertained, as these Companies, and also the Knott's Princes Line, do not enter in their passenger lists the different nationalities; it is, however, calculated that probably from 100 to 150 have arrived within the past year, and it appears that most of these have now left the island.

6. The ostensible purpose given by these Armenians for visiting Cyprus is to ascertain, if possible, news of their relations and friends, as they are prohibited from landing in Asia Minor.

7. Mr. Ansell, the Acting Collector of Customs at Larnaca, the port where these Armenians have landed, gives reasons for considering that Cyprus has simply been used as a basis for obtaining information and distributing relief, and I attach an extract from his Report of the 22nd September, 1895, referring to this subject.

8. Sir Walter Sendall, by his Confidential despatch of the 4th June last, stated that it would be easy, without running the risk and trouble of landing the reshipment, for Cyprus boats to take on board arms and ammunition from vessels at sea, and I think it may be probable that Cyprus is made use of by the Armenians as a basis for this purpose, and also for the purposes mentioned in the

previous paragraph, but I do not think that arms are actually smuggled into Cyprus for the purpose of being conveyed to the opposite coast.

9. Early in December last eight Armenians left Papho in a lighter avowedly bound for the port of Karovostassi, but is stated that they were transhipped in the neighbourhood of that port into a smaller lighter and taken to the Karamanian coast; the vessel in which they sailed to Karamania was said to have been a small Cypriot lighter; it is not known whether she was loaded with arms; but if so, the arms must have been transferred to her from some vessel when out at sea.

10. Sir Walter Sendall, by his Confidential despatch of the 4th June last, informed you that a telegram had been received from Her Majesty's Ambassador at Constantinople stating that four boats, with fire-arms from Cyprus, had attempted to land on the coast between Alexandretta and Latakia, one of which, containing 400 rifles, had been seized, the others escaping; also that the Consul at Aleppo had telegraphed on the 2nd June last, that arms and ammunition had been landed from a sailing-vessel from Cyprus.

11. On further inquiry, it was, however, found that no actual seizure had taken place and that the information was premature.

12. Likewise, the statement made by the United States' Consular Agent to the effect that twenty Armenians, some from the United States and some from England, has met at Cyprus, and had sailed from there in a small boat which they had loaded with arms, may possibly be based upon exaggerated information of the particulars given in paragraph 9 of this despatch.

(Signed) ARTHUR YOUNG.

F. O. 424/184, pp. 106-107, No. 148/1

Inclosure 2 in No. 288

*Extract from a Report of the Acting Collector of Customs, Larnaca,
to the Chief Collector, Nicosia.*

Confidential.   CUSTOM-HOUSE, LARNACA, *September 25, 1895.*

MENTIONED in my last Report that I doubted whether any smuggling of arms or ammunition had taken place. My impression is that Cyprus has simply been used as the means of obtaining information and distributing relief. My reasons for so thinking are as follows:-

A Mr. Houssepain, watchmaker, who used rarely to be seen away from his shop, has, during the past year, and still does, pay frequent visits to the Pier, Customs, Post Office, and the Bank, generally in company with other Armenians. I am informed privately from the Bank that he has presented Bank of England notes of 100*l.* each, and that he receives drafts from Constantinople, &c., all of which are exchanged for gold.

A certain O'Lannes, who bought his discharge from the Police, has for months past made several voyages by steamers trading between Cyprus, the Syrian, and Caramanian coasts; his baggage is always well rummaged, and we have seen nothing suspicious about it. When not travelling, he never fails to be about when steamers are in, and frequently goes on board. The last occasion was when the "Dunkeld" was in, he went off immediately. Shortly afterwards some Armenians brought his baggage to the Customs, but O'Lannes returned from the steamer, and his baggage was taken back into the town.

I therefore assume that the money can only be used among the Armenians in Cyprus, or more likely in Turkey, through the medium of O'Lannes when travelling.

F. O. 424/184, p. 107, No. 148/2

No. 289

Sir E. Monson to the Marquess of Salisbury.

No. 304.   VIENNA, *October 22, 1895.*
My Lord,   *(Received October 25.)*

I CALLED this morning on Baron Pasetti, who, in the absence of Count Goluchowski at Budapest, has been carrying on the business at the Ministry of Foreign Affairs, and communicated to him the substance of your Lordship's telegrams Nos. 63 and 64 of yesterday's date.

Baron Pasetti said that Baron Calice had acted on his own initiative in his intimation to Sir P. Currie that the Powers composing the Triple Alliance would probably claim the right of having the reforms officially made known to them and of communicating with the Commission of Control, through the Dragomans of their Embassies, on the same footing as Great Britain, France, and Russia. Baron Calice had not reported his having done this as yet, but would undoubtedly do so by next messenger. In the absence of Count Goluchowski, Baron Pasetti said that he must limit himself to giving his own personal opinion that it would be desirable that all Great Powers should be on the same footing in regard to the right of communicating with the Commission of Control.

I answered that I expected that there would be a general agreement on this head; and asked the Baron whether there had been any discussion on this subject between the Cabinets of Vienna, Berlin, and Rome.

His Excellency replied in the negative, and concluded the conversation by expressing his admiration of the way in which British diplomacy had carried the day, in the face of overt and covert obstacles.

My interview with Baron Pasetti was necessarily brief, as I interrupted him in the task of handing over his charge to Count Welsersheimb, his successor at the Ministry of Foreign Affairs.

I shall send a copy of this despatch by messenger to-morrow to Constantinople.

I have, &c.

(Signed) EDMUND MONSON.

F. O. 424/184, p. 113, No. 166

No. 290

Sir P. Currie to the Marquess of Salisbury.

No. 702.   THERAPIA, *October 22, 1895.*
My Lord,   *(Received October 29.)*

I HAVE the honour to transmit to your Lordship herewith copy of a Report which I have received from the Rev. R. Chambers, a British clergyman attached to the American Mission, giving the details of a massacre which took place at Akhissar.

I have called the serious attention of the Grand Vizier to the state of affairs in the Ismidt Sandjak, and have urged the removal of the Military Commandant, who is said to be one of the chief causes of danger there.

I have, &c.

(Signed) PHILIP CURRIE.

F. O. 424/184, p. 126, No. 195

Inclosure in No. 290

The Rev. R. Chambers to Sir P. Currie.

Your Excellency,   BAGHCHEJIK (ISMIDT), *October 16, 1895.*

HEARING that some of our Protestant people were wounded in the affray at Akhissar, and that all were in great terror, I went to that village on Sunday, the 13th instant. I expected to meet our Mutessarif there, but he had departed before my arrival.

The Military Pasha was very angry when he found that I had gone. He and the Mutessarif called the Protestant Vakeel on Monday evening, and treated him very rudely, rating him for not having warned them of my intention to go. Their treatment of the Vakeel has produced a very bad impression in the minds of the Christians of Nicomedia (Ismidt).

Immediately on my return I called on the Mutessarif, who received me with great honour, and talked with the utmost freedom of the whole situation.

As I entered the village of Akhissar on Sunday a fearful stench greeted me. Several bodies that had that morning been recovered from a well were being buried. I visited four wells: from one of them—ten minutes' walk from the scene of the slaughter—fourteen bodies had been recovered; from another, two; from another, five. One had not yet been opened; there were blood-marks on the stones covering it. In all, twenty-three bodies have been recovered for burial. Of these, nine were the bodies of Akhissar merchants; six of traders from Kunjilar; six from Koordbeleng; and two from Arslanbeg. At least six others are known to have been killed. There are thirty-three wounded, while about fifty persons, most of whom were expected to be present in Akhissar on that day, have not been heard from.

The murders were committed in the most inhuman manner: cudgels, knives, axes, swords and fire-arms were used. Young boys helped in the slaying. Ropes were tied to the feet of the dead, and the bodies were dragged through the streets (leaving clots of blood on the stones over which they were dragged), and thrown into the wells. One old man of 75 years was tumbled in without being killed, and was left to die among the corpses of his friends.

The stones about the mouths of the wells were carefully washed or covered over with earth and manure.

There were about 200 Armenian shops, 63 of which were permanently occupied by merchants of the place, while the rest were occupied on market days by the traders from the villages. But one shop, where ketchag (thick native felt) was kept for sale, escaped. Of the rest, every window was smashed, and not so much as a pin or needle left. I was amazed to see what a clean sweep was made. The merchants' money, watches, and other valuables were first secured, then the men killed, and their acount books, notes of hand, and valuable papers torn to shreds. Sometimes the murderers would scatter a handful of shredded accounts upon the body of the merchant, saying, "Aha, receive what I owe you." The loss in goods must be not less that 15,000 liras, and, perhaps, much over that sum.

The killers were the survivors and sons of immigrants who came from Bosnia, Bulgaria, and Roumelia at the close of the late war. They lived in the village of Akhissar and in the vicinity, and were known as friends and neighbours.

There were sixteen armed officials present—Mudir, Kol-Aghasi, zaptiehs, and soldiers—but their presence was evidently an encouragement to the killers. They could have stopped the slaughter at its inception or at any time during its course, as the Mutessarif and Attorney-General confessed to me. Instead of attempting to do so they acted as follows: the Kol-Aghassi observed the killing for forty minutes, and then taking with him three zaptiehs rode to Gueve, 5 miles away, to give word to the Kaïmakam, who, four hours after the slaughter commenced arrived on the scene. This shows fiendish deliberation of movement. Ibrahim on-Bashi stood watching, and when piteously appealed to by name by perishing men paid no attention. Ismidli Mehemet, a zaptieh, took money from two men on the promise to save them, and then killed one of them. This zaptieh was arrested by the authorities, but soon released. Men in hiding and women in the houses heard the Mudir shouting encouragement to the killers. Hadji Bosh Chaoush, member of the Belidieh Court, mounted on a horse and brandishing an axe, encouraged the killers. Deli Hafans visited the Government house just before the affair began, and on his return began the work. Viazim Effendi (Imam) was supposed to be giving signs, directing the killing or sparing of victims. Warnings were given to some in outside places that the "infidels" religion was to be destroyed that day. On the preceding Tuesday a prominent Armenian told the Kaïmakam that the Mudir (Hussein) and the Kol-Aghassi (Racim) were dangerous men, and entreated that ten or fifteen soldiers be stationed in Akhissar to protect the people. This was not done. The killing of so many, the disposing of the bodies, the careful covering up of the wells, the washing of blood-stains, the complete disappearance of such a quantity of goods, and the destruction of notes of hand and account books, all show a perfection of plan and a deliberation of action impossible to an unprepared and suddenly aroused mob.

There has never been the slightest trace of Hunchagism in Akhissar, the Armenians had no arms and made no resistance, nor, as the Attorney-General confessed to me, did they do anything to bring on the affray (though the Mutessarif asserts that two young Armenians early in the day, having pistols, fired them off seven times and thus frightened the Mohammedans, who resorted to arms to save themselves). An Armenian was arrested as the cause of the affair, but was soon released. The Mudir was arrested, examined, and released, but on Monday last he was again arrested and placed on the train under guard. The soldiers left the train at Adabazar, and the Mudir was next day reported as at large at Sabanja. About sixty have been arrested.

The whole Armenian population of this province is in a state of intense anxiety. I spent Monday afternoon and night at Adabazar. Monday was market day, but the Armenians had opened very few of their shops. An attack was expected, as many threats had been made. Threats and alarming rumours have been heard in Ismidt, and the people are excited and full of fear.

If a dozen of the Akhissar killers could be court-martialled and promptly shot confidence would be restored.

Baghchejik is quiet and safe. We have no fear here if only left alone by the Government. Yesterday a spy, professing to be survivor of Sasun and Constantinople, was caught and returned to the Governor. If soldiers are sent here, and an attempt made to deprive the people of the few arms they have in their houses, serious trouble will be sure to follow.

I have, &c.

(Signed) R. Chambers.

F. O. 424/184, pp. 126-128, No. 195/1

No. 291

Sir P. Currie to the Marquess of Salisbury.

No. 703.   THERAPIA, *October 22, 1895.*
My Lord,   *(Received October 29.)*
        IN my despatch No. 694 of the 17th instant I had the honour to forward to
your Lordship the French text of the scheme of reforms as agreed upon between the
three Ambassadors and the Minister for Foreign Affairs. The Sublime Porte
subsequently prepared first a Turkish and then a second French text. The
differences between this document and the original (which are given in the inclosed
Memorandum) are mostly unimportant, but two deserve notice.
        In treating of the Permanent Commission of Control, Article 32, the Turkish
text inserts the words, "with a Mahommedan President," but this phrase is not
found in either of the French versions. The Ambassadors have raised no objection
to the appointment of a Mussulman President, and the Grand Vizier has informed
us of his intention to propose Hassan Fehmi Pasha, Governor of Smyrna, for the
post.
        Secondly, in the French text of the Porte the last of the "paragraphes figurant
dans le Décret" runs as follows:-
        "Des mesures conformes aux principes ci-dessus seront appliquées dans les
cazas tels que Zéitoun et Hadjin."
        When the issue of the Imperial Iradé was communicated to the Embassies
they were verbally informed that the Sultan desired the *insertion* of the words, "tels
que Zéitoun et Hadjin," but it was understood that the words, "où les non-
Musulmans forment une partie notable de la population," would remain. An effort
was made to induce Saïd Pasha to consent to their reinsertion, but his Excellency,
who declared that they had dropped out by a mistake, begged that the text adopted
by the Porte might be accepted, on the ground that discussion of the wording, if
once commenced, might last an indefinite period and delay the settlement of the
question. The three Embassies therefore agreed to take note in their reply to the
Sublime Porte of the difference of reading, and to reaffirm the principle that the
reform scheme is to be adopted in localities where a considerable proportion of the
inhabitants are Christians.
        I would suggest that this French version of the Porte, in conjunction with the
note of the three Embassies, should be regarded as the authoritative text of the
reform scheme.
                                I have, &c.
                                                (Signed) PHILIP CURRIE.

F. O. 424/184, p. 128, No. 196

Inclosure in No. 291

Differences between French texts of Scheme of Reforms as prepared by the three Embassies and accepted by the Porte.

Text of three Embassies.	*Text of Porte.*
CHAPITRE III, Art. 5: ". . . de l'Empire . . ."	Omit these words.

Chapitre VI, Art. 19.

Both texts omit the reference, but it appears from the Turkish text, after the words, "conformément au réglement des," should be inserted, "prescription du II Chapitre de la Loi sur la Formentation des Tribunaux Civils."

Chapitre XV, Art. 31.	After the words, "en cas de difficulté ceux-ci pourront recourir aux Tribunaux." Add— "Dans le cas où personne ne se présenterait pour l'affermage des dîmes de certains villages, ou bien si le prix offert était inférieur à la valeur réelle des dîmes à adjuger, ces dîmes seront administrées en régie conformément au Règlement sur la matière."

Dispositions qui doivent figurer dans le Décret de Promulgation.

IV. Des mesures conformes aux principes ci-dessus seront appliquées dans tous les cazas où les non-Musulmans forment une partie notable de la population.	IV. Des mesures conformes aux principes ci-dessus seront appliquées dans les cazas tels que Zéitoun et Hadjin.

F. O. 424/184, p. 129, No. 196/1

No. 292

Sir P. Currie to the Marquess of Salisbury.

No. 704.
My Lord,

THERAPIA, *October 22, 1895.*
(Received October 29.)

WITH reference to my despatch No. 694 of the 17th instant, forwarding the scheme of reforms as agreed upon by the Ambassadors of the three Powers with

Saïd Pasha, and also to my last preceding despatch, I have now the honour to inclose a copy of a *note verbale* from the Porte officially communicating the text of a Vizirial letter which has been addressed to Shakir Pasha, inclosing the scheme, and instructing him to superintend its execution. The letter adds that the reforms have at the same time been communicated to the Governors of Erzeroum, Van, Bitlis, Sivas, Kharput, and Diarbekir, and that measurers in conformity with the principles laid down will be applied to other cazas, such as Zeitoun and Hadjin. We have, in reply, sent a collective note, of which a copy is inclosed, taking act of the arrangements made, and reserving to ourselves the right of calling the attention of the Sublime Porte to any unfit persons who may be designated for posts in the provincial Administration. We have also taken act of the intention of the Porte to extend the reforms to all cazas in Asia Minor where the Christians may be in a majority.

Saïd Pasha will formally acknowledge the receipt of this note.

I have, &c.

(Signed) PHILIP CURRIE.

F. O. 424/184, p. 129, No. 197

Inclosure 1 in No. 292

Note Verbale.

SA Majesté Impériale le Sultan ayant bien voulu, dans sa haute sollicitude pour le bien-être de ses sujets sans distinction de race ni de religion, sanctionner spontanément le plan des réformes à introduire dans l'administration des vilayets d'Erzeroum, Sivas, Van, Diarbékir, Bitlis, et Mamouret-el-Aziz, le Ministre des Affaires Étrangères a l'honneur d'en transmettre ci-jointe une copie à son Excellence M. l'Ambassadeur de Sa Majesté Britannique, avec le texte du Décret y relatif.

Le 20 October, 1895.

F. O. 424/184, p. 130, No. 197/1

Inclosure 2 in No. 292

Vizirial Order addressed to the Valis of Erzeroum, Van, Bitlis, Diarbekir, Mamouret-el-Aziz, and Sirvas, and to the Inspector, his Excellency Shakir Pasha.

Translation.

IN accordance with the glorious provisions of the Hatti-Humayoun of Gulkhané, promulgated on the 26th of Shaaban, 1255, by His late Imperial Majesty Abdu-el-Mejid Khan, the illustrious father of the Sovereign, as well as the terms of the Firman of Reforms issued in the beginning of Jemazirel-Akhiri, 1272, and in pursuance of the laws actually laid down and in force, as all men know, the selection and appointment of the officials and employés of the Imperial Government, is effected by virtue of an Imperial Iradé, and in due compliance with the special Regulations on the point, and all classes of Ottoman subjects to whatsoever nationality they may belong, are to be admitted to the service of the State. Accordingly it has been decided that these shall be employed according to their merits and capacity, in accordance with Regulations which shall be observed in respect of all classes alike, and also that all Ottoman subjects who comply in point of age and attainments with the existing Regulations of the State schools shall be received into such schools without any distinction being made.

Moreover, just as from time to time a number of measures and Regulations have been introduced of a nature to bring about the necessary reforms in proportion as these are requisite and possible in every part of the Ottoman dominions, and to improve the well-being of the subjects, and increase the prosperity of the country so since the auspicious accession of His Imperial Majesty, his thoughts have been directed towards the complete realization of these benevolent designs.

It is, therefore, intended by the Imperial Government to carry out gradually useful reforms throughout His Majesty's dominions, corresponding with local requirements and the nature of the inhabitants, and accordingly, it has been decided to effect reforms in the Asiatic vilayets of Erzeroum, Van, Bitlis, Diarbekir, Mamouret-el-Aziz, and Sivas, to comprise the application of the Laws and Regulations contained in the Destour, as well as the provisions of the aforesaid Hatti-Humayoun of Gulkhané, and the Firman of Reforms.

This decision being submitted by a special Council of Ministers to the Sultan, has been sanctioned by His Majesty in an Imperial Iradé, and certified copies obtained from the Imperial Divan of the schedule containing the points of reform decided upon having been transmitted to each of the six vilayets mentioned. A copy is inclosed to your Excellency herewith.

Besides this, four other Articles included in the decision and sanctioned by the Imperial Iradé are subjoined as follows:—

1. An official in every respect worthy of regard shall be appointed by the Imperial Government, with the title of General Inspector, to attend to the carrying out of the reforms and superintend their application, and shall proceed to his post. In the event of the absence of the Inspector, or of any impediment, another high Mussulman official will be temporarily appointed by His Majesty to replace him. The inspector will be accompanied during the execution of his duties by a non-Mussulman Assistant.

2. As the Armenians accused or convicted of being implicated in political events were granted an Imperial pardon on the 11th (23rd) July, 1895, this measure will be applied to all Armenians who shall not be proved to be directly

concerned in any offence at common law, and who having been imprisoned before that date still remain in confinement.

3. Armenians exiled from the country, or who have fled for refuge to foreign countries shall, upon proving their Ottoman nationality, and their good behaviour, be allowed to return freely to the Ottoman dominions.

4. In cazas, such as Zeitoun and Khachin, measures similar to the aforesaid rules shall be applied. It is unnecessary to explain or repeat that the most ardent desire of His Imperial Majesty the Sultan, the bounteous benefactor, is the increase of the prosperity of the Ottoman dominions, and, in general, of all his subjects, and the insuring of their comfort and happiness, and these Articles and Enactments will still further assure the realization of this aim.

His Excellency Shakir Pasha, one of His Majesty's Aides-de-camp, who has been appointed to the important post of General Inspector, has been named in accordance with an Imperial Order to the six vilayets aforesaid, and the appointment of the Assistant who is to accompany him, as well as the Commission of Inspection to be named in accordance with the schedule already mentioned, are in course of progress, and I have to desire you to proceed to carry out the matters decided upon with extraordinary zeal, attention, and care in your district, and to report in due course upon the results thus attained.

30 Rebi-ul-Akhir, 1313 (October 8 (20), 1895)
F. O. 424/184, pp. 130-131, No. 197/2

Inclosure 3 in No. 292

Collective Note addressed by the Ambassadors of Great Britain, France, and Russia to Saïd Pasha.

LES Soussignés, Ambassadeurs de Russie, de France, et de Grande-Bretagne ont reçu la note verbale que la Sublime Porte leur a adressée le 20 de ce mois. et ont l'honneur d'en accuser réception à son Excellence M. le Ministre des Affaires Étrangères.

Ils ont pris connaissance du texte de Décret relatif aux réformes dont Sa Majesté Impériale le Sultan vient de décider l'application ainsi que du plan qui en contient l'exposé, et c'est avec satisfaction qu'ils constatent que le Gouvernement Impérial a résolu de mettre en pratique les Règles solennellement formulées dans les Hatts précédents des Souverains Ottomans et les mesures découlant des principes exposés par la Sublime Porte dans ses communications des 2 Juin, 17 Juin, 5 Août, 17 Août, et 5 Octobre de la présente année.

En prenant acte de ces dispositions et de l'intention de la Sublime Porte de les étendre outre les vilayets mentionnés dans le Décret à tous les cazas d'Anatolie où les Arméniens forment une partie notable de la population, les Ambassadeurs de France, de Grande-Bretagne, et de Russie ne doutent pas que les fonctionnaires chargés d'exécuter et d'appliquer les réformes n'assurent par leur intelligence, leur zéle, et leur désintéressement, à tous les sujets Ottomans sans distinction les bienfaits d'une Administration soucieuse du bien-être général et de la prospérité de l'Empire.

Les garanties dont le Gouvernement Impérial déclare dans ses communications susmentionnées vouloir entourer le choix et la nomination des fonctionnaires de tous ordres, témoignent de l'importance que la Sublime Porte attache à ce que ses Agents dans les provinces remplissent leur mission à la satisfaction de toutes les communautés et à ce que les Valis, notamment, donnent à l'administration de chaque vilayet une impulsion conforme aux vues que vient d'affirmer à nouveau Sa Majesté Impériale.

C'est dans cette confiance que les Ambassadeurs de France, de Grande-Bretagne, et de Russie croient pouvoir le mieux servir les intentions manifestées par la Sublime Porte en se réservant de lui signaler lors de leur désignation les personnes dont les antécédents et le caractère ne sembleraient pas répondre aux conditions indiquées comme nécessaires par le Gouvernement Ottoman lui-même.

C'est aussi, dans cette confiance qu'ils seront heureux de prêter, à l'occasion, tout leur concours au Gouvernement de Sa Majesté Impériale pour la réalisation des réformes qu'elle vient de décréter.

Les Soussignés prient son Excellence M. le Ministre des Affaires Étrangères de vouloir bien accuser réception de la présente communication et saisissent, &c.

(Signé) NÉLIDOW.

P. CAMBON.

PHILIP CURRIE.

Le 24 Octobre, 1895.
F.O. 424/184, pp. 135-136, No. 197/4

No. 293

Sir P. Currie to the Marquess of Salisbury.

No. 706. THERAPIA, *October 22, 1895.*
My Lord, *(Received October 29.)*
IN consequence of the action of the Armenian Revolutionary Committees in sustaining the agitation amoung their countrymen in this city by means of the compulsory closing of their shops, and consequent suspension of all tráde and commerce, the Ambassadors agreed to make a joint communication to the Patriarch on this state of affairs through the Dragomans of the Austrian, Russian, and British Embassies.

I instructed Mr. Marinitch to explain at the same time to his Beatitude that our main object in taking the present step was to stengthen his hands in the difficult circumstances in which he was placed. His Beatitude replied that he would continue as in the past to advise the prominent members of the Armenian community to do their utmost to prevent acts of violence, though it was impossible for him to influence directly the instigators of the proceedings of which we complained, as they were unknown to him.

Mgr. Ismirlian expressed great satisfaction at learning that the Iradé authorizing the reform scheme had been issued, and his earnest hope that they would be faithfully executed.

The Patriarch said that the only object of the moderate and sensible portion of the Armenians was that the safety of their lives and property should be secured by good administration, and if the reforms would produce this result, he could declare, in the name of his nation, that all Armenians would be satisfied with them, and would show their gratitude for doing their utmost to bring about a return to a normal condition of affairs.

His Beatitude requested the Dragomans to convey to the Ambassadors the expression of his warmest acknowledgements for the service they had rendered to the Armenian people, and he expressed the earnest hope that the Great Powers would continue to show the same sympathy and interest towards the Armenians, who would on their part do their best to prove that they were not undeserving of the benefits conferred upon them.

I have, &c.

(Signed) PHILIP CURRIE.

F. O. 424/184, p. 136, No. 198

Inclosure in No. 293

Joint Communication to the Armenian Patriarch.

EN réponse aux instances du Patriarche les Ambassadeurs s'inspirant de sentiments d'humanité et désireux de contribuer au rétablissement de la paix publique, sont intervenus pour faire évacuer les églises. Cette intervention a en pour effet de rétablir la tranquillité dans les esprits. Mais il résulte de nouvelles informations que l'effervescence renaîtrait et setait entretenue par des agitateurs qui déterminent à l'aide de leurs menaces la fermeture des magasins, l'interruption des relations commerciales et qui fomentent de nouvelles manifestations.

Les Ambassadeurs signalent ces manœuvres à sa Béatitude et la prient d'user de toute son influence pour combattre une agitation qui peut avoir des conséquences funestes et compromettre de succès de l'intervention des Puissances.

F. O. 424/184, p. 137, No. 198/1

No. 294

Sir P. Currie to the Marquess of Salisbury.

No. 521.   CONSTANTINOPLE, *October 23, 1895, 2.30 p.m.*
Telegraphic.   *(Received October 23.)*
MR. HAMPSON telegraphs from Mush to-day that he considers the success of the relief work is now secure, and that the essential question now remaining is the protection of Armenians against the Kurds.
F. O. 424/184, p. 107, No. 149

No. 295

Sir P. Currie to the Marquess of Salisbury.

No. 523.   CONSTANTINOPLE, *October 23, 1895, 5 40 p.m.*
Telegraphic.   *(Received October 23.)*
THREATENING letters have been addressed by Turks to the Minister of Marine, who is a tool of the Sultan. Guards have been placed round his house.

According to circumstantial reports which reach me from several sources, Mussulmans who have taken part in the agitation against the present system have been arrested and confined in the prisons at Yildiz, and it is positively asserted that many of them have been put to death secretly.
F. O. 424/184, p. 108, No. 151

No. 296

Sir P. Currie to the Marquess of Salisbury.

No. 524.   CONSTANTINOPLE, *October 23, 1895, 5.30 p.m.*
Telegraphic.   *(Received October 23.)*
I MADE a representation to the Grand Vizier as to the situation at Rodosto, the Vice-Consul having reported that the Christians were in danger owing to the fanatical attitude of the Turks. His Highness has telegraphed to the Vali of Adrianople to take precautionary measures.
F. O. 424/184, p. 108, No. 152

No. 297

Sir P. Currie to the Marquess of Salisbury.

No. 525.   CONSTANTINOPLE, *October 23, 1895, 5.50 p.m.*
Telegraphic.   *(Received October 23.)*

WITH reference to my despatch No. 692 of the 17th instant respecting the Akhissar massacre, a Circular is sent to-day to the Ottoman Representatives abroad giving an entirely false account of the occurrence.

A Circular will also be sent on the affair at Erzinghian, where, according to the Grand Vizier, the Armenians attacked the Mussulmans, and sixty Turks and Armenians were killed in the affray, including the Inman. Military measures have been taken to prevent a recurrence of attacks.

F. O. 424/184, p. 108, No. 153

No. 298

Sir P. Currie to the Marquess of Salisbury.

No. 526.   CONSTANTINOPLE, *October 23, 1895, 5.30 p.m.*
Telegraphic.   *(Received October 23.)*

THE Sultan has expressed concurrence with the views of the Grand Vizier and Foriegn Minister as to the importance of selecting good men for the Reforms Commission. A Committee of Ministers for drawing up proposals will meet to-morrow.

F. O. 424/184, p. 108, No. 154

No. 299

Sir P. Currie to the Marquess of Salisbury.

No. 527.   CONSTANTINOPLE, *October 23, 1895, 6 p.m.*
Telegraphic.   *(Received October 23.)*

WITH reference to my telegram No. 520 of yesterday, Mr. Marinitch was informed this morning by the Grand Vizier that the Armenians of Zeitoun had made a raid in the Andrin district, carrying off cattle and property belonging to Turks, and that two gendarmes and thirty Mussulmans had been wounded. The Armenians were now collecting at Deredin, and their numbers daily growing. Mr. Marinitch spoke strongly to the Grand Vizier in my name, and warned him against the danger of allowing furhter massacres. His Highness replied that he had urged he Armenian Patriarch to instruct the clergy at Zeitoun and Marash to give quieting advice, and expressed the hope that the publication of the reforms would calm the excitement in the provinces. I proposed to my colleagues to address a joint warning to the Porte, but they preferred to make separate representations.

F. O. 424/184, pp. 108-109, No. 155

No. 300

Sir P. Currie to the Marquess of Salisbury.

No. 528.   CONSTANTINOPLE, *October 23, 1895, 6.15 p.m.*
Telegraphic   *(Received October 23.)*

MR. CUMBERBATCH telegraphs from Erzeroum that on Monday a disturbance occurred at Erzinghian, at which a few Mussulmans and about sixty Armenians were killed. The official version states that the conflict was started by an Armenian shooting a Mollah.

Bands of Lazes and of Kurds continue to pillage Armenian villages in the neighbourhood of Erzeroum, but things remain quiet in the town itself.

F. O. 424/184, p. 109, No. 156

No. 301

The Marquess of Salisbury to the Marquess of Dufferin.

No. 141.   FOREIGN OFFICE, *October 23, 1895.*
Telegraphic.

WITH reference to my preceding telegram, repeating Sir P. Currie's telegram No. 520 of yesterday, I request you to communicate to the Government to which you are accredited what is stated by his Excellency as to the condition of affairs in the Vilayet of Aleppo, and to express the hope of Her Majesty's Government that the Ambassadors of the other Powers will be instructed to join his Excellency in impressing upon the Porte the necessity of issuing the most stringent orders to the provincial authorities, with a view to prevent the repetition at Zeitoun or elsewhere of the shocking occurrences which have led all to the recent trouble.

The following is secret. The Admiralty will probably receive authority to detach vessels to the coast of the Vilayet of Aleppo, but nothing should be said about this at present.

F. O. 424/184, p. 109, No. 157

No. 302

Foreign Office to Admiralty.

Confidential.   FOREIGN OFFICE, *October 23, 1895*
Sir,
    I AM directed by the Marquess of Salisbury to transmit to you, to be laid
before the Lords Commissioners of the Admiralty, a copy of a telegram from Her
Majesty's Ambassador at Constantinople, reporting that disturbances had taken
place between the Armenians and Turks at Zeitoun and Anderin, in the Vilayet of
Aleppo, which his Excellency fears may lead to a massacre of the Armenians of
Zeitoun and the vicinity, and suggesting that the Commander-in-Chief on the
Mediterranean Station should, in case of necessity, be authorized to send some
ships to Alexandretta or one of the neighbouring ports.
    I am to say that, in view of the critical state of affairs, Lord Salisbury is of
opinion that authority should at once be given to the Admiral as recommended by
Sir. P. Currie.
                                    I am, &c.
                                            (Signed) T. H. SANDERSON
    F. O. 424/184, p. 109, No. 158

No. 303

Sir P. Currie to the Marquess of Salisbury.

No. 710.   THERAPIA, *October 23, 1895*
My Lord,   *(Received October 29.)*
    HER Majesty's consul at Erzeroum reported to me recently that the ex-Chief
of the Mush Police, Mohammed Farzi, whose dismissal I demanded, in concert
with my French and Russian colleagues, as a punishment for the unauthorized
entry of the police into the house occupied by the Consular Delegates with the
Sasun Commission, had been appointed to the more important post of Tabur-
Agassi, or Chief of Battalion of Police at Trebizond, immediately afterwards.
    I at once called the attention of the Grand Vizier and the Minister for Foreign
Affairs to this flagrant case of rewarding an offender against Consular privileges
under the pretence of punishing him, and asked what I was to think of such a
proceeding. They both expressed deep regret at the occurrence, and promised that
the officer in question should be at once dismissed.
                                    I have, &c.
                                            (Signed) PHILIP CURRIE
    F. O. 424/184, p. 137, No. 199

No. 304

Sir P. Currie to the Marquess of Salisbury.

No. 711. CONSTANTINOPLE, *October 23, 1895.*
My Lord, *(Received October 29.)*

WITH reference to my despatch No. 666 of the 9th October, I have the honour to forward to your Lordship herewith copy of a despatch which I have received from the Acting British Consul at Angora, reporting the result of the Vali's enquiry into the recent affray at Cæsarea.

I have, &c.

(Signed) PHILIP CURRIE.

F. O. 424/184, p. 137, No. 200

Inclosure in No. 304

Acting Consul Fontana to Sir P. Currie.

Sir, ANGORA, *October 15, 1895.*

WITH reference to my despatch to your Excellency of the 2nd instant, reporting that no steps had so far been taken by the Cæsarea authorities to investigate the affray at Talas, in which four Armenians were wounded by a Turkish mob, and that the Vali had consequently promised to inquire into the matter and inform me of the result, I now have the honour to report to your Excellency that Memdouh Pasha read to me yesterday a telegram he had received from the Kaïmakum of Talas, having reference to the incident in question.

The telegram was to the effect that the four Armenians were intoxicated at the time the disturbance had taken place, and while watering their horses at a fountain had jeered at certain Turks and reviled the Mahommedan religion; that in the scuffle which ensued, they had drawn their knives and wounded a Bekji and a policeman; and that, although summonses have subsequently been served by the local Correctional Court both upon the Armenians and upon such Turks as had taken part in the broil, none of the former had as yet put in an appearance at the Court.

My own private information leads me, however, to believe that the attack made on these four men was entirely unprovoked, and originated simply in a desire for retaliation on the part of the Turks, who were incensed at the outcome of the demonstration made, shortly before, by other Armenians at the Deverenk Monastery, as set forth in Mr. Consul Cumberbatch's despatch to your Excellency of the 2nd ultimo.

I have, &c.

(Signed) RAPHAEL A. FONTANA.

F. O. 424/184, pp. 137–138, No. 200/1

No. 305

Sir P. Currie to the Marquess of Salisbury.

No. 712.   CONSTANTINOPLE, *October 23, 1895*
My Lord,   *(Received October 29.)*
WITH reference to my despatch No. 641 of the 2nd October, I have the
honour to forward to your Lordship herewith copy of a despatch which I have
received from the Acting British Consul at Angora, reporting the arrival of a further
number of Circassian immigrants into the Angora district.

I have, &c.

(Signed) PHILIP CURRIE.

F. O. 424/184, p. 138, No. 201

Inclosure in No. 305

Acting Consul Fontana to Sir. P. Currie.

Sir,   ANGORA, *October 17, 1895.*
WITH reference to my despatch to your Excellency of the 24th ultimo
reporting the arrival in Angora of 1,200 Circassian Mahommedans from the
Caucasus, I now have the honour to report that contrary to the belief expressed by
the Vali that no immigration would take place, 2,800 Circassians have, since the
date of the despatch referred to, been conveyed to Angora from Ismidt for
distribution within this vilayet.

A Commission has been formed by Memdouh Pasha, under the presidency of
the Mektoubju, to inquire into the condition of the immigrants, and provide for
their well-being; to furnish the poorer among them with farming implements, and
with money for their more immediate necessities.

Of these settlers, 1,073 have already been dispatched to Boghazlian and Ak-
Tagh Maden, and 440 to Kir Shehr, in waggons drawn by mules or oxen, and
under an escort of police, who have received orders to see that the travellers are
provided with food and shelter on the way.

A special Committee will be called in the chief town of each caza, where a
settlement is to be effected, whose duty it will be to portion out land to the settlers
and to provide them with timber and other building material; and further, to report
every week to the Vali the progress of their installation.

An impression is prevalent among the Armenians here that the settlement of
these foreign Mahommedans in the vicinity of Ak-Tagh Maden and Boghazlian
will be a direct menace to their Armenian co-religionists, who are especially
numerous in those towns.

As an instance of the predatory habits of the Circassian settlers in Turkey, I may mention that quite recently a band of five men belonging to a former generation of immigrants from the Caucasus attacked, near a bridge called "Chok Ghieuz Kiupru," a caravan of twenty carriers who were engaged in transporting various merchandize to the yearly fair at Changira, and succeeded in carrying off all that was of value; none of the robbers have, as far as I am aware, been hitherto arrested.

I have, &c.

(Signed) RAPHAEL A. FONTANA.

F. O. 424/184, pp. 138–139, No. 201/1

No. 306

Sir P. Currie to the Marquess of Salisbury.

No. 713.　　　　　　　　　　　　　　　　CONSTANTINOPLE, *October 23, 1895.*
My Lord,　　　　　　　　　　　　　　　　　*(Received October 29.)*

I HAVE the honour to forward to your Lordship herewith copy of a despatch which I have received from Her Majesty's Consul at Trebizond respecting apprehended disturbances at Sivas.

I have, &c.

(Signed) PHILIP CURRIE.

F. O. 424/184, p. 139, No. 202

Inclosure in No. 306

Consul Longworth to Sir P. Currie.

Sir,　　　　　　　　　　　　　　　　　　TREBIZOND, *October 13, 1895.*

DR. JEWETT, in his letter of the 9th instant, reports as follows on the situation at Sivas:-

"I am told by Armenians that the Karslis of this city and region, assisted by some of the Karslis belonging to the Hamidieh Regiment, are contemplating an attack on the Armenians. My informers say they have positive knowledge that the Karslis have had some meetings in which they have discussed the plan. I do not place much importance in this report. The Turks are too disunited to plan any concerted action, and the Karslis of this region are too careful of their own skins to take any great risk. The Armenians are pretty well armed, and would give the Karslis a warm reception.

"I am informed that the Armenians have a plan to come in a great crowd to the

Consulate ostenisbly to present a Petition, but really with the anticipation that the police will interfere; there will be a riot; the Armenians will have cause for complaint.

"The Armenians are not yet ready to make martyrs of themselves, and I do not think they will carry out this plan. However, being forewarned I am forearmed, and I will not get pulled into this plot."

I have, &c.

(Signed) H. Z. LONGWORTH.

F. O. 424/184, p. 139, No. 202/1

No. 307

Sir P. Currie to the Marquess of Salisbury.

No. 529.   CONSTANTINOPLE, *October 24, 1895.*
Telegraphic.   *(Received October 24.)*

I WAS granted an audience by the Sultan this morning on the occasion of my leaving for England.

His Majesty expressed a hope that Her Majesty's Government would be satisfied with the steps he had taken in the matter of Armenian reforms, and would consider that the question was now finally closed.

I observed, in reply, that a great deal would depend on the manner in which the reforms were carried out, and, in particular, I urged the necessity for the appointment of good and reliable men to the Governorships and to the Commission of control.

His Majesty assured me that this would be done, and that the reforms would be carried out faithfully. He said that he hoped that Her Majesty's Government would show their good-will by expressing their approval publicly. He complained bitterly of the hostility of the English press, and said that such an expression of approval might have the effect of modifying it.

F. O. 424/184, p. 110, No. 159

No. 308

Sir P. Currie to the Marquess of Salisbury.

No. 530.   CONSTANTINOPLE, *October 24, 1895, 7 p.m.*
Telegraphic.   *(Received October 24.)*

ACCORDING to the arrangement mentioned in my telegram No. 527 of yesterday's date, the Dragomans of the other Embassies to-day made representations to the Grand Vizier, and pointed out the urgent necessity of adopting measures to prevent further massacres at Zeitoun and other places. The Grand Vizier stated, in reply, that the precautions adopted had resulted in the re-establishment of tranquillity. No further news of disturbances had reached the Porte since yesterday. The Patriarch's advice had produced a good effect, and the well-affected Armenians had undertaken to hand over the disturbers of the public peace to the local authorities. The town of Aintab, in the Vilayet of Aleppo, had been illuminated on receipt of the news of the acceptance of the reforms. Some danger was, however, still to be apprehended from the Armenians collected at Deredin.

F. O. 424/184, p. 110, No. 160

No. 309

The Marquess of Salisbury to Sir P. Currie.

No. 359.

Sir,   FOREIGN OFFICE, October 24, 1895.

I HAVE received and laid before the Queen your despatches Nos 681 and 685 of the 15th and 16th instant respectively, reporting your audience of the Sultan, and the communication made to you by Marshal Zeki Pasha respecting the question of Armenian reforms.

I approve your Excellency's language on the subject to the Sultan and to Marshal Zeki Pasha, and your refusal to make any communication to His Imperial Majesty relative to reforms except in concert with your French and Russian colleagues.

I am, &c.

(Signed) SALISBURY.

F. O. 424/184, p. 111, No. 164

No. 310

Sir P. Currie to the Marquess of Salisbury.

No. 717.   CONSTANTINOPLE, October 24, 1895.

My Lord,   (Received November 4.)

I HAVE the honour to transmit herewith copy of a letter which I have received from a M. Pisani respecting the critical state of affairs at Kerassunde, in the Sandjak of Trebizond.

I am calling the attention of the Sublime Porte to the subject.

I have, &c.

(Signed) PHILIP CURRIE.

F. O. 424/184, p. 160, No. 273

Inclosure in No. 310

M. Pisani to Sir P. Currie.

Your Excellency,   KERASSUNDE, *October 4 (16), 1895.*

I THINK it my duty to inform your Excellency that the frightful events of Constantinople, and especially those of Trebizond, provoked the excitement of the Turks to a high pitch here too, and since a week people is in a state of terror, waiting any moment for the slaughter to begin.

To-day about 11 o'clock A.M. the alarm was given, and in a second everything was pell-mell: shops closing in hurry, people running right and left panic-stricken, others rushing into Foreign Offices asking refuge, and so on. Fortunately enough the Kaïmakam rushed on the spot, and before a shot was fired, which evidently would have frightful consequences, appeased a little the minds for the time being, though what may happen in another second is quite unknown.

The authorities are taking apparently steps to keep order, but, being powerless, they will not be able to check the rush in case of emergency.

They have not but thirty soldiers against that horrible mob.

I remain, &c.

(Signed) W. G. PISANI.

F. O. 424/184, p. 160, No. 233/1

No. 311

Sir E. Monson to the Marquess of Salisbury.

No. 75.   VIENNA, *October 25, 1895.*
Telegraphic.   *(Received October 25.)*

I HAVE the honour to report, with reference to my telegram No. 74, that the Austrian Ambassador at Constantinople has received instructions from Count Goluchowski in the sense desired by your Lordship.

F. O. 424/184, p. 113, No. 167

No. 312

Sir E. Monson to the Marquess of Salisbury.

No. 76.   VIENNA, *October 25, 1895.*
Telegraphic.   *(Received October 25.)*

ON being asked by Count Goluchowski whether our fleet would, for the present, remain at the Island of Lemnos, I stated to his Excellency, in reply, that there was, I believed, no question of withdrawing it at the present moment.

I am authorized by his Excellency to tell your Lordship, in the strictest confidence, that the greatest importance is attached by him to the squadron being kept, for the present, at or in the immediate neighbourhood of the station now occupied by it.

F. O. 424/184, p. 114, No. 168

No. 313

Sir E. Monson to the Marquess of Salisbury.

No. 77.   VIENNA, *October 25, 1895.*
Telegraphic.   *(Received October 25.)*

WITH reference to the despatch No. 98 addressed to me by your Lordship on the 16th instant, I have the honour to report that County Goluchowski has declared his entire satisfaction with the assurances given by your Lordship to the Austrian Ambassador, to the effect that no change of policy in the Mediterranean is meditated by Her Majesty's Government.

I think he feels his responsibility heavily, and that he has been very nervous over recent events, although he affirms that he, personally, had never believed in the change of policy in question, but that he had wished to be in a position to reassure others who did.

He again repeated to-day his anxiety that Austria-Hungary should act in entire community with England, and I reaffirmed that your Lordship's sentiments on this head were reciprocal.

F. O. 424/184, p. 114, No. 169

No. 314

Admiralty to Foreign Office.

ADMIRALTY, *October 25, 1895.*
Sir,   *(Received October 26.)*
    WITH reference to your letter of the 23rd October inclosing copy of a telegram from Her Majesty's Ambassador at Constantinople, reporting that disturbances have taken place between the Armenians and Turks at Zeitoun and Anderin, in the Vilayet of Aleppo, which his Excellency fears may lead to a massacre of the Armenians, I am commanded by my Lords Commissioners of the Admiralty to request that you will state to the Marquess of Salisbury that the Commander-in-chief in the Mediterranean has been authorized by telegram to send ships to Alexandretta, or one of the neighbouring ports, if the Ambassador represents it as necessary.

I am, &c.

(Signed) EVAN MACGREGOR.

F. O. 424/184, p. 114, No. 170

No. 315

Sir P. Currie to the Marquess of Salisbury.

No. 532.   CONSTANTINOPLE, *October 26, 1895, 6.20 p.m.*
Telegraphic.   *(Received October 26.)*
    HER Majesty's Vice-Consul at Mush telegraphs that serious disorders took place in Bitlis yesterday, but that no details have as yet reached him. He adds that the situation in Mush is critical, and that no confidence is felt in the soldiers. However, the new Mutessarif authorizes him to say that he will guarantee that no disturbances shall be begun from the side of the Mussulmans.

F. O. 424/184, p. 114, No. 171

No. 316

Sir P. Currie to the Marquess of Salisbury.

No. 533.   CONSTANTINOPLE, *October 26, 1895, 7 p.m.*
Telegraphic.   *(Received October 26.)*
    THE Grand Vizier to-day stated that at Marash, in the Vilayet of Aleppo, the Armenians had attacked the patrols in the streets and killed some Mussulmans; in

the Vilayets of Erzeroum and Bitlis they were making attacks on the Moslem population, provoking retaliation on the part of the latter. At Bitlis they had attacked the mosques during the hour of prayer, but no details were to hand.

I cannot but regard with suspicion the marked similarity in the reports received from the authorities in different parts of the Asiatic provinces, all accusing the Armenians of taking the initiative.

His Highness added that the Sublime Porte had taken preventive measures, and had given orders to call out some Reserves in the six vilayets.

He had requested the Patriarch to address a Circular to his clergy instructing them to restrain the people, but his Beatitude made his consent conditional on the publication of the reforms.

His Highness asked me to urge the Patriarch to send a Circular at once.

F. O. 424/184, p. 115, No. 172

No. 317

The Marquess of Salisbury to Sir P. Currie.

No. 360.

Sir,   FOREIGN OFFICE, *October 26, 1895.*

I HAVE received your despatch No. 684 of the 16th instant, reporting the steps taken to prevail on the Armenians, who had taken refuge in the various churches in Constantinople after the recent disturbances, to disperse and return to their homes, and the successful result of their proceedings.

Your Excellency's action in this matter has my entire approval, and I request that you will express to Mr. Marinitch my satisfaction at the manner in which he discharged the difficult duty intrusted to him.

I am, &c.

(Signed) SALISBURY.

F. O. 424/184, p. 115, No. 173

No. 318

The Marquess of Salisbury to Sir P. Currie.

No. 361.

Sir,   FOREIGN OFFICE, *October 26, 1895.*

I HAVE received your Excellency's despatch No. 693 of the 17th instant forwarding a copy of a Report by Mr. Lister on the state of the prisons in Constantinople, and the treatment of the Armenian prisoners.

I request you to convey my thanks to Mr. Lister for this Report, which has been read with interest.

I am, &c.

(Signed) SALISBURY.

F. O. 424/184, p. 115, No. 174

No. 319

Saïd Pasha to Rustem Pasha.

CONSTANTINOPLE, *le 26 Octobre, 1895.*

Télégraphique.   *(Communicated by Rustem Pasha, October 27.)*

LE Gouverneur-Général de Bitlis nous télégraphie que, dans la journée d'hier, les Arméniens ont attaqué, les armes à la main, les mosquées de la ville au moment même où tous les Musulmans s'y trouvaient réunis pour la prière du Vendredi.

Les Musulmans, surpris par cette attaque, et sans armes, durent défendre leurs vies contre leurs agresseurs en se servant de pierres et de bâtons.

Les autorités prévenues de ces faits envoyèrent immédiatement dans tous les quartiers de la ville des détachements de police, de gendarmerie, et de soldats pour rétablir l'ordre et la tranquillité.

Une partie des Arméniens se sont barricadés dans les Khans et ont continué à se servir de leurs armes.

Pendant la bagarre il y a cu des morts et des blessés des deux côtés.

F. O. 424/184, pp. 115-116, No. 175

No. 320

Mr. Gosselin to the Marquess of Salisbury.

No. 240.   BERLIN, *October 26, 1895.*

My Lord,   *(Received October 28.)*

ON the receipt of the instructions contained in your Lordship's telegrams Nos. 92 and 93 of the 23rd instant, I called on Baron von Marschall, and informed his Excellency of the serious state of affairs in the Vilayet of Aleppo.

Baron von Marschall said that he had not received any information from the German Ambassador as to the state of affairs in that special district, but that, some ten days ago, his Excellency had reported that he considered the situation throughout the whole Ottoman Empire as grave, the more so as the agitation was no longer confined to the Christian population, but seemed to be spreading among the Mussulman subjects of the Sultan.

Baron von Marschall promised to telegraph at once to his Excellency instructing him to report immediately on the matter, and, if the news were confirmed, to act in concert with the other Ambassadors in order to prevent, as far as possible, any repetition of the massacres.

I was unable to see Baron von Marschall this morning, as his Excellency has accompanied the Emperor to Leipzig; but Baron von Rotenhan informed me that the Foreign Office had received no telegrams from Constantinople during the last few days, and that the German courier, who was on his way home with despatches, had been delayed by floods, and was not expected to reach Berlin till the 30th instant.

I have, &c.

(Signed) MARTIN GOSSELIN.

F. O. 424/184, p. 117, No. 180

No. 321

Sir F. Monson to the Marquess of Salisbury.

No. 308.   VIENNA, *October 26, 1895.*
My Lord,   *(Received October 28.)*

NOT having seen Count Goluchowski for ten days in consequence of his absence in Hungary, I called upon him yesterday, and spoke to him upon the instructions telegraphed to me by your Lordship on the 23rd instant in regard to the common action of the Ambassadors of the Great Powers at Constantinople in warning the Porte not to allow the renewal of massacres.

His Excellency said that, in consequence of my communication to Count Welsersheimb (the new Under-Secretary of State or First Chief of Section, as is the title given here to the immediate subordinate of the Minister for Foreign Affairs), the desired orders had been at once telegraphed to Baron Calice.

Count Goluchowski proceeded to say that, although the concessions obtained by England, France, and Russia are well enough in their way, they can only serve to dissipate for the moment the most pressing of the dangers, to the existence of which it is impossible for the Powers to close their eyes.

It is essential that the Sultan and his Government should take steps for the amelioration of the condition of Macedonia, otherwise troubles are certainly to be expected in that province in the spring, and the contingency of their occurrence cannot but be viewed by the Austro-Hungarian Government with the greatest apprehension.

I have, &c.

(Signed) EDMUND MONSON.

F. O. 424/184, pp. 117-118, No. 181

No. 322

Sir Clare Ford to the Marquess of Salisbury.

No. 174.   ROME, *October 26, 1895.*
My Lord,   *(Received October 29.)*

I HAVE the honour to inform your Lordship that I duly carried out your Lordship's instructions as conveyed to me in your Lordship's telegram No. 50 of the 23rd instant.

Baron Blanc, Minister for Foreign Affairs, was absent from Rome at the time, but I have this day received a reply, a copy of which is herein inclosed, to the communication which I had made him.

I have, &c.
(Signed) FRANCIS CLARE FORD.

F. O. 424/184, p. 139, No. 203

Inclosure in No. 322

Baron Blanc to Sir Clare Ford.

Cher Ambassadeur,   ROME, *le 26 Octobre, 1895.*

NOTRE nouvel Ambassadeur à Constantinople, M. Pansa, y a trouvé à son arrivée, le 24 courant, nos instructions portant que la période de l'action à trois de l'Angleterre avec la Russie et la France dans les affaires d'Arménie pouvant être considérée comme terminée par la communication, quelle qu'en doive être la valeur effective, du Règlement Ottoman pour les réformes en Arménie, l'Ambassade Royale doit, en présence de la continuation des massacres qui nous est annoncée par notre Consul à Trébizonde, s'entendre avec les Ambassades d'Autriche-Hongrie et d'Allemagne pour appuyer les démarches que l'Ambassade d'Angleterre de son côté croient opportunes ou nécessaires.

Je reçois, en ce moment, de M. Pansa, information que des nouvelles inquiétantes continuant à arriver de divers points de l'Asie-Mineure, il a fait avec ses collègues d'Autriche-Hongrie et d'Allemagne des démarches auprès de la Sublime Porte pour qu'elle avise promptement à prévenir de nouveaux excès.

Croyez-moi, &c.
(Signé) BLANC.

F. O. 424/184, p. 140, No. 203/1

No. 323

Sir P. Currie to the Marquess of Salisbury.

No. 721.   CONSTANTINOPLE, *October 26, 1895.*
My Lord,   *(Received November 4.)*
    I HAVE the honour to forward to your Lordship herewith copy of a despatch which I have received from the Acting British Vice-Consul at Angora, expressing the satisfaction of the Armenians of that district at the acceptance of the scheme of reforms.

I have, &c.

(Signed) PHILIP CURRIE.

F. O. 424/184, p. 163, No. 276

Inclousure in No. 323

Acting Consul Fontana to Sir P. Currie.

Sir,   ANGORA, *October 19, 1895.*
    I HAVE the honour to acknowledge, with my best thanks to your Excellency, the receipt of your Excellency's telegram of yesterday's date, informing me that the Sultan has at length consented to adopt the scheme of reforms for the six Armenian vilayets, as proposed by the Representatives of England, France, and Russia.
    Some of the leading Armenians in Angora called upon me to-day, and requested me to convey to your Excellency, in the name of the Armenians of this vilayet in general, their heartfelt thanks and respectful congratulations upon the success which has crowned your Excellency's representations on behalf of their kindred in Armenia, to the Sultan, and to the Sublime Porte.

I have, &c.

(Signed) RAPHAEL A. FONTANA.

F. O. 424/184, p. 163, No. 276/1

No. 324

Sir P. Currie to the Marquess of Salisbury.

No. 725.   THERAPIA, *October 26, 1895.*
My Lord,   *(Received November 4.)*
    IN my despatch No. 719 of the 24th October, I have already had the honour to transmit to your Lordship reports which seem to prove that the Turkish troops at

Trebizond took part in the recent massacre of Armenians. I have now received some further details on this subject from my Russian colleague.

It would appear that the night before the massacre the Secretary of the Russian Consulate visited the Vali, and heard orders being given to arm certain Lazes who had come in from the country. He subsequently saw the arms being issued. When M. de Nélidoff mentioned this story to Saïd Pasha, the latter said that it explained a telegram from the Governor of Trebizond, which he had hitherto been unable to understand. Kadri Bey had telegraphed to know if he could have arms and uniforms for 300 extra soldiers, and the Minister of War had replied that there were no uniforms forthcoming, but that he could have the arms. Kadri Bey's object, Saïd Pasha added, had doubtless been to increase the forces available for the protection of the town.

M. de Nélidoff also said there was evidence that the massacre had been perpetrated in a very deliberate manner. Only Gregorian Armenians had been killed, and in many cases where one house in a street belonged to an Armenian who was a Catholic or a Russian subject, it and its inmates had been left untouched, though every other house had suffered.

He did not believe a report which had been current, that eight Armenians had been executed for the disturbance. Three Commissions had been formed at Trebizond: one military and exclusively Turkish, for investigating the massacre and discovering the guilty parties; the second, composed of Turks, Greeks, and Armenians, for estimating the damage done to property, and considering the best method of giving compensation; the third, also mixed, for giving aid to the widows and children of the victims of the disaster.

I have, &c.

(Signed) PHILIP CURRIE.

F. O. 424/184, pp. 168-169, No. 279

No. 325

Mr. Herbert to the Marquess of Salisbury.

No. 726.   THERAPIA, *October 26, 1895.*
My Lord,   *(Received November 4.)*

IN accordance with instructions from their respective Ambassadors, the Dragomans of the British, French, and Russian Embassies called upon the Minister for Foreign Affairs on the 26th instant, and handed to his Excellency the collective note drawn up in acknowledgment of the plan of reforms and Decree received from the Sublime Porte, copies of which were inclosed in Sir P. Currie's despatch No. 704 of the 22nd instant.

Saïd Pasha, to whom Mr. Marinitch read the collective note, made one reservation with regard to the references made in it to various previous communications of the Sublime Porte therein.

His Excellency maintained that all earlier schemes of reforms had been superseded on the acceptance by the Sublime Porte of the final Schedule drawn up by the Ambassadors.

The Dragomans pointed out to his Excellency that the communications referred to, having been addressed by the Sublime Porte to the Embassies, could not contain any points which had not received the sanction of the Turkish Government, but promised to lay the matter before their respective Ambassadors.

The Minister for Foreign Affairs at once submitted the collective note to the consideration of the Grand Vizier.

I am informed by M. de Nélidoff that Saïd Pasha made a further objection with regard to the extension of the reforms to cazas containing a considerable non-Mussulman population. This reservation appears, however, to have been made only to the Dragoman of the Russian Embassy, who remained with the Minister for Foreign Affairs after the others had left.

This reservation may possibly be alluded to in the acknowledgment of the collective note which the Sublime Porte has promised to send.

I have, &c.

(Signed) MICHAEL H. HERBERT.

F. O. 424/184, p. 169, No. 280

No. 326

Sir P. Currie to the Marquess of Salisbury.

No. 534.   CONSTANTINOPLE, *October 27, 1895, 2.45 p.m*
Telegraphic.   *(Received October 27.)*

IN reply to my inquiries, Her Majesty's Consul at Aleppo telegraphs that he will ascertain as soon as possible whether it was the Armenians who were the aggressors at Marash; as yet he has no direct information on the subject.

It is also reported at Aleppo that there have been disturbances at Zeitoun, but Mr. Barnham has received no details as yet. It is said that some Reserves have also been called out in the Vilayet of Aleppo.

F. O. 424/184, p. 116, No. 176

No. 327

Sir P. Currie to the Marquess of Salisbury,

No. 535.   CONSTANTINOPLE, *October 27, 1895.*
Telegraphic.   *(Received October 27.)*

HER Majesty's Vice-Consul at Mush telegraphs that he believes the news contained in his telegram of the 25th October is correct, but that till last night no further news had been received from Bitlis, as the telegraph wires had been cut. In Mush, so far, there had been no disorder, but the situation was most critical, and all the shops were shut.

Mr. Hampson has urged the Muterssarif to issue orders that no one shall carry arms in the town, but the latter again assures him that there will be no disorder.

The Vali of Bitlis has telegraphed to the Mutessarif viâ Van that things are quieter, and advised him to take precautions to prevent any trouble in Mush or Boulanik.

F. O. 424/184, p, 116, No. 177

No. 328

Sir P. Currie to the Marquess of Salisbury.

No. 536.   CONSTANTINOPLE, *October 27, 1895, 5.15 p.m.*
Telegraphic.   *(Received October 27.)*

THE Mussulman agitation mentioned in my telegram No. 523 of the 23rd instant continues. I hear from a reliable source that proofs have come into the hands of the authorities that the agitators contemplate joint action against the Palace with the Armenian Hintchak Society, with whom they are in communication.

F. O. 424/184, p. 116, No. 178

No. 329

Sir P. Currie to the Marquess of Salisbury.

No. 537.   CONSTANTINOPLE, *October 27, 1895.*
Telegraphic.   *(Received October 27.)*

HER Majesty's Consul at Trebizond telegraphs that there were disturbances at Gumush-Khane the day before yesterday, but he cannot ascertain the number of the killed.

F. O. 424/184, p. 117, No. 179

No. 330

Morel Bey to Foreign Office.

1, BRYANSTON SQUARE, LONDRES, *le 28 Octobre, 1895.*
Cher Sir Thomas,   *(Received October 28.)*
RUSTEM PACHA me charge de vous envoyer, pour votre information, la copie ci-jointe d'un télégramme qu'il a reçu ce matin de la Sublime Porte, et qui annonce de nouveaux conflits entre Musulmans et Arméniens.

Bien sincèrement à vous.

(Signé) G. MOREL.

F. O. 424/184, p. 118, No. 182

Inclosure in No. 330

Saïd Pasha to Rustem Pasha.

Télégraphique.   CONSTANTINOPLE, *le 27 Octobre, 1895.*
LES Arméniens continuent leurs tentatives criminelles partout où ils le peuvent en attaquant sans aucune provocation les populations Musulmanes.

Avant-hier, c'était à Bitlis que les émeutiers attaquaient les Musulmans dans leurs mosquées au moment de la prière du Vendredi. Hier, c'était à Baïbourt, à Zeitoun, et à Marache que d'autres émeutes ont éclaté.

En effet, suivant un télégramme du Commandant Militaire et du Caïmacam, une dizaine de coups de feu ont été tirés du quartier Arménian de Baïbourt sur des Musulmans, dont plusieurs furent mortellement atteints.

A la vue des cadavres de leurs corcligionnaires, les Musulmans fermèrent leurs boutiques et coururent aux armes pour défendre leurs vies.

Il y a eu pendant l'échauffourée des morts et des blessés des deux côtés.

Les autorités locales ont envoyé immédiatement des détachments de police, de gendarmes, et de soldats pur rétablir la tranquillité, et elles sont parvenu à calmer l'agitation de la population Musulmane.

F. O. 424/184, p. 118, No. 182/1

No. 331

Mr. Herbert to the Marquess of Salisbury.

No. 539.   CONSTANTINOPLE, *October 28, 1895, 7 p.m.*
Telegraphic.   *(Received October 28.)*

SIR P. CURRIE has requested the Consuls concerned to send a telegraphic report on the statements of the Porte that the Armenians in the Provinces of Bitlis, Erzeroum, and Aleppo were attacking the Mahommedans.

F. O. 4124/184, p. 118, No. 183

No. 332

Mr. Herbert to the Marquess of Salisbury.

No. 541.   CONSTANTINOPLE, *October 28, 1895, 7.50 p.m.*
Telegraphic.   *(Received October 28.)*

IN reply to P. Currie's instructions, reported in my telegram No. 539 of to-day's date, Her Majesty's Consul at Trebizond telegraphs that there is no reason to believe that the Armenians in that town contemplated an attack on the Mussulmans, though it is probable that it was Armenians who attacked Bahri Pasha on the 2nd instant.

As, however, an Armenian Revolutionary Committee undoubtedly exists in Trebizond which advocates violence, it is possible that some Armenians may have written and spoken about creating disturbances in the event of the reforms being rejected, and some of them may even have acted rashly.

F. O. 424/184, pp. 118–119, No. 184

No. 333

Mr. Herbert to the Marquess of Salisbury.

No. 542.   CONSTANTINOPLE, *October 28, 1895, 7.55 p.m.*
Telegraphic.   *(Received October 28.)*

IN reply to Sir P. Currie's instructions, as reported in my telegram No. 539 of to-day's date, the Acting British Consul at Erzeroum telegraphs that the Armenian Revolutionary Committees have recently sent agents to these parts from Russia and from Constantinople, viâ Trebizond, with the undoubted object of provoking disturbances wherever possible, but that the community in general disapprove of this.

Mr. Cumberbatch considers that the disturbances which have occurred at Erzinjan and Trebizond support this view.

News had also reached Erzeroum of troubles at Bitlis which had been similarly provoked. There an Armenian armed band had made an attack on the Mussulmans while gathered together in prayer at the mosque.

At Baiburt also some Armenians fired yesterday from their houses on peaceable Turks. Both there and at Bitlis there had been serious fighting in consequence, but Mr. Cumberbatch had received no details.

If necessary the Reserves were to be called out, but so far this had not been done anywhere except at Erzinjan.

F. O. 424/184, p. 119, No. 185

No. 334

Mr. Herbert to the Marquess of Salisbury.

No. 543. CONSTANTINOPLE, *October 28, 1895, 8 p.m.*
Telegraphic. *(Received October 28.)*

VICE-CONSUL HAMPSON has telegraphed to me, with reference to my telegram to your Lordship of to-day No. 539, that the authorities say that the affair at Bitlis began by the Armenians attacking the mosques. He thinks this most improbable, and says that the Armenians at Mush are in a terrible panic, and have certainly no idea of attacking Mussulmans, nor does he believe in its existence elsewhere.

He has urged Armenians to reopen shops to-morrow. He adds that no further details have reached him from Bitlis, but the Mutessarif repeats that he thinks that at least 500 were killed.

F. O. 424/184, p. 119, No. 186

No. 335

Mr. Herbert to the Marquess of Salisbury.

No. 544. CONSTANTINOPLE, *October 28, 1895, 11 p.m.*
Telegraphic. *(Received October 28.)*

HER Majesty's Consul at Aleppo telegraphs that he hears that the attitude of the Armenians at Ourfa is threatening, and that it is rumoured that there are disturbances there. He is making inquiries.

F. O. 424/184, p. 119, No. 187

No. 336

Mr. Herbert to the Marquess of Salisbury.

No. 545.   CONSTANTINOPLE, *October 28, 1895.*
Telegraphic.   *(Received October 28.)*

MR. HAMPSON telegraphs from Mush that he has received information from Bitlis that the Mussulmans, on coming out of the mosques last Friday, attacked the Armenians; that 630 persons were killed.

This information, he says, tallies with what he knew respecting the plans of the Mussulmans for the previous Friday, which were, however, frustrated.

The Mussulmans and Kurds in Mush were still carrying arms, the authorities asserting that they were in fear of attacks from the Christians.

From what he hears on all sides, Mr. Hampson fears that the Kurds are rising to join in an attack on the Armenians, which he thinks would create a most serious situation.

F. O. 424/184, p. 120, No. 188

No. 337

Mr. Herbert to the Marquess of Salisbury.

No. 546.   CONSTANTINOPLE, *October 28, 1895, 8 p.m.*
Telegraphic.   *(Received October 28.)*

MR. DRUMMOND HAY telegraphs to-day from Beyrout that the Mussulman excitement has decreased, and the population has been tranquillized by the publication of the news by the Vali that the Sultan intends to introduce reforms in Armenia, and to extend them for the purpose to other provinces.

F. O. 424/184, p. 120, No. 189

No. 338

Mr. Herbert to the Marquess of Salisbury.

No. 547.   CONSTANTINOPLE, *October 28, 1895, 11.15 p.m.*
Telegraphic.   *(Received October 28.)*

I WAS informed to-day by the Minister for Foreign Affairs that the Armenians have been the aggressors in the disturbances which he tells me have taken place at

Marash, Zeitoun, Bitlis, Gumush-Khane, Baibourt and Karpout. He stated that at Bitlis the Mussulmans had been attacked by the Armenians while in the mosques; 173 Mussulmans and 179 Armenians had been killed and wounded.

Fresh troubles are apprehended from Zeitoun, where a band of 2,000 Armenians killed five gendarmes and their Commander, and also from Baibourt, but order has been restored in the other places.

F. O. 424/184, p. 120, No. 190

No. 339

Saïd Pasha to Morel Bey.

CONSTANTINOPLE, *le 28 Octobre, 1895.*

Télégraphique.   *(Communicated by Morel Bey, October 29.)*

LE 24 courant, quinze Arméniens armés ont tué sans motif un jeune Musulman de Marache. Les meurtriers ont été pris vivants avec une cinquantaine d'armes. Le 26, une discussion futile servit de prétexte aux Arméniens pour susciter une émeute au bazar; le Gouverneur parvint pourtant par ses conseils à les calmer, mais vers le soir, douze Arméniens blessèrent grièvement dans les quartiers excentriques deux Musulmans sans défense. La plupart des coupables furent arrêtés; mais ceux qui parvinrent à s'enfuir revêtirent ensuite des costumes Musulmans avec turbans et tuèrent pendant la nuit un Notable Arménien.

Six autres Arméniens qui avaient tiré de leurs maisons des coups de feu sur les patrouilles furent également arrêtés, et grâce aux mesures prises la tranquillité règne dans la ville.

Quant aux agitateurs d'Alabach (Zéitoun) ils ont attaqué et pillé le village Musulman de Camarly en blessant quelques villageois.

Le Commandant de la Gendarmerie de Marache, qui avait été envoyé sur les lieux pour faire une enquête, a été, à son retour, attaqué par une bande de 2,000 émeutiers et mis à mort avec quatre des cinq gendarmes qui l'escortaient. Les meneurs sont les Arméniens de Marache et de Zéitoun.

Ils se proposeraient d'envahir bientôt différentes régions et de fomenter dans la ville de Marache une nouvelle émeute.

D'après les renseignements fournis par le Vali d'Alep, la surexcitation dans ces parages serait provoquée par quelques étrangers qui sont arrivés dernièrement.

Le 28 Octobre.—Une certaine agitation parmi les Arméniens ayant été signalée Gumuchbané, le Gouverneur-Général de Trézibond a immédiatement pris des mesures pour le maintien de l'ordre et de la tranquillité.

Le 28 Octobre.—Les meneurs Arméniens ayant voulu provoquer de l'agitation à Kharpout en faisant fermer précipitamment les boutiques, le Gouverneur-Général, aidé par les Notables et le missionnaire Américain, Mr. Barmen [?] est parvenu sans aucune effusion de sang à calmer les esprits et à faire rouvrir les boutiques fermées. Le calme y est complètement rétabli.

Le 29 Octobre.—D'après les renseignements reçus du Vilayet de Bitlis, le nombre des tués et des blessés tant de la part des Musulmans que des Arméniens, monte au chiffre total de 352, dont 173 Musulmans et 179 Arméniens.

Le 29 Octobre.—Les Arméniens qui avaient massacré près de Zéitoun le Commandant de la Gendarmerie de Marache ainsi que son escorte, ont brûlé les corps de deux de ces gendarmes.

F. O. 424/184, p. 140, No. 204

No. 340

Mr. Herbert to the Marquess of Salisbury.

No. 551.   CONSTANTINOPLE, *October 29, 1895, 11.15 p.m.*
Telegraphic.   *(Received October 29.)*

THE list of persons proposed as suitable to serve on the Commission of Control, or as Moavins in the six vilayets, has been submitted to the Sultan, and it is expected that the appointments will shortly be gazetted.

Acting on direction received from Sir P. Currie, I yesterday protested to the Grand Vizier against the Minister for Foreign Affairs being appointed President of the Commission, a step which the Sublime Porte was contemplating. The French and Russian Ambasssadors have contented themselves with advising the Porte, while raising no personal objection to Saïd Pasha, not to appoint the Minister for Foreign Affairs as President of the Commission of Control, and have not formally protested, as they say that they have no right to do so.

At the end of my interview with the Grand Vizier his Highness stated that the Minister for Foreign Afffairs would not be appointed. I understand, however, that the Sultan is very desirous to make this appointment, and I fear that His Majesty will have his way.

An Iradé has been issued sanctioning the appointment of Fethy Bey as Assistant to Shakir Pasha. Fethy Bey is a Maronite, and was for some time Secretary of Embassy at St. Petersburgh when Shakir Pasha was Ambassador. His appointment is considered to be a very good one.

F. O. 424/184, p. 142, No. 207

No. 341

The Marquess of Salisbury to Mr. Herbert.

No. 198.   FOREIGN OFFICE, *October 29, 1895, 11 p.m.*
Telegraphic.

I HAVE received your telegram No. 548 of to-day, repeating telegrams Nos. 1, 2, and 3 from Mr. Hampson, in which he refers to the recent massacre at Bitlis, and reports on the present condition of affairs at Mush and Sasun.

The representations which you propose to make to the Turkish government cannot be too strong respecting the impression which will be produced in this country if these massacres continue, or if the Turks persist in the attempt to stop the relief of the distressed Armenians, and to intimidate the missionaries into leaving the district.

The latter, I think, should consult their safety by withdrawing till the excitement has abated.

F. O. 424/184, p. 142, No. 208

No. 342

Mr. Herbert to the Marquess of Salisbury.

No. 727.   CONSTANTINOPLE, *October 29, 1895.*
My Lord,   *(Received November 4.)*

I HAVE the honour to forward to your Lordship herewith a copy of a despatch which I have received from Her Majesty's Acting Consul at Erzeroum, inclosing a despatch from Vice-Consul Hallward, reporting a partial improvement in the state of affairs at Van. I am pressing for the dismissal of the officers mentioned, and for the appointment of a good Mutessarif to Hekkiari.

I have, &c.

(Signed) MICHAEL H. HERBERT.

F. O. 424/184, p. 16, No. 281

No. 343

Mr. Herbert to the Marquess of Salisbury.

No. 731. Confidential.   CONSTANTINOPLE, *October 29, 1895.*
My Lord,   *(Received November 4.)*

I HAVE the honour to forward to your Lordship herewith copy of a despatch which I have received from Her Majesty's Acting Consul at Erzeroum, reporting on the critical state of things in that town.

I have approved Mr. Cumberbatch's action.

I have, &c.

(Signed) MICHAEL H. HERBERT.

F. O. 424/184, p. 169, No. 281

Inclosure in No. 343

Consul Cumberbatch to Sir P. Currie.

Confidential.

Sir,   ERZEROUM, *October 10, 1895.*

WITH reference to my previous despatch of this day's date, I have the honour to report that the news of the Constantinople disturbances, which your Excellency kindly communicated to me on the 3rd instant, did not get known here till a day or two ago through Turkish official channels, but all the details are not yet publicly known.

In the present critical state of things it is anticipated that the news, as it spreads, will act as an incentive to Armenian agitation on the one hand, and as an encouragement for a display of Mussulman resentment on the other, should any incident arise locally to provoke it.

The military authorities have been ordered to stand by in case of an emergency, and, among other preparations, fifty rounds of cartridges have been served out to each soldier of this garrison, whilst the members of the police force have received special instructions to act with caution and tact.

The ostensible object is to prevent any Mussulman assault, though experience has shown that any move on the part of the Armenians would be suppressed with a strong and harsh hand.

In accordance with the express desire of Hakki Pasha, who does not conceal his anxiety, I have taken upon myself to strongly advise Mgr. G. Shismanian, the enlightened and energetic Armenian Archbishop of Erzeroum, whose official relations with the Vali are very strained owing to his attitude towards Shakir Pasha, to use whatever influence he and his Council may possess to restrain his co-religionists from committing any rash act which may, under the circumstances, lead to a conflict, and which would not in any way help towards a peaceable settlement of the questions at issue.

I have received that prelate's assurances that he had used, and will continue to use, every means in his power to preserve public peace on their side as he fully recognizes the danger and futility of such conduct, but he had to admit that neither he nor his Council had any control over the desperate actions of the "Hintchakists," now in such force in this town and district, and that the otherwise peaceably-disposed Armenians, especially those in the outlying districts, were so exasperated by the sufferings they are made to bear at the hands of Turks and Kurds, that there is no knowing what reckless action they may not be capable of taking part in.

I have, &c.

(Signed) H. A. CUMBERBATCH.

F. O. 424/184, p. 174, No. 285/1

No. 344

Mr. Herbert to the Marquess of Salisbury.

No. 732. CONSTANTINOPLE, *October 29, 1895.*

My Lord, *(Received November 4.)*

I HAVE the honour to forward to your Lordship herewith copy of a despatch which I have received from Her Majesty's Acting Consul at Erzeroum reporting the assassination of alleged informers by agents of the Revolutionary Committee.

I have, &c.

(Signed) MICHAEL H. HERBERT.

F. O. 424/184 p. 184, No. 286

Inclosure in No. 344

Consul Cumberbatch to Sir P. Currie.

Sir, ERZEROUM, *October 11, 1895.*

I HAVE the honour to report that the emissaries of the revolutionary or "Hintchakist" party are credited with the murder on the 5th instant of two Armenians of some position in this town named Artin Effendi Serkissian, a lawyer, and Simon Agha Bosoyan, a merchant. They were stabbed in a most daring manner in a crowded thoroughfare, and both died immediately afterwards. One man, a Russian Armenian, of this place, has been arrested on suspicion.

It is generally thought that Artin Effendi was killed because he was suspected of having acted as an informer, and because he had quite recently refused to join the Secret Committee being formed here. It was not intended to injure Simon Agha, but he must have got mortally wounded in defending his friend.

At Erzinghan, some ten days ago, another Armenian, called Garabet Der Garabet, was also murdered. He was considered a spy of Zekki Pasha, and the same agency is credited with his death.

In addition to forbidding any Armenian to retain any sort of administrative employ, these men try to extort money from the richer Armenians, one man having three days ago been summoned to hand over 300*l.* to their funds.

Even an Armenian youth of 20, the only Christian student at the "Idadieh" College here, has this week had an anonymous letter put into his hand when he was standing alone at the door of the establishment, threatening him with death from the same hands which had so recently killed Artin Effendi if he did not leave the school at once.

These cases will suffice to show the audacity and determination of the dangerous faction the authorities have now to deal with.

I have, &c.

(Signed) H. A. CUMBERBATCH.

F. O. 424/184, p. 175, No. 286/1

No. 345

Mr. Herbert to the Marquess of Salisbury.

No. 733.   CONSTANTINOPLE, *October 29, 1895.*
My Lord,   *(Received November 4.)*

I HAVE the honour to forward to your Lordship herewith copy of a despatch which I have received from Her Majesty's Acting Consul at Erzeroum, reporting that there is no abatement in Kurdish lawlessness, and inclosing a threatening letter addressed by Kurdish Chiefs to Armenian villagers.

I am causing the matter to be mentioned at the Sublime Porte.

I have, &c.

(Signed) MICHAEL H. HERBERT.

F. O. 424/184 p. 175, No. 287

Inclosure 1 in No. 345

Consul Cumberbatch to Sir P. Currie.

Sir,   ERZEROUM, *October 11, 1895.*

I HAVE the honour to report that, from information reaching me from all sides, the depredations of the lawless Kurds show no signs of abatement.

Without troubling your Excellency with a detailed list of the numerous acts of violence and robbery laid to their charge within the last few weeks, I will merely transmit, as an interesting specimen of their arbitrary behaviour, a translation of a letter, the Turkish original of which I have seen, sent, on or about the 6th instant, to the villages of Khalil Tchaoush and Kaghkig, near Khinous, a small town some eighteen hours to the south-east of Erzeroum. Both these villages are entirely or mostly inhabited by Armenians, and the threatening letter is due to the disappearance of a Sheikh called Haidar Effendi, whom the Armenians are accused of having done away with.

I, this day, handed Hakki Pasha a copy of the document, and represented the necessity of immediate steps being taken to prevent the menace from being carried out, and his Excelllency assured me that he had already sent an officer to the spot to inquire, and would take measures to protect the villagers.

I have, &c.

(Signed) H. A. CUMBERBATCH.

F. O. 424/184, p, 176, No. 287/1

Inclosure 2 in No. 345

Letter from Kurdish Chiefs to Armenian Villagers.

Translation

To the Armenians of the villages of Khalil Tchaoush and Kaghkig:

SOME days ago you caused to disappear our Sheikh, Haidar Effendi. If he is not found, we give you notice that you will all be put to the edge of the sword. Know it well.

We write you this in the name of all our tribes.

(Seals of Mohamed, Ali, Kadir, Meto.)

F. O. 424/184, p. 176, No. 287/2

No. 346

Mr. Herbert to the Marquess of Salisbury.

No. 734.   CONSTANTINOPLE, *October 29, 1895.*

My Lord,   *(Received November 4.)*

I HAVE the honour to forward to your Lordship herewith copy of a despatch which I have received from Her Majesty's Acting Consul at Erzeroum, reporting upon the critical state of things at Kharput.

I have, &c.

(Signed) MICHAEL H. HERBERT.

F. O. 424/184, p. 176, No. 288

Inclosure in No. 346

Consul Cumberbatch to Sir P. Currie.

Sir,   ERZEROUM, *October 14, 1895.*

OWING to a letter received by me from Dr. Barnum, American missionary at Kharput, dated the 28th September, I had the honour to telegraph to your

Excellency to-day that the situation in that place was such that the immediate departure of the new Vali for the Vilayet of Maamuret-ul-Aziz was highly advisable.

Dr. Barnum reports that there were unmistakable signs of hostile preparations on the part of the Turkish and Kurdish populations, and that, during the thirty-six years of his residence there, he has never seen anything approaching the present condition of terror.

I have, &c.

(Signed) H. A. CUMBERBATCH.

F. O. 424/184, pp. 176–177, No. 288/1

No. 347

Mr. Herbert to the Marquess of Salisbury.

No. 735.   THERAPIA, *October 29, 1895.*
My Lord,   *(Received November 4.)*

I HAVE the honour to transmit to your Lordship herewith copy of a despatch which I have received from Her Majesty's Acting Consul at Erzeroum, reporting the death of another Talori prisoner, and stating the imperative necessity of the dismissal of the Mudir of the Mush prison, Sadil Effendi, and of one of the officials, Meh Tchaoush.

I have since learnt that a new system has been introduced in the Mush prison, according to which the Governor is changed every month. The present Governor is a certain Abdul Kadir, who enjoys the very worst reputation, and I am causing strong representations to be made at the Sublime Porte for his dismissal from the service of the Ottoman Government.

I have, &c.

(Signed) MICHAEL H. HERBERT.

F. O. 424/184, p. 177, No. 289

Inclosure in No. 347

Consul Cumberbatch to Sir P. Currie.

Sir, ERZEROUM, *October 14, 1895.*

WITH reference to your Excellency's despatch of the 18th ultimo, the contents of which I have communicated to Her Majesty's Vice-Consul at Mush, I have the honour to inform you that Mr. Hampson reports that the Talori prisoner, whose case was last referred to in the inclosure of my despatch of the 1st instant, died in the first week of this month, and that now only five out of the sixteen prisoners from that district survive.

Mr. Hampson also states that, up to the 8th instant, he had not received permission to visit the prison, and adds that he learns, from both Christian and Mussulman sources, the dismissal of the Mudir of the prison, Sadil Effendi, and of his abettor in ill-doing, Meh Tchaousch, is imperatively needed.

I have, &c.

(Signed) H. A. CUMBERBATCH.

F. O. 424/184, p. 177, No. 289/1

No. 348

Mr. Herbert to the Marquess of Salisbury.

No. 739. Confidential. CONSTANTINOPLE, *October 29, 1895.*

My Lord, *(Received November 4.)*

I HAVE the honour to forward to your Lordship herewith copy of a despatch which I have received from Her Majesty's Acting Consul at Erzeroum, reporting on the state of things at Erzeroum and in the district.

I have, &c.

(Signed) MICHAEL H. HERBERT.

F. O. 424/184, p. 180, No. 292

Inclosure in No. 348

Consul Cumberbatch to Sir P. Currie.

Sir,   ERZEROUM, *October 17, 1895.*

I HAD the honour to telegraph to your Excellency yesterday that the state of things in Erzeroum and the outlying districts continued in a very critical state, and that the greatest anxiety prevailed on all sides; also that it would encourage the Armenians to maintain the attitude of forbearance which they have so far maintained, and to continue to resist pernicious counsels, if some hope of a favourable turn in affairs in the near future could be held out to them.

To-day I received your Excellency's answer, which will materially assist me in persuading them of the folly of any rash act on their part under present circumstances.

In the meantime the authorities are fully alive to the danger, and the greatest precautions are being taken to prevent a conflict between Christians and Mussulmans.

Strong military patrols are on foot day and night, and a strict watch is kept on the movement of the Turkish as well as the Armenian inhabitants of the town.

The same is the case in towns where there is a garrison, but in the outlying districts matters are in a deplorable state of disorder and confusion. Caravans and smaller parties of Armenians as well as villagers are being mercilessly attacked in all directions by Kurds. The much-frequented road between Erzeroum and Trebizond is infested with marauding bands, chiefly composed of Lazes, who have scattered themselves all over that region after taking part in the sacking of Trebizond, a significant fact being that, before each onslaught, they call upon any Moslems who may be in the party to separate themselves from their Christian fellow-travellers.

Though the authorities have the wish to prevent disturbances, and to put down the unruly Kurds and Lazes, it is more than doubtful if they have the power, and they must be aware of the fact.

I have, &c.

(Signed) H. A. CUMBERBATCH.

F. O. 424/184, p. 180, No. 292/1

No. 349

Mr. Herbert to the Marquess of Salisbury.

No. 740. Confidential.   CONSTANTINOPLE, *October 29, 1895.*
My Lord,   *(Received November 4.)*
    I HAVE the honour to forward to your Lordship herewith copy of a despatch which I have received from Her Majesty's Acting Consul at Erzeroum, giving further details with regard to Shakir Pasha's mission. I am calling the attention of the Grand Vizier to the desirability of the removal of Ismaïl Bey from his staff.
              I have, &c.
                        (Signed) MICHAEL H. HERBERT.
F. O. 424/184, p. 180, No. 293

Inclosure in No. 349

Consul Cumberbatch to Sir P. Currie.

Confidential.
Sir,   ERZEROUM, *October 18, 1895.*
    AS mentioned in my telegram of the 15th instant, Marshal Shakir Pasha returned here from Bayazid that day, after an absence of three weeks.
    He appears to have devoted most of his time to trying to settle quarrels between the Kurdish tribes, and in attempting to instil into the minds of their Chiefs a better respect for the Government. How far he succeeded remains to be seen.
    The peaceful Turkish and Kurdish inhabitants, believing that he had come to redress their wrongs, plied him with Petitions against Kurdish violence, but as a rule he referred them to the permanent authorities.
    No Armenian either dared or was allowed to approach him to set forth his grievances.
    He inspected the various administrative Departments at Hassan-Kaleh and Bayazid, and dismissed the "Mal-Mudiri" (Financial Secretary) of the former place, who was shown to have caused the burning down of the Government offices some time ago in order to destroy the documentary proofs of his defalcations on a large scale.
    Being the originator of the "Hamidieh" corps, it was only natural that he should receive the hearty welcome he did from them all along the route. Reviews were held in his honour, and he had frequent consultations with the officers.
    He has made several reports, recommending, among other things, certain administrative reorganizations and reforms in the Law Courts and Public

Education Department, besides suggesting a plan for the permanent settlement of Kurdish tribes in specially defined districts, and for the institution of a Commission, composed of the Kurdish Chiefs, to decide questions that may arise amongst themselves.

During an unofficial visit I paid him this afternoon the subject of the present disturbed state of things was discussed, but nothing touching his mission, and he mentioned to Raouf Pasha, the new Vali, who was present, that he considered it necessary to remove the notorious Chief of the Haidaranei tribe, Hussein Pasha, of Patnoz, who, I hear, actually defied him, but that the question was how to manage it.

A member of his staff was Ismaïl Bey, Colonel on the staff of the IVth Army Corps, whose Sasun fame is known to your Excellency. This clever and unscrupulous officer did much to thwart independent inquiry, especially in Armenian quarters, as it was he who acted as the Marshal's chief guide and counsellor.

Shakir Pasha considerably helped towards the inquiry into the murder of Mr. Lenz, the American cyclist—in fact, without his assistance the little that has so far been done would not have been otherwise accomplished.

It is probable that he has learnt enough of the principal and most flagrant evils that exist, but, apparently, having little or no executive power, it is difficult to see what immediate benefits are to accrue from his visit.

A Persian complainant at one of the places, not getting the satisfaction he expected out of his Excellency, replied in a most determined tone: "If you, one of the Sultan's most powerful Pashas, are unable to redress our wrongs, there is only His Majesty left to do so, and he will never come here. After your departure our condition will be worse than it ever was, and will end disastrously. I warn you!" This characteristic reply pretty accurately describes the situation as regards Shakir Pasha's tour in the Bayazid district.

He returned through the Khinous Caza, and his arrival in the vicinity of the town of that name at a critical moment no doubt helped to prevent the attack on that town and neighbouring villages, which was contemplated by certain Kurdish tribes, as reported in my despatch of the 11th instant.

The future movements of the Special Mission are not definitely known, but it is expected to proceed shortly to Sivas viâ Erzinghan.

I have, &c.

(Signed) H. A. CUMBERBATCH.

F. O. 424/184, p. 181, No. 293/1

No. 350

Mr. Herbert to the Marquess of Salisbury.

No. 741. Confidential.   CONSTANTINOPLE, *October 29, 1895.*
My Lord,   *(Received November 4.)*

I HAVE the honour to forward to your Lordship herewith copy of a despatch which I have received from Her Majesty's Acting Consul at Erzeroum, announcing that precautionary measures have been maintained to prevent excitement at the news of the acceptance of the reforms.

I have approved Mr. Cumberbatch's action.

I have, &c.

(Signed) MICHAEL H. HERBERT.

F. O. 424/184, p. 182, No. 294

Inclosure in No. 350

Consul Cumberbatch to Sir P. Currie.

Confidential
Sir,   ERZEROUM, *October 18, 1895.*

I HAVE the honour to acknowledge the receipt of your Excellency's telegram, informing me of the acceptance by His Majesty the Sultan of the reforms proposed by the three Powers for the Armenian provinces.

Having heard at the same time that the news had been transmitted from Constantinople by both official and private sources, I considered it necessary under the circumstances to advise the Armenians, through their influential ecclesiastical chief, to carefully abstain from any kind of demonstration which might give rise to a misinterpretation of their intentions in Turkish circles, and I received assurances that my counsels would be followed.

At the same time, I informed the Vali of what I had done, and I expressed a conviction that he would continue to maintain the precautionary measures taken by the authorities to suppress the slightest incident on either side which might lead to a conflict.

I afterwards saw Raouf Pasha, who thanked me for my action, and assured me that he would vouch for the tranquillity of the Turks so long as the Armenians remained quiet.

A more active patrolling of the streets by soliders has been visible to-day, and it is hoped that if both sides persevere in the repression of an expression of feeling, matters will calm down to their normal state.

I have, &c.

(Signed) H. A. CUMBERBATCH.

F. O. 424/184, p. 182, No. 294/1

No. 351

Mr. Herbert to the Marquess of Salisbury.

No. 742.   CONSTANTINOPLE, *October 29, 1895.*
My Lord,   *(Received November 4.)*
    I HAVE the honour to forward to your Lordship herewith copy of a despatch which I have received from Her Majesty's Consul at Trebizond, inclosing a despatch from the Consular Agent at Samsun, reporting apprehensions of disturbances at Samsun, and an attack on the Armenians at Charshamba.
    I am calling the attention of the Porte to the matter.

I have, &c.

(Signed) MICHAEL H. HERBERT.

F. O. 424/184, p. 182, No. 295

Inclosure 1 in No. 351

Consul Longworth to Sir P. Currie.

Sir,   TREBIZOND, *October 18, 1895.*
    I HAVE the honour to inclose herewith copy of a despatch from our Consular Agent at Samsoun, reporting apprehensions of disturbances at Samsoun and an attack on the Armenians at Charshamba.

I have, &c.

(Signed) H. Z. LONGWORTH.

F. O. 424/184, p. 183, No. 295/1

Inclosure 2 in No. 351

Mr. Cortanze to Consul Longworth.

M. le Consul, SAMSOUN, *le 16 Octobre, 1895.*

AUSSITÔT arrivé j'ai été aux renseignements, il en résulte ce qui suit:-

Les Arméniens d'ici ne sont pas en nombre suffisant pour oser tenter l'aventure d'une révolte quelconque. De plus, ils sont presque tous de petits marchands nés dans le pays, et comme tous ceux des villes, d'une lâcheté à nulle autre pareille.

Il n'y a que 200 hommes environ au plus susceptibles de marcher si l'ordre leur en était donné. Une seule chose est à craindre c'est qu'il en vienne de l'intéreur. Les routes sont bien gardées mais ces gens-là ne voyagent pas par les grands chemins. Les bruits les plus divers circulent et les plus absurdes sont ceux qui ont le plus de crédit. Il en résulte donc une surexcitation extrême dans tous les clans et la panique est à son comble. Toutes les affaires, principalement du côté des Arméniens sont arrêtées. Plusieurs magasins sont fermés et tous ceux qui peuvent partent. Beaucoup ne restent qu'à cause que les autorités ne leur donnent point de Teskéré. Il résulte de ce qui précède que pour ce qui concerne les Arméniens je ne crois pas qu'ils oseront quoique cela soit. Il n'y a que de ce côté qu'une crainte, c'est qu'un membre du Comité ne fasse une démonstration quelconque pour amener l'effusion du sang comme ils le disent.

Du côté des Ottomans dans ce cas cela serait le signal des massacres qui seraient, j'en suis certain, plus importants que ceux de Stamboul et de Trébizonde, et cela à cause des 800 Lazes environ qui forment la population marine, sur lesquels les autorités n'ont absolument aucun pouvoir. Ils sont très bien armés et ils n'attendent qu'un signal pour se jeter sur les Arméniens et principalement piller leurs maisons. Outre cela la population Musulmane, qui est la dominante, est très fanatique et déteste cordialement tous les Chrétiens et plus encore peut-être même les autorités.

En un mot, toute cette population, qui est bien armée, n'attend qu'un signal pour le pillage et pour s'offrir des têtes de l'ennemi détesté.

Quant aux autorités, le Mutessarif en tête, elles paraissent animées du ferme désir de maintenir l'ordre, [*sic*] quelques mesures qui me paraissent devoir être de bien peu d'efficacité en cas de conflit, ce n'est pas sur cela que je base ma croyance dans le maintien de l'ordre dans notre ville, mais bien plus sur la faiblesse des uns et sur la force des autres qui démontrent aux deux parties mieux que tous les raisonnements qu'il n'y a rien à espérer et rien à craindre.

Veuillez, &c.

(Signé) H. DE CORTANZE.

P.S. *Le 17 Octobre.*—Je viens à l'instant d'apprendre qu'il y a eu hier à 3 heures du soir à Charshamba des troubles assez importants. Les Arméniens auraient fermés leurs magasins et se seraient portés en masse chez le Caïmacam. Il y a eu, dit-on, plusieurs morts; je ne puis encore en savoir le nombre. Aussitôt que j'aurai des renseignements je vous en ferai part.

H. De C.

F. O. 424/184, p. 183, No. 295/2

No. 352

Mr. Herbert to the Marquess of Salisbury.

No. 744.   THERAPIA, *October 29, 1895.*
My Lord,   *(Received November 4.)*
    I HAVE the honour to transmit to your Lordship herewith copy of a despatch which I have received from Her Majesty's Consul at Trebizond reporting on the situation, and stating that his Turkish scribe, an Armenian, had been imprisoned.
    Strong representations were at once made at the Sublime Porte to the effect that the servants of Her Majesty's Consulate were not to be interfered with, and telegraphic instructions have been sent accordingly to the Vali of Trebizond.
                        I have, &c.
                                        (Signed) MICHAEL H. HERBERT.

F. O. 424/184, p. 184, No. 296

Inclosure in No. 352

Consul Longworth to Sir P. Currie.

Sir,   TREBIZOND, *October 17, 1895.*
    THE situation here is not yet one to inspire confidence. The two Armenian lads, Gasparoglou and Stephanoglou, who, it is said, wounded the Pashas on the 2nd instant and a Turk on the night of the 4th instant, have not been discovered either among the dead or living. So long as they are at large, it is feared that by their firing at some one disturbances may break out again.
    The Russian gun-boat is still in port without allowing any one to land, while the Russian Consulate, I hear, has closed its gates to outsiders.
    As I telegraphed to your Excellency this morning, the court-martial is occupied entirely in arresting and examining Armenians. It is even said that some of them will be shot. No Turks have as yet been arrested, and this Consultate is viewed with suspicion by the military. I am quite helpless under the circumstances, and it is in vain that the poor people are appealing to me for protection. There are three Armenian gentlemen connected with this Consulate: my Dragoman, Mr Gomidas Hekimian, my supernumerary clerk, Mr. Vartan Fetradjian, and my

Turkish scribe, Mr. Joseph Mikaëlian. The last-named is in gaol, but the other two are at present under my roof. Convinced as I am of their not having taken part in any conspiracy, I sincerely trust that your Excellency, on receipt of my this day's telegram, will have caused an order to be issued that they should not be even questioned without my being present, at least during their examination.

As public security is being maintained in town, I am thinking of sending away the guard of soldiers placed at my disposal. Such a move on my part I believe would inspire confidence among the Christians, conciliate the Turks, and please the authorities. Before doing so, however, I shall first consult the Vali as to whether he can guarantee the non-recurrence of troubles in the immediate future.

I have, &c.

(Signed) H. Z. LONGWORTH.

F. O. 424/184, p. 184, No. 296/1

No. 353

Mr. Herbert to the Marquess of Salisbury.

No. 552.   CONSTANTINOPLE, *October 30, 1895, 10 a.m.*
Telegraphic.   *(Received October 30.)*

THE Representatives of the six Great Powers have received a Circular letter from the Armenian Patriarch begging them to make representations to the Sublime Porte with a view to having a stop put to the massacres of Armenians now taking place in the provinces.

F. O. 424/184, p. 142, No. 209

No. 354

Mr. Herbert to the Marquess of Salisbury.

No. 553.   CONSTANTINOPLE, *October 30, 1895, 10.10 a.m.*
Telegraphic.   *(Received October 30.)*

A LETTER from the Minister of the Interior to the Minister for Foreign Affairs, requesting that the missionaries should be recalled from Sasun on the ground that the Bitlis authorities regarded their distribution of relief as giving rise to serious objections, was yesterday communicated by the Porte to the Acting First Dragoman.

Mr. Marinitch expressed his regret that the Bitlis authorities should so misunderstand the charitable intentions of the missionaires, and deprecated the receipt of such a communication.

I do not propose to take any notice of this communication of the Sublime Porte.

F. O. 424/184, pp. 142-143, No. 210

No. 355

Mr. Herbert to the Marquess of Salisbury.

No. 554.   CONSTANTINOPLE, *October 30, 1895, 7.30 p.m.*
Telegraphic.   *(Received October 30.)*

HER Majesty's Consul at Aleppo telegraphs that the Armenians in the city are being disarmed, but not the Mussulmans, that the calling out of the Reserves has caused great excitement, and that Europeans have been insulted and windows broken.

Mr. Barnham adds that disturbances are reported at Beilan.

F. O. 424/184, p. 143, No. 211

No. 356

Mr. Herbert to the Marquess of Salisbury.

No. 555.   CONSTANTINOPLE, *October 30, 1895, 8.10 p.m.*
Telegraphic.   *(Received October 30.)*

YOUR Lordship's telegram No. 198 of yesterday.

I had already anticipated your Lordship's instructions, and have to-day renewed my representations to the Porte. I also insisted that orders should be sent for the protection of the Armenians of Sasun after the departure of the missionaires, and, further, that the latter, if compelled to withdraw temporarily, should be allowed to return to their relief work as soon as the promised reinforcements arrive.

I have asked the United States' Minister to support my representations, which he has done.

F. O. 424/184, p. 143, No. 212

No. 357

Mr. Herbert to the Marquess of Salisbury.

No. 556. Confidential. CONSTANTINOPLE, *October 30, 1895, 11.25 p.m.*
Telegraphic. *(Received October 30.)*

WITH reference to my telegram to your Lordship No. 551 of yesterday, I have the honour to state that I was confidentially asked this morning by Saïd Pasha whether I had any objection to his proposed appointment as President of the Commision of Control.

I replied that we objected to the post being combined with that of Minister for Foreign Affairs, and we desired that the Commission should be of an administrative, and not of a political, character, and entirely independent of the Porte; if, however, he was ready to resign the Ministry for Foreign Affairs, we should no doubt welcome his appointment as President of the Commission. Saïd Pasha, after long discussion, said that, in view of my objections, his appointment would not be proceeded with. I thanked his Excellency for showing so much deference to the wishes of Her Majesty's Government, and expressed the hope that the Porte would be able to find for the post a good independent man whose appointment would meet with the approval of the Powers.

F. O. 424/184, p. 143, No. 213

No. 358

Mr. Herbert to the Marquess of Salisbury.

No. 557. CONSTANTINOPLE, *October 30, 1895, 11.40 p.m.*
Telegraphic. *(Received October 30.)*

I HAVE sounded the Ambassadors as to what answer should be returned to the Patriarch's Circular letter which formed the subject of my telegram No. 552 of to-day.

The situation in the provinces is very bad, though no fresh disturbances have been reported during the last twenty-four hours, and I think something ought to be done besides individual representations, of which little notice is taken by the Porte.

F. O. 424/184, p. 144, No. 214

No. 359

Mr. Herbert to the Marquess of Salisbury.

No. 558.   CONSTANTINOPLE, *October 30, 1895, midnight.*
Telegraphic.   *(Received October 30.)*

IN view of the action of the Porte in persisting, in spite of our representations, in their refusal to communicate the plan of reforms to the Armenian Patriarch, I, to-day, having previously obtained the approval of the Russian and French Ambassadors, handed to his Beatitude printed copies of the reforms, and of the correspondence accompanying them.

I propose to-morrow to renew my request to the Grand Vizier to have the reforms communicated to the Patriarch, and, in the event of his refusing, I shall request permission for his Beatitude to print an Armenian translation of the reforms in the form of a pamphlet for distribution among his people.

F. O. 424/184, p. 144, No. 215

No. 360

Mr. Herbert to the Marquess of Salisbury.

No. 561 A.   CONSTANTINOPLE, *October 30, 1895, 11.50 p.m.*
Telegraphic.   *(Received October 30.)*

MY telegram of to-day No. 555.

I have to ask for your Lordship's instructions as to whether I should continue to take the initiative in measures for the protection of the missionaries, who, although distributing English Relief Fund, are all American citizens. The United States' Minister appears to think it is for me to take the first steps.

F. O. 424/184, p. 144, No. 216

No. 361

Sir E. Monson to the Marquess of Salisbury.

No. 78.   VIENNA, *October 30, 1895.*
Telegraphic.   *(Received October 30.)*

WITH reference to the telegram addressed to me by your Lordship No. 69, I have the honour to report that His Majesty the Emperor has expressed his qualification at these assurances through Count Goluchowski, and also His Majesty's personal wish that in questions connected with the Mediterranean and

South-East Europe there should be the most thorough understanding with Her Majesty's Government.

F. O. 424/184, p. 144, No. 217

No. 362

Mr. Herbert to the Marquess of Salisbury.

No. 747.   THERAPIA, *October 30, 1895.*

My Lord,   *(Received November 4.)*

WITH reference to the telegram No. 550 of the 29th instant, I have the honour to report that on the receipt of Mr. Hampson's telegram of the 28th instant respecting the threats of the chief Mussulmans of Mush, I called on the United States' Minister, and asked him what action he proposed to take in regard to the American missionaries at Sasun. Mr. Terrell, after consultation with Mr. Dwight, the head of the Bible House at Stamboul, decided that in view of the risk mentioned by Mr. Hampson, it would be better to ask the missionaries to withdraw temporarily, and it was agreed that I should send a telegram to Mr. Hampson in this sense. I subsequently called on the Grand Vizier, whom I found at the Palace in company with the Minister for Foreign Affairs, and protested most strongly at the threats used by the Mussulmans at Mush, informing them at the same time that I should hold the Ottoman Government responsible for the lives and property of every missionary at Sasun and for any disturbances which might occur there. I also pointed out what a deplorable effect the enforced withdrawal of the missionaries from their charitable and humane work would produce in England.

The Grand Vizier promised to send instant orders to the local authorites at Mush for the protection of the missionaries, and he stated that if he learnt that there were not enough soldiers on the spot to insure their safety more troops would be dispatched there. In the latter event, he suggested that the missionaries should withdraw temporarily to Mush until the reinforcements arrived, when they could return to Sasun and resume their relief work.

I told his Highness, in reply, that if it was found necessary to withdraw the missionaries temporarily, it must be distinctly understood that they should be allowed to return to Sasun directly the reinforcements arrived.

The United States' Minister said, at our interview in the morning, that he would make similar representations.

I have, &c.

(Signed) MICHAEL H. HERBERT.

F. O. 424/184, pp. 184-185, No. 297

No. 363

Mr. Herbert to the Marquess of Salisbury.

No. 748.   THERAPIA, *October 30, 1895.*
My Lord,   *(Received November 4.)*
WITH reference to my telegram of the 30th instant, I have the honour to
transmit to your Lordship herewith a copy of a letter addressed by the Gregorian-
Armenian Partiarch to the Embassies of the Powers at Constantinople, asking for
their intervention to prevent the continuance of massacres in Asia Minor.

I told his Beatitude yesterday that Her Majesty's Embassy were making, and
would continue to make, strong representations to the Porte on the subject of the
massacres in the provinces, but that I could not tell him whether any collective
action would be taken until I had seen the Representatives of the other Powers.

I have, &c.

(Signed) MICHAEL H. HERBERT.

F. O. 424/184, p. 185, No. 298

Inclosure in No. 363

The Armenian Patriarch to Mr. Herbert.

M. le Chargé d'Affaires,   CONSTANTINOPLE, *le 16 (28) Octobre, 1895.*
PAR notre précédent écrit que nous avons eu l'honneur d'adresser à votre
Excellence le 27 du mois dernier, nous avions pris la liberté de solliciter votre
bienveillante attention sur le besoin de mesures immédiates et radicales, propres à
ramener une complète sécurité dans la capitale, et à empêcher le renouvellement
dans les provinces des massacres dont tant de personnes non armées et innocentes
tombèrent victimes à Constantinople.

Nous regrettons de nous voir dans la nécessité de revenir aujourd'hui sur la
même question et d'établir que la crainte éprouvée par nous à l'endroit des
provinces se change désormais en une navrante réalité, et que la vie des Arméniens
Chrétiens s'y trouve vouée à des carnages et leur propriété à la déprédation.

Selon nos premières informations reçues des provinces de Trébizonde et dans
les bourgades environnantes une grande quantité d'Arméniens Chrétiens ont été
égorgés sans merci, et leurs biens, pour une valeur totale considérable, livrés au
pillage; de même, dans le village d'Akhissar d'Ismidt, nombre d'Arméniens ont été
tués par la populace Turque, leurs marchandises et leurs effets ont été enlevés, et il
paraît que ce soit au su du Moudir lui-même qui, avant le massacre, avait fait

fouiller les Arméniens s'assurant qu'ils étaient sans armes et incapables de se défendre; les autres villages d'Ismidt, ainsi que l'Évêque du diocèse venu à Constantinople nous l'a déclaré en personne, et le confirme par écrit de son diocèse, sont exposés aux mêmes dangers, et déjà on mentionne le village Khendek, habité par les Arméniens, comme étant sous menace.

Un télégramme daté du 14 (26) Octobre, et signé par les chefs spirituels des communautés Arménienne, Arméno-Catholique, et Protestante de Marache, informe que les Musulmans de cette ville, attaquant les Chrétiens en ont blessé un grand nombre, et quoique les chefs spirituels aient sollicité par les démarches auprès du Gouverneur Commandant Militaire des mesures de nature à prévenir l'agitation, leur demande n'a pas été prise en considération et la populace, encouragée par cette insouciance, a commencé le massacre qui continue. On informe de l'Évêché de Baybourd, que des Lazes venus de Surméné et la population Turque ont attaqués les villages environnants et commis des meurtres, des viols, et des pillages. On mande du diocèse de Kharput que des armes sont distribuées aux habitants Turcs de la ville et des villages, et en demande aide pour prévenir un massacre imminent.

Des renseignements venus d'Eghin il résulte que toute la ville ainsi que les campagnes sont en butte au même danger; enfin, on annonce successivement d'Amassia, de Kemakh, de Hassan Ova, et de diverses autres contrées l'armememt des Musulmans, les préparatifs de massacre, et des pillages déjà commencés.

D'un autre côté à Constantinople même et, comme conséquence du récent massacre, les familles éloignées de leurs demeures, les gens de province ayant dû abandonner leurs gîtes se trouvent toujours en proie à la même terreur; des manœuvres, dépouillés, restent sand manger et demandent assistance; des parents éplorés réclament leurs enfants disparus; de ceux qui avaient été arbitrairement arrêtés, il en existent qui n'ont pas été encore relâchés; les arrestations continuent; et le chiffre des tués, qui paraît considérable, demeure indeterminé.

Nous pensons, Excellence, que la situation aiguë actuelle et l'extension, tous les jours plus menaçante, des massacres, à raison même de leur caractère exceptionnel et de l'imminence d'un formidable péril, exigent, pour avoir une fin, des dispositions exceptionnelles, urgentes et énergiques, grâce auxquelles les massacres entrepris contre les Chrétiens s'arrêtent sans retard; une enquête soit ouverte, qui soit susceptible d'aboutir à la découverte des malfaiteurs et à leur châtiment selon la justice, et pour exemple aux autres, afin qu'ils ne soient point encouragés à de nouveaux crimes; les personnes éprouvées touchent quelque réparation, qui les aide à procurer de quoi subsister; les détenus soient mis en liberté; les rigueurs, occasionnées par la perception des impôts, cessent; en un mot, la tranquillité soit rétablie.

Nous nous permettons, Excellence, de recommander de nouveau à votre haute attention cet état de choses, et ces quelques considérations, et d'implorer de vous la grâce de continuer à prêter en vue de résultat désiré votre concours et vos soins précieux, dont nous avons déjà enregistré avec gratitude les effets beinfaisants dans les circonstances difficiles que nous traversons.

En confiant, &c.

(Signé) MATTÉAS,
Patriarche des Arméniens de Turquie.

F. O. 424/184, pp. 185-186, No. 298/1

No. 364

Mr. Herbert to the Marquess of Salisbury.

No. 559.   CONSTANTINOPLE, *October 31, 1895, 12.15 a.m.*
Telegraphic.   *(Received October 31.)*

WITH reference to Sir P. Currie's telegram No. 516 of the 21st instant, I have the honour to report that I have been informed by the Russian Ambassador that he considered that the claim which, as he understood, was being advanced by the Representatives of the other Powers to the right of communicating with the Commission of Control through their Dragomans would only increase the difficulty of arriving at a joint decision as to recommendations to be made to the Porte, and that he was therefore opposed to it.

M. de Nélidoff also said that he did not see why the advantages which had been obtained by the efforts of France, Russia, and England should be shared by the other Powers. He had, however, received no instructions on the subject from his Government, and was expressing only his personal opinion.

In a conversation with Mr. Marinitch, the Russian First Dragoman uttered a similar opinion.

F. O. 424/184. p. 145, No. 218

No. 365

Mr. Herbert to the Marquess of Salisbury.

No. 560.   CONSTANTINOPLE, *October 31, 1895, 12.30 a.m.*
Telegraphic.   *(Received October 31.)*

MY telegram of yesterday No. 558.

At my interview with the Patriarch I asked him to distribute copies of the plan of reforms which I had given him, and made an earnest appeal to his Beatitude to do all in his power to tranquillize his people, and induce them to keep the peace.

The Patriarch promised me that he would do his utmost to carry out my wishes, and said that, now that the three Embassies had communicated to him officially a copy of the reforms, he would telegraph to the Armenian Bishops in the Anatolian provinces informing them of the issue of the reforms, and instructing them to advise the people not to resort to violence, but await with confidence the execution of the reforms.

He then went on to point out with considerable warmth that the question of the reforms had become now only of secondary importance; that we had now a question of life and death confronting us; that unless the Powers at once took some action to prevent the recurrence of the massacres which were occuring in all quarters of the Empire the entire Armenian population of Turkey would soon be exterminated.

F. O. 424/184, p. 145, No. 219

No. 366

Mr. Herbert to the Marquess of Salisbury.

No. 561.   CONSTANTINOPLE, *October 31, 1895, 10 a.m.*
Telegraphic.   *(Received October 31.)*

HER Majesty's Vice-Consul at Mush telegraphed yesterday that he had received no further news from Bitlis during the day, and that things at Mush were quiet, and some shops were open, but that the town was full of Kurds.

Mr. Hampson reports that the Kurds are murdering and robbing in every direction, and that six villages in the plain were pillaged during the night of the 29th. He had also heard that the Kurds had pillaged the large village of Koultouk, two hours from Bitlis, and had killed many Armenians.

F. O. 424/184, p. 145, No. 220

No. 367

Mr. Herbert to the Marquess of Salisbury.

No. 562.   CONSTANTINOPLE, *October 31, 1895, 10.15 a.m.*
Telegraphic.   *(Received October 31.)*

MR. HAMPSON telegraphed from Mush last night that the situation is most serious in that vilayet, and that he fears much for Sasun. He believes the authorities are unable to control the Kurds, who are everywhere attacking the Armenian villages, murdering the chief men, and committing every excess.

F. O. 424/184. p. 146, No. 221

No. 368

Mr. Herbert to the Marquess of Salisbury.

No. 563.   CONSTANTINOPLE, *October 31, 1895, 11.10 a.m.*
Telegraphic.   *(Received October 31.)*

THE Acting British Consul at Erzeroum telegraphs that disturbances occured there yesterday, that the Turkish mob pillaged the Armenian shops, and that the number of killed and wounded on both sides was considerable. The Armenians, he says, were still continuing a desultory fire from their houses.

The military authorities appear to have displayed great activity in restraining the Mussulman mob.

F. O. 424/184, p. 146, No. 222

No. 369

Mr. Herbert to the Marquess of Salisbury.

No. 564.   CONSTANTINOPLE, *October 31, 1895.*
Telegraphic.   *(Received October 31.)*

WITH reference to the withdrawal of the American missionaries from Mush, Vice-Consul Hampson telegraphs to-day as follows:-

"The Mussulmans pretend to believe that the missionaries are inciting the Armenians of Sasun to attack Mussulmans of Mush, and this is the reason why they demanded their recall. I fear I did not make this clear in my telegram of the 28th October.

"Missionaries themselves are most unwilling to leave Sasun, fearing the worst results from panic which would ensue there. Mutessarif, who is violently anti-Protestant, absolutely refused to take any responsibility or give an opinion. All the principal Mussulmans adhere to their demand. The Armenians dread a massacre next Friday.

"I hope I shall be excused, under these circumstances, for having this evening made the following communications to the Mutessarif, as if from the Embassy:

" 'If the Mutessarif states that the recall of missionaries is necessary for the tranquillity of Mush, you may recall them temporarily. Anyhow, the Mutessarif is responsible for the safety of missionaries, and for the tranquillity of Mush.'

"Mutessarif at last gave a formal answer, which I told him I would communicate to you. He said that although inhabitants of Mush demanded recall of missionaries, he saw no necessity for it, and in any case he would guarantee there would be no disturbance here.

"I think, under the circumstances, that the recall of the missionaries would risk a panic in Sasun, and would be humiliating."

Mr. Hampson reports that from all sides he hears of more murders and outrages by Kurds.

F. O. 424/184, p. 146, No. 223

No. 370

Mr. Herbert to the Marquess of Salisbury.

No. 565.   CONSTANTINOPLE, *October 31, 1895.*
Telegraphic.   *(Received October 31.)*

MR. BARNHAM telegraphs that the attitude of Mussulmans at Aleppo is very threatening, and the general situation becomes worse every day,

The Zeitounlis have surrounded the Turkish troops between Zeitoun and Marash and reinforcements of Reserves are still leaving Aleppo.

It will have very serious consequences if, as is possible, the Turkish troops are beaten. The Ferik of Acre will arrive at Aleppo to-morrow to take command of the expedition.

The disturbances at Beilan have not been confirmed.

F. O. 424/184, p. 147, No. 224

No. 371

Mr. Herbert to the Marquess of Salisbury.

No. 566.   CONSTANTINOPLE, *October 31, 1895, 6.45 p.m.*
Telegraphic.   *(Received October 31.)*

I HAVE sent the following telegram to Mr. Hampson with reference to my telegram to your Lordship No. 564 of the 31st October:-

"In view of promise of Mutessarif, American Minister desires missionaries to decide for themselves whether they will leave at present."

F. O. 424/184, p. 147, No. 225

No. 372

The Marquess of Salisbury to Mr. Herbert.

No. 199.
Telegraphic.   FOREIGN OFFICE, *October 31, 1895, 4.30 p.m.*
    I HAVE received your telegram No. 553 of yesterday, stating that the Porte
had communicated to the Dragoman of Her Majesty's Embassy an application
from the Minister of the Interior for the recall of the American missionaries from
the Sasun district.
    I approve your intention to leave this communication unnoticed.
    F. O. 424/184, p. 147, No. 226

No. 373

The Marquess of Salisbury to Mr. Herbert.

No. 200.
Telegraphic.   FOREIGN OFFICE, *October 31, 1895, 11 p.m.*
    I ENTIRELY approve your proceedings in connection with the question of
communicating to the Armenian Patriarch the plan of reforms, as reported in your
telegram No. 558 of yesterday.
    F. O. 424/184, p. 147, No. 227

No. 374

Mr. Herbert to the Marquess of Salisbury.

No. 754,   CONSTANTINOPLE, *October 31, 1895.*
My Lord,   *(Received November 4.)*
    I HAVE the honour to forward to your Lordship herewith copy of a despatch
which I have received from the Acting British Consul at Angora, reporting upon
the recent state of affairs in that town.
                            I have, &c.
                                          (Signed) MICHAEL H. HERBERT.
    F. O. 424/184, p. 188, No. 301

Inclosure in No. 374

Acting Consul Fontana to Sir P. Currie.

Confidential.

Sir,   ANGORA, *October 26, 1895.*

I HAVE the honour to report to your Excellency that from the date of the recent demonstrations at Constantinople up to that of the acceptation by the Sultan of the scheme of reforms great anxiety prevailed among the Christians of all sects in this town. As soon as the news of the slaughter of Armenians at Stamboul and Kassim Pasha was received here, the Mussulmans began secretly to purchase arms and ammunition, and threatened openly in the market-place to exterminate, when sufficiently armed, every Christian in Angora.

The son of Attar Bashi Ali Effendi, a local Turk of some note, is said to have sold within two weeks £ T. 50 worth of ammunition alone. Government officials, merchants, and labourers alike purchased from him; he refused, however, to sell to any but Mussulmans.

A Committee, composed of six fanatical Turks, met in private to arrange for a sudden and simultaneous attack upon the Christians in the various quarters of the town and in the suburbs; and its members did their best individually to excite the fanaticism of the lower class Turks against their Christian neighbours.

The Vali has made strenuous and hitherto successful efforts to prevent disturbances of any kind. He forbade the sale of arms, and upon hearing of the proceedings of the six men referred to sent them off, one by one, under police escort, to various parts of the vilayet. He formed a special guard to patrol the town both day and night, under strict orders to at once arrest any disorderly Christian or Turk, and sent injunctions to the various café proprietors in the town to forbid any discussion upon, or even allusion to, political questions among the customers on their premises.

Memdouh Pasha informed me, however, that he would be powerless to restore order should a collision once take place between Turks and Armenians; that the regular troops stationed at Angora amounted, all told, to less than 100, and that the local police force was insufficient even in ordinary times. He requested me to do my best to prevent any rash act on the part of the Armenians; but the efforts I made to that end were quite unnecessary.

At Yuzgat and at Cæsarea the tension has been very great. The Armenians in the latter town barricaded, until a few days ago, their shops and dwellings, and comparatively few ventured into the streets. At Yuzgat, I am informed, there are some twenty-eight Mussulmans who returned last year from Mecca, and certain of whom have received decorations from the Sultan. These pilgrims are the chief cause for anxiety to the local Christians owing to their fanaticism, and to the influence they possess over their Mahommedan fellow-townsmen.

There is, however, a battalion of reserves stationed there, which would suffice, under wise leadership, to nip in the bud any preliminary hostilities between Christians and Turks.

I have, &c.

(Signed) RAPHAEL A. FONTANA.

F. O. 424/184, p. 189, No. 301/1

No. 375

Mr. Herbert to the Marquess of Salisbury.

No. 752.   CONSTANTINOPLE, *October 31, 1895.*
My Lord,   *(Received November 4.)*

I HAVE the honour to forward to your Lordship herewith copy of a despatch which I have received from Her Majesty's Consul at Aleppo respecting the revolutionary movement in the vilayet. I propose to speak to the Grand Vizier respecting the character of the present Vali, as reported in Mr. Barnham's despatch.

I have, &c.

(Signed) MICHAEL H. HERBERT.

F. O. 424/184, p. 187, No. 300

Inclosure in No. 375

Consul Barnham to Sir P. Currie.

Confidential.
Sir,   ALEPPO, *October 14, 1895.*

I HAVE the honour to inform your Excellency that a few days ago I received a visit from an Armenian gentleman, a respected resident of Aleppo, who showed me a letter which he had received from an Armenian Notable at Aintab, in which he was requested to call upon me as British Consul, and ask for my authority that the revolutionary party in Aintab should make a demonstration on the grounds and under the conditions given below.

The writer stated that he was requested by the members of the party to ask me the following question:-

"As they had no hope that in the reforms which would be granted by the Imperial Government special guarantees would be given for the protection of Armenians in outlying districts, such as Aintab, Marash, and Zeitoun, they asked me if I was of opinion that they would further the cause of the Armenians in that region by causing a demonstration to be made immediately in that part of the vilayet, and, if so, would I authorize it?"

My visitor was requested, in the event of receiving an answer in the negative, to communicate it to his correspondent by the following code telegram: "Hadji Yemé" ("Do not take the medicine").

After taking notes of this letter, I requested my visitor to burn it in my presence, which he at once did, and I told him to send by a trusty messenger such an answer as would convey to these misguided persons in the most emphatic manner that the English Government does not approve of any such act, and to use every endeavour to dissuade them from taking a course which would inevitably bring upon them great suffering, and must hamper the Powers in endeavouring to bring about a solution of the question.

This happened three days ago. I have heard nothing since, and trust that my action will have had the desired effect, and that it meets with your Excellency's approval.

A proposal of a similar nature was recently made to the British Vice-Consul at Alexandretta as regards a demonstration at Pyas.

The situation is extremely dangerous at Aintab, Marash, Zeitoun, and at Pyas, in the Vilayet of Adana.

I have already reported how many Armenians had recently joined the revolutionary party in Aintab owing to the continued presence in that city of Aghasé, the Hunchag leader.

While the attention of the Government is directed to the movement in Suedia, there is no question that the paramount danger exists in the north of the vilayet, where the Armenian population is considerable, that in the cities of Aintab and Marash being, in each case, 15,000 approximately.

I am inclined to think that the danger of an accidental collision between Moslems and Christians is greater at Marash than at Aintab, where the Mussulman population is more Turkish than Arab, and therefore more sensitive about the Armenian question. Where, as in the city of Aleppo, the Arab element predominates, and the Armenian population is insignificant, that question is not likely to provoke a spontaneous conflict.

At Aintab, the Government is drawing the enmity of both sects upon itself. An order has been promulgated for the immediate collection of the road tax—now five years in arrear—the sum demanded from Aintab alone amounting to 9,000 Turkish liras. This is a special tax, which has been assessed and paid with some irregularity for the past twenty-eight years.

Under the régime of Djemil Pasha a similar collection of arrears was ordered, and 42,000 medjidiés were sent from Aintab to Aleppo.

The only work to show for all this money is some 5 or 6 miles of road built from the city in the direction of Killis, and over ground requiring very little labour. In view of this, the people are at last refusing to pay the tax any longer, without assurance that it will be expended on the object for which it is assessed. The local authorities, under urgent demands from Aleppo, are resorting to the severest measures, and many have been imprisoned.

The authorities are in the meantime preoccupied with the situation at Suedia, where they anticipate an explosion when they commence to collect the taxes.

The Commandant recently informed me that some bombs had been discovered in the district and forwarded to Constantinople. Troops have been gradually drafted into the district from Aleppo and from Damascus, and six pieces of cannon have recently left for Suedia. A Turkish corvette is off the coast. If the Ansariyeh take part against the authorities there may be serious fighting, otherwise the movement would be immediately suppressed.

Whatever abuses exist in this vilayet, and whatever troubles are impending, have been greatly provoked by the personal action of the present Vali of Aleppo, whose presence here at this time is, in the public opinion, a source of great danger, owing to his inveterate hatred of Christians, and the universal prayer of the people throughout the province is that he may be removed.

His Highness, the present Grand Vizier, who was formerly Vali here and knows the vilayet well, is aware of the character of the present Vali and of the mischief he has done here, and it is therefore greatly hoped that he will soon be dismissed.

On the other hand, if the public peace has not been disturbed in the neighbourhood of Aleppo, it is certainly due to his Excellency Edhem Pasha, the Commander of the Troops, whose conduct in the present critical state of affairs is deserving of the greatest praise.

I have, &c.

(Signed) HENRY D. BARNHAM.

F. O. 424/188, pp. 187-188, No. 300/1

No. 376

Mr. Herbert to the Marquess of Salisbury.

No. 750.   THERAPIA, *October 31, 1895.*
My Lord,   *(Received November 4.)*

MGR. AZARIAN, the Catholic Armenian Patriarch, called at this Embassy yesterday afternoon, and was received in my absence by Mr. Eliot.

He said he was visiting all the Embassies with the view of ascertaining whether it was true, as he had heard, that the Catholic Armenian Bishops at Mush and Erzeroum had been killed during the recent disturbances. He was informed that Her Majesty's Embassy had received no information to this effect.

He then spoke in strong terms of the terrible situation in the provinces, and expressed the hope that the Powers would use their influence to prevent the continuance of massacres. His language, however, was vague, and he did not definitely ask for the intervention of Her Majesty's Embassy.

In alluding to the recent events in Zeitoun and Marasch, he stated that, according to information received from his Bishops there, the Armenians had been attacked by the Turks, and had only fired on the latter in self-defence.

The greater part of his visit, however, was occupied by an eulogy of Sakis Ohannes Effendi, whom he desired to see named as Catholic member of the Commission of Control about to be established. I have not as yet any detailed information about this gentleman, but his candidature is supported by the French Ambassador.

Mgr. Azarian was till lately regarded as the tool of the Turkish Government, and certain publications which he made after the Sasun massacres, exculpating the Turkish authorities, and throwing the blame on the Armenians, made him an object of hatred to most of the latter. It is said, however, that the very direct menaces of assassination which he has received from the Hindchag Committee have inspired him with more patriotic views.

I have, &c.

(Signed) MICHAEL H. HERBERT.

F. O. 424/184, pp. 186-187, No. 299

No. 377

Mr. Herbert to the Marquess of Salisbury.

No. 751.   THERAPIA, October 31, 1895.
My Lord,   (*Received November 5.*)

I HAVE the honour to transmit to your Lordship herewith a copy of a letter which Sir Philip Currie addressed to the Gregorian Armenian Patriarch, communicating to him the scheme of reforms and other documents.

I am also urging the Sublime Porte, at the request of his Beatitude, to communicate to him officially the text of the reforms, and permit him to publish and circulate it in an Armenian translation.

I have also, at the desire of the French Ambassador, addressed to the Armenian Catholic Patriarch a letter identical with that sent to Mgr. Ismirlian.

I have, &c.

(Signed) MICHAEL H. HERBERT.

F. O. 424/184, p. 193, No. 315

Inclosure in No. 377

Sir P. Currie to the Patriarch of the Armenians of Turkey and the Patriarch of the Armenian Catholics.

Monseigneur,   THERPIA, *October 28, 1895.*
WITH the consent of the Russian and French Ambassadors, I have the honour to transmit to your Beatitude herewith copies of a *note verbale* addressed to me by the Sublime Porte, and containing the schedule of the reforms to be introduced in the six vilayets of Van, Sivas, Erzeroum, Bitlis, Kharput, and Diarbekir, as well as the Vizierial letter ordering their execution.

I also inclose a copy of the note addressed by the three Ambassadors to the Sublime Porte, acknowledging the receipt of this communication, and formulating certain reserves with respect to the extension of the reforms to Cazas outside the six vilayets, and the right of the three Embassies to object to the nomination of unsuitable officials.

I have, &c.

(Signed) PHILIP CURRIE.

F. O. 424/184, pp. 193-194, No. 315/1

No. 378

Saïd Pasha to Morel Bey.

                                                   CONSTANTINOPLE, *le 1 Novembre, 1895.*
Télégraphique.   *(Communicated by Morel Bey, November 1.)*
LE 30 Octobre, quelques jeunes Arméniens se sont rendus à l'Hôtel du Gouvernement à Erzeroum et ont tiré sur le Commandant de la Gendarmerie, sans l'atteindre; mais l'un d'eux ayant tué un sous-officier à coups de revolver, les fonctionnaires de garde ont riposté, et pendant la fusillade les dits Arméniens furent tués.

Une panique s'en est suivie, et dans la bagarre qui eut lieu entre Musulmans et Arméniens, une cinquantaine de personnes furent tuées et blessées de part et d'autre.

Grâce aux mesures promptes et énergiques prises par les autorités Impériales, l'ordre et la sécurité sont rétablis.

Un Arménien qui avait, pendant l'incident, recommandé à ses coreligionnaires de fermer leurs boutiques, a été arrêté.

Une enquête est ouverte à propos de ces événements.

F. O. 424/184, pp. 147-148, No. 228

No. 379

Saïd Pasha to Morel Bey.

CONSTANTINOPLE, *le 1 Novembre, 1895.*
Télégraphique.   *(Communicated by Morel Bey, November 1.)*

D'APRÈS des nouvelles reçues de Marach le Colonel Commandant de la caserne de Zéitoun et les 400 soldats qui s'y trouvent sont cernés par un nombre très considérable d'insurgés Arméniens.

Les Arméniens de Marach, armés, se seraient de leur côté réunis par groupes dans leurs maisons et n'attendent qu'un signal de Zéitoun pour se livrer à des excès.

D'autres Arméniens arrivant de tous les côtés incendient et détruisent les villages Musulmans des districts d'Andrine et d'Elbistan.

Le Vali d'Alep télégraphie de son côté qu'avant-hier le prêtre Khorène, domicilié à Seferelias, s'est rendu de nuit à Ourfa pour se concerter clandestinement avec les Arméniens de la ville.

Dès son retour vingt Arméniens sont sorti de la maison qu'il venait de quitter et ont tiré des coups de feu sur la patrouille qui passait et ont blessé un zaptié.

F. O. 424/184, p. 148, No. 229

No. 380

Mr. Herbert to the Marquess of Salisbury.

No. 567.   CONSTANTINOPLE, *November 1, 1895, 11 a.m.*
Telegraphic.   *(Received November 1.)*

I AM making urgent representations to the Sublime Porte about the following telegram which I received from Mush to-day:-

"A letter dated yesterday states that the missionaries in Bitlis are in imminent peril. Unless help arrives quickly for both Bitlis and elsewhere, I fear few Christians will be spared. The Protestant pastor at Boulanik was killed last night. Many of the former pupils of missionaries have been killed. Being practically besieged by Kurds, the missionaries are unable to telegraph."

F. O. 424/184, p. 148, No. 230

No. 381

Mr. Herbert to the Marquess of Salisbury.

No. 568.   CONSTANTINOPLE, *November 1, 1895, 11 a.m.*
Telegraphic.   *(Received November 1.)*
 MR. HAMPSON telegraphs to-day that neither the authorities nor others have detailed news from Bitlis, but he fears that number killed is very large, and the town is in a most unsafe condition. In one church alone he hears that there are over 400 bodies not yet claimed.
 At Mush the disorder is worse again to-day, and all the shops are shut. Mr. Hampson adds that the Mussulmans now demand not only the recall of missionaries, but that the Armenians should sign a Petition for his own recall.
 F. O. 424/184, p. 148, No. 231

No. 382

Mr. Herbert to the Marquess of Salisbury.

No. 756.   CONSTANTINOPLE, *November 1, 1895.*
My Lord,   *(Received November 11.)*
 WITH reference to my despatch No. 747 of the 30th October, I have the honour to forward to your Lordship herewith copy of a despatch which I have received from the United States' Minister informing me of the representations he has made to the Sublime Porte respecting the safety of the American missionaries at Sasun.

            I have, &c.

            (Signed) MICHAEL H. HERBERT.

 F. O. 424/184, p. 207, No. 367

Inclosure in No. 382

Mr. Terrell to Mr. Herbert.

    LEGATION OF THE UNITED STATES OF AMERICA, CONSTANTINOPLE,
Sir,   *October 30, 1895.*
 I HAVE the honour to inform you that representations have been made to the Sublime Porte for an efficient force to protect Americans engaged in distributing relief in the district of Sasun [*sic*] was expected by my Government, and who would return to resume their charitable work; that my Government would look to Turkey

alone as responsible for their safety, and when this was assured they would resume their labours.

Accept my thanks for your promptness in advising me of the danger of my fellow-citizens now in Sasun.

Very truly yours,

(Signed) A. W. TERRELL.

F. O. 424/184, p. 207, No. 367/1

No. 383

Mr. Herbert to the Marquess of Salisbury.

No. 569. CONSTANTINOPLE, *November 1, 1895, 11 a.m.*
Telegraphic. *(Received November 1.)*

ON 31st October Mr. Hampson telegraphed as follows:-

"I had a meeting this evening with the chief Armenians and Mussulmans of the town, at the invitation and in the presence of the Mutessarif, to discuss the question of the public peace and the missionaries. We finally agreed that the missionaries should leave Sasun as soon as possible, and direct the relief work from Mush, that the Mutessarif should send two officials to be present at the distribution of relief, and that, in this way, peace would be insured, and all suspicion averted.

"This gives us all we ask for, as it appears that the missionaries already intended to leave for Mush in a fortnight to direct operations from there, and the Turkish Committee was always supposed to have cognizance of the proceedings of the missionaries.

"This meeting has, in my opinion, contributed greatly towards assuring the maintenance of order here."

F. O. 424/184, p. 149, No. 232

No. 384

Mr. Herbert to the Marquess of Salisbury.

No. 570. CONSTANTINOPLE, *November 1, 1895, 11 a.m.*
Telegraphic. *(Received November 1.)*

IN continuation of his telegram repeated in my telegram No. 565 of yesterday, Her Majesty's Consul at Aleppo now telegraphs that, in view of the fact that the present garrison of Aleppo, which is composed entirely of people of the town, would, in the event of a rising there, probably refuse to fight against their fellow-citizens, he considers it most urgent that it should be at once sent away, and replaced by troops from another vilayet. I will urge the Sublime Porte to adopt the suggestion put forward by Mr. Barnham.

F. O. 424/184, p. 149, No. 232

No. 385

Mr. Herbert to the Marquess of Salisbury.

No. 571.   CONSTANTINOPLE, *November 1, 1895, 11 a.m.*
Telegraphic.   *(Received November 1.)*

THE Acting British Consul at Erzeroum telegraphed yesterday that the number of those killed is estimated at about sixty, of whom the large proportion were Armenians. There were a great many wounded, and many Armenian shops were plundered.

He reports that things are now quieter, though occasional firing still continues from Armenian houses.

F. O. 424/184, p. 149, No. 234

No. 386

Mr. Herbert to the Marquess of Salisbury.

No. 572.   CONSTANTINOPLE, *November 1, 1895, 11.10 a.m.*
Telegraphic.   *(Received November 1.)*

THERE was a partial run on the Ottoman Bank yesterday, and a regular panic in local financial circles. The situation is very serious, but fortunately the fact of to-day being a holiday will give time to the Bank.

F. O. 424/184, p. 149, No. 235

No. 387

Mr. Herbert to the Marquess of Salisbury.

No. 573.   CONSTANTINOPLE, *November 1, 1895, 9.40 p.m.*
Telegraphic.   *(Received November 1.)*

I HAVE this morning sent the following telegram to Her Majesty's Consul at Aleppo in reply to his telegram repeated to your Lordship in my telegram No. 570 of to-day's date:-

"The Grand Vizier states that, according to his information, Aleppo is quiet, and, the number of Armenians there being inconsiderable, his Highness does not anticipate trouble.

"As to your suggestion for changing the entire garrison at Aleppo, he does not see how that can be done, but there is probably a movement of troops there, as some are being sent to relieve Zeitoun, and others will take their place.

"His Highness hopes to be able to change the Vali of Aleppo, with whom he is not at all pleased."

F. O. 424/184, p. 150, No. 236

No. 388

Mr. Herbert to the Marquess of Salisbury.

No. 574.   CONSTANTINOPLE, *November 1, 1895, 9.55 p.m.*
Telegraphic.   *(Received November 1.)*

WITH reference to my telegram No. 560 of the 30th ultimo, I have the honour to inform your Lordship that, as the reports received from some of Her Majesty's Consuls accuse the Armenians of having been the aggressors in many places, I renewed my representations to the Patriarch to-day, requesting him to do all in his power to calm his people.

His Beatitude pleaded that he could not control the revolutionary movement, the magnitude of which he freely admitted, and added that it was inspired by Russian agents, and that money was sent from Tiflis to Erzeroum to support the agitation.

After much pressure, however, his Beatitude consented to send a Circular telegram exhorting the Armenians to be patient and remain quiet in view of the approaching publication and execution of the reforms.

F. O. 424/184, p. 150, No. 237

No. 389

Mr. Herbert to the Marquess of Salisbury.

No. 575. Very secret.   CONSTANTINOPLE, *November 1, 1895, 10.4 p.m.*
Telegraphic.   *(Received November 1.)*

IN order to relieve the financial situation, as reported in my telegram No. 572 of to-day's date, Sir Edgar Vincent has applied to the Turkish Government to decree a three or six months' *moratorium*, and makes any further advance of money, of which the Porte is urgently in need, dependent on their complying with his request, which the Council of Ministers met this afternoon to consider. A general

financial crash here is inevitable should the government refuse to grant the
moratorium, or to relieve the situation in some other way.

F. O. 424/184, p. 150, No. 238

No. 390

Mr. Herbert to the Marquess of Salisbury.

No. 577.   CONSTANTINOPLE, *November 1, 1895, 10.40 p.m.*
Telegraphic.   *(Received November 1.)*

WITH reference to my telegram of the 30th ultimo No. 556, I have the honour
to state that the Russian and French Ambassadors and myself have been sounded
by the Porte as to our opinion respecting the proposed appointment of Shefik Bey as
President of the Commission of Control. Shefik Bey was formerly President of the
Court of Appeal in Constantinople, and was last year appointed President of the
Mush Commission.

We have replied that, in our opinion, the fact of his having served on the Mush
Commission was an objection to his appointment, and that we did not consider him
a man of sufficient importance for the post.

F. O. 424/184, p. 151, No. 240

No. 391

Mr. Herbert to the Marquess of Salisbury.

No. 578.   CONSTANTINOPLE, *November 1, 1895, 11.15 p.m.*
Telegraphic.   *(Received November 1.)*

IN reply to Mr. Hampson's three telegrams of yesterday, repeated to your
Lordship in my telegrams Nos. 567, 568, and 569 of the 1st November, I have
informed him that the Grand Vizier, while admitting the difficulty of dealing with
the Kurds, states that no news has reached him of the disorders, and that troops are
being sent as quickly as possible into the disturbed districts.

I have approved the arrangements made by Mr. Hampson with the
Mutessarif as regards the missionaries, and have told him to apply to the
authorities for a guard if he considers himself to be in any danger.

F. O. 424/184, p. 151, No. 241

No. 392

Mr. Herbert to the Marquess of Salisbury.

No. 579. CONSTANTINOPLE, *November 1, 1895, 11.15 p.m.*
Telegraphic. *(Received November 1.)*

MY telegram of 31st October No. 560.

I renewed my request to the Grand Vizier to-day for the publication of the reforms in the newspapers. If this were not done, I begged his Highness to allow the Patriarch to have an Armenian translation made for distribution among his people. His Highness replied that he hoped to be able to obtain permission from the Sultan within a day or two for the publication of the full text of the reforms in the Turkish official press. As soon as this was done, there could be no objection to the Patriarch printing an Armenian translation.

F. O. 424/184, p. 151, No. 242

No. 393

Mr. Herbert to the Marquess of Salisbury.

No. 580. CONSTANTINOPLE, *November 1, 1895, 11.25 p.m.*
Telegraphic. *(Received November 1.)*

VICE-CONSUL HAMPSON telegraphs that, in view of the agreement arrived at with the Mutessarif as reported in my telegram to your Lordship No. 564 of yesterday, he will await further instructions before summoning the missionaries to Mush. The missionaries themselves think that, considering the anti-Protestant views of the Mutessarif, they are safer in Sasun than in Mush. Mr. Hampson recommends the transfer of the Military Commandant at Mush, Rahmi Pasha, who he says is old, incapable, and a fanatic.

F. O. 424/184, p. 152, No. 243

No. 394

Mr. Herbert to the Marquess of Salisbury.

No. 581. CONSTANTINOPLE, *November 1, 1895.*
Telegraphic. *(Received November 1.)*

ACTING on my instructions, Mr. Block called on the Grand Vizier to-day, and again drew his Highness' serious attention to the gravity of the situation in the provinces.

His Highness gave him the most emphatic assurances that the Government were doing their best to restore order, and had sent orders to the Moslems in all parts of the Empire not to resort to vengeance, but to keep quiet. His Highness was fully alive to the dangers which threaten the Ottoman Empire if the present state of affairs was allowed to continue, but he maintained that the Armenians had been the aggressors in every instance, acting under orders from the Armenian Societies, and that they did everything to provoke the Mussulmans to violence in the hope of forcing the foreign Powers to intervene. It was with the Armenians, therefore, that the responsibility for the disturbances lay.

The Turkish Government were honestly anxious to put a stop to the movement, but the gendarmerie and police alone were not equal to the task. Orders had therefore been given for calling out forty battalions of Reserves, and he trusted that on their arrival they would be able to restrain the Mussulman population.

My own impression is that both the Turkish Government and the Patriarch find themselves for the moment powerless to control the movement.

F. O. 424/184, p. 152, No. 244

No. 395

The Marquess of Salisbury to Mr. Herbert.

No. 202.
Telegraphic.   FOREIGN OFFICE, *November 1, 1895.*

IN reply to the inquiry made in your telegram No. 561 A of the 30th ultimo, I see no objection to your taking the initiative in obtaining protection for the work of the American missionaries while they are engaged in distributing to the Armenians the relief funds subscribed in England.

As regards their personal safety generally, however, it is clearly the United States' Minister who ought to make representations, and who can do so most effectively.

F. O. 424/184, p. 152, No. 245

No. 396

Mr. Herbert to the Marquess of Salisbury.

No. 758.   CONSTANTINOPLE, *November 1, 1895.*
My Lord,   *(Received November 11.)*

I HAVE the honour to forward to your Lordship herewith copy of a despatch which I have received from Her Majesty's Consul-General at Beyrout transmitting translation of a telegram received by the Vali of Beyrout respecting the introduction of reforms in Armenia.

I have, &c.

(Signed) MICHAEL H. HERBERT.

F. O. 424/184, p. 209, No. 369

Inclosure 1 in No. 396

Consul-General Drummond Hay to Sir P. Currie.

Sir, BEYROUT, *October 24, 1895.*

I HAVE the honour to transmit to your Excellency herewith a translation of a telegram received yesterday by the Governor-General of Beyrout from the Grand Vizier relating to the introduction of reforms in the Armenian provinces.

This communication has been published in all the newspapers of Beyrout.

I have, &c.

(Signed) R. DRUMMOND HAY.

F. O. 424/184, p. 209, No. 369/1

Inclosure 2 in No. 396

The Grand Vizier to the Vali of Beyrout.

Translation. CONSTANTINOPLE, *October 21, 1895.*

WE have learned that the Armenians have circulated misleading rumours regarding the reforms which it has been decided to introduce in some provinces. The steps taken for the introduction of reforms are not intended exclusively for the Armenians, but for the application within the Vilayets of Van, Mamouret-el-Aziz, Erzeroum, Bitlis, Diarbekir, and Sivas, of the Laws and Regulations contained in the Destour, and the useful Decrees and Articles promulgated in the Imperial Order of Gulhané and in the Firman of reforms.

The said reforms will be for the benefit of all the subjects of His Majesty, Mussulmans and non-Mussulmans, and measures will be taken with the view of generalizing them throughout all the Imperial provinces as far as they are required. I have therefore hastened to communicate to you the truth of the case.

The Grand Vizier.

(Signed) KIAMIL.

F. O. 424/184, p. 209, No. 369/2

No. 397

Mr. Herbert to the Marquess of Salisbury.

No. 760.   CONSTANTINOPLE, *November 1, 1895.*
My Lord,   *(Received November 11.)*
     I HAVE the honour to forward to your Lordship herewith copy of a despatch
which I have received from Her Majesty's Consul at Trebizond respecting the
apprehension felt as to disturbances in other parts of the vilayet.
                              I have, &c.
                                   (Signed) MICHAEL H. HERBERT.

F. O. 424/184, p. 209, No. 370

Inclosure 1 in No. 397

Consul Longworth to Sir P. Currie.

Sir,   TREBIZOND, *October 21, 1895.*
     WITH reference to the inclosure in my despatch of the 18th instant, I have to
inclose herewith copy of another from M. de Cortanze, stating that the report of a
disturbance at Charshamba is refuted.
     I may be allowed to state in this connection that similar rumours, followed by
contradictions, are reaching me from other parts of the vilayet.
     They serve to indicate an exceptional state of disquietude, arising probably
from the impression that the lamentable events at Trebizond form one of a series
accompanying or reflecting those of Constantinople. The country is, no doubt,
passing through a severe political crisis. The maintenance of order, I think all the
same, depends on the good-will of the Executive. There are lawless characters
everywhere, who can and should be kept within restraint. In the case of Trebizond,
this was not done effectively, and the consequences were heart-rending.
     Ottoman officials, indeed, cannot understand that, in critical times, quick and
decisive action is of paramount necessity.
     The acceptance by the Sultan of the reforms which your Excellency kindly
announced to me by wire will very likely prove propitious when made public, but I
do not think it will meet the exigencies of the situation in these parts. The bad men
among the Turks are now obviously becoming more arrogant and the good men
more timid, so that it is scarcely questionable at present which party has the upper
hand.
     It is these impressions that induced me to telegraph to your Excellency this
morning the opinion, that attacks on Armenians throughout the province are to be
apprehended is condign punishment is not meted out to the ringleaders of the

Trebizond massacre, adding that, to do this in safety, precautionary measures against the renewal of riots would have to be taken preliminarily.

I would like to point out here that any injudicious action may possibly bring about another outbreak, and this though it is generally believed that what was done was done on orders from Constantinople.

There seems to me only one way out of the difficulty. It is the dispatch here, without unnecessary delay, of a strong Commission of Inquiry, and the replacement of the troops here by such as have taken no part whatever in the disturbances.

I have, &c.

(Signed) H. Z. LONGWORTH.

F. O. 424/184, p. 210, No. 370/1

Inclosure 2 in No. 397

Mr. Cortanze to Consul Longworth.

M. le Consul,   SAMSOUN, *le 18 Octobre, 1895.*

J'AI l'honneur de porter à vote connaissance que contrairement à ce que je vous ai annoncé dans ma précédente lettre, il ne s'est produit aucun trouble à Charshamba. Ce bruit a été répandu par un officier de la garnison de Charshamba qui a télégraphié de son autorité privée à notre Mutessarif et à la Sublime Porte.

Cet officier a été arrêté pour avoir donné cette fausse nouvelle.

Les bruits les plus divers et les plus sinistres circulent à chaque instant et l'on ne sait réellement plus à quoi et à qui croire.

Veuillez, &c.

(Signé) H. DE CORTANZE.

F. O. 424/184, p. 210, No. 370/2

No. 398

Mr. Herbert to the Marquess of Salisbury.

No. 582.   CONSTANTINOPLE, *November 2, 1895, 8 p.m.*
Telegraphic.   *(Received November 2.)*

MR. BARNHAM has received the following information as to the state of affairs at Ourfa from the Armenian Bishop at Aleppo, who says he begs Embassy to communicate these facts to the Patriarch, as his telegram would not be forwarded.

On Sunday, the 27th October, some Turks entered the Armenian quarter of Ourfa, and killed an Armenian. The aggressors were imprisoned, but a mob of

Arabs, Kurds, and Turks sacked the Armenian quarter next day, wounding and killing a great many. This mob was then joined by some Hamidieh, and broke open shops which had been closed at the disturbance, and looted everything.

Only thirty or forty regular troops and a few police were in the town at the time, the total population being 32,000. The authorities then called out the Reserves from villages near, but they joined the others in killing and plundering.

F. O. 424/184, pp. 152-153, No. 246

No. 399

Mr. Herbert to the Marquess of Salisbury.

No. 583.   CONSTANTINOPLE, *November 2, 1895, 8 p.m.*
Telegraphic.   *(Received November 2.)*

BRITISH Vice-Consul at Van reports that the Kurds have plundered the villages of Arjish, and several men have been murdered. The tradesmen of Arjish have closed their shops and come to Van. Large numbers of Armenians—men, women, and children—have arrived in boats from villages of Adeljevaz, having been plundered of everything by Haideranli Kurds. Mr. Hallward says that the arrest and punishment of responsible Kurdish chiefs is absolutely necessary to prevent other serious outrages. In districts of Bashkale and Garzan, in the Vilayet of Van, and in Khizan and Bitlis Vilayet, extensive robberies and several murders have occurred.

F. O. 424/184, p. 153, No. 247

No. 400

Mr. Herbert to the Marquess of Salisbury.

No. 584.   CONSTANTINOPLE, *November 2, 1895, 8.10 p.m.*
Telegraphic.   *(Received November 2.)*

ORDERS to the effect that, if Christians were touched by Mussulmans, latter would be fired upon, were sent by the Grand Vizier to Governors of provinces last night.

F. O. 424/184, p. 153, No. 248

No. 401

Mr. Herbert to the Marquess of Salisbury.

No. 585.   CONSTANTINOPLE, *November 2, 1895, 10.25 p.m.*
Telegraphic.   *(Received November 2.)*

I RECEIVED this evening a telegram from Mr. Cumberbatch, who reports that yesterday the state of Erzeroum was quiet. On 30th October forty-one soldiers and two officers were wounded slightly, and six soldiers were killed; number among Mussulman civilians not yet reported.

Last night the dead bodies of Armenians amounted to over 300. The participation in excesses by soldiers has been established by personal visit to the pillaged houses and interrogation of surviving inmates.

Mr. Cumberbatch asks for Consular assistance.

F. O. 424/184, p. 153, No. 249

No. 402

Mr. Herbert to the Marquess of Salisbury.

No. 586.   CONSTANTINOPLE, *November 2, 1895, 10.25 p.m.*
Telegraphic.   *(Received November 2.)*

HER Majesty's Consul at Aleppo telegraphs that an attack was made on the 31st ultimo by Hamidiehs on a large caravan belonging to Armenian merchants on the road between Sooroodj and Ourpat. Sixty-two bales of merchandize, valued at 1,000*l.*, fifteen mules, and 90*l.* in cash carried off.

F. O. 424/184, p. 153, No. 250

No. 403

Mr. Herbert to the Marquess of Salisbury.

No. 587.   CONSTANTINOPLE, *November 2, 1895, 10.45 p.m.*
Telegraphic.   *(Received November 2.)*

I COMMUNICATED Mr. Hampson's telegram of 1st November, repeated to your Lordship in my telegram No. 569 of the same date, to the American Minister, at whose request I have now sent the following telegram to Mr. Hampson:-

"Inform missionaries in name of United States' Minister that, in view of the agreement arrived at between you and the Mutessarif, they should do whatever in their opinion offers the least risk, and must consult their own safety."

F. O. 424/184, p. 154, No. 251

No. 404

Mr. Herbert to the Marquess of Salisbury.

No. 588.   CONSTANTINOPLE, *November 2, 1895, 10.50 p.m.*
Telegraphic.   *(Received November 2.)*

THE Sultan has to-day decreed the *moratorium* for four months referred to in my telegram No. 575 of yesterday. This step has produced a deplorable moral effect, though there appears to be a quieter feeling in financial circles. The run on the Ottoman Bank to change their notes for gold still continues, and it is possible that if it does not cease by Monday the Bank may have temporarily to suspend payment of bank notes pending the arrival of the gold which is on its way here.

In return for the *moratorium* Vincent will make an advance to the Government.

F. O. 424/184, p. 154, No. 252

No. 405

Mr. Gosselin to the Marquess of Salisbury.

No. 37.   BERLIN, *November 2, 1895, 4.15 p.m.*
Telegraphic.   *(Received November 2.)*

YOUR Lordship's telegram of yesterday has been acted on. The Imperial Secretary of State for Foreign Affairs stated that he yesterday received a telegram from Constantinople, reporting that the agitation in the Turkish provinces was increasing. No further details, however, were given.

Baron von Marschall repeated that the Imperial Government earnestly desired to co-operate with other Powers in order that this alarming state of affairs might be brought to an end.

F. O. 424/184, p. 154, No. 254

No. 406

Mr. Goschen to the Marquess of Salisbury.

No. 106.   ST. PETERSBURGH, *November 2, 1895.*
Telegraphic.   *(Received November 2.)*

PRINCE LOBANOFF, to whom I have communicated the substance of your Lordship's telegram No. 215, told me that Mr. Herbert would, no doubt, be supported in his representations by M. de Nélidoff, whose instructions were to act with his colleagues in all cases where loss of life could be prevented by prompt action.

According to reports received from M. de Nélidoff, Prince Lobanoff continued, serious disturbances were apprehended, as the excitement among the Turks in Constantinople against the Government, and even the Sultan, was daily increasing. In consequence of this, instructions had been sent to the Russian Ambassador at Constantinople to concert with his colleagues as to the proper measures to be taken, in the event of any serious outbreak, for the protection of their respective nationals; and Prince Lobanoff had also impressed upon his Excellency the importance of conducting such deliberations with the greatest prudence, in order to avoid any premature alarm. He added that he hoped Mr. Herbert would receive similar instructions from your Lordship.

F. O. 424/184, p. 155, No. 255

No. 407

Sir E. Monson to the Marquess of Salisbury.

No. 80.   VIENNA, *November 2, 1895.*
Telegraphic.   *(Received November 2.)*

WITH reference to your Lordship's telegram No. 74 of the 1st instant, I am informed by Count Goluchowski that, as the Ambassadors are doing their utmost to save the Turkish Government from the consequence of its own apathy, it appears to him useless to send them any further instructions.

F. O. 424/184, p. 155, No. 256

No. 408

Sir E. Monson to the Marquess of Salisbury.

No. 81.   VIENNA, *November 2, 1895.*
Telegraphic.   *(Received November 2.)*
I HAVE the honour to report, with reference to the scheme of Armenian reforms, that the Powers of the Triple Alliance will formally demand that it should be communicated to their respective Embassies, unless the Porte does so officially and of its own accord.

This attitude is based by Count Goluchowski upon the rights given to the Signatory Powers by the Treaty of Berlin, with the provisions of which it is necessary to conform.

F. O. 424/184, p. 155, No. 257

No. 409

Sir J. Pauncefote to the Marquess of Salisbury.

No. 62.   WASHINGTON, *November 2, 1895.*
Telegraphic.   *(Received November 2.)*
I HAVE communicated the substance of your Lordship's telegram No. 53 to the United States' Government, who have received from their Minister at Constantinople the following telegram, dated the 2nd November:

"The missionaries at Bitlis inform me, by telegraph, that they are in great danger, but still safe. I have secured the renewed issue of orders for their protection by telegraph."

F. O. 424/184, p. 155, No. 258

No. 410

The Marquess of Salisbury to Mr. Herbert.

No. 203.
Telegraphic.   FOREIGN OFFICE, *November 2, 1895.*
I APPROVE your action, as reported in your telegram No. 577 of the 1st instant.

The connection of Shefik Bey with the Sasun Commission of Inquiry would render his appointment as President of the Commission of Control very objectionable.

Recall to the notice of the Grand Vizier his suggestion of Hassan Fehmi Pasha as President (see Sir P. Currie's telegram No. 517 of the 21st ultimo), and express the great disappointment of Her Majesty's Government at the abandonment of this proposal, as a high opinion was formed of Hassan Fehmi Pasha when he came on a Special Mission to this country.

You will, in Sir P. Currie's opinion, find that both the French and Russian Ambassadors will be ready to support you strongly in advocating Hassan Fehmi Pasha's qualifications.

F. O. 424/184, p. 156, No. 259

No. 411

The Marquess of Salisbury to Mr. Herbert.

No. 364.

Sir, FOREIGN OFFICE, *November 2, 1895.*

I HAVE received Sir P. Currie's despatch No. 706 of the 22nd ultimo, reporting the representation made to the Armenian Patriarch by the Austrian, Russian, and British Embassies at Constantinople with a view to checking, through his intervention, the continuance of the agitation fostered in the capital by the Armenian Revolutionary Committees.

His Excellency's action in this matter is approved.

I have, &c.

(Signed) SALISBURY.

F. O. 424/184, p. 156, No. 260

No. 412

The Marquess of Salisbury to Mr. Herbert.

No. 366.

Sir, FOREIGN OFFICE, *November 2, 1895.*

I HAVE received Sir P. Currie's despatch No. 710 of the 23rd ultimo, reporting the protest made by him on learning the promotion to a higher appointment at Trebizond of Mohammed Farzi, whose dismissal from his post as head of the police at Mush had been demanded in consequence of the forcible entry by the police into the house occupied by the Consular Delegates with the Sasun Commission.

His Excellency's action in this matter is approved by Her Majesty's Government.

I am, &c.

(Signed) Salisbury.

F. O. 424/184, p. 156, No. 261

No. 413

Saïd Pasha to Rustem Pasha.

Constantinople, *le 2 Novembre, 1895.*

Télégraphique.   *(Communicated by Rustem Pasha, November 3.)*

LE Vali de Diarbékir télégraphie que le 20 Octobre courant (v. s.) les Arméniens ont attaqué les mosquées du chef-lieu pendant que les Musulmans y faisaient leurs prières du Vendredi, et ayant tiré des coups de feu, il en est résulté des désordres dans la ville. Il y a eu de part et d'autre quelques morts et blessés; mais des mesures énergiques sont prises pour rétablir l'ordre. Un incendie qui avait éclaté au bazar a été étouffé aussitôt.

Le Gouverneur de Marache télégraphie de son côté que le Lieutenant Hassan Agha, sa femme et ses enfants en bas âge, au moment oú ils se rendaient de Keulksoun à Marache, ont été attaqués en route par les Arméniens de Zéitoun, qui les ont mis à mort de la manière la plus cruelle et se sont emparés de leurs effets. 300 de ces émeutiers ont aussi fait irruption sur le village de Goucherké et enlevé aux villageois 300 têtes de betail et leurs effets domestiques.

Le Vali d'Erzeroum télégraphie que les autorités Impériales l'ayant informé que quelques Chefs de tribus Kurdes de Ploumer s'étaient rendus à la tête d'un certain nombre d'individus à l'endroit appelé Tchaltché, à une heure de distance de Kighi, dans le but d'attaquer les Arméniens, un certain nombre de Musulmans ont été armés, et aidés par les gendarmes et les soldats, se sont mis à la poursuite de ces Kurdes, et les ont dispersés avant qu'ils aient pu réaliser leur projet.

F. O. 424/184, pp. 156-157, No. 262

No. 414

Mr. Herbert to the Marquess of Salisbury.

No. 589.   Constantinople, *November 3, 1895.*
Telegraphic.   *(Received November 3.)*

HER Majesty's Consul at Aleppo telegraphs that yesterday afternoon two individuals, neither being an Armenian, had some trifling quarrel, whereupon a large mob of Mussulmans armed with clubs suddenly assembled from every quarter of the city. They raised a cry that now was the moment to kill the Christians and plunder their houses, and nothing but the energy of the Ferik prevented a massacre.

Mr. Barnham reports that the town is still in a state of panic.

F. O. 424/184, p. 157, No. 263

No. 415

Mr. Herbert to the Marquess of Salisbury.

No. 590.   CONSTANTINOPLE, *November 3, 1895, 11.20 a.m.*
Telegraphic.   *(Received November 3.)*

THE Representatives of the Powers are to meet at 4 o'clock to-morrow to discuss the present situation.

Does your Lordship wish to send me any instructions?

F. O. 424/184, p. 157, No. 264

No. 416

Mr. Herbert to the Marquess of Salisbury.

No. 592.   CONSTANTINOPLE, *November 3, 1895, 12.15 p.m.*
Telegraphic.   *(Received November 3.)*

MY immediately preceding telegram.

Shefik Bey has been appointed President of the Commission in spite of our strong representations. The appointments of Sakys and Carathéordory are considered good ones.

Djelal was, like Shefik, a member of the Mush Commission. Abdullah and Dilber seem to have no special qualifications to serve on the Commission, Dilber's chief title to fame being his great experience at cards.

I will consult the Russian and French Ambassadors as to what attitude we should adopt.

F. O. 424/184, p. 157, No. 265

No. 417

Mr. Herbert to the Marquess of Salisbury.

No. 591.   THERAPIA, *November 3, 1895, 12.15 p.m.*
Telegraphic.   *(Received November 3, 3 p.m.)*
    AN Iradé is published to-day appointing Shefik Bey President of the
Commission of Control. The other Mussulman members are Djemal Bey, Director
of the Agricultural Bank; Abdullah Bey, Member of the Council of State; Djemal
Bey, President of Criminal Section of Court of Appeal. Christian members are
Constantine Carathéodori, Member of the Council of State, Greek; Sakyz Ohannes
Effendi, Public Prosecutor for Acountant-General's Office, Catholic Armenian;
and Dilber Effendi, formerly Assistant Under-Secretary of Minister of Justice, and
one of Legal Advisers of the Porte, Armenian Gregorian.
    F. O. 424/184, p. 157*, No. 264*

No. 418

Mr. Herbert to the Marquess of Salisbury.

No. 593.   CONSTANTINOPLE, *November 3, 1895, 7.35 p.m.*
Telegraphic.   *(Received November 3.)*
    ACCORDING to a telegram received by M. Cambon from the French Consul
at Diarbekir, that town has been for three days the scene of continuous fighting, and
many people have been killed.
    Five hundred Christians have taken refuge in the French Consulate, which is
practically besieged.
    M. Cambon has made strong representations to the Grand Vizier, who has
made his usual reply that the Armenians were the aggressors, having attacked the
Mussulmans in the mosques.
    The French Consul, however, declares that there is absolutely no truth in this
statement.
    F. O. 424/184, p. 158, No. 266

No. 419

Mr. Herbert to the Marquess of Salisbury.

No. 594.   CONSTANTINOPLE, *November 3, 1895, 7.30 p.m.*
Telegraphic.   *(Received November 3.)*

WITH reference to my telegram No. 592 of to-day, I have the honour to inform your Lordship that I have spoken to the French Ambassador respecting Shefik Bey's appointment.

M. de Nélidoff is gone for a trip to Prince's Islands, but returns to-morrow morning, and M. Cambon wishes to consult him before expressing an opinion. We are all three to have a meeting to-morrow.

F. O. 424/184, p. 158, No. 267

No. 420

Mr. Herbert to the Marquess of Salisbury.

No. 595.   CONSTANTINOPLE, *November 3, 1895, 7.30 p.m.*
Telegraphic.   *(Received November 3.)*

THE Acting British Consul at Erzeroum telegraphs that there have been no further disorders there, but that all the Armenian villages in the surrounding districts have been plundered by large marauding bands; that at Erzinjian over 260 Armenians and a few Turks were killed; at Bitlis over 120 Armenians and 39 Turks.

Mr. Cumberbatch reports that at Erzeroum some Mussulman rioters and several supposed Armenian revolutionists have been arrested.

He says that Shakir Pasha and the Vali are making efforts to recover loot, and have acted humanely in connection with the recovery of dead bodies and the attendance of the wounded Armenians, which Mr. Cumberbatch and his colleagues had at once taken in hand.

F. O. 424/184, p. 158, No. 268

No. 421

Mr. Herbert to the Marquess of Salisbury.

No. 596.   CONSTANTINOPLE, *November 3, 1895.*
Telegraphic.   *(Received November 3.)*

THE Acting British Consul at Erzeroum telegraphs that a slight disturbance occurred there this afternoon.

He further reports that a meeting of the Consular Body had been held, when it was unanimously decided that, in view of the undoubted participation of the soldiers in the recent massacre and pillage, they should inform their respective Embassies that it was necessary for the re-establishment of tranquillity that their immediate trial and punishment should be demanded of the Turkish Government, and that a stop should be put to the wholesale imprisonment of supposed revolutionary Armenians.

F. O. 424/184, pp. 158-159, No. 269

No. 422

The Marquess of Salisbury to Mr. Herbert.

No. 206.
Telegraphic.   FOREIGN OFFICE, *November 3, 1895.*

I HAVE repeated to you Mr. Goschen's telegram No. 106 of yesterday, reporting the instructions sent to M. de Nélidoff to concert with his colleagues as to measures for the protection of foreigners in the event of serious disturbances at Constantinople.

You will, of course, be ready to take part in any deliberations which the Russian Ambassador may invite for this purpose, and you should report to me the result of any such consultation.

You are at liberty, if you think it desirable, to inform your colleagues that it is proposed to move the British Squadron to Salonica from Lemnos, and you may also acquaint the Grand Vizier.

F. O. 424/184, p. 159, No. 270

No. 423

The Marquess of Salisbury to Mr. Herbert.

No. 208.
Telegraphic.   FOREIGN OFFICE, *November 3, 1895.*

I HAVE received your telegram No. 590 of to-day, requesting instructions in view of the proposed meeting of foreign Representatives to-morrow to consider the situation.

Your proceedings hitherto have my entire approval, and you should continue to act on the same lines. You should associate yourself with your colleagues in any representation or other action which may be judged by the meeting to be desirable with the object of saving further loss of life.

The missionaries should be induced, as far as possible, to avoid exposing themselves to danger.

F. O. 424/184, p. 159, No. 271

No. 424

The Marquess of Salisbury to Mr. Goschen.

No. 216.
Telegraphic.   FOREIGN OFFICE, *November 3, 1895.*

I HAVE received your telegram No. 106 of the 2nd instant, reporting the instructions sent to M. de Nélidoff, with a view to the adoption of measures for the protection of foreigners in case of a renewal of disorders at Constantinople, and Prince Lobanoff's hope that Her Majesty's Representative might receive similar instructions.

You can inform his Excellency that I have telegraphed to Mr. Herbert in the sense desired.

F. O. 424/184, p. 159, No. 272

No. 425

Mr. Herbert to the Marquess of Salisbury.

No. 603.   CONSTANTINOPLE, *November 4, 1895, 10 p.m.*
Telegraphic.   *(Received November 4.)*

I HAVE sent the following telegram to Her Majesty's Consuls at Trebizond, Erzeroum, Mush, Van, Aleppo, and Angora in view of the present state of affairs in the provinces:

"The Porte has, at my request, instructed Vali to give you all necessary protection in view of disturbances reported in your district.

"Missionaries should be quietly informed not to expose themselves to risk."

F. O. 424/184, p. 192, No. 309

No. 426

Mr. Herbert to the Marquess of Salisbury.

No. 605.   CONSTANTINOPLE, *November 4, 1895, 10.30 p.m.*
Telegraphic.   *(Received November 4.)*

TWENTY-FIVE THOUSAND men have been sent to Marash and Zeitoun.
At the latter place 420 are prisoners in the hands of the Armenians, and the garrison
have capitulated.

In the 4th and 5th Army Corps districts twenty more battalions have been
called out. Total number now 60,000 men.

F. O. 424/184, p. 192, No. 310

No. 427

Mr. Herbert to the Marquess of Salisbury.

No. 606. Secret.   CONSTANTINOPLE, *November 4, 1895 10.40 p.m.*
Telegraphic.   *(Received November 4.)*

THE air is full of rumours of a Mussulman revolution, but as far as I can
ascertain as yet there are no men of importance ready to head the movement, which
seems to be without any proper organization.

Grand Vizier admitted to-day, both to Baron Calice and Mr. Block, that
serious discontent prevailed among the Mussulmans, but the Sultan, who is well
aware of the danger, is adopting every precaution.

The Representatives of the Powers at their meeting to-day agreed that the
moment was not opportune for taking collective action for the safety of foreign
residents.

F. O. 424/184, p. 192, No. 311

No. 428

Mr. Herbert to the Marquess of Salisbury.

No. 607.   CONSTANTINOPLE, *November 4, 1895, 10.15 p.m.*
Telegraphic,   *(Received November 4.)*

MR. HAMPSON telegraphed yesterday that snow had commenced to fall at
Mush, which will probably have more effect in restoring order than any measure
which could be devised.

There was a heavy fall last night, which continues to-day.

F. O. 424/184, p. 192, No. 312

No. 429

Mr. Herbert to the Marquess of Salisbury.

No. 608.   CONSTANTINOPLE, *November 4, 1895, 10.20 p.m.*
Telegraphic.   *(Received November 4.)*

I RECEIVED the following telegram from Mush to-day:-

"Missionaries urge necessity for measures to protect Sasun against the Kurds.

"Dr. Reynolds request to be relieved from work, and Mr. Cole requests permission to go to Bitlis, as they consider their presence in Sasun no longer necessary for the distribution of relief. Mr. Cole would return shortly and direct further work from here.

"They both ask for safe-conduct to their homes, and for the doctor to take the ladies from Bitlis to Van if it seems best."

F. O. 424/184, p. 193, No. 313

No. 430

Mr. Herbert to the Marquess of Salisbury.

No. 609.   CONSTANTINOPLE, *November 4, 1895, 10.30 p.m.*
Telegraphic.   *(Received November 4.)*

THE French Ambassador received last night further telegram in regard to disturbances at Diarbekir referred to in my telegram No. 593, in which it was stated that French Consul's life was in great danger.

M. Cambon immediately sent to inform the Grand Vizier (at 2 A.M)that he would ask his Government to occupy some Syrian port if the guilty parties were not punished, and would require the head of the Vali if anything happened to the Consul.

This report describes the Sheikh of Zeilan as the principle instigator of the massacre, in comparison with which all other disturbances in the provinces sink into insignificance, especially as it would appear that not only Armenians, but Christians of every Church, were indiscriminately slaughtered.

As a telegram was received from the Consul this afternoon to say that things are quiet, it would seem that the threats of the French Ambassador have produced their desired effect.

F. O. 424/184, p. 193, No. 314

No. 431

Mr. Goschen to the Marquess of Salisbury.

No. 255. Confidential.   St. Petersburgh, *November 4, 1895.*
My Lord,   *(Received November 12.)*

I DULY communicated to Prince Lobanoff the substance of Mr. Herbert's telegram to your Lordship respecting the alarming position of the missionaries at Bitlis, and, as I informed your Lordship by telegraph, his Excellency stated that M. de Nélidoff would be sure to support Mr. Herbert's representations to the Porte if called upon to do so, as he had full instructions to join with his colleagues in any endeavour to secure tranquillity and prevent loss of life.

His Excellency expressed himself as being much perturbed, though not surprised, at the continual reports of disturbances and massacres in Asia Minor, which reached him from Constantinople. He was of opinion that, notwithstanding the publication of the "Iradé" granting the reforms, it would take some time before the situation would improve, owing to the fever of excitement under which both the Mahommedans and the Armenians were labouring. This excitement was, he said, the natural result of the uncompromising manner in which the Armenian question had been taken up. He spoke very warmly on the subject, and did not conceal from me his opinion that England was chiefly responsible for this state of things, owing to the encouragement given to the Armenian Committees by so many of her leading men.

Where was this going to stop? his Excellency continued; paper reforms had been granted, but in the meantime, the blood of both Mahommedans and Armenians was up, and attacks on the one side and reprisals on the other were taking place day by day. Now, to crown all, there was the growing agitation among Turks of all classes against the Sultan's Government and the Sultan himself—a danger of which the gravity could hardly be exaggerated.

In speaking further of this agitation among the Mahommedans, he told me that he had received a very alarming account of the state of affairs in Constantinople from M. de Nélidoff, who was of the opinion that disturbances might break out there at any moment. As, in the event of such disturbances taking place, the Christians would surely be the first to be attacked, he had instructed M. de Nélidoff to lose no time in taking every precaution and to consult with his colleagues as to the best means of saving the lives of their respective fellow-countrymen should they be in danger. At the same time, as he knew from his own experience the difficulty of keeping anything secret in that "nid de commérages," Constantinople, he had impressed upon his Excellency the importance of avoiding premature alarm, and had begged him to exercise the greatest prudence, both in his consultations with his colleagues and in any preparations for saving the lives of his countrymen, which he might deem it his duty to make.

Prince Lobanoff expressed to me the hope that your Lordship would send similar instructions to Her Majesty's Chargé d'Affaires.

I have, &c.

(Signed) W. E. GOSCHEN.

F. O. 424/184, p. 220, No. 380

No. 432

Saïd Pasha to Rustem Pasha.

CONSTANTINOPLE, *le 5 Novembre, 1895.*

Télégraphique.   *(Communicated by Rustem Pasha, November 5.)*

LES autorités de Marache ayant été avisées qu'à la suite de quelques coups de feu tirés par des Arméniens sur des Musulmans dont un a été tué et un autre grièvement blessé, la population Musulmane se préparait à des représailles, ont pris des mesures, grâce auxquelles le calme a été rétabli. Dans cette affaire un Lieutenant de Gendarmerie et cinq Musulmans ont été grièvement blessés et quatorze Arméniens tués et blessés.

Le nommé Mighirditch et son frère Nazaret, impliqués dans l'incident de Bitlis, ayant dernièrement à Khuntz menacé de leurs revolvers et injurié deux Musulmans ont été arrêtés et désarmés.

F. O. 424/184, p. 194, No. 316

No. 433

Mr. Herbert to the Marquess of Salisbury.

No. 610.   CONSTANTINOPLE, *November 5, 1895.*

Telegraphic.   *(Received November 5.)*

HER Majesty's Consul at Aleppo reports that the Armenians took the citadel of Zeitoun about four days ago, putting the garrison to flight, and capturing two guns. Ten battalions, mostly Reserves, and all considerably under their proper establishment, had been dispatched against them.

The Officer Commanding at Zeitoun stated that the Armenians were 8,000 strong.

Mr. Barnham says that the Military Commander is doing all he can to prevent an outbreak at Aleppo, and that, in consequence of the news received on Friday of the disturbances at Diarbekir, two battalions have been left at Aleppo instead of one.

F. O. 424/184, p. 194, No. 317

No. 434

Mr. Herbert to the Marquess of Salisbury.

No. 611. Secret.   CONSTANTINOPLE, *November 5, 1895, 12.20 p.m.*
Telegraphic.   *(Received November 5.)*
   THE feeling against the Sultan in Constantinople is said to be growing more and more intense in all circles.
   I am informed that His Majesty, who, in the opinion of even the Palace, is now at the mercy of any accident, may throw the blame for the present situation on the Grand Vizier and dismiss him.
   F. O. 424/184, p. 194, No. 318

No. 435

Mr. Herbert to the Marquess of Salisbury.

No. 612.   CONSTANTINOPLE, *November 5, 1895, 6.15 p.m.*
Telegraphic.   *(Received November 5.)*
   WITH reference to my telegram to your Lordship No. 604 of 4th November, the Representatives of the six Powers made to-day to the Minister for Foreign Affairs the communication agreed upon at yesterday's meeting.
   Saïd Pasha promised to give us a formal answer in a day or two.
   After repeating arguments in regard to attacks by Armenians, his Excellency said that his Government were doing their best to cope with the disturbances, as the calling out of the Redifs in various parts of the Empire proved. But he admitted that the situation was very serious.
   F. O. 424/184, p. 195, No. 319

No. 436

Mr. Herbert to the Marquess of Salisbury.

No. 613.   CONSTANTINOPLE, *November 5, 1895, 6.30 p.m.*
Telegraphic.   *(Received November 5.)*
   IDENTIC representations were made at the Porte to-day by the French, Russian, and Italian Ambassadors and myself in the sense of Mr. Cumberbatch's suggestion, as reported in my telegram to your Lordship No. 596 of the 3rd instant.
   I have telegraphed the above information to Mr. Cumberbatch.
   F. O. 424/184, p. 195, No. 320.

No. 437

Mr. Herbert to the Marquess of Salisbury.

No. 614.   CONSTANTINOPLE, *November 5, 1895, 6.46 p.m.*
Telegraphic.   *(Received November 5.)*

MY representations to the Porte in regard to the safety of missionaries at Bitlis and in the Mush district have been supported by M. de Nélidoff, who had received instructions from his Government to do so.

F. O. 424/184, p. 195, No. 321

No. 438

Mr. Herbert to the Marquess of Salisbury.

No. 615.   CONSTANTINOPLE, *November 5, 1895, 11.45 p.m.*
Telegraphic.   *(Received November 5.)*

I INSTRUCTED Mr Block to-day to call at the Palace and warn the Sultan, through the First Secretary, of the danger of the present situation, and to point out how necessary it was that the existing disorders should be put an end to. His Majesty has sent me this evening the following message in reply:-

"The strictest instructions have been sent to the provinces enjoining the authorities to take every possible step to prevent Moslems attacking Christians and *vice versa*, and to punish indiscriminately the authors of disturbances.

"The reforms will be published in to-morrow's newspapers, and will be followed by an Iradé stating that all possible measures will be taken to secure prosperity and welfare of all classes.

"It has unfortunately been found necessary to call out large numbers of troops at great expense in order to preserve order, but the authorities have been instructed at the same time to use every effort to induce the people to discontinue hostilities, and the troops will only receive orders to use their arms if disturbances continue in spite of this warning."

Secret.

I am desired by Sultan to inform your Lordship that, in spite of the utterances of the British press, His Majesty is well aware of your friendly disposition towards him; that a few weeks ago Zeki Pasha, a man in whom His Majesty had full confidence, was sent by him to Sir P. Currie to explain his good intentions and his friendship towards England; that His Majesty is certain your Lordship will approve his language, and continue to extend to himself and to Turkey your friendly offices and assistance; and that your Lordship should be convinced, whoever his Ministers may be, His Majesty's policy remains unchanged.

F. O. 424/184, pp. 195-196, No. 322

No. 439

The Marquess of Salisbury to Mr. Herbert.

No. 209. Secret.
Telegraphic.   FOREIGN OFFICE, *November 5, 1895.*
   THE following is secret.
   You should try to ascertain what view the French and Russian Ambassadors take in regard to the course to be followed if a revolution breaks out at Constantinople. The contingency of serious disturbances there must evidently be looked upon as a possible one.

F. O. 424/184, p. 196, No. 323

No. 440

Mr. Herbert to the Marquess of Salisbury.

No. 765.   CONSTANTINOPLE, *November 5, 1895.*
My Lord,   *(Received November 11.)*
   I HAVE the honour to forward to your Lordship herewith copy of a despatch which I have received from Her Majesty's Consul at Trebizond respecting the attitude of the Armenians in the recent disturbances.

                                   I have, &c.
                            (Signed) MICHAEL H. HERBERT.

F. O. 424/184, p. 212, No. 372

Inclosure in No. 440

Consul Longworth to Sir P. Currie.

Sir,   TREBIZOND, *October 28, 1895.*
   I RECEIVED your Excellency's telegram of the 26th instant, asking me to wire any information I may have on the attitude of the Armenians, as reports from the authorities of the Bitlis, Erzeroum, and Aleppo Vilayets state that they are

provoking retaliation by attacking Mussulmans. I am therein further informed that some of the reserves in the six Armenian vilayets were about to be called out.

My reply by telegraph will have reached your Excellency this morning. It was to the effect that an Armenian Committee advocating violence doubtless exists, that a few among those who spoke and wrote of causing disturbances, if reforms were not granted, may have acted rashly; but that apart from the probability that Armenians wounded the two Pashas on the 2nd instant, there is no reason to think that at Trebizond itself Armenians contemplated an attack on the Moslems.

I should like to give here a little more fully my views on the subject, based on information taken from different sources.

It cannot be denied that of late years weapons from the Caucasus and seditious prints from Europe have been surreptitiously introduced and sedulously distributed among the Armenians in Asiatic Turkey. They may have influenced the minds of the people elsewhere, but in this vilayet even a ripple was not observable of a possible agitation. Secret agents, I believe, were to be found here, as in other Armenian centres. They were selected, doubtless, from among the more reckless and unscrupulous. Assassination of at first informers only, but now of Government officers and others obnoxious to the Society, appears to be the vow taken by these men. The basis of operations, which was a few months ago Athens, is now believed to be in London. Nazarbeck, the editor of the "Huntchak", is probably one of the chief originators and promoters of this baneful organization. Whoever they may be they are directing the movement from abroad, and, with all safety to themselves, are rendering existence for their countrymen unbearable in Turkey. The object may, or may not, be to rouse the Moslems against the Christians, and bring about such massacres as would horrify Europe. That it is anarchical in character must be patent to all, for in its conception enters the creation of political confusion and lawlessness through violent means, the aim being to further thus the cause of Armenia, securing for it not only reforms, but independence as a barrier or buffer State between Russia and Turkey in Asia.

National aspirations are legitimate enough perhaps, so long as they do not interfere with public order and security. The Armenians as a people would be content, I believe, if they could only have the enjoyment of safety to life, honour, and property. The Mussulmans are equally anxious to secure ameliorations, though it irritates them to find that their own sufferings and grievances are ignored, while those of the Armenians are championed by the Powers, especially England. The governing classes can, if they like, restrain them from causing disturbances. They did not do so at Trebizond. They, on the contrary, encouraged the massacre by enhancing in the eyes of the Turks a street assault into the importance of a general insurrection. The authorities unfortunately still persist in taking the one-sided view that a revolution was imminent, though the Vali has up to now been able to produce to me very insufficient proofs, and this after imprisoning the Armenians and searching thoroughly their houses.

The most important discovery is a seal bearing in Armenian words and letters what may be rendered thus in English: "A. R. Alliance. The Trebizond Committee." It was found in the house of a joiner, named Manouk Tateosian, now in prison, who declares it to have been left in his safe-keeping by a certain Armenian killed in the massacre.

I cannot offer any opinion as to other parts, but here, at least, the Armenians were, and are still, in great stress: killed in cold blood, robbed of their goods, flung into gaol, not allowed to emigrate, blackmailed by the Moslems, and persecuted by the authorities, the poor people are in the deepest despair. There is a limit, however, to human endurance, and if therefore they really [?], who can blame them? One more remark, in conclusion. It is satisfactory to know that a portion of the reserves in the interior are about to be mobilized. The Executive will then have no excuse in any failure to maintain order. At Trebizond the troops were declared insufficient, but had they been more, their conduct was such that the carnage would have been greater.

I have, &c.

(Signed) H. Z. Longworth.

F. O. 424/184, pp. 212-213, No. 374/1

No. 441

Mr. Herbert to the Marquess of Salisbury.

No. 766.   Constantinople, *November 5, 1895.*
My Lord,   *(Received November 11.)*
I HAVE the honour to forward to your Lordship herewith copy of a despatch which I have received from the Acting British Consul at Erzeroum, reporting the release of certain Armenian prisoners at Van and Bitlis.

I have, &c.

(Signed) Michael H. Herbert.

F. O. 424/184, p. 213, No. 373

Inclosure in No. 441

Consul Cumberbatch to Sir P. Currie.

Sir,   Erzeroum, *October 21, 1895.*
I HAVE the honour to inform your Excellency that Mr. Vice-Consul Hallward reports that seven more Armenian prisoners at Van, viz., Nos. 12, 13, 14,

15, 94, 96, and 99 in the list which accompanied Mr. Graves' despatch of the 2nd May, have been released; and that Ohan Effendi, of Shattakh, referred to in Mr. Graves' despatch of the 21st May has been again imprisoned.

Mr. Hallward again insists on the necessity of some decision being arrived at with regard to the remaining prisoners, especially those of Shattakh, as they are simply being kept in prison indefinitely without trial.

Her Majesty's Vice-Consul at Mush also writes, that the six young Armenians in the Bitlis prison, referred to in your Excellency's despatch of the 18th September, have been released.

Mr. Hampson had spoken to the Acting Vali on the subject when he was at Bitlis, and he had promised that they would be set free as soon as it could safely be done. He further adds that the accusation that they attempted to rape a Moslem woman is absurd. What they did was to endeavour to rescue from the hands of certain Kurds a girl whom they were led to believe was an Armenian. They failed, however, to prove their case, and their rashness resulted in their being imprisoned for some months.

I have, &c.

(Signed) H. A. CUMBERBATCH.

F. O. 424/184, p. 213, No. 373/1

No. 442

Mr. Herbert to the Marquess of Salisbury.

No. 616. Secret. CONSTANTINOPLE, *November 6, 1895, 3.50 p.m.*
Telegraphic. *(Received November 6.)*

WITH reference to my telegram to your Lordship No. 598 of 4th November, I hear that the French Ambassador has hinted to Munir Bey that your Lordship may possibly refuse to accept Shefik Bey as President of the Commission of Control, and has himself made a strong protest against the manner in which the appointment was made.

F. O. 424/184, p. 196, No. 324

No. 443

Mr. Herbert to the Marquess of Salisbury.

No. 617. Secret. CONSTANTINOPLE, *November 6, 1895, 6.45 p.m.*
Telegraphic. *(Received November 6.)*

YOUR Lordship's telegram of the 5th instant No. 209.

The Russian and French Ambassadors are of opinion that it would be advisable that the Representatives of the Powers here should be authorized by their respective Governments to act together, and be given *carte blanche* as to the measures to be taken in the event of disturbances breaking out. M. de Nélidoff is further of the opinion that, should joint action become necessary, all the foreign Representatives here should take part in it.

Neither he nor M. Cambon, however, consider the danger of revolution to be imminent, though they regard it as possible, and they think that it would be premature, and indeed impossible, to concert measures of protection at this moment.

F. O. 424/184, p. 196, No. 325

No. 444

Sir E. Monson to the Marquess of Salisbury.

No. 324.   VIENNA, *November 6, 1895.*

My Lord,   *(Received November 8.)*

COUNT GOLUCHOWSKI read to me this afternoon a telegram from Baron Calice, reporting the decision taken by the Representatives of the Great Powers yesterday at Constantinople, to make fresh and serious representations to the Porte respecting the massacres of Christians in Asia Minor.

His Excellency said that he expected to see the Turkish Ambassador after my interview, and that he should tell him plainly that there is abundant proof that, in some of the recent massacres, the butchery has been committed under the direct orders of the authorities, and that, unless the Turkish Government takes without loss of time efficacious steps to protect the Christians and punish those who ill-treat them, the public opinion in every country in Europe will be so much aroused, that it will be impossible to prevent outside intervention in some form or another, thus opening the whole Eastern question, and producing a state of things which, however disagreeable and perhaps prejudicial to the interests of some of the Great Powers, will certainly have the most serious consequences for Turkey.

I have, &c.

(Signed) E. MONSON.

F. O. 424/184, p. 203, No. 348

No. 445

Mr. Herbert to the Marquess of Salisbury.

No. 767.   PERA, *November 6, 1895.*
My Lord,   *(Received November 11.)*

WITH reference to my telegram No. 612 of the 5th instant, I have the honour to transmit herewith copy of the identic communication to the Porte in regard to the state of affairs in the Turkish provinces, which was made verbally to the Minister for Foreign Affairs by the Representatives of the six Powers yesterday.

In making this communication to Saïd Pasha I pointed out that the five Ambassadors and myself were absolutely united in asking and even insisting, in the name of humanity, that order should be re-established, and I again expressed the hope that the Turkish Government would take every means in their power to put an end to the present state of affairs, which was becoming a menace to Europe and to the existence of the Turkish Empire.

Saïd Pasha said that he would give me a formal answer in a day or two. In the meantime he could assure me that the Turkish Government were doing their best to cope with the disturbances, and to that end had called out 60,000 more troops. His Excellency admitted that the situation was very serious, but he complained once more that it had been brought about by the attacks and aggressions of the Armenians, whom he described somewhat bitterly as our protégés.

I replied that it was not a question of who began the disturbances—that both Turks and Armenians were Ottoman subjects— and that the master ought to be able to keep order in his own house.

I have, &c.

(Signed) MICHAEL H. HERBERT.

F. O. 424/184, p. 214, No. 374

Inclosure in No. 445

Identic Communication addressed to the Porte, November 5, 1895.

LES Représentants des six Grandes Puissances ont échangé leurs vues sur la sitation dont la gravité leur est signalée par tous leurs Agents. Ils sont très inquiets de l'état des provinces, où règne une anarchie complète qui n'a plus de rapport avec l'agitation Arménienne et qui menace les Chrétiens de toute nationalité.

A Diarbékir le massacre et le pillage ont frappé indistinctement les Chrétiens des différents rites sans aucune provocation de leur part.

A Mossoul, à Bagdad, en Syrie, où il n'y a pas d'Arméniens, l'effervescence prend des proportions inquiétantes.

La Porte doit savoir par l'exemple de ce qui s'est passé en Syrie en 1860 que cette anarchie ne peut durer impunément.

Les Représentants des Puissances sont obligées d'en référer à leurs Gouvernements, qui Se concerteront dans le cas où la Porte ne prendrait pas immédiatement des mesures efficaces.

Ils prient le Ministre des Affaires Étrangères de leur faire savoir ce que le Gouvernement Ottoman compte faire pour mettre un terme aux désordres actuels.

F. O. 424/184, p. 214, No. 374/1

No. 446

Mr. Herbert to the Marquess of Salisbury.

No. 768.   CONSTANTINOPLE, *November 6, 1895.*
My Lord,   *(Received November 11.)*

I HAVE the honour to transmit to your Lordship herewith copy of an account of the Trebizond massacres, signed by the local authorities civil and military, by the Ulemas, and by the Notables of the Mussulman, Orthodox, and Catholic religions, which has been communicated to me by the Grand Vizier.

I have, &c.

(Signed) MICHAEL H. HERBERT.

F. O. 424/184, p. 214, No. 375

Inclosure in No. 446

Account of the Trébizond Massacres.

LE Général de Division Bahri Pacha, ex-Vali de Van, qui a passé quelques jours à Trébizonde en rentrant de Van, et Ahmed Hamdi Pacha, Commandant des Rédifs de Trébizonde, traversaient, Mercredi, le 20 Septembre, 1895 (v.s.), vers les 11 heures à la Turque du soir, en compagnie du Consul de Perse à Trébizonde, Razi Han; du Directeur des Postes et Télégraphes, Hadji Omer Effendi; et du Commandant de la Gendarmerie du vilayet, Suleiman Bey, qu'ils avaient rencontrés chemin faisant, la Rue Ouzoun Sokak, débouchant à la Place Charki, dans la ville même de Trébizonde, lorsqu'un certain Armenak, domestique à l'Évêché Arménien, que l'on soupçonnait être affilié aux Comités révolutionnaires, et un autre individu, également Arménien, ont tiré sur eux plusieurs coups de revolver, et ont blessé Bahri Pacha à la cheville et Hamdi Pacha au pied. Armenak et son complice ont été arrêtés sur le champ.

Ce fait ayant eu lieu à Trébizonde pour la premièr fois depuis que des

Arméniens, sujets Ottomans, ont commencé à commettre des crimes, et à se mettre en rébellion dans quelques parties de l'Empire, a provoqué naturellement une certain émotion parmi la population, mais il n'a pas été suivi heureusement ce jour-là d'autre incident. Deux jours plus tard, soit le Vendredi, vers les 2 heures à la Turque de la nuit, quelques Musulmans appartenant au corps des métiers, ayant rencontré au quartier Aï Vassil un certain Hatchik, fils d'un coiffeur nommé Stépan, qui était recherché par la police sous la prévention d'avoir participé à l'agression contre les deux Pachas, lui ont adressé la parole dans les termes suivants: "L'autorité te cherche parce que tu es accusé de coups et blessures; où te sauves-tu?" Hatchik, saisissant aussitôt son arme, a fait feu sur eux à plusieurs reprises. Un certain Rahmi Effendi, qui passait en ce moment dans une rue voisine, ayant entendu la détonation, et voulant en connaître la cause, est entré dans la rue d'où venait le bruit, mais aperçu par Hatchik, il a été assailli à coups de revolver et tué.

Ce second incident succédant à l'autre à deux jours d'intervalle a produit une grande effervescence, et au bruit des coups de feu entendu des quartiers avoisinants, tout le monde s'est précipité dans les rues, les uns armés, et les autres sans armes. Une rumeur, suivant laquelle les Arméniens auraient attaqué le siège du Gouvernement et assassiné le Vali, ayant été répandue aux villages Musulmans situés à proximité de la ville, la population a commencé aussi à y affluer, et il en est résulté un grand encombrement et une très forte agitation. Cependant, les autorités civiles et militaires, ainsi que les zaptiés et les agents de police, aidés des Notables de la ville, ont occupé l'entrée de chaque rue, et ont réssui, avec beaucoup de difficulté, it est vrai, à calmer les esprits et à disperser la foule, en lui expliquant que les coups de feu entendus n'avaient aucune gravité, et que les Arméniens n'avaient fait rien de fâcheux.

La répétition des coups et blessures par les conjurés Arméniens, et la non-arrestation de l'un des agresseurs et de son complice, ont eu pourtant pour effet d'entretenir l'agitation publique. D'autre part, la méfiance témoignée à l'égard des Musulmans et de l'autorité par les Arméniens, qui n'ouvraient plus leurs boutiques et magasins, a nécessairement accentuée la tumulte. En présence de cette situation le prêtre Mesrob, représentant de l'évêque la tumulte. En présence de cette situation le prêtre Mesrob, représentant de l'Évêque Arménien, et les Notables de la communauté, ont été convoqués au siège du Gouvernement, mais deux seuls se sont présentés: le représentant de l'Évêque et le négociant Mahouhian. Ils ont été priés de déployer tous leurs efforts pour prévenir le renouvellement de pareilles scènes, qui sont de nature à détruire la confiance mutuelle entre les différents habitants, et pour découvrir et signaler à l'autorité le lieu où se cachaient les deux prévenus, dont l'arrestation devait amener le calme et la tranquillité. En réponse à ces exhortations Mahouhian a déclaré qu'il ne s'est jamais mêlé, et qu'il ne se mêlerait pas non plus dans l'avenir, des affaires de la communauté. La prêtre a répondu de son côté qu'il ne connaissait pas les prévenus, que, d'après ce qui se disait, les deux Pachas auraient été blessés par un soldat, et que Rahmi Effendi aurait été tué par un Musulman. Il a ajouté qu'il serait juste de mcttre en état d'arrestation les vrais coupables et élargir les Arméniens emprisonnés par haine personnelle.

Il leur a été fait observer que les deux faits étaient de notoriété publique, constituaient même des cas de flagrant délit. Le premier avait eu lieu en plein jour, les agresseurs avaient été aperçus par plusieurs personnes, et Hatchik Stépan, non encore arrêté, habitait la ville même. On était par conséquent mal venu à simuler l'ignorance et à prendre ainsi le parti des coupables. Mesrob et Mahouhian ont été donc engagés de nouveau à prendre en considération les conseils de l'autorité et convoquer les Notables de la communauté à conférer entre eux sur la situation, signaler confidentiellement le lieu oú se cachaient Hatchik et son complice, et contribuer ainsi à calmer l'effervescence qui avait gagné la population.

Ces deux incidents ayant été suivis de la nouvelle des troubles suscités à Constantinople par quelques vagabonds Arméniens, la préoccupation du public s'est accrue davantage. Tout le monde a été alarmé et les Arméniens en général ont commencé à se promener tout armés et à ne plus ouvrir leurs magasins. Comme depuis le jour de l'incident, les Arméniens des villages environnants avaient commencé à affluer dans la ville, le Gouverneur-Général, voulant prévenir des rixes sanglantes et des actes de pillage, s'est rendu au marché accompagné du Président de la Municipalité, le Mardi, 26 Septembre au matin et rassemblant dans un magasin un grand nombre de notables Musulmans et Chrétiens pris dans le corps des métiers, il leur a adressé des conseils, les exhortant à ne pas troubler l'ordre et la tranquillité et à cesser le tumulte. C'est précisément en ce moment que des coups de fusil et de revolver se sont fait entendre subitement de tous côtés sur la Place Charki. Il était alors environ 3 heures et demie à la Turque. Au milieu du trouble qui régnait, il n'a pas été possible de déterminer le lieu où la bagarre avait tout d'abord éclaté. Le fait est que plus les troupes Impériales, les agents de police, et les zaptiés travaillaient à réprimer l'émeute, plus l'audace des Arméniens augmentait. C'est de leurs boutiques et magasins, des chambres de dessus, des fenêtres donnant sur les rues et de partout où il se trouvaient qu'ils tiraient sans cesse sur les soldats, les zaptiés, et la population indistinctement. Le Vali apprenant l'emeute, s'est rendu en toute hâte sur les lieux. Malgré sa présence, le feu a continué, dirigé contre les officiers de l'armée régulière et du corps des zaptiées qui, postés devant les hans et les boutiques, engageaient les émeutiers à quitter leurs armes et à se mettre sous la protection de l'autorité qui saurait les défendre. On n'a pas épargné non plus la personne du Gouverneur contre lequel on a tiré plusieurs coups. A la vue d'un soldat et de deux ou trois particuliers Musulmans blessés ainsi que de deux autres gisant raides morts, l'agitation de Musulmans et des gens qui s'étaient rassemblés est arrivée à son paroxysme. Ce n'est que vers les 9 heures seulement à la Turque que l'on a pu à grand'peine rétablir l'ordre. Les cadavres éntendus dans les rues et les boutiques ont été transportés cetter même nuit dans les magasins inoccupés et les blessés ont été installés dans leurs maisons et à l'hôpital.

Après que la bagarre eut pris fin, les Arméniens qui étaient restés enfermés dans les maisons, les hans, et les magasins en ont été retirés et débarrassés de leurs armes. Jusqu'à ce que même la surexcitation fût calmée, ils ont été installés dans les hôtels des autorités civiles et militaires, et ceux qui parmi eux et parmi les familles réfugiées dans quelques maisons Musulmanes et à l'école Catholique étaient dépourvus de moyens, ont reçu du pain et tout ce qui leur était nécessaire. Quand l'ordre a été complètement rétabli, les récidivistes et les prévenus qui ont pu être saisis ont été déférés à la cour martiale et tous les autres ont regagné leurs foyers.

Les sujets Ottomans et les étrangers qui avaient cherché un asile chez les Consuls au moment de la bagarre ont été transportés par groupes chez eux et en vue de protéger pendant l'action contre toute attaque les Consulats étrangers, les écoles et les établissements du culte ainsi que les habitations des sujets étrangers, tous ces édifices ont été gardés par des troupes régulières et des zaptiés. Quelques familles même ont été mises en sûreté dans des maisons de Notables Musulmans et partout où la troupe et les zaptiés ont fait ddefant, ce sont les Primats Musulmans et partout où la troupe et les zaptiés ont fait défaut, ce sont les Primats Musulmans et Chrétiens qui y ont suppléé. Pour aider l'autorité dans son œuvre de pacification, une Commission a été instituée sous la présidence du Recceveur-Général du vilayet, composée de notables Musulmans, Orthodoxes, et Catholiques. Sa mission consiste à rassurer les esprits, pourvoir à la subsistance des nécessiteux, faire soigner les blessés, faire rendre les objets qui auraient été volés pendant la bagarre tant au marché que dans les maisons, prévenir toute attaque des villages Arméniens aux alentours de la ville par d'autres villages, découvrir les objets qu y auraient été perdus et si l'on venait à apprendre quelque projet d'attaque de villages Musulmans et Chrétiens ou loin de la ville de Trébizonde par des villages voisins Arméniens, aviser aux mesures nécessaires de concert avec la force armée et le corps des zaptiés ainsi que des Primats de ces villages. L'effectif existant de ce dernier corps n'étant pas suffisant, 200 nouveaux zaptiés ont été enrôles provisoirement. En un mot, ce que la prévoyance indique a été exécuté en vue de parer à toute éventualité.

Après la complète répression des troubles, il a été procédé à une enquête minutieuse en vue de découvrir les auteurs des premières fusillades. Il a été ainsi constaté que le Mardi matin, 6 Septembre, jour de l'émeute, quelques conjurés étaient attendu de Constantinople sur le bateau Autrichien. Un rassemblement inusité d'Arméniens ayant eu lieu au débarcadère près de la Place Charki, la curiosité de la population s'est éveillée. Parmi les lettres apportées par ce bateau et distribuées par la poste il y en a eu une à l'adresse de l'homme d'un certain Chvarch d'Erzindjan, demeurant au han, vis-à-vis de l'Hôtel Municipal, qui se trouve sur la même Place Charki. Cette lettre contenait des détails sur l'incident de

Constantinople et rendait compte de la mort du frère du destinataire. Celui-ci, aussitôt qu'il a lu la lettre, s'est mis, de la fenêtre de la chambre qu'il occupait, à tirer sur les passants des coups de revolver, en disant qu'on devait agir ainsi en pareille occurrence. Immédiatement après, quatre ou cinq coups de fusil et de revolver sont partis du magasin des Diradourian, en face du han et au-dessous de l'Hôtel Municipal. Ces coups ont été suivis de plusieurs autres tirés par les Arméniens rassemblés au débarcadère. C'est ainsi que la foule qui se trouvait sur cette place et dans les rues a été forcée bon gré mal gré de riposter.

Le fait que quelques-uns des individus ayant fait feu pendant l'émeute de l'intérieur des maisons Arméniennes étaient des habitants des villages environnants descendus en ville le matin; que les premiers coups ont été tirés par eux et de différents points; qu'avant la bagarre les boutiques et les magasins avaient été fermés; que les Arméniens eux-mêmes reconnaissent ces faits; et qu'enfin les officiers de l'armée et du corps des zaptiés, en les exhortant à faire leur soumission et à déposer leurs armes, ont été accueillis par des coups de fusil et de pistolet, ainsi qu'il a été exposé plus haut, prove surabondamment que les émeutiers avaient résolu de produire dans le pays un grand carnage.

Il est digne de remarque que le susnommé Chvarch d'Erzindjan, de la chambre duquel est parti le premier coup, bien qu'affilié au Comité révolutionnaire, et quoique coupable de plusieurs crimes, a bénéficié de l'amnistie accordée par Sa Majesté Impériale le Sultan. De même, les Diradourian comptent parmi les individus les plus suspects.

Comme il est impossible aux Arméniens de nier qu'ils ont été les auteurs de ces troubles, ne trouvant rien à dire, ils se bornent à maudire les misérables qui ont agi et les vouent à la vengeance Divine.

F. O. 424/184, pp. 215-217, No. 375/1

No. 447

Mr. Gosselin to the Marquess of Salisbury.

No. 38. BERLIN, *November 7, 1895, 2.40 p.m.*
Telegraphic. *(Received November 7.)*

I HAVE acted on your Lordship's telegram No. 104 of to-day.

Some days ago the Minister for Foreign Affairs telegraphed to the German Ambassador at Constantinople asking his Excellency to report whether, in his opinion a revolution or the Sultan's desposition was imminent. The Ambassador has stated, in reply, that there is no doubt as to the existence at Constantinople of increasing disaffection amongst not only the Christian, but also the Mahommedan population. He did not, however, think an outbreak imminent as, in view of the network of spies which the Sultan had organized, no one dared to make a move. No special instructions have therefore been sent by the German Government.

The Minister for Foreign Affairs told me that he would telegraph the substance of the Greek Government's report as given in your Lordship's telegram, and ask the Ambassador's opinion.

A telegram, apparently identic to that repeated to me in your Lordship's telegram No. 102 of yesterday, has been received here from the German Ambassador at Constantinople, who reports the state of the whole Turkish Empire as one of the utmost gravity.

Baron von Marschall fears that the new Grand Vizier (Rifaat Pasha) is now too old to be of much use in the present serious crisis, though he gained great credit some years ago by his successful organization of a Christian gendermerie at Janina.

F. O. 424/184, p. 200, No. 338

No. 448

Sir E. Monson to the Marquess of Salisbury.

No. 82.   VIENNA, *November 7, 1895.*
Telegraphic.   *(Received November 7.)*

WITH reference to the telegram addressed to me by your Lordship No. 77, I am informed by Count Goluchowski that he has not received any such information, and that he regards as generally untrustworthy any news coming through Greek channels.

The Austrian Ambassador at Constantinople telegraphs that a more tranquil feeling prevails in the capital, and that the action taken by the Sublime Porte in consequence of the last representations made by the Embassies is satisfactory.

F. O. 424/184, p. 200, No. 339

No. 449

The Marquess of Salisbury to Mr. Herbert.

No. 212.
Telegraphic.   FOREIGN OFFICE, *November 7, 1895.*

URGENT representations have been made by Mr. Bompas, Q.C., on behalf of M. Knajian, a young Armenian clergyman, educated in England. He was arrested recently at Marsovan and taken to Yuzgat, whence it is believed he was transferred to Sivas, where it is feared he may be kept in chains.

I understand that communications in regard to him took place between Sir P.

Currie and the Grand Vizier, and that the latter said that if there was no serious charge against the prisoner he should be taken back to Marsovan.

I request you to inquire how the matter now stands, and to telegraph any information you can obtain.

F. O. 424/184, p. 201,* No. 341*

No. 450

Mr. Herbert to the Marquess of Salisbury.

No. 632.   CONSTANTINOPLE, *November 8, 1895, 12.30 p.m.*
Telegraphic.   *(Received November 8.)*

IN reply to your Lordship's telegram No. 212 of yesterday, I have the honour to state that Knajian was arrested at Marsovan on the 16th October, and has been conveyed to Sivas. He is charged with continuing the propaganda of Thoumaian.

Sir P. Currie made representations about his case to the Grand Vizier, who promised that he should be sent back if there was no serious charge against him, and the Vali of Angora informed Her Majesty's Consul that he would be well treated, and merely sent back to his native town of Orfa, on reaching which he would be set at liberty. It is at the present moment very difficult to insure the safety and proper treatment of individual Armenians in the provinces, but I will make fresh inquiries respecting Knajian of the present Grand Vizier.

F. O. 424/184, p. 201*, No. 342*

No. 451

Mr. Herbert to the Marquess of Salisbury.

No. 769.   PERA, *November 7, 1895.*
My Lord,   *(Received November 11.)*

AS an impression is prevalent here, and to some extent confirmed by Consular reports, that the Armenians have on several occasions taken the initiative against the Mahommedans in the provinces, and that the revolutionary movement among them is growing more aggressive, I instructed Mr. Eliot to call on the Armenian Patriarch and urge him to send a further Circular exhorting his people to tranquillity.

I have the honour to inclose herewith a report by Mr. Eliot of the Patriarch's language.

I have, &c.

(Signed) MICHAEL H. HERBERT.

F. O. 424/184, p. 217, No. 376

Inclosure in No. 451

Memorandum.

I INFORMED the Armenian Patriarch this afternoon that the reports received from our Consular officers accused the Armenians of several districts, particularly the inhabitants of Zeitoun and Marash, of taking the initiative in provoking disturbances, and urged him as instructed, to send a second Circular to the Armenian ecclesiastical authorities. At last, after great pressure and with evident unwillingness, his Beatitude promised to immediately dispatch a telegram to all the Armenian vilayets exhorting his people to remain quiet and patient until the reforms granted by the Sultan should be published and executed.

He said he did not deny the importance of the revolutionary movement among the Armenians, but what gave it its present force? Some influence was at work which was not under his control. The Armenians, as he knew them, were poor broken-spirited people, too timid to raise their hands against the Turks. Yet in many places they seemed to have become possessed of money and misplaced courage. He attributed this state of things to the action of Russian agents, who brought money and arms into Armenia from Tiflis. Whenever the Turks attempted to arrest them, the Russian Embassy intervened, and they merely left the country, or even returned to the scene of their exploits. He had no pretensions to understand politics, but he imagined the explanation of Russia's conduct to be as follows:-

By the Treaty of San Stefano she had arranged the affairs of the East, but all Europe had objected to that arrangement. Russia was therefore determined to do nothing to ameliorate the state of Christians in Turkey until every one in the East, as well as the West, should turn to her as the only Power capable of dealing with the problem, and beg her to settle it as she thought best. He believed she was encouraging massacres in Asia Minor at present in the hope that she would be invited to occupy Armenia. He hated the Russians as a selfish and tyrannical nation, who desired to stamp out the Armenian language and religion, but, if the next fortnight should witness as many massacres as the last, he could only implore them to march to Erzeroum and save his people from slaughter.

He contrasted the action of the Powers in regard to Bulgaria and Armenia. The Bulgarians had attacked the Turks and massacred them wholesale, but this conduct had not alienated the sympathies of Europe. Now, whenever Armenians, driven to desperation, killed a few Turks, the Powers seemed to think that the whole nation had forfeited all claim to assistance.

He would send the telegram in order to show the Embassy, the Porte, and the English people that he was against every form of revolutionary movement, but he feared that its effect would be small. He had no influence over the agitators, and the Turkish Government had done their best to destroy his prestige with his own people. He could not even write his telegram in effective language; for instance, the police would not let him telegraph that the Embassies had communicated to him the scheme of reforms. He could only urge the necessity of having confidence in the benevolent wisdom of the Sultan, and he knew that the impression produced on Armenians in the provinces would be that he had been forced by the Porte to send the telegrams, just as they were forced to sign loyal and thankful Addresses.

I have, &c.

(Signed) C. N. E. ELIOT.

CONSTANTINOPLE, *November 1, 1895.*
F. O. *424/184, pp. 217-218, No. 376/1*

No. 452

Mr. Gosselin to the Marquess of Salisbury.

No. 255.   BERLIN, *November 7, 1895.*
My Lord,   *(Received November 11.)*
IN compliance with the instructions contained in your Lordship's telegram No. 104 of to-day, I communicated to Baron von Marschall the substance of the information communicated to your Lordship by the Greek Chargé d'Affaires, with regard to the critical state of affairs in the Turkish capital, and inquired of his Excellency whether similar news had reached Berlin; and, if so, what instructions the Imperial Government proposed to send to Constantinople.

His Excellency replied that some days ago rumours had reached him—he did not say from what source—as to the likelihood of a rising in Constantinople, or at all events a deposition of the Sultan, and he had consequently telegraphed to Baron de Saurma to inquire whether he considered either event probable.

His Excellency had replied that there was no doubt that the disaffection of all classes and creeds in Constantinople to the Sultan's rule was increasing in volume, but that in view of the network of spies and the army of informers with which His Majesty had succeeded in surrounding the Palace, no one dared to make the first move; and that he considered that for this reason, but not from any spark of loyalty, amongst either the Christian or Mahommedan population, there was no immediate fear of an outbreak.

Baron von Marschall said that under these circumstances he had not sent any special instructions to Constantinople—in case of a revolution—"Indeed, I do not quite see what could yet be done."

His Excellency begged me to express his thanks for your Lordship's communication, which he would transmit by telegraph to Baron von Saurma, and ask for his immediate opinion thereon.

He said that the German Government considered the state of things, not only in Constantinople itself, but throughout the whole Empire, as exceedingly grave, and proceeded to give me a report of the meeting of the Representatives of the Powers on the 5th instant, confirming entirely the news transmitted to your Lordship by Mr. Herbert in his telegram No. 590 of the 5th.

His Excellency said that the new Grand Vizier, Rifaat Pasha, gained some credit some years ago by his successful administration in Albania, where he organized a Christian gendarmerie for the district of Janina, but he feared that he had now reached an age when it would be hopeless to expect from him much energy in surmounting the numberless difficulties which he would have to face.

His Excellency added that Tewfik Pasha, the Ottoman Ambassador here, had called on him the day he left Berlin to say that he had received the Sultan's orders to come as quickly as possible to Constantinople; but Baron van Marschall seemed to doubt whether the Ambassador's counsels would be of much service to his Imperial Master, an opinion in which any one who knows the amiable Ambassador will most certainly concur.

Since our interview a telegram has been received here saying that Tewfik Pasha has been nominated Minister for Foreign Affairs.

Tewfik Pasha is considered here as an "homme du Palais," with little or no initiative of his own; he is a personal friend of the Sultan, and in as far as he has any independent views, he is credited with being in favour of a Russian alliance.

I have, &c.

(Signed) MARTIN GOSSELIN.

F. O. 424/184, pp. 218-219, No. 377

No. 453

Mr. Herbert to the Marquess of Salisbury.

No. 772.   CONSTANTINOPLE, *November 8, 1895.*
My Lord,   *(Received November 18.)*

I HAVE the honour to forward to your Lordship herewith copy of a despatch which I have received from the Acting British Consul at Erzeroum, reporting on the uneasiness prevailing throughout this district.

I have, &c.

(Signed) MICHAEL H. HERBERT.

F. O. 424/184, p. 242, No. 451

Inclosure 1 in No. 453

Consul Cumberbatch to Sir P. Currie.

Sir,   ERZEROUM, *October 21, 1895.*

WITH reference to my despatch of the 17th instant on the subject of the critical state of affairs in this town and vilayet, I have the honour to report that I have received information from Van, Mush, and Kharput, showing that the same uneasiness exists in those parts, principally in consequence of the recent disturbances at Constantinople and elsewhere.

I inclose copy of Mr. Vice-Consul Hallward's despatch, in which he alludes to the danger of an outbreak should the delay in the introduction of the long-expected reforms be prolonged.

Mr. Vice-Consul Hampson stated on the 6th instant that, as telegraphed to your Excellency, there was considerable uneasiness in Mush, rumours of the events in Constantinople giving rise to fears of disorders there, but that the town was being carefully patrolled.

I send copy of his despatch of the 16th instant reporting the state of feeling at the time.

At Kharput it is shown, by the accompanying extract from a private leter, that the situation is much the same, as already mentioned in my despatch of the 14th instant.

I have, &c.

(Signed) H. A. CUMBERBATCH.

F. O. 424/184, p. 242, No. 451/1

Inclosure 2 in No. 453

Vice-Consul Hallward to Consul Cumberbatch.

Confidential.

Sir,   ERZEROUM, *October 15, 1895.*

FROM a conversation which I had yesterday with the Vali, I gathered distinctly that he had no instructions to deal effectively with the Kurds; and, in fact, none of the criminals who have so long been the plague of this vilayet have been brought to justice, and robbery and crime continue almost unchecked.

As his Excellency remarked, it is useless to talk about reform unless the Kurds are brought under control, and quite unnecessary to send Shakir Pasha to do this. Were the necessary authority given to the Valis, the thing could be done at once. The fact that this step is not taken shows, I fear, that the authorities in Constantinople are determined to allow the present state of things to continue.

There is, on the other hand, a very decided and wide-spread feeling among the Armenians that this state of things must not be allowed to continue, but that a change of some sort must be wrought at any price. It is a common thing to hear said by ignorant peasants that immediate death would be preferable to the present slow system of extermination, and I have no doubt that this idea is being fostered among them. There is far more general sympathy with revolutionary ideas among all classes of the population than formerly; as, though bad government has existed here from time immemorial, it is only within the last year or two that the Armenians have become convinced that the Turks are aiming at their extermination.

I do not wish to exaggerate the importance of these sentiments, as I am by no means convinced that the Armenians have sufficient courage or devotion to a common cause to set on foot anything like an active general movement against the Government. But if the solution of this question is delayed much longer, and the Armenians lose hope of their legitimate demands being satisfied through the intervention of the Powers, there will be considerable danger of serious disturbances arising in this province.

I have, &c.

(Signed) C. M. HALLWARD.

F. O. 424/184, pp. 242–243, No. 441/2

Inclosure 3 in No. 153

Vice-Consul Hampson to Consul Cumberbatch.

Sir, MUSH, *October 16, 1895.*

I AM glad to be able to report that perfect tranquillity continues to exist in this town and neighbourhood, and, as far as I can learn, throughout the vilayet. In spite of the rumours of disturbances at Constantinople, Trebizond, Sivas, &c., and the consequent tension of public feeling, which is undoubtedly great, not the smallest outbreak has so far occurred.

This is much to the credit of the Mutessarif, who is taking every precaution in the way of patrols, &c. It is an anxous moment, but I hope that we may escape here without trouble.

I have, &c.

(Signed) CHARLES S. HAMPSON.

F. O. 424/184, p. 243, No. 451/3

Inclosure 4 in No. 453

Extract from Private Letter from Kharput, dated October 7, 1895.

THE anxiety of the Christians over the reported distribution of arms and ammunition has deepened; scarcely any one doubts the truth of the rumour. The shopkeepers in the town, nearly all of them, decided not to open their shops on Saturday (5th October) last, because of the report that an uprising was to occur on that day, but some of the more intelligent men, with great difficulty, prevented the closing so as not to rouse the Turks.

A Protestant woman, who goes from this part of the town to the other to give lessons, has been advised by a friendly Turkish woman not to pursue her labour for the present.

F. O. 424/184, p. 243, No. 451/4

No. 454

Mr. Herbert to the Marquess of Salisbury.

No. 773.   CONSTANTINOPLE, *November 8, 1895.*
My Lord,   *(Received November 18.)*
    I HAVE the honour to forward to your Lordship herewith copy of a despatch which I have received from the Acting British Consul at Erzeroum respecting the assassination of two Armenian informers at Van and Mush.

I have, &c.

(Signed) MICHAEL H. HERBERT.

F. O. 424/184, p. 243, No. 452

Inclosure in No. 454

Consul Cumberbatch to Sir P. Currie.

Sir,   ERZEROUM, *October 21, 1895.*
    WITH reference to my despatch of the 11th instant on the subject of the assassination of certain Armenian informers, I have the honour to report that Her Majesty's Vice-Consul at Mush announces the murder of a priest, Parsekh by name, in that town on the 6th instant.

Mr. Hampson says that this man was a notorious spy and agent of the authorities, and was deservedly hated by the Armenians.

Her Majesty's Vice-Consul at Van also reports the stabbing to death in that town, on the 7th instant, of Ohannes Derbogossian.

Mr. Hallward states that he was a clever man, who no doubt used his abilities chiefly to his own advantage, and possibly to the detriment of his co-religionists.

In both instances Armenian revolutionary agents are credited with the crime, though no evidence had yet been forthcoming to that effect.

I have, &c.

(Signed) H. A. CUMBERBATCH.

F. O. 424/184, p. 244, No. 452/1

No. 455

Mr. Herbert to the Marquess of Salisbury.

No. 774.   CONSTANTINOPLE, *November 8, 1895.*
My Lord   *(Received November 18.)*

I HAVE the honour to forward to your Lordship herewith copy of a despatch which I have received from the Acting British Consul at Erzeroum reporting the satisfactory progress of the relief work at Sasun.

I have, &c.

(Signed) MICHAEL H. HERBERT.

F. O. 424/184, p. 244, No. 453

Inclosure 1 in No. 455

Consul Cumberbatch to Sir P. Currie.

Sir,   ERZEROUM, *October 22, 1895.*

I HAVE the honour to transmit copy of a further report of Her Majesty's Vice-Consul at Mush, together with a letter from Mr. Cole to the Constantinople Committee, on the subject of relief operations in Sasun.

Mr. Hampson says that much still remains to be done to adequately provide for the destitute Armenians against the coming winter, and he lays stress on the necessity of the dispatch at once of any further funds that may be available.

The missionaries charged with the work wish to have their gratitude conveyed to the Marquess of Salisbury for his Lordship's kind appreciation of their labours.

I have, &c.

(Signed) H. A. CUMBERBATCH.

F. O. 424/184, p. 244, No. 453/1

Inclosure 2 in No. 455

Vice-Consul Hampson to Consul Cumberbatch.

Sir,   Mush, *October 16, 1895.*

I HEAR good accounts of the way in which the relief work in Sasun is progressing. A considerable number of houses in the villages are completed, though I fear that the present cold and wet weather must cause much suffering and sickness among those for whom no shelter is as yet provided. It is much to be regretted that the military authorities have not lent some tents, as suggested in my despatch of the 29th ultimo.

Necessary clothing, grain, and cattle are also being collected and sent up to the villages as fast as the means and the money will permit, and the 3,000*l.* already sent from England were nearly expended. To-day I have received Sir P. Currie's telegram informing me that a further sum of 1,000*l.* is at our disposal, and as the Armenian Committee has also now expressed the intention of confiding considerable sums to the missionaries, we can now go ahead boldly. Much, however, still remains to be done to make anything like adequate provision for the destitute against the coming winter, and the time is now very short. The more rapidly funds can reach us now the more hope there is of obtaining a really satisfactory result.

Mr. Cole and Dr. Reynolds wish me to express the pleasure they feel at the Marquess of Salisbury's kind appreciation of their work, conveyed to me in Sir Philip Currie's despatch of the 30th ultimo.

I have, &c.

(Signed) Charles S. Hampson.

P.S.—I inclose an interesting report from Mr. Cole on his recent visit to the Talori district. I would call special attention to the fact that the Kurdish Aghas are again demanding tribute from the villages. Prompt steps are needed to stop this evil, and to keep Kurd Sasun in order. (*Vide* my despatch of yesterday.)

C. S. H.

F. O. 424/184, pp. 244-245, No. 453/2

No. 456

Mr. Herbert to the Marquess of Salisbury.

No. 775.

CONSTANTINOPLE, *November 8, 1895.*

(Received November 18.)

My Lord,

WITH reference to Sir P. Currie's telegram No. 528 of the 23rd ultimo, I have the honour to forward to your Lordship herewith copy of a despatch which I have received from the Acting British Consul at Erzeroum respecting the recent disturbances at Erzinghian.

I have, &c.

(Signed) MICHAEL H. HERBERT.

F. O. 424/184, p. 245, No. 454

Inclosure in No. 456

Consul Cumberbatch to Sir P. Currie.

Sir,

ERZEROUM, *October 24, 1895.*

I HAD the honour to telegraph to your Excellency yesterday that disturbances had occurred on the 21st instant at Erzinghian, during which about sixty Armenians and a dozen Turks had been killed, besides many on both sides wounded, and that the official report was to the effect that the troubles arose from the shooting of a Mollah. I also added that, though the pillaging of Armenian villages by both Kurdish and Laz bands continued very actively all round, things in this town remained quiet.

No detailed account has yet been received from Erzinghian, but it appears that the Mollah, or rather Imam, was shot in the market-place by an Armenian, who was then and there set upon and beaten to death by the Turks.

This incident naturally led to reprisals on both sides, some Armenians firing from their houses on the Turks.

The number of wounded on both sides is not yet known, but must be considerable.

The conflict was stopped and further bloodshed prevented, for the present at least, by the interference of the soldiers under the orders of Zekki Pasha, Commander-in-chief of the 4th Army Corps.

I have, &c.

(Signed) H. A. CUMBERBATCH.

F. O. 424/184, p. 245, No. 454/1

No. 457

Mr. Herbert to the Marquess of Salisbury.

No. 776.   CONSTANTINOPLE, *November 8, 1895.*
My Lord,   *(Received November 18.)*
    WITH reference to my despatch No. 740 of the 29th ultimo, I have the honour
to forward to your Lordship herewith copy of a despatch which I have received
from the British Acting Consul at Erzeroum giving further details respecting the
mission of Shakir Pasha.
                                    I have, &c.
                                              (Signed) MICHAEL H. HERBERT.
    F. O. 424/184, p. 246, No. 455

Inclosure in No. 457

Consul Cumberbatch to Sir P. Currie.

Confidential.
Sir,   ERZEROUM, *October 24, 1895.*
    WITH reference to my despatch of the 18th instant, I have the honour to
inform your Excellency that Shakir Pasha is still at Erzeroum, and that no date is
yet fixed for his departure.
    Whether his detention here is due to superior instructions, in order that he
may assist the Vali in re-establishing order in the vilayet amongst the Kurds and
Lazes, or that he may receive fresh instructions necessitated by the latest turn of
events, I am unable to discover.
    He has been very busy writing reports on the subject of the various
Government Departments of this vilayet, as mentioned in my above-named
despatch, including one in connection with the collection of taxes.
    In most, if not all, of his schemes he has evidently been guided by the project of
the 11th May of the three Powers, though he claims them to be the results of his own
inquiries and deliberations.
                                    I have, &c.
                                              (Signed) H. A. CUMBERBATCH.
    F. O. 424/184, p. 246, No. 455/1

No. 458

Mr. Herbert to the Marquess of Salisbury.

No. 777. Confidential.   CONSTANTINOPLE, *November 8, 1895.*
My Lord,   *(Received November 18.)*

WITH reference to my telegram No. 632 of to-day's date, I have the honour to forward to your Lordship herewith copy of a despatch which I have received from the Acting British Consul at Angora reporting the arrest of the Protestant pastor at Marsovan named Knajian.

I have, &c.

(Signed) MICHAEL H. HERBERT.

F. O. 424/184, p. 246, No. 456

Inclosure in No. 458

Acting Consul Fontana to Mr. Herbert.

Confidential.
Sir,   ANGORA, *November 2, 1895.*

I HAVE the honour to report, for your information, that the Rev. Mugherditch Khajian, pastor of the Protestant church at Marsovan, was suddenly arrested in that town on the 16th ultimo without receiving any intimation as to the nature of the charge brought against him, and was hurried off during the night to Yuzgat; he was prevented, moreover, from communicating with his friends before leaving, and even from providing himself with money and clothes for the journey.

The Vali, to whom I spoke upon the subject to-day, informed me that Knajian was suspected of being the follower, and, in fact, the successor of the Armenian patriot Tomaian, who is believed to be at present in England; that the Marsovan authorities further complained of his unbridled tongue and general restlessness, and that it had consequently been decided to banish him to his native town of Orfa, in the Vilayet of Aleppo.

Memdouh Pasha assured me, however, that he had telegraphed to the Vali of Sivas requesting that the pastor might be well cared for upon his arrival there, and added that he would be set at liberty as soon as he reached Orfa.

The Rev. Knajian is considered by the Armenians in this city to have done good work in Marsovan by using every effort to bring to light covert official abuses and acts of oppression committed in that town; and he is said to have journeyed to Constantinople last year with the express purpose of presenting either to Her Majesty's Embassy or to the Porte a petition signed by many of his fellow-townsmen, protesting agains the wholesale imprisonment of Armenians, and the ill-treatment they suffered at thc hands of the Turks.

I have, &c.

(Signed) RAPHAEL A. FONTANA.

F. O. 424/184, pp. 246-247, No. 456/1

No. 459

Mr. Herbert to the Marquess of Salisbury.

No. 780.   CONSTANTINOPLE, *November 8, 1895.*
My Lord,   *(Received November 18.)*

AS I had the honour to report to your Lordship in my telegram No. 615 of the 5th instant, the Sultan sent me on that day a message containing, amongst other things, a promise that the reforms should be published in the press of the capital "to-morrow." As they did not appear in the papers of either the 6th or 7th, I sent Mr. Block yesterday to the Palace to express to the First Secretary my astonishment and regret at His Majesty's failure to carry out his promises.

In reply, I received the following message: His Majesty had intended to make the publication, but he now hesitated from fear that the result would be an increase of jealousy on the part of his Moslem subjects, who would perhaps visit their resentment on the Christians; in fact, His Majesty had decided that this was not the moment. Even were they published, what good would it do? A résumé had been published in the press, and the Armenians should thus know that reforms would be given them. What advantage would it be to the Armenian peasant to know that such and such an Article of the law would be carried out? People could not go about with the "Destour" open searching for various Articles of the law.

The Sultan complained that, although the Powers were satisfied with the reforms, the Patriarch had never expressed a word of thanks or gratitude.

His Majesty desired me to telegraph to your Lordship that deeds and not words were, in his opinion, what was necessary at the moment. He had already said he would carry out the reforms, and he intended totally to do so, but the first thing was to put an end to this deplorable bloodshed in the provinces, provoked by the Armenians. This he was striving to do by sending the strongest instructions, holding the authorities responsible, and enjoining upon them the necessity of first using conciliatory measures before allowing the troops to use their arms. He trusted your Lordship would instruct the Consuls to urge the Armenians to return to their vocations, and not provoke disorders and arouse the Turks, and that the Embassy would also urge the Patriarch to use his influence. With regard to the reforms being communicated in detail to the Patriarch officially, the same objections held good, as the Patriarch would publish them in the Armenian press.

The First Secretary suggested a way out of the difficulty, viz., that the Patriarch should be called to the Ministry of Public Worship, and the reforms read to him, but this does not seem very practicable.

I have, &c.

(Signed) MICHAEL H. HERBERT.

F. O. 424/184, p. 247, No. 457

No. 460

The Marquess of Salisbury to Mr. Herbert.

No. 215.
Telegraphic. FOREIGN OFFICE, *November 8, 1895, 4.30 p.m.*

I HAVE received your telegram No. 627 of yesterday, relating to the selection of the President of the Commission of Control. I should certainly approve of the appointment of Saïd Pasha, the late Minister for Foreign Affairs, to the Presidency, but I concur in the opinion of your French and Russian colleagues that it will be refused if suggested by the three Powers.

F. O. 424/184, p. 203, No. 349

No. 461

The Marquess of Salisbury to Mr. Gosselin.

No. 315.
Sir, FOREIGN OFFICE, *November 8, 1895.*

COUNT METTERNICH called at this Office to-day and stated that the German Ambassador at Constantinople had reported, in reply to an inquiry addressed to him, that, in his opinion, the situation there was far from satisfactory, that the new Ministry had no authority, and that what was more serious was that the troops on which reliance could be placed were those stationed at Yildiz.

I am, &c.

(Signed) SALISBURY.

F. O. 424/184, p. 203, No. 350

No. 462

Mr. Herbert to the Marquess of Salisbury.

No. 644. Very Secret.   CONSTANTINOPLE, *November 9, 1895, 10.30 p.m.*
Telegraphic.   *(Received November 9.)*
THE Representatives of the Powers met to-day and discussed at length the question of what measurers should be taken if disturbances arose here. We arrived at no conclusion, but the Russian Ambassador stated that a proposal had been submitted by him to his Government, and that if this were approved he would submit it to us at our next meeting on Monday.

We also decided that we should consult with the Captains of the "stationnaires" and report at the same meeting as to the number of men which could be landed to guard the Embassy buildings.

F. O. 424/184, p. 204, No. 355

No. 463

Mr. Herbert to the Marquess of Salisbury.

No. 647.   CONSTANTINOPLE, *November 10, 1895, 10.30 a.m.*
Telegraphic.   *(Received November 10.)*
VICE-CONSUL HAMPSON telegraphs that the Kurds who are still pillaging the villages of the Mush plain have pillaged the village of Hitenk, in Sasun.

F. O. 424/184, p. 206, No. 360

No. 464

Mr. Herbert to the Marquess of Salisbury.

No. 648.   PERA, *November 10, 1895, 11.55 a.m.*
Telegraphic.   *(Received November 10, 5 p.m.)*
MY telegram No. 640.

Following appointments are gazetted this morning:-

Kiamil Pasha to be Governor of Smyrna, Governor of Smyrna to be Governor of Salonica, Governor of Salonica to be Governor of Aleppo.

F. O. 424/184, p. 206, No. 361

No. 465

Mr. Herbert to the Marquess of Salisbury.

No. 649. Secret.   CONSTANTINOPLE, *November 10, 1895, 11 a.m.*
Telegraphic.   *(Received November 10.)*

WITH reference to my telegrams Nos. 643 and 644 of the 9th November, the most reliable and best informed people here think that if a Mussulman revolution takes place it will be effected quietly, and that the movement will be directed against the Sultan alone, and not against Christians.

Two other dangers exist, however: the possibility of the Sultan in his present state of mind exciting the Mussulmans against the Christians, and the danger of another rising by Armenians, who are again desperate, with the view of bringing about foreign intervention.

The former danger is much feared by the Greek Minister and the five Ambassadors, who are now all anxious to face the situation, and to discuss measures to be taken in the event of an outbreak, as during the last forty-eight hours they have become much more alarmed.

Personally, I am of opinion that no additional cause for alarm has arisen during the last three days, but that, although nothing may occur, we should be prepared for every contingency.

F. O. 424/184, p. 206, No. 362

No. 466

Mr. Herbert to the Marquess of Salisbury.

No. 650. Secret.   CONSTANTINOPLE, *November 10, 1895, 11.10 a.m.*
Telegraphic.   *(Received November 10.)*

M. DE NÉLIDOFF has heard, though he cannot vouch for the truth of the information, that leaders have been found for the Mussulman revolutionary movement. Two Generals and four Colonels are spoken of in connection with it.

F. O. 424/184, p. 206, No. 363

No. 467

Mr. Herbert to the Marquess of Salisbury.

No. 651.   CONSTANTINOPLE, *November 10, 1895, noon.*
Telegraphic.   *(Received November 10.)*

AS "Cockatrice" usually passes through here at this time of year, and her arrival would presumably excite no comment, I have suggested to Admiral that she, should at once be ordered here from the Danube.

F. O. 424/184, p. 207, No. 364

No. 468

Mr. Herbert to the Marquess of Salisbury.

No. 652.   CONSTANTINOPLE, *November 10, 1895, 6.25 p.m.*
Telegraphic.   *(Received November 10.)*

WITH reference to my telegram No. 646, I have the honour to state that the Porte has telegraphed to the Vali of Syria instructing him to put a stop to disturbances, and to insure the safety of missionaries.

F. O. 424/184, p. 207, No. 365

No. 469

Mr. Gosselin to the Marquess of Salisbury.

No. 41.   BERLIN, *November 10, 1895, 3 p.m.*
Telegraphic.   *(Received November 10.)*

YESTERDAY the German Imperial ship "Moltke" left Brindisi for Smyrna.

F. O. 424/184, p. 207, No. 366

No. 470

Mr. Herbert to the Marquess of Salisbury.

No. 781.   CONSTANTINOPLE, *November 10, 1895.*
My Lord,   *(Received November 18.)*
    I HAVE the honour to forward to your Lordship herewith copy of a despatch which I have received from Her Majesty's Consul at Trebizond reporting further on the situation in that town.

I have, &c.

(Signed) MICHAEL H. HERBERT.

F. O. 424/184, p. 248, No. 458

Inclosure in No. 470

Consul Longworth to Mr. Herbert.

Sir,   TREBIZOND, *November 2, 1895.*
    SINCE the outbreak of the 8th ultimo, there have been at times false alarms in town, but no disturbances.
    Public confidence in the situation is, however, by no means entertained. Apart from other causes, the authorities still threaten the Armenians with another massacre if they fail to discover and deliver over to them shortly the suspects Gasparoglou and Stephanoglou. They, moreover, persist in the make-belief that there was an insurrectionary movement at Trebizond, unable though they are to name a single Turk as killed or wounded by Armenians on the occasion of the outbreak. Such dogged obduracy and perversity can only be possible in a shameless and despotic Government, supported by a people who had shown themselves to be murderers and robbers of the helpless and innocent.
    All but fifty of the Armenian prisoners have been released. It is questionable, however, whether most of them were not better off in gaol, for boycotted as they are by even Greeks out of fear of the Turks, they are virtually outcasts, bereft of their belongings, reduced to beggary, and expelled from their hired houses. In the villages I hear distress is greater, for their houses were sacked and burnt, and their cattle and grain stolen. No reliable information has, however, reached me from the near, much less from the distant, localities.
    Not one Turk has as yet been arrested for having taken part in the riot. What does this mean? Are they to consider themselves beyond the reach of the law? If so it is only fair to allow the Armenians wholesale emigration.
    As in the past so in the present, I am doing my utmost to inspire in the governing classes a more conciliatory spirit and a greater sense of justice. My efforts

have unfortunately met with very poor success. Every move of mine, in fact, to befriend the oppressed and to mitigate their sufferings is regarded with suspicion. Humanitarian sentiments, it would seem, are only too readily misconstrued into political machinations. I must of necessity therefore be prudent. I must advance gradually and cautiously, as any injudicious action on my part may precipitate matters and aggravate the situation. In other words, the moment is not propitious for any open interference in behalf of the persecuted people. The animosity created by false reports of England's policy in the Anatolian question, named unhappily the Armenian question, is at present too acute. We must therefore wait patiently for a reversion of feelings before venturing to urge more energetically the display of greater equity in this God-forsaken country.

I have, &c.

(Signed) H. Z. LONGWORTH.

F. O. 424/184, p. 248, No. 458/1

No. 471

Mr. Herbert to the Marquess of Salisbury.

No. 784.   CONSTANTINOPLE, *November 10, 1895.*
My Lord,   *(Received November 18.)*
    I HAVE the honour to forward to your Lordship herewith copy of a despatch which I have received from Her Majesty's Consul in Trebizond respecting the state of affairs in the Sivas Vilayet.

I have, &c.

(Signed) MICHAEL H. HERBERT.

F. O. 424/184, p. 251, No. 461

Inclosure in No. 471

Consul Longworth to Mr. Herbert.

Sir,   TREBIZOND, *October 30, 1895.*
    DR. JEWETT reports as follows in his letter to me, dated Sivas, the 23rd instant:-
    "Up to last Sunday threats of a massacre here were quite common, and caused considerable uneasiness. Extra precautions to prevent disturbances were taken by the Vali, and now the danger seems to be past.
    "When it became generally known on Sunday that I had received a telegram from Mr. Terrell announcing that the scheme of reforms had been accepted, the

general alarm subsided, and the Armenians began to rejoice. It appears quite certain that all of this talk of a massacre was instigated by the revolutionists, who have been planning and trying to start some disorder here. However, the Turks became persuaded that they were to go for the Christians, and they were prepared to do their duty.

"Three hundred Christians of Azizieh, hearing that there were serious disorders here, started for Sivas one day last week ostensibly to assist the Government, but really, I suppose, for the sake of plunder. They were turned back by a company of zaptiehs.

"I think the majority of Turks are pleased that the Armenian question is apparently settled, and that there are to be reforms. Of course, the corrupt officials are not pleased. Some Turks who want reforms are angry that they should come from the cries of the Armenians.

"The Armenian Archbishop received the following telegram, dated the 21st October, from his representative at Divrik:-

"'About 400 Dersim brigands, after having entirely ruined the Armenian Cariehs of Hassova and Armoudan, and killed many people, they attacked yesterday the Armenian Cariehs of Zoumara and Puigian, killed many people, and destroyed their property. It is certain they will attack others, and we are all in great danger. Some zaptiehs sent from here to check these brigands are reported to have been killed.'"

I have, &c.

(Signed) H. Z. LONGWORTH.

F. O. 424/184, p. 251, No. 461/1

No. 472

Mr. Herbert to the Marquess of Salisbury.

No. 787.   CONSTANTINOPLE, *November 10, 1895.*
My Lord,   *(Received November 18.)*

I HAVE the honour to inform your Lordship that a question has arisen lately as to the right of British Consuls, who are charged with Armenian interests, to protect naturalized American subjects of Ottoman origin.

From the correspondence herewith inclosed, it appears that the Turkish authorities entirely deny any such right.

I have also received a telegram from Her Majesty's Consul at Trebizond, asking whether, during the existence of martial law, a Consul may extend protection to a naturalized British subject or an American citizen of Ottoman origin.

As under ordinary circumstances Her Majesty's Consular officers do not extend protection to naturalized British subjects of Orroman origin when they return to Turkey, I have the honour to request your Lordship's instructions as to the position that should be taken up by British Consuls in the matter.

I have, &c.

(Signed) MICHAEL H. HERBERT.

F. O. 424/184, p. 252, No. 462

Inclosure 1 in No. 472

Consul Cumberbatch to Sir P. Currie.

Sir,   ERZEROUM, *October 22, 1895.*

WITH reference to Mr. Consul Graves' despatched of the 8th and 11th July and 17th September and his telegram of the 25th September, as well as your Excellency's telegrams of the 9th and 12th July, I have the honour to forward, for the information of the United States' Minister, a translation of a letter received by me from the Vali of Erzeroum, in reply to one addressed to his predecessor by Mr. Graves last July, refusing to recognize the claims of Aroutine Simonian to the protection of the United States.

I have, &c.

(Signed) H. A. CUMBERBATCH.

F. O. 424/184, p. 252, No. 462/1

Inclosure 2 in No. 472

Note Verbale.

Translation.

AROUTINE SIMONIAN, mentioned in your letter of the 13th July last, who declares himself to be American subject, is a native of the Mamouret-el-Aziz Vilayet, and is an Ottoman subject. In 1303 (1887), when he was about 17 years of age, he went to America, remained there six years, and became an American subject; he afterwards returned.

When a Turkish subject wishes to become the subject of a foreign country, it is absolutely necessary for him to obtain the permission of the Ottoman Government; this permission has not been given to Aroutine.

If any one who is by birth a Turk wishes to become a foreign subject according to the Regulations of the foreign country, his papers must be examined and confirmed, and this can only be done for those who have become foreign subjects prior to the Ottoman Regulation published in 1285 (19th January, 1869).

Therefore the aforesaid Aroutine's claim to foreign protection cannot be accepted, as has been stated in the letter of the Minister of Foreign Affairs, dated the 7th (19th) September, 1311 (1895), and decided by the "Idaré Medjliss" of the vilayet and by the "Terdjamé Odassi" (Dragoman's office).

Dated Rebi-ul-Akhir 28, 1311, and Tishruni-Evvel 5, 1311 (October 17, 1895).

(Signed) RAOUF PASHA,
Vali of Erzeroum Vilayet.

F. O. 424/184, p. 252, No. 462/2

No. 473

Mr. Herbert to the Marquess of Salisbury.

No. 654. CONSTANTINOPLE, *November 11, 1895, 11.10 a.m.*
Telegraphic. *(Received November 11.)*

I INFORMED Her Majesty's Consul at Aleppo of a rumour which had come to my ears that the Zeitounlis had offered to capitulate, and I have now received the following answer:-

"The Ferik has informed me confidentially that the Zeitounlis have offered to capitulate peaceably. He sincerely hopes that this offer will not be refused."

F. O. 424/184, p. 219, No. 378

No. 474

The Marquess of Salisbury to Mr. Herbert.

No. 216.
Telegraphic. FOREIGN OFFICE, *November 11, 1895, midnight.*

I HAVE received your telegram No. 653 of to-day, in which you transmit a further message from the Sultan expressing surprise at having received no answer to his former message, in which His Imperial Majesty renewed his promises respecting the execution of reforms in the Armenian provinces, and appealed to Her Majesty's Government for assistance in his task.

In reply, you should explain to His Imperial Majesty that my answer to his last message was deferred until he had fulfilled the promise conveyed in it to publish immediately the scheme of reforms with a further Iradé, and you may express my great regret and disappointment at the postponement of the publication.

You will convey to His Imperial Majesty my respectful acknowledgements for his assurances of friendship to this country, and inform him that Her Majesty's Government are still desirous of assisting him, but that they consider it indispensable that measures should be taken to repress and prevent the attacks on the Christian population by the Mohammedans, which are taking place in various portions of the Ottoman dominions. The reports which have reached us show that the Sultan is mistaken in his belief that the Armenians have provoked these disorders. We are informed that on nearly every occasion this was not the case, and that in too many instances the Turkish authorities and troops have encouraged and even taken part in the outrages which have occurred.

The fact that the Sultan recently decorated an officer, whom he had dismissed on the ground of gross misgovernment, does not encourage Her Majesty's Government to feel any confidence in the earnestness of His Imperial Majesty's intention to give serious effect to the promised measures of reform.

F. O. 424/184, pp. 219-220, No. 379

No. 475

Tewfik Pasha to Rustem Pasha.

CONSTANTINOPLE, *le 11 Novembre, 1895.*
Télégraphique.   *(Communicated by Rustem Pasha, November 12.)*

LES nouveaux renseignements qui nous parviennent de Diarbékir établissent d'une manière évidente que les derniers désordres survenus dans cette ville ont été provoqués par les agitateurs Arméniens seuls. Les coups de revolver tirés par ceux-ci sur les mosquées au moment où les Musulmans faisaient leurs prières de Vendredi et leurs attaques à main armée contre les Musulmans ont été l'unique cause de ces troubles.

Quant à l'incendie qui a éclaté dans la ville, il a été également provoqué par des Arméniens; car il avait pris naissance à un endroit contigu aux maisons arméniennes d'où partaient continuellement des coups de fusil. Les Musulmans peuvent d'autant moins être accusés d'être les auteurs de cet incendie que les 90 pour cent des magasins et boutiques détruits leur appartenaient. De même que la très grande partie des marchandises brûlées étaient aussi leur propriété.

Le Vali d'Adana nous informe de son côté qu'environ 200 Arméniens déguisés en Circassiens ont attaqués les villages Musulmans de Zéitoun, Beli, et de Narl, en commettant toutes sortes de déprédations. Des mesures efficaces sont adoptées pour leur répression.

F. O. 424/184, p. 221, No. 381

No. 476

Tewfik Pasha to Rustem Pasha.

Télégraphique.

CONSTANTINOPLE, *le 11 Novembre, 1895.*
(Communicated by Rustem Pasha, November 12.)

LES émeutiers de Zéitoun ont attaqué le village de Tchoukour-Hissar, tué trente-cinq Musulmans, commis des actes de pillage, enlevé les armes, bestiaux, et objets des habitants du village Musulman de Deunghel, et assassiné le Secrétaire de la Direction des Impôts à Zéitoun. On ignore le sort de la femme et des quatre enfants de ce fonctionnaire.

F. O. 424/184, p. 221, No. 382

No. 477

Mr. Herbert to the Marquess of Salisbury.

No. 791.
My Lord,

CONSTANTINOPLE, *November 11, 1895.*
(Received November 15.)

I HAVE the honour to transmit to your Lordship herewith the translation of a message which was sent to me last night from the Sultan through His Imperial Majesty's First Secretary.

The Sultan also inquired if I could tell him where the Russian fleet was, and whether an alliance had been concluded between England and Austria. He had heard that an Austrian man-of-war had joined our fleet at Salonica.

I have, &c.

(Signed) MICHAEL H. HERBERT.

F. O. 424/184, pp. 229-230, No. 409

Inclosure in No. 477

Message to Mr. Herbert by His Majesty the Sultan.

"HOW is it that after all my messages of friendship, and the expressions of my good intentions, I get no answer from Lord Salisbury?" (The First Secretary here told His Majesty that you had sent his message, but that, evidently, there had been no time for an answer.)

His Majesty's message continued:-

"I hope for assistance from England, and I repeat that England should be convinced of my earnest desire to carry out my promises. The reforms have been granted; there is no reason in the world to suppose that they will not be faithfully carried out. It is to my interest and that of this country that the reforms should be introduced, and naturally we look to our own interests in this respect. The execution of reforms, however, is dependent on the re-establishment of order, and they can only be put in force when quiet exists.

"The Armenians, by their intrigues and sedition, and by provoking disorders, have delayed, and are still delaying, the reforms. Directly Shakir Pasha got to Erzeroum, he began to enrol Christian gendarmes. This is a proof that I desired to set to work at once. Then the trouble began at Erzindjian, followed by that at Baïbourt and Erzeroum, and I do not know if Shakir Pasha has been able to do anything more, but he began to work on the day of his arrival, and if he has been unable to continue it, it is only the troubles which have stopped him.

"To put an end to disorder I have had to call out at great sacrifice large numbers of troops with the ultimate object of executing the reforms as soon as possible, and I think I shall be able to complete them directly order is restored in less than two months. Thus I do not anticipate that much time will elapse before being able to get the reforms into working order.

"To further this end I am sending to-morrow two Feriks, Abdallah Pasha and Saad-ed-din Pasha, with some civil functionaires, the first to go to the Erzeroum district, the second to the Bitlis district, and their first efforts will be employed in restoring order by conciliatory means, if possible, and advise to all classes of the population. This is a still further proof of my good faith.

"Let then England help me by giving good advice to the Armenians, or even threatening them that nothing will be gained by their present conduct, and by telling them that, on the contrary, reforms cannot be carried out as long as they continue to agitate and create disorder.

"Why is it that England will not help me? I cannot understand it. Does Lord Salisbury not wish to help me? In spite of all my sincerest efforts I see that the English papers still abuse me. Can they not see that I am earnestly striving to put things straight? Cannot something be done to stop them? I expect Englnad to give me great assistance."

F. O. 424/184, p. 230, No. 409/1

No. 478

Mr. Herbert to the Marquess of Salisbury.

No. 656.   CONSTANTINOPLE, *November 12, 1895, 10.15 a.m.*
Telegraphic.   *(Received November 12.)*

I WAS informed yesterday by M. Cambon that he had asked his Government that French fleet should be sent to the Levant.

The French will probably send ships to the Syrian coast if the Catholics are attacked by the Druses, who, according to French Consuls in Syria, have hoisted the English flag.

F. O. 424/184, p. 221, No. 383

No. 479

Mr. Herbert to the Marquess of Salisbury.

No. 658. CONSTANTINOPLE, *November 12, 1895, 10.25 a.m.*
Telegraphic. *(Received November 12.)*

ACCORDING to the instructions contained in your Lordship's telegram No. 210 concerning the appointment of Shefik Bey to the Presidency of the Commission of Control, I told the Minister for Foreign Affairs that this appointment would not be accepted by Her Majesty's Government.

I was informed, in reply, that another person would be appointed, as Shefik Bey had resigned.

F. O. 424/184, p. 221, No. 384

No. 480

Mr. Herbert to the Marquess of Salisbury.

No. 659. CONSTANTINOPLE, *November 12, 1895, 10.25 a.m.*
Telegraphic. *(Received November 12.)*

THE American Vice-Consul at Sivas has telegraphed to the United States' Minister here that the village round Sivas have been pillaged. Great alarm prevails in Sivas itself, and at Malatia a serious massacre has taken place, four Jesuits having been killed.

F. O. 424/184, p. 222, No. 385

No. 481

Mr. Herbert to the Marquess of Salisbury.

No. 660. Secret. CONSTANTINOPLE, *November 12, 1895, 10.35 a.m.*
Telegraphic. *(Received November 12.)*

THERE was another meeting of the Representatives of the Great Powers last night, when M. de Nélidoff made the following proposal: That each Representative should apply to his Government to hold a gun-boat or light-armed vessel in readiness to dispatch to Constantinople to act as second "stationnaire," such vessel to have a crew of not less than 100 or more than 200 men; that as soon as we have all received answers from our Governments, and if they approve, another meeting will be held to decide whether the vessels shall be sent at once or not.

M. de Nélidoff insisted that the presence of six gun-boats with 600 men must produce a great moral effect here, and hinted that the adoption of his proposal might obviate the necessity of having recourse to measures involving political complications.

I believe a similar measure was adopted in 1876, when each Government had two "stationnaires" here.

As the other Representatives approved of the proposal, I agreed to submit it to your Lordship, but, if the danger here is imminent, I do not consider it very practical, as the Sultan has it in his power to delay the granting of the Firmans for the passage of the Straits for weeks, and, unless great pressure is brought to bear upon him, he will probably do so.

If your Lordship approves the proposal, will you inform me of the name of the vessel designated, and of her whereabouts?

We also agreed upon the arrangements for landing the crews and arms from the "stationnaires" in the event of disturbances.

F. O. 424/184, p. 222, No. 386

No. 482

Mr. Herbert to the Marquess of Salisbury.

No. 661.   CONSTANTINOPLE, *November 12, 1895, 11.30 a.m.*
Telegraphic.   *(Received November 12.)*

I REPEATED yesterday to the new Grand Vizier the arguments used on former occasions in regard to the publication of reforms, and pressed his Highness to proceed with it.

In reply, the Grand Vizier used language similar to that employed by the Sultan in his message to your Lordship of the 10th instant, and stated that it would be absolutely dangerous to publish reforms at this moment in view of the present effervescence among the Mussulmans.

An appeal was also made to me by his Highness that at this critical juncture the Turkish Government might receive the assistance of England.

I reminded him that the friendly advice which Her Majesty's Embassy had repeatedly offered had been hitherto steadfastly ignored by the Turkish Government, that every measure which had been suggested by us for the better government in the provinces had been opposed by them step by step, and that the present state of affairs was entirely due to the policy which they had though fit to pursue in spite of all our warnings.

F. O. 424/184, pp. 222-223, No. 387

No. 483

Mr. Herbert to the Marquess of Salisbury.

No. 662.   CONSTANTINOPLE, *November 12, 1895, 11.25 a.m.*
Telegraphic.   *(Received November 12.)*

MR. HAMPSON telegraphs that the news of the disturbances in Diarbekir has caused a return of the panic in Mush, and that the situation in Sasun and Talori is very bad. The Kurds have pillaged several villages and are threatening others, and complete panic reigns. If preventive measures are not taken at once the whole of the relief work will be wiped out. Mr. Hampson has again made urgent representations to the Mutessarif, who promised to send soldiers to Sasun; he cannot, however, send them to Talori, which is in the Sandjak of Guendj.

F. O. 424/184, p. 223, No. 388

No. 484

Mr. Herbert to the Marquess of Salisbury.

No. 664.   CONSTANTINOPLE, *November 12, 1895, 7.15 p.m.*
Telegraphic.   *(Received November 12.)*

HER Majesty's Vice-Consul at Van telegraphs as follows:-

"The village of Serai, which is principally inhabited by Nestorians, has been sacked by the Kurds. The bazaar and private houses were plundered, and every sort of property was swept away. No interference was attempted by the Kaïmakam or the small military force there. Several other villages have been sacked by the Kurds, and no attempt is made by the Government to check them. Indeed, they appear to tacitly approve proceedings by which thousands of Armenians have become destitute and homeless, and they have done nothing whatever to punish authors of outrages reported in my telegram of 2nd November. In the town great alarm is felt, and no business is being carried on. There is urgent need for strong measures in order that the state of anarchy may be put an end to."

I have brought this telegram to the notice of the Turkish Government.

F. O. 424/184, p. 223, No. 389

No. 485

Foreign Office to Admiralty.

Secret.

Sir,   FOREIGN OFFICE, *November 12, 1895.*

I AM directed by the Marquess of Salisbury to transmit to you, to be laid before the Lords Commissioners of the Admiralty, a copy of a telegram from Mr. Herbert, Her Majesty's Chargé d'Affaires at Constantinople, reporting that the Representatives of the six Great Powers, at a meeting held yesterday evening, had agreed, on the proposal of the Russian Ambassador, to apply to their respective Governments to hold in readiness for dispatch to Constantinople a gun-boat or light-armed vessel to act as second "stationnaire."

A telegram has been addressed to Mr. Herbert in reply, inquiring whether the arrival of the "Cockatrice," suggested by him, as their Lordships are aware from the telegram communicated in my letter of yesterday, would satisfy the proposal of the Russian Ambassador so far as the presence of Her Majesty's ships is concerned.

Lord Salisbury will be glad to be favoured with the observations of the Lords Commissioners on the Russian Ambassador's proposal.

I am, &c.

(Signed) T. H. SANDERSON.

F. O. 424/184, p. 223*, No. 389*

No. 486

Mr. Herbert to the Marquess of Salisbury.

No. 674.   CONSTANTINOPLE, *November 13, 1895, 6.45 p.m.*
Telegraphic.   *(Received November 13.)*

I RECEIVED the following telegram from Her Majesty's Consul at Aleppo dated yesterday:-

"The British Vice-Consul at Mersyna has received two telegrams from Missionary Martin requesting him to proceed to Hadjin, but I have instructed him not to comply with Mr. Martin's request, who has been informed that troops are at his disposal either to protect him at Hadjin or to escort him and his family to the coast.

"If the missionary is in personal danger, the presence of the Vice-Consul would do no good, and his life would be equally in danger.

"Mr. Martin would, I think, be unwilling to leave Hadjin without orders from the Society, but he ought to leave while it is still possible."

I have to-day telegraphed to Mr. Barnham approving his action, and informing him that the Bible House, though they refuse to order Mr. Martin to leave Hadjin, have authorized him to do so. I have at the same time instructed Mr. Barnham to insist on troops being sent to protect him in any case.

F. O. 424/184, p. 226, No. 399

No. 487

Sir E. Monson to the Marquess of Salisbury.

No. 84.   VIENNA, *November 13, 1895.*
Telegraphic.   *(Received November 13.)*

COUNT GOLUCHOWSKI has informed me that the Austro-Hungarian Ambassador in London had been instructed by him to inquire your Lordship's views as to what should be done to insure the safety of foreign residents at Constantinople in case of a revolutionary outbreak, and his Excellency read to me your Lordship's reply, which had been transmitted to him by Count Deym.

Count Goluchowski entirely approves the arrangement as to a second "stationnaire," but if massacres began in the town this alone would not suffice.

As the six Powers will shortly all have a naval force in the neighbourhood of Constantinople, and as they agree in acting for the general interest, Count Goluchowski thinks that an understanding should be arrived at that they are entitled, in case of need, to exact from the Turkish Government the right to send their ships of war through the Dardanelles. In his Excellency's opinion the Powers have a clear right to impose this view upon Turkey, being her protectors; and that Constantinople should be as accessible to their squadrons as Beyrout or Smyrna at a moment of such grave peril.

The Admirals of the various squadrons should receive instructions to dispatch them immediately on being warned by the Diplomatic Representatives at Constantinople, and each Power should bind itself to send a limited number of ships.

His Excellency feels sure that it is only prudent to arrive at an understanding beforehand, and not to leave everything to be arranged at the last moment, but he hopes that the danger against which it is desirable to provide is not imminent.

Count Goluchowski further informed me that the other Powers will be addressed by him in the same sense.

F. O. 424/184, pp. 226-227, No. 400

No. 488

Sir E. Monson to the Marquess of Salisbury.

No. 85.   VIENNA, *November 13, 1895.*
Telegraphic.   *(Received November 13.)*
  WITH reference to my preceding telegram No. 84 of this day's date, I have the
honour to report, most confidentially, that orders will be given this afternoon for
the dispatch to the Levant of an Austrian squadron consisting of four or five ships.
  A binding agreement limiting the number of ships to be sent through the
Dardanelles, on receipt of a summons from the Diplomatic Representatives at
Constantinople, is considered by Count Goluchowski to be essential. If such an
understanding be not arrived at, Russia might dispatch to the Golden Horn her
entire Black Sea fleet if she found that England sent a proportionately greater
number of ships than the Mediterranean Powers.
  His Excellency trusts that a squadron will be sent to the Levant by Germany
without loss of time.
  F. O. 424/184, p. 227, No. 401

No. 489

Sir E. Monson to the Marquess of Salisbury.

No. 86. Secret.   VIENNA, *November 13, 1895.*
Telegraphic.   *(Received November 13.)*
  WITH reference to the two preceding telegrams of this day's date, Nos. 84 and
85, which I had the honour to address to your Lordship, I beg to report that Count
Goluchowski informed me, in the strictest secrecy, that a revolution at
Constantinople, in which the Sultan would disappear, would not be absolutely
unacceptable, as it is difficult to see how he can be deposed by the Powers, and as
the best, if not the only, chance of restoring tranquillity seems now to depend upon
His Majesty's dethronement.
  F. O. 424/184, p. 227, No. 402

No. 490

The Marquess of Salisbury to Sir E. Monson.

No. 111.

Sir,   FOREIGN OFFICE, *November 13, 1895.*

YESTERDAY the Austrian Ambassador called upon me by special appointment, and stated that the object of the interview was to put to me two questions which he had been instructed by his Government to ask. In the first place, he wished to know whether I thought that a revolutionary crisis in Constantinople was impending; and secondly, if so, to know what proposals I was prepared to make for meeting it.

I replied that, without expressing any very confident opinion, it was my impression that, for the moment, the danger of revolution had passed by, though it would probably recur. I did not, however, anticipate immediate danger. To the second request I mentioned to him the proposal of the Russian Ambassador that each Power should call up to the Bosphorus two "stationnaires" instead of one, which it is believed that, under the Treaties, they have the power to do. I said that it seemed to be the opinion of those most competent to judge that the Embassies with that protection would not be in serious peril.

His Excellency replied that there were large bodies of Christians outside the Embassies, some of them belonging to other European nations, some of them subject of the Porte, who would be placed in very considerable jeopardy if the existing order in Constantinople was overthrown by any outburst of Mussulman fanaticism. What remedy had I to suggest for this danger? I asked him whether he contemplated acting through the Sultan, or in despite of the Sultan. He replied that, of course, his Government only contemplated acting through the Sultan. My answer was that, while I did not, in any way, question the expediency of restricting European interference to that extent, at least, for the present, I was very apprehensive that no change for the better in the administration of Turkish affairs was likely to take place during the reign of the present Sultan. I thought, however, that, to some extent, his impracticability was due to his belief that the Powers would never consent to do without him; and that, if he once was convinced that it was not safe for him to reply on the continuance of this policy on their part, his attitude would change considerably. I said that the mere impression, if it ever gained ground, that so conservative a Government as Austria was prepared to act with the unanimous concurrence of the Powers, but without the assent of the Sultan, that assent would not then be difficult to obtain.

I am, &c.

(Signed) SALISBURY.

F. O. 424/184, pp. 227-228, No. 403

No. 491

Tewfik Pasha to Rustem Pasha.

CONSTANTINOPLE, *le 13 Novembre, 1895.*
Télégraphique.   *(Communicated November 14.)*

LES autorités Impériales de Mamouret-ul-Aziz, avisées qu'une rixe avait éclatée à Kessik entre Musulmans et Arméniens, à la suite des coups de revolvers tirés par ces derniers, y ont envoyé aussitôt une compagnie de réservistes qui y a établi l'ordre. Dans cette affaire deux Musulmans et deux Arméniens ont été blessés légèrement. Bagdji Oghlou Kirkor, provocateur de l'incident, a été arrêté.

Grâce aux mesures prises par les autorités locales l'ordre et la sécurité ont été assurés à Malatia.

Dans le nuit du 26 au 27 courant, les émeutiers Arméniens d'Arabkir ont mis le feu à une mosquée, à une medressé (école) et au bazar et provoqué ainsi un grand incendie qui a détruit plusieurs boutiques et un nombre de maisons appartenant tant aux Musulmans qu'aux Chrétiens. Ils ont en outre attaqué le quartier Musulman d'Ouloupinar et tué ses habitants.

Les mesures nécessaires sont adoptées par les autorités Impériales pour l'arrestation des agitateurs.

F. O. 424/184, p. 228, No. 404

No. 492

Tewfik Pasha to Rustem Pasha.

CONSTANTINOPLE, *le 13 Novembre, 1895.*
Télégraphique.   *(Communicated November 14.)*

LE 27 courant, les émeutiers Arméniens d'Erzindjan ont tiré sur des Musulmans et attaqué l'hôtel du Gouvernement, le corps de garde, et d'autres endroits. Les forces militaires envoyées sur les lieux ont pu disperser les agitateurs et rétablir l'ordre et la sécurité.

Les révolutionnaires Arméniens d'Arabkir ayant attaqué le quartier Musulman d'Iknepinar une rixe eut lieu entre eux et les Musulmans. Il y a eu des tués de part et d'autre.

Un engagement a eu lieu aux environs du village de Saroy (Van) entre une bande de brigands Arméniens qui battait la campagne et les gendarmes. Les malfaiteurs s'étant enfuis et retirés dans le village de Bogazkessen, les gendarmes les ont poursuivis et sont parvenu à les disperser. Plusieurs gendarmes ont été tués et blessés.

Les émeutiers Arméniens de Sivas, après avoir enlevé clandestinement les marchandises se trouvant dans leurs boutiques les ont fermées et ont attaqué les Musulmans. Une rixe se produisit entre ceux-ci et les agresseurs.

Les autorités Impériales ont pris les mesures nécessaires pour rétablir l'ordre.

Les autorités d'Arabkir ont découvert dans les maisons de Tamgadji Oghlou Serkis et un autre Arménien des bombes à incendie qu'ils avaient fabriquées pour allumer des incendies et ainsi que des bombes à dynamite.

Les agitateurs Kirkor et Kevork, du village de Kemer (Sivas) qui avaient tiré des coups de feu, et dans les maisons desquels les autorités Impériales ont découvert des armes et des cartouches, ont été arrêtés.

Plus de 5,000 révolutionnaires Arméniens se sont réunis à Tchoukmerzen (Adana) et se préparent à commettre des agressions.

F. O. 424/184, pp. 228-229, No. 405

No. 493

Tewfik Pasha to Rustem Pasha.

CONSTANTINOPLE, *le 13 Novembre, 1895.*
Télégraphique   *(Communicated November 14.)*

SA Majesté Impériale le Sultan a donné des ordres pour que toutes les personnes, tant Musulmanes que Chrétiennes, qui ont eu à souffrir durant ces dernières rixes survenues dans les provinces, soient nourries et logées aux frais de l'État. Des instructions à cet effet ont été envoyées par télégraphe aux Gouverneurs-Généraux.

F. O. 424/184, p. 229, No. 406

No. 494

Mr. Howard to the Marquess of Salisbury.

No. 367. Confidential.   PARIS, *November 13, 1895.*
My Lord,   *(Received November 15.)*

BETWEEN 2 and 6 this afternoon M. Berthelot received forty of the Chefs de Missions, and, therefore, had naturally but little time to devote to each, especially as the Russian Ambassador took considerably more than his proper share.

I consequently only asked his Excellency the following questions: What instructions had been sent M. Cambon on the subject of the Russian proposal to send a second "stationnaire" to Constantinople? and whether the rumour in the press as to the intention of the French Government to strengthen their squadron already sent to the Levant was well founded?

M. Berthelot to my first question replied, as I have had the honour to telegraph to your Lordship, that the French Ambassador at Constantinople had been instructed to inform his colleagues that France was willing to hold a vessel in readiness to act as a second "stationnaire," provided that all the other Powers were unanimous in agreeing to do the same.

In answer to my second inquiry, his Excellency stated that the rumour I had mentioned was virtually correct, inasmuch as the French Government would send additional ships to the Levant should the situation there require such a step, but he added that it was to be hoped that the fleet of the Powers would burn coal and not powder.

I have, &c.

(Signed) HENRY HOWARD.

F. O. 424/184, pp. 230-231, No. 410

No. 495

Mr. Herbert to the Marquess of Salisbury.

No. 793. Confidential.   CONSTANTINOPLE, *November 13, 1895.*
My Lord,   *(Received November 18.)*

I HAVE the honour to transmit to your Lordship herewith a Memorandum by Mr. Eliot on some information respecting the present position of the Armenian Patriarch.

M. de Nélidoff spoke to me yesterday about the incident of the pastoral letter, which had also been communicated to him by the Patriarch's Secretary, and said he thought the Patriarch had acted quite rightly, and that even the Minister of Police admitted the force of his Beatitude's argument.

I have, &c.

(Signed) MICHAEL H. HERBERT.

F. O. 424/184, p. 254, No. 464*

Inclosure in No. 495

Memorandum by Mr. Eliot.

Confidential.

THE Secretary of the Armenian Patriarch informed me this morning that his Beatitude had, in consequence of the representations made to him by the Sublime

Porte and this Embassy, prepared a pastoral letter exhorting his people to keep quiet, which was to have been made in the churches of the capital last Sunday.

The letters, however, which we received from Erzeroum gave so terrible a picture of the atrocities which had been perpetrated there and in the surrounding districts that the Patriarch sent to the Minister of Police to say that under the circumstances his pastoral would be a mockery and would provoke excitement among the Armenians, and he must therefore withdraw it.

The Secretary added that the Patriarch was now very unpopular with a large section of Armenians. He did not think it true, as had been rumoured in England, that there was any risk of assassination, but feared that a hostile demonstration might be made before the Patriarchate or in the Church of Koum Kapou. He thought that unless things improved the Patriarch's resignation was only a question of time, perhaps of days.

(Signed) C. N. E. ELIOT.

November 11, 1895.
F. O. 424/184, p. 254, No. 464*/1

No. 496

Sir E. Monson to the Marquess of Salisbury.

No. 333.   VIENNA, *November 14, 1895.*
My Lord,   *(Received November 18.)*
COUNT GOLUCHOWSKI informed me yesterday that he had, twenty-four hours previously, telegraphed to the Austro-Hungarian Ambassadors at the capitals of the Great Powers, instructing them to communicate to the respective Ministers of Foreign Affairs his views as to the urgency of arriving at a clear understanding as to joint action towards Turkey.

There were three points upon which it seemed to him most important to agree: the measures to be taken at once for the protection of the foreign Embassies and Colonies at Constantinople, the open display of European unison, and the decision as to concerted employment of force in the event of a serious revolutionary outbreak in the Turkish capital.

For the first, the adoption of M. de Nélidoff's proposal for the summons of a second "stationnaire" for each Power would be sufficient provision. For the second, the dispatch of a squadron into the Levant by France, Italy, Germany, and Austria would be patent evidence of a European agreement; and each of those Powers was taking steps to be so represented, the orders for the departure of the Austro-Hungarian Squadron being given by telegraph that afternoon. For the third, it seemed to his Excellency urgent that the Powers should come to a decision.

County Goluchowski had just received from Count Deym a telegram, reporting your Lordship's reply to his application; and I understood him to say that you had not given any specific opinion on this last point. His Excellency, however, considered its discussion by no means premature, saying that, although he hoped that extreme peril was not imminent, it would be imprudent to delay to provide against it until the last moment, when the horror inspired by possible massacres on a large scale would prevent calm consideration.

As the principle on which the Great Powers act involved the exclusion of individual interests, it would, in County Goluchowski's opinion, be essential that, in the event of the employment of foreign ships of war becoming necessary, each Power should be represented by a certain number of ships only, to be limited by previous agreement. Otherwise, said his Excellency, the preponderance of British ships in the Levant might induce Russia to make a still more ponderous display of force from the Black Sea.

As regards the right of passage through the Dardanelles, County Goluchowski considers that Europe, which has sanctioned the existing arrangement, and constituted the Sultan guardian of the Straits and adjacent waters in the interests of peace, has an absolute right, when those interests are threatened, to impose upon His Imperial Majesty the suspension of that arrangement, and exact from him free admission of their naval forces.

Count Goluchowski pointed out further that, as any local outbreak on the Turkish coasts of the Levant, as, for instance, at the important seaports of Smyrna or Beyrout, would justify foreign Powers in sending ships of war for the protection of their countrymen, it would be absurd that, in the event of a supreme emergency of a similar kind, an exception should be made in favour of the capital, and that Constantinople should not be accessible to foreign squadrons.

Should events render such a step necessary as the concentration of a combined naval force in the waters of the Bosphorus, the Embassies should of course be authorized to issue the summons. It would be for the Diplomatic Representatives on the spot to decide upon the necessity and opportuneness of such action, and there should be no question of referring home for instructions, and thus risking the extension of a calamity which might be minimized by resolute promptitude.

As, however, the presence of a combined force representing the great navies of Europe might in the meantime arouse the susceptibilities of the Mussulmans, and precipitate the very catastrophe which it is desirable to avert, Count Goluchowski stated that it would be better that the various squadrons now on their way should not unite in one anchorage, but station themselves separately at convenient points accessible by telegraph from Constantinople.

There was a question which had occurred to him which might give trouble, but the preliminary solution of which he feared might not be feasible, that, namely, of the precedidence of the officers in supreme command of the ships to be detached for the special purpose of protecting Constantinople. He hoped that mutual jealousies and rivalries might not cause friction between the Commanders, but he could not help feeling that there might be danger in this quarter.

Count Goluchowski asked me to report at once to your Lordship briefly by telegraph, and in detail by writing, all that he had said to me, which I undertook to do at once, although I presumed that you would have already been placed in complete possession of his Excellency's views by Count Deym.

With regard to the possibility of friction between the Naval Commanders, I said that I imagined that, even if their own good sense and discretion did not suffice to avert such a state of feeling, there must be well-recognized rules of conduct to be observed in such contingencies as that contemplated, which would reduce to a minimum the risk of any serious trouble resulting from individual rivalries.

I have, &c.

(Signed) EDMUND MONSON.

F. O. 424/184, pp. 256-257, No. 467

No. 497

Mr. Herbert to the Marquess of Salisbury.

No. 676.   CONSTANTINOPLE, *November 14, 1895, 10.30 a.m.*
Telegraphic.   *(Received November 14.)*
IN reply to your Lordship's telegram No. 218 of yesterday, I have the honour to state that I do not consider that it would be of much use at the present moment to dispatch a ship to Alexandretta, as all the disturbances up till now have occurred in the interior. I will, however, consult Consul Barnham by telegraph.

F. O. 424/184, p. 229, No. 408

No. 498

Tewfik Pasha to Rustem Pasha.

CONSTANTINOPLE, *le 14 Novembre, 1895.*
Télégraphique.   *(Communicated November 14.)*
LES révolutionnaires Arméniens de Sivas après avoir enlevé de leurs boutiques les marchandises qui s'y trouvaient, ont attaqué les Musulmans. Plusieurs d'entre eux ont tiré de leurs maisons des coups de feu dont un a atteint un soldat qui fût blessé grièvement. Des balles ont atteint le fenêtre de la chambre occupée par le Gouverneur-Général.

Ils ont, en outre, attaqué le village de Mandjilik, tué des Musulmans et commis des actes de pillage.

Les autorités d'Arabkir ont découvert quarante bombes que les agitateurs Arméniens avaient enfouies pour faire sauter les édifices publics spéciaux, tels que casernes, hôtels du Gouvernement, dépôts militaires.

L'incendie qui a éclaté dans la ville a été causé par l'explosion d'autres bombes à incendie.

La population Musulmane d'Arabkir attaquée par les émeutiers Arméniens armés et equipés et au nombre de 1,500, vient d'adresser au Gouvernement Impérial un télégramme pour solliciter sa protection.

Les autorités Impériales ont pris toutes les mesures nécessaires grâce auxquelles l'ordre et la sécurité ont été rétablis sur ces dits points.

F. O. 424/184, p. 229, No. 407

No. 499

Admiralty to Foreign Office.

Secret.   ADMIRALTY, *November 14, 1895.*
Sir,   *(Received November 15.)*

WITH reference to your letter of the 12th instant, transmitting copy of a telegram from Her Majesty's Chargé d'Affaires at Constantinople reporting that the Representatives of the six Great Powers had agreed on the proposal of the Russian Ambassador to apply to their respective Governments to hold in readiness for dispatch to Constantinople a gun-boat or light-armed vessel to act as second "stationnaire," I am commanded by my Lords Commissioners of the Admiralty to request that you will state to the Marquess of Salisbury that a vessel can be dispatched from the Mediterranean Fleet for this service if Her Majesty's Government desire it, and that the Admiral in command has been requested to name the ship he would propose to employ.

I am to ask whether it would be necessary to withdraw the "Cockatrice" in that case.

I am, &c.

(Signed) EVAN MACGREGOR.

F. O. 424/184, p. 231, No. 411

No. 500

Mr. Egerton to the Marquess of Salisbury.

No. 134.   ATHENS, *November 15, 1895.*
My Lord,   *(Received November 20.)*
     NONE of the foreign Representatives here appear to have been informed by
M. Skouzés of his intention to represent to the Powers the gravity of the situation at
Constantinople, neither did M. Delyanni, when questioned by one of my colleagues
subsequently, appear to think that any official appeal had been made by his
Government to the Powers on the subject; indeed, the Greek Prime Minister
seemed to be more optimistic and to consider that there seemed a lull in the bad
news and a good hope that things may calm down.
     I do not think that M. Skouzés, to judge by his language, indulges in such
hopes; indeed, he seems to anticipate the deposition of the Sultan, of whom nearly
all the leading men of the State are thoroughly wearied. Even the army, he learns, is
not so perfectly loyal as it was; and, though the Albanians and the great mass of the
army are faithful still, public opinion appears to have been at length aroused in the
distracted capital, and that public opinion is so unfavourable to the Sultan that a
dynastic catastrophe seems probable.
                         I have, &c.
                                          (Signed) EDWIN H. EGERTON.

F. O. 424/184, p. 267, No. 502

No. 501

Mr. Herbert to the Marquess of Salisbury.

No. 803.   CONSTANTINOPLE, *November 15, 1895.*
My Lord,   *(Received November 22.)*
     THE Sublime Porte made yesterday a communication to the Dragomans of
the Embassies respecting the forces called out in Asia Minor to restore order, and
the dispatch of a Commission to the disturbed districts.
     The same communication was officially published in the press to-day, and I
have the honour to inclose a translation herewith.
     It would appear that, in spite of the official notice to the contrary, the
Commission of Control has not met yet.
                         I have, &c.
                                          (Signed) MICHAEL H. HERBERT.

F. O. 424/184, p. 275, No. 527

Inclosure in No. 501

Extract from the "Terjuman-i-Hakikat" of November 3 (15), 1895.
Official Communication.

Translation.

ON account of the disturbances which have occured in certain vilayets in Anatolia, and as the first of the measures adopted under the directions of His Imperial Majesty, besides the 4th and 5th Corps d'Armée, 128 battalions of Redifs have been called under arms, and are being gradually dispatched to the necessary places.

Similarly, for the complete re-establishment of order and tranquillity, the dispatch of officials to carry out the requisite administrative, military, and judicial undertakings to the places where such are necessary has been approved, and by Iradé of His Majesty, Sami Effendi, Councillor of State, Lieutenant-Generals Saaded-din and Abdullah Pashas, Jemal Bey, of the Commission of Control, and Ibrahim Bey, of the Requests Department of the Court of Cassation, and Hussein Rushdi Effendi, member of the Criminal Section of the Court of Cassation, have been appointed.

They are divided into two sections, one of which is to visit Trebizond, Gumushkhane, Baibourt, Erzeroum, Mush, Bitlis, and the other Samsoun, Amasia, Tokat, Sivas, Molatia, Kharput, Erghana Madeni, and Diarbekir. Both sections proceeded to their posts on Tuesday last on steamers specially provided for that purpose.

F. O. 424/184, p. 276, No. 527/1

No. 502

Mr. Herbert to the Marquess of Salisbury.

No. 804.   CONSTANTINOPLE, *November 15, 1895.*
My Lord,   *(Received November 22.)*

TO-DAY'S papers contain a list of thirty-nine officers of the Hamadié cavalry who have received promotion.

This has attracted much attention in connection with the statement that Shakir Pasha has telegraphed to say he found it impossible to disarm the Kurds.

I have, &c.

(Signed) MICHAEL H. HERBERT.

F. O. 424/184, p. 276, No. 528

No. 503

Tewfik Pasha to Rustem Pasha.

CONSTANTINOPLE, *le 15 Novembre, 1895.*
Télégraphique.   *(Communicated November 15.)*

UN certain nombre d'émeutiers Arméniens de Zéitoun, ayant à leur tête le Sergent de Gendarmerie Nazaret, ont attaqué et pillé le village Musulman de Bechansis aux environs de Zéitoun et incendié cinquante-sept maisons.

Les insurgés de Zéitoun ont fait aussi irruption dans le village Musulman de Kourtel, incendié toutes les maisons avec les effets qui s'y trouvaient, brûlé vif un habitant et blessé grièvement un autre.

Le nombre de Musulmans des deux sexes tués par ces rebelles à Tchoukour-Hissar est de quatre-vingts et celui de blessés de quinze. Le village est entiérement détruit.

F. O. 424/184, p. 231, No. 412

No. 504

Tewfik Pasha to Rustem Pasha.

CONSTANTINOPLE, *le 15 Novembre, 1895.*
Télégraphique.   *(Communicated November 15.)*

EN vue de mettre fin aux désordres surgis sur certains points en Anatolie et de sauvegarder complèment l'ordre et la tranquillité publique, le Gouvernement Impérial, entre autres mesures, a appelé sous les armes 128 bataillons de réserves, independammendes contigents des 4ᵉ et 5ᵉ Corps d'Armée Impériaux, et a adressé de nouvelles recommandations fermes et péremptoires aux Valis et Commandants pour que le calme de l'ordré soient promptement et définitivement assurés par l'application d'un traitement égal et juste envers tous les sujets de Sa Majesté Imperialé sans distinction de race ni de religion. Il n'y a pas de doute que, grâce à ces dispositions, l'apaisement des esprits no soit sous peu obtenu partout.

En outre, le Conseiller d'État Samy Effendi, les Généraux de Division Saadeddin et Abdullah Pachas, Djemal Bey, membre de la Commission de personnel, et Ibrahim Edhem Bey et Hussein Ruchdi Effendi, Conseillers à la Cour de Cassation, ont été chargés d'appliquer les mesures administratives et militaires pour le maintien de la sécurité et de l'ordre publics. Ces fonctionnaires formeront deux corps dont l'un se rendra à Trébizonde, Gumuchhané, Baïbourt, Erzeroum, Mouche, et Bitlis, et l'autre à Samsoun, Amassia, Tokat, Sivas, Malatia, Mamouret-ul-Aziz, Diarbékir. Ils sont partis hier par bateau spécial pour ces destinations.

La Commission chargée de veiller à l'application des réformes arrêtées pour les six vilayets a, de son côté, commencé dès aujourd'hui ses travaux et les dites réformes se trouvent déjà en cours d'exécution.

F. O. 424/184, pp. 231-234, No. 413

No. 505

Tewfik Pasha to Rustem Pasha.

CONSTANTINOPLE, *le 15 Novembre, 1895.*
Télégraphique.   *(Communicated November 15.)*

LES émeutiers Arméniens de Zéitoun et de Marach ont attaqué les villages de Fersakh et de Bitchli.

Ceux d'Azirlou et de Tchokmerzemenk ont saccagé Pias et d'autres villages Musulmans, tué un grannd nombre de leurs habitants, mis le feu à plusieurs maisons. Des mesures ont été prises pour le rétablissement de l'ordre.

Le Vali de Sivas nous informe de son côté que grâce aux dispositions adoptées par les autorités Impériales les maraudeurs qui étaient venus au chef-lieu pour se livrer au pillage ont été arrêtés.

Nonobstant les fausses rumeurs répandues au sujet de la situation à Hadjin, la tranquillité n'y a point été troublée.

La Vali d'Erzeroum télégraphie aussi que des Commissions spéciales instituées au chef-lieu de vilayet et à Passinler pour la découverte et la restitution à leurs propriétaires des objets enlevés pendant da dernière bagarre fonctionnent activement, et qu'un grand nombre de ces objets ont été restitués.

La Maréchal Chakir Pacha informe que la Commission formée dans le même but à Khouns a déjà découvert et rendu à leurs propriétaires les objets qu'ils avaient perdus et que le calme et la tranquillité sont rétablis dans la ville.

F. O. 424/184, p. 232, No. 414

No. 506

Tewfik Pasha to Rustem Pasha.

CONSTANTINOPLE, *le 15 Novembre, 1895.*
Télégraphique.   *(Communicated November 15.)*

LE Vicaire de Patriarcat Syrien et quelques Notables de sa communauté viennent d'envoyer de Kharpout à Sublime Porte le télégramme suivant:-

"Que le Très-Haut daigne prolonger les jours précieux de notre auguste Souverain et accroître sa puissance! Depuis 600 ans que nous avons le bonheur de vivre sous la protection de Gouvernement Impérial, nous n'avons jamais été l'objet d'aucune injustice ni de la part des autorités ni de celle de la population Musulmane. Aujourd'hui encore nous n'avons qu'à nous louer de nos rapports avec nos compatriotes Musulmans et nous affirmons sous serment que notre unique désir est de conserver toujours notre nationalité Ottomane."

F. O. 424/184, p. 232, No. 415

No. 507

Mr. Herbert to the Marquess of Salisbury.

No. 679.   CONSTANTINOPLE, *November 15, 1895, 11.30 a.m.*
Telegraphic.   *(Received November 15.)*
    IN spite of the official "Communiqué" in the newspapers which I reported to your Lordship in my telegram No. 677 of yesterday, the Commission of Control did not hold a sitting yesterday.

    Notwithstanding the statement of the Minister for Foreign Affairs, there seem to be doubts as to Shefik Bey's resignation. I hear, however, that he is not well, and that he shows great reluctance to accept the Presidency of the Commission.

F. O. 424/184, p. 233, No. 416

No. 508

Mr. Herbert to the Marquess of Salisbury.

No. 680.   CONSTANTINOPLE, *November 15, 1895, 11.30 a.m.*
Telegraphic.   *(Received November 15.)*
    WITH reference to my telegram No. 676, my opinion that ship is unnecessary at present is shared by Mr. Barnham.

F. O. 424/184, p. 233, No. 417

No. 509

Mr. Herbert to the Marquess of Salisbury.

No. 681.   CONSTANTINOPLE, *November 15, 1895.*
Telegraphic.   *(Received November 15.)*
    I RECEIVED a further message from the Sultan last night, stating that His Majesty has never hesitated to accept our advice, and that he is ready to do so now;

that it is untrue, as is alleged, that His Majesty opposed the proposals made by the ex-Grand Vizier, Saïd Pasha, in regard to the reforms, but, on the contrary, the Porte, who refused to carry out His Majesty's orders, is to blame. Message also recapitulates measures which have been taken to restore order in the provinces, and expresses hope that they will be successful.

F. O. 424/184, p. 233, No. 418

No. 510

Mr. Herbert to the Marquess of Salisbury.

No. 683.   CONSTANTINOPLE, *November 15, 1895, 12.10 p.m.*
Telegraphic.   *(Received November 15.)*

I HAVE through Her Majesty's Vice-Consul at Van received the following message from the Armenian Bishop there for communication to the Patriarch:-

"In answer to your telegram of congratulations on the introduction of the reforms, I beg to inform your Beatitude that the Kurds have suddenly fallen like wolves on the districts of Adeljevaz, Arjest, Khizan, Sparghird, Gargar, Shatlak, Khoshaf, Bergheri, Elbak, and Van, and plundered the Armenian villages. Many have been murdered, and more than ten thousand persons are scattered abroad without food and shelter. The state of things gets worse every day; if it continues our people will be forced to change their religion.

"I have sent six telegrams to your Beatitude and one to the Sultan and the Grand Vizier to the above effect, but have received no answer."

F. O. 424/184, p. 233, No. 419

No. 511

Mr. Herbert to the Marquess of Salisbury.

No. 684.   CONSTANTINOPLE, *November 15, 1895.*
Telegraphic.   *(Received November 15.)*

POLICE officers and Palace officials have lately been engaged in registering, in Pera, Stamboul, and the suburbs, houses inhabited by Armenians. The Armenians here consider this as the prelude to an attack on them, and are in a state of panic.

I hear that some of the Notables have held a meeting, and that a deputation will ask for the intervention of the Russian Ambassador, and implore him to prevent them from being massacred.

There can be no doubt that the state of panic among the Armenians is a source of danger.

F. O. 424/184, p. 233*, No. 419*

No. 512

Mr. Herbert to the Marquess of Salisbury.

No. 685.   CONSTANTINOPLE, *November 15, 1895, 1.5 p.m.*
Telegraphic.   *(Received November 15.)*

THE British Vice-Consul at Alexandretta reports serious disturbances in the district of Pias, and begs me to communicate the following message from the Armenian Vicar to the Patriarch:-

"According to a report dated yesterday from the priest of Chokmerzime, the Turks, three days ago, destroyed Odjakli, an Armenian village of 300 houses, and have burnt over 30 Armenian farms in the neighbourhood.

"Yesterday they marched to the village of Uzuli and destroyed it, and they have attacked the village of Chokmerzime. The number of killed and wounded on both sides is considerable, and over 7,000 have taken refuge at Chokmerzime. There are 200 regular Turkish soldiers there, but they do nothing to check the ferocity of the Mussulman population. If nothing is done to put a stop to the excesses of the Turks, the Christians will not stand it very long."

An American subject, resident at Chokmerzime, has telegraphed a similar report to his Consul at Alexandretta. I have telegraphed to Mr. Catoni to ask whether he considers the presence of a ship of war necessary.

The Porte has also received intelligence of disturbances in these places, but accuses the Christians of being the aggressors.

F. O. 424/184, p. 234, No. 420

No. 513

Mr. Herbert to the Marquess of Salisbury.

No. 687.   CONSTANTINOPLE, *November 15, 1895, 6.50 p.m.*
Telegraphic.   *(Received November 15.)*

WITH reference to my telegram No. 669 of the 13th instant, proposal of Russian Ambassador has been approved by the Austrian, French, and Italian Governments. They have also designated ships, each having over 100 men.

I should be glad of your Lordship's instructions as soon as possible, as we meet again to-morrow at 5 to decide whether the extra vessels shall be asked for at once or not.

F. O. 424/184, p. 234, No. 422

No. 514

Mr. Herbert to the Marquess of Salisbury.

No. 688. Secret.   CONSTANTINOPLE, *November 15, 1895, 7 p.m.*
Telegraphic.   *(Received November 15.)*

AUSTRIAN Ambassador informs me that, at an audience which he had with the Sultan to-day, he laid great stress on the absolute unanimity of the Powers at the present juncture, and that His Majesty appeared much disturbed thereat.

The Turkish Government have also be informed by their Representatives at Paris, Vienna, and Rome, that the Powers are in complete accord in regard to their Oriental policy.

F. O. 424/184, p. 235, No. 423

No. 515

Mr. Herbert to the Marquess of Salisbury.

No. 689.   CONSTANTINOPLE, *November 15, 1895.*
Telegraphic.   *(Received November 15.)*

HER Majesty's Vice-Consul at Mush telegraphs me the following message from the missionaries at Bitlis for communication to the United States' Minister here:-

"We consider that our families must leave Bitlis for Van; we beg that measures should be taken for our safe escort, and that, if possible, the British Vice-Consul at Van come to Bitlis for that purpose. It will be necessary, after our departure, to adopt strong measures for the protection of our property and of the Protestant community."

Mr. Hampson adds that the situation at Bitlis is still very critical, though the missionaries have now a military guard. He says that they wish him to go to Bitlis, but that he cannot well leave Mush in view of the critical position of events there.

I have, in reply, informed him that it is not advisable for him to leave Mush, and that, in consequence of representations made by the United States' Minister and myself, telegraphic instructions in the sense derived have been sent to the authorities at Bitlis.

I have also sent to Mr. Hampson the following message from the United States Minister:-

"Safe escort for Van demanded, and measures for protection of property and Protestants at Bitli. Am informed that British Vice-Consul cannot go to Bitlis."

F. O. 424/184, p. 235, No. 424

No. 516

Mr. Herbert to the Marquess of Salisbury.

No. 691.   CONSTANTINOPLE, *November 15, 1895, 7.20 p.m.*
Telegraphic.   *(Received November 15.)*

I AM informed by the French Ambassador that a man-of-war will be sent to the Syrian coast by the French Government.

F. O. 424/184, p. 235, No. 425

No. 517

Mr. Herbert to the Marquess of Salisbury.

No. 693.   CONSTANTINOPLE, *November 15, 1895, 7.50 p.m.*
Telegraphic.   *(Received November 15.)*

HER Majesty's Consul at Aleppo telegraphs as follows:-

"The Turks are encamped in force on the River Jehan, seven hours from Zeitoun. I have just received a Petition from Zeitoun, dated the 3rd November, stating that provisions there are running short, and calling on Her Majesty's Government to intervene and prevent hostilities."

At an interview with Minister of Foreign Affairs last Monday, I expressed the hope that the Government would treat the Zeitounlis with leniency if they capitulated, and, in the absence of any instructions from your Lordship, I hesitate to do more at present.

F. O. 424/184, p. 235, No. 426

No. 518

Mr. Gosselin to the Marquess of Salisbury.

No. 45.   BERLIN, *November 15, 1895, 7.5 p.m.*
Telegraphic.   *(Received November 15.)*

WITH reference to Mr. Herbert's telegram No. 660, Secret, and to your Lordship's answer No. 217, both of the 12th instant, I was informed by Baron von Marschall to-day that His Majesty's ship "Moltke," which is now at Smyrna, is the only German ship available to be sent to the Levant.

F. O. 424/184, p. 236, No. 428

No. 519

Mr. Gosselin to the Marquess of Salisbury.

No. 269.   BERLIN, *November 16, 1895.*
My Lord,   *(Received November 18.)*

AT my interview with Baron von Marschall yesterday I asked his Excellency whether he had received any recent news from Constantinople.

Baron von Marschall replied that no improvement in the state of things was visible in any part of the Turkish Empire, and that he had two days ago received a telegram from Baron von Saurma stating that all the Ambassadors had agreed to recommend their respective Governments to send each a second "stationnaire" to Constantinople to afford additional protection in case of an outbreak.

His Excellency said that personally he did not think that this proposal would have much practical effect, but that the Imperial Government had no objection whatever to make to the suggestion; as far as Germany is concerned, the only available ship for service in the Levant is His Majesty's ship "Moltke," which is already at Smyrna; but he believed that both Italy and Austria-Hungary intended to send strong squadrons to the Levant.

Last night's papers announced that the Austrian squadron under orders for the Levant consists of the "Empress Elizabeth," "Tegetthof," "Donau," and "Meteor," under the command of Rear-Admiral Seemann, and that besides these vessels the "Sebenico" had already arrived at Smyrna, and the "Taurus" at Constantinople.

I have, &c.

(Signed) MARTIN GOSSELIN.

F. O. 424/184, p. 258, No. 468

No. 520

Sir Clare Ford to the Marquess of Salisbury.

No. 180. ROME, *November 16, 1895.*
My Lord, *(Received November 19.)*
    I HAVE the honour to transmit to your Lordship herewith a report which I have received from Colonel Needham, Military Attaché to Her Majesty's Embassy, respecting the dispatch of Italian vessels of war to the Eastern Mediterranean.

               I have, &c.

               (Signed) FRANCIS CLARE FORD.

F. O. 424/184, p. 262, No. 483

Inclosure in No. 520

Colonel Needham to Sir Clare Ford.

Sir, ROME, *November 16, 1895.*
    I HAVE the honour to report, for the information of your Excellency, that at an interview with Admiral Morin, Minister of Marine, this day, I was informed that the movement of a portion of the Italian fleet to Eastern waters has no political signification beyond the natural wish of the Italian Government to act in concert with the other Powers for the protection of their subjects, in view of the disturbed condition of affairs at Constantinople.

    The squadron under orders forms the 1st Division, or one-half of the Italian fleet, and consists of six vessels, under the command of Admiral Accinni. Their probable destination is Smyrna, but different orders may be given if circumstances render them necessary.

               I have, &c.

               (Signed) CHARLES NEEDHAM,
               Colonel, Military Attaché.

F. O. 424/184, p. 262, No. 483/1

No. 521

Mr. Herbert to the Marquess of Salisbury.

No. 806.   CONSTANTINOPLE, *November 16, 1895.*
My Lord,   *(Received November 25.)*
    I HAVE the honour to forward to your Lordship herewith copy of despatch which I have received from Her Majesty's Consul at Trebizond respecting the state of affairs in the Sivas Vilayet.

                        I have, &c.
                          (Signed) MICHAEL H. HERBERT.

F. O. 424/184, p. 278, No. 537

Inclosure in No. 521

Consul Longworth to Mr. Herbert.

Sir,   TREBIZOND, *November 5, 1895.*
    THE following contents of a letter from Dr. Jewett, dated Sivas, the 30th October, show a very alarming and deplorable state of affairs in that vilayet:-

    "This province has been in a ferment of an excitement. Sanguinary encounters between Turks and Armenians have with good reason been anticipated at Sivas, Tokat, Amassia, and Marsovan. However, up to the present moment, I have not heard of anything serious at these places. The Vali has sent the Protestant preacher of Marsovan to Oorfa because he preached too boldly, and protested to the Kaïmakam against the arming of the Turks and disarming of the Armenians. The people are much excited by this event. The kurds are now the chief disturbers of the peace. About two months ago they began operating in the region of Divrik. They attacked the villages of Pengan, Zumara, Armoudan, Hassova, and others. From Pengan they carried off 800 sheep. They are said to be from the Dersim district, and the number is variously estimated from 200 to 400."

    The Armenian Archbishop received the following information from his deputy at Karahissar:-

    "Telegraphed 26th October:-

    "For some days past Beys of Soushehir, Mahommedans and Kurds by hundreds, attacked the Cariehs of Aghovances, Iban, Toretz, Sarindick, Ezbeder, Agrakous, and Ilamlick, openly plundered the whole of their property, killed and wounded some, and committed other outrages. They are still going on. The lives, property, and honour of the Armenians is in danger.

    "Telegraphed on the 28th October:-

    "In the last few days Mahommedans and Kurds attacked eighteen Armenian cariehs, plundered everything, killed, wounded, and beat some of the people.

"Also, yesterday, they attacked the quarters of the city (Karahissar), and up to 12 o'clock in the evening they plundered about forty Armenian houses, they killed a priest, and killed and wounded others, burnt one house. Therefore, most of the people from the villages and city gathered in the church for security.

"The Vali has sent about seventy newly-collected Redifs to Karahissar. He directs the Archbishop to order the Armenians at Karahissar to give up their arms. Without arms I think they would quickly be slaughtered by Mahommedans. Similar affairs are reported near Gergenis and Enderes. At the latter place 400 are said to have been killed, which is probably an exaggeration.

"Yesterday it was reported that 1,500 Kurds had appeared near Dousla-hissar. About seventy-five Redifs and zaptiehs were sent to the Divrik region.

"At Gurun the city is excited over the imprisonment of an Armenian refugee from Sasun. Trouble is feared there. Fifty Redifs have been sent there from here, and a lot of Circassians are reported to have been sent to Gurun from Azizieh. Sending the Circassians I regard as a very bad omen.

"The Redifs are an untrained lot, without any adequate conception of responsibility. Two days ago 100 new zaptiehs were hastily picked up and put on duty. They embrace all varieties of unsuitable men. I think the situation is very dangerous and critical."

I have, &c.

(Signed) H. Z. LONGWORTH.

F. O. 424/184, pp. 278-279, No. 537/1

No. 522

Mr. Herbert to the Marquess of Salisbury.

No. 807. Confidential.   CONSTANTINOPLE, *November 16, 1895.*
My Lord,   *(Received November 25.)*

WITH reference to my despatch No. 794, Confidential, of the 13th instant, I have the honour to forward to your Lordship herewith copy of a despatch which I have received from Her Majesty's Consul at Trebizond, giving his views on the recent massacres of Armenians.

I have, &c.

(Signed) MICHAEL H. HERBERT.

F. O. 424/184, p. 279, No. 538

Inclosure in No. 522

Consul Longworth to Mr. Herbert.

Strictly Confidential.
Sir,
                                                        TREBIZOND, *November 6, 1895.*
    THE series of massacres in the interior resemble much, I hear, the one that was experienced by the Armenian population at Trebizond.

That such outbreaks are spontaneous is hard to believe, while the connivance in them of men in responsible positions is scarcely questionable.

Hence the effect is only too visible, and while the cause must be sought for elsewhere the medium may well be suspected. From what I have heard and seen indeed there appears to be in all this a secret agency at work, which, while exciting the Mahommedan element, is paralyzing the action of the authorities. It doubtless wields an enormous power to bring about such convulsions, a power far beyond that of Armenian revolutionists, who at worst can only become insurgents and break out into a guerilla warfare.

I have given the subject my best attention, and I have arrived at only one conclusion. It is briefly this. The spies of the Palace infesting the country are the chief instigators of the massacres. In the absence of conclusive evidence, however, it is a mere conjecture on my part, but any unbiassed mind, I believe, would think the same by giving some thought to all the circumstances attending the lamentable events in these regions.

It will be admitted, I think, that shooting, slashing, and looting inoffensive Armenians for a political rather than a religious cause are not exactly deeds commendable to the usually law-abiding Turks of Asia Minor. Now we hear of such butcheries from all quarters. What is strange is the control under which this hideous work is done. Even ferocious men mad with excitement spared women and children, and distinguished one race of Christians from another. More than this, when calm again they excused themselves for having carried out what they were made to believe was a mandate of their Sovereign. This is surely significant enough when taken with the fact that the killing and sacking were commenced by the troops.

Before the night disturbance of the 4th ultimo, which, as reported in my despatch of the following day, was checked successfully, no one could have conceived the possibility of a massacre at Trebizond, though troubles such as riots on a small scale were for some time apprehended. I was out on that occasion, and was surprised to find the Turks under the impression that Armenians were assaulting the Mussulmans. I then assured many of them that they were deceived, and persuaded some of them to return to their homes. It was soon discovered that the false alarm arose from a recruit having received a mortal wound from an officer. It was an affair of a woman, as the authorities subsequently stated, such brawls being rather common at Trebizond. The town became almost at once full of absurd rumours about the Armenians and about this Consulate. Who started them I could never find out. On the 7th ultimo I saw the Vali, and found him during the interview extremely nervous. I once more impressed upon him the gravity of the situation, and urged him to carry out speedily my own suggestions and those of the Consular Body. He promised to do so, but left his promises unfulfilled. The massacre took place on the following day. It was then that cries were raised, "On the English Consulate," but happily the armed bands could not be led to the attack.

A day or two before, and after the outbreak, it was evident that the Moslems were in great terror of the Armenians. This was remarkable, as it was inexplicable. Only now, indeed, are they beginning to understand that their fears were without foundation. Furthermore, they no longer glare or look askance at those of this Consulate, though the officials continue to avoid being seen speaking to us publicly. All this tends to show that the hatred of the Turks against the Armenians is not genuine. Much less so that evinced by them against England. There are indeed many signs that a turn in our favour has taken place, indications that may lead one to think the ill-feeling was superficial if not artificial. I have some hope, therefore, that before long the influence of this Consulate will be regained, an influence exercised to some degree over the governed as well as the governing.

I find the better Turks in private not only ashamed but apprehensive. They seem all to be in a state of suspense, and some of them had gone so far as to drop me words of a treasonable significance. The Vali, for instance, remarked to me latterly in a mysterious whisper, "Change the shaft of the machinery, and all will go well."

I need only, in conclusion, refer to my despatch of the 17th June, and remark that the espionage system in Turkey is a curse which apparently benumbs the Executive and incites the populace.

I have, &c.   (Signed) H. Z. LONGWORTH.

F. O. 424/184, pp. 279-280, No. 538/1

No. 523

Mr. Herbert to the Marquess of Salisbury.

No. 808.   CONSTANTINOPLE, *November 16, 1895.*
My Lord,   *(Received November 25.)*

I HAVE the honour to forward to your Lordship herewith copy of a despatch which I have received from Her Majesty's Consul at Trebizond, reporting that affairs at Trebizond have improved.

I have, &c.

(Signed) MICHAEL H. HERBERT.

F. O. 424/184, p. 280, No. 539

Inclosure in No. 523

Consul Longworth to Mr. Herbert.

Sir,   TREBIZOND, *November 9, 1895.*
    IT is not, I hope, too early for me to say that an improvement in the situation is manifesting itself at Trebizond.

The Vali I found lately more amenable to good advice, while the generality of the Turks it would seem are displaying a kindlier disposition towards the Armenians.

Cadri Bey, however, though much less unreasonable, still maintains that there was an insurrectionary movement at Trebizond. His stubbornness on this point leads one almost to think that he is afflicted with a peculiar kind of insanity. I had often enough admitted to him that revolutionists in and out of the country were greatly to blame. This was not enough, so I though it best now to avoid speaking to him of the past, and to confine myself as much as possible to the present and the future. Our conversations have thus become once more free and cordial.

The measures taken to inspire confidence may, I think, on the whole, be considered satisfactory. An Armenian exodus is no longer forbidden, stolen property is gradually restored, while the suspects in prison, now numbering thirty-six, are allowed the solace of seeing their families and obtaining some comforts from their homes. More than this, any one molesting any one is promptly carried off to gaol, and more than this again, arms carried by even Turks, if seen in the streets, are at once confiscated.

For the maintenance of public order and security sixteen battalions of the Reserves have been called out in the vilayet, each one being formed 1,000 strong by enrolling with the Redifs some of the Mustaphuz. The Nizam soldiers will be shortly leaving for Erzinghian, while the new levies of infantry are to be so disposed as to insure safety to life and property throughout the province. The Vali tells me he has confidence in these men, and further that he has money to feed and clothe them.

I have, &c.

(Signed) H. Z. LONGWORTH.

F. O. 424/184, p. 281, No. 539/1

No. 524

Mr. Herbert to the Marquess of Salisbury.

No. 692. CONSTANTINOPLE, *November 16, 1895, 11.45 a.m.*
Telegraphic. *(Received November 16.)*

HER Majesty's Consul at Aleppo has sent me the following telegram:-

"The town of Andrin has been burnt by the Zeitounlis. The Ferik informs me that he hopes that the Zeitounli trouble will be satisfactorily settled within ten days, as otherwise it will have become a most serious matter. I do not, however, know what means are being employed to secure so speedy a settlement.

"Meanwhile, the Ferik has ordered that no offensive measures shall be taken against the Zeitounlis, and if any military steps are absolutely necessary he will employ only regular troops, of whom there are three battalions with the expedition."

F. O. 424/184, p. 236, No. 429

No. 525

Mr. Herbert to the Marquess of Salisbury.

No. 697. Secret. CONSTANTINOPLE, *November 16, 1895, 8.10 p.m.*
Telegraphic. *(Received November 16.)*

PORTE has been informed by Turkish Chargé d'Affaires at Berlin that he has been told by the German Minister for Foreign Affairs that the Great Powers are losing patience in consequence of the situation in the Turkish provinces and in Constantinople, and that Turkish Government must be prepared for a joint naval demonstration.

In view, however, of the friendship existing between the Sultan and the Emperor, the German Government will not take part in it, but they advise His Majesty before it is too late to take energetic and immediate steps, both in the provinces and in the capital, to restore tranquillity.

F. O. 424/184, p. 236, No. 430

No. 526

Mr. Herbert to the Marquess of Salisbury.

No. 698.   CONSTANTINOPLE, *November 16, 1895, 10 p.m.*
Telegraphic.   *(Received November 16.)*
WITH reference to my telegram No. 687 of the 15th instant, it was agreed at meeting of the Representatives of the Six Powers to-day to postpone decision as to "stationnaires" until German Ambassador and myself received instructions.

I gather that there may be a difference of opinion at our next meeting as to the necessity for having extra vessels here at once. General impression at meeting to-day was that the situation had slightly improved.

F. O. 424/184, p. 237, No. 431

No. 527

Mr. Herbert to the Marquess of Salisbury.

No. 699.   CONSTANTINOPLE, *November 16, 1895.*
Telegraphic.   *(Received November 17.)*
THE Turkish Minister for Foreign Affairs has informed the Russian and French Ambassadors and myself officially of the measures which the Sultan's Government has taken to prevent massacres in the provinces. The other Ambassadors, however, have had no reply to the identic representation. This is in consequence of an order from the Sultan, who wishes to ignore the union of the Six Powers. In these circumstances it was decided at a meeting to-day that the English, Russian, and French Dragomans should inform the Porte on Monday that we should not consider that we had received any reply to our identic representation until all six Representatives had received a similar official communication from the Minister for Foreign Affairs.

F. O. 424/184, pp. 237, No. 431

No. 528

Mr. Herbert to the Marquess of Salisbury.

No. 700.   CONSTANTINOPLE, *November 16, 1895, 10.35 a.m.*
Telegraphic.   *(Received November 16.)*
YOUR Lordship's telegram No. 219 of the 16th instant.

In view of arrival of "Cockatrice" here, Turkish Government, if we ask for a second "stationnaire," may object that we have two already, although, according to the Treaty, there is no limit as to number.

Shall I suggest exchange of "Imogene," which is of no use, for another vessel, or shall I simply ask for another "stationnaire"?

Until German Ambassador receives his instructions, no decision can be come to.

F. O. 424/184, p. 237, No. 432

No. 529

Sir E. Monson to the Marquess of Salisbury.

No. 87.   VIENNA, *November 16, 1895.*
Telegraphic.   *(Received November 16.)*

IT is announced that the Austro-Hungarian squadron proceeding to the Levant under the command of Rear-Admiral Seeman von Trauenwart will consist of the "Kaiserin Elisabeth" as flag-ship, the "Tegetthot," "Donau," and "Meteor;" the "Sebenico" is already at Smyrna.

F. O. 424/184, p. 237, No. 433

No. 530

The Marquess of Salisbury to Mr. Herbert.

No. 219.
Telegraphic.   FOREIGN OFFICE, *November 16, 1895.*

I HAVE received your telegram No. 687 of yesterday, and I authorize you to agree to the Russian Ambassador's proposal relative to a second "stationnaire" for the Embassies, and to request the British Admiral to have a vessel in readiness. Instructions have been sent to him by the Admiralty.

The Sultan's Firmans to enable the ships to come to Constantinople should, in my opinion, be applied for as soon as possible.

F. O. 424/184, p. 237, No. 434

No. 531

The Marquess of Salisbury to Mr. Herbert.

No. 220.
Telegraphic.   FOREIGN OFFICE, *November 16, 1895, 3.40 p.m.*
    THE French Government having dispatched a ship of war to the coast of
Syria, it is desirable that you should communicate with the Admiral commanding
the Mediterranean Squadron, and request him to dispatch one of the vessels under
his command to Alexandretta.
    F. O. 424/184, p. 237, No. 435

No. 532

The Marquess of Salisbury to Mr. Herbert.

No. 221.
Telegraphic.   FOREIGN OFFICE, *November 16, 1895.*
    ACCORDING to a telegram received from the Admiral in Command of the
Mediterranean Squadron, Her Majesty's ship "Barham" is held in readiness for
service as second "stationnaire" at Constantinople. She is a third-class cruiser of
1,830 tons, and has a complement of 170 officers and men.
    Do you apprehend that any objections will be raised on account of her size?
    Do you propose that the "Cockatrice" should also remain at Constantinople?
    F. O. 424/184, p. 237*, No. 435*

No. 533

The Marquess of Salisbury to the Marquess of Dufferin.

No. 152.
Telegraphic.   FOREIGN OFFICE, *November 16, 1895, 5 p.m.*
    HER Majesty's Government approve the proposal that Her Majesty's
Representative at Constantinople should be authorized to summon a second
"stationnaire," and they are of opinion that the Imperial Firmans to enable to ship
to pass through the Dardanelles should be applied for and obtained as soon as
possible.

You should make a communication in this sense to the Government to which you are accredited.

Mr. Herbert has been instructed accordingly.

F. O. 424/184, p. 238, No. 436

*Also to Mr. Gosselin (No. 115), Mr. Goschen (No. 226), Sir Clare Ford (No. 65), and Sir E. Monson (No. 82).

No. 534

The Marquess of Salisbury to Sir P. Currie.

Separate.

Sir,   FOREIGN OFFICE, *November 16, 1895.*

IN accordance with the recommendation made by the Representatives of the six Powers at Constantinople, I have authorized Her Majesty's Chargé d'Affaires to call up a second "stationnaire," which will be at your Excellency's disposal.

In the event of the state of affairs in Turkey becoming so serious as to make it necessary, in your opinion and that of your colleagues, to take further measures for the protection of the interests committed to your charge, I request your Excellency to communicate with the Admiral in Command of the Mediterranean Squadron.

He will place at your disposal for employment in any manner on which the Ambassadors at Constantinople may determine, such vessels as they may consider to be necessary.

I am, &c.

(Signed) SALISBURY

F. O. 424/184, p. 238, No. 437

No. 535

Foreign Office to Admiralty.

Secret.

Sir,   FOREIGN OFFICE, *November 16, 1895.*

WITH reference to your letter of the 14th instant, and to the telegraphic correspondence with Her Majesty's Ambassador at Constantinople since forwarded to you, I am directed by the Marquess of Salisbury to state, for the information of the Lords Commissioners of the Admiralty, that upon the arrival of the gun-boat selected for service as second "stationnaire" at Constantinople, it may be necessary to withdraw Her Majesty's ship "Cockatrice," but that, in Lord Salisbury's opinion, this matter may best be left to be settled between Her

Majesty's Chargé d'Affaires at Constantinople and the Admiral in Command of the Mediterranean Squadron.

I am, &c.

(Signed) T. H. Sanderson.

F. O. 424/184, p. 238, No. 438

No. 536

Tewfik Pasha to Rustem Pasha.

Constantinople, *le 17 Novembre, 1895.*

Télégraphique.   *(Communicated November 19.)*

LES émeutiers Arméniens de Hasnimensour ayant tué deux Musulmans, une rixe est survenue entre eux et les Musulmans. Il y a eu des tués et des blessés de part et d'autre. Grâce aux mesures prises par les autorités Impériales l'ordre a été rétabli.

Les Arméniens rebelles de Marsovan et d'Amassia, après avoir fermé leurs boutiques, se sont réunis dans l'église et les khans, d'où ils tirent sur les Musulmans.

F. O. 424/184, p. 262, No. 484

No. 537

Tewfik Pasha to Rustem Pasha.

Constantinople, *le 17 Novembre, 1895.*

Télégraphique.   *(Communicated November 19.)*

LES insurgés Arméniens de Zéitoun (de Fernès) et de Kemban, au nombre de plus de 800, ont attaqué de district d'Enderin, incendié le local du Gouvernement et les maisons appartenant aux Musulmans, et capturé celles des familles Musulmanes qui n'ont pu s'enfuir.

Les émeutiers ont fait une nouvelle incursion dans le village de Kurtler à Marach, et incendié dix maisons ainsi que les effets qui s'y trouvaient.

F. O. 424/184, p. 262, No. 485

No. 538

Tewfik Pasha to Rustem Pasha.

CONSTANTINOPLE, *le 17 Novembre, 1895.*

Télégraphique. *(Communicated November 19.)*

VOICI le résumé de deux lettres envoyées par l'Évêque Arménien d'Alep à celui d'Ourfa, par l'intermédiaire d'un Arménien déguisé en Arabe, et saisi par les autorités de cette dernière ville, et qui prouvent d'une façon incontestable l'existence d'une entente parfaite entre les révolutionnaires Arméniens des différents centres de l'Asie-Mineure:-

"Envoyez de la poudre aux émeutiers de Zéitoun pour les mettre à même de résister aux autorités Impériales, et procurez-nous une certaine quantité de salpêtre pour fabrication de la poudre.

"Baronaga, de Zéitoun, formera une armée.

"Nous nous sommes rapprochés des jours où des événements sanglants auront lieu.

"Les Arméniens de Marach sont prêts à combattre et le désirent vivement. Ils demandent des armes et des munitions et comptent prêter leur assistance aux autres rebelles."

Ces informations ont été portées à la connaissance de tous les Comités.

F. O. 424/184, p.263, No. 486

No. 539

Mr. Herbert to the Marquess of Salisbury.

No. 701. CONSTANTINOPLE, *November 17, 1895, 11 a.m.*

Telegraphic. *(Received November 17.)*

HER Majesty's Consul at Aleppo telegraphs that great uneasiness prevails there. A serious outbreak occurred at Aintab yesterday morning, and fighting is still proceeding there.

F. O. 424/184, p. 238, No. 439

No. 540

Mr. Herbert to the Marquess of Salisbury.

No. 702.   CONSTANTINOPLE, *November 17, 1895.*
Telegraphic.   *(Received November 17.)*
    MY telegram of yesterday, No. 692.
    I have to-day informed Mr. Barnham by telegram to do all he can to persuade
both the military and civil authorities to treat the Zeitounlis with leniency if they
are ready to cease hostilities and submit.
    F. O. 424/184, p. 239, No. 440

No. 541

Mr. Herbert to the Marquess of Salisbury.

No. 703.   CONSTANTINOPLE, *November 17, 1895, 12.40 p.m.*
Telegraphic.   *(Received November 17.)*
    WITH reference to your Lordship's telegram No. 221 of the 16th instant,
dispatch of Her Majesty's ship "Barham" here would, I fear, frighten my
colleagues as she is much too large to meet M. de Nélidow's proposal. I do not know
the size of the Russian boat, but Austrian Government are sending a torpedo gun-
boat, 57 metres in length, of 800 tons, and with a crew of 130 men.
    The Italians are sending a gun-boat and the French a torpedo-catcher, neither
being quite so large as the Austrian.
    Admiral has been informed by telegraph.
    F. O. 424/184, p. 239, No. 441

No. 542

Mr. Herbert to the Marquess of Salisbury.

No. 704. Secret.   CONSTANTINOPLE, *November 17, 1895, 1.45 p.m.*
Telegraphic.   *(Received November 17.)*
    WITH reference to my telegrams Nos. 692 and 702 of the 16th and 17th
instant respectively, the Vali of Aleppo, according to secret information which I
have just received, has reported confidentially to the Sultan, in reply to a telegram
from His Majesty, that orders have been given to completely exterminate the
Armenians at Marash, Hadjin, and Zeitoun.
    The Sultan's request for our good offices with the Armeniens, contained in my

telegram No. 695, gives us an opening for intervention, whether the above news be true or not, but it must be borne in mind that the Armenians in those districts are undoubtedly in a state of open rebellion, and according to the Turks, have burned villages and attacked regular troops.

F. O. 424/184, p. 239, No. 442

No. 543

Mr. Herbert to the Marquess of Salisbury.

No. 705.   CONSTANTINOPLE, *November 17, 1895, 1.50 p.m.*
Telegraphic.   *(Received November 17.)*

UNITED STATES' Minister here has received a telegram from American Vice-Consul at Sivas reporting that massacres have begun at Amassia and also at Marsovan.

F. O. 424/184, p. 239, No. 443

No. 544

Mr. Herbert to the Marquess of Salisbury.

No. 706.   CONSTANTINOPLE, *November 17, 1895, 2 p.m.*
Telegraphic.   *(Received November 17.)*

WITH reference to my telegram No. 696 of the 16th instant, Turkish newspapers publish reassuring articles this morning in regard to public tranquillity and the execution of reforms.

These articles are evidently inspired by the Turkish Government.

F. O. 424/184, p. 240, No. 444

No. 545

Mr. Herbert to the Marquess of Salisbury.

No. 707.   CONSTANTINOPLE, *November 17, 1895.*
Telegraphic.   *(Received November 17.)*

HER Majesty's Vice-Consul at Mush telegraphed as follows yesterday:-

"No. 13. All is quiet to-day. Yesterday there were six deaths, and the wounded are about forty in number, all Armenians. There is on all sides nothing but praise for the conduct of the Mutessarif.

"I think the effect would be excellent if some signal mark of the approval of the Turkish Government could be sent to him. There have been several arrests of Mussulmans, and the authorities are making a strict investigation."

I will make the suggestion contained in the second paragraph of the above.

F. O. 424/184, p. 240*, No. 444*

No. 546

Sir Clare Ford to the Marquess of Salisbury.

No. 44.   ROME, *November 17, 1895.*
Telegraphic.   *(Received November 17.)*

I HAVE carried out the instructions contained in your Lordship's telegram No. 65 of the 16th instant, and have been informed by the Minister for Foreign Affairs that he entirely agrees with your Lordship, and considers that the necessary Firmans for the second "stationnaires" should be asked and obtained as speedily as possible. Baron Blanc has received a telegram from the Italian Ambassador at Constantinople, whom his Excellency has authorized to make the demand for the Italian ship "Archimede," reporting that it has been unanimously agreed among the Ambassadors to await the notification of the dispatch of second "stationnaires" before making a simultaneous demand, as some of the Ambassadors have not yet received such notification from their respective Governments.

According to information he has received, Baron Blanc considers it doubtful whether the dispatch of the Russian and French "stationnaires" could take place so early, and would be glad to know if, in the opinion of Her Majesty's Government, the duty incumbent on each Power to protect its own subjects would justify a demand for each Firman being made at the moment when its second "stationnaire" has sailed.

I have been asked by Baron Blanc to let him know confidentially what your Lordship's views on this point may be.

F. O. 424/184, p. 240, No. 445

No. 547

Sir E. Monson to the Marquess of Salisbury.

No. 89.   VIENNA, *November 17, 1895.*
Telegraphic.   *(Received November 17.)*

THE message which your Lordship transmitted to Count Goluchowski, through the Austro-Hungarian Ambassador in London, accepting his views, has evidently afforded his Excellency the greatest satisfaction.

I am informed that the Italian Government fully concur.

The answer given by Prince Lobanoff before he had seen the Emperor is also of a satisfactory nature.

I am informed that the Austro-Hungarian Ambassador in Paris believes that the French Government entirely agree, but he will not see the Minister for Foreign Affairs till to-morrow.

Count Goluchowski's point of view is absolutely accepted by Germany, but it is not certain that a squadron will be sent by her to Turkish waters.

Count Goluchowski considers that ships of war should only be sent by the Powers signatory of the Berlin Treaty, and that small Powers, such as Greece, should not send any. The advice given by the Italian Government to Greece, to the effect that the latter should not make any movement to take part in a display of naval force, meets with Count Goluchowski's approval.

F. O. 424/184, pp. 240-241, No. 447

No. 548

Mr. Gosselin to the Marquess of Salisbury.

No. 46. BERLIN, *November 17, 1895, 5.30 p.m.*
Telegraphic. *(Received November 17.)*

YOUR Lordship's telegram No. 115 of yesterday, upon which I have acted.

The Imperial Secretary of State for Foreign Affairs begs me to thank your Lordship for the communication contained therein, and to state that there are no German ships which would be available for this purpose.

Baron von Marschall is afraid that the Sultan will delay the issue of Firmans as long as he can.

F. O. 424/184, p. 241, No. 448

No. 549

Mr. Gosselin to the Marquess of Salisbury.

No. 47. BERLIN, *November 17, 1895, 5.30 p.m.*
Telegraphic. *(Received November 17.)*

I WAS informed this morning by Baron von Marschall that the Imperial Government have accepted the Austrian proposal for joint action of fleets in principle, should the necessity arise at Constantinople for such action.

As explained in my foregoing telegram, His Majesty's ship "Moltke," now at Smyrna, is the only vessel available to represent the German flag.

I informed his Excellency that your Lordship has not communicated with me on the subject of the proposal made by the Austrian Government.

F. O. 424/184, p. 241, No. 449

No. 550

Mr. Goschen to the Marquess of Salisbury.

No. 112. Confidential.   St. Petersburg, *November 17, 1895.*
Telegraphic.   *(Received November 17.)*

I HAVE received, on good authority, the information that the Ministry of Finance has allowed a considerable supplementary credit for the more rapid mobilization of the Russian Mediterranean and Black Sea Squadrons.

The latter is reported to be ready to go to sea in twenty-four hours.

The "Rurik" and "Dimitri Donskoi" left Cronstadt on the 10th instant, and are said to be bound for the Mediterranean, where they will join the "Groziashchi."

Orders have also been sent to Cronstadt to expedite the fitting out of the "Peter-Veliki" and two other ships, all of which are to proceed to Reval before the ice comes, in order to be ready to sail in the early spring for the Mediterranean, if required. It is also reported that the Black Sea Squadron is in readiness to go to sea in twenty-four hours.

In conversation yesterday with Prince Lobanoff his Excellency told me that he had heard that the British Mediterranean Squadron was about to be reinforced by fourteen of Her Majesty's ships that had recently been dispatched there. Considering how large the squadron in question already was, this report, he said, had caused him some surprise.

F. O. 424/184, p. 241, No. 450

No. 551

Admiralty to Foreign Office.

Admiralty, *November 18, 1895.*
Sir,   *(Received November 18.)*

WITH reference to previous correspondence respecting "stationnaires" at Constantinople, I am commanded by my Lords Commissioners of the Admiralty to transmit the accompanying decypher of a telegram, dated the 17th instant, from the Commander-in-chief on the Mediterranean Station, from which it appears that the gun-boat "Dryad" is the only other ship besides the "Barham" available for second "stationnaire" at Constantinople.

I am to observe that the "Dryad's "Navy List" tonnage is 1,070 and her complement 120, but this seems to be the nearest approach to the desired conditions; and I am to request you will move the Marquess of Salisbury to cause their Lordships to be informed whether the "Dryad" will do.

I am, &c.

(Signed) EVAN MACGREGOR.

F. O. 424/184, p. 258, No. 469

Inclosure in No. 551

Admiral Sir M. Culme-Seymour to Admiralty.

Telegraphic.   SALONICA, *November 17, 1895.*

FOLLOWING telegram received from Chargé d'Affaires at Constantinople:-

"Fear that 'Barham' is much too large to send here. Austrians have selected torpedo gun-boat 57 metres long, 800 tons, 130 men. French will send torpedo-catcher, Italians gun-boat, both trifle smaller than Austrian.

"Have you nothing about the size Austrian? Am informed that 'Hebe' or 'Skipjack' are about the necessary size."

Have informed him "Barham" specially ordered by Admiralty, and that I have telegraphed to you "Dryad" only other ship available.

F. O. 424/184, p. 258, No. 469/1

No. 552

Mr. Herbert to the Marquess of Salisbury.

No. 709.   CONSTANTINOPLE, *November 18, 1895, 10.45 1 a.m.*
Telegraphic.   *(Received November 18.)*

WITH reference to your Lordship's telegram No. 220 of the 16th instant, I have received a telegram from Admiral Seymour stating that the "Arethusa" will be sent to Alexandretta, and that she ought to arrive there by Wednesday.

The United States' cruiser "San Francisco" is also being sent there by the American Government, who have already a man-of-war on the Syrian coast.

F. O. 424/184, p. 259, No. 470

No. 553

Mr. Herbert to the Marquess of Salisbury.

No. 710.   CONSTANTINOPLE, *November 18, 1895, 10.45 a.m.*
Telegraphic.   *(Received November 18.)*

IN reply to an inquiry which I addressed to him yesterday, Her Majesty's Consul at Aleppo telegraphs as follows:-

"The Vali is such a fanatic that it is quite possible that he should have suggested to the Sultan the destruction of the Armenians at a distance from Aleppo. Fear is often expressed here lest the Vali should give orders for a Mussulman rising without the Ferik knowing anything about it.

"I asked the latter what he thought about this last week, and his reply was that the Vali was wicked enough, but had not the necessary courage to take this step.

"I shall take the first opportunity of speaking to the Ferik about the treatment of the Zeitounlis in the event of their submission, as instructed by you, and I may perhaps be able to ascertain whether he is cognizant of anything extraordinary."

F. O. 424/184, p. 259, No. 471

No. 554

Mr. Herbert to the Marquess of Salisbury.

No. 711.   CONSTANTINOPLE, *November 18, 1895.*
Telegraphic.   *(Received November 18.)*

MR. HAMPSON telegraphs that the village of Ishkensor has been completely pillaged by the Kurds of Guendj, under Suleiman, and everything that has been distributed there by the Relief Committee has been carried off.

F. O. 424/184, p. 259, No. 472

No. 555

The Marquess of Salisbury to Mr. Herbert.

No. 222.
Telegraphic.   FOREIGN OFFICE, *November 18, 1895, 10.30 p.m.*

I HAVE received your telegrams Nos. 693, 702 and 704 of the 16th and 17th instant respectively relative to the position of the Armenians of Zeitun, and the reported issue of orders for their wholesale destruction.

Her Majesty's government earnestly hope that in the event of the Zeitunlis surrendering they will be treated with clemency. If, in the present state of feeling in this country and in Europe, the Turkish troops are guilty of any massacres or acts of unnecessary violence, an effect will be produced entailing consequences for which Her Majesty's Government could not answer.

You should convey messages in this sense to the Sultan and to the Grand Vizier.

In case, it should be maintained that punishment of those who are responsible for acts of violence is necessary, you may state that they should only be punished on sufficient evidence after a fair trial.

F. O. 424/184, p. 260, No. 478

No. 556

The Marquess of Salisbury to Mr. Herbert.

No. 223.
Telegraphic.   FOREIGN OFFICE, *November 18, 1895, 10.30 p.m.*

WITH reference to your telegram No. 700 of the 17th instant, I think that the Powers who intend to apply for Firmans for the passage of second "stationnaires" should do so in terms as nearly as possible identical, and that the applications should be presented simultaneously.

In the event of the Porte raising any objection on the ground that there are already two vessels attached to the British Embassy, you may state that Her Majesty's ship "Cockatrice" is detailed for service at the mouth of the Danube, and that her stay, therefore, at Constantinople is only temporary. You may add that by Treaty no limit is fixed to the number of vessels, but that it is intended, in order to pursue exactly the same course as the other Powers, that either she or Her Majesty's ship "Imogene" should leave as soon as the other vessel arrives.

You should then communicate with the Admiral in command of the Mediterranean Squadron with a view to settle which is the most convenient of these two courses.

F. O. 424/184, p. 261, No. 479

No. 557

The Marquess of Salisbury to Sir E. Monson.

No. 84. Secret.
Telegraphic.   FOREIGN OFFICE, *November 18, 1895, 11.30 p.m.*

IN my immediately preceding telegram I repeated to you a telegram from Her Majesty's Chargé d'Affaires at Constantinople, No. 697 of the 16th instant, reporting a communication made to the Porte by the Turkish Respresentative at Berlin respecting the attitude of Germany.

You may communicate this information in strict confidence to Count Goluchowski, stating that it has reached Her Majesty's Government indirectly, and not indicating its origin.

F. O. 424/184, p. 261, No. 480

No. 558

The Marquess of Salisbury to Sir Clare Ford.

No. 66.
Telegraphic.   FOREIGN OFFICE, *November 18, 1895, 9.30 p.m.*

I HAVE received your Excellency's telegram No. 44 of the 17th instant relative to Baron Blanc's inquiries as to the date when the Imperial Firmans for second "stationnaires" should be applied for at Constantinople.

In reply, you may tell his Excellency that, in my opinion, it would be desirable that the Representatives of the Powers should apply simultaneously for the Firmans to the Sultan independently of the time of the departure of the ships for Constantinople, or of their arrival at the Straits.

As far as I am aware, there is no rule which prevents such a request being brought forward until the vessel has arrived, and, in any case, I think that on this occasion the sooner the application is made the better.

It should, as far as possible, be left to the Ambassadors at Constantinople to settle the details of procedure.

F. O. 424/184, p. 261, No. 481

No. 559

The Marquess of Salisbury to Mr. Goschen.

No. 227.
Telegraphic.   FOREIGN OFFICE, *November 18, 1895, 11 p.m.*

I HAVE received your telegram No. 112, Confidential, of yesterday, reporting that Prince Lobanoff had expressed his surprise at a report which had reached him that fourteen more vessels had been dispatched to reinforce the British Mediterranean Squadron.

I should wish you to inform his Excellency that there is absolutely no foundation for the report. Two second-class cruisers only are being dispatched to take the place of ships which have been ordered to join the British Squadron in Chinese waters.

F. O. 424/184, pp. 261-262, No. 482

No. 560

Mr. Gosselin to the Marquess of Salisbury.

No. 270.   BERLIN, *November 18, 1895.*
My Lord,   *(Received November 20.)*

IN compliance with the instructions conveyed to me by your Lordship's telegram of the 16th instant, I called on Baron von Marschall yesterday, and informed his Excellency that Her Majesty's Government agreed to the proposal that Mr. Herbert should be empowered to summon a second "stationnaire" to Constantinople, and that the sooner the Firmans were applied for and granted the better; adding that instructions in this sense had already been sent to Her Majesty's Embassy at the Porte.

Baron von Marschall, in begging me to thank your Lordship for this communication, said that Germany had no ship of the "stationnaire" class available for the purpose; that, personally (as he had stated to me two days ago), he did not think the proposal would be of much practical use, and that the Sultan would probably do all in his power to delay granting the Firmans for the passage of the additional "stationnaire" through the Straits for as long a time as possible.

His Excellency then asked me whether I had heard anything of Count Goluchowski's proposal for combined action in certain eventualities on the part of the fleets of the Great Powers. I replied that I had seen the proposal mentioned in German newspapers, but had heard nothing from your Lordship on the subject.

Baron von Marschall said that the Imperial Government had accepted in principle the Austro-Hungarian proposal as to joint action of the fleets in case of an outbreak in Constantinople itself; but that the only ship which could represent Germany was His Majesty's ship "Moltke," now at Smyrna.

It would take, said his Excellency, from three to four weeks to get a second ship ready at Kiel; and no orders had as yet been sent to put another German cruiser in commission.

I have, &c.

(Signed) MARTIN GOSSELIN.

F. O. 424/184, p. 268, No. 503

No. 561

Admiralty to Foreign Office.

Confidential.   ADMIRALTY, *November 19, 1895.*
Sir,   *(Received November 19.)*

IN reply to your letter of this day's date, expressing the request of the

Secretary of State that a telegram should be sent at once to the Commander-in-chief in the Mediterranean, instructing him to place the "Dryad" at the disposal of Her Majesty's Chargé d'Affaires at Constantinople as second "stationnaire," I am commanded by my Lords Commissioners of the Admiralty to request that you will inform the Marquess of Salisbury that the following telegram has this day been received, in cypher, from Sir Michael Culme-Seymour, viz.:-

"Referring to your telegram No. 112, I have informed the British Chargé d'Affaires that the 'Dryad' will be held in readiness instead of ships previously named."

Telegram No. 112, from this Office to the Commander-in-chief, was as follows:-

"Arrangement about 'Barham' is cancelled, as the ship is too large—800 tons is now considered limit of size. Make arrangements with Chargé d'Affaires, and report."

I am, &c.

(Signed) EVAN MACGREGOR.

F. O. 424/184, p. 263, No. 487

No. 562

Mr. Herbert to the Marquess of Salisbury.

No. 717.   CONSTANTINOPLE, *November 19, 1895, 10.55 a.m.*
Telegraphic.   *(Received November 19.)*

WITH reference to my telegram No. 703 of the 17th instant, other Powers are asking for Firmans to-day. Please telegraph whether the "Dryad" is the vessel selected.

F. O. 424/184, p. 263, No. 488

No. 563

Mr. Herbert to the Marquess of Salisbury.

No. 723.   CONSTANTINOPLE, *November 19, 1895, 10.5 p.m.*
Telegraphic.   *(Received November 19.)*

YOUR Lordship's telegram No. 222.

Sultan has sent following reply to your Lordship's message:-

The Turkish Government cannot make the first advances after the manner in which the Zeitounlis are known to have acted. The Military Commandants in all parts of the Empire have already received orders not to touch any one who does not resist the authorities. His Majesty will give orders to the troops and guns which are ready at Marash not to move for two days. If on their arrival at Zeitoun the rebels consent to submit, hand over the authors of the outrages and deliver up their arms, nothing will be done to them.

Sultan again requests your Lordship to make a public declaration that the reforms will be carried out by His Majesty without delay in accordance with His Majesty's repeated assurances contained in previous messages, and an answer from your Lordship is pressed for.

A rumour that the "stationnaires" are to be doubled has reached His Majesty. Sultan hopes your Lordship will not take this step, as it might excite public feeling and prevent the tranquillity which is necessary to enable him to carry out the reforms.

His Majesty also urges that your Lordship should strongly advise the Armenians through the Patriarch to remain quiet, and not to make any fresh troubles.

F. O. 424/184, p. 265, No. 493

No. 564

Mr. Herbert to the Marquess of Salisbury.

No. 724.   CONSTANTINOPLE, *November 19, 1895, 10.40 p.m.*
Telegraphic.   *(Received November 19.)*

MY telegram No. 723 of to-day.

I have telegraphed to Mr. Barnham repeating portion of Sultan's message relating to the Zeitounlis, and instructing him to see what he can do in conjunction with the Ferik. I have warned him at the same time not to make himself in any way responsible for the promises which either side may give.

F. O. 424/184, p. 265, No. 494

No. 565

Sir E. Monson to the Marquess of Salisbury.

No. 91. Secret.   VIENNA, *November 19, 1895.*
Telegraphic.   *(Received November 19.)*

I HAVE the honour to report to your Lordship that I communicated to the Austro-Hungarian Minister for Foreign Affairs the substance of your telegram of yesterday No. 83, Secret, but made no allusion to the source from which the information was derived.

I am informed by his Excellency that the Austro-Hungarian Ambassador at Berlin describes the Emperor's language to him as entirely satisfactory and loyal, and that that used by the German Ambassador at Constantinople to the Sultan is reported by Baron Calice as being downright and straightforward.

Consequently, his Excellency does not believe that a message such as that reported can have been sent by the German Government.

In a conversation with me last night the German Ambassador insisted to me that the co-operation of his Government in the dispatch to the Levant of foreign squadrons is only prevented by want of ships. I do not think that this is really believed by Count Goluchowski, and I could not readily admit it to be the case.

F. O. 424/184, p. 265, No. 495

No. 566

The Marquess of Salisbury to Mr. Egerton.

No. 12.

Telegraphic.   FOREIGN OFFICE, *November 19, 1895, 1.25 p.m.*

THE Austrian Government are of opinion that the Powers only who signed the Treaty of Berlin should join in the naval measures for the protection of European interests at Constantinople and in other parts of the Ottoman Empire, and that lesser Powers, such as Greece, should take no part in them. The Italian Government have, I understand, given advice in this sense to Greece.

If consulted, you may express the same opinion, and if two or three of your colleagues should wish it, you may join in a representation on the subject to the Greek Government.

F. O. 424/184, p. 267, No. 500

No. 567

Foreign Office to Admiralty.

Confidential.

Sir,   FOREIGN OFFICE, *November 19, 1895.*

I AM directed by the Marquess of Salisbury to state, for the information of the Lords Commissioners of the Admiralty, that a telegram has been received from Mr. Herbert, Her Majesty's Chargé d'Affaires at Constantinople, reporting that the Representatives of the other Great Powers intend to apply to-day for Firmans granting passage through the Dardanelles of the vessels selected for service as second "stationnaires" to the Embassies.

Mr. Herbert stated in his telegram No. 713 of yesterday's date, a copy of which was communicated to you, that Her Majesty's ship "Dryad" would be suitable for the purpose, and Lord Salisbury requests that a telegram may be sent at once to the Admiral, instructing him to place that vessel at Mr. Herbert's disposal.

I am, &c.

(Signed) T. H. SANDERSON.

F. O. 424/184, p. 267, No. 501

No. 568

Mr. Herbert to the Marquess of Salisbury.

No. 810.   CONSTANTINOPLE, *November 19, 1895.*

My Lord,   *(Received November 25.)*

I HAVE the honour to forward to your Lordship herewith copy of a despatch which I have received from the Acting British Consul at Erzeroum, inclosing Reports on the state of affairs in Bitlis, Van, Kharput, Diarbekir, and the surrounding districts.

I have, &c.

(Signed) MICHAEL H. HERBERT.

F. O. 424/184, p. 281, No. 540

Inclosure 1 in No. 568

Consul Cumberbatch to Mr. Herbert.

Sir,   ERZEROUM, *November 4, 1895.*

I HAVE the honour to forward copy of a despatch received from Her Majesty's Vice-Consul at Mush reporting that disorders took place at Bitlis on the 25th and 26th ultimo resulting in the death of several hundred Armenians and the pillaging of their shops, and that the greatest fear existed at Mush lest similar disturbances should break out in that town and district.

I also inclose copy of a despatch from Her Majesty's Vice-Consul at Van reporting the insecurity existing in that vilayet, and extracts from a private letter from Kharput as to the condition of things in that place and Diarbekir.

All these reports depict a state of things which existed at Erzeroum before the disorders which took place on the 30th ultimo as duly reported by me at the time.

I have, &c.

(Signed) H. A. CUMBERBATCH.

F. O. 424/184, p. 281, No. 540/1

Inclosure 2 in No. 568

Vice-Consul Hampson to Consul Cumberbatch.

Sir,   MUSH, *October 29, 1895.*

IT is with deep regret that I have to report that a very serious disturbance took place in Bitlis on Friday last the 25th instant, resulting, I fear, in the death of very many persons. The telegraph line between Mush and Bitlis having been cut—it is supposed by Kurds—we have, so far, very few reliable details, either as to the origin and course of the events, or as to the number killed. On the latter point, the Mutessarif told me, until yesterday, that he believed the victims to be at least 500. Now the authorities are endeavouring to make out that they are only about 100; while the latest Armenian report gives the number at 800. From my knowledge of the place, I am disposed to fear that the latter number is at least nearer the truth.

The disturbances began when the Mussulmans were coming from the Mosques, and lasted at least four hours that day. According to what I hear, the whole bazaar was pillaged and wrecked by Kurds on the following day.

As to the origin, the Turks say that the Armenians attacked the Mosques. This is most improbable, as is allowed by the Turks themselves, the cowardly character of the Bitlis Armenians being a by-word in these parts. I have reliable information that, on the previous Friday, 18th October, the Mussulmans went to the Mosques fully armed, with the avowed intention of attacking the Christians; but the acting Vali, having been warned, sent sufficient troops to prevent any disorder. It is probable that, on the 25th, matters got beyond his control; which view is supported by his appeals for more troops. I think that there is also little doubt that the Kurds from Modeki came into Bitlis to join in the massacre.

For further details I must wait until reliable information arrives.

I am glad to be able to state that all the Americans in Bitlis are, so far, safe.

The result of the news from Bitlis was to produce a terrible panic in Mush, which has as yet but little abated. All shops were closed last Saturday, and very few are open even to-day. Mussulmans and Kurds parade the streets fully armed; and though I have repeatedly urged the Mutessarif to issue an order that no one shall carry arms in the streets, it has been ineffectual. The Mussulmans believe, or pretend to believe, that the Armenians intend to attack them; and their fears are (so they say) especially directed to Sasun, from which district the Armenians—fully armed by means of the pretended relief supplies sent them by the English Committee—are advancing in large numbers against Mush. They (the Mussulmans) on their side are calling in the Kurds from the neighbouring mountains to protect them.

As the Armenians (who certainly have not the least idea of attacking the Mussulmans) are in an abject state of terror, and, in spite of my strong advice, declare they dare not open their shops so long as the Mussulmans carry arms and

Kurds are in the neighbourhood, it is difficult to see a peaceful end to this situation, which is most critical.

Yesterday evening the chief Mussulmans and Christians of the town met to discuss the means of restoring confidence. The result was an ultimatum on the part of the former that the American missionaries must leave Sasun; that, if this were done, they would abandon their fears of an attack from that quarter, and cease to carry arms; but if not, the present panic would continue, and, very probably, result in a repetition of the Bitlis affair. Three days' delay was given to the Christians for an answer.

I am in doubt what view to take of this demand. If the Mussulmans are honest in their ideas, they are showing a crass ignorance and fanaticism which seems almost hopeless; if they are not honest, their intentions must be most sinister.

I had a long interview with the Mutessarif last night on the subject. It is evident that, since his arrival here, the views of his co-religionists have been carefully instilled into him. I said that, if he assured me that the return of the missionaires was the only means of securing freedom from disorders, I would ask Her Majesty's Ambassador to authorize me to recall them, at least temporarily; but at the same time warned him that, if this became necessary, the recall of the missionaires from the scene of their disinterested and humane labours on behalf of Ottoman subjects would, I thought, create a very bad impression in the civilized world; and also that if—which I entirely disbelieved—there were any idea of sedition among the people of Sasun and Talori, the recall of the missionaires would remove one of the chief restraints. Eventually the Mutesarrif promised to endeavour to persuade the Mussulmans that their suspicions were unfounded.

The Kurds are profiting by the situation to commit outrages in every direction. I hear that the large village of Coultonk, two hours from Bitlis, has been entirely wrecked, and a large number of the inhabitants killed. In the plain of Mush alone, ten villages were pillaged last night, not without loss of life I fear. The followers of Ibo, of Varto (*vide* my despatch of the 9th instant), attacked the village of Avram; also in the plain of Mush, killed two men and wounded six, and carried off a large number of sheep.

The outlook is very black, and the improvement of the last few months is, I fear, more than undone; and this must largely be attributed to the criminal folly and impatience of the Armenians in Constantinople and elsewhere where they were the cause of disorders.

I have kept Her Majesty's Embassy fully informed by telegraph of the main facts contained in this despatch.

I have, &c.

(Signed) CHARLES S. HAMPSON.

P.S. *October 30.*—The position here is unchanged to-day. From all sides come stories of Kurd outrages, villages robbed, Armenians murdered, &c. In Boulanik things are very bad. The two leading Christians of that caza were murdered at Liss yesterday. I am very anxious at Sasun and Talori.

The Kurds are, I fear, now beyond the control of the Government, and the situation throughout the vilayet is most serious.

C. S. H.

F. O. 424/184, pp. 281-283, No. 540/2

Inclosure 3 in No. 568

Vice-Consul Hallward to Consul Cumberbatch.

Sir,   VAN, *October 30, 1895.*

THERE has been a very uneasy feeling among all classes of the population here for the last week, caused on the one hand by rumoured preparations among the Turks for a hostile movement against the Christians, and on the other hand by exaggerated reports which were current among the Moslems of an intended rising of the Armenians. The anxiety was intensified, and reached something like a panic, especially among the Armenians, on the 26th instant, when a report came from Bitlis of a serious conflict between the Moslems and Christians there. Hitherto, however, no disturbance has occurred, thanks in great measure to the precautions taken both by the civil and military authorities, and the anxiety in the town has somewhat diminished in the last two days.

On the other hand, the state of things in the villages is deplorable. Threats of massacre are continually being made by the Kurds against the Armenians, and the latter know that if these threats were carried out they would be completely at the mercy of the Kurds, who are nearly all well armed, while the Armenians have practically no arms at all.

The report that reached here ten days ago of the acceptance of the scheme of reforms has not tended to improve matters, as the Kurds declare that they will not accept any reforms, whether approved by the Sultan or not, and meantime there are no signs whatever of the enforcement of any reforms. Were a serious attempt made to carry out reforms I do not believe for a moment that there would be any real resistance on the part of the Moslem population, which would largely benefit by any measures taken to insure greater security for life and property, and a better administration; but the condition of uncertainty prevailing in the minds of all, and the excited state of feeling manifested throughout the province by a large population of armed Kurds are very dangerous elements in the present situation, and it is most desirable that immediate steps should be taken for a settlement of affairs.

I have, &c.

(Signed) C. M. HALLWARD.

F. O. 424/184, p. 283, No. 540/3

Inclosure 4 in No. 568

Extracts from a Private Letter from Kharput, dated October 21, 1895.

Kharput.—This region is quiet, and general confidence is largely restored, although the knowledge of the riots in Constantinople has excited the Turks a good deal. The Armenians about us show no disposition to disturb the peace, although their patience is greatly tried.

Diarbekir.—About three weeks ago Enis Pasha was appointed Vali, and upon that the Christian Notables of Diarbekir sent thanks to the Porte, praising his efficiency, &c. This act of the Notables offended the common people among the Christians, and they sent a counter-statement to the Patriarchates saying that his administration had been a failure, &c. At the same time they closed every church and all the Christian schools, and there was a good deal of excitement. The shops occupied by Christians were also closed for three days. Meanwhile it is said that the Turks planned to burn the market, but the military Pasha heard of the plan, and went to the mosque where they were congregated at night, and persuaded them to desist from their undertaking. This is confidently believed. The churches were closed about two weeks, but it was expected they would be opened yesterday— Sunday.

F. O. 424/184, p. 284, No. 540/4

No. 569

Mr. Herbert to the Marquess of Salisbury.

No. 814.   CONSTANTINOPLE, *November 19, 1895.*
My Lord,   *(Received November 25.)*
    I HAVE the honour to forward to your Lordship herewith copy of a despatch which I have received from the Acting British Consul at Erzeroum respecting the recent disorders at Baiburt, and stating that he has no confirmation of the report that the Armenians were the aggressors.

I have, &c.

(Signed) MICHAEL H. HERBERT.

F. O. 424/184, p. 287, No. 544

Inclousre in No. 569

Consul Cumberbatch to Mr. Herbert.

Sir,   ERZEROUM, *November 5, 1895.*
    WITH reference to your telegram of the 28th ultimo, instructing me to make inquiries as to whether Armenians were the aggressors on the occasion of the disorders at Baiburt, I have the honour to state that, owing to the disturbances that have taken place here and the disordered state of this region in general, it has been impossible to obtain any details about those occurrences beyond those I gave in my telegrams of the 27th and 28th ultimo (which must have crossed yours), to the effect that certain Armenians had fired on some Turkish peasants, and that over 160 Armenians and 11 Mussulmans had lost their lives in the reprisals that ensured.
    My information was, however, derived from Turkish official sources, and needs confirmation.
                              I have, &c.
                                        (Signed) H. A. CUMBERBATCH.
    F. O. 424/184, p. 287, No. 544/1

No. 570

Mr. Herbert to the Marquess of Salisbury.

No. 816.   CONSTANTINOPLE, *November 19, 1895.*
My Lord,   *(Received November 25.)*
    I HAVE the honour to forward to your Lordship herewith copy of despatch which I have received from the Acting British Consul at Erzeroum, reporting extensive raids by Kurds and Lazes on Armenian villages throughout the vilayet.
                              I have, &c.
                                        (Signed) MICHAEL H. HERBERT.
    F. O. 424/184, p. 288, No. 546

Inclosure in No. 570

Consul Cumberbatch to Mr. Herbert.

Sir,   ERZEROUM, *November 6, 1895.*
    AS mentioned in several recent telegrams and despatches, raids by Kurds and Lazes on Armenian villages in this vilayet have been going on simultaneously with the disorders in the chief towns. Details are not yet forthcoming, but it is generally

feared that the devastation has been widespread, though not always accompanied by murder. The entire districts of Terdjan, Khinis, and Passim have been pillaged by these marauding bands as well as the Erzeroum plain.

The authorities, being taken up with the disorders in the towns, have been unable to adequately protect the villagers, except a little at first, and, when matters are more settled, stories of ravages that have been, and are being, committed will pour in from all sides.

As stated in my telegram of this day's date, Shakir Pasha left hurriedly this morning for Khinis, where the Kurds in strong force were reported as having fallen on that town and its neighbouring villages.

I have, &c.

(Signed) H. A. CUMBERBATCH.

F. O. 424/184, p. 288, No. 546/1

No. 571

Mr. Herbert to the Marquess of Salisbury.

No. 818.   CONSTANTINOPLE, *November 19, 1895.*
My Lord,   *(Received November 25.)*

WITH reference to my telegram No. 655 of the 11th November, I have the honour to forward to your Lordship herewith copy of a despatch which I have received from the Acting British Consul at Erzeroum, recommending the removal of the Armenian Archbishop of that town.

I have, &c.

(Signed) MICHAEL H. HERBERT.

F. O. 424/184, p. 290, No. 548

Inclosure in No. 571

Consul Cumberbatch to Mr. Herbert.

Secret.
Sir,   ERZEROUM, *November 8, 1895.*

WITH reference to my telegram of this day's date, I have the honour to state as follows:-

Mgr. Ghévant Shishmanian, Metropolitan Archbishop of Erzeroum, was formerly looked upon as a Turcophil. Some months ago he changed his tactics, presumably under instructions from the present Patriarch, and he favoured the "Tashnaktzagan" organization, but without showing any leaning towards the "Hintchakists." Recently, however, he has been accused, even by Armenians, of submitting to the influence of the latter, more through fear, probably, than through approval of their reckless plans.

His conduct of late has certainly not been judicious. When Shakir Pasha arrived here as Inspector-General for the Armenian vilayets, Mgr. Shishmanian received instructions from the Patriarch not to recognize the Marshal's mission, but, obeying the orders of the "Hintchakists," he abstained from calling on his Excellency as he should have done.

The withdrawal at the same time of all the Armenian members of the Administrative Council and Tribunals, &c., though due to the threats of the revolutionary party, was laid to his charge, and, in fact, he was looked upon by the authorities as the chief conspirator.

The publication in the newspapers of his telegraphic appeal to Her Majesty's Secretary of State made his position still worse.

He has made no attempt, either before or since the disorders of the 30th ultimo, to reconcile himself with the authorities, but rather takes up a defiant attitude, which is not conducive to allay the suspicions of the Mussulmans, or to strengthen the confidence in him of his community.

He remains shut up in his private residence, as he thinks his life is in danger.

Both Shakir Pasha and the Vali are personally ill-disposed towards him, owing to his conduct towards the former, and his relations with the authorities are suspended.

Under these circumstances, I have thought it my duty, in the interests of all concerned, to suggest that this Prelate should be quietly recalled, if only temporarily, in order to remove the suspicions of the authorities, which are shared by the Mussulman population, and to facilitate the execution of the contemplated reforms.

Personally, I am on the best terms with Mgr. Shishmanian, and I will regret his departure if it is decided upon.

I have, &c.

(Signed) H. A. CUMBERBATCH.

F. O. 424/184, p. 290, No. 548/1

No. 572

Tewfik Pasha to Morel Bey

Télégraphique.

CONSTANTINOPLE, *le 20 Novembre, 1895.*
(Communicated by Morel Bey, November 20.)

TÉLÉGRAMME adressé au Maréchal du 4ᵉ Corps d'Armée et aux Commandants Militaires d'Alep, Bitlis, Adana, Trébizonde, Diarbékir, Sivas, Mamouret-ul-Aziz, et autres parties de la Turquie d'Asie, en date du 5 (17) Novembre, 1895:-

"La volonté formelle de notre auguste Maître étant que l'on veille plus que jamais et d'une façon tout à fait spéciale au maintien de la tranquillité du pays, de façon à prévenir absolument tout acte, tel que: incendie, menée séditieuse, effusion de sang, ou attaque de la part d'une classe de la population contre l'autre ou contre les Consulats et sujets étrangers, des instructions en conséquence ont été déjà transmises aux fonctionnaires de l'Administration Civile. Conformément à un Iradé Impérial, les autorités Impériales militaires doivent se concerter avec les Valis et les Mutessarifs pour tâcher d'assurer la tranquillité publique et veiller à ce que les officiers et soldats de l'armée agissent dans les limites des règlements militaires en s'abstenant soigneusement de se porter à des actes pouvant provoquer des plaintes. Tout manquement à ces ordres, toute négligence et tout procédé contraire à la discipline entraînera une grave responsabilité."

F. O. 424/184, p. 268, No. 504

No. 573

Mr. Herbert to the Marquess of Salisbury.

No. 725.
Telegraphic.

CONSTANTINOPLE, *November 20, 1895, 2.40 p.m.*
(Received November 20.)

SULTAN sent last night to my colleagues similar message to that contained in my telegram No. 723 of yesterday in regard to the demand for extra "stationnaires." We have all replied that, in our opinion, it is in His Majesty's interest not to make objections, and to grant the necessary Firmans at once, in order to prevent stronger measures being resorted to, and that, moreover, we are convinced that the pressure of extra vessels here will have a tranquillizing effect.

I fear, however, that His Majesty will not give way without a struggle.

Following are the names of the vessel designated by the other Powers:-

Austrian, "Selenico;" French, "Faucon;" Italian, "Archimede;" Russian, "Donetz."

Austrian, Italian, and Russian Ambassadors and myself have applied for Firmans to-day. French Ambassador, who is awaiting some communication from his Admiral, will apply to-morrow, and German Ambassador as soon as he receives instructions as to the name of vessel designated by his Government.

F. O. 424/184, pp. 268-269, No. 505

No. 574

Mr. Herbert to the Marquess of Salisbury.

No. 726.   CONSTANTINOPLE, *November 20, 1895, 3.15 p.m.*
Telegraphic.   *(Received November 20.)*

MR. HAMPSON has telegraphed to me suggesting the formation of a corps of mountain police from among the Armenians of Sasun and Talori, under Turkish officers. He considers they would prove most effective in keeping the Kurds in order. Shall I instruct Mr. Cumberbatch to communicate this suggestion, which seems to me a good one, to Shakir Pasha?

F. O. 424/184, p. 269, No. 506

No. 575

Mr. Herbert to the Marquess of Salisbury.

No. 727.   CONSTANTINOPLE, *November 20, 1895, 3.40 p.m.*
Telegraphic.   *(Received November 20.)*

WITH reference to my telegram No. 559 of the 30th ultimo, plan of reforms was officially communicated yesterday by the Porte to German, Austrian, and Italian Ambassadors.

F. O. 424/184, p. 269, No. 507

No. 576

Mr. Herbert to the Marquess of Salisbury.

No. 728.   CONSTANTINOPLE, *November 20, 1895, 3.55 p.m.*
Telegraphic.   *(Received November 20.)*

HER Majesty's Consul at Aleppo telegraphs as follows:-

"The Ferik shares my opinion that it would be possible to prevent bloodshed among the Zeitounlis if the Sultan would at once dispatch a Commission, consisting of five or six suitable persons, to Zeitoun to persuade the rebels to accept the conditions of surrender laid down by His Majesty. There would be no difficulty in finding suitable persons here.

"The Ferik begs us not to divulge his knowledge of this proposal."

F. O. 424/184, p. 269, No. 508

No. 577

Sir Clare Ford to the Marquess of Salisbury.

No. 45.   ROME, *November 20, 1895.*
Telegraphic.   *(Received November 20.)*

I HAVE communicated the substance of your Lordship's telegram of the 18th instant to Baron Blanc, who, in expressing his thanks, states that "tout est bien d'accord au sujet du second stationnaire."

F. O. 424/184, p. 269, No. 509

No. 578

The Marquess of Salisbury to Mr. Herbert.

No. 226.
Telegraphic.   FOREIGN OFFICE, *November 20, 1895, 12.40 p.m.*

I HAVE received your telegram No. 718 of yesterday, requesting instructions on behalf of Consul Longworth as to extending protection to the Armenians of Ottoman origin who are naturalized as American citizens, and are now being tried before a court-martial at Trebizond.

You should consult your United States' colleague as to whether he is aware of any sufficient ground on which to base a claim for their protection.

Our rules lay down that unless naturalization has been effected with the sanction of the Porte, no claim for protection can be sustained, and the Consul can only watch the case and intervene in an unofficial manner.

F. O. 424/184, p. 270, No. 510

No. 579

The Marquess of Salisbury to Mr. Herbert.

No. 228.
Telegraphic.   FOREIGN OFFICE, *November 20, 1895, 6.30 p.m.*

I HAVE received your telegram No. 726 of to-day respecting a proposal made by Her Majesty's Vice-Consul at Mush for the formatiorn of a corps of mountain police composed of Armenians from Sasun and Talori, and commanded by Turkish officers.

The suggestion had better be reserved for the consideration of Her Majesty's Ambassador on his arrival at Constantinople.

F. O. 424/184, p. 270, No. 511

No. 580

The Marquess of Salisbury to Sir E. Monson.

No. 87.
Telegraphic.   FOREIGN OFFICE, *November 20, 1895, 3 p.m.*

I HAVE received your telegram No. 91, Secret, of yesterday, stating that satisfactory information had reached Count Goluchowski as to the language held by the German Ambassador to the Sultan.

The telegram from Her Majesty's Chargé d'Affaires at Constantinople which I repeated to you on the 19th instant will show your Excellency that equally satisfactory information on the subject has been received by Mr. Herbert.

As regards the communication sent home by the Turkish Chargé d'Affaires at Berlin, if correctly stated, it probably represents the alternations which he deemed it wise to make in any message which he received for transmission to the Porte.

F. O. 424/184, p. 270, No. 512

No. 581

Tewfik Pasha to Morel Bey.

                                                CONSTANTINOPLE, *le 20 Novembre 1895.*
Télégraphique.   *(Communicated November 21.)*

TÉLÉGRAMME adressé aux vilayets de Van, Bitlis, Erzeroum, Alep, Diarbékir, Trébizonde, Sivas, et Mamouret-ul-Aziz, en date du 5 (17) Novembre, 1895:-

"Bien que les instructions itératives qui vous ont été déjà données prescrivent l'adoption dans votre vilayet de mesures propres à prévenir tout fait pouvant troubler l'ordre public ainsi que toute effusion de sang et d'empêcher qu'une classe de la population attaque l'autre et que des actes contraires à la justice soient commis, de pareils cas continuent cependant à se produire. L'une des attributions les plus importantes des Valis étant de maintenir et d'assurer la tranquillité dans les provinces, je viens, conformément aux ordres formels de notre auguste Maître, vous prévenir que si après que le présent télégramme vous sera parvenu on laisse se produire des méfaits, tels que: incendies, menées séditieuses, perturbation publique, ou effusion de sang, une pareille infraction aux devoirs qui incombe aux autorités ne pourrait en aucune façon être pardonné et entraînerait une grave et absolue responsabilité. Cette responsabilité s'étend également aux Mutessarifs et aux Caïmacams. Vous devez vous concerter aussi avec les Commandants pour l'adoption de dispositions en conséquence.

"Vous aurez surtout à veiller avec la plus grande vigilance à la protection des Consulats et des sujets étrangers, de façon à les mettre à l'abri de tout danger et à écarter tout motif de plainte de leur part. Tous les coupables devront être arrêtés et punis conformément à la loi.

"Vous télégraphierez en clair toutes les vingt-quatre heures au Ministère de l'Intérieur, au Sérasккérat, au Grand Vizirat, et au Palais Impérial la situation de vilayet."

F. O. 424/184, pp. 270-271, No. 513

No. 582

Tewfik Pasha to Morel Bey.

CONSTANTINOPLE, *le 20 Novembre, 1895.*
Télégraphique.   *(Communicated November 21.)*

TÉLÉGRAMME adressé aux Gouverneurs-Généraux des vilayets de Trébizonde, d'Erzeroum, Bitlis, Van, Diarbékir, Mamouret-ul-Aziz, Sivas, Adana, et Alep, en date du 3 (15) Novembre, 1895:-

"Les Commandants de Brigade, en expédiant des corps volants pour la répression des désordres surgis dans leurs circonscriptions, lanceront une Proclamation aux populations pour engager ceux qui tentent de troubler à main armée la sécurité publique, à renoncer à leur attitude et à s'abstenir de tous faits qui seraient contraires à la volonté manifeste de Sa Majesté Impériale le Sultan.

"Ils auront à sévir immédiatement par les armes contre ceux qui ne se conformeraient pas à cette injonction et s'empresseraient d'empêcher, en faisant stationner des troupes sur divers points, tout mouvement des émeutiers pour attaquer à main armée les bourgs et villages.

"Si des meurtres et des actes d'insurrection venaient à être commis inopinément dans la sphére d'évolution d'un corps volant, les dits Commandants auront à en poursuivre immédiatement les auteurs sans délai et sans leur faire aucune sommation.

"Le Commandant-en-chef du 4ᵉ Corps d'Armée Impériale aura à prêter au moyen des troupes du dit corps, l'assistance nécessaire aux Commandants de brigade susmentionnés qui se trouveront sous ses ordres en vue d'assurer le succés le leur tâche.

"Le Séraskérat a été invité à transmettre des ordres télégraphiques dans ce sens tant au Muchir de dit corps d'armée qu'aux commandants précités.

"La ligne de conduite à suivre par les autorités civiles à l'égard des agitateurs ayant été précédemment indiquée par télégraphe, conformément à un Iradé Impérial, vous aurez à faire à qui de droit des recommandations dans le sens du dit télégramme avant l'envoi de troupes pour la répression des actes attentatoires à la sécurité publique.

"Ces dispositions ayant été revêtues de la sanction Impériale et des instructions en conséquence ayant été transmises au Séraskérat et aux Valis je vous engage encore une fois à vous y conformer strictement en ce qui concerne votre vilayet.

"Notre auguste Maître exigeant vivement que l'ordre soit rétabli au plus tôt dans les localités où il a été troublé, que la vie, l'honneur, et les biens de tous soient sauvegardés et que tous faits et actes contraires à la justice et à l'équité soient empêchés, vous aurez à veiller jour et nuit pour assurer la réalisation de la dite volonté souveraine en mettant sans retard fin aux désordres."

F. O. 424/184, p. 271, No. 514

No. 583

Mr. Herbert to the Marquess of Salisbury.

No. 827.   CONSTANTINOPLE, *November 20, 1895.*
My Lord,   *(Received November 25.)*

AS your Lordship is aware, the Ministry was changed shortly after the six Embassies made the representations respecting the state of the Asiatic Provinces, communicated to your Lordship in my telegram No. 604 of the 4th instant.

On the 9th instant it was decided to repeat these representations to the new Minister for Foreign Affairs, which was accordingly done by my colleagues and myself on the 11th November. Tewfik Pasha replied that an answer was drafted, and that we should receive it almost immediately. The same evening I had the honour to receive your Lordship's telegram No. 216, containing a message to the Sultan, which I caused to be translated into Turkish, and presented to His Imperial Majesty through his First Secretary on the morning of the next day.

His Imperial Majesty replied that the only explanation he could offer of the situation and of your Lordship's language, was that, on the one hand, his orders were not obeyed by the Valis, and, on the other, were not communicated to the Embassies by the Porte. He would send the Minister of Foreign Affairs to me to explain the measures he had taken, or was still taking.

For the last month His Majesty had been sending numberless instructions to the provincial authorities, bidding them prevent outbreaks, and punish the guilty, without distinction of creed. He held them responsible for what had occurred in their provinces; had told them he had no more confidence in them, and intended to send Aides-de-camp to inquire into their conduct. He could but express his deep sorrow and pain at what had occurred, and the only explantion he could give was that the movement was well organized through a very large extent of country, and it was impossible to deal with it quickly.

In accordance with this promise, the Minister for Foreign Affairs called on me the same evening to inform me of the measures which His Majesty was taking to restore order. They were as follows:-

One hundred and twenty battalions of reserves have been called out.

The Valis have received categorical orders to punish any Moslems who attack Armenians, and not to ill-treat the latter.

Special Commissioners are being sent to various parts of Armenia to see that the provincial authorities obey these instructions.

The sufferers from the recent disturbances, whether Christian or Moslem, are to be housed and fed at the expense of the State.

His Excellency also said that a telegram had been received from Shakir Pasha, stating that perfect order now prevailed, and eulogizing the conduct of the Hamidié regiments who had protected the Armenians against the Mahommedans.

The same communication was made to the French and Russian Ambassadors, but by order of the Sultan, who is determined to ignore, and hopes to destroy the union of the six Powers, no communication was made to the Austrian, German, and Italian Ambassadors, who thus remained without any reply to the representations they had made on the 4th and 11th instant.

It was accordingly decided that the British, French, and Russian Embassies should send their Dragomans to the Porte, and state through them that they could not consider they had had any reply to their identic representations of the 11th instant, until all six Embassies had received similar communications from the Minister for Foreign Affairs. This was done on the 17th November, and the French Dragoman added that in M. Cambon's opinion the Porte had committed a great mistake, and incurred the displeasure of the three other Ambassadors.

It is said that an Iradé has been issued, instructing the Porte to reply in writing to the six Embassies.

I have, &c.

(Signed) MICHAEL H. HERBERT.

F. O. 424/184, pp. 298-299, No. 554

No. 584

Mr. Goschen to the Marquess of Salisbury.

No. 270. Confidential.   ST. PETERSBURGH, *November 20, 1895.*
My Lord,   *(Received November 26.)*

I HAVE the honour to report that, on the occasion when I communicated to Prince Lobanoff the substance of your Lordship's telegram of the 17th instant,* his Excellency, after giving me his reply, proceeded to discuss the question of the intervention on the part of the Powers to put an end to the disorders in Asia Minor.

His Excellency's ideas on the subject are as follows: it is presumably the object of every Power to get the Sultan to restore peace and order in his dominions; to do this in the present state of excitement among his subjects His Majesty must have time, and his moral authority must be unimpaired. Threats of intervention cannot but undermine that authority, and will therefore defeat the object the Powers have in view, as, no matter how much the Sultan may wish and strive to restore order, without prestige and moral authority he can do nothing. As things stand at present the Sultan has accepted all our demands and we should now give ample time to allow the excitement to subside, and await patiently the result of His Majesty's efforts to tranquillize the disturbed districts.

I said that, as far as I understood the matter, it appeared to me that if intervention took place at all, it would only be as a last resort, and after it was clearly proved that the Sultan had not the requisite authority to cope with the situation himself, but that I supposed that, if the horrible scenes enacted daily in Asia Minor should happen to continue without any effectual measures being taken to put them down, the time might come when patience might be exhausted, and the Powers feel it their duty to put an end to a state of things which was clearly intolerable.

Prince Lobanoff then made use of a phrase which he had used to one of my colleagues a short time ago: "My experience in the East tells me that such disturbances as are now taking place soon die a natural death, except in cases when the opposing elements are stirred up to continued action by some Power for her own political interests."

I ventured to observe, in reply, that happily this could not be the case at present, as the Powers concerned in the question of Armenian reforms had been all along in such complete accord. I added that I had no authority to discuss the question of ultimate intervention with his Excellency, and that any remarks I might have made were merely expressive of my personal views suggested by his own observations. His Excellency replied that he quite understood that, but that he had wished to place before me his own view of what would be the result of intervention, namely, that it would so weaken the authority of the Sultan as to render him powerless to cope with the difficulties of the situation.

His Excellency then proceeded to discuss the practical difficulties of any forcible intervention in Asia Minor, the greatest of which was, he observed, the large extent of territory where the disturbances are taking place. When France received the mandate of Europe to restore order in Damascus, this difficulty did not exist, as the disturbances were confined to one district; but in the present case, supposing the Powers undertook a similar task they would have the whole of Asia Minor to tranquillize, and how could it be done? Riots might be quelled in Zeitoun, they would crop out again say at Diarbekir, and so on through the whole country, and it was not difficult to forsee the enormous force that would be required to carry out such a tremendous undertaking effectually.

The keynote, however, of Prince Lobanoff's whole conversation was the fear that the more intervention was threatened the more would the Armenians be encouraged to endeavour to bring about that intervention by formenting disturbances, and provoking the Turks to sanguinary reprisals.

I have, &c.

(Signed) W. E. GOSCHEN.

F. O. 424/184, pp. 307-308, No. 570

* ? 16th instant.

No. 585

Mr. Herbert to the Marquess of Salisbury.

No. 729.   CONSTANTINOPLE, *November 21, 1895, 10.13 a.m.*
Telegraphic.   *(Received November 21.)*

I HAVE received the following telegram from Her Majesty's Consul at Aleppo:-

"The outbreak at Marash yesterday was most serious, but I have no information yet as to the number of killed and wounded.

"The disturbances originated in the death of a Mussulman, which the Turks attributed to the Armenians, the result being an outbreak on the part of the Mussulman population. The troops were called out, and the Armenians fired on them from their houses, and killed many. The town was set fire to in four different quarters. The outbreak was suppressed in the afternoon, and the town was not bombarded. Large numbers of Mussulman refugees are crowding into Aleppo from the surrounding villages which have been burnt by the Zeitounlis. Their presence is a source of great danger, as whenever the troops advance against the Zeitounlis, they are sure to follow in their wake, and wreak vengeance on their enemies.

"At Aintab there were 200 killed and more wounded; an explosion occurred in a house where some dynamite was kept, and part of the town was burnt.

"All the Americans and English in Aleppo are safe."

F. O. 424/184, p. 272, No. 516

No. 586

Mr. Herbert to the Marquess of Salisbury.

No. 731.   Constantinople, *November 21, 1895, 10.45 a.m.*
Telegraphic.   *(Received November 21.)*

THE Acting British Consul at Angora telegraphs as follows:-

"Great uneasiness prevails throughout this vilayet, and it is urgently necessary that a new Vali should be at once appointed.

"There was a serious disturbance last Sunday at Marsovan, where it is reported that the Armenians slaughtered large numbers of Turks.

"At Choroun, the Turks wounded two Armenians, whereupon the Armenians all took refuge in their church, and up to last night, in spite of the assurances of Mutessarif, they refused to move."

F. O. 424/184, p. 272, No. 517

No. 587

Mr. Herbert to the Marquess of Salisbury.

No. 734. Secret.   Constantinople, *November 21, 1895, 10.15 p.m.*
Telegraphic.   *(Received November 21.)*

ACCORDING to information received by the Russian Ambassador, a secret message from the Palace enjoining the authorities not to fire on Mussulmans accompanied the recent orders to the Valis to put a stop to the massacres.

F. O. 424/184, p. 273, No. 520

No. 588

Mr. Herbert to the Marquess of Salisbury.

No. 735.   CONSTANTINOPLE, *November 21, 1895, 10.35 p.m.*
Telegraphic.   *(Received November 21.)*

SIX Representatives have again received further message from the Sultan stating that His Majesty wishes the Council of Ministers which meets next Sunday to consider our request for Firmans for the extra "stationnaires." We have urged the necessity of Firmans being granted at once, replying in much the same terms as those contained in my telegram No. 725. Unless we use much stronger language, this sort of thing is likely to go on for some time. As there is no German vessel available in the Mediterranean, German Ambassador has not asked for a Firman, but he is energetically supporting our request, and he may apply for a Firman later. I have received a telegram from Admiral Seymour, requesting me, if it is impossible to keep both, to send away the "Cockatrice," and keep the "Imogene." As my colleagues are fussing about our having three ships, and as Minister for Foreign Affairs has also raised objections, I fear I shall have to send the "Cockatrice" to Salonica. On the other hand we shall have much fewer men here than the other Powers, if the "Cockatrice" leaves.

F. O. 424/184, p. 273, No. 521

No. 589

Sir E. Monson to the Marquess of Salisbury.

No. 93.   VIENNA, *November 21, 1895.*
Telegraphic.   *(Received November 21.)*

THE following has been received by me from Sir P. Currie:-

"I called upon the French Minister for Foreign Affairs, but his Excellency confined himself to generalities as to the necessity that the understanding between the Powers at Constantinople should be maintained.

"The refusal by Russia of his proposal that authority should be given to the Ambassadors to summon the fleets is, professedly, not considered final by Count Goluchowski, though he is evidently much disappointed.

"He considered that the one essential point was that the concert of the Ambassadors at Constantinople should be maintained, and that there was no occasion for excitement. Full powers to act in the sense indicated had been given to the Austrian Ambassador. Satisfactory assurances had been received by Count Goluchowski, through the Italian Ambassador, that Germany would thoroughly support Italy, England, and Austria in the second line.

"Count Goluchowski agreed that the necessity of using our efforts to obtain from the Sultan the nomination of some such responsible Minister as Saïd Pasha, and the delegation to him of some measure of authority, should be kept in view by us."

F. O. 424/184, pp. 273-274, No. 522

No. 590

Sir E. Monson to the Marquess of Salisbury.

No. 94.   VIENNA, *November 21, 1895.*
Telegraphic.   *(Received November 21.)*

THE reply of the French Government to Count Goluchowski's proposals was received by his Excellency to-day. They accept the first two points, but with regard to the third, viz., the passage of the Dardanelles by ships of war, they state that such a proposal demands mature consideration.

For the present, at any rate, his Excellency hopes that this third point may be permitted by circumstances to remain in abeyance.

F. O. 424/184, p. 274, No. 523

No. 591

The Marquess of Salisbury to Mr. Herbert.

No. 229.
Telegraphic.   FOREIGN OFFICE, *November 21, 1895, 3.30 p.m.*

I HAVE received your telegram No. 728 of yesterday respecting a suggestion made by Her Majesty's Consul at Aleppo, after consultation with the Ferik, for the appointment of a Commission to arrange for the surrender of the Zeitounlis on the terms laid down by the Sultan.

I authorize you to bring this suggestion forward in any manner which you may consider most judicious.

F. O. 424/184, p. 274, No. 524

No. 592

The Marquess of Salisbury to Sir E. Monson.

No. 116.
Sir,   FOREIGN OFFICE, *November 21, 1895.*

THE Austro-Hungarian Ambassador called here on the 15th instant and stated that his Government, in compliance with the recommendations made by the Representatives of the six Powers at Constantinople, had at once placed a second "stationnaire" at the disposal of Baron Calice, and had instructed him to apply to the Porte for the necessary Firman to enable the vessel to pass the Dardanelles without waiting for her arrival.

Count Goluchowski hoped that Her Majesty's Government would take the same course.

I have informed Count Deym that Her Majesty's Chargé d'Affaires at Constantinople has also been authorized to agree to the Russian proposal, and to communicate with the Admiral in command of the British squadron as to the dispatch of a suitable vessel.

I said I thought that the sooner application was made for the necessary Firmans for the passage of these vessels through the Dardanelles the better.

I am, &c.

(Signed) SALISBURY.

F. O. 424/184, p. 274, No. 525

No. 593

The Marquess of Salisbury to Sir E. Monson.

No. 117. Confidential.
Sir,   FOREIGN OFFICE, *November 21, 1895.*

AFTER making the communication recorded in my immediately preceding despatch, the Austro-Hungarian Ambassador went on to say that Count Goluchowski hoped that the dispatch of a second "stationnaire" to Constantinople by all the Great Powers would be sufficient to calm the agitation prevailing there, and would make an impression on the Porte. But he was of opinion that the Powers ought also to contemplate the possibility of this step not sufficing to prevent the danger of anarchy, and of other measures being necessary for the protection of foreign interests. Collective action for this purpose could scarcely be unanimous and efficacious unless concerted beforehand, and unless the means to carry it out were already available.

The Austro-Hungarian Government had consequently decided also to send four ships of war to the Levant. Russia had already a fleet at her disposal there, and it was supposed that, besides the English and French squadrons, the German and Italian flags would be represented in Turkish waters.

If events should occur threatening European life and property at Constantinople, and the Turkish Government should be unable to restore order, the Austro-Hungarian Government thought that the Ambassadors there should concert together for calling up an equal number of vessels from each squadron to protect European interests. In such case it would be desirable that no regard should be paid to any refusal on the part of the Porte to let the ships pass the Dardanelles, but that any resistance to their entry should be overcome by common action.

Count Goluchowski agreed with Baron Calice that it would not be prudent to bring the squadrons too near the Dardanelles, which would be considered as a threat, and would cause increased excitement. He was further of opinion that it would be advisable to avoid grouping the squadrons according to alliances between the countries, and that above all the unanimity of the Powers should be made clearly evident.

Count Deym was instructed to inquire whether Her Majesty's Government would be disposed to give instructions in this sense to Her Majesty's Representative at Constantinople.

I saw his Excellency on the 16th instant, and told him that Her Majesty's Government were ready to concur in the course proposed by Count Goluchowski, if the other Great Powers did so. I said that Sir P. Currie, who was returning at once to Constantinople, would receive authority to join in any measures which the six Representatives might consider necessary for the protection of the interests confided to their charge, and to communicate with the Admiral in command of the British squadron as to the dispatch of the ships required for the purpose.

I am, &c.

(Signed) SALISBURY.

F. O. 424/184, p. 275, No. 526

No. 594

Mr. Herbert to the Marquess of Salisbury.

No. 828.   CONSTANTINOPLE, *November 21, 1895.*
My Lord,   *(Received November 25.)*

ON the 12th instant I received a telegram from Her Majesty's Vice-Consul at Mush, informing me that the three police officers, Reshid, Iskender, and Hajji Fehim, mentioned in Sir P. Currie's despatch No. 660 of the 9th October, had been reinstated, and sent to Bitlis. As your Lordship is aware, Her Majesty's Embassy had insisted on the dismissal of these men on account of the gross cruelty and rapacity shown by them in collecting taxes, and Mr. Hampson reported that their reappointment was fatal to British influence, and had produced the worst impression in Mush, as being the first fruits of the reforms.

I, therefore, sent a message to the Sultan through His Majesty's First Secretary, giving a brief account of the crimes of the officers, and insisting on their immediate redismissal.

On the 15th instant the Sultan's Chief Secretary sent word to me to say that the three officers in question should not be reappointed, but recalled in this direction.

I have, &c.

(Signed) MICHAEL H. HERBERT.

F. O. 424/184, p. 299, No. 555

No. 595

Mr. Herbert to the Marquess of Salisbury.

No. 828A.   CONSTANTINOPLE, *November 21, 1895.*
My Lord,   *(Received November 25.)*

OWING to the strong language recently used to the Sultan by the German Ambassador, who hinted at the possibility of his dethronement, and informed him that this was possibly the last warning he would receive, His Imperial Majesty expressed a wish to have the advice of the Representatives of the six Powers as to what steps he should take to restore confidence.

A meeting of Ambassadors was accordingly called on the afternoon of the 18th instant, at which it was decided to send the following message through the Doyen, Baron Calice:-

"The only means of restoring confidence is to put a stop to the massacres, which we are convinced the Sultan can do if he is sincere in his professions. It is not for us to indicate the measures to be taken, but we venture to make the following suggestions:-

"That the functionaires responsible for the massacres should be dismissed.

"That an inquiry should be held as to the participation of soldiers in the outrages, and the guilty be punished.

"That the orders recently sent to the Valis and Military Commanders should be published, and assurances given that previous orders have been cancelled.

"That a Hatt should be issued by the Sultan ordering his subjects to obey his wishes, and abstain from creating disturbances."

Baron Calice was also charged to say that, in view of the general alarm, each Embassy was sending for a second "stationnaire," and that Firmans for their passage would be requested the next day.

It was further suggested that Military Commanders should be assigned to the different districts of Constantinople, and be held responsible for the safety of the Christian population.

I have the honour to inclose a copy of the letter from Baron Calice reporting the reply made by Tewfik Pasha to this message.

I have, &c.

(Signed) MICHAEL H. HERBERT.

F. O. 424/184, pp. 299-300, No. 556

Inclosure in No. 595

Baron Calice to Mr. Herbert.

Mon cher Collègue,   CONSTANTINOPLE, *le 18 Novembre, 1895.*

J'AI fait part à Tewfik Pasha de nos suggestions en lui laissant prendre quelques notes. Il n'a soulevé d'objections contre aucun point, ayant plutôt l'air de trouver le tout parfaitement fondé et en règle. Il ne prévoyait non plus de difficultés quant à l'admission des stationnaires mais ce qui l'intéressait le plus c'était de savoir si la présence d'un second stationnaire pour chaque Ambassade empêcherait l'arrivée des flottes. J'ai cru devoir le rassurer sur ce point en lui disant que certes le redoublement des stationnaires calmerait beaucoup les appréhensions et qu'à moins de nouveaux dangers pour la sécurité des étrangers et des Chrétiens, la venue de nouvelles forces navales ne me paraissait aucunement probable.

Tewfik Pasha a beaucoup insisté sur l'efficacité—certaine d'après lui—des mesures que la Porte venait de prendre pour l'apaisement des Provinces d'Anatolie, tout en regrettant que tout cela n'ait pas été fait plus tôt. Comme une preuve de l'énergie et de l'impartialité du Gouvernment Impérial, il m'a communiqué un télégramme de Shakir Pacha, daté de Erzeroum, 18 Novembre, et portant que "Husséin Pacha, de Haideranli (un chef Kurde redoutable), a été arrêté d'après les lois militaires en vigueur, et qu'il sera jugé bientôt," qu'en outre, "il a ordonné que toutes choses pillées soient rendues."

Tewfik Pacha m'a prié de porter "ce fait important" à la connaissance de messieurs mes collègues.

Je vous prie, mon cher collègue, de communiquer ces lignes à l'Ambassadeur de France, avec prière de les faire passer aux autres collègues.

Votre tout dévoué,

(Signé) CALICE.

F. O. 424/184, p. 300, No. 556/1

No. 596

Mr. Herbert to the Marquess of Salisbury.

No. 829.
My Lord,

PERA, *November 21, 1895.*
(Received November 25.)

TEWFIK PASHA called on me this afternoon and informed me that the Sultan desired to express his thanks for the advice tendered him by Baron Calice on behalf of the Representatives of the Powers at Constantinople.

His Excellency went on to say that the instruction to the Valis which we had asked for had already been communicated to the several Embassies, and a list of the functionaries at places where disturbances had broken out was being prepared. As regards the publication of a Hatt, His Majesty was of the opinion that it was unnecessary, as the instructions to the Valis which had been communicated to us had all been published in the newspapers, and Her Majesty's subjects would be able to judge from them how much in earnest he was in his desire to put an end to the disturbances in the provinces. There had been now no fresh news from the disturbed districts for three days, and this proved how effective were the measures which His Majesty had taken to that end.

I expressed the hope to Tewfik Pasha that the Sultan would not oppose the grant of Firmans for the passage up the Dardanelles of the additonal "stationnaires," but his Excellency evaded the question by stating that His Majesty had not yet received the Takrirs made by the different Embassies for the Firman.

I have the honour to inclose herewith copies of the instructions sent by the Porte to the Valis and Military Commissioners above referred to, and also of the comments made on them in the Turkish paper "Sabah."

I have, &c.

(Signed) MICHAEL H. HERBERT.

F. O. 424/184, pp. 300-301, No. 557

Inclousre 1 in No. 596

*Telegram addressed to the Governors-General of the Vilayets of Trebizond, Erzeroum, Bitlis,
Van, Diarbekir, Mamouret-ul-Aziz, Sivas, Adana, and Aleppo, dated November 3, 1895
(o.s.).*

LES Commandants de Brigades, en expédiant des corps volants pour la répression des désordres surgis dans leur circonscription, lanceront une Proclamation aux populations pour engager ceux qui tentent de troubler à main armée la sécurité publique à renoncer à leur attitude et à s'abstenir de tous faits qui seraient contraires aux hautes volontés de Sa Majesté Impériale le Sultan.

Ils auront à sévir immédiatement par les armes contre ceux qui ne se conformeraient pas à cette injonction et d'empresseront d'empêcher en faisant stationner des troupes sur divers points, tout mouvement des émeutiers pour attaquer à main armée les bourgs et villages.

Si des meurtres et actes d'insurrection venaient à être commis inopinément dans la sphère d'évolution d'un corps volant les dits Commandants auront à en poursuivre immédiatement les auteurs sans leur faire aucune sommation.

Le Commandant-en-chef du 4ᵉ Corps de l'Armée Impériale aura à prêter au moyen des troupes du dit corps, l'assistance nécessaire aux Commandants de brigade susmentionnés qui se trouveront sous ses ordres en vue d'assurer le succès de leur tâche.

Le Séraskérat a été invité à transmettre des ordres télégraphiques dans ce sens tant au Muchir du dit corps d'armée qu'aux Commandants précités.

La ligne de conduite à suivre par les autorités civiles à l'égard des agitateurs ayant été précédemment indiquée par le télégraphe, conformément à un Iradé Impérial, vous aurez à faire à qui de droit des recommandations dans le sens du dit télégramme Circulaire avant l'envoi de troupes pour la répression des actes attentatoires à la sécurité publique.

Ces dispositions ayant été revêtues de la sanction Impériale et des instructions en conséquence transmises au Séraskérat et aux autres Valis, je vous engage encore une fois à vous y conformer strictement en ce qui concerne votre vilayet.

Notre auguste Maître désirant vivement qui l'ordre soit rétabli au plus tôt dans les localités où il a été troublé, que la vie, l'honneur, et les biens de tous soient sauvegardés et que tous faits et actes contraires à la justice et à l'équité soient empêchés, vous aurez à veiller jour et nuit à assurer la réalisation de la volonté souveraine en mettant sans retard fin aux désordres.

F. O. 424/184, p. 302, No. 557/1

Inclosure 2f in No. 596

Telegram addressed to the Major-General of the 4th Army Corps and to the Military Commanders of Aleppo, Bitlis, Adana, Trebizond, Diarbekir, Sivas, Mamouret-ul-Aziz, and in other parts of Asiatic Turkey, dated November 5, 1895 (o.s.).

LA volonté formelle de notre auguste Maître étant que l'on veille plus que jamais et d'une façon tout à fair spéciale au maintien de la tranquillité du pays de façon à prévenir absolument tous actes tels qu'incendies, menées séditieuses, effusion de sang ou attaques de la part d'une classe de la population contre l'autre ou contre les Consultats et sujets étrangers, des instructions en conséquence ont été déjà transmises aux fonctionnaires de l'Administration Civile. Conformément à un Ordre Impérial, les autorités militaires doivent se concerter avec les Valis et les Mutessarifs pour tâcher d'assurer la tranquillité publique et veiller strictement à ce que les officiers et soldats et l'armée Impérial agissent dans les limites des règements militaires en s'abstenant soigneusement de se porter à des actes pouvant provoquer des plaintes, tout manquement à ces prescriptions, toute négligence et tous procédés contraires à la discipline devant entraîner une grave responsabilité.

Telegram addressed to the Vilayets of Van, Bitlis, Erzeroum, Aleppo, Diarbekir, Trebizond, Sivas, and Mamouret-ul-Aziz, dated November 5, 1895 (v.s.).

Bien que les Iradés Impériaux itératifs qui vous ont été déjà communiqués prescrivent l'adoption dans votre vilayet de mesures propres à prévenir tout acte pouvant troubler l'ordre public ainsi que toute effusion de sang, et d'empêcher qu'une classe de la population attaque l'autre ou que des actes contraires à la justice soient commis, de pareils cas continuent cependant à se produire. L'une des attributions les plus importantes des Valis étant de maintenir et d'assurer la tranquillité dans les provinces, je viens, conformément aux ordres formels de notre auguste Maître, vous prévenir que si après que le présent télégramme vous sera parvenu on laissait se produire des méfaits tels qu'incendie, menées séditieuses, perturbation de l'ordre public ou effusion de sang, un pareil manquement aux devoirs ne pourrait en aucune façon être pardonné et entraînerait une grave et absolue responsabilité. Cette responsabilité devant aussi s'étendre aux Mutessarifs et aux Caïmacams vous devez vous concerter aussi avec ces Commandants pour l'adoption de dispositions en conséquence. Vous aurez surtout à veiller avec la plus grande vigilance à la protection des Consulats et des sujets étrangers de façon à les mettre à l'abri de tout danger et à écarter tout motif de plainte de leur part. Tous les coupables devront être arrêtés et punis confirmément à la loi.

Vous télégraphierez en clair toutes les vingt-quatre heures, au Ministère de l'Intérieur, au Séraskérat, au Grand Vizirat, et au Palais Impérial la situation du vilayet.

F. O. 424/184, pp. 301-302, No. 557/2.

Inclosure 3 in No. 596

Extract from the "Sabah" of November 8 (20), 1895.

Translation.

THE following is a continuation of our previous articles respecting the action of the Imperial Government in putting an end to the troubles in certain Anatolian vilayets and restoring public order.

It is well known that the scene of these disorders was chiefly the district of the 4th and 5th Corps d'Armée. Now as the corps d'armée in question consist of four brigades and that, besides these, eight brigades of Redifs have been called under arms, the troops in those parts are amply sufficient to prevent any disorders. Moreover, the Imperial Government is determined to use its troops for this purpose, so as to speedily re-establish order, His Imperial Majesty's chief desire being that all his subjects should enjoy security for their lives, honour, and property. The necessary measures to this end have consequently been determined upon, and the requisite orders and instructions have been sent to the vilayets in question. These may be summarized as follows:-

The fundamental duty of the military forces being to put a stop at once to all crimes and attacks on the part of all who, impelled by private animosity or a desire for vengeance, seek to destroy the peace and institute massacres, either amongst themselves or by making an armed attack on the adminsitrative or military authorities,

[Here follow the instructions communicated by the Sublime Porte.]

It is hoped that these instructions, whose wisdom is undeniable, will be properly appreciated by those who have given rise to these disorders, and that they will return to peaceful pursuits, and thereby render themselves worthy of the Imperial clemency.

F. O. 424/184, p. 302, No. 557/3

No. 597

Mr. Herbert to the Marquess of Salisbury.

No. 830. Very Confidential.   CONSTANTINOPLE, *November 21, 1895.*
My Lord,   *(Received November 25.)*

I HAVE the honour to transmit to your Lordship herewith a Confidential Memorandum addressed to me by Colonel Chermside respecting the number of troops which Turkey could send to reinforce the Dardanelles in from one to six weeks.

I have, &c.

(Signed) MICHAEL H. HERBERT.

F. O. 424/184, p. 302, No. 558

Inclosure in No. 597

Memorandum

The Estimated Capacity of Turkish Military Organization to reinforce the Garrisons of the Dardanelles and Gallipoli Peninsula.

Strictly Confidential.

THESE garrisons normally consist of three regiments of fortress artillery of four, four, and two battalions respectively, and a battalion or half-battalion of infantry at Gallipoli.

The four battalion regiments are stationed respectively in the forts and batteries of the European and Asiatic shore defences, and the two battalion regiment in the lines of Boulair.

The regiments have been recently reinforced by 500 to 600 artillery men in all.

The following estimates are based on rather complicated data, and in my opinion represent the fair average probability of Turkish power of reinforcement by the different routes.

It is assumed that the garrison of Yildiz Kiosk and its precincts and environs will remain untouched. The Ordous considered as available to contribute reinforcements are Nos. 1, 2, 3, and 4.

If unrestricted sea communication outside the Dardanelles remains available for Turkey, she could in one week concentrate in the Straits:-

	Battalions	Number of Men	Squadrons	Field Guns
One week	38	20,000	20	180

If sea communication outside the Dardanelles was not available, Turkey could concentrate on the shores of the Straits and in the Gallipoli Peninsula:-

Weeks	Battalions	Number of Infantry	Squadrons	Field Guns	Total in round Numbers
1	18	9,000 to 10,000	20	84	15,000
2	62	37,200	30	180	45,000
3	145	87,000	35	240	97,000
6	228	160,000 to 200,000	40	360	175,000 to 215,000

As regards the last line, this concentration would consist of 48 battalions Nizam, 180 battalions Redif, 8 cavalry regiments Nizam, and 60 field, mountain, and horse batteries. It is assumed that no Redif battalion is mobilized under seven days, a space of time in which on various occasions from 1885 to 1895 inclusive Redif battalions have actually been mobilized.

If Turkish forces in the 2nd, 3rd, and 4th Ordous were retained owing to contemplated action of Bulgaria, Servia, Montenegro, Greece, and Russia, the numbers of these concentrations would be very considerably affected.

It is therefore very evident that Turkey could mobilize in a short time very large field forces on both sides of the Straits, which would not be hampered in the same way for want of transport and supply services as concentration at a distance from the sea.

(Signed) HERBERT CHERMSIDE,
Colonel.

CONSTANTINOPLE, *November 15, 1895.*
F. O. 424/184, p. 303, No. 558/1

No. 598

Mr. Goschen to the Marquess of Salisbury.

No. 272.   ST. PETERSBURGH, *November 21, 1895.*
My Lord,   *(Received November 26.)*

I HAVE the honour to report that, in compliance with your Lordship's instructions, I have duly informed Prince Lobanoff that the report that fourteen of Her Majesty's ships had been dispatched to the Mediterranean to reinforce the

British Squadron there was entirely devoid of truth, and that only two second-class cruisers had been sent to replace ships that had been moved elsewhere.

I may mention that, on the occasion when Prince Lobanoff alluded to the report in question, I told his Excellency that, although I was unacquainted with the movements of Her Majesty's ships, I was quite sure that the rumour was incorrect, and that if any vessels were being sent to the Mediterranean, it was probably only in consequence of some contemplated rearrangement of the squadron.

In thanking me yesterday for the information I had given him, Prince Lobanoff alluded generally to the size of our squadron in the Mediterranean, and said that Russia has only three or four "miserable little ships" on that station; he added, however, that the little squadron which left Cronstadt on the 10th instant, viz., the "Rurik" and the "Dmitri Donskoi", had orders, after touching at Portsmouth and Brest, to go to Algiers, and there to await instructions as to whether they were to remain in the Mediterranean or proceed elsewhere.

With reference to the orders given for the "Peter Veliki" and two other ships to go to Reval with all possible dispatch, to which I alluded in my telegram to your Lordship of the 17th instant, I am informed that at a conference of the Marine General Staff, held on the 12th instant, Admiral Kremer stated that this step had been decided upon as a measure of precaution, but that he did not consider it probably that the services of the ships in question would be required in the Mediterranean before the spring.

I have, &c.

(Signed) W. E. GOSCHEN.

F. O. 424/184, p. 308, No. 571

No. 599

Mr. Egerton to the Marquess of Salisbury.

No. 137.   ATHENS, *November 21, 1895.*

My Lord,   *(Received November 27.)*

I LEARN that the Austrian Minister, while explaining to the Greek Minister for Foreign Affairs that it was not (as falsely described by the newspapers) a naval demonstration which his Government had proposed to the Powers signatory of the Treaty of Berlin, discouraged this Government from making any attempt to join in the action proposed.

The Italian Minister, more directly instructed, spoke to M. Skouzès in the same sense, and M. Onou, the Russian Minister, while conveying Prince Lobanoff's explanation that the dispatch of the European war-vessels to Turkish waters was not a hostile measure, but one for an iminently peaceful purpose, gave his own personal view that it would be a great mistake on the part of the Hellenic

Government to dispatch any war-ships. The flags of the men-of-war of the Great Powers were familiar in the ports of Turkey, but that of Greece might arouse fanatical excitement, and create the very evil which it is desired to prevent.

I have not seen the French and the German Representatives, but I have no reason to think that the Greek Government would not receive similar advice from them.

When I last saw M. Skouzés I was not aware that any of my colleagues had spoken to him on the subject, and as our conversation was on other matters I did not introduce it, the less so as I did not see signs that M. Delyanni was about to take any immediate naval action.

To-day, however, when I had the honour to see the King, I let His Majesty know that my Government agreed with the opinion expressed by the Austrian Government that the naval measures for the protection of European interests in Turkey should be taken by those Powers only who signed the Treaty of Berlin.

His Majesty made no remark as to the limiation, but seemed very fearful of the insufficienty of the step to be taken by the Powers. To send ships as proposed was, in his opinion, a half measure which would not stop the massacres inland.

I answered that here in Athens we were in the dark as to much that was going on, but fortunately he could rely on the Powers acting in unison and suiting their action to the necessities of the case.

His Majesty, after speaking on the subject of the Greek populations in Turkey, whose interests should, no less than those of the Armenians, be considered, reverted to the correct and prudent attitude of his Prime Minister, who had done all in his power here to allay excitement on foreign questions, and to whom, for this conduct, he had expressed his approval on his return.

I agreed with His Majesty that M. Delyanni had apparently been acting with sense and prudence, though no doubt much tried by the violence of a press which advocated so much foolish adventure.

In fine, the Hellenic Government has been made aware that their war-ships are not invited to join those of the Great Powers, and I trust that it may not be necessary to say more to them on the subject of the movement of those vessels; but, if it should appear so, I will act with my colleagues in dissuasion from imprudent action.

I have, &c.

(Signed) EDWIN H. EGERTON.

F. O. 424/184, pp. 313-314, No. 584

No. 600

Mr. Herbert to the Marquess of Salisbury.

No. 831.   CONSTANTINOPLE, *November 21, 1895.*
My Lord,   *(Received December 2.)*

WITH reference to my telegram No. 725 of the 20th instant, I have the honour to inclose a list of vessels designated by the Powers to act as second "stationnaires" at Constantinople, together with a description of their tonnage, length, armament, and crews.

As your Lordship will observe, both the "Donetz" and the "Faucon" have a greater displacement, carry more men, and are more heavily armed than the "Dryad." In fact, the dispatch of the "Faucon" is not consistent with the agreement come to by the Representatives of the six Powers at their meeting on the 12th instant, when it was distinctly stipulated that cruisers should not be sent.

M. Cambon, whom I spoke to on the subject, informed me confidentially that the French Government had offered him the choice of the "Faucon" and the "Flèche," a torpedo-catcher of about 400 tons; that he had at first meant to apply for a Firman for the "Flèche," but, as the news on the morning of the day the application was sent in was disquieting, he had determined to have the larger vessel, and had accordingly substituted the name of the "Faucon" for that of the "Flèche" in the Takrir.

If the "Cockatrice" leaves when the "Dryad" arrives, we shall have considerably fewer men here than the other Powers, as the "Imogene" also carried a smaller crew than the other "stationnaire" at present in the harbour.

I have, &c.

(Signed) MICHAEL H. HERBERT.

F. O. 424/184, p. 322, No. 606

Inclosure in No. 600

LIST of Vessels designated by England, France, Russia, Austria, and Italy to act as second "stationnaires" in the Bosphorus.

Name of Vessel	No. of Men	Tonnage	Length	Armament	Speed
			Feet		Knots
Dryad	120	1070	250	2 4.7-in. guns, 4 6-prs. Q.F., 3 torpedo tubes	19
Faucon (French)	148	1220	223	5 10-centim. guns, 4 47-millim. Q.F., 6 37-millim. Hotchkiss revolvers, 1 65-millim. for landing	17
Donetz (Russian)	161	1224	210	2 8-in. guns, 1 6-in., 1 Q.F., 6 47-millim.	13
Sebenice (Austrian)	146	856	186	5 light guns, 7 mitrailleuses, 1 torpedo tube	
Archimede (Italy)	114	771	229	4 light guns, 5 torpedo tubes	

F. O. 424/184, p. 323, No. 606/1

No. 601

Mr. Herbert to the Marquess of Salisbury.

No. 832. Very Confidential.   CONSTANTINOPLE, *November 21, 1895.*
My Lord,   *(Received December 2.)*

WITH reference to my telegram No. 722 of the 19th instant, I have the honour to report the following details in regard to the language held to the Sultan by Baron Saurma, the German Ambassador.

It appears that his Excellency was invited to an audience, but he declined, thinking that the fact of his being received alone might produce the impression that Germany was not in complete agreement with the other Great Powers. He, however, sent through Kiazim Bey a message to the Sultan from the German Emperor, couched in the following terms:-

"The state of anarchy which prevails throughout the Empire has caused the Powers to lose all confidence, and induced them to unite a powerful fleet in Turkish waters to be ready for any eventuality. The German Emperor, from a friendly and personal feeling for His Majesty, had abstained from joining in this movement. But the Sultan should not be under any delusion on that account. Germany was in complete accord with Europe in regard to the Oriental question, and the Emperor desired to warn His Majesty that there was great danger of his deposition if he did not adopt a line of policy which would restore the confidence of Europe. His Majesty might take this as a last warning, and the Emperor trusted that he would take heed to it."

After delivering this message, which was couched in perhaps the strongest language ever held to the Sultan, Kiazim Bey was put under surveillance, and the Sultan's First Secretary, with the Minister for Foreign Affairs, were sent to the German Embassy to inquire whether the language he had used was accurate.

They were informed, in reply, by Baron Saurma, that the message had been correctly and faithfully delivered by Kiazim Bey, who seems to have behaved with dignity and courage.

His Majesty was in consequence very much perturbed, and appealed to Baron Saurma for his advice. His Excellency replied that His Majesty had better consult all the Ambassadors, and not one alone, and this, as I have had the honour to report in my despatch No. 827 of the 20th instant, His Majesty decided to do

I have, &c.

(Signed) MICHAEL H. HERBERT.

F. O. 424/184, p. 323, No. 607

No. 602

Mr. Herbert to the Marquess of Salisbury.

No. 836.   CONSTANTINOPLE, *November 21, 1895.*
My Lord,   *(Received December 2.)*

WITH reference to my telegrams Nos. 681, 684, 686, and 695, I have the honour to inclose copies of Memoranda by Mr. Block, reporting the various messages sent to me on the 15th and 16th instant by the Sultan in regard to the efforts made by His Majesty to execute the reforms and to repress the disorders in Anatolia.

I have, &c.

(Signed) MICHAEL H. HERBERT.

F. O. 424/184, p. 325, No. 611

Inclosure 1 in No. 602

Memorandum by Mr. Block.

THE Sultan's First Secretary sent again for me last night, and said the Sultan desired to know if his last message to the Marquess of Salisbury had been telegraphed, and if there was any reply. The Sultan had again yesterday given fresh instructions to the Ministers to take every means for restoring order, to have any one who is to blame punished without distinction of race or creed. His Majesty had also instructed the Ministry to ascertain what were the complaints of the people, and to suggest to him means of satisfying them, as well as to have officials who had not done their duty removed, and to appoint good men in their stead. The sum of £T. 110,000 had been sent off that afternoon for the troops, and there were no news of fresh disturbances in the provinces. His Majesty hoped that his measures would be successful.

The First Secretary said he thought it looked as if there was a cessation of outbreaks except in the Adana district, where the Armenians had pillaged some Moslem villages, although there was no fresh news from there at the Palace.

The First Secretary then gave me the following extraordinary message from the Sultan: that His Majesty had never hesitated to accept our advise; that it had been alleged that it was he who opposed the reforms, whereas he had accepted the scheme of the 11th May, with the exception of a few clauses which he had proposed to discuss immediately that scheme was presented; that it had been alleged that the ex-Grand Vizier, Saïd Pasha, had repeatedly made proposals with respect to the reforms which His Majesty had refused to adopt; that this was untrue, that Saïd Pasha had made no single proposal, that there was no paper of his to prove such an allegation; but that, on the contrary, the Porte had on various occasions declined to carry out His Majesty's orders, and His Majesty instanced a case where he had told the Ministry to write a note to the Embassies, which the Porte refused to do, although clear proof of His Majesty's instructions remained on record.

Further, His Majesty added that he hoped any complaints and suggestions would be made to him by the Embassy, and he would at once endeavour to follow our advice. His Majesty concluded by reiterating that the inauguration of the reforms would be at once proceeded with, and that he had given instructions to the Ministers to that end.

(Signed) ADAM BLOCK.

CONSTANTINOPLE, *November 15, 1895.*
F. O. 424/184, p. 325, No. 611/1

Inclosure 2 in No. 602

Memorandum by Mr. Block.

IN accordance with your instructions, I told the First Secretary that the American Legation had just informed Her Majesty's Embassy that, according to telegraphic news just received, 4,000 Christians had been killed at Gurun (Vilayet of Sivas); that a number of villages had been burned in the neighbourhood of Mardin, that at Kharput from 500 to 800 persons had been killed, that eight out of twelve missionary buildings had been pillaged and burned, that the Kaïmakam of Hajin had threatened to burn the town; that at Sivas 800 Armenians had been killed and ten Turks. I warned His Majesty that if these disturbances and massacres continued there was every probability that the Powers would collectively intervene, and that the result might be the disappearance of the Ottoman Empire. I used the strongest language possible to convince His Majesty of the imminent danger of the present situation. His Majesty replied that there was no news of further disturbances in the provinces; that he hoped order was now restored, that the only news from Gurun was to the effect that the Kurds had twice attacked the town, but that the Kaïmakam had with the help of the troops driven them off; that from Kharput the Governor General had telegraphed only yesterday that the Kurds and tribes in the plain of Kharput had gone away, that order had been restored, that measures had been taken to prevent the Kurds renewing their attack, that a Commission had been formed to restore the Armenians to their homes and provide for their comfort; that the Vali of Sivas had telegraphed that day to say that 130 Armenians had been killed. The First Secretary at the same time showed me a telegram addressed to the Sultan by the villagers of the Moslem villages of Bechan, Kourtel, and Kurtler, consisting respectively of fifty-six, fifty-seven, and eight houses, stating that Armenians in large numbers had attacked their villages, had pillaged and burnt them, that some of the men (Moslems) had been burnt alive, that the Armenian had cut off the breasts of women and strangled the children, and they prayed the Sultan for help. The First Secretary showed me a telegram also from Marash, stating that at Choukour Hissar the Armenians had killed eighty men and wounded fifteen, and that troops were being sent to restore order.

During the night the Sultan sent for me, and this morning, by His Majesty's orders, the First Secretary informed me that the Ministers had been at the Palace till 5 this morning, and all the Valis had been called to the telegraph offices; that under His Majesty's personal supervision communication had been held with them, and they had received fresh instructions, warnings, threats, &c., to maintain or restore order. The First Secretary said that there was no fresh news since yesterday, and it seemed as if tranquillity had been re-established. The Commandant at Kharput had telegraphed that at that place 150 Christians had been killed, 10 wounded; 37 Moslems killed and 18 wounded, as well as two soldiers killed, that the Kurds had been driven off, and that confidence had been restored; that 119 Christian families had been protected in the "dépôt," that the American missionaries had been protected by soldiers, and that numbers of Christians had taken refuge and had been protected in the mosques and in Moslem houses; that the Kurds were now some two or three hours distant, and that 100 of them or more had been arrested. The First Secretary showed me a telegram from Jurun, to the effect that 1,000 Christians had been protected and had now returned to their homes; the Kaïmakam had been asked to state the number of killed, and his report was expected; in fact, all the Valis, Mutessarifs, and Governors had been instructed to send reports of numbers killed and wounded, either Moslem or Christian.

The First Secretary showed me also a telegram from Diarbekir, saying quiet existed at Mardin, Lijé, Sichan (?), Direk, Severek, Chirmek, Jeziré, and Midial; only at Silvan had the Kurds attacked the town, but had been driven off.

(Signed) ADAM BLOCK.

CONSTANTINOPLE, *November 16, 1895.*
F. O. 424/184, pp. 325-326, No. 611/2

Inclosure 3 in No. 602

Memorandum by Mr. Block.

Extract.

BUT it was necessary that the discontented Armenians should know that England will not help them further to realize their dreams and aspirations, and will not demand further privileges for them. His Majesty therefore begs that Lord Salisbury will instruct the Embassy and the Consuls to inform all Armenians, from the Patriarch downward, that it is no use their looking for further exceptional privileges. His Majesty begs that an end should be put to their illusions that by a Congress or intervention they will obtain autonomy or anything more than they have already got. This would have a good effect if the Armenians could be made to remain quiet; at present they go about boasting that the English fleet is to be increased by six ships, that the French fleet is coming to the Levant, and thus by all kinds of illusions and beliefs are a source of disquietude, thinking that whatever is being done by Europe is for their special benefit. If they could be made to understand that the first thing before reforms can be put into force is to restore order and tranquillity, and that if they do not remain quiet they will not be able to get the reforms, it would have a good effect. Whilst His Majesty is making every effort and sacrifice to re-establish order, the Armenians continue aspiring to and talking of further privileges; this renders His Majesty's task much more difficult, and if once they could be made to understand through their spiritual Chiefs or otherwise—Lord Salisbury knows best in what manner that they must be contented and remain quiet, Mussulman effervescence would die away, and the task of restoring order and commencing reforms much simpler.

(Signed) ADAM BLOCK.

CONSTANTINOPLE, *November 16, 1895.*
F. O. 424/184, pp. 326-327, No. 611/3

No. 603

Mr. Herbert to the Marquess of Salisbury.

No. 836A.   CONSTANTINOPLE, *November 21, 1895.*
My Lord,   *(Received December 2.)*

I HAVE the honour to transmit the text of a message which was sent me by the Sultan on the night of the 13th November, with a request that I would at once forward it to your Lordship.

I have, &c.

(Signed) MICHAEL H. HERBERT.

F. O. 424/184, p. 327, No. 612

Inclosure in No. 603

Message from His Majesty the Sultan.

I AM very grateful for Lord Salisbury's message with regard to the assistance he is ready to afford me, and I desire Mr. Herbert to convey my sincere thanks for the same, and for the expressions of friendship in that message. I have, however, seen a résumé of a speech of Lord Salisbury, in which this phrase occurs: "I have little confidence that the promised reforms will be executed." This statement has pained me very much indeed, as the carrying out of the reforms is a matter decided upon by me, and, further, I am desirous of executing them as soon as possible. I have already repeatedly told my Ministers so. This being so, the only reason why Lord Salisbury should thus throw doubts on my good intentions must be the intrigues of certain persons here, or else false statements have been made to cause such an opinion. The execution of reforms is absolutely decided upon, but it is first necessary that quiet should exist in the country. The most complete measures have been taken, and are being taken, to restore order and re-establish tranquillity. There is no doubt that the result of these measures will soon be apparent, if they have not already become so.

For instance, at Trebizond, Erzeroum, Bitlis, and Diarbekir, there have been no fresh disorders for some days past. But I repeat I will execute the reforms. I will take the paper containing them, place it before me, and see myself that every article is put in force. This is my earnest determination, and I give my word of honour. I wish Lord Salisbury to know this, and I beg and desire that his Lordship, having full confidence in these declarations, will make another speech by virtue of the friendly feeling and dispositions he has for me and my country. I shall await the result of this message with the greatest anxiety. I further ask that the Embassy will itself advise the Armenians, and instruct its Consuls to advise them in the strongest manner possible, to remain satisfied with the reforms, as Lord Salisbury says in his speech that they should be, and to keep quiet. And they ought to be made to understand that the reforms cannot be carried out if they create disturbances.

F. O. 424/184, p. 327, No. 612/1

No. 604

Mr. Herbert to the Marquess of Salisbury.

No. 837.   Constantinople, *November 21, 1895.*
My Lord,   *(Received December 2.)*
      WITH reference to my telegram No. 723 of the 19th instant, I have the honour to inclose copy of a Memorandum by Mr. Block, reporting the message which the Sultan sent to me in reply to the communication which, in accordance with your Lordship's instructions, I made to His Majesty on that day, expressing the hope of Her Majesty's Government that the Zeitounlis would be treated with clemency.
                                                              I have, &c.
                                           (Signed) Michael H. Herbert.
      F. O. 424/184, pp. 327-328, No. 613

Inclosure in No. 604

Memorandum by Mr. Block.

      IN accordance with your instructions, I showed Lord Salisbury's message concerning the Zeitounlis to the Grand Vizier, and afterwards delivered the same to the First Secretary for transmission to the Sultan.
      The Sultan replied that his illustrious ancestors and predecessors had never failed to show clemency to those who submitted and asked for pardon; he himself had always followed the same course, as could be proved by numbers of instances. At the same time, every one must know how the Zeitounlis had acted and were acting at the present moment. If pardon is extended to them, it must be done in

such a way as not to sully the honour of the Ottoman Government. His Majesty could not under the circumstances make the first advances. The Zeitounlis should apply to the Government or the Commandant. In any case, the Sultan had already given orders to the military and civil authorities in the provinces to use their efforts to restore order by conciliatory means; to treat the submissive with clemency, and not to harm those who did not resist the troops. His Majesty would now instruct the Commandant of Marash, who was ready to march with artillery, to wait two days; if the Zeitounlis submit when the troops advance, will give up their arms without further hostilities, will give up also those guilty of outrages to be tried by the Tribunals and punished, the affair will end; if not, the Zeitounlis must take the consequences.

The Sultan in return desires something from Lord Salisbury. His Majesty has had no answer yet to his last messages, nor has Lord Salisbury done what His Majesty asked him to do. His Majesty has stated again and again that he will carry out the reforms without delay; if any difficulty arises he will consult the Powers as to the manner of overcoming it; by this His Majesty does not mean that difficulties may prevent the reforms being carried out, nor does he wish to shelter himself behind any such excuse; if any one has such an idea, His Majesty strongly protests against it from this moment.

Lord Salisbury has publicly stated that he had no confidence that His Majesty would carry out the reforms. The Sultan now desires Lord Salisbury to say, in view of the declarations and promises so often reiterated by the Sultan, that his Lordship has confidence in the Sultan's good faith with regard to the reforms.

Further, His Majesty stated that "there was a rumour that the 'stationnaires' were to be increased." This would cause people to talk, and might excite the mind of the public, and thus prevent the attainment of that tranquillity which the Sultan was endeavouring to establish with a view to the prompt execution of the reforms. He trusted Lord Salisbury would not increase the "stationnaires."

Lastly, the Sultan again desired Lord Salisbury to give strong advice to the Patriarch to exhort the Armenians to remain quiet and satisfied with the reforms.

(Signed) ADAM BLOCK.

CONSTANTINOPLE, *November 20, 1895.*
F. O. 424/184, p. 328, No. 613/1

No. 605

Mr. Gosselin to the Marquess of Salisbury.

No. 48.   BERLIN, *November 22, 1895, 4 p.m.*
Telegraphic.   *(Received November 22.)*
    THE Imperial Secretary of State for Foreign Affairs states that yesterday a
Council was held at the Palace on the question of granting Firmans, but that no
decision was arrived at, as the Sultan opposed the matter.
    Baron von Marschall added that, as the request was in accordance with the
Treaties, His Majesty would have to give way.
    F. O. 424/184, p. 276, No. 529

No. 606

The Marquess of Salisbury to Mr. Herbert.

No. 233.
Telegraphic.   FOREIGN OFFICE, *November 22, 1895.*
    WITH reference to your telegram No. 735 of yesterday, you will, of course,
retain both Her Majesty's ships "Cockatrice" and "Imogene" until Her Majesty's
ship "Dryad" has arrived at Constantinople.
    F. O. 424/184, p. 276, No. 530

No. 607

The Marquess of Salisbury to Mr. Herbert.

No. 234.
Telegraphic.   FOREIGN OFFICE, *November 22, 1895.*
    I APPROVE the language which, as reported in your telegram No. 738 of to-
day, you held in reply to the inquiry made by Ismaïl Kemal Bey, in the Sultan's
name, as to whether the request for a second "stationnaire" would be withdrawn if
His Imperial Majesty were to make proposals to the Embassies for assistance in
establishing a liberal form of government.
    Her Majesty's Government cannot believe that any excitement could really be
caused by the arrival of five small ships coming in singly at intervals.
    F. O. 424/184, p. 277, No. 531

No. 608

The Marquess of Salisbury to Mr. Gosselin.

No. 118.
Telegraphic.   FOREIGN OFFICE, *November 22, 1895.*

I REQUEST you to state to the German Minister for Foreign Affairs that Her Majesty's Government have heard with great satisfaction of the language held by the German Ambassador at Constantinople to the Sultan, by which an excellent effect appears to have been produced. You will express our best acknowledgments for the friendly support of the German Government.

I have been glad to learn from Count Hatzfeldt that the German Ambassador has also joined in endeavouring to obtain clemency for the Armenian insurgents of Zeitoun. If barbarities were committed there by the Turkish troops, a very serious effect would be produced on public opinion in this country and in Europe generally.

F. O. 424/184, p. 277, No. 532

No. 609

Mr. Herbert to the Marquess of Salisbury.

No. 839.   CONSTANTINOPLE, *November 22, 1895.*
My Lord,   *(Received December 2.)*

WITH reference to my telegram No. 729 of the 20th instant, I communicated the information contained in Mr. Barnham's telegram of the same date in regard to the disturbances at Marash to the Turkish Government who have received the following telegram from the Vali of Aleppo giving this version of the outbreak:-

"Although the spiritual chiefs and Notables of the Christian population were over and over again counselled and exhorted to keep quiet, and although the strongest assurances were given them, the Christians declined to open their shops to Moslems, and by their action showed that they would not cease from bringing about a disturbance. During the night a Moslem, and in the morning several soldiers and gendarmes were murdered, and firing took place from the houses. Brigadier-General Ziner Pasha and Major Ali Effendi had the streets patrolled with soldiers and gendarmes, and to a certain extent restored quiet. Fire was set to the town in three or four places, but was extinguished and guards were placed within and without the bazaar in various quarters. Firing still continued from time to time, but the disturbance was eventually quelled and measures were taken to prevent any recurrence of it. The number of dead and wounded will be ascertained and reported later."

The Turkish Government have denied the rumour which reached the United States' Legation here that Marash had been bombarded.

I have, &c.

(Signed) MICHAEL H. HERBERT.

F. O. 424/184, p. 329, No. 615

No. 610

Mr. Herbert to the Marquess of Salisbury.

No. 840.   CONSTANTINOPLE, *November 22, 1895.*
My Lord,   *(Received December 2.)*

I HAVE the honour to inclose a translation of a telegram from Shakir Pasha, published in the "Sabah", stating that Hussein Pasha, of Patnotz, is to be tried by court martial. The misdeeds of this individual are notorious, and are referred to in Mr. Graves' despatch No. 41 of the 8th June, 1894, copy of which was sent to the Foreign Office in Sir P. Currie's despatch No. 307 of the 22nd of the same month.

Mr. Block has been informed by the First Secretary that the Sultan has censured the Commandant of Mush and the Vali of Sivas for not preventing the outbreaks at these places, and the Major commanding at Gurun has also been placed under arrest for his conduct during the disorders there.

I have, &c.

(Signed) MICHAEL H. HERBERT.

F. O. 424/184, p. 329, No. 616

Inclosure in No. 610

Extract from the "Sabah" of November 20, 1895.

Traduction.

COPIE d'un télégramme reçu de son Excellence Shakir Pacha, chargé de l'inspection des provinces Asiatiques se trouvant à Erzeroum:-

"Je suis arrivé à Erzeroum le 2 (14) Novembre, 1895. Les plaintes du Catholicos d'Aghtamar disant que certains villages dans les Vilayets de Van et de Bitlis ont été pillés, ne sont que les dégâts et les dommages causés précédemment par Hussein Pacha Haidaranli et dont j'avais déjà informé votre Excellence. Le pillage avait complètement cessé lorsque je me suis rendu à Khouns, et le Vali de Van m'informe que les effets et objets enlevés ayant été repris, on a procédé à les restituer à leurs propriétaires.

"Conformément à la teneur de l'Iradé Impérial, le dit Pacha sera jugé d'après la loi martiale et recevra la punition qu'il mérite.

'Comme dans ces parages, rien n'est arrivé de la part des régiments Hamidiés qui soit contraire à la volonté Impériale, à part les Haidaranlis, les plaintes du dit Catholicos, dans leur ensemble, ne sont donc pas conformes à la vérité.

Le 4 (16) Novembre, 1895.

F. O. 424/184, p. 330, No. 616/1

No. 611

Mr. Herbert to the Marquess of Salisbury.

No. 841.   CONSTANTINOPLE, *November 22, 1895.*

My Lord,   *(Received December 2.)*

WITH reference to my telegram No. 738 of to-day, I have the honour to inform your Lordship that I received a visit at 3 o'clock this morning from Ismaïl Kemal Bey, who had, he told me, been sent to me by the Sultan.

Ismaïl Kemal Bey, who is a follower of Midhat, and who has for some time past been pressing the Sultan to change his policy, began by stating that His Majesty was disgusted with Russia, in whom he had hitherto trusted, and now wished to turn to England and adopt a more liberal policy. His Majesty was accordingly seriously contemplating publishing a "Hatt" confirming all previous "Hatts" promulgated by former Sultans from that of Gulhané to the present day, and making proposals to the Powers for assistance in establishing a more liberal form of government. If, he went on to say, I would give him an assurance that our demand for a second "stationnaire" would be withdrawn, he was convinced that His Majesty, who was under the impression that the presence of extra "stationnaires" was intended as a personal menace, would at once act on his advice and take the above steps.

I replied to Ismaïl Kemal Bey that I had no doubt that His Majesty would be quite right in taking his advice, and I was sure a change in His Majesty's policy such as was contemplated would have an excellent effect in restoring confidence. The Powers were, however, absolutely determined to insist on their right to call up second "stationnaires" here immediately. There was no question of personally threatening the Sultan, and their dispatch here was only meant to tranquillize the foreign colonies, and restore confidence among them. If there was any delay in granting the Firmans, the question, which was now a small one, might be magnified, and the news that His Majesty was raising difficulties would excite public opinion both here and in Europe. It was therefore in His Majesty's interest to let the boats come up to Constantinople without any further delay.

Ismaïl Kemal Bey then asked me whether, if His Majesty made these proposals to the other Ambassadors, I would authorize him to state that I would support His Majesty's request that the "stationnaires" should not be insisted upon.

I stated that my colleagues were absolutely united in insisting upon the necessity for the dispatch of second "stationnaires" at once, and that I could not for a moment think of acting independently. I further pointed out that such proposals, if made at all, should be made to all the Embassies, and not to this one alone.

I have, &c.

(Signed) MICHAEL H. HERBERT.

F. O. 424/184, p. 330, No. 617

No. 612

Mr. Herbert to the Marquess of Salisbury.

No. 842.   CONSTANTINOPLE, *November 22, 1895.*
My Lord,   *(Received December 2.)*

ON the 15th instant a persistent rumour spread among the Armenians of Constantinople that officials from the Palace and police had been visiting the houses inhabited by Armenians in Pera, Stamboul, and the suburbs, and making a list, with a view to a general massacre.

It was further stated that a meeting of Armenian Notables had been held, and that it was in contemplation to send a deputation to the Russian Ambassador begging for his intervention.

There seemed to be no doubt that inquiries such as those described were being made, as the house of an Armenian employé of this Embassy was visited by persons whose exact official status was not known, but who behaved as if they had a right to question the inhabitants. The Russian Ambassador had also information that the priests of an Armenian church in Galata had been interrogated respecting their parishioners, which looked as if something more was going on than an ordinary collection of rates and taxes.

I accordingly sent a message to the Sultan, through His Majesty's First Secretary, in which, after mentioning the rumours current, I said that, whether they were true or not, the Armenians were undoubtedly in a state of panic which constituted a menace to public tranquillity, and imperatively demanded the adoption of reassuring measures. I further reminded His Majesty of the union of the Powers, and warned him that any fresh disturbances in Constantinople might bring about an European intervention and endanger the existence of the Ottoman Empire.

His Majesty replied he knew nothing of the report, but would make inquiries of the Minister of Police. He subsequently sent a second message to the Embassy saying that the Minister of Police had officially reported there was no truth in the rumours. It would appear that in a secret report the Minister ascribed the agitation to the conduct of an Armenian who had dressed up as a Mahommedan fruit-seller and gone about taking notes of Armenian houses.

The next day the Grand Vizier called on me, and I drew his attention to these disquieting rumours, and urged that some notice should be published in the papers to restore confidence among the Armenians. The Russian Ambassador spoke to His Highness in the same sense, and also made strong representations to the Minister of Police.

In the next few days several inspired articles of a generally reassuring character appeared in the Turkish press, but no particular reference was made to this story of the registration of Armenian houses, and the rumours of preparations for a massacre continued.

M. de Nélidoff took the matter much to heart, because the mysterious officials in the pursuit of their inquisitorial inquiries did not spare the sister of the wife of his Third Dragoman, and when that lady asked their reasons, replied, "You will know in a day or two." Accordingly, on the 20th November, the Dragomans of the Russian, French, and British Embassies made another representation to the Sultan's First Secretary, requesting the insertion of an official Notice in the papers of the capital to calm the apprehensions of the Armenians.

The Sultan sent back a reply through his Secretary, saying he would order the Prefect of the town to discover and punish the offenders, and also give orders for the publication of the required Notice in the paper next day.

I inclose a translation of this communication. It is characteristic that the word "Armenian" does not occur it in.

I have, &c.

(Signed) MICHAEL H. HERBERT.

F. O. 424/184, p. 331, No. 618

Inclosure in No. 612

Extract from the "Sabah" of November 21, 1895.

Communication Officielle.

Traduction.

AYANT appris que ces jours-ci une ou deux personnes se sont livrées à des actes d'agitation en enregistrant les maisons dans certaines localités et les personnes qui y demeurent, et comme ces actes n'ont d'autre but que celui de donner lieu à de vains propos, nous venons porter à la connaissance du public que l'autorité Impériale, à la suite des recherches qu'elle a faites, vient d'arrêter les individus en question, lesquels seront traduits en justice pour qu'il soit sévi contre eux conformément à la loi.

F. O. 424/184, p. 332, No. 618/1

No. 613

Sir E. Monson to the Marquess of Salisbury.

No. 343. Most Confidential.   VIENNA, *November 22, 1895.*
My Lord,   *(Received November 26.)*

COUNT GOLUCHOWSKI called on me yesterday afternoon, and expressed himself as much gratified at the nature of the conversation which he had had in the morning with Sir Philip Currie.

His Excellency proceeded to say that he had just received the answer of the French Government to his communication of the 12th instant, in which the Austro-Hungarian Government proposed the three points, since accepted by England, Italy, and Germany. The French Government agreed in regard to the first two, but stated that the third, empowering the Ambassadors at Constantinople to summon the foreign squadrons without further application to their respective Governments, was of such weighty importance that it required mature consideration. The refusal was, in fact, said Count Goluchowski, not so positive in langauge as that of Russia, but sufficiently plain in its meaning.

Count Goluchowski went on to observe that the situation at Constantinople appears so far improved as to inspire the hope that the crisis, for which the third point was intended to provide, need no longer be feared as imminent; and he spoke vaguely of the possibility that the Russian reserve in regard to that point might not prove to be insuperable.

His Excellency was very anxious to impress upon me that there is no reason to doubt the sincerity of the German Government in regard to their adhesion to the necessity of putting the utmost pressure upon the Sultan. The language of their Ambassador at Constantinople to His Imperial Majesty, and the assurances given by the Emperor William to M. de Szögyeni, at Berlin, and by Count Eulenburg here had been identic in their spirit, and thoroughly satisfactory to the Austro-Hungarian Government.

The general accord between the six Powers was, therefore, thoroughly established; and the minor divergence of opinion in regard to the entry of the foreign squadrons into the Dardanelles by no means disturbed it.

Upon this point I may as well report to your Lordship that I have, within the last two or three days, had several opportunities of conversing with my German colleague, and I have not scrupled to tell him that the pretext alleged by his Government of having no ships which can be spared to be sent to the

Mediterranean does not appear to me to be a valid one. After the recent naval display at Kiel, at which he (Count Eulenburg) had himself been present as a spectator, he was making far too little of the maritime resources of his country, if he considered that she had not the means of sending a few representative ships to join the squadrons of the other Powers in cruising in the Levant.

Count Eulenburg, however, persisted that Germany really cannot do this from lack of the requisite vessels; and that his Imperial Master is always complaining of the inadequacy of his fleet for all the purposes required of it.

Count Nigra, who called here yesterday to see Sir Philip Currie, had, he told me, been speaking in the same strain to Count Eulenburg; and entirely agreed with me as to the unfortunate effect which this excuse has produced. No one, said my Italian colleague, could accept it as a sufficient reason for the non-participation of Germany; and the latter Power had consequently no right to express surprise if doubts had been felt as to her sincere adoption of the standpoint of the other Powers.

In his conversation yesterday afternoon with me, Count Eulenburg stated that, in his belief, the stories in circulation as to the backwardness of Germany were the mischievous work of Russia.

I have, &c.

(Signed) EDMUND MONSON.

F. O. 424/184, pp. 308-309, No. 572

No. 614

Mr. Gosselin to the Marquess of Salisbury.

No. 273. BERLIN, *November 22, 1895.*
My Lord, *(Received November 26.)*

BARON VON MARSCHALL told me this morning that, according to the last news he had received from Constantinople, a Council had been held yesterday at the Palace at Constantinople to deliberate on the question of the issue of the Firmans for the passage through the Straits of the additional "stationnaires," but that no decision had been come to.

The Sultan was much opposed to the proposed step, but his Excellency considered that His Majesty must yield sooner or later, as the contemplated measure was strictly in accordance with the Treaties.

He asked me whether I had seen the reply sent by M. Nélidoff to the Armenian Catholicos, in reply to the appeal for protection forwarded by his Beatitude to the Russian Government.

On my replying in the affirmative, his Excellency remarked: "Il me semble que la réponse est un peu forte."

Baron von Marschall said that the proposal put forward by Count Goluchowski for combined action on the part of the fleets had practically fallen through, in consequence of the opposition of Russia, "who as usual is backed up by France;" but his Excellency thinks that the dispatch of such a large naval force to the Levant may still have a salutary effect in keeping the agitation in Constantinople itself within bounds.

I have, &c.

(Signed) MARTIN GOSSELIN.

F. O. 424/184, p. 309, No. 573

No. 615

Mr. Herbert to the Marquess of Salisbury.

No. 845.   CONSTANTINOPLE, *November 22, 1895.*
My Lord,   *(Received December 2.)*

WITH reference to Sir P. Currie's telegram No. 537 of the 27th October, I have the honour to forward to your Lordship herewith copy of a despatch which I have received from Her Majesty's Consul at Trebizond giving his views as to the origin of the disturbances at Gumush-Khaneh.

I have, &c.

(Signed) MICHAEL H. HERBERT.

F. O. 424/184, p. 333, No. 620

Inclosure in No. 615

Consul Longworth to Mr. Herbert.

Sir,   TREBIZOND, *November 15, 1895.*

ON the 26th ultimo I telegraphed to the Embassy the fact that on the day preceding a disturbance had occurred at Gumush-Khaneh.

It now seems, from independent and reliable sources of information, that the affair was an unprovoked attack on the Armenians in the town and villages around.

The Vali's version, however, does not confirm this altogether. He wishes me to believe that the killing and sacking arose out of a spirit of retaliation felt by the Mussulman populace on hearing that a Turk was fired at in the street by an Armenian, shortly after a rumour had received credence to the effect that an invalided gendarme had died of a drug sold by an Armenian chemist.

In the town itself, the number of persons killed is variously estimated from ten to thirty, the lower figure being the one given to me by the Governor-General. I am told that seven Turks lost their lives in assaulting the house of the rich Armenian, Hadji Nishan. The building was subsequently destroyed by fire and all its inmates either shot or burnt. The losses sustained by the villages are not known, but it is generally believed there were many deaths, and the looting was as complete as that in the town.

The Sandjak of Gumush-Kaneh has a population of about 118,500 souls, of which 2,500 are Armenians. Forming as they do a very small minority, it would be suicidal on their part, one would think, to raise a hand against the Moslems. The authorities, however, are inclined to take, on apparently insufficient evidence, the one-sided view that in all Armenian communes, large and small, there are a number of men who are ready to make martyrs of themselves and their people. Such blind patriotism, calculated to extinguish the whole race, does not seem incredible to them. Even the Vali, from the contents of some intercepted letters written mostly in invisible ink, is convinced that such is the case, though who these desperate characters are within this vilayet, he does not pretend to know positively. The letters, if really compromising, are very likely such as may prove, I think, the existence among the Armenians of not an active but a passive disaffection.

I have, &c.

(Signed) H. Z. LONGWORTH.

F. O. 424/184, p. 333, No. 620/1

No. 616

Mr. Gosselin to the Marquess of Salisbury.

No. 49.   BERLIN, *November 23, 1895, 12.30 p.m.*
Telegraphic.   *(Received November 23.)*

ACCORDING to a telegram received yesterday by Baron von Marschall from the Imperial Ambassador at Constantinople, Tewfik Pasha has stated that the Sultan has promised to sign the Firman for the additional "stationnaires."

F. O. 424/184, p. 277, No. 533

No. 617

Sir P. Currie to the Marquess of Salisbury.

No. 741.   CONSTANTINOPLE, *November 23, 1895, 10.20 p.m.*
Telegraphic.   *(Received November 23.)*

MR. HALLWARD telegraphs that Van is in a state of panic, and that the Kurds are still pillaging the villages round about, and murdering the inhabitants. The Vali, according to his own confession, is helpless to do anything.

F. O. 424/184, p. 277, No. 534

No. 618

Sir Clare Ford to the Marquess of Salisbury.

No. 46.   ROME, *November 23, 1895.*
Telegraphic.   *(Received November 23.)*

BARON BLANC made the following communication to me to-day:-

He says that information has reached him indirectly from Constantinople to the effect that since the 21st instant energetic orders are being sent to the provinces by the Sultan both with regard to the suppression of the disorders, which must be put an end to inexorably and at all hazards, and respecting the mobilization which the Mussulmans are told is with a view to the eventual necessity of offering resistance to the joint action which the Western Powers are threatening.

The Zeitounli Armenians will not lay down their arms unless they are pardoned by the Sultan, and it appears that Her Majesty's Government have insisted on their receiving the necessary guarantees in view of the massacres which justify them in the defensive attitude they have taken up, and of fresh massacres which are likely to occur, and for which the directions issued by the Sultan to repress disorders may serve as a pretext.

Baron Blanc adds that, as he was not in possession of direct information with regard to the steps Her Majesty's Government were taking, he has only desired Signor Panza to carry out his general instructions, and to support his colleagues in any action they may take in the matter.

F. O. 424/184, pp. 277-278, No. 535

No. 619

Mr. Herbert to the Marquess of Salisbury.

No. 851.   CONSTANTINOPLE, *November 23, 1895.*
My Lord,   *(Received December 2.)*

AS I have already had the honour to report to your Lordship in my telegram No. 736 of the 21st instant, the Ephors of the Armenian Church in Pera sent to the Embassy the evening before last to inform me that placards, written in Armenian and Turkish, had been posted that day in Psamatia, a suburb of Stamboul.

The first warned the Armenians that they were going to be attacked, and urged them to take measures at once to arm and defend themselves; the second was addressed also to the Armenians informing them that if they made any movement they would be exterminated. The Ephors added that panic prevailed among the Armenians in consequence of these placards, and that a large number of their shops would be closed on the following day.

In view of this information, I at once sent Mr. Block to the Palace, and desired him to point out to the Sultan, through the First Secretary, how dangerous any disturbances in Constantinople would be at this moment, and to request His Majesty to cause immediate steps to be taken to insure order and to tranquillize both parties. At the same time I requested M. Stavrides to make a similar communication to the Minister of Police in Stamboul.

His Majesty replied that he would at once send categorical orders to the Minister of Police to take every possible precaution to prevent an outbreak. His Majesty did not believe that the Moslems would attack the Christians, but the Minister of Police would be called upon to redouble his vigilance. In His Majesty's opinion this was a move of the Armenian Committees who desired to create disturbances and attract attention, and he therefore suggested that I should advise the Armenian Patriarch to give good advice to his flock and urge them to keep quiet.

I accordingly sent for the Patriarch's Secretary early yesterday morning, and requested him to ask his Beatitude from me to do all in his power to prevent any disturbances on his side.

I have the honour to inclose copy of an official communication which, owing to my representations, was published in yesterday's papers with the view of tranquillizing both parties. The words "neighbours" and "fellow-countrymen" have not been applied to the Armenians for some years past, and this communication has created a very good effect among them.

The Minister of Police has since sent a message to the Embassy to say that the story of the placards is only an invention, but there appears to be no doubt that such placards were posted.

I have, &c.

(Signed) MICHAEL H. HERBERT.

F. O. 424/184, pp. 337-338, No. 623

Inclosure in No. 619

Extract from the "Sabah" of November 22, 1895.

Translation.

INFORMATION has been received by the Government to the effect that placards containing threats both on the part of the Armenians against the Mussulmans and from the latter against Armenians, had been posted up in certain streets in the direction of Psamatia, and that certain persons had got into a state of alarm on that account. Now it is obvious that this is the work and concoction of evil-disposed persons, both for the reason that there is no former instance of aggressive conduct on the part of the Mussulmans, and also because there is no cause or state of things which would lend probability to such conduct now. Nor has it ever occured to the mind or imagination of the latter to place themselves in opposition to the dictates of humanity with regard to the Christians who are their neighbours and fellow-countrymen. Further, good relations between the classes of the population have continued up to the present, and in particular as regards the police force the greatest care is ordained, and it is a fixed order that no occasion for any act of aggression of one class of the population against another is to be allowed, and that all persons committing such acts shall be admonished and corrected. This being so, it is evident, as stated above, that the authors of the above publications are a set of evil-disposed persons who are striving to inspire suspicion among the people, and to create troubles in the country. It is announced, therefore, that, the truth being known, every one can attend to his business with his mind at ease, and that, as the Government is in search of the evil-disposed persons, the authors of this kind of seditious concoctions, any one who may facilitate their capture by giving information to the Government will be rewarded, and will besides receive overwhelming marks of the Imperial favour.

F. O. 424/184, p. 338, No. 623/1

No. 620

Mr. Gosselin to the Marquess of Salisbury.

No. 275.   BERLIN, *November 23, 1895.*
My Lord,   *(Received November 26.)*
        IN compliance with the instructions conveyed to me in your Lordship's telegram No. 118 of yesterday's date I called this morning on Baron von Marschall, and told his Excellency that your Lordship had heard with much satisfaction of the language held by Baron von Saurma to the Sultan, which seemed to have produced a very good effect, and that I had been instructed to convey to his Excellency the best acknowledgments of Her Majesty's Government for the friendly support thus given by Germany.

        I further stated that your Lordship was glad to learn that Baron von Saurma has joined Mr. Herbert in endeavouring to obtain generous treatment for the Zeitoun insurgents, and added that if a massacre ensued, the effect on public opinion would be very serious.

        Baron van Marschall begged me to express his cordial thanks for your Lordship's message.

        He said that Baron von Saurma had used the plainest possible language to the Sultan, and had told him in so many words that, if he wished to preserve his Throne, it was absolutely necessary for him to follow the advice of the Six Powers, and put an end to the lawless proceedings of the Kurds, which are a disgrace to any civilized Government.

I have, &c.

(Signed) MARTIN GOSSELIN.

F. O. 424/184, p. 310, No. 574

No. 621

Mr. Gosselin to the Marquess of Salisbury.

No. 276. Confidential. BERLIN, *November 23, 1895.*

My Lord, *(Received November 26.)*

IN the Telegram Section for the 16th-18th instant, I observe a despatch from Mr. Herbert, stating that the Turkish Chargé d'Affaires at Berlin has telegraphed to the Porte that Baron von Marschall informed him that a joint naval demonstration was imminent, but that in view of the friendship existing between the Emperor and the Sultan, Germany will not take part in it.

I do not believe it at all probable that any such language was ever held by Baron von Marschall to Rifaat Bey, the Ottoman Chargé d'Affaires.

I happened to call at the Foreign Office on the 16th instant, and Baron von Marschall told me that he had seen Rifaat Bey on the previous day, and had spoken to him in the strongest possible way of the dangers which the Sultan was incurring, by disregarding the counsels of all Europe.

"Whether he will repeat my remarks at Constantinople is perhaps doubtful, but at all events I gave him some very good advice."

I inquired yesterday of Baron von Marschall whether anything was known as to Tewfik Pasha's successor.

His Excellency replied that he had heard nothing at all about it; but his own impression is that Tewfik Pasha, bearing in mind the kaleidoscopic changes which follow each other with such startling rapidity at the Porte, is very anxious to keep the Berlin Embassy open for himself, as a haven of rest when his Master shall have grown tired of his services.

I have, &c.

(Signed) MARTIN GOSSELIN.

F. O. 424/184, p. 310, No. 575

No. 622

Sir P. Currie to the Marquess of Salisbury.

No. 852.   CONSTANTINOPLE, *November 25, 1895.*
My Lord,   *(Received December 2.)*
    I HAVE the honour to forward to your Lordship herewith copy of a despatch
which I have received from Her Majesty's Acting Consul at Erzeroum,
transmitting a copy of a despatch from Her Majesty's Vice-Consul at Van,
reporting extensive raids by Kurds near that town, and also an encounter between
zaptiehs and a band of revolutionists near Boghaz-Kessen.
                            I have, &c.
                                            (Signed) PHILIP CURRIE.

    F. O. 424/184, p. 338, No. 624

Inclosure in No. 622

Consul Cumberbatch to Mr. Herbert.

Sir,   ERZEROUM, *November 11, 1895.*
    WITH reference to my despatch of the 6th instant, I have the honour to send
you a copy of a despatch received by me from Her Majesty's Vice-Consul at Van,
reporting extensive raids by Kurds near that town, and the flight of the Armenian
villagers.
    Mr. Hallward also mentions an encounter between zaptiehs and a band of
revolutionists, in which one of the latter was killed, near Boghaz-Kessen.
                            I have, &c.
                                            (Signed) H. A. CUMBERBATCH.

    F. O. 424/184, p. 338, No. 624/1

No. 623

Memorandum communicated by Morel Bey, November 25, 1895.

    LES Représentants des Puissances ont officiellement demandé à la Sublime
Porte l'autorisation pour le passage à travers Détroits des Dardenelles et du
Bosphore d'un second stationnaire.
    La Sublime Porte croit devoir faire remarquer à ce propos que la présence au
moment actuel de ces bâtiments dans les eaux de Constantinople peut être de
nature à encourager les agitateurs, et peut-être même, à donner occasion à des

désordres tant dans la capitale que dans les provinces; et, en outre, que les étrangers habitant les différentes parties de la capitale n'ont pas été molestés et n'ont absolument rien eu à souffrir pendant les derniers désordres, qui ont été fomentés, comme on le sait, par des agitateurs Arméniens.

La Sublime Porte espère que le Gouvernement de Sa Majesté Britannique prendra en considération les observations qui précàdent, et voudra bien autoriser le Représentant de Sa Majesté à ne pas insister sur sa demande, qui, au moment où la sécurité et la confiance commencent à renaître, paraît au Gouvernement Impérial peu justifiée.

F. O. 424/184, p. 304, No. 559

No. 624

The Marquess of Salisbury to Sir P. Currie.

No. 237.
Telegraphic.   FOREIGN OFFICE, *November 25, 1895, 6.25 p.m.*

I HEAR from Count Hatzfeldt that the German Ambassador at Constantinople has given his support to the representations made by Her Majesty's Government relative to the necessity of treating the Zeitoun insurgents with leniency in the event of their surrendering to the Imperial troops.

The Italian Minister for Foreign Affairs states that your Italian colleague will be willing also to support the efforts of her Majesty's Embassy.

I have expressed my thanks for this assurance, and have said that if your colleague will consult you, he will receive full information.

F. O. 424/184, p. 304, No. 560

No. 625

The Marquess of Salisbury to Sir P. Currie.

No. 238.
Telegraphic.   FOREIGN OFFICE, *November 26, 1895, 6.25 p.m.*

MOREL BEY, the Turkish Chargé d'Affaires, called at this Office to-day, and communicated a request from the Porte that Her Majesty's Government should withdraw the application for a Firman for a second "stationnaire" at Constantinople, as the security of the European residents there was not threatened. He stated that the fanatical feeling amongst the Mahommedan population was solely directed against the Armenians, and was not roused against foreigners or other classes of Christians.

In reply, I told Morel Bey that Her Majesty's Government had not initiated the demand for second "stationnaires" to be attached to the Embassies, but that they thought it a desirable measure, that the circumstances thoroughly warranted the proposal, and that I was unable to agree to its withdrawal.

I refused to enter into any attempt at discriminating precisely the objects of the outbreaks on the part of the Mussulmans.

F. O. 424/184, p. 304, No. 561

No. 626

The Marquess of Salisbury to Sir Clare Ford.

No. 70.
Telegraphic.   FOREIGN OFFICE, *November 25, 1895.*

I REQUEST your Excellency to thank the Italian Minister for Foreign Affairs for his friendly communication and promises of support reported in your telegram No. 46 of the 23rd instant.

Her Majesty's Government have strongly urged that if the Zeitoun Armenians surrender they should be treated with clemency by the Turkish Government, and that if any fresh massacres or excesses by Turkish troops should take place, the effect on public opinion in England and in Europe generally would be very serious. Her Majesty's Representative at Constantinople has been authorized to suggest the dispatch of a Commission, by which the terms of surrender might be arranged. If the Italian Ambassador will consult Sir P. Currie he will receive full information.

F. O. 424/184, pp. 304-305, No. 562

No. 627

Sir P. Currie to the Marquess of Salisbury.

No. 745.   CONSTANTINOPLE, *November 25, 1895, 11.15 p.m.*
Telegraphic.   *(Received November 25.)*

I INSTRUCTED the Acting British Consul at Erzeroum to speak to Shakir Pasha about the critical position of affairs at Van and Talori, and I have now received the following telegram in reply:-

"I spoke to Shakir Pasha in the sense of your Excellency's telegram of the 23rd November, calling his attention to the serious position at Van and Talori. His Excellency replied that he was not aware of the danger at the former place, and has at once taken the necessary measures. The whole of the reserves of the 4th Army

Corps have been called out, amounting in all to 60,000 men, and Sadedin Pasha, who is now on his way from Constantinople, will be placed in command of them."

F. O. 424/184, p. 305, No. 564

No. 628

Sir P. Currie to the Marquess of Salisbury.

No. 746.   CONSTANTINOPLE, *November 25, 1895, 11 p.m.*
Telegraphic.   *(Received November 25.)*

AT the meeting of Ambassadors to-day, a suggestion was made that the International Red Cross Society might be willing to organize a system of relief work among the suffering Armenians, and it was agreed that we should communicate this idea to our Governments.

The Armenian Patriarch has communicated to the Embassies here an appeal to the Powers for the destitute Armenians in the Asiatic provinces, who, after being exposed to massacre and pillage, are threatened with extermination by famine.

F. O. 424/184, p. 305, No. 565

No. 629

Sir P. Currie to the Marquess of Salisbury.

No. 747.   CONSTANTINOPLE, *November 25, 1895, 11 p.m.*
Telegraphic.   *(Received November 25.)*

I RAISED a discussion at the Ambassadors' meeting to-day as to whether it would not be feasible for us to urge the Sultan to appoint a responsible Ministry.

Most of my colleagues received my suggestion well, but the Russian Ambassador held that the attempt would be sure to fail, and objected to it as an undue interference in the internal affairs of Turkey.

F. O. 424/184, p. 306, No. 566

No. 630

Sir P. Currie to the Marquess of Salisbury.

No. 748.   CONSTANTINOPLE, *November 25, 1895, 11.15 p.m.*
Telegraphic.   *(Received November 25.)*

IN view of the refusal of the Porte to grant Firmans for the passage of the "stationnaires" and of the direct appeal made by the Turkish Government to the various Governments to withdraw the demand, it was agreed, at the Ambassadors' meeting this afternoon, that we should telegraph to our respective Governments in the following terms:-

"The Ambassadors are unanimously of the opinion that the dignity of the Powers and the security of the foreign Colonies require that they should insist on their demand for Firmans for the passage of the second 'stationnaire,' and, in the event of a refusal, that they should fix on a date, after which they will take measures to insure the concession of a right which has been formally recognized in the Treaties."

The measures to be taken will remain to be discussed when the Powers have concurred in the above telegram.

I proposed that we should ask authority to say that the "stationnaires" would appear at the Dardanelles on a given day, and, if the Firmans were not then granted, would be escorted through by the squadrons, but this was negatived by the French and Russian Ambassadors.

F. O. 424/184, p. 306, No. 567

No. 631

The Marquess of Salisbury to the Marquess of Dufferin.

No. 551.

My Lord,   FOREIGN OFFICE, *November 25, 1895.*

THE French Ambassador called here this afternoon, and stated that he was instructed to thank Her Majesty's Government for the communication which your Excellency had made as to our concurrence in the proposal that second "stationnaires" should be attached to the Embassies at Constantinople.

He was further instructed to state that the French Government had also agreed to this proposal, and had authorized their Ambassador to take the necessary steps at the Porte.

I am, &c.

(Signed) SALISBURY.

F. O. 424/184, p. 306, No. 568

No. 632

The Marquess of Salisbury to the Marquess of Dufferin.

No. 552.

My Lord,   FOREIGN OFFICE, *November 25, 1895.*

AFTER informing me of the course taken by his Government for attaching a second "stationnaire" to the Embassies at Constaninople, the French Ambassador went on to inform me that the Turkish Ambassador at Paris had, on the 23rd instant, made a communication to the French Minister for Foreign Affairs to the effect that as tranquillity is now restored at Constantinople, and the safety of Europeans is in no way threatened, the Porte consider that the presence of second "stationnaires" is unnecessary, and must decline to grant Firmans for their entrance into the Straits.

Baron de Courcel said that his Government would be glad to know whether a similar communication had been made to Her Majesty's Government, and what view they took of it.

I have informed his Excellency that the Turkish Chargé d'Affaires had called here this afternoon and had requested that Her Majesty's Government would withdraw their application for a Firman, giving the same grounds for considering it to be unnecessary. I had replied that Her Majesty's Government did not initiate the proposal for second "stationnaires," but that they entirely concurred in its expediency, and that I must decline to withdraw our application.

I am, &c.

(Signed) SALISBURY.

F. O. 424/184, pp. 306-307, No. 569

No. 633

Sir E. Monson to the Marquess of Salisbury.

No. 95.   VIENNA, *November 26, 1895.*

Telegraphic.   *(Received November 26.)*

WITH reference to the telegram addressed to me by your Lordship No. 89 I have to state that the request of the Turkish Ambassador that Count Goluchowski should withdraw the application for a second "stationnaire" was yesterday categorically refused by the latter, who advised that the demand should be complied with promptly.

Through the French Ambassador, Count Goluchowski had heard the day before yesterday that the French Government had already received the request, but as yet it is not known here what answer they have returned.

F. O. 424/184, p. 311, No. 576

No. 634

Sir E. Monson to the Marquess of Salisbury.

No. 96. Most Confidential.   VIENNA, *November 26, 1895.*
Telegraphic.   *(Received November 26.)*

COUNT GOLUCHOWSKI being absent at a shooting party, Count Welsersheimb, the Under-Secretary of State for Foreign Affairs, showed two telegrams to me to-day in the strictest confidence. In the first of these was conveyed the text of the identic telegram which the six Ambassadors had addressed to their respective Governments, in which it was proposed that a date should be fixed before which the Turkish Government must grant Firmans for second "stationnaires," and threatening, in case of refusal, to take further measures. In the second telegram it was stated confidentially as Baron Calice's idea that the Ambassadors in the latter case may declare that iron-clads will escort these "stationnaires" through the Dardanelles.

I hope to-morrow to be able to report to your Lordship the views held on this point by Count Goluchowski.

F. O. 424/184, p. 311, No. 577

No. 635

Sir P. Currie to the Marquess of Salisbury.

No. 749.
Telegraphic.   CONSTANTINOPLE, *November 26, 1895, 2.30 p.m.*

I WAS informed to-day by the Minister for Foreign Affairs that we were at liberty to send for the "Dryad" in exchange for one of the two "stationnaires" now lying there.

His Excellency added that Firmans would be issued for an additional "stationnaire" for the four other Powers.

I have informed the Admiral that as the "Cockatrice" has a larger crew, I would prefer that she should remain here, and have proposed to send the "Imogene" to the Dardanelles to await the arrival of the "Dryad", and then proceed to join the fleet.

F. O. 424/184, p. 311, No. 578

No. 636

Sir P. Currie to the Marquess of Salisbury.

No. 750.   CONSTANTINOPLE, *November 26, 1895, 1.45 p.m.*
Telegraphic.   *(Received November 26.)*

YOUR Lordship's telegram No. 237 of yesterday.

The Grand Vizier informs me that instructions have been sent to Marash to form a Commission of Christian Notables, who are to proceed to Zeitoun to treat with the inhabitants.

The German Ambassador has supported the representations made by his Embassy about the Zeitounlis.

Mr. Consul Barnham fears an outbreak at Aleppo. I have been assured by the Minister for Foreign Affairs to-day that he will make inquiries as to the state of affairs there.

F. O. 424/184, pp. 311-312, No. 579

No. 637

Sir P. Currie to the Marquess of Salisbury.

No. 751.   CONSTANTINOPLE, *November 26, 1895, 5 p.m.*
Telegraphic.   *(Received November 26,)*

THE Acting British Consul at Erzeroum telegraphs to me as follows:-

"I do not consider that Mr. Hampson's suggestion for the formation of an Armenian Mountain Police is at present feasible. Shakir Pasha is doing his best to stop Kurdish raids, and will succeed if he is allowed a free hand.

"We have had a slight disturbance here to-day, owing to a false alarm which created a panic, but quiet was promptly restored by the authorities, who arrested several Turks. So far as I can learn, two Armenians were killed, and two wounded.

"Shakir Pasha has communicated to me a telegram from the Vali of Van, reporting that tranquillity has been restored in the neighbourhood, and that there is no need for special anxiety about the danger of the town. The Vali says that the Kurds in the Hekkiari district are not yet under control, and that Kurds have been crossing the frontier from Persia, and that the Persian Ambassador has been requested to have a stop put to this.

F. O. 424/184, p. 312, No. 580

No. 638

The Marquess of Salisbury to Sir P. Currie.

No. 384.

Sir,   FOREIGN OFFICE, *November 26, 1895.*

I HAVE received Mr. Herbert's despatch No. 767 of the 6th instant relative to the identic verbal communication made on the 5th instant by the Representatives of the Six Powers to the Porte on the subject of the condition of the Asiatic provinces of Turkey.

I approve the terms of the communication, and the language held by Mr. Herbert to Saïd Pasha when making it.

I am, &c.

(Signed) SALISBURY.

F. O. 424/184, p. 312, No. 581

No. 639

The Marquess of Salisbury to Mr. Goschen.

No. 358.

Sir,   FOREIGN OFFICE, *November 26, 1895.*

THE Russian Ambassador called here to-day and communicated a message from his Government in the terms of the inclosed Memorandum,* stating that the Sultan had requested that the demand made by the Powers for second stationnaires at Constantinople might at least be deferred, if it could not be withdrawn. His Excellency was instructed to say that the Russian Government were ready to agree, and hoped that Her Majesty's Government would do so.

In reply, I have informed M. de Staal that the Turkish Chargé d'Affaires here had presented a request that Her Majesty's Government should withdraw their application, but that I had replied that I must refuse to do so, and that I gathered from a telegram just received from Sir P. Currie, that the Minister for Foreign Affairs had informed him that the Firmans would be granted. I hoped, therefore, that the question was settled, and it seemed to me that the arrival at Constantinople of five vessels of comparitively small size was not a matter to create any serious excitement or alarm.

I am, &c.

(Signed) SALISBURY.

F. O. 424/184, p. 312, No. 582

* Memorandum communicated by M. de Staal, November 26, 1895.

No. 640

The Marquess of Salisbury to Sir E. Monson.

No. 118.

Sir, FOREIGN OFFICE, *November 26, 1895.*

THE Austro-Hungarian Ambassador called here to-day and stated that his Government had received no communication from the Porte on the subject of the second "stationnaire" for the Embassies at Constantinople. The French Government had, however, consulted them respecting the communication made by the Turkish Representative at Paris to the effect that the Sultan refused to grant the necessary Firmans. Count Goluchowski thought that the Powers ought to stand firm, and that if they gave way the impression produced on the Porte and on the population in Turkey, Mussulmans and Christians alike, would be unfortunate.

Count Deym was informed, in reply, that the Turkish Chargé d'Affaires had yesterday communicated to me a request that Her Majesty's Government would withdraw their application for a Firman, but that I had replied that I must decline to do so, and that the Turkish Minister for Foreign Affairs had now told Sir P. Currie that the Firmans would be granted.

I am, &c.

(Signed) SALISBURY.

F. O. 424/184, p. 313, No. 583

No. 641

Admiralty to Foreign Office.

Confidential. ADMIRALTY, *November 27, 1895.*

Sir, *(Received November 27.)*

I AM commanded by my Lords Commissioners of the Admiralty to transmit, for the information of the Secretary of State for Foreign Affairs, decypher of a telegram, dated this day, from the Commander-in-chief in the Mediterranean.

I am, &c.

(Signed) EVAN MACGREGOR.

F. O. 424/184, p. 314, No. 585

Inclosure in No. 641

Admiral Sir M. Culme-Seymour to Admiralty.

Telegraphic. SALONICA, *November 27, 1895.*
AT request of Ambassador "Dryad" leaves to-day to replace "Imogene;" latter will come here, and shortly go to Malta to be docked and cleaned, and await further orders. Arrange mails.

F. O. 424/184, p. 314, No. 585/1

No. 642

Sir P. Currie to the Marquess of Salisbury.

No. 752. CONSTANTINOPLE, *November 27, 1895, 11.30 a.m.*
Telegraphic. *(Received November 27.)*
THE Sultan has sent me a message proposing the appointment of Sirri Pasha, late Governor of Diarbekir, as President of the Commission of Control, in the place of Shefik Bey, who has been removed from the post. Sirri Pasha bears a good character, and I do not therefore intend to make any objections to his appointment.

F. O. 424/184, p. 314, No. 586

No. 643

Sir P. Currie to the Marquess of Salisbury.

No. 753. CONSTANTINOPLE, *November 27, 1895, 12.53 p.m.*
Telegraphic. *(Received November 27.)*
IT appears that the Foreign Minister misled me yesterday in stating that permission had been given for the passage of the "stationnaires," as reported in my telegram No. 749 of yesterday.

The Sultan persists in his refusal apparently from fear that the vessels will be used against him, though the Ministers profess that they have advised him to yield.

F. O. 424/184, p. 314, No. 587

No. 644

Sir E. Monson to the Marquess of Salisbury.

No. 97.   VIENNA, *November 27, 1895.*
Telegraphic.   *(Received November 27.)*

IN continuation of my telegram of yesterday, I beg to report that the proposal contained in the identic telegram of the six Ambassadors at Constantinople was at once agreed to by Count Goluchowski.

A suggestion of Prince Lobanoff that the Firmans for the passage of the second "stationnaires" should not be acted on when granted was communicated yesterday to Count Goluchowski by Count Kapnist. The former replied that such a course would not only make the Powers ridiculous in the eyes of the Turks, but would also prove to the Sultan the non-existence of the unanimity of the Powers which had been so loudly proclaimed.

F. O. 424/184, p. 315, No. 588

No. 645

Sir E. Monson to the Marquess of Salisbury.

No. 98. Confidential.   VIENNA, *November 27, 1895,*
Telegraphic.   *(Received November 27.)*

COUNT GOLUCHOWSKI informs me that he has told Count Kapnist that Prince Lobanoff's opinion that the Ambassadors at Constantinople are unduly impressed by being on the spot, and that a sounder estimate can be formed by their respective Governments at a distance, is in no way shared by him.

On the contrary, the fifteen years' local experience gained by Baron Calice renders him a far better judge of the situation than he (Count Goluchowski) can be, and the most widely-extending full powers have been in consequence given to the Austro-Hungarian Ambassador at Constantinople.

Count Kapnist was further told by Count Goluchowski that he should for himself, and he thought that all the other Governments should also for themselves, shrink from refusing to concur in a course which the six Ambassadors at Constantinople has unanimously recommended, such a refusal being, in his Excellency's opinion, too great a responsibility to undertake.

Prince Lobanoff's suggestion as to not acting on the Firmans was, I understand, made before the decision of the Ambassadors formulated in their identic telegram came to his knowledge.

F. O. 424/184, p. 315, No. 589

No. 646

The Marquess of Salisbury to Sir P. Currie.

No. 241.
Telegraphic.   FOREIGN OFFICE, *November 27, 1895, 3.30 p.m.*

I HAVE received your telegram No. 752 of to-day, reporting that the Sultan proposes to appoint Sirri Pasha, late Vali of Diarbekir, to the Presidency of the Armenian Commission of Control, in the place of Shefik Bey, who has been removed from that post.

I agree that your Excellency need not raise any objection to Sirri Pasha's appointment.

F. O. 424/184, p. 315, No. 590

No. 647

The Marquess of Salisbury to Sir P. Currie.

No. 242.
Telegraphic.   FOREIGN OFFICE, *November 27, 1895, 6.35 p.m.*

M. DE STAAL communicated on the 26th instant a message from Prince Lobanoff to the effect that the Sultan had requested that the application by the Powers for Firmans for second "stationnaires" at Constantinople might at least be deferred, if it could not be withdrawn. His Excellency added that his Government were willing to grant this request, and hoped that Her Majesty's Government would also agree to it.

In reply, I stated that the Turkish Chargé d'Affaires here had presented a request that the application made by Her Majesty's Government for a Firman should be withdrawn, but that I had refused to do so; that I understood from your Excellency that Tewfik Pasha had promised that the Firmans would be issued, and that I therefore hoped that this question might be regarded as already settled. From your telegram No. 753 of to-day, however, I fear that it has not been possible to overcome the Sultan's objections.

I hear that the Austro-Hungarian Government have accepted the proposal of the Ambassadors that they should be authorized to name a date for the issue of the Firmans, after which action should be taken to obtain the concession of a right which the Treaties formally recognize.

F. O. 424/184, pp. 315-316, No. 591

No. 648

The Marquess of Salisbury to Sir P. Currie.

No. 243. Confidential.
Telegraphic.   FOREIGN OFFICE, *November 27, 1895, 6.40 p.m.*

THE Admiral in command of the Mediterranean Squadron reports that Her Majesty's ship "Dryad" will replace Her Majesty's ship "Imogene," and will leave Salonica to-day for the purpose.

I shall be glad to learn whether your Excellency will still be able to make arrangements for this exchange. If so, the Porte can hardly continue to refuse the application of the other Ambassadors to be placed on the same footing as the British Embassy.

F. O. 424/184, p. 316, No. 592

No. 649

Mr. Gosselin to the Marquess of Salisbury.

No. 281.   BERLIN, *November 27, 1895.*
My Lord,   *(Received November 29.)*

WITH reference to my despatch No. 276, Confidential, of the 23rd instant, I have the honour to inform your Lordship that the semi-official "Norddeutsche Allgemeine Zeitung" of yesterday calls attention to a statement published on the 23rd of this month by the "Hamburgische Correspondent," in the form of a telegram from Constantinople, that "a Declaration made by the German Emperor that His Majesty does not sympathize with the naval demonstration has been gratefully received in Turkish circles. The Sultan declared to his Ministers that he fully appreciates Germany's friendship for Turkey."

Commenting upon this, the "Norddeutsche" states that, according to inquiries which they have made, the alleged Declaration of His Imperial Majesty is a pure fabrication.

I have, &c.

(Signed) MARTIN GOSSELIN.

F. O. 424/184, p. 321, No. 601

No. 650

Sir P. Currie to the Marquess of Salisbury.

No. 876.   CONSTANTINOPLE, *November 29, 1895.*
My Lord,   *(Received December 3.)*
    I HAVE the honour to forward to your Lordship herewith copy of a despatch
which I have received from Her Majesty's Consul at Trebizond, reporting on the
situation at Samsoun.

I have, &c.

(Signed) PHILIP CURRIE.

F. O. 424/184, p. 356, No. 648

Inclosure 1 in No. 650

Consul Longworth to Mr. Herbert.
Sir,   TREBIZOND, *November 20, 1895.*
    I HAVE the honour to annex herewith copy of a despatch from our Consular
Agent at Samsoun, alluding therein to the disturbed condition of the inland
districts.

    Mr. de Cortanze, it will be seen, refers to the talk of those he styles as "les
agents provocateurs Arméniens," and I am this day writing to him, therefore, to
furnish me with all available information respecting these individuals.

    The opinion expressed by him that if the Mutessarif were allowed a free hand
disorders at Samsoun would be averted, appears to me very significant.

I have, &c.

(Signed) H. Z. LONGWORTH.

F. O. 424/184, p. 356, No.648/1

Inclosure 2 in No. 650

Consular Agent Cortanze to Consul Longworth.
M. le Consul,   SAMSOUN, *le 18 Novembre, 1895.*
    J'AI l'honneur de porter à votre connaissance qu'il y a eu des troubles à
Amassia, Tokat, Mersifon, et Uniah.

A Amassia il y a eu des victimes la chose est sûre. Les autorités donne le chiffre de dix, les agents provocateurs Arméniens parlent de 200; la vérité est entre ces deux chiffres, mais à quel degré?

Quant aux autres villes ci-dessus mentionnées, je ne puis vous donner pour le moment aucun renseignement précis. Les bruits les plus sinistres circulent. Le fait certain est qu'il y a partout une très violente surexcitation, et, pour ma part, je suis convaincu que s'il n'y a point encore des massacres réguliers, il n'y a pas moins de nombreux crimes isolés et enfantés par la sécurité de l'impunité, et je dirai même de l'approbation officieuse de l'autorité.

Ici pour le moment tout est calme. Les Arméniens ont une grande frayeir, et les Musulmans attendent, non sans impatience, le moment du pillage; la chose se déclare assez ouvertement.

Notre Mutessarif, plein de zèle et d'activité, prend toutes les mesures possibles pour conjurer tout danger, et je suis certain que si on lui laisse toute initiative et liberté d'agir, il n'y aurait rien ici, mais j'ai tout lieu de supposer qu'on l'entrave souvent, et que sa séverité et son impartialité soient mal vues en haut lieu.

Veuillez, &c.

(Signé) II. DE CORTANZE.

F. O. 424/184, p. 356, No. 648/2

No. 651

The Marquess of Salisbury to Sir P. Currie.

No. 244.
Telegraphic.   FOREIGN OFFICE, *November 29, 1895, 9 a.m.*

I HAVE received your telegram No. 746 of the 25th instant, communicating a suggestion made at a meeting of the Ambassadors on that day that the International Red Cross Society might be willing to organize Missions for the relief of the destitute Armenians in the Asiatic provinces.

Her Majesty's Government are in favour of the proposal if agreed to by the other Powers.

I should be glad to learn what replies have been received from the other Governments, and what steps they propose should be taken to carry out the suggestion.

F. O. 424/184, p. 321, No. 602

No. 652

Mr. Gosselin to the Marquess of Salisbury.

No. 50.   BERLIN, *November 29, 1895, 6 p.m.*
Telegraphic.   *(Received November 29.)*

AT an interview with Baron von Marschall this morning the Turkish Chargé d'Affaires asked that the Emperor should exert his good offices with the other five Powers with a view to the demand for second "stationnaires" being abandoned; he said that the Sultan was prepared to guarantee order and the security of life and property at Constantinople.

His Excellency categorically refused this request, and again impressed on the Turkish Chargé d'Affaires that the Sultan's best chance of maintaining order was at once to yield to the request which the Great Powers had unanimously put forward.

Baron von Marschall informed me in strict confidence that Russia had recently sounded the German Government as to whether it would be advisable to withdraw the demand, but that they had delined to do so, and that Russia will now join in concerted action of the other Powers.

F. O. 424/184, p. 321, No. 603

No. 653

Acting Consul Fontana to Sir P. Currie.

Confidential.
Sir,
                                            ANGORA, *November 29, 1895.*

ACCORDING to a letter I have received, dated the 19th instant, from a trustworthy correspondent at Cæsarea, the Armenians in the south-westerly portion of the Sivas Vilayet, especially at Ghemerek and the surrounding villages, are undergoing great sufffering and loss. Seven villages in particular, of which Boorhan, Lisanlu, Chepné, and Ala-Kilissé are the more important, have been pillaged by mixed bands of Circassians, Kurds, and Turcomans—"everything having been taken, even to the matting and the wooden spoons."

In Boorhan one man was killed, but on the whole there appears to have been, comparatively, but little loss of life. Dendil (?), another village in the same neighbourhood, was, up to the 17th instant, surrounded by Kurds and Circassians, who threatened a raid. The Armenians sent to the Kaïmakam of Sharkishla for assistance. His only reply was, "Defend yourselves; I have no soldiers to lend you;" thereupon they provisioned their church, and placed their women and children there for safety. My informant is unaware of what happened in this village subsequent to the date referred to.

I hear from another source that the villagers have been flocking into Ghemerek for safety; but that even there the Kurds managed to seize and carry off some 9,000 sheep which had been driven in from the surrounding hamlets.

I have called the attention of the Acting Vali to the deplorable condition of a district in the immediate vicinity of his own vilayet. He professes, however, to have no cognizance of the matter, and states that, in any case, he could not interefere with the affairs of any other vilayet than his own without special instructions to that effect.

I have, &c.

(Signed) RAPHAEL A. FONTANA.

F. O. 424/184, p. 377, No. 689/1

No. 654

Sir P. Currie to the Marquess of Salisbury.

No. 884A. Confidential.   CONSTANTINOPLE, *November 29, 1895.*
My Lord,   *(Received December 9.)*

I HAD the honour of being received this afternoon by the Sultan in a private audience, which lasted two and a-half hours.

His Imperial Majesty began by inquiring after the health of the Queen. I replied that Her Majesty was well, and had charged me to present her compliments to the Sultan, and to thank him for the messages he had sent. Her Majesty had heard with great grief of the events which had occurred in Turkey during the last few weeks, and trusted that the Sultan would do all in his power to prevent their continuance.

His Imperial Majesty replied that I was doubtless already aware that order had been restored, as the Porte had been instructed to communicate to the Embassies all news received from the provinces, as well as copies of the orders sent to the local authorities for the maintenance of order. Troops had also been dispatched to prevent a recurrence of disorder, and, in fact, everything that could be done had been done. I must have heard from our Consular officers, said His Imperial Majesty, in conclusion, that since some days quiet prevailed.

I said the reports I had received confirmed His Majesty's statements, but that in some places disturbances still continued, though on a relatively small scale.

His Majesty went on to say that there still existed a regrettable impression that he was not sincere in his desire to execute the reforms without delay. Such a scheme had naturally required prolonged discussion, but, once approved and adopted, he was resolved it should be carried out in its entirety. The first things, however, needful was to restore order, for only then could the reforms be taken in hand. Nevertheless, a beginning had already been made: certain Inspectors had been chosen, as well as Muavins for the Valis and Mutessarifs. Shakir Pasha had begun to enrol a Christian gendarmerie, and but for the disturbances would have introduced it by now in all the six vilayets.

I said that Her Majesty's Government had heard with satisfaction of the Sultan's fixed resolve to execute reforms, but, unfortunately, late events could not but shake their confidence. The acceptance of the reforms had been followed by massacres throughout the Armenian provinces, and thousands of people who had lost their homes and property must starve during the winter unless relief was forthcoming. Just before leaving the Embassy I had received news which was far from reassuring, namely, that several Armenians had been forced to accept Mahommedanism to escape death.

His Majesty remarked that he had no sympathy with any one who changed his religion, and he cited the case of a well-known Armenian, a high functionary in the Ministry of Justice, who had turned Mahommedan. He had no consideration whatever for this man. He asked me to give him details respecting the forced conversions I had mentioned, and I promised to do so.

I then informed His Majesty that I had that day received a telegram from Her Majesty's Vice-Consul at Mush, saying that Armenians had been threatened and tortured at Bitlis in order to force them to telegraph to Constantinople that the massacres at that place had been begun by Armenians. The Sultan at first expressed incredulity, and asked who forced the Armenians to make such statements. I replied it was the authorities, who wished to disown all responsibility for what had occurred. The Sultan said he would make inquiries, but asked what evidence would convince me. I said His Majesty had no doubt officials whom he could trust, on which he suggested Abdullah Pasha, or Saad-ed-Din Pasha, President of the Commission, lately dispatched as suitable persons, but I declined to interfere in the choice of functionaries to be sent, and confined myself to suggesting that one of Her Majesty's Vice-Consuls should take part in the inquiry. The Sultan agreed to this.

I then said that there were two circumstances which Her Majesty's Government had learned with much regret: one was, that no one had as yet been punished for the massacres; the other, that His Majesty had not yet issued the promised Hatt.

The Sultan, replying only to the latter of these observations, said that deeds were more important than words or Proclamations; he would communicate to me through the Porte his reasons for not publishing a Hatt. He had repeatedly stated that he would execute the reforms; he was an obstinate man, he said, and having once taken a determination he intended to carry it through. I continued, however, to press the point, and said that, in the opinion of Her Majesty's Government, the promulgation of the Hatt was necessary for three reasons: (1) to convince the Powers of His Majesty's sincerity;(2) to convince the Armenians they were really to have reforms; (3) to convince the Moslems that the reforms contained nothing injurious to their interests. The Sultan replied that he would instruct his Ministers to give me explanations respecting the second and third points, which he hoped would convince me that his refusal to publish a Hatt was justified. With regard to the first point, the reforms had been officially communicated to all the Ambassadors, and it depended on them to inform their respective Governments of the determination he had expressed to execute them, and of the practical measures he was taking for this purpose. He then reverted to my second and third points, and observed that, in spite of what he had said, he would like to discuss them with me as a friend.

He then entered into a long historical disquisition with the object of showing that the issue of a new Hatt would be futile. He referred to the Hatt of Gulhane, and the Hatt-i-Shereef of his father; the latter had been a bone of contention between the French partisans, Ali and Fuad Pashas, on the one hand, and Reschid Pasha, an English partisan, on the other, and, when finally promulgated, had led to much hostile feeling on the part of the Sheikh-el-Islam and other Moslem leaders. Yet, after all, the practical result had been small. When he came to the Throne, he had put into force some clauses of his father's Hatt; he had instituted a Parliament in which were a certain number of ignorant and childish people, and which had to be superseded. He had reformed the administration of justice and inaugurated a new Code. The present reforms were only an elaboration of the former Hatt-i-Shereef, and, in his opinion, there was no need to publish them in extenso. He had caused a notice to be put in the press that certain reforms would be taken in hand, and that was sufficient; a further publication would not carry conviction to any one. His object was to adopt the reforms in practice, and then people would learn what their nature was.

In reply, I still pressed the matter, and said that in every civilized country laws that were to be enforced were first published. It was, in the opinion of Her Majesty's Government, essential that the details of the reforms should be made generally known, that they should be published in every vilayet, and posted up in every Armenian village and house.

The Sultan replied he would explain the situation still further. He had intended to publish the reforms. They has been copied in extenso for the press, with references showing to which Article of the Law on the vilayets each clause referred. I had doubtless read a translation of the existing Laws, and therefore was aware that the scheme of reforms contained nothing new.

I replied I was well aware of this, and reminded His Majesty that some months ago, when he had asked me what the reforms we intended to propose were, I had told him they contained nothing which was not already in the Code. It was accordingly highly desirable that the public, both Moslem and Christian, should know this. The Sultan replied that, notwithstanding this, he had not ventured to make any publication. He would, however, again consult his Ministers and Saïd Pasha about the Hatt, and would let me know the result. He hoped I would be reasonable, and believe in the sincerity of the arguments adduced should the promulgation of a Hatt be again recognized as unadvisable. If I would examine these questions with an open mind, it would be greatly to the advantage of both Turkey and England.

I then touched upon the question of the "stationnaires," and expressed deep regret that His Imperial Majesty showed such unfounded suspicion of the intention of the Powers in demanding Firmans for additional vessels.

Under the Treaty of Paris they had a distinct right to two "stationnaires;" they had exercised this right on many occasions, and their sole object in claiming to exercise it now was to afford adequate protection to the foreign Colonies in case of need. Notwithstanding the assurances given by the Imperial Government that perfect security existed, the confidence which had been destroyed by recent events here and in the provinces could not be restored, and constant panics prevailed.

The Sultan replied that, as everything had been done to restore order, and as tranquillity now reigned, there was no necessity to press this point any more. Disturbances had, it was true, broken out at Constantinople, and been followed by others in the provinces, but there was now no further danger. His wish was to take advantage of the present calm to execute the reforms, and the step now taken by the Powers only rendered his task more difficult, and might provoke disorders.

"There is no danger," he said. "Has even one foreigner's nose bled either in the capital or in the provinces?"

I said I could not admit there was no danger. The step taken by the Powers was in the interests of Turkey as well as of the foreign subjects, for if an outbreak occurred here it might lead to the entrance of the fleets.

The Sultan answered that every measure had been taken to insure order, that the greatest vigilance was exercised wherever Europeans dwelt, and that, though ordinary crimes might be committed, as in London, Paris, and every city of the world, a revolt was improbable.

He did not agree with the reasoning of the Ambassadors; they argued that the presence of the "stationnaires" would prevent an outbreak, but the Minister of Police and other authorities reported to him that it would probably provoke one. He hoped, therefore, that England would not insist on this step.

I replied that all the Powers were absolutely agreed on its necessity, but the Sultan insisted that if England would abandon the idea, she was quite able to induce the others to follow her. He trusted that I would telegraph to your Lordship his views on the subject, and that Her Majesty's Government would persuade the others to withdraw their demand.

I replied that His Majesty misjudged the situation; England did not stand alone in this matter, and the Powers were acting in strict concert; there was no intention of injuring His Majesty or the interests of the Empire.

The suspicions which seemed to fill His Majesty's mind must have been inspired by his enemies, with the object of bringing about a naval intervention. Although an attack on foreigners might not be probable, it was not impossible, and there could be no doubt that if such an event occurred the fleets would at once come to Constantinople to protect the lives of foreign subjects. The only guarantee against such an eventuality was the presence of the armed "stationnaires" which the Powers demanded. They did not require the vessels for the purpose of making a naval demonstration; their sole object was to restore confidence and assist His Majesty in maintaining order. I therefore, as a friend of His Majesty and of Turkey, earnestly begged him to let the ships pass the Dardanelles. They would come through one by one, and attract no attention; but I warned him that if the permission was refused the Powers were united, and resolved to carry the matter through. His Majesty said he would again consult his Ministers and Saïd Pasha, who had already been sent round to the Embassies with a message on the subject. But in the meantime he begged me to support his request, that Her Majesty's Government should abandon the proposal.

I said I would report His Majesty's language, but that considering the instructions I had received, I could hold out no hope that Her Majesty's Government would alter their decision.

His Majesty sent Munir Pasha to me after the audience to again press the point.

I then spoke of the attack on our Consuls at Jeddah, and said I wished to remind His Imperial Majesty that, though some months had elapsed since the outrage had occurred, no reparation whatever had been made by the Ottoman Goverment. The Sultan said that this was a matter to be treated by the Sublime Porte, but that, as far as he was aware, it had been decided with the assent of the Embassics that the best means of laying hands on the perpetrators of the outrage was by giving hostages. I said that no answer had yet been returned to the notes on the subject addressed by the Powers to the Sublime Porte, and that I wished to impress on His Majesty the gravity of the matter. Whether soldiers should be sent or the criminals be captured by negotiations was a question of detail for His Majesty to decide, but reparation was necessary, and must be obtained in some way or another. His Majesty replied that he was endeavouring to induce the culprits to surrender, but they had taken refuge in inaccessible mountains. If I thought it necessary he would send troops after them, but the Grand Shereef and the Vali were trying to capture them by other means, and this, he understood, was the cause of the delay. If he sent troops the men would probably not be taken alive, and, if they were shot, how would it be possible to convince the Ambassadors they were the real culprits? He would, however, inquire of the Porte how the matter stood, and inform me of the result.

I have, &c.

(Signed) PHILIP CURRIE.

F. O. 424/184, pp. 369-372, No. 684

No. 655

Mr. Gosselin to the Marquess of Salisbury.

No. 284. Very Confidential.   BERLIN, *November 30, 1895.*
My Lord,   *(Received December 2.)*

BARON VON MARSCHALL told me yesterday that Rifaat Bey, the Turkish Chargé d'Affaires, had called a few hours previously at the Foreign Office with a personal message from his Sovereign to the Emperor, to the following effect:-

The Sultan pointed out that no recent disturbances had occurred in Constantinople. He was ready to give guarantees for the preservation of order and the security of the life and property of all his subjects, Christian and Mahommedan alike, residing in his capital. He feared that the arrival of the second "stationnaires" would inevitably excite ill-feeling amongst the Mahommedans, and might, on the other hand, increase the disaffection of the Armenians; and, under these circumstances, His Majesty appealed to the good offices of his old friend and ally, the German Emperor, to induce the other five Powers to withdraw, or at all events to suspend, their demand for the Firmans authorizing the second "stationnaires" to pass through the Straits.

Baron von Marschall told me that he had categorically refused to comply with this request, and had "once more" impressed on the Turkish Chargé d'Affaires that the best chance the Sultan had of preserving order in his dominions was to yield at once to the unanimous request of the Great Powers with regard to the "stationnaires."

His Excellency informed Rifaat Bey that Baron de Saurma had been instructed to support the demand, and would continue to do so, and that if his Excellency had not applied for a Firman for a second German stationnaire, the only reason for his not having done so is the fact that the Imperial Government have no available vessel in commission of the calibre required.

"I thought," said Baron von Marschall, "it as well to explain this very clearly, for fear that the absence of a second German 'stationnaire' might be misrepresented at the Porte."

His Excellency further told me, in strict confidence, that the German

Government has been recently sounded by the Russian Government as to the advisability of withdrawing the demand, in consequence of an urgent appeal in this sense addressed by the Sultan to the Emperor Nicholas, but that they had delined to do so, and that he was convinced that the Russian Ambassador at Constantinople would now act in entire harmony with his colleagues in support of a measure which was originally proposed by the Russian Ambassador himself.

Baron von Marschall, in reply to my inquiry, said that he had yesterday morning telegraphed to Constantinople to say that His Majesty would be pleased to receive Turkhan Pasha as Ottoman Ambassador at this Court.

I have, &c.

(Signed) MARTIN GOSSELIN.

F. O. 424/184, p. 353, No. 642

No. 656

Sir E. Monson to the Marquess of Salisbury.

No. 100. Very Confidential.   VIENNA, *November 30, 1895.*
Telegraphic.   *(Received December 4.)*

COUNT KAPNIST communicated the contents of a telegram to Count Goluchowski, which he had received from Prince Lobanoff, stating that Russia would join in maintaining the demand for Firmans for the second "stationnaires" in view of the insistance of England and Austria, and at the same time he gave his Excellency to understand that M. de Nélidoff is considered at St. Petersburgh to have exaggerated apprehensions and to have shown unnecessary nervousness.

M. de Nélidoff and his colleagues appear to have been warmly defended against this charge by Count Goluchowski, but Count Kapnist declared that on no account would M. de Nélidoff be allowed by his Government to dictate the action to be adopted by them.

The conversation which ensued was in the sense reported by me to your Lordship in my telegram No. 98.

This afternoon Count Goluchowski said to me that the Russian Government do not only allow him to be bitterly abused by their press, but have done all in their power to make difficulties at Constantinople and to nullify his action.

F. O. 424/184, p. 361, No. 654

No. 657

The Marquess of Salisbury to Sir P. Currie.

No. 385.

Sir,   Foreign Office, *November 30, 1895.*

I HAVE received Mr. Herbert's despatch No. 828A of the 21st instant, stating that the Sultan had expressed a wish to have the advice of the Representatives of the Powers as to what measures he should take to restore confidence, and reporting the message which, at a meeting of the Ambassadors on the 18th instant, it was decided to send in reply through Baron Calice, the Doyen of the Corps Diplomatique.

Her Majesty's Government concur generally in the steps recommended to His Imperial Majesty in this message.

I am, &c.

(Signed) Salisbury.

F. O. 424/184, p. 322, No. 604

No. 658

Sir P. Currie to the Marquess of Salisbury.

No. 763.   Constantinople, *December 1, 1895.*

Telegraphic.   *(Received December 1.)*

THE Foreign Minister called on me this morning to inquire, on the part of the Sultan, whether your Lordship had yet sent any message in answer to His Majesty's observations as to the "stationnaires" at the audience granted me last Friday.

The Foreign Minister added that His Majesty still hoped that England would return to her former footing of intimate friendship with Turkey, and would induce the other Powers to waive their demands.

I replied that I had received no message from your Lordship, and that I did not expect one, as your reply had already been given to the Turkish Chargé d'Affaires in London. As to Her Majesty's Government intervening to induce the Powers to waive their demand, there could be no question of their adopting such a course; all the Powers were agreed to insist on their demand, and England was acting in concert with them.

F. O. 424/184, p. 322, No. 605

No. 659

Sir P. Currie to the Marquess of Salisbury.

No. 764. CONSTANTINOPLE, *December 2, 1895.*
Telegraphic. *(Received December 2.)*

THE time seems to have come for acting on the Ambassadors' recommendation reported in my telegram No. 748 of the 25th November, that a delay should be fixed for the granting of the Firmans for the "stationnaires," after which measures would be taken in insure the concession of a right formally recognized in the Treaties.

The French Ambassador has received no instructions from his Government as yet, but the Turkish Ambassador in Paris has been informed that the French Government adhere to the Resolution adopted by the six Powers. Till M. Cambon receives his instructions our hands are tied, and I would therefore suggest that the French Government should be pressed to authorize his Excellency to act on the recommendation above referred to.

F. O. 424/184, p. 353, No. 643

No. 660

Sir P. Currie to the Marquess of Salisbury.

No. 765. CONSTANTINOPLE, *December 2, 1895, 9.5 p.m.*
Telegraphic. *(Received December 2.)*

THE Acting British Consul at Angora telegraphs as follows:-

"There were serious disturbances at Cæsarea last Saturday, which lasted for many hours. The official report puts the number of deaths at between fifty and sixty.

"The Mutessarif telegraphed to the Vali that the disturbance was commenced by some Armenians who wounded a Turk, and that the Turks were assisted by foreign Mussulmans, probably Circassians and Kurds."

F. O. 424/184, p. 354, No. 644

No. 661

The Marquess of Salisbury to Sir E. Monson.

No. 92. Confidential.
Telegraphic.   FOREIGN OFFICE, *December 2, 1895.*

DURING a conversation which I had to-day with the Austro-Hungarian Ambassador on the present situation in Turkey I observed to his Excellency that, as the Russian Government declined to agree to any attempt on the part of the other Governments to force the passage of the Dardanelles, the Powers would be compelled, in the event of the Sultan continuing to refuse the Firmans the second "stationnaire," either to accept a complete defeat at his hands, or to inform His Imperial Majesty that, if one of the "stationnaires" attempting to proceed to Constantinople were fired at, this would be considered as a hostile act, which would give rise to reprisals in other parts of his dominions.

I stated, however, to Count Deym that this was not to be considered as a formal proposal, but only as an idea which suggested itself to me on reflecting over the situation, and which I offered for his Excellency's consideration.

F. O. 424/184, p. 354, No. 645

No. 662

The Marquess of Salisbury to the Marquess of Dufferin.

No. 160.
Telegraphic.   FOREIGN OFFICE, *December 2, 1895.*

I HAVE just repeated to you a telegram from Her Majesty's Ambassador at Constantinople, No. 764, of to-day, stating that his French colleague has received no instructions on the subject of the Ambassadors' proposal that a delay should be fixed for compliance with their demand for Firmans for second "stationnaires," after which measures should be taken to secure the concession of a right which is formally recognized by the Treaties.

I request that you will communicate with the Minister of Foreign Affairs, and urge that M. Cambon be authorized to act in concert with his colleagues in this matter.

F. O. 424/184, p. 354, No. 646

No. 663

Sir E. Monson to the Marquess of Salisbury.

No. 101.   VIENNA, *December 3, 1895.*
Telegraphic.   *(Received December 4.)*
WITH reference to the telegram received from your Lordship No. 92, I have the honour to report that Count Goluchowski had been informed of the nature of your Lordship's observations by the Austro-Hungarian Ambassador in London.

Count Goluchowski is of opinion that the Sultan cannot remain obstinate now that the reiteration of the demand for Firmans is agreed to by Russia.

It is probable that His Majesty's definite decision will be known within the next forty-eight hours. It will then be time for the Cabinets to consult as to further action if it is a refusal.

(The following is confidential.)
To the above remarks his Excellency added that Russia feared the consequences of leaving a free hand to England, and that she had undoubtedly foreseen that she would do so if she broke up the European concert.

F. O. 424/184, p. 361, No. 655

No. 664

Sir E. Monson to the Marquess of Salisbury.

No. 102.   VIENNA, *December 3, 1895.*
Telegraphic.   *(Received December 4.)*
THE report, alleged to be current at Athens, to the effect that the Austro-Hungarian Government have been requested by the Sultan not to send their squadron to Salonica is entirely untrue. They do not intend to send it to that port.

F. O. 424/184, p. 361, No. 656

No. 665

The Marquess of Salisbury to Sir P. Currie.

No. 249.
Telegraphic.   FOREIGN OFFICE, *December 4, 1895, 5.30 p.m.*
I REPEATED to Her Majesty's Ambassador at Paris your telegram No. 764 of the 2nd instant respecting the application of the Ambassadors of Firmans for

second "stationnaires," and I instructed his Excellency to speak to the Acting Minister for Foreign Affairs, and urge that M. Cambon should be authorized to act in concert with his colleagues in this matter.

Lord Dufferin has spoken on the subject to M. Ricard, who stated that he must ask for a short delay in order to acquaint himself with the elements of the question.

F. O. 424/184, p. 362, No. 657

No. 666

Sir E. Monson to the Marquess of Salisbury.

No. 356.   VIENNA, *December 4, 1895.*
My Lord,   *(Received December 7.)*

IN a conversation which I had yesterday with Count Goluchowski, his Excellency said that now that Russia had again placed herself completely in line with the other Powers in regard to reiterating the demand for the Firmans for second "stationnaires," it was impossible for the Sultan to continue his refusal to accede to it.

His Ottoman Majesty's obstinacy on this point seemed due, said his Excellency, not only to the promptings of Izzet Bey, the Prefect of Police, but to his own superstitious dread of the possible consequences to his own person, founded on the fact that a similar concession on the part of Abdul Aziz was very quickly followed by that Sultan's tragic end.

Count Goluchowski, however, feels so persuaded that the Sultan must now give way, that he declares that it would be absolutely premature to discuss what is to be done in the opposite event.

Referring to the action of the French Government, his Excellency said that he had reason to believe that their views in regard to the repetition of the demand for Firmans had all along been in accord with those of the majority of the Powers.

I have, &c.

(Signed) EDMUND MONSON.

F. O. 424/184, p. 367, No. 667

No. 667

Sir P. Currie to the Marquess of Salisbury.

No. 772.   CONSTANTINOPLE, *December 5, 1895, 3.15 p.m.*
Telegraphic.   *(Received December 5.)*

HER Majesty's Vice-Consul at Mush has sent me the following telegram:-

"The Mutessarif begs me to say that his chief difficulty in dealing with the Kurds comes from the fact that he has no command of military forces. He expresses entire disbelief in Shakir Pasha, especially with regard to his recent telegram putting all the blame on the Haideranli Kurds. The Private Secretary of the Mutessarif, whilst dining with me to-night, begged me semi-officially on behalf of his chief to state that the entire blame for any miscarriage of justice in connection with the recent riots in Mush rests with the Cadi, who also constitutes the chief danger of possible future disturbances. I believe that this remark is fully justified."

F. O. 424/184, p. 363, No. 664

No. 668

Sir P. Currie to the Marquess of Salisbury.

No. 773.   CONSTANTINOPLE, *December 5, 1895, 3.10 p.m.*
Telegraphic.   *(Received December 5.)*

HER Majesty's Consul at Aleppo telegraphs that the Commandant of Marash has been removed from the control of the Ferik, and placed under the direct control of the Palace. In consequence of the Minister for Foreign Affairs having informed me that the Zeitounlis had killed all the Turks still remaining prisoners in their hands, I sent a telegram to Mr. Barnham, asking whether this was true. Mr. Barnham now replies that they have killed seven of their prisoners, and have refused to receive the Commission.

F. O. 424/184, pp. 363-364, No. 665

No. 669

Sir P. Currie to the Marquess of Salisbury.

No. 775.   CONSTANTINOPLE, *December 5, 1895, 7.55 p.m.*
Telegraphic.   *(Received December 5.)*

MY telegram No. 767 of yesterday.

It appeared at to-day's meeting of Ambassadors that my French and Russian colleagues had not yet received any instructions as to the second "stationnaires," and they were therefore unwilling to discuss the question.

F. O. 424/184, p. 364, No. 667

No. 670

Sir P. Currie to the Marquess of Salisbury.

No. 776.   CONSTANTINOPLE, *December 5, 1895, 8 p.m.*
Telegraphic.   *(Received December 5.)*

NOTWITHSTANDING the assurance of the Sultan, the massacres in Asia Minor still continue. At the Ambassadors' meeting to-day I suggested the adoption of some such step as the dispatch of our Military Attachés to hold an investigation. My colleagues did not seem to give much support to my suggestion, and the Russian Ambassador, who is evidently instructed to oppose all joint action, distinctly discouraged it.

F. O. 424/184, p. 364, No. 668

No. 671

Sir P. Currie to the Marquess of Salisbury.

No. 897.   CONSTANTINOPLE, *December 5, 1895.*
My Lord,   *(Received December 9.)*

I HAVE the honour to report to your Lordship that I have been informed by Mr. Cobb, the British Postmaster at Constantinople, that on the 2nd instant he stamped "Interdit" and returned to London seven heavy packets of the Armenian publication, the "Hinchag," printed on red paper.

The number was dated the 20th November, and there must have been several hundred copies.

Mr. Cobb believes that if the "Hinchag" has hitherto been introduced into Turkey in large quantities, it must have been by some other means, as he does not remember having ever seen any in the Post Office.

I avail, &c.

(Signed) PHILIP CURRIE.

F. O. 424/184, p. 381, No. 694

No. 672

Sir P. Currie to the Marquess of Salisbury.

No. 778.   CONSTANTINOPLE, *December 6, 1895, 11.30 a.m.*
Telegraphic.   *(Received December 6.)*

MY telegram No. 751 of the 26th November.

Her Majesty's Vice-Consul at Van sent me the following telegram, dated the 3rd December:-

"Shakir Pasha's remarks about the Kurds have no special point just now, as they apply to a state of things existing for years past. It is, of course, possible that some Persian Kurds have crossed the frontier, but it is the Turkish Kurds who have done practically all the mischief. Things are rather quieter about here now."

F. O. 424/184, p. 366, No. 673

No. 673

The Marquess of Salisbury to Sir E. Monson.

No. 96.

Telegraphic. FOREIGN OFFICE, *December 6, 1895.*

THE following is very confidential.

From the intelligence that reaches Her Majesty's Government as to the attitude of the other Powers in the question of the second "stationnaires" at Constantinople, it appears that the Russian Ambassador has instructions not to take any joint action, that the French officiating Minister for Foreign Affairs refuses to send the French Ambassador any instructions tending to action, and that the German Ambassador is instructed as far as possible to avoid moving in the matter.

I should be glad if your Excellency could ascertain what is the view taken of the present position of the question by the Austro-Hungarian Minister for Foreign Affairs.

F. O. 424/184, p. 367, No. 676

No. 674

Sir P. Currie to the Marquess of Salisbury.

No. 904. CONSTANTINOPLE, *December 7, 1895.*

My Lord, *(Received December 16.)*

WITH reference to my despatch No. 876 of the 29th November, I have the honour to forward to your Lordship herewith copy of a despatch which I have received from Her Majesty's Consul at Trebizond, reporting on the situation at Samsoun.

I have, &c.

(Signed) PHILIP CURRIE.

F. O. 424/184, p. 404, No. 735

Inclosure 1 in No. 674

Consul Longworth to Sir P. Currie.

Sir,   TREBIZOND, *November 26, 1895.*
    IN mine of the 20th instant copy of a despatch from our Consular Agent at
Samsoun was annexed.
    On the following day I received a telegram from him worded thus:-
    "Reçu lettre.
    "Vous communiquerai renseignements demandés par prochain. Panique très
grande, mais, grâce mesures prises, Gouverneur espère encore aucun accident. Je
demande, pour tranquilliser esprits, faire afficher une Proclamation claire et nette
faisant bien comprendre intention Gouvernement. Gouverneur répondu
outrepasser ses droits. Obtenez cela du Vali. Juge cette mesure indispensable.
Vous confirme cette dépêche par lettre."
    The contents of this telegram, together with that of the despatch, will account,
I hope, for my having on its receipt wired to the Embassy in the sense that
disturbances were apprehended at Samsoun, that full discretionary power should
be allowed to its Governor, and that a ship of war was desirable there without
removing the one here.
    The Vali, I need scarcely say, granted at once the permission required, and I
have this day received the following telegram from Mr. de Cortanze:-
    "Proclamation à la population pour maintien ordre affichée dans toute la ville.
L'effet produit excellent."
    Copy and translation of the Notice referred to therein as posted up at Samsoun
is herewith inclosed for your Excellency's perusal. The Russian gun-boat
"Uraletz," I further understand, is on her way there, while her sister ship "Teretz"
returned here last night—after coaling at Batoum.
    Allow me, before ending, to make a few remarks of an explanatory character. I
should not like it to be supposed that I have given the question undue importance
and urgency. My opinion has always been that no serious disturbances were
possible without the connivance of the authorities. It is an opinion which I
expressed clearly enough in my despatch of the 2nd July. The sad events which
have since happened have not tended greatly to modify this impression. I, indeed,
still hold to the belief that the Turks are by nature and precept obedient, law-
abiding, and orderly. This was sufficiently proved on the occasion of the Armenian
demonstration reported in my despatches of the 25th and 27th May. The blame of
wholesale massacres must therefore rest with the governing classes, in whose hands
the people are mere tools, sharpened or blunted according to political exigencies
and personal interests. It follows from this that the majority of the officials are
wanting in humane sentiments; there are, however, others, though in small
minority, who, if encouraged, could keep the unscrupulous within bounds. Our

aim must therefore be to weaken the hands of the bad and strengthen those of the good. This was one of my objects, but I had another in venturing to suggest the dispatch of a war-vessel to Samsoun and the investment of the Governor there with absolute power. It is the potent reason that, should a riot break out in that town, the safety of the Christians along the whole coast would be affected by arousing into activity those violent passions which are kept at present with such difficulty in check.

I have, &c.

(Signed) H. Z. LONGWORTH.

F. O. 424/184, pp. 404-405, No. 735/1

Inclosure 2 in No. 674

Official Proclamation.

Translation.

IT is the wish of His Imperial Majesty the Sultan that all his subjects and other inhabitants under his Imperial protection should live in peace, confidence, and tranquillity. The Imperial wish is emphatically reiterated by several Imperial Orders and Decrees. Whoever, therefore, of whatever class or religion, attempts the live, honour, or property of any one, in opposition to the Sheri and Imperial will, shall, according to the orders of His Imperial Majesty, be punished severely and summarily. The local authorities, having taken all measures for the maintenance of public peace by appointing and establishing patrols and guard-houses with Imperial soldiers, are watching attentively even the most insignificant movement of the people. Hence every one must set aside fear and excitement, and live like before, honestly and honourably attending to his own work and business. This we officially declare in the name of the local authorities.

(Signed) HAMDI,
The Mutessarif of Djanik.

SAMSOUN, *November 10 (22), 1895.*
F. O. 424/184, p. 405, No. 735/2

No. 675

Sir P. Currie to the Marquess of Salisbury.

No. 909.   CONSTANTINOPLE, *December 9, 1895.*
My Lord,   *(Received December 16.)*

I HAVE the honour to transmit herewith copy of a communication which I, in common with the other Embassies, have received from the Armenian Patriarch, stating that the Patriarchate has no information respecting a rumoured demonstration of Armenians at Constantinople, disclaiming all responsibility for such a demonstration, and requesting that the influence of Her Majesty's Embassy may be directed towards preventing the recurrence of the unhappy events which followed the last demonstration.

In acknowledging the receipt of the Patriarch's communication I have informed his Beatitude that the influence of Her Majesty's Embassy is unceasingly exerted for the object he mentions.

The letter will be considered at the next meeting of Ambassadors, which will take place to-morrow.

I have, &c.

(Signed) PHILIP CURRIE.

F. O. 424/184, p. 409, No. 740

Inclosure in No. 675

The Armenian Patriarch to Sir P. Currie.

M. l'Ambassadeur,   CONSTANTINOPLE, *le 25 Novembre (7 Décembre), 1895.*

IL nous a été part d'un bruit parvenu aux Ambassades d'aprés lequel les Arméniens prépareraient une manifestation à Constantinople, et il nous a été demandé de faire ce qui serait necessaire pour la prévenir.

Considérant d'une part qu'avant les incidents de 18 (30) Septembre, une recommandation semblable nous a été faite par la Sublime Porte et que sans tenir compte de notre résponse, on a cherché à faire retomber sur nous les responsabilités, de l'autre, que ces incidents ont servi de raison aux horribles massacres accompagnés de pillage et d'incendie qui se continuent encore dans les provinces, nous regardons comme le devoir sacré de notre conscience et de notre mission de prier votre Excellence qu'elle veuille bien considérer que sauf les rumeurs en question, nous n'avons aucune information touchant les préparations d'une manifestation quelconque, ni ses auteurs, et si malheureusement le bruit communiqué est fondé, nous exprimons le regret que nos moyens seuls, purement moraux, ne suffisent nullement, eu égard surtout aux douloureuses coujonctures actuelles, à amener le résultat désiré.

Il incombe aux autorités de remplir leur devoir avec la prudence et la sagesse nécessaires pour qu'il ne se produise rien de contraire à l'ordre et que, par-dessus tout, les désastres qui ont frappé la nation ne se renouvellent pas.

Pour nous, nous implorons de votre Excellence la grâce d'user de sa haute et tutélaire influence pour prévenir le retour de nouveaux malheurs.

Invoquant des bénédictions, &c.

(Signé) Madtéos,
Le Patriarche des Arméniens de Turquie.

F. O. 424/184, p. 409, No. 740/1

No. 676

Sir P. Currie to the Marquess of Salisbury.

No. 785.
Telegraphic.   CONSTANTINOPLE, *December 10, 1895, 3.15 p.m.*
SULTAN has given way about "stationnaires" in consequence of representations of Russian Ambassador.

Admiral has been informed, and has been asked to make arrangements.

F. O. 424/184, p. 385, No. 701

No. 677

Sir P. Currie to the Marquess of Salisbury.

No. 786.
Telegraphic.   CONSTANTINOPLE, *December 10, 1895, 10 p.m.*
WITH reference to my immediately preceding telegram, I have the honour to inform your Lordship that, at the meeting of Ambassadors to-day, the question was raised as to when we should call up the "stationnaires." On my stating that I had already telegraphed for the "Dryad," my Austrian, French, and Italian colleagues said that they would follow my example, but the Russian Ambassador said that it might not be convenient for the Russian "stationnaire" to be ordered to come at once.

F. O. 424/184, p. 386, No. 702

No. 678

Sir P. Currie to the Marquess of Salisbury.

No. 787.   CONSTANTINOPLE, *December 10, 1895, 10.20 p.m.*
Telegraphic.   *(Received December 10.)*

AT to-day's meeting of Ambassadors, I insisted on the necessity of something being done with regard to the massacres and pillage in Asia Minor.

I proposed that we should recommend our Governments to appoint an International Commission, which should proceed to the spot, investigate what has taken place, arrange for the restitution of the plunder to the rightful owners, and point out the guilty for punishment.

In the subsequent discussion of my proposal, my views were supported by my Austrian and Italian colleagues, but M. de Nélidoff said that, according to his instructions, the concert of the Powers only applied to measures for the protection of foreigners, and he had therefore no authority to discuss the question.

He suggested instead that we should address further representations to the Porte, but had to admit the utter futility of any such proceeding.

Finally, he said that if my proposal were adopted by Her Majesty's Government, and a formal proposal made by them to the Cabinets for the appointment of an International Commission, the question would no doubt be referred to us, and we should then be able to discuss it.

The necessity of taking some action was admitted by all, but nobody made any other suggestion, except that we should draw up a Tabular Statement in common from the information in the possession of the various Embassies, and this we agreed to do.

If this idea of an International Commission of Inquiry were actually carried out, the mere presence of European Commissioners in the disturbed districts would not fail to do good, as we have seen how valuable the influence of Consular officers, wherever they were stationed, has been. But the mere proposal, if it had not other result, would at all events frighten the Sultan into taking more strenuous action himself.

F. O. 424/184, p. 386, No. 703

No. 679

Memorandum communicated by Morel Bey, December 11, 1895.

UN Iradé Impérial autorise le passage par les Détroits des seconds stationnaires que les Ambassades ont demandé à faire venir à Constantinople, à la condition que leur séjour ici sera provisoire, et que leurs formes, forces, et dimensions seront les mêmes que celles des bâtiments qui stationnent déjà dans la capitale, et lesquelles ont toujours été, d'après les Traités et suivant l'usage, bien définies.

Il va sans dire que cette autorisation spéciale ne devra affecter en aucune manière le droit de Gouvernement Impérial, consacré par les Traités, au sujet de la fermeture des Détroits de Bosphore et des Dardanelles aux bâtiments de guerre étrangers, droit qui est et demeure comme par le passé strictement intact.

Il va sans dire également que les seconds stationnaires en question ne franchiront pas en bloc les Détroits, et que chacun d'eux devra entrer isolément et à des époques séparées, après que les Ambassades auront, suivant l'usage, présenté à la Sublime Porte les listes des noms, dimensions, et autres des bâtiments précités, et obtenu chacune le Firman d'autorisation de son navire.

F. O. 424/184, p. 387, No. 705 ·

No. 680

Sir P. Currie to the Marquess of Salisbury.

No. 920.   CONSTANTINOPLE, *December, 11, 1895.*
My Lord,   *(Received December 16.)*

I HAVE the honour to inclose a translation of a placard which has been widely circulated in Constantinople.

It appears to represent the views generally entertained by Mussulmans of every class. But I do not see any probability at present of active steps being taken by the Sultan's subjects to depose him. The Turks seem unable to carry out a combined plan of action, and they have no leaders. The precautions taken by the Sultan for his own safety appear, moreover, to make any direct attack upon him hopeless.

The only plan of which I have heard which seems to offer any chance of success is that some member of the Imperial family should be proclaimed Sultan in Stamboul, and that Abdul Hamid should be left to his own devices at Yildiz. But it would be essential to success that the army should first be gained over, and although there is undoubtedly much discontent among the officers, there is no reason to suppose that the men would not remain faithful to the reigning Sovereign.

I have been informed on very good authority that the Sultan gave privately as his real reason for refusing the new "stationnaires" that they might cut him off from Stamboul. It is probably that a movement such as I have mentioned may have been in his mind, and that he feared that if it took place the foreign vessels would station themselves in the Golden Horn, and prevent the access of his troops to Stamboul across the bridges.

I have, &c.

(Signed) PHILIP CURRIE.

F. O. 424/184, p. 423, No. 749

Inclosure in No. 680

Placard.

Traduction.

Compatriotes!

La patrie se perd et se sacrifie pour le plaisir d'une personne. Nos âmes et nos biens sont en danger. La cruauté et l'absolutisme minent et mettent en déroute notre pays. Le peuple depuis la dernière guerre n'a pas pu se remettre encore. Le Padichah, au lieu d'améliorer la situation des paysans affamés et nus, ne s'efforce qu'à s'emparer de leurs terres ainsi que de leurs bœufs, moyen de leur existence. Il accapare les droits de la nation. Il souille sa dignité et son honneur. Il tue les hommes et philanthropes dans les prisons, à l'exil et en les torturant par des chaînes. Il exil et fair mourir de chagrin ceux qui demandent la Constitution pour le salut et le bonheur de la patrie ainsi que pour la tranquillité générale. La souveraineté d'un Padichah qui se conduit contrairement au Chéri et à la loi qui ne pense qu'à son bonheur et `son plaisir, qui gaspille annuellement 3,000,000 de livres de la nation pour les espions et les flatteurs, ne peut pas être légitime. Continuerons-nous encore à obéir à ceux qui détruisent la patrie? Continuerons-nous encore à nous fléchir le cou à ceux qui sucent le sang de la nation? Continuerons-nous encore à voir patiemment ceux qui aiment la patrie et qui travaillent à l'amélioration de l'adminstration actuelle être avilis et tourmentés? Il est vrai que tout le monde voit cet énorme danger. Chacun, à l'exception de ceux qui profitent du pillage, se plaint contre le Gouvernement actuel. Mais, vi l'absence d'accord entre nous, la plainte reste ensevelie et ne produit aucun son. Unissons-nous, au lieu de rester misérables et méprisables en gardant le silence. Formons des Comités composés des Ulémas, des Chefs Militaires, et des dignitaires du Gouvernement, sans distinction de nationalité et de religion. Envoyons des députations aux Valis et à la Sublime Porte. Faisons savoir la situation et l'opinion des Osmanlis. Obligeons le Padichah à agir conformément au Chéri et à la loi. Que notre plus grand chef soit la loi et la justice. Nous n'avons point l'intention de provoquer le monde à des massacres et à des insurrections et de faire une distinction entre les Musulmans et les Chrétiens. Tant que la discorde existe, on ne peut prévenir la cruauté et l'absolutisme. On ne peut pas s'imaginer un Gouvernement despotique qui puisse résister devant l'Union. Les militaires ne sont des bourreaux. Il ne tirent pas sur leurs compatriotes et leurs frères. Un Souverain cruel ne peut jamais donner de son propre désir une liberté à ses sujets. Nous avons droit à la liberté. Demandons ce droit. Exigeons instamment une réunion composée des gens bien renseignés sur la situation et des philanthropes et la nomination des hommes possédant les faveurs du peuple, l'honnêteté, la capacité et le zéle à la tête des affaires du Gouvernement. Si le Padichah qui accepte l'humiliation et la bassesse de se mettre sous le joug des étrangers sans daigner demander le concours d'une Commission composée des enfants de la patrie, refuse la présente demande qui est faite au nom des intérêts et du salut de tous les Osmanlis, dans ce cas, enlevons d'une autre manière les souillures approtées au nom de notre nation.

Que l'union, la persévérance, et le courage soient les compagnons de notre conduite.

(Comité Ottoman du Progrès et de l'Union.)

F. O. 424/184, pp. 423-424, No. 749/1

No. 681

Sir P. Currie to the Marquess of Salisbury.

No. 921.   CONSTANTINOPLE, *December, 11, 1895.*
My Lord,   *(Received December 16.)*

IN continuation of my despatch No. 908 of the 8th instant, I have the honour to state that at the meeting of Ambassadors which was held at the French Embassy yesterday, I called the attention of my colleagues to the continuance of massacres and pillage in the provinces of Asia Minor, and asked whether, in their opinion, we were not bound to take some steps to put an end to such a state of things.

The Austrian Ambassador spoke in favour of a discussion of the question, and expressed in eloquent terms his view of the responsibility that would fall upon us if we remained indifferent to what was taking place.

The Italian Ambassador followed in the same sense, and read an interesting letter from a Turkish officer to his friends in Constantinople, of which I am forwarding a copy in another despatch, and which gives a vivid picture of the state of the country, and of the wholesale slaughter carried on by the Kurds.

M. de Nélidoff was strongly pressed to state his views, and, while admitting the gravity of the situation, said the only suggestion he could offer was that we should press the Porte for a reply to the communication made by the Ambassadors more than a month ago, and should ask what steps were being taken.

I pointed out that such a representation would have no satisfactory results, that we should only receive in reply the usual denials and fictitious accounts of the events which were taking place.

I urged the necessity, for our own credit, and that of our Governments, of taking some more decided steps. The fact that the six Ambassadors were acting in concert had been widely proclaimed, and public opinion would, I thought, look for some results of our co-operation.

The only means, in my opinion, of exercising any control under existing circumstances was by the presence of Europeans on the spot; the salutary influence exerted by the Consuls proved this; and I cited the cases of Mush and Van, where, owing mainly to Messrs. Hampson and Hallward, there had been no outbreaks.

I suggested that we might recommend to our Governments the appointment of an International Commission, which should make an investigation on the spot, should point out the persons responsible for the massacres with a view to punishment being inflicted on them, and should devise means for restoring to those who had been robbed such property as could be recovered.

M. de Nélidoff replied that a proposal such as I had suggested could not properly be recommended by the Ambassadors, but must be initiated by the Cabinets. He added that, so far as he was concerned, his instructions did not authorize him to act in concert with the other Ambassadors for any purpose except that of securing the safety of the foreign colonies in Constantinople and its neighbourhood. He admitted that the presence of an International Commission would be beneficial if it could be carried out, but he saw great difficulties in the way, especially at this season of the year. He added, however, that if Her Majesty's Government were on my suggestion to make a proposal to the Cabinets, it would, no doubt, be referred to the Representatives here, who would then be at liberty to discuss it with their colleagues.

On the suggestion of M. Cambon it was agreed that a tabular statement of the places where massacres had taken place, with the numbers of those who were believed to have perished, and such particulars as we possessed of the conduct of the authorities, should be drawn up. For this purpose it was arranged that one of the Secretaries of each Embassy should be deputed to meet his colleagues, and that all the information in the possession of the various embassies should be combined in one document, which would serve as a basis for further communication to the Porte.

Beyond this co-operation in setting forth the facts, it is clear that there will be no concerted action of the Ambassadors in regard to the troubles in Anatolia unless your Lordship should see fit to make some proposal to the Powers. Should the plan I have suggested meet with your approval, it would at any rate serve as a basis for discussion.

There may be insurmountable difficulties in carrying it out, but the mere mention of it would have a salutary effect on the Sultan, and might induce him to take more effective measures than he has hitherto done for the restoration of order and security.

It must be borne in mind that since the commencement of the disturbances in the Asiatic provinces no Turkish officer, civil or military, has been punished for the outrages inflicted on the Christians. Some few officials have been dismissed in consequence of our representations, but they have been subsequently appointed to other offices, or have had decorations conferred upon them.

The President of the Bible House, in the Report which I forwarded to your Lordship in my despatch No. 869, stated his belief that 300,000 Christians are in a state of entire destitution.

This estimate may be an exaggerated one, but there can be no doubt that there will be a terrible loss of life by starvation if steps are not promptly taken to provide the destitute population with necessaries, and to restore the property of which they have been plundered.

I have, &c.

(Signed) PHILIP CURRIE.

F. O. 424/184, pp. 424-425, No. 750

No. 682

Sir P. Currie to the Marquess of Salisbury.

No. 792.   CONSTANTINOPLE, *December, 13, 1895, 1.50 p.m.*
Telegraphic.   *(Received December 13.)*

I AM informed that, by order of the Sultan, reports are being drawn up for publication, proving that, during the massacres in the Anatolian provinces, more Mussulmans were killed than Christians.

F. O. 424/184, p. 391, No. 716

No. 683

Sir P. Currie to the Marquess of Salisbury.

No. 801.   CONSTANTINOPLE, *December 16, 1895.*
Telegraphic.   *(Received December 16.)*
   FRENCH, Russian, Italian, and Austrian "stationnaires" have now arrived.
F. O. 424/184, p. 427, No. 754

No. 684

Sir P. Currie to the Marquess of Salisbury.

No. 803. Confidential.   CONSTANTINOPLE, *December 16, 1895, 11 p.m.*
Telegraphic.   *(Received December 16.)*
   IN a conversation which Costaki Pasha had with the Sultan, in consequence of
my having warned his Excellency that he would find in England a strong feeling
about the massacres, His Majesty informed him that he intended to appoint a
Commission to inquire into them, that this Commission would be composed of
persons inspiring the highest confidence, and that His Majesty himself would be its
President.
   I pressed for names, and was informed that Musurus Bey, formerly
Ambassador at Rome, was the only one selected. He is quite incapable, and it was
obviously the idea that his name would be popular in England which caused him to
be suggested.
   It cannot be doubted that this Commission will not be less shadowy than most
of the others appointed here.
F. O. 424/184, p. 427, No. 755

No. 685

Sir P. Currie to the Marquess of Salisbury.

No. 925.   CONSTANTINOPLE, *December 13, 1895.*
My Lord,   *(Received December 23.)*
   I HAVE the honour to forward to your Lordship herewith extract from a
private letter which I have received from Her Majesty's Consul acting at
Erzeroum, respecting the state of affairs in that town.
                              I have, &c.
                                           (Signed) PHILIP CURRIE.

F. O. 424/184, p. 442, No. 782

Inclosure in No. 685

Acting Consul Cumberbatch to Sir P. Currie.

Private.
Extract. *Undated.*

MY mediation between Mgr. Shishmanian and the two Pashas has succeeded, and they have "shaken hands" but the game of the latter appears to be to ignore that Prelate's right to represent and interfere on behalf of the Armenian community, except in matters purely spiritual. They will deal with the leading men of the place, and have already commenced *pourparlers*. Some eight of them were induced to telegraph to the Patriarch for the Archbishop's removal, but without effect, so there is virtually a split in the Armenian camp, which for their sakes is to be regretted, but then there never was unity among them.

As to reforms, nothing is heard about their introduction.

Shakir's visit to Khinis was too late. One or two tribes of Kurds there had refrained from attacking some four or five villages, and he recommended them for decorations forthwith, only to find out from me on his return here that their abstention had been paid for at the price of 200*l*. He was somewhat disgusted.

I hear to-day that the Americans have started relief funds, and have wired to the missionary here (Chambers) to dispose of 100*l*. at once. Are we going to do anything in this line?

Funds are at a very low ebb in Turkish provincial coffers, and I don't see how they are going to defray their extra military expenses. Unless it is in view of foreign complications, there was no necessity for the hurried mobilization of the Reserves. The regular troops would be able to tackle the Kurds if business in that quarter was really meant, and as for the Armenians, they haven't got a "kick" in them.

F. O. 424/184, p. 442, No. 782/1

No. 686

Sir P. Currie to the Marquess of Salisbury.

No. 927. PERA, *December 13, 1895.*
My Lord, *(Received December 23.)*

WITH reference to my despatch No. 926, forwarding a Report from Mr. Barnham of events which took place at Aintab, in the Vilayet of Aleppo, on the 16th and 17th ultimo, I have the honour to state that Mr. Terrell, United States' Minister, has to-day shown me a Report from Mr. Sanders, an American missionary at Aintab, giving a favourable report of the protection afforded to the missionaires and to the college and girls' school at Aintab by the Turkish troops during the disturbances. He also speaks very highly of the conduct of two Mussulman Aghas in watching over their safety.

Mr. Sanders does not allude to the use of bombs and vitriol ascribed to the Armenians by Mr. Barnham's canvass. He estimates the dead as over 300 in number. Many of the wounded were brought to the American hospital, and were treated by the Mission doctors, of whom several are ladies.

The strong representations made by Mr. Terrell have produced a good result so far as the missionaries are concerned, and none of them have been injured during the massacres in the Asiatic provinces; but Mr Terrell speaks of the conduct of the Aghas and soldiers at Aintab as the one bright spot in a terrible record of slaughter. He has expressed his acknowledgment to the Turkish Government.

I have, &c.

(Signed) PHILIP CURRIE.

F. O. 424/184, p. 450, No. 784

No. 687

Sir P. Currie to the Marquess of Salisbury.

No. 928.   CONSTANTINOPLE, *December 13, 1895.*
My Lord,   *(Received December 23.)*

WITH reference to my despatch No. 872 of the 27th November, I have the honour to forward to your Lordship herewith copy of a despatch which I have received from Her Majesty's Consul acting at Erzeroum, transmitting a despatch from Her Majesty's Vice-Consul at Mush reporting the recent attempt by Moslems to massacre Armenians in that town, and its prompt suppression by the Mutessarif.

I have, &c.

(Signed) PHILIP CURRIE.

F. O. 424/184, p. 451, No. 785

Inclosure 1 in No. 687

Consul Cumberbatch to Sir P. Currie.

Sir,   ERZEROUM, *November 25, 1895.*

WITH reference to my despatch of the 20th instant, I have the honour to transmit a copy of a despatch from Mr. Vice-Consul Hampson, reporting the attempt at a massacre of Armenians at Mush on the 15th instant, which was frustrated by the energetic and courageous conduct of Féham Pasha, the

Mutessarif. I also hear that Brigadier-General Ahmed Pasha, the Military Commander, and the Mufti, acted well on that occasion.

I have, &c.

(Signed) H. A. CUMBERBATCH.

F. O. 424/184, p. 451, No. 785/1

Inclosure 2 in No. 687

Vice-Consul Hampson to Consul Cumberbatch.

Sir,
MUSH, *November 16, 1895.*

I HAVE the honour to report that some of the lower Mussulmans started a massacre of the Armenians in this town yesterday morning. Thanks, however, to the prompt action of the authorities, and especially to the energy and personal courage of the Mutessarif, order was restored in little over half-an-hour.

The following account of the origin of the disturbance I have from an Armenian boy in my service, who was in the market at the time, and narrowly escaped being cut down. He and some thirty other Armenians were saved by a Turkish "han" keeper, Mourad by name, who took them in and boldly held the door against the mob. I caused the boy to repeat his statement to the Mufti when the latter called on me yesterday evening.

About 11 A.M. the sound of a pistol-shot was heard from the shop of an Armenian locksmith of rather bad character. It is said that the pistol went off by accident. It seems not improbable that it was a preconcerted signal, especially when it is remembered that it was Friday morning, and that this was, according to Mr. Knapp's account, exactly the manner in which the Bitlis massacre was started. Moreover, the man has been arrested, and is said to have confessed that he fired the pistol in obedience to the orders of certain Turks. However this may be, directly the shot was heard a crowd of armed Mussulmans rushed into the market, shooting and cutting down any Armenians they met. Luckily, the latter were on their guard, and comparatively few were in the streets. My servant saw three cut down: one by a Softa, who, after running his sword through the body, drank the blood, a second by a Turkish butcher, and a third by a young Turk. Then the soldiers came. The Mutessarif himself rode into the market and gave orders to the troops to shoot any man, Mussulman or Christian, who attacked a person or a shop, and the mob was dispersed. My servant then returned home, guarded by a zaptieh. Meanwhile, the riot had spread more or less all over the town, and shots were heard on every side. Two Armenians running past my house fell, one shot, the other cut down. However, very shortly patrols appeared in every direction; the Mutessarif himself scemed to be everywhere, dispersing the rioters and reassuring the Armenians, and soon everything was quiet again.

Up to this evening six deaths are known to have resulted, and there are about forty wounded, most of them not seriously. They are all Armenians.

About twenty Mussulmans, including two zaptiehs, have been arrested for taking part in the riot, and the Government is making a strict inquiry.

Of the conduct of the Mutessarif I cannot speak too highly, and I trust that it will be recognized in the proper quarter. I was an eye-witness of his riding, attended only by one zaptieh, into a crowd of Softas and dispersing them with blows of his whip. He told the Armenians that he must be killed before they were. Undoubtedly, but for him, a repetition of the Bitlis affair, perhaps even on a more serious scale, would have occurred. As soon as order was restored he came and rested at my house, evidently very indignant at such an attempt having been made, the possibility of which, being newly arrived here, he had, in spite of warnings, refused to admit.

The measures taken by the military authorities to provide against such an emergency seem also to have been excellent. The soldiers were in the market in a very short time, and not more than twenty minutes had elapsed since the first shot before a guard was at my door and patrols everywhere.

I trust that this will have been a lesson to the evilly-disposed that the authorities do not intend to allow disorders here, and that no further attempt will be made.

The better class Mussulmans behaved very well in saving life, and I hope that an improvement in the relations between the Christian and Mussulman inhabitants may result from yesterday's experiences.

Immediately after the riot the Mutessarif took measures to inform the neighbouring villages of the true facts, in order to prevent excessive panic. An example of his prompt and wise conduct is that, through me, he begged the missionaries to write to Sasun and give the people there the true story, telling them to keep quiet and not fear. The messenger, an Armenian of Sasun, was sent off at once under the escort of two zaptiehs.

All has been quiet here to-day, though naturally there is great uneasiness.

I have, &c.

(Signed) CHARLES S. HAMPSON.

P.S. *November 20.*—There has been no further attempt at disorder so far, but no shops are open, and there is considerable discontent among certain classes of the Mussulmans because the Mutessarif acted with such energy last Friday.

C. S. H.

F. O. 424/184, pp. 451-452, No. 785/2

No. 688

Sir P. Currie to the Marquess of Salisbury.

No. 926.   CONSTANTINOPLE, *December 14, 1895.*
My Lord,   *(Received December 23.)*

I HAVE the honour to transmit to your Lordship herewith two despatches from Mr. Barnham on the massacres which have occured at Marash, Aintab, and other places in the Vilayet of Aleppo.

It is, I think, evident that the authorities of this province behaved in a different manner from those in the six vilayets named in the scheme of reforms, and have exerted themselves to prevent massacres. If this view is correct, it would confirm the view generally entertained that in the six vilayets the officials received orders from Constantinople for the destruction of the Armenian population.

I have, &c.

(Signed) PHILIP CURRIE.

F. O. 424/184, pp. 442-443, No. 783

Inclosure 1 in No. 688

Consul Barnham to Sir P. Currie.

Confidential.
Sir,   ALEPPO, *November 24, 1895.*

I HAVE the honour to submit herewith, for the information of Her Majesty's Government, a Report upon the massacres which have recently occurred in this Consular district.

Events have succeeded each other so rapidly that I have hitherto restricted myself to a free use of the telegraph, trusting that within a reasonable time I should find leisure to write a full and accurate Report. I have, however, found so great a difficulty in communicating with the scenes of disturbance that I cannot venture to call this a complete narrative of what has taken place. Very much unquestionably remains to be told.

The authorities, fearing to increase the general panic by allowing the news to spread, have withheld the delivery of the post from Urfa, Aintab, and Marash. Special messengers bearing letters addressed to myself and to the American Vice-Consul have been arrested and imprisoned, and my letters restored to me after so long delay, and in such a condition, as to warrant the belief that they have been opened. Friends at the various Missions, apprised of these facts, and unwilling to expose their messengers to ill-treatment, are deterred from writing frequently. They are compelled to write by post, trusting that their letters will ultimately be delivered, and, moreover, to write in cypher. Telegrams received by private individuals are valueless, as they are subject to the Censure, and nothing allowed to pass which has not the approval of the Government. These difficulties are enhanced by the wild rumours fabricated in the city, especially by the Christians and Jews, whose brains appear to have become addled by fear. Nine-tenths of the reports which reach me by word of mouth are senseless, and without a shadow of foundation.

One source of information has always been open to me—the facts brought to my knowledge by the Lieutenant-General commanding the troops. I would, judging by experience, be most distrustful of information derived from a Turkish source, but I shall have occasion during the present Report to refer more than once to the services rendered by Edhem Pasha to the people of Aleppo during the present crisis, from which your Excellency will, I feel sure, recognize in him an officer of rare ability and devotion to duty. He is a man who knows no distinction between Mussulman and Christian, and who does not adpot the reports of his subordinates and communicate them to Constantinople without testing their accuracy.

I would acknowledge, with gratitude, on behalf of those whose interests I have the honour to protect, that the authorities have made every effort to secure their safety, and that up to the present date no European has been molested.

It would, perhaps, be of interest and useful for future reference that I should state the number and place of residence of those under British protection. Of natural-born British subjects there are in the city of Aleppo 13, in Alexandretta 20, in Aintab 1, in Marash 4, in Antioch 2; total, 40. The number of protected subjects is about 250, mostly resident in Aleppo.

The scenes of disturbance have been Zeitoun, Marash, Aintab, and Urfa in the Vilayet of Aleppo, and Pyas, with its surrounding villages, in the Vilayet of Adana.

Zeitoun.

This town is situated 56 hours or 168 miles north of Aleppo, and 12 hours or 36 miles from Marash, and is approached from Aleppo through the towns of Aintab and Marash. It stands 2,700 feet above the sea, and is built in terraces on the slope of a mountain 3,700 feet above the sea-level. It has a population of between 8,000 and 9,000 Armenians, who in time of peace earn their living as muleteers or as shoesmiths, but who take to the road and plunder when harsh treatment by the Government makes it difficult for them to earn money by lawful means. Their past history is notorious, and has stamped them as an independent and warlike people, the use of arms being familiar to the women as well as to the men. The town is divided into Upper and Lower Zeitoun, which are separated by a small ravine traversed by a mountain torrent, called Zeitoun-Sou, and spanned by a bridge. About a mile from the town there is a flat-topped hill, on which stands the fort of

Zeitoun, and in this fort there was, at the time these troubles commenced, a garrison of 400 soldiers, commanded by a Binbashi, and the position was defended by two pieces of cannon.

During the present year the Zeitounlis, who are among the poorest of the people in Asia Minor, have been treated by the Government with unusual severity in the collection of taxes, and it was when they were exasperated to the utmost that Aghassé and other Hunchag agents appeared among them and organized them for rebellion. Around Zeitoun, and forming part of that district, are numerous villages, Armenian and Kurdish, and it was the people of Alabash, one of these Armenian villages, who commenced hostilities by attacking a convoy proceeding from Marash to Zeitoun, killing the officer in command and ten soldiers. The troops then attacked Alabash (15th October), and a fight ensued, which lasted six hours, and resulted in heavy loss on both sides. It is, however, evident that the troops were worsted in the action, for they were compelled to retreat to the fort, where they were besieged. Their water supply was cut off, and after two days' severe fighting they surrendered. Four hundred rifles, a large supply of ammunition, and two guns thus fell into the hands of the rebels. The news of this success caused considerable consternation here and in Constantinople, and, simultaneously with the calling out of the Reserves in other vilayets, those from the Vilayet of Aleppo were at once mobilized, and five battalions reached Marash at the commencement of the month. It is unknown to what extent the Hunchag organization has been adopted by the Zeitounlis. At Suedia last summer the villagers drilled in uniform, wearing a cap, distinguished by a number of red crosses on a dark ground, and displaying a Hunchag flag, the main feature of which was also a red cross. Large quantities of arms were landed at Suedia, and forwarded to Aintab and Zeitoun, and empty bomb-shells, of which I have written in earlier reports, were loaded at Aintab.

The command of the expedition against Zeitoun having been intrusted to Mustafa Remzy Pasha, the Commandant of Acre, that officer arrived in Marash about the 5th November, and at the same time the Turks established an outpost on the River Jehan, about seven hours from Zeitoun.

Marash.

Marash stands about 2,000 feet above the sea, at the foot of a mountain called the Akhor-Dagh. It has a total population of 54,000, of whom 15,000 are Armenians, and the remainder (excepting only a handful of Jews and nondescripts) are Mussulmans. The latter are of Turkish origin, and fanatical. The town is commanded by a ruined citadel, which is now manned with artillery and garrisoned. The expeditionary force for Zeitoun is under canvas outside town.

Marash, owing to its proximity to Zeitoun, has been the scene of repeated massacres of a terrible nature. On Wednesday, the 23rd October, a quarrel occured between an Armenian and a Turk, both of the lowest class, on which occasion the

Turk was stabbed and he died of his wounds on the following Friday morning. Just then another quarrel occurred between a Turk and an Armenian butcher in the market-place, when the Turk called the Moslems to his aid, and a fight ensued with sticks and knives. That night there was a riot at Karaman, a suburb in the west end of the town, when Garabed Agha Topalian, one of the most prominent, wealthy, and highly esteemed Protestants of Marash, met his death, and his body was horribly mutilated. In their efforts to restore order the authorities then, and in subsequent events, seemed to act wholly on the assumption that Christians were the only disturbers of the peace. The soldiers made a cruel use of their whips, and the prison was filled with Armenians. The excitement caused by this first massacre spread rapidly through the villages on the road to Aleppo, and it became an exceedingly dangerous thing for a Christian to travel alone. An Armenian gentleman employed as medical officer to the troops left Marash on the 27th October, two days afterwards, and reported that the road was thronged with people hastening to Marash to share the plunder. Their general talk was that permission had come to kill the Giaours, and they were eager to be at the work. Isolated cases of murder now became frequent, especially at the mills on the wayside, and all of them are now deserted.

On the 15th November I received a cypher from Marash referring to this massacre. It stated that the results so far as known were 40 killed and about 300 wounded, of whom many would die; that twenty houses outside Karaman had been plundered, and four or five burned down. At that date all the churches were closed and all the shops. A general massacre of the Christians had taken place in the surrounding villages, especially those toward Zeitoun. A few days later I received a letter from the Armenian priest of Zeitoun, dated the 27th October, in which, after relating the events which had occurred there (described above), the writer stated that provisions were running short, that they would soon be in desperate straits, and begged for the intervention of our Government to save them from the massacre which would probably follow their surrender.

At the same time I had news that the Zeitounlis were raiding in every direction and no doubt collecting provisions. About the 12th November they attacked and burned Andrin, a group of villages to the north-west of Marash, and several Kurdish villages nearer that town, which now became the goal of hundreds of panic-stricken and destitute people, who crowded into the streets and constituted a fresh source of danger. Orders were sent from Aleppo to prevent the entry of these refugees by placing a cordon round the town.

Urfa.

This city is 41 hours or 126 miles north-east of Aleppo, beyond the Euphrates. It is inclosed by a massive wall in the form of an irregular triangle, with a castle at the north-east angle, and it is surrounded by gardens watered by the Kara Chai

River. It has a population of about 32,000, of whom 8,000 are Armenians. Both the American Protestants and the Franciscans have Mission schools at Urfa. Disturbances took place in this town on the 27th and 28th October under the following circumstances:-

An Armenian money-changer demanded payment of a debt from a Mussulman, of Beredjik, who murdered him in consequence. He went to the Armenian's house on the Saturday night, and called him out into the street, where he shot him. He was arrested, but on the following morning, when the Armenians, proceeding to church, saw the body of the murdered man lying before his doorway, they lost control over themselves, and rushed to the guard-house, dragged out the murderer, and lynched him.

A mob of Turks, Arabs, and Kurds, armed with knives and clubs, now invaded the Armenian quarter, and in the fight, which lasted throughout the day, about forty were killed and many more wounded. The loss of life was, under the circumstances, not considerable, but the whole town was given up to loot during Sunday and Monday. The Mutessarif was absent when the outbreak commenced, and only reached Urfa on Monday when the fighting was over.

There were only about forty soldiers in the town at the time, who, of course, were powerless against the mob, and looked on whilst the Kurds, Hamidié, and Circassians made a clean sweep of everything. More than 1,500 shops were pillaged.

The last news received from Urfa shows that the shops remain closed, and the Armenians remain shut up in their houses.

Aintab.

Aintab is 24 hours or 76 miles north of Aleppo, and resembles this city in the massive structure of its houses and khans, and in the aspect of the citadel at the west end of the town. The castle, though in an advanced stage of decay, is now mantled with guns, and garrisoned. A massacre of a very savage description occurred here on Friday, the 15th November.

I had greatly hoped that Aintab would have escaped this calamity, because it was generally believed that more reliance could be placed upon the self-control of the Mussulman inhabitants that is the case in Marash. But I think it probable that mischief was done among the Armenians by Aghassé, the Hunchag leader, who spent the months of August and September in Aintab, and that some of the younger Armenians may have from time to time betrayed themselves into acts provoking retaliation. It was, moreover, a terrible strain upon the self-control of a people so situated to witness the constant passage of troops through the city, followed by crowds of Mussulman women weeping and cursing the infidels—scenes which must infallibly have stirred up the fanaticism of the Mussulman inhabitants.

The outbreak originated, as usual, in a private quarrel; but the rapidity with which the fight became general, and the number of villagers from a distance who poured into the city at that moment, almost suggests that the attack had been planned beforehand.

Abour 200 are said to have been killed, and more wounded, while the city was pillaged, and fires broke out in several quarters. A quantity of dynamite exploded in the house of an Armenian, destroying the occupants and causing a conflagration. It is to be noted that some of the Moslem inhabitants behaved with great humanity in protecting Christians, and it is said that nearly 2,000 Armenians took refuge in their houses.

The city was full of strangers loaded with plunder; and to prevent their escaping, orders were issued that, as there were not sufficient troops to form a cordon round the city, mounted patrols should be organized at all points where it was possible to find an exit. These arrangements were explained to me by his Excellency the Ferik, who informed me that two more battalions would soon be sent to Aintab.

His Excellency showed me a telegram which had been received from the Kaïmakam of Aintab, accusing the Armenians of having poisoned the water which supplies the city. He showed me at the same time the telegram which he had sent in reply, which instructed the Kaïmakam to ask Dr. Shepard and his assistants at Aintab College to examine the water; and if they reported that it had been poisoned, he would then give the matter his attention, but not otherwise. I do not suppose that anything more will be heard from the Kaïmakam on the subject. He evidently did not realize that the management of affairs has, during the past fortnight, practically passed from the hands of the fanatical Vali, who has just been dismissed, into those of the Ferik.

Had the massacre of Aintab happened a month ago, this accusation would at once have been indorsed by the Vali, and telegraphed to the Palace.

This Kaïmakam, and practically all the Sub-Governors of the vilayet, have become unfit for their work at this critical time, because they have been the willing servants of the late Vali, and are incapable of treating the Armenians with justice. The prisons of Marash and Aintab are now crammed with Armenians, and there being no accommodation there, prisoners are now being forwarded to Aleppo.

Aleppo.

I pass on to a consideration of the measures which have been taken for the preservation of order in the vilayet, and especially in the city of Aleppo.

When the news of the earlier massacres at Marash and Urfa were reported at Constantinople orders were sent here that all arms in the possession of private persons should be collected. A descent was accordingly made upon the gunsmiths' shops in the city, and guns which are commonly used by gardeners and caretakers for the purpose of warning off smugglers were confiscated. This measure was enforced in the other towns of the vilayet; but everywhere much complaint was made that arms were taken from the Christians rather than from the Turks.

There was great uneasiness here while the Reserves were assembling outside the town, and many an unpleasant incident occured which gave rise to panic. There was great difficulty in obtaining transport animals to accompany the troops, so that wherever it was possible to do so camels and horses were seized for the purpose. On two occasions caravans were stopped outside the town, and it was discovered that large quantities of revolvers and cartridges were concealed among the loads. One evening, when Edhem Pasha was at home conversing with his staff officer, some one rushed in with the news that several cases of Martini-Henry rifles had been seized outside the town, and that there was great confusion and fear of an outbreak. The Pasha mounted his horse, and accompanied only by three or four house servants and Refaat Bey, his staff officer, arrived on the scene to meet an excited mob of Arab men, women, and children, who had gathered together from the outlying quarter of the town, their number calculated at 6,000. What had been seized was in fact only some cheap sporting guns, which had been ordered from Damascus by a Christian gun-merchant in the city in the ordinary course of business, but it was of course useless to explain that to an infuriated mob. The women took the leading part in the demonstration, clapping their hands and shouting out curses on the Giaours, and insisting upon following the Pasha into the city to see the guns deposited at the Konak. One called out that arms were hidden in the Khan Saboon, another in the Khan Gumruk, and with every moment the mob increased. The Ferik had no arms with him, having forgotten to take his revolver, and the mob became very dangerous. So, bidding his staff officer run off and bring soldiers immediately, he remained parleying with the crowd, with great difficulty no doubt, as he could not speak Arabic. His great anxiety was that troops should arrive before he reached the city gate, for he knew that once the mob entered the city with the guns the whole Mussulman population would come out and there would be serious trouble. Luckily troops were quickly found and brought on to the scene, with the result that the mob was dispersed. Edhem Pasha that night saved the town from a riot, and his conduct then and since has inspired the Christian population with confidence that so long as he remains in Aleppo we have a reasonable hope that all will be well.

Three days afterwards, in consequence of a dispute between a Christian tax-collector and a soldier, a Mussulman mob collected in the streets of Aleppo, armed with clubs and knives, shouting out "Death to the Christians," but nothing serious happened, thanks to the promptness with which the troops were called out. The guards were now doubled at the city gates, at all the guard-houses in the town, and in the suburb of Azizié, where the Russian and English Consulates are situated, and during many nights the Ferik himself patrolled the city until morning, thus instilling in the minds of all classes his determination to allow no breach of the peace. The Mukhtars of the city wards and the Religious Heads of sects were assembled at the Konak, and charged under heavy penalties to keep order. Proclamations were made by crier in the streets, and public notice given to the Moslems, when at midday prayer, that they should not molest Christians. Within the last few days placards have been posted up in prominent parts of the city announcing that those who cause disturbance will be subject to martial law. Special arrangements have been made for the protection of the Consulates and of the Ottoman Bank.

Troops have arrived at Alexandretta from Tripoli of Barbary and the Vilayet of Aidin, and there will soon be a force of 50,000 men in the province.

Vilayet of Adana.

In a letter from Hadjin, dated the 16th November, the Rev. Mr. Martin reports that almost all the Christian villages within a radius of twelve hours from Hadjin had been sacked by Circassians. He mentions the following villages: Geokson, Kiriz, Dash, Oloong, Roomloo, Khasta Khana, Shar, Kar Sorran, as being stripped of everything, and abandoned by the villagers.

In a letter written the following day Mr. Martin reports further that the village of Sharbazleen (?), three hours from Hadjin, had been attacked by a force of 2,000 Circassians and Turks, and the inhabitants massacred, and that he feared an attack upon the Mission.

I have since received a reassuring telegram, in which he informs me that a new Kaïmakam having arrived, there was a greater feeling of security in the town.

Villages of Pyas.

Pyas is on the coast, four hours north-west of Alexandretta, and the scenes of disturbance have been the three villages of Tchoukmerdziven, Uzurlu, and Ojaklu, near that town. The two last villages were attacked and destroyed by the Turks, and the villagers fled to Tchoukmerdziven, where heavy fighting was reported on the 13th November. It continued apparently for several days, but, as I learn from Vice-Consul Catoni, the Armenians have laid down their arms and peace is restored. I have no information as to how this was brought about.

I have, &c.

(Signed) HENRY D. BARNHAM.

F. O. 424/184, p. 443-448, No. 783/1

Inclosure 2 in No. 688

Consul Barnham to Sir P. Currie.

Confidential.

Sir,   ALEPPO, *November 28, 1895.*

IN continuation of my Confidential despatch of the 24th instant, I have the honour to submit a further Report upon the recent disturbances at Aintab, Marash, and Zeitoun.

About a fortnight ago I had occasion to send one of the Consular cavasses (a Circassian) to the Armenian missionaries at Aintab and Marash, and he has now returned, having been unable to communicate with the missionaries; but has brought back much interesting and, I think, reliable information.

The massacre at Aintab occurred on Saturday, the 16th, not Friday, the 15th instant, as reported. The cavass arrived in Aintab on the Friday evening, and the fight broke out at 8 o'clock on the following morning, and continued until 4 o'clock in the afternoon.

I conclude that the loss of life was much greater than at first estimated, for the fighting was exceptionally savage, guns, revolvers, knives, and even penknives being used. Great loss of life was caused by the explosion of bombs thrown from the windows of the Armenian houses, and especially from the house of a certain Babik Oghlou. This man kept a store of bomb-shells, dynamite, &c., in the adjoining house, which exploded the following night, killing the occupants. This incident has been already referred to as it had occured during the fight on Saturday. From another Armenian house vitriol was squirted into the faces of people passing by, and the cavass saw two zaptiehs carried away with their faces practically destroyed.

As regards the statement that the water had been poisoned, the cavass states that in two or three quarters of the town there are open cisterns, supplied by water from the hills, and that when he went to one of these on Saturday he was warned by a zaptieh not to drink, and shown the carcasses of two dogs which had died immediately after drinking. On the following day he saw four dogs dead near another cistern, and saw two men removed to the hospital in a state of collapse. I concluded that those who were barbarous enough to throw vitriol and bomb-shells were also capable of this outrage.

In short, although the looting of the market was in a great measure the work of Kurds, Arabs, and Turkomans from outside, the atrocities of the fight were committed by Armenians, who appear to have used every infernal device that is known in the annals of anarchy.

At one moment Aintab College was in great danger. It stands a little above the city, and the cavass tells me that he met a Yuzbashi with a party of soldiers running towards the College, and inquiring the reason, was told that the mob was coming up to attack the place, and that their orders were to protect the College by every means.

Immediately after the mob came in sight, and as they paid no attention to the summons of the Yuzbashi, he gave orders to the soldiers to fire. Three of those in the front rank were shot dead, and the crowd then retired.

The cavass proceeded to Marash on Thursday, the 21st instant, where he was again unable to communicate with the missionaries, and finally decided to destroy the letters which I had given to him.

He informs me that there are at the present moment four battalions in Marash, three in the Hamidié Kyuprusu, the first bridge on the River Jehan, and three at the second bridge, which was destroyed by the Zeitounlis some weeks ago, and which is apparently only four hours from Zeitoun.

Four battalions are employed in the neighbourhood of Andrin under the command of Colonel Ali Bey, lately Commander of the Desert in the Vilayet of Aleppo. Another battalion is distributed among the villages near Marash, and another was expected to arrive in Marash immediately. The direction of the campaign is in the hands of Circassian officers.

Edhem Pasha, the Ferik at Aleppo, is a Circassian, so also are Mustafa Remzi Pasha, the Ferik at Marash, and his staff, Major-Generals Saïd Pasha and Ziver Pasha.

A great many Circassians and Hamidiés arrived in Marash at the same time as my cavass with the object of offering their services to the Government. When they went before the Ferik to make their offer, the cavass, acting apparently under the belief that his identity was not known, went with them. He states that the Ferik received them with great kindness, but said that the Government had no need of their services, and begged them to return quietly home, as Marash was in a disturbed state, and if any outbreak occurred it would probably be said that they had been the cause of it. It appears that hundreds of Circassians from every part of the vilayet had been to Marash on the same errand, but their services had been refused.

The cause of the massacre at Marash on the 18th instant is stated to have been the exasperation produced in that city by the news that Andrin had been taken by the Zeitounlis. The people of Andrin were mostly Moslems employed in Marash, and these and the troops were the authors of the massacre. I have no description of the massacre from an eye-witness, but probably the Armenians made quite as desperate a resistance as at Aintab.

A large quantity of loot was recovered by the authorities, both at Marash and Aintab, and stored in the mosques, whence it is delivered over to the owners on receipt of proof.

The burial of the dead is undertaken by the Municipality. The burial party in the case of the Armenians consists of a priest, a few leading Armenians, one or two officials, and an escort of soldiers, and a similar arrangement is made in the case of Mussulmans.

When the cavass returned to Aintab on the 26th all the dead had been removed, with the exception of one poor Jew, who apparently had no one to look after him. Three small churches were burnt at Marash during the massacre of the 18th, and a Christian quarter below the citadel, known as Shekerli Deré, was completely destroyed by fire.

Zeitoun.

It appears that after the garrison of Zeitoun surrendered the prisoners, soldiers, and zapteihs were stripped of their uniforms and finally set at liberty. A party of Zeitounlis then donned these uniforms, and disguised as a troop of Turkish soldiers proceeded to Andrin, which was immediately captured and burnt. On receiving news of the burning of Andrin, Ali Bey advanced in pursuit of the Zeitounlis and captured the villages of Bounduk and Jebeen, but on approaching Fernouz, which is a large village, very difficult of access, he found it necessary to halt and send to Marash for guns, which were sent to him on the 24th instant. In the meantime it appears that he was attacked by the Zeitounlis outside Fernouz and compelled to retreat in the direction of Hadjin.

I would point out that there is a delusion among the people that the operations of the Zeitounlis are directed by Englishmen. I hear that two men who speak English and wear European hats are in Fernouz at present. They are no doubt Armenian Hunchag agents, who purposely allow this impression to go abroad.

With regard to the information furnished by my cavass Mehemet, I think that the fact that he is a Circassian might convey the impression that his report is exaggerated. It is therefore right to state why I think him an honest and reliable witness. I have known him for eleven years, and before he entered my service he was with Sir Charles Wilson, Consul Richards, and Mr. Cameron. He is a man known very widely for his courage, truthfulness, and sound common sense, and, moreover, his statements, so far as they affect Aintab and Marash, are confined to what he has seen with his own eyes.

I have, &c.

(Signed) HENRY. D. BARNHAM.

F. O. 424/184, pp. 448-450, No. 783/2

No. 689

Sir E. Monson to the Marquess of Salisbury.

No. 369.   VIENNA, *December 15, 1895.*
My Lord,   *(Received December 18.)*

THE "Neue Freie Presse" of this morning published a statement of the motives which, according to the correspondent of that paper at St. Petersburgh, have actuated the Russian Government in the policy pursued by them in regard to the question of the demand for second "stationnaires" formulated by the Representatives of the Powers at Constantinople.

It is alleged in this statement (a summary of which is given in the inclosed extract from the "Correspondance Politique") that the policy of the Cabinet of St. Petersburgh had been devoted to the object of preserving the interests of the Sultan against any eventualities due to English policy. The correspondent explains that the French and Russian naval forces in Turkish waters are as nearly as possible equal in number and strength to those of England and Italy, and that as the German ships may be counted upon to act also in defence of the Sultan, there would be no question of the superiority of force being found on the side of the Anglo-Italian fleet.

Under these circumstances, it was reasonably hoped at St. Petersburgh that the Sultan would be convinced that he would be wise in yielding to the demand of the Powers, since the presence of additional "stationnaires" would, in case of necessity, insure protection for himself. Such a contingency was by no means regarded at the Russian capital as not to be taken into account.

The reproduction of this statement in the "Correspondance Politique" invests it with a sufficient importance to make it worth reporting to your Lordship.

I have, &c.

(Signed) EDMUND MONSON.

F. O. 424/184, p. 437, No. 766

Inclosure in No. 689

Extract from the "Correspondance Politique" of December 15, 1895.

LA Nouvelle Presse libre reçoit de Saint-Pétersbourg un Exposé des Motifs qui auraient guidé la politique Russe dans la question des deuxièmes stationnaires. Il en résulte que le Gouvernement Russe se serait toujours efforcé de préserver les intérêts du Sultan contre des surprises éventuelles de la politique Anglaise. "Les navires Russes et Français rassemblés dans les eaux Turques sont à peu près égaux en nombre et en force à ceux de l'Angleterre et de l'Italie. De plus, on peut s'attendre à ce que les vaisseaux Allemands servent également à protéger le Sultan, de sorte que la supériorité ne se trouverait nullement du côté de la flotte Anglo-Italienne. On espère avec certitude à Saint-Pétersbourg que le Sultan acquerra la conviction que ce qu'il avait de mieux à faire, c'était de céder à la demande des Puissances, puiseque les sconds stationnaires peuvent, le cas échéant, lui assurer à lui aussi de la protection. La possibilité d'une pareille éventualité n'était aucunement regardée comme exclue dans la capitale Russe."

F. O. 424/184, p. 438, No. 766/1

No. 690

Sir P. Currie to the Marquess of Salisbury.

No. 932. CONSTANTINOPLE, *December 15, 1895.*

My Lord, *(Received December 23.)*

I HAVE the honour to inform your Lordship that on Thursday morning a panic occurred in Galata and Pera. It lasted in the latter place for about an hour, people flying along the street to escape from the imaginary danger, and all the shops being at once closed. The most conflicting rumours were abroad, that a revolution had broken out in Galata owing to the arrival of the "stationnaires," and that there was firing in the streets; that an attack was to be made on the British Embassy, or that a demonstration was to be made at Yildiz.

It appears that the real 'origin of the panic was a quarrel between two Armenians in Stamboul, one of whom had brought an action for forgery against the other, who thereupon revenged himself by firing four shots from a revolver at his adversary. A policeman, with drawn sword, pursued the would-be assassin, and a *sauve qui peut* and general panic ensued. The Minister of Police took every means possible to allay the fears of the population, but it is said that, in Galata, shouts were at once raised telling the Armenians to close their shops, as the Turks had risen and were about to massacre them.

I have not heard of any lives lost, or of any damage done to property.

The Mutessarif of Pera, with an ingenuity which did credit to his imagination, caused a report to be circulated that a lion had escaped from a menagerie, and that some shots which were fired at him had caused the panic.

Some people maintain that it was deliberately caused by the police; others that its premature occurrence prevented a rising of the Softas, which had been prepared; but these reports do not appear to have any foundation, and only show the excited state of the inhabitants, which disposes them to listen to any rumour, however improbable.

I have, &c.

(Signed) PHILIP CURRIE.

F. O. 424/184, p. 455, No. 788

No. 691

Sir P. Currie to the Marquess of Salisbury.

No. 933.   CONSTANTINOPLE, *December 15, 1895.*
My Lord,   *(Received December 23.)*
    I HAVE the honour to transmit to your Lordship herewith a summary of an
article which appeared in the "Sabah" on the 13th instant denying the rumours
which are current as to the arrival of the foreign fleets at Constantinople, and giving
an explanation of the demand of the Powers for a second "stationnaire."
                        I have, &c.
                                            (Signed) PHILIP CURRIE.
    F. O. 424/184, p. 455, No. 789

Inclosure in No. 691

Extract from the "Sabah" of December 13, 1895.

Translation.
    WE much regret the baseless and improbably rumours which find an echo in
the foreign press and in public gossip. Thus, a statement has lately been current to
the effect that the fleets of the Powers were coming to Constantinople. Fortunately,
perfect order and tranquillity prevail not only at the capital, but also throughout
the whole of the Ottoman dominions. Such a step would, therefore, have no object,
nor, indeed, has the rumour any foundation, save the fact that the Powers have
applied for permission for a second "stationnaire" each to be allowed to come, as
their vessels may, in case of necessity, go on duty in the Danube. Under these
circumstances, the Imperial Government has acceded to their request.
    F. O. 424/184, p. 455, No. 789/1

No. 692

Sir P. Currie to the Marquess of Salisbury.

No. 804.   CONSTANTINOPLE, *December 16, 1895, 11.10 p.m.*
Telegraphic.   *(Received December 16.)*
    I CONFERRED to-day with my Russian and French colleagues about the
Commission of Control. The new President, Sirri Pasha, died a few days ago, and
was never appointed.

Shefik Bey, whose appointment was objected to by your Lordship, has not been removed.

Meetings of the Commission are occasionally held, but they have been given no business to transact, and no information has been communicated to them.

We agreed that our Dragomans should be sent separately to inquire who is their President, and what they are doing.

F. O. 424/184, p. 428, No. 756

No. 693

Consul-General Mockler to Sir P. Currie.

Sir,   BAGDAD, *November 16, 1895.*

I HAVE the honour very respectfully to forward, for your Excellency's information, copy, in translation, of a news-letter, dated the 29th ultimo, from Mr. Rassam, British Consular Agent at Mosul, together with copy, in Turkish and translation, of the paragraph in the "Mosul" newspaper referred to in such news-letter.

I have, &c.

(Signed) E. MOCKLER, *Colonel.*

F. O. 424/184, p. 467, No. 801/1

Inclosure 1 in No. 693

Mr. Rassam to Consul General Mockler.

Extract.   MOSUL, *October 29, 1895.*

ON Friday last his Excellency Saleh Pasha, the Vali, communicated to the head clergy a telegram which he had received from the Grand Vizier, contradicting rumours spread by the Armenians about the reforms which have been decided upon to be carried out, which telegram is published in the paper "Mosul," of which I herewith submit a copy of same for your information. His Excellency the Vali on the morning of the same day sent away as exiles to the Vilayet of Conea the sons of Karha, the notorious ruffian, as also Naamat-Ullah Hanna Bunni to Aleppo, for this man has been found to have committed adultery with the wife of a Mulazim (Lieutenant) in the Turkish army; the proceedings adopted have been under orders obtained from the Porte, but the Patriarch of the Syrian Catholics has been exceedingly aggrieved at the Vali's proceedings in the matter, and more so for his having mentioned in his letter to the Vizier that the man in question was the nephew of the Patriarch, instead of describing him by his father's name. The Patriarch, therefore, intends to make a complaint against the Vali, and institute a suit for libel against him.

About a fortnight ago, when a caravan of Christians of the district of Tal, a dependency of the Government of Julamirg, was going to Amadieh, it was attacked at a place about an hour and a-half from Amadieh by twenty-five men from the followers of Fatah Agha, of Zibar, the Kurdish rebel, who plundered twenty-four mules and 24 Turkish liras, with several articles; they killed one man named Dawood, and wounded three named Rabbo, Winan, and Fito. This occurred below the village Khamria, a dependency of the district of Amadieh; these rebels passed to Zibar, taking with them what they had plundered. The party so plundered went to Amadieh, and reported to the Kaïmakam what had befallen them, who, having declared his inability to give them any assistance, directed them to go to Mosul and report their case there; so two of the party named Abdal and Khoshaba arrived here on Saturday last. On relating to me what had happened to their caravan, and I finding I was unable to assist them in the way they wished, they submitted a Petition to his Excellency the Vali, but I have not as yet learnt what answer has been given them, or what steps have been proposed to be taken in the matter.

F. O. 424/184, p. 467, No. 801/2

Inclosure 2 in No. 693

Extract from the "Mosul" of October 24, 1895.

Translation.

IT has come to our notice that the Armenians are spreading rumours contrary to facts in connection with the reforms decided upon to be carried out in certain vilayets. The true state of the matter is therefore herewith explained: that the measures adopted with respect to reforms does not concern Armenians only, but being with the object of establishing conformity in the Vilayets of Van, Mamooret-al-Aziz, Erzeroum, Bitlis, Diarbekir, and Sivas, with the rules and regulations set down in the Dastoor (Code), as well as with the Ordinances and beneficial clauses given in the Hatti-humayoun of Gulkhanah, and the High Firman respecting reforms, the said measures comprehend all subject of the Imperial Government, whether Moslem or non-Moslem, and that preparation is being made to bring about conformity with this, and make it common in all other vilayets also, according to their local requirements.

F. O. 424/184, pp. 467-468, No. 801/3

No. 694

Sir. P. Currie to the Marquess of Salisbury.

No. 958.   CONSTANTINOPLE, *December 16, 1895.*
My Lord,   *(Received December 23.)*

IN consequence of information supplied to me by the Ephas of the Armenian church in Pera respecting the continued arrests of Armenians in the city, I instructed Mr. Shipley to bring the matter to the notice of Nazim PAsha, Minister of Police, informing his Excellency that I attached great importance to it, and had already made represetations direct to the Sultan on the subject.

Mr. Shipley accordingly presented to the Minister a list of the Armenians recently arrested, and drew his particular attention to certain alleged cases of death in prison from ill-treatment at the hands of other prisoners.

This latter accusation the Minister denied with great warmth, adding that in none of these cases of alleged torture could the persons making the accusation bring any proofs in support of their statements. Nazim Pasha admitted that twenty Armenians had been arrested by night at Tophane, but said that this was due to the stupidity of the Mutessarif of Pera, whom he had called to account.

With regard to the alleged wholesale repatriation of Armenians, his Excellency said that there was no truth in the allegation; he had no wish to repatriate the 3,000 or 4,000 Armenians of the provinces resident in the capital, but only such as he knew to be revolutionists. He knew, for instance, that in the Armenian church in Galata there were some fifty or sixty disreputable Armenians who were trying, by intimidation, and even torture, to force other Armenians to join in the seditious movement. What was he to do with such people, if for political reasons he was not allowed to arrest or repatriate them?

I also instructed Mr. Shipley to bring to his Excellency's notice a report that had reached me that arms were being sold to Mussulmans while they were refused to Christians. This report the Minister also characterized as misleading. The sale of arms was now permitted to any one of respectable position, but he had prohibited it to both Christians and Mussulmans alike who were of the poorer classes, such as porters, fireman, &c. His Excellency added that he personally was in favour of a general measure of disarmament applying to all classes of the population, both Christian and Mussulman.

I have, &c.

(Signed) PHILIP CURRIE.

F. O. 424/184, p. 475, No. 807

No. 695

Sir F. Lascelles to the Marquess of Salisbury.

No. 314. Confidential.   BERLIN, *December 16, 1895.*
My Lord,   *(Received December 23.)*

I CALLED upon Baron von Marschall this morning for the purpose of communicating to him, as instructed by your Lordship's telegram No. 135 of the 15th instant, the substance of the telegram from Her Majesty's Vice-Consul at Mush, which your Lordship did me the honour to repeat to me in your telegram No. 134 of the 15th instant.

Baron von Marschall observed that the information contained in Mr. Hallward's telegram, and also in Sir P. Currie's telegram No. 136, of which I also communicated the substance to his Excellency, corresponded with that which he had received from other quarters. There could be no doubt as to horrible massacres having been committed, although he had been under the impression that in some places there had been some provocation on the part of the Armenians. His Excellency then asked whether Her Majesty's Government had any suggestions to propose, and on my replying that I had no instructions on the subject, said that he thought it probable that things would go on much as they were during the winter, but he feared that complications might arise in the spring. The increasing weakness of the Sultan's authority would encourage the agitation in Macedonia, and the state of affairs in Bulgaria was not calculated to inspire confidence. It was probable that the Bulgarian Government would be unwilling or unable to put a stop to the activity of the Macedonian Committees, and, in his Excellency's opinion, a Macedonian agitation might give rise to greater complications than the Armenian question.

I have, &c.

(Signed) FRANK C. LASCELLES.

F. O. 424/184, p. 482, No. 813

No. 696

Mr. Goschen to the Marquess of Salisbury.

No. 284. Confidential.   ST. PETERSBURGH, *December 16, 1895.*
My Lord,   *(Received December 23.)*

IMMEDIATELY on the receipt of your Lordship's telegram on the subject of the forced conversion of Armenian villagers in Vilayet of Diarbekir, reported by Her Majesty's Vice-Consul at Mush, I called upon Prince Lobanoff and asked him, in accordance with your Lordship's instructions, whether he had received similar intelligence. His Excellency replied that he had heard nothing on the subject.

I then informed him that your Lordship would be glad to learn the views of the Imperial Government as to a joint remonstrance on the part of the Powers against such proceedings.

His Excellency answered that, before any joint remonstrance could be made, it would be necessary that the facts should be fully verified, which appeared to him a very difficult matter.

In the first place, what constituted a forced conversion? If an Armenian in fear of death promised that if his life was spared, would that be a forced conversion? And even if it was regarded as such, what would it matter, as the moment his persecutors turned their backs he would immediately renounce his new religion and revert to his own faith. From his own experience in such cases in the East, there was nothing so difficult to prove as alleged forced conversions to Mahommedanism.

I ventured to observe, in reply, that his Excellency probably referred to isolated cases, chiefly of women taken off to Turkish harems and obliged to embrace the Mahommedan religion. I myself had known of many such cases when in Turkey, and it had certainly always been difficult to ascertain the truth; but in the present instance it appeared to be the whole Armenian population of large districts who were to be compelled to turn Mahommedans. That was a very different matter, as it would mean wholesale persecution under the direction, or at least with the connivance, of the Turkish authorities; and in such a case evasion would not be so easy as his Excellency appeared to think.

Prince Lobanoff said that the fact that the Turkish authorities would necessarily be at the head of such a movement rendered the report all the more incredible, as religion had nothing to do with the Armenian persecutions. It was a national and not a religious question, as was proved by the fact that throughout the troubles Christians of other nationalies had never been attacked.

I then expressed to his Excellency the hope that he would authorize me to inform your Lordship that in the event of the report being corroborated the Imperial Government would join in a remonstrance on the subject to the Ottoman Government.

His Excellency replied that although he was in favour of interfering as little as possible in Turkish internal affairs at present, he saw no objection to joining in the proposed remonstrance, so long as the forced conversions alleged to have taken place were fully proved and the other Powers were agreed on the subject. He added, however, that he thought the best plan would be to place the matter in the hands of the Ambassadors at Constantinople, who were in a position to inquire into the truth of the report, and to decide whether a joint remonstrance was necessary.

I have, &c.

(Signed) W. E. GOSCHEN.

F. O. 424/184, pp. 482-483, No. 814

No. 697

Sir E. Monson to the Marquess of Salisbury.

No. 370.   VIENNA, *December 16, 1895.*
My Lord,   *(Received December 23.)*

AS instructed by your Lordship's telegram No. 104 of the 14th instant, I communicated yesterday to Count Goluchowski, by means of a French paraphrase, the statements telegraphed by Her Majesty's Vice-Consul at Mush to Sir. P. Currie on the 13th instant as to the massacres in his district being deliberately organized by the Turks, and being unprovoked by any rebellious movement on the part of the Armenians; and that in his (the Vice-Consul's) opinion these massacres will continue until the surviving Armenians become Mussulmans, unless they are stopped by foreign intervention.

Count Goluchowski at once admitted the probable accuracy of these statements, but said that there is nothing to be done, except to wait and see whether the Sultan will really carry out his promises and re-establish order in the disturbed districts. The most serious admonitions have again and again been made to His Imperial Majesty, and he has undertaken to meet with wishes of the Powers. Time must be given him to carry out his promises.

As for any foreign intervention, the experience of the original intervention of England, France, and Russia had not been encouraging, for, in fact, the action of those three Powers had only resulted in disaster to the Armenians themselves.

I have, &c.

(Signed) EDMUND MONSON.

F. O. 424/184, p. 454, No. 816

No. 698

Mr. Goschen to the Marquess of Salisbury.

No. 285. Very Confidential.   ST. PETERSBURGH, *December 17, 1895.*
My Lord,   *(Received December 23.)*

WITH reference to my immediately preceding despatch, I have the honour to report that I took an opportunity to-day of communicating to Prince Lobanoff the further telegram from Her Majesty's Vice-Consul at Mush on the subject of the forced conversions of Armenians to the Mahommedan religion. In doing so I again alluded to the strong feeling that such proceedings would inevitably rouse in England when they became known.

Prince Lobanoff said, in reply, that he was afraid that would be the case, and after a pause added, "I was only two years in England, but in that short time I realized the fact that the English are the most inflammable people in the world; much more so than the French or Italians, who usually enjoy that reputation, and in this Armenian question they have proved my ideas to be correct. I must admit at the same time that they have 'une forte dose—très forte même de philanthropie.' But when they let their philanthropic ideas run riot, they not only get excited themselves but cause excitement amongst others with very disturbing results, as in the present instance; for it cannot be denied that the encouragement given to the Armenian Committees by public men, and public opinion in England, has stimulated the Armenians to revolt and roused the fanaticism of the Turks."

I replied, that I could by no means admit what he appeared to imply, namely, the responsibility of England for the state of affairs in Asia Minor; that responsibility rested with the authors and perpetrators of the cold-blooded massacres at Sasun, and it had not required any promptings of the Armenian Committees to make England and all other civilized Powers regard those events with the greatest possible horror. But in any case, I said, I was glad to hear that his Excellency attributed the hearty manner in which England had taken up the matter to philanthropy, as I had noticed that Russian public opinion, as represented by the press, attributed the action of Her Majesty's Government to other and less laudable motives. I told him that scarcely a day passed without some violent and hostile article appearing in the most important and most widely circulated Russian journals, the gist of which was usually to the effect that, for selfish political motives of her own, England had stirred up the Armenian question and was still doing all she could to keep up the excitement and fan the flames of murder and rapine.

His Excellency admitted that unfortunately articles of that description constantly appeared, but made the usual excuse that no one paid any attention to them. I replied that, judging from what I heard, they were, on the contrary, very much read and that the opinions of the press were freely adopted by a large class, and I hinted that it was all the more unfortunate that these articles should appear so constantly as, rightly or wrongly, it was generally believed that the press in Russia was under strict official supervision.

His Excellency reiterated his opinion that the press had no influences on public opinion in Russia, and the conversation dropped.

I have, &c.

(Signed) W. E. GOSCHEN.

F. O. 424/184, pp. 483-484, No. 815

No. 699

Sir P. Currie to the Marquess of Salisbury.

No. 807. Confidential.   CONSTANTINOPLE, *December 18, 1895, 10.30 a.m.*
Telegraphic.   *(Received December 18.)*

THERE is now a greater disposition on the part of my colleagues to recommend that pressure should be exerted for the establishment in Turkey of a responsible Ministry.

The French and Russian Ambassadors insist strongly on the importance of carefully preparing the ground before any definite proposal is made.

As a first step they will, I hope, write to their Governments by courier recommending that instructions shall be sent to the Ambassadors at Constantinople to consult together and propose some remedy for the existing state of disorder, which is left uncontrolled must lead to a breakdown of the entire machinery of government, and to a reopening, in an aggravated form, of the Eastern question.

It is thought better that nothing should be said at Rome at present, as M. Blanc's discretion is doubted.

The German Ambassador is well disposed, and if the French Government are favourable, it is possible that their influence may induce Russia to agree.

F. O. 424/184, pp. 438-439, No. 768

No. 700

Sir P. Currie to the Marquess of Salisbury.

No. 808.   CONSTANTINOPLE, *December 18, 1895, 11 a.m.*
Telegraphic.   *(Received December 18.)*

MR. CUMBERBATCH telegraphed yesterday from Erzeroum that large numbers of destitute Armenians are arriving there from Constantinople, whence they have been expelled, and that the Mustafis soldiers have been disbanded. He adds that there is no intention of executing the reform scheme until the pacification of the country is considered as sufficiently established.

F. O. 424/184, p. 439, No. 769

No. 701

The Marquess of Salisbury to Sir P. Currie.

No. 266.
Telegraphic. FOREIGN OFFICE, *December 18, 1895.*

I HAVE received your Excellency's despatch No. 914 of the 10th instant, relative to the work of relieving the distressed Armenians of the Sasun district.

The Armenian Relief Committee, as mentioned in my telegram No. 257 of the 13th instant, are anxious to learn your views as to the further distribution of assistance outside that district, and I should be glad if you would telegraph your recommendations on this point.

F. O. 424/184, p. 439, No. 771

No. 702

Sir P. Currie to the Marquess of Salisbury.

No. 965. Confidential. CONSTANTINOPLE, *December 18, 1895.*
My Lord, *(Received December 23.)*

I HAVE the honour to forward to your Lordship herewith copy of two despatches which I have received from Her Majesty's Consul acting at Erzeroum respecting the attitude of Russian Consular officers towards Armenians.

I have, &c.

(Signed) PHILIP CURRIE.

F. O. 424/184, p. 480, No. 812

Inclosure 1 in No. 702

Consul Cumberbatch to Sir P. Currie.

Confidential.
Sir, ERZEROUM, *December 3, 1895.*

I HAVE the honour to send your Excellency copy of a despatch received from Her Majesty's Vice-Consul at Van on the attitude of Russian Consular officers towards Armenians.

As regards Mr. Hallward's remarks on the non-interference in matters concerning Ottoman subjects, I have to state that such is not the case with the Russian Consul-General here, who has shown the greatest willingness to act in concert with his colleagues in connection with the succour of the Armenians wounded during the disorders of the 30th and 31st, the recovery and burial of those that were killed, the measures necessary for the security of the town, and the stopping of wholesale arrests of suspected persons. In fact, it was he who proposed our collective telegram to our respective Embassies recommending the punishment of the soldiers who participated in the riots here, and the cessation of indiscriminate arrests of Armenians. Since then he has followed the same line.

With regard to the other side of the question, his attitude of late can best be defined in the following words: "I told you so. Why did you rely on the English?"

Only a few days ago he received instructions to try and calm Mussulman feelings by explaining, in Turkish circles, the real tenor of the scheme of reforms, and by showing how erroneous the idea was that only Armenians will benefit by their introduction.

At the same time, however, I have learnt that he has prevented the conveyance, by the Russian post, of a sum of money sent by the Catholicos to the Armenian Bishop here, as reported in my other despatch of this day's date.

I have, &c.

(Signed) H. A. CUMBERBATCH.

F. O. 424/184, p. 480, No. 812/1

Inclosure 2 in No. 702

Vice-Consul Hallward to Consul Cumberbatch.

Confidential.

Sir,   VAN, *November 26, 1895.*

SOME of the foreign residents here lately suggested that the Consuls should collectively urge the local authorities to take proper measures for the security of the town, and in the course of a conversation I had with the Russian Vice-Consul on this subject he informed me that he had strict orders not to interfere in local politics, and that he could do nothing beyond demanding security for himself and his subjects. I have every reason to believe that he was perfectly sincere in what he said, and that as a matter of fact he entirely abstains from interesting himself in matters concerning Ottoman subjects. This attitude has, I believe, been constantly maintained here by Russian Agents for the last five years.

Local Turks, officers, and officials, have maintained throughout the present crisis that the attitude of Russia towards Turkey was friendly as contrasted with that of England. The one thing the Turks here fear from foreigners is a Russian occupation, and as long as there is no question of that they feel that they are free to treat the Christians as they like, though some of the better class Turks do not approve of the policy of exterminating the Armenians, which they consider contrary to their own interests, and many of them think that a Russian occupation is inevitable sooner or later.

Another point worthy of remark is the vigilance exercised by the Russian Government in preventing armed Armenians from crossing the frontier. A considerable service is thereby rendered to the Turkish Government, for were the Russian Armenians free to carry arms across the frontier there can be little doubt that they would utilize the privilege in such a way as to cause considerable annoyance to the Turkish authorities.

In fact, the attitude of the Russian Government from a local point of view has been throughout strictly "correct," but perhaps the indifference they have shown (locally speaking) to the Armenian side of the question has tended to encourage the Turkish Government in its sense of impunity and irresponsibility in dealing with its Christian subjects.

I have, &c.

(Signed) C. M. HALLWARD.

F. O. 424/184, p. 481, No. 812/2

Inclosure 3 in No. 702

Consul Cumberbatch to Sir P. Currie.

Confidential.

Sir, ERZEROUM, *December 3, 1895.*

I HAVE the honour to inform your Excellency that yesterday I received a letter from the Armenian Archbishop here telling me that a sum of money (2,000 roubles), on its way to him from the Catholicos of Etchmiadzin, and destined for the relief of the destitute Armenians, has been stopped at Sarıkamish by the interference of the Russian Consul-General here.

Mgr. Shishmanian, under the impression that there was a British Consular officer at Tiflis, requested me to ask him to receive the money and forward it to me.

I told the Archbishop that the nearest British Consul resides at Batoum, and that he could only give his assistance if authorized to do so by Her Majesty's Government.

The action of my Russian colleague is probably due to instructions issued at the request of the Turkish Government, who, no doubt, think that the money is destined for seditious purposes, which I have no reason to think is the case.

I have, &c.

(Signed) H. A. CUMBERBATCH.

F. O. 424/184, p. 481, No. 812/3

No. 703

Sir E. Monson to the Marquess of Salisbury.

No. 374. Confidential.   VIENNA, *December 18, 1895.*
My Lord,   *(Received December 23.)*

IN accordance with your Lordship's orders, telegraphed to me the night before last, I asked Count Goluchowski yesterday to send instructions to Baron Calice to associate himself with his colleagues in taking steps to verify the assertion that the surviving Armenian villagers in Saird Chabakhcor and in certain districts of Diarbekir are being compelled to adopt the Mussulman religion.

His Excellency consented to do so; but said that it did not seem to him to be worth taking much trouble about people who are so ready to change their faith as the Armenians appear to be.

I answered that, in view of the destitution and persecution to which so many of them are exposed, I could not wonder at the fact that numbers of them yielded to the temptation to save themselves; to which his Excellency rejoined that, after all, the crown of martyrdom is always within their reach.

I have, &c.

(Signed) EDMUND MONSON.

F. O. 424/184, p. 485, No. 818

No. 704

Sir P. Currie to the Marquess of Salisbury.

No. 810.   CONSTANTINOPLE, *December 19, 1895, 11.10 a.m.*
Telegraphic.   *(Received December 19.)*

I RECEIVED a visit from the Foreign Minister yesterday, who informed me that the troops had now surrounded the Zeitounlis, but that the Sultan, still hoping that they may be induced to surrender, delays ordering the attack to be made.

His Excellency added that the Porte had received reports that the Zeitounlis had burned and plundered Mussulman villages, had massacred their Ottoman prisoners, and had committed outrages on women and children who had fallen into their hands.

F. O. 424/184, p. 440, No. 773

No. 705

Sir P. Currie to the Marquess of Salisbury.

No. 811. CONSTANTINOPLE, *December 19, 1895, 11.10 a.m.*
Telegraphic. *(Received December 19.)*

MR. HAMPSON reports that the missionaries who were carrying on the relief work in Sasun, having expended 2,955*l.* there, have now left for Bitlis.

F. O. 424/184, p. 440, No. 774

No. 706

Sir P. Currie to the Marquess of Salisbury.

No. 812. CONSTANTINOPLE, *December 19, 1895, 12.30 p.m.*
Telegraphic. *(Received December 19.)*

IN reply to your Lordship's telegram No, 266 of yesterday, I have the honour to state that on the 30th ultimo I approved the proposal of the Constantinople Relief Committee to send 1,000*l.* to Erzeroum, 1,000*l.* to Kharput, 500*l.* to Trebizond, and 500*l.* to Mardin.

Further, on the 15th instant I agreed, subject to the approval of the Duke of Westminster's Committee, that sums of 500*l.* each should be granted to Cæsarea, Marash, and Aintab.

The selection of the places to which money should be sent should, I consider, be left to the judgment of the Local Committee, who should communicate with me on the subject. In making their choice they must be guided not only by the information they receive, but also by the facilities offered for the distribution of relief. At present, the missionaries who inhabit the towns are both their principal sources of information and means of distribution. It would be necesssary to send special agents to distribute relief in the country district, and the organization of the Red Cross Society might be very useful for this purpose.

F. O. 424/184, p. 440, No. 775

No. 707

Sir P. Currie to the Marquess of Salisbury.

No. 967. Confidential.　　　　　　　　　　CONSTANTINOPLE, *December 19, 1895.*
My Lord,　　　　　　　　　　　　　　　　　　　*(Received December 24.)*

I REGRET to say that I am unable to report any improvement in the state of affairs here.

The Ministry appointed after the fall of Kiamil Pasha remains nominally in office, but appears to exercise no control over the affairs of the Empire. Such orders as are given emanate directly from the Sultan.

The accounts from the Asiatic provinces show that the ravages of the Kurds continue unchecked. The perpetrators of the massacres remain unpunished, while innocent Armenians are committed to prison on frivolous charges.

The Redifs who have been called out are quite undisciplined; the Treasury is unable to find money for them, and, instead of restoring order, they will only swell the ranks of the robbers who prey upon the unfortunate population.

At Zeitoun the Turkish troops are closing round the Armenians, and the Sultan is justifying himself beforehand for the extermination of the Zeitounlis by accusing them of killing and mutilating Mussulman women and children.

Disturbances have commenced in Crete, and are threatened in Macedonia. The financial state is desperate, and it seems probable that by next spring the Turkish Government will find itself unable to cope with its difficulties.

This condition of affairs would appear not only to justify, but to call for interference on the part of the Treaty Powers, in order to restore order and to prevent disturbances which would be dangerous to peace. But, unfortunately, the concert of the Ambassadors, as far as the Russian Ambassador is concerned, is limited to the protection of foreigners, and M. de Nélidoff does not consider himself authorized to enter into discussion with his colleagues as to the general state of the Empire.

I have had many private conversations with my other colleagues, who appear to be strongly impressed with the critical position of affairs, and I have suggested that if we were, each of us, to report our opinions to our Governments, they might possibly, if they concurred in our views, be able by united pressure to induce the Russian Government to modify to some extent their present attitude.

I have drawn up the following statement, showing the limits within which my colleagues would appear to be prepared to act on my suggestion:-

"The disorder and discontent which reign in all parts of the Empire and in all Departments of the Administration, if some means are not found to remedy them, must before long lead to a breakdown of the entire machinery of Government, and so bring the whole Eastern question on the *tapis*. The mental condition of the Sultan is such that he is powerless to bring about an improvement, even if he were willing to do so, and the men who surround him are too corrupt and incapable to contribute to the task.

"It is clear, therefore, that unless some influence is brought to bear from without, Europe is exposed to serious risk.

"Under these circumstances, if the Powers of Europe are agreed that something ought to be done, the best course would appear to be that they should instruct their Ambassadors at Constantinople to concert as to the nature of the remedy which they can jointly recommend to their Governments."

I have shown this paper to Baron Calice and M. Cambon, who expressed generally their concurrence, and gave me to understand that they would write to-day by courier to their Governments in the sense indicated.

It will be seen that the recommendation goes no further than to suggest that the Ambassadors should be authorized to consult together and propose a remedy for the existing state of things. We are of opinion that if the Russian Government could be induced to give such an instruction to their Ambassador, we should have a better chance of bringing them into line through the influence of M. de Nélidoff, who, being on the spot, is naturally more impressed by the gravity of the situation that the Russian Minister for Foreign Affairs.

Baron Calice and M. Cambon are both strongly impressed with the importance of carefully preparing the ground before any definite proposal is made. They attribute the failure of Count Goluchowski's well-meant efforts to the neglect of this precaution.

My French colleague personally attaches great importance to an interference on the part of the Powers, and will, I doubt not, exert his influence in that sense with his Government. Unfortunately, the present French Foreign Minister is not so well acquainted with the circumstances as M. Hanotaux, nor does he rely so much as his predecessor on M. Cambon's advice.

If the Russian Government has finally made up its mind that Turkey should be allowed to go from bad to worse until it suits their convenience to intervene, our efforts will be fruitless; but my French colleague, who has good opportunities of judging, is of opinion that Russia's backwardness is, in great part, due to the conviction entertained by Prince Lobonoff, that the state of affairs at Constantinople is the same as when he held the post of Ambassador here many years ago—that everything will right itself if affairs are left to take their course, and that the reports of the Russian Representative show unnecessary nervousness and alarm.

I have, &c.

(Signed) PHILIP CURRIE.

F. O. 424/184, pp. 487-488, No. 822

No. 708

Sir E. Monson to the Marquess of Salisbury.

No. 111. Secret.   VIENNA, *December 20, 1895.*
Telegraphic.   *(Received December 20.)*

WITH reference to Sir P. Currie's telegram No. 807, I took the opportunity to-day to remind Count Goluchowski that Sir P. Currie, during his stay in Vienna, had in a conversation with him alluded to the desirability of establishing a responsible Ministry at Constantinople, and as I said that his Excellency would in all probability soon hear from Baron Calice on the subject, as I knew that Sir Philip had lately conferred with his Austrian colleague in regard to this question.

While fully agreeing as to the expediency of the proposal, Count Goluchowski seems to be strongly of the opinion that the opposition of Russia would frustrate any attempt in this direction, Russia being only too ready to avail herself of any opportunity of proving to the Sultan that she is his only true friend, and thus bringing about the destruction of the European concert.

His Excellency thinks that the Sultan should be allowed to carry on his affairs in his own way for the present, but that, of course, any suggestion made by Baron Calice, in conjunction with Sir P. Currie and M. Cambon, would receive his best consideration

From what I gather, he does not feel disposed for the present to take any action in the matter.

F. O. 424/184, p. 441, No. 777

No. 709

Sir E. Monson to the Marquess of Salisbury.

No. 382. Secret.   VIENNA, *December 20, 1895.*
My Lord,   *(Received December 23.)*

IN a conversation which I had this afternoon with Count Goluchowski, I took occasion to remind his Excellency that Sir P. Currie, on his way through Vienna, had mentioned to him the desirability of taking steps at Constantinople for the establishment of a responsible Ministry, headed by a Grand Vizier with genuine administrative powers.

I said that the condition of affairs in that city seemed to show a steady increase in the confusion at the Palace; and that, in Sir Philip's opinion, the inevitable and not-long-delayed result would be the complete breakdown of the existing administrative machinery.

Under these circumstances, it was probable that his Excellency would very soon receive from Baron Calice a report of the exchange of views which had taken place between him and his British, and, I believe, also his French, colleague.

Count Goluchowski replied that he had assented to Sir Philip Currie's views on this subject as far as the principle goes; but that he must confess that since then he had seen such evident proof of the intention of Russia to seize upon every chance of persuading the Sultan that she is his only friend, and that she alone holds back the other Powers from depriving him of his sovereign rights, that he is of opinion that it would be highly dangerous to broach the subject. If submitted to Russia and rejected by her the proposal would come to the ears of the Sultan, would convince him of the existence of differences of opinion between the Powers, and might, in fact, break up the European concert, to which he (Count Goluchowski) continues to ascribe the greatest importance. He therefore advocates the leaving of the Sultan to carry on affairs in his own way, and prefers to await his breaking down, if the collapse is really inevitable, as the best moment for inaugurating another system.

He added that for eight days he had received nothing from Constantinople, that his mail is due to-morrow, and that he will give his best consideration to any proposal made by Baron Calice and Sir Philip Currie.

I remarked that sooner or later the collapse must apparently come, and that it might be as well to reflect upon the expediency of making it as little mischievous as possible; but I can see that Count Goluchowski is, as matters stand, persuaded that it is expedient that the Powers should continue to stand aloof from interference of every kind.

I have, &c.

(Signed) EDMUND MONSON.

F. O. 424/184, pp. 486-487, No. 820

No. 710

Sir P. Currie to the Marquess of Salisbury.

No. 813. CONSTANTINOPLE, *December 21, 1895, 11.45 a.m.*
Telegraphic. *(Received December 21.)*

I AM informed by her Majesty's Consul at Aleppo that the suffering in his district is already great, and will become appalling as winter advances. Money is urgently needed for the relief of the destitute, especially at Marash.

There is great need for warm clothing. Grain can be obtained if only money is provided to purchase it. I have communicated the above to the Armenian Relief Committee here.

F. O. 424/184, p. 441, No. 780

No. 711

Sir P. Currie to the Marquess of Salisbury.

No. 814.   CONSTANTINOPLE, *December 21, 1895, 6.30 p.m.*
Telegraphic.   *(Received December 21.)*

IT appears that the Zeitounlis have offered to submit, but that the Turks insist on their laying down their arms and handing over their leaders. This they will probably refuse to do, and will then be slaughtered.

I have made representations to-day at the Porte through Mr. Block, and have urged that, at any rate, measures should be taken to prevent indiscriminate slaughter.

The German Emperor instructed the Ambassador to make similar representations in His Majesty's name.

F. O. 424/184, p. 442, No. 781

No. 712

Sir P. Currie to the Marquess of Salisbury.

No. 815.   CONSTANTINOPLE, *December 23, 1895, 10 p.m.*
Telegraphic.   *(Received December 23.)*

THE Ambassadors have been appealed to by both the Gregorian and Catholic Armenian Patriarchs to use their good offices with the Porte in favour of the Zeitounlis. It is suggested that the foreign Consuls might act as intermediaries in the same way as the Dragomans did when they persuaded the Armenians to evacuate the churches in Constantinople, as it is thought that the Zeitounlis might be willing to accept the assurances of the Turkish Government if conveyed to them by the foreign Consuls, though they refused to trust the Notables who were first sent to them. At a meeting of Ambassadors, which was held at my suggestion this afternoon to discuss this proposal, we all agreed to ask authority from our Goverments to propose to the Porte that we should send the Consuls at Aleppo to Zeitoun to act as intermediaries between the Porte and the Zeitounlis.

Have I your Lordship's authority to send Barnham?

I have just heard that snow has fallen at Zeitoun, and this will make if impossible for the troops to make their attack at once.

F. O. 424/184, p. 487, No. 821

No. 713

Sir P. Currie to the Marquess of Salisbury.

No. 994.
My Lord,

CONSTANTINOPLE, *December 24, 1895.*
(Received December 30.)

I HAVE the honour to forward to your Lordship herewith copy of a despatch which I have received from Her Majesty's Consul at Trebizond, reporting a remark made by Abdullah Pasha to Mr. Jewett respecting the opposition of Russia to the execution of any real reforms in Anatolia.

I have, &c.

(Signed) PHILIP CURRIE.

F. O. 424/184, p. 510, No. 855

Inclosure in No. 713

Consul Longworth to Sir P. Currie.

Confidential.
Sir,

TREBIZOND, *December 17, 1895.*

IN connection with my despatch of the 25th ultimo, I beg leave to quote the following paragraph from Dr. Jewett's letter to me of the 10th instant:-

"Abdullah Pasha told me that when Russia agreed to the scheme of reforms she gave Turkey to understand that they must not be carried out. He said that if reforms had been seriously introduced in Anatolia ten years ago it would have been the signal for a war with Russia. When asked why Turkey did not brace up and introduce real reforms now, he replied, with a smile: "Il faut avoir un Gouvernement pour cela."

I have, &c.

(Signed) H. Z. LONGWORTH.

F. O. 424/184, p. 510, No. 855/1

No. 714

Sir P. Currie to the Marquess of Salisbury.

No. 995.   CONSTANTINOPLE, *December 24, 1895.*
My Lord,   *(Received December 30.)*
    WITH reference to my despatch No. 862 of the 26th ultimo, I have the honour
to forward to your Lordship herewith copy of a despatch which I have received
from the Acting British Consul at Erzeroum respecting the origin of the disorders at
Erzinghian.

I have, &c.

(Signed) PHILIP CURRIE.

F. O. 424/184, p. 510, No. 856

Inclosure in No. 714

Consul Cumberbatch to Sir P. Currie.

Sir,   ERZEROUM, *December 9, 1895.*
    WITH reference to my despatches of the 6th and 12th ultimo, on the subject of
the disorders at Erzingian, I have the honour to inform your Excellency that,
according to a letter received from a person who can be trusted, the official version
as to the attack on Armenians in that place having been provoked by the killing of
an Imam is incorrect.
    The first Turk to be killed was a shopkeeper, who—like most of the
Mussulman mob there and in other towns—had bound a white turban round his
head, and may have been taken for a Mollah or even an Imam. He, moreover, was
only killed after fifteen or twenty Armenians had lost their lives.

I have, &c.

(Signed) H. A. CUMBERBATCH.

F. O. 424/184, p. 510, No. 856/1

No. 715

Sir P. Currie to the Marquess of Salisbury.

No. 1002.   CONSTANTINOPLE, *December 24, 1895.*
My Lord,   *(Received December 30.)*
    In the Sultan's message communicated to your Lordship in Mr. Herbert's
despatch No. 791 of the 11th November, His Majesty stated that, with a view to

restoring order in the Anatolian provinces, he was sending Generals Shakir Pasha and Saadeddin Pasha, together with some civil functionaries, to the Erzeroum and Bitlis districts respectively. Your Lordship is already acquainted with the movements of the Commission under Shakir Pasha; and I have now the honour to report that Her Majesty's Vice-Consul at Mush telegraphed to me on the 20th December that Saadeddin Pasha, accompanied by the civilians Ibrahim and Jemal Beys, had arrived at Mush; and on the 22nd December, that after inquiring into the situation in that town, and recommending the inhabitants to keep quiet, they had left for Bitlis.

Her Majesty's Vice-Consul added that the dangerous situation in the district was represented to the Commission in forcible terms by the Mutessarif, but that their visit had had no practical result, and the Cadi, whose removal both Mr. Hampson and the Mutessarif consider indispensable for the public safety, remained unchanged.

Under my instructions Mr. Block made inquiries of the Grand Vizier and the Minister for Foreign Affairs as to the object and powers of Saadeddin Pasha's Commission, and he was informed in reply that they were sent to take measures for the restoration and maintenance of order, and to see whether the civil and military authorities had faithfully carried out the instructions given to them. The Porte had as yet received no Report from the Commission.

Mr. Block at the same time urged the Porte to consider the advisability of removing the Cadi of Mush (see my telegram to your Lordship No. 772 of the 5th December). The Grand Vizier replied that, in answer to his inquiries, the Vali of Bitlis reported that the Cadi was the most loyal, devoted, and excellent of all officials, and that the reason why the Mutessarif objected to his remaining at Mush was a private quarrel between the two men; the Grand Vizier added that he had given them both to understand that they must live in harmony. Mr. Block then spoke very strongly on the subject, and again urged him to remove the Cadi, dwelling on the grave responsibility which would be incurred by the Porte in the event of further disturbances at Mush. His Highness finally said that he would apply for information to Saadeddin Pasha.

On my informing Mr. Hampson by telegraph of the Grand Vizier's language, he has replied that all the respectably Turks and Armenians at Mush declare the Cadi to be a more unscrupulous and dangerous man. He adds that the Commission threatened the Armenians with extermination if they intrigued, and warned them against expecting foreign intervention.

I have now instructed Mr. Block to bring the Cadi's character to the notice of the Sultan's Chief Secretary.

I have, &c.

(Signed) PHILIP CURRIE.

F. O. 424/184, p. 519, No. 863

No. 716

Sir P. Currie to the Marquess of Salisbury.

No. 1004.   PERA, *December 24, 1895.*
My Lord,   *(Received December 30.)*
WITH reference to my despatch No. 986 of the 24th December, I have the
honour to state that I met my Russian and French colleagues on the 24th instant in
order to discuss the steps that we should take with a view of having the Commission
of Control placed on a proper footing.

As it appeared evident that the Porte was neither willing nor able to deal with
the matter, we decided to make a direct representation to the Sultan through his
First Secretary.

We have accordingly instructed our three Dragomans to call together on
Tahsin Bey, and, after informing him of the unsuccessful communications which
they have made to the members of the Commission and to the Porte, to request him
to call His Imperial Majesty's immediate attention to the following points:-

1. The nomination of a President of the Commission.

2. The enlargement of the powers of the Commission, so as to make it in fact
what it is in name, a Commission of Control.

3. Authority to be given to the Commission to communicate direct with the
local authorities and not, as at present, with the Ministry of the Interior.

4. That the Judicial Inspectors sent to the provinces be instructed to cause
judicial inquiries to be held into recent events.

5. That the instructions given to Shakir Pasha be communicated to us.

6. That a Christian Muavin be at one attached to Shakir Pasha.

                                I have, &c.

                                            (Signed) PHILIP CURRIE.

F. O. 424/184, p. 521, No. 865

No. 717

Sir P. Currie to the Marquess of Salisbury.

No. 820.   CONSTANTINOPLE, *December 25, 1895, 11.10 a.m.*
Telegraphic.   *(Received December 25.)*
HER Majesty's Consul at Aleppo telegraphs as follows:-

"The Turkish troops took Zeitoun on the 23rd December. They shelled and
burnt the fort, and the town will probably be destroyed.

"The troops have eight guns in action, but the Armenians had none, as the two
which they had previously captured had been disabled.

"The defenders fled from the fort into the town, and then made for the open country in the direction of Killis, near which place several have been taken prisoners.

"The number of Zeitounlis killed is not known, but it is no doubt considerable.

"According to the official account, ten Turkish soldiers and one officer were killed and ten wounded.

"The Ferik says that the non-combatants will be given a safe escort to Marash; but considering the large numbers of Kurds and Circassians who are waiting on the road for an opportunity to fall on them, I very much doubt their safety."

F. O. 424/184, p. 490, No. 828

No. 718

Sir P. Currie to the Marquess of Salisbury.

No. 823.   CONSTANTINOPLE, *December 26, 1895, 7 p.m.*
Telegraphic.   *(Received December 26.)*

MY telegram No. 820 of yesterday.

Turkish Government state that, although the troops have destroyed the barracks at Zeitoun and surrounded the town, so that all serious opposition may be considered to be at an end, instructions have been sent to the Commander to advance very slowly so as to allow the Zeitounlis time to surrender, and, in any case, to spare all non-combatants.

I have repeated this telegram to Her Majesty's Consul at Aleppo.

F. O. 424/184, p. 491, No. 830

No. 719

Sir P. Currie to the Marquess of Salisbury.

No. 1008.   CONSTANTINOPLE, *December 26, 1895.*
My Lord,   *(Received December 30.)*

I HAVE sent Mr. Block twice during the past week to the Porte to make representations respecting the people of Zeitoun. In addition to the usual inhabitants of the town, many thousands of Armenians from the surrounding districts have, it is said, crowded into the valley, and it is to be feared that the usual excesses will be committed as soon as the resistance of the armed Zeitounlis has been overcome. My German colleague had received instructions to make an urgent protest on the subject, and the First Dragoman of the German Embassy and Mr.

Block expressed our earnest hope that no efforts would be spared to induce the Zeitounlis to submit by conciliatory means before having recourse to arms.

The Grand Vizier accused the Zeitounlis of having killed the soldiers of the garrison whom they had taken prisoners, and of having committed fearful atrocities in the Turkish villages in the neighbourhood.

No confirmation has been received of the truth of these charges, but the Zeitounlis, when preparing for resistance, appear to have forcibly collected provisions from the country districts which are inhabited by Mussulmans.

On the 23rd instant I received a visit from the Armenian Catholic Patriarch, Mgr. Azarian, who made a communication on behalf of the religious Heads of the Catholic, Gregorian, and Protestant Armenian communities at Aleppo. It was to be effect that they had at the request of the Turkish authorities sent Notables to Zeitoun to urge the Armenians to surrender, and then to offer them guarantees for their safety on certain conditions. The Zeitounlis had replied that they had no confidence in the guarantees, and persisted in their armed resistance to the troops. It was believed that they could not hold out much longer, and that there would be a terrible slaughter of the peaceful inhabitants and of the refugees. The Patriarch made an earnest appeal for the intervention of the Ambassadors, and urged that we should send our Consuls from Aleppo to negotiate a surrender. I called at once on Baron de Calice, the Doyen, and asked him to summon a meeting of the Ambassadors. He did so, and on my proposal my colleagues agreed to ask for the necessary authority.

The Austrian Ambassador undertook meanwhile to sound the Porte as to their willingness to consent, and he accordingly made a communication to the Foreign Minister on the 24th instant. The Ambassadors having received the sanction of their respective Governments, a further meeting was summoned for yesterday evening, but meanwhile I received Mr. Barnham's telegram announcing the capture of Zeitoun. When we assembled at the French Embassy M. de Nélidow stated that he had just been received in audience by the Sultan, and that His Majesty has spoken to him about Zeitoun, and had referred to the communication made on the previous day by the Austrian Ambassador. His Majesty had said that he was most anxious to avoid unnecessary bloodshed, and that he had given orders to his troops to advance with deliberation so as to give time to the Zeitounlis to come to terms. But he added that they had already three times refused the proposals made to them, and it was necessary that they should be subdued. The terms offered were that they should surrender all the arms of precision which they possessed, that they should give up their leaders, and that they should rebuild the barracks which had been destroyed. M. de Nélidow spoke of the proposed mission of the Consuls, which His Majesty considered unnecessary, though he did not absolutely reject it.

The Sultan in his conversation with the Russian Ambassador had ignored the fact that Zeitoun had already been captured two days previously, and my colleague heard with some surprise the contents of Mr. Barnham's telegram.

The objects which His Majesty had in view in concealing the truth are not clear, but the fact of his doing so diminished the reliance which some of us might have been ready to place on his assurances.

I suggested that, notwithstanding the capture, we should ask for safe-conducts for our Consuls and send them to Zeitoun to make arrangements for the protection of the unarmed inhabitants and refugees.

M. de Nélidow stated that the authority he had received to send his Consul to negotiate would not extend to such a mission as I proposed, and my suggestion, though it met with some approval from my other colleagues, was not adpoted by them.

M. de Nélidow stated his intention of sending his Dragoman to-day to the Palace to remind the Sultan of his assurances, and to urge that strict orders be given to the troops to spare the non-combatants. The other Dragomans will make similar representations.

I have, &c.

(Signed) PHILIP CURRIE.

F. O. 424/184, pp. 524-525, No. 868

No. 720

Sir. P. Currie to the Marquess of Salisbury.

No. 1010. Confidential.   CONSTANTINOPLE, *December 26, 1895.*
My Lord,   *(Received December 30.)*

I LEARN from an authoritative source that the deficit in the Turkish Budget up to the end of October amounted to £T.1,485,000, and that this deficit may be expected to be largely increased in view of the distrubed state of the Anatolian Provinces, and the difficulty of obtaining any further revenue for them

The revenues in the Vilayets of Roumelia as well as in Anatolia show a considerable falling-off, and with the sole exception of the Vilayet of Aidin, the Minister of Finance has been unable to draw any money from them, but on the contrary, has been obliged to supply funds to certain places in order to meet local requirements.

The revenues of the Public Debt were £T.20,000 lower last month than during the corresponding month last year. The receipts of the Régie are from £10,000 to £20,000 lower for the same period, and they are, so I am informed, diminishing in every province of Asiatic Turkey except Aidin, Angora, Sivas, Castamouni, and Trebizond.

The Customs revenues are already £ T.100,000 short for this year, and it is estimated that they will fall off about 40 per cent next year.

In short, the financial situation is becoming exceedingly serious, and with the constantly increasing expenditure owing to the calling out of the reserves, it is difficult to foresee how the Turkish Government will make both ends meet.

Hopes have been held out that extraordinary resources would be obtained by the grant of monopolies on petroleum, spirits, cigarette-papers, and other commodities, and negotiations have been going on with private individuals and syndicates with a view of carrying such arrangements into effect.

I have sounded my colleagues as to the support which some of them were said to have given to these schemes, but they were all of opinion that it would be impossible to put them in force without the unanimous consent of the Treaty Powers, which there is no prospect of obtaining at present.

The state of the money market will postpone indefinitely the proposed conversion of the Customs and Railway Loans, and there remains only the renewal of the Régie Concession.

The Ottoman Bank and the Government have hitherto been unable to come to terms about this, and under present circumstances it could only be carried out on conditions very unfavourable to the Turkish Government.

I have, &c.

(Signed) PHILIP CURRIE.

F. O. 424/184, pp. 527-528, No. 870

No. 721

Sir E. Monson to the Marquess of Salisbury.

No. 114. Secret.   VIENNA, *December 26, 1895.*
Telegraphic.   *(Received December 26.)*

WITH reference to my telegram No. 111, I have been informed by Count Goluchowski that he has received Baron Calice's report of the discussion on the subject of a responsible Ministry, which had taken place at Constantinople between the latter and his English and French colleagues.

It is still Count Goluchowski's conviction that a question of such importance can only be approached with safety if all the Powers are unanimous on the subject; such unanimity he thinks impossible to obtain at the present moment.

Although no reply has as yet been sent to Baron Calice, it is my conviction that Count Goluchowski will answer in the negative.

F. O. 424/184, p. 490, No. 829

No. 722

Sir P. Currie to the Marquess of Salisbury.

No. 825.   CONSTANTINOPLE, *December 27, 1895, 7.15 p.m.*
Telegraphic.   *(Received December 27.)*
    MY telegram No. 823 of the 26th December.
    Her Majesty's Consul at Aleppo telegraphs as follows:-
    "The Ferik says that after the capture of the fort on the 23rd the Zeitounlis retired to a height from which they can command the town, at a distance of about 2,000 yards from the Turkish position. He estimates their number at over 5,000 men.
    "A battle is imminent, and upon its issue depends the surrender of the town."
    F. O. 424/184, No. 491, No. 831

No. 723

The Marquess of Salisbury to Sir. P. Currie.

No. 414.
Sir,   FOREIGN OFFICE, *December 27, 1895.*
    I HAVE received your despatch No. 958 of the 16th instant, reporting the answers returned by the Turkish Minister of Police to communications addressed to him by Mr. Shipley on your Excellency's instructions, with reference to the continued arrests of Armenians in Constantinople, their treatment in prison, and the report that arms are sold to Mussulmans, while they are refused to Christians.
    I approve your Excellency's action in calling the attention of Nazim Pasha to these proceedings.
                                        I am, &c.
                                                (Signed) SALISBURY.

    F. O. 424/184, p. 491, No. 832

No. 724

The Marquess of Salisbury to Sir P. Currie.

No. 415.
Sir,   FOREIGN OFFICE, *December 27, 1895.*
    I HAVE received your despatch No. 954 of the 17th instant, stating that your Excellency had represented to the Sultan the importance of supporting the

Mutessarif of Mush against the opposition offered to his authority by the Cadi and the military authorities, of which you had heard from Mr. Vice-Consul Hampson.

I approve your Excellency's action in this matter.

I am, &c.

(Signed) SALISBURY.

F. O. 424/184, p. 491, No. 833

No. 725

Sir E. Monson to the Marquess of Salisbury.

No. 390. Secret.   VIENNA, *December 27, 1895.*
My Lord,   *(Received December 30.)*

I ASKED Count Goluchowski yesterday whether he had received from Baron Calice the report of his consultations with Sir Philip Currie and M. Cambon respecting the possibility of taking steps to induce the Sultan to appoint a responsible Ministry, and whether he had at all changed his mind in regard to the expediency of making an effort in this direction since I mentioned the subject to him on the 20th instant.

His Excellency replied tht he had heard from Baron Calice, whose Report had been, in fact, entirely in the sense in which I had given him to understand it would be drawn up. As regards his own opinion, however, he had found no reason to alter it. He felt strongly that in a matter of such importance success would be impossible without the absolute unanimity of all the Powers, and upon that unanimity it was useless to reckon.

"There will be," said he, "some one Power, it is not necessary to be precise as to which it will be, which from motives, I will not say of bad faith, but of excess of prudence, will not care to join the others in such a step; and the effect of this dissent will be such as I described in our last conversation on this subject."

Count Goluchowski, in reply to a further inquiry on my part, explained that although his opinion is fixed, he had not yet made any communication, in consequence, to Baron Calice; and I gathered from his language that he might delay doing so, probably because he wishes, first of all, to know what effect will have been produced at Paris by M. Cambon's representations. At the same time, I have no expectation that his view on the inexpediency of raising the question of a responsible Turkish Ministry will be materially affected by anything he may hear from Count Wolkenstein, who had not up till yesterday furnished any information in regard to it.

I have, &c.

(Signed) EDMUND MONSON.

F. O. 424/184, p. 528, No. 871

No. 726

Sir P. Currie to the Marquess of Salisbury.

No. 827. CONSTANTINOPLE, *December 28, 1895, 3.15 p.m.*
Telegraphic. *(Received December 28.)*

IN view of the fact that the Zeitounlis have not yet surrendered, it was decided, at a meeting of the Ambassadors this morning, that we should offer to the Porte the mediation of the Consuls at Aleppo. If our offer is accepted, we shall urge them to grant an armistice. Meanwhile, I have telegraphed to Barnham to consult him confidentially as to what arrangements should be made in the event of the Porte accepting our proposal.

F. O. 424/184, p. 492, No. 834

No. 727

The Marquess of Salisbury to Sir P. Currie.

No. 276.
Telegraphic. FOREIGN OFFICE, *December 28, 1895.*

INFORMATION has reached the Armenian Relief Committee, with regard to Kurdish depredations in the relieved districts, of a similar nature to that contained in Vice-Consul Hampson's report, forwarded in your Excellency's despatch No. 914 of the 10th instant.

The Committee ask if we have any later information to give them.

I should be glad to know whether any of the plundered villages have received further relief, and whether the instructions which your Excellency demanded have been issued by the Porte.

F. O. 424/184, p. 492, No. 835

No. 728

Admiralty to Foreign Office.

ADMIRALTY, *December 28, 1895.*
Sir, *(Received December 30.)*

I AM commanded by the Lords Commissioners of the Admiralty to transmit, for the information of the Secretary of State for Foreign Affairs, extracts from a letter from the Commanding Officer of Her Majesty's ship "Arethusa," dated at

Alexandretta, the 10th December, respecting the state of affairs and the massacres at Marash.

I am, &c.

(Signed) EVAN MACGREGOR.

F. O. 424/184, p. 528, No. 872

Inclosure in No. 728

Captain Langley to Admiral Sir M. Culme-Seymour.

Extract.   "ARETHUSA," AT ALEXANDRETTA, *December 10, 1895.*

I HAVE the honour to report that affairs in the town of Alexandretta are quiet, but according to reports from the interior the conditions have not altered, as fresh outbursts on the part of the Mahommedan population at both Kaiseryah and Marash have taken place.

As there are several men in the town here who took part in the massacres at Marash, and have returned, we have got pretty authentic details of the horrors that the Christians inhabitants were subjected to. The soldiers in this case were the perpetrators of the massacred ordered by the Pasha.

F. O. 424/184, pp. 528-529, No. 872/1

No. 729

Sir P. Currie to the Marquess of Salisbury.

No. 828.   CONSTANTINOPLE, *December 29, 1895, 12.45 p.m.*
Telegraphic.   *(Received December 29.)*

THE proposal of the Ambassadors to send the Consuls to Zeitoun will probably be refused by Sultan unless his hand is forced, as he does not wish to miss this opportunity of exterminating the Zeitounlis in the same way as he did the Sasunlis. It is not likely that Russia will join in pressing the proposal seriously unless we show her that we mean to carry it through.

If the consent of the Porte is refused or delayed beyond to-morrow evening, have I your Lordship's authority to inform my colleagues that Her Majesty's Government cannot calmly be a witness of the extermination of the Zeitounlis without making an effort to save them, and that I have been instructed to send Colonel Chermside to the head-quarters of the Turkish troops before Zeitoun to do his best to arrange terms, whether the Turkish Government consent or not? He was successfully employed on a similar errand in 1879 (see "Turkey No. 1: 1880").

The other Powers will probably force the Sultan to accept our joint proposal if they see that we mean business.

F. O. 424/184, p. 492, No. 836

No. 730

Sir P. Currie to the Marquess of Salisbury.

No. 829.   CONSTANTINOPLE, *December 30, 1895, 4.45 p.m.*
Telegraphic.   *(Received December 30.)*

WITH reference to your Lordship's telegram No. 277 of the 30th December respecting Zeitoun mediation, I wanted authority to send Colonel Chermside both as pressure on the Sultan to make him accept the proposal of the mediation of the Consuls and also as a lever to move my colleagues to insist on the joint proposal. If both fail, I should send Colonel Chermside to Alexandretta or Messina in the "Imogene." He does not anticipate any difficulty in getting from thence to the scene of action, and, even if his mediation is not accepted, his presence there would exercise a controlling influence on the Sultan as well as on the Military Commander.

F. O. 424/184, p. 529, No. 873

INDEX

A

S